IRISH UNIVERSITY PRESS

*British*
*Parliamentary Papers*

# NEWSPAPER STAMPS
[ 1851 (558) VOL XVII ]

Newspapers 1

*This Series*
*is published with the active co-operation of*
SOUTHAMPTON UNIVERSITY

IRISH UNIVERSITY PRESS SERIES

OF

# *British Parliamentary Papers*

## REPORT FROM THE SELECT COMMITTEE ON NEWSPAPER STAMPS WITH PROCEEDINGS MINUTES OF EVIDENCE APPENDIX AND INDEX

## *Newspapers*

## *1*

SHANNON · IRELAND

## PRINTER'S NOTE

The Printer wishes to draw attention to the many variations in the graphic quality of this series: broken type, ink set-off, poor impression and background blemishes are to be found in the original copy.

Every effort has been made to minimise these faults and to make the reprint copy as legible as possible.



*Microforms*

*Microfilm, microfiche and other forms of micro-publishing*


SBN 7165 0456 1

## PUBLISHER'S NOTE

The Irish University Press Series of British Parliamentary Papers is a facsimile reproduction. The original documents in this volume have been reproduced by photo-lithography and are unabridged even to the extent of faithfully retaining the printer's imprint.

The contents of this volume have been printed in their entirety by Robert Hogg, Printer to the Irish University Press, Shannon, Ireland.

As a result of the arrangement of the documents in subject sets and of the bringing together in a single book of a number of papers, some volumes in the Irish University Press Series may include the imprints of more than one printer.

*Irish University Press Shannon Ireland*

DUBLIN CORK BELFAST LONDON NEW YORK

*Captain T M MacGlinchey Publisher*

*Robert Hogg Printer*

# REPORTS

FROM

# COMMITTEES:

*FIFTEEN VOLUMES.*

—*(11.)*—

NEWSPAPER STAMPS.

Session

4 *February* —— 8 *August* 1851.

VOL. XVII.

1851.

# REPORT

FROM THE

SELECT COMMITTEE

ON

# NEWSPAPER STAMPS;

TOGETHER WITH THE

PROCEEDINGS OF THE COMMITTEE,

MINUTES OF EVIDENCE,

APPENDIX, AND INDEX.

---

*Ordered, by* The House of Commons, *to be Printed,*
18 *July* 1851.

---

558.

NEWSPAPER STAMPS:

# REPORTS FROM COMMITTEES:

1851.

*FIFTEEN VOLUMES:—CONTENTS OF THE*

ELEVENTH VOLUME.

N.B.—*THE* Figures *at the* beginning of the line, *correspond with the* N° *at the foot of each* Report; *and the* Figures *at the* end of the line, *refer to the* MS. Paging *of the Volumes arranged for The House of Commons.*

NEWSPAPER STAMPS:

*Lunæ,* 7° *die Aprilis,* 1851.

*Ordered,* THAT a Select Committee be appointed to inquire into the present State and Operation of the LAW relative to NEWSPAPER STAMPS; also, into the Law and Regulations relative to the Transmission of Newspapers and other Publications by Post, and to report their Opinion thereupon to The House.

*Veneris,* 11° *die Aprilis,* 1851.

Committee nominated, of—

Mr. Milner Gibson.
Mr. Tufnell.
Mr. Ker Seymer.
Mr. Rich.
Mr. Stafford.
Mr. Cobden.
Mr. George Alexander Hamilton.
Sir Joshua Walmsley.
Sir Thomas Frankland Lewis.
Mr. Chichester Fortescue.
Colonel Mure.
Mr. Shafto Adair.
Mr. Ewart.
Mr. Sotheron.
Sir William Molesworth.

*Veneris,* 18° *die Julii,* 1851.

*Ordered,* THAT the Committee have power to Report the Minutes of Evidence taken before them to The House.

# REPORT.

THE SELECT COMMITTEE appointed to inquire into the present State and Operation of the LAW relative to NEWSPAPER STAMPS; also, into the Law and Regulations relative to the Transmission of Newspapers and other Publications by Post, and to Report their Opinion thereupon to The House; and who were also empowered to Report the Minutes of Evidence taken before them to The House;——HAVE considered the Matters to them referred, and have agreed to the following REPORT:

IN conformity with the object for which Your Committee was appointed, they have examined witnesses competent to give information upon the state of the law affecting Newspaper Stamps, and the operation of that law upon the Newspaper Press and the public welfare.

Your Committee have further taken evidence respecting the transmission of newspapers and other printed matter by the Post Office.

Upon the interpretation which the Board of Inland Revenue put upon the law, and the practice which has been pursued by that department, Your Committee have examined the Solicitor and the Assistant Secretary of the Board. Among the witnesses practically cognizant of the details involved in the publication of newspapers Your Committee have examined the manager of "The Times," one of the editors of "The Daily News," and other gentlemen connected with the metropolitan and the provincial press; and upon the policy of imposing a direct tax on the diffusion of a knowledge of current events through newspapers, they have examined several gentlemen who have given attention to the subject.

The duty on newspapers is imposed by the Act 6 & 7 Will. 4, c. 76, and is as follows:

For every sheet or other piece of paper whereon any newspaper shall be printed, 1 *d.*

A further additional duty of ½ *d.* and 1 *d.* is imposed in case the paper exceeds certain sizes specified in the Act. These additional duties are, practically, not incurred.

On supplements not exceeding a certain size, ½ *d.*

These duties are declared to be payable on—

1st. Any paper containing public news, intelligence or occurrences printed in any part of the United Kingdom, to be dispersed and made public.

2d. Also, any paper printed weekly or oftener, or at intervals not exceeding 26 days, containing only, or principally, advertisements.

3d. Also, any paper containing any public news, intelligence or occurrence, or any remarks or observations therein, printed for sale, and published periodically, or in parts or numbers, not exceeding 26 days between the publication of any two such papers, parts or numbers when any of the said papers, parts or numbers respectively shall not exceed two sheets of the dimensions specified, or shall be published for sale for a less price than 6 *d*, exclusive of the duty by the Act imposed.

The net produce of these duties, in the year 1850, was 350,418 *l.*; and, on an average of the years 1848, 1849 and 1850, amounted to 350,545 *l.* per annum.

It appears from the evidence of Mr. Keogh and Mr. Timm, that in the opinion of the Board of Inland Revenue, there are three classes of publications legally liable to the newspaper stamp: 1. Any paper containing public news, without reference to price, size, interval of publication, or to its being published more than once. 2. Any paper printed at less intervals than 26 days, containing only or principally advertisements. 3. Any paper containing remarks on public news printed at less intervals than 26 days, where the price is less than 6 *d.*, or the size less than two sheets.

With regard to publications of the first class, Your Committee would remark upon the difficulty which must necessarily exist in determining what the taxable article "news" is, and whether any or how much of it may be contained in an unstamped

unstamped publication; and therefore they were not surprised to find that the officers of the Board of Inland Revenue were unable to define the character of the intelligence which may legally be published on unstamped paper, or that the practice of the Board had not been uniform as to the kind of publications upon which they had felt themselves bound from time to time to enforce the stamp. In proof of the difficulty of defining the meaning of the term "news," Your Committee would point to the evidence of the Solicitor of the Board of Inland Revenue, who states (Ev. 100–165), that the Queen's Speech is "news," and he thinks that any one who printed the Queen's Speech on a piece of unstamped paper would be liable to a penalty of 20 *l.*, but he doubts whether the Chancellor of the Exchequer's speech is news, (Ev. 159–170); and in the case of the Queen's Speech being printed on unstamped paper, he says (Ev. 100), "that it is done almost immediately after every speech is delivered, but when we have notice of that, we write and tell the parties they have infringed the law; if we had a copy of it, so that we could bring the offence home to the party, we should prosecute him." Further, the Board of Inland Revenue, as it appears from the evidence of their Secretary, recognise a difference hard to be understood between public and private news, and draw a distinction unknown to the law between public and class news. Respecting private news, the secretary states (Q. No. 407) that a paper containing nothing but records of proceedings in private families, and calumnious insinuations as to the conduct of individuals, is not liable to the stamp; and as to class news, it is understood that a paper addressed to one particular subject, for instance, architecture, or law, &c., and giving news bearing on that particular subject only, or on persons connected with it, is not considered a newspaper; thus the "Legal Observer" publishes without a stamp an account of a meeting of lawyers upon any subject, as class news; but if it had published an account of a meeting of clergymen (Q. 469), then the secretary "would not have had the slightest doubt" as to its liability to the stamp duty, as it would then have been a report of a meeting of persons not connected with the class subject.

It appears that the Board of Inland Revenue have not usually interfered with class publications confined to particular objects, in consequence of the insertion therein of some trifling paragraphs of public news; yet, there are exceptions to this rule, for in the case of an unstamped class monthly

monthly publication, called the "Norwich Reformer," where only one-sixteenth of the contents came under the description of news, the solicitor to the Board thought it necessary to intimate to the publishers that they were infringing the law.

On the second class of publications, Your Committee have not much information before them. It appears, however, that the circulation of these papers must be restricted by the stamp, and the facilities to the public of advertising thereby considerably lessened. This is especially true in regard to the cases of advertising sheets which are given away, where the point at which expenditure and receipts balance each other, and beyond which no circulation can take place without absolute loss, is sooner arrived at where each copy is compelled to bear the stamp than if it were free from that tax.

As to the third class of publications, which are held by the Board to be liable to the stamp, Your Committee would observe that if it is difficult to make clear the meaning of the term "news," the difficulty is greatly increased in attempting to define remarks upon news, and in drawing the distinction between remarks upon news and news itself, a distinction necessary to be made, because the former may, under certain conditions, be published without a stamp, while the latter is always liable to the duty. The object for which the third class of publications was rendered liable to the provisions of the Newspaper Act appears to have been to subject to restrictions small and cheap publications issued at frequent intervals, not considered as newspapers, but merely containing essays on political subjects; the solicitor to the Board of Inland Revenue states (Q. 32) that there has been "very little practice at all" in reference to this class of publications, "because the publications that have come under the notice of the Board have generally contained public news, and therefore they have come under the first definition of newspapers. Parties have attempted to excuse themselves by stating that their paper is not a newspaper within the third definition; but our reply to that is, 'It is a newspaper within the first definition, because it contains public news, intelligence, and occurrences.'"

It appears to Your Committee, that with respect to comments on news in cheap publications, the law has been allowed to some extent to sleep. One witness, extensively engaged in publishing periodicals of various kinds, pointed out the difficulty

ficulty of keeping within the law about commenting upon events, and it is notorious that a great number of publications issued at intervals of less than 26 days, and at prices less than 6*d.*, by philanthropic, religious, political, and other societies, are published without a stamp, and contain comments and observations upon public events.

It appears to your Committee that if the law, imposing a stamp on public intelligence and on observations thereon, were carried out, nearly all periodical printed matter, and a large portion of occasional printed matter would be subjected to the stamp duty; whilst, if it be understood that the law is not to be fully observed, much unequal competition must continue to arise between different publishers, and the Board of Inland Revenue will continue to be placed in the undesirable position of having to decide upon what periodicals the law is to be enforced, and in what cases its provisions may be dispensed with.

A want of uniformity in the practice of the Board, even as to the sort of publications on which they appear to intend to enforce the law, is shown by the Evidence. As an instance that might be cited, the Committee would point to the case of the "Wakefield Examiner," a provincial paper, where a prosecution was instituted against, and a penalty of 10*l.*, being rather more than the duty incurred, inflicted upon the publisher for reprinting separately, on unstamped paper, the report of a trial which had previously appeared in his own stamped newspaper, whilst it appears that in the Metropolis and elsewhere speeches in Parliament and accounts of public meetings are issued without stamps in a similar manner.

With regard to the operation of the stamp on the established newspapers, it is of course obvious, that by increasing their cost, it limits the field of their circulation; and, moreover, it has been shown (A. 2755-2756) that the penny stamp on each copy of a newspaper generally raises the price to the public beyond the mere addition of that sum. The effect of the Newspaper Act by restricting the superficial extent of letter-press in newspapers, and affixing an additional stamp on supplements to newspapers, is to make it necessary for the proprietors of "The Times," as stated by its manager, in order to avoid loss, not only to reject advertisements, but to prevent the circulation of that paper from exceeding certain limits. The manager of "The Times" also states (Ev. 2043,) that "if there were no considerations but that of supplying the

the public demand for that paper, it would probably double its circulation within two years."

Some opinions are expressed that the proprietors of existing newspapers have an interest in the maintenance of the stamp, and would be injured by its abolition. Were these views correct they could not be considered to furnish a good ground for retaining the stamp if the public interests required its repeal; but Your Committee find little evidence in support of those opinions, and they point to the testimony of the manager of "The Times," who states (Ev. 2225), "his conviction that if the stamp duty be taken off, the commercial advantages to 'The Times' would be enormous."

It is stated to Your Committee by the editor of "The Scotsman" (Ev. 1471), that the penny stamp is "a favourable arrangement for newspapers on the whole;" that he does not "consider it a tax," but "a payment made to the Post Office for services which he does not think could be so efficiently performed in any other way for much more cost." Other witnesses do not participate in this opinion, nor is it supported by the Post-office authorities. It appears to Your Committee that newspapers do not practically enjoy such favourable terms for transmission by post as other printed matter; for whilst newspapers are compelled to stamp every copy of their impression, whether sent by post or not, other publications, up to the weight of two ounces, obtain by virtue of a Treasury Minute, the same freedom from postage as newspapers, by registering as newspapers, and by stamping only so many copies as are actually required to be sent by post. If the newspaper stamp were allowed to be affixed only to such copies of newspapers as go through the post, it might then assume the character of a mere equivalent for postal services, but in those cases, especially in that of provincial papers where the post is little used, the compulsory stamp upon every copy can be viewed in no other light than that of a tax. In reality, however, the freedom from postage charge is not always accorded to newspapers in return for the newspaper stamp. Your Committee think it right to advert to an anomaly that exists with regard to the transmission of newspapers by post, viz., that, in the London district, a circle of three miles round the General Post Office, and where the post might be of much use for the distribution of newspapers, a stamped newspaper is charged a penny if posted in one part of that district to be transmitted to another. Your Committee

Committee do not see any good reason for this regulation, and would therefore recommend that it be abolished.

Your Committee find that considerable evasions of the postage charge take place under cover or pretence of stamped newspapers; that letters and unstamped publications and parcels are sent concealed within rolls of stamped newspapers; and that unstamped and foreign newspapers are occasionally passed without being subjected to charge. This is partly admitted by the Post-office authorities, who attribute much of the 1694.
evasion to the papers which pass through the Post-office by virtue of the Treasury Minute of 1838. It is clear that in a department transmitting daily from 120,000 to 260,000 papers, and which are despatched within two or three hours after the greater portion of them are received, nothing but an extravagantly large force of examiners could prevent evasion.

If a revenue is to be derived from the postage of newspapers, it is worthy of consideration whether it would not be simpler and more economical that the collection of such revenue should be managed, as in the case of letters, directly by the Post Office, rather than indirectly by another department. Were this suggestion adopted, and the present newspaper stamp abolished, your Committee see no reason to doubt that the Post Office authorities would devise means of regulating the transmission and distribution by post of newspapers, if not of all printed matter, at a small charge, not exceeding a penny for each packet, up to a weight equal to that of the largest existing newspaper, without exposing the revenue to the frauds to which the present system unavoidably renders it subject. In passing, it may be right to mention the peculiar use which is sometimes made of the existing privilege of sending papers within the United Kingdom, free from postage charge for ever, in virtue of the original Somerset House stamp. Mr. Parkhurst, senior clerk in the office of the Secretary of the Post Office (Ev. 1677), says, "We know that newspapers are sent as waste paper very often through the post; there have been cases of very old bundles of papers being sent in that way."

There is, however, a consideration connected with the additional cost supposed to be caused by the imposition of the stamp on newspapers, which requires a particular notice; viz., the right of gratuitous transmission of newspapers through post. Mr. Smith, the head of a London newspaper agency firm, which has been established for the last 60 years, and which

2813. which transmits about one-seventh of all the London daily
2832. papers, states distinctly that the re-transmission of newspapers is carried on to a "most enormous" extent, so as greatly to reduce the cost of their newspaper to those least able to pay for it. He gives instances in which the cost of "The Times" is thus reduced to 2*d.* and to even 1*d.*, and yet read by the last
2840. person in the series on the second morning after publication, and he adds, that the number of persons thus receiving the best newspapers at a very cheap rate, is exceedingly numerous, and that the proposed charge of 1*d.* for each re-transmission would, in fact, prevent them, probably, from taking any paper at all, unless it was a weekly paper.

On the whole, considering on the one hand the various modes now in use by railways and private agency of distributing newspapers through the country, and on the other, the frauds upon the Post Office from unstamped publications being now unavoidably carried post-free; seeing, in short, that in many cases the stamp is paid where no postal advantages are received, and in other cases the stamp is not paid where postal advantages are obtained, Your Committee are of opinion that immediate steps should be taken to place the regulations affecting the transmission of newspapers and other printed matter by post, on a more satisfactory footing.

In examining witnesses as to the operation of the law on the newspaper press, it is found that an opinion prevails to some small extent, that the maintenance of the stamp has the effect of rendering newspapers more respectable than they would be if free from that restriction. After weighing the reasons for such opinion, Your Committee conclude that it does not rest on any good foundation. No deterioration of the newspaper press, but, on the contrary an improvement followed the reduction of the stamp which took place in 1836; and doubtless the character of newspapers would continue to improve in proportion to the advance in public taste and morals, although the stamp should be entirely abolished. It is stated by one of the witnesses, as an objection to the removal of the stamp, that a new class of journals would spring up, if the stamp were repealed, in the smaller towns and country districts, and that it would be (Ev. 1555) "a misfortune that there should be local papers of a more petty character than at present exist." The general bearing of nearly all the other evidence is of a contrary tendency; and the unanimous opinion of those

those gentlemen who, being persons who had devoted attention to the education and social improvement of the working classes, were specially examined on this branch of the subject, was to the effect that moral advantages might be expected to follow the establishment of cheap local newspapers.

Your Committee concur with the proprietor of the "Liverpool Journal" in thinking that the cheapening the cost of existing provincial papers would extend their circulation and improve their quality; whilst they also believe that, should a new class of small and cheap local papers arise, they would occupy a field hitherto not reached by existing newspapers, and be the vehicles of knowledge to large classes of persons who otherwise would get no newspaper at all. The present extensive sale of penny publications, as shown by the evidence (Evidence 2494 and 2509), abundantly proves the desire among the humbler classes for some kind of reading and mental improvement; but the stamp prevents the penny paper from containing a record of the current events of life, thus depriving the readers of small periodicals, who are for the most part persons living by labour or of limited means, of that most useful knowledge, the news of the day; for which, as is stated by Mr. Abel Heywood, a gentleman extensively engaged in supplying cheap literature, "as the result of his experience" amongst the class of readers alluded to, there is a greater desire than for any other kind of information. It may be said with truth, that the newspaper stamp prohibits the existence of such newspapers as from their price and character would be suitable to the means and wants of the labouring classes.

The question of pirating articles of intelligence by one newspaper from another has been brought under the notice of Your Committee by witnesses conversant with the newspaper press, and favourable to the abolition of the duty. The established newspapers, particularly the London daily press, collect the valuable information which they report to the public at a very great expense, and publish it at a very costly celerity. It has been stated, that if the newspaper duty were abolished, there would be great temptation to the numerous halfpenny and penny publications which would then spring up, to pirate the public intelligence collected at so much cost and exertion. It has been proposed, that some short privilege of copyright should therefore be conferred.

In conclusion, Your Committee consider it their duty

to

to direct attention to the objections and abuses incident to the present system of newspaper stamps, arising from the difficulty of defining and determining the meaning of the term "news;" to the inequalities which exist in the application of the Newspaper Stamp Act, and the anomalies and evasions that it occasions in postal arrangements; to the unfair competition to which stamped newspapers are exposed with unstamped publications; to the limitation imposed by the Stamp upon the circulation of the best newspapers, and to the impediments which it throws in the way of the diffusion of useful knowledge regarding current and recent events among the poorer classes, which species of knowledge, relating to subjects which most obviously interest them, call out the intelligence by awakening the curiosity of those classes.

How far it may be expedient that this tax should be maintained as a source of revenue, either in its present or in any modified form, Your Committee do not feel themselves called upon to state; other considerations, not within their province, would enter into that question. But, apart from fiscal considerations, they do not consider that news is of itself a desirable subject of taxation.

18 *July* 1851.

# PROCEEDINGS OF THE COMMITTEE.

*Lunæ*, 14° *die Aprili* 1851.

Present:

Mr. Milner Gibson.
Mr. Ewart.
Mr. Shafto Adair.
Sir Joshua Walmsley.
Mr. Cobden.
Mr. Stafford.

Right Hon. T. MILNER GIBSON called to the Chair.

Committee deliberate on their course of proceeding.

[Adjourned till Friday, 2 May, at One o'clock.

*Veneris*, 2° *die Maii*, 1851.

Present:

Right Hon. T. MILNER GIBSON, in the Chair.

Mr. Rich.
Sir J. Walmsley.
Mr. Stafford.
Mr. Ewart.
Mr. Tufnell.
Mr. Cobden.
Mr. Geo. A. Hamilton.
Mr. Sotheron.

Mr. *Timm*, examined.

[Adjourned till Tuesday next, at One o'clock.

*Martis*, 6° *die Maii*, 1851.

Present:

Right Hon. T. MILNER GIBSON, in the Chair.

Sir T. Frankland Lewis.
Mr. Shafto Adair.
Mr. Cobden.
Mr. Hamilton.
Sir J. Walmsley.
Mr. Rich.
Mr. Ewart.
Mr. C. Fortescue.
Mr. Sotheron.

Mr. *Keogh*, examined.

[Adjourned till Friday, at One o'clock.

*Veneris*, 9° *die Maii*, 1851.

Present:

Right Hon. T. MILNER GIBSON, in the Chair.

Mr. Rich.
Mr. Ewart.
Mr. Sotheron.
Mr. Tufnell.
Mr. C. Fortescue.
Sir Joshua Walmsley.
Mr. Hamilton.
Mr. Stafford.
Mr. Cobden.

Mr. *M. J. Whitty* and Mr. *C. D. Collet*, examined.

[Adjourned till Tuesday next, at One o'clock.

---

*Martis*, 13° *die Maii*, 1851.

Present.

Right Hon. T. MILNER GIBSON, in the Chair.

Mr. C. Fortescue.
Mr. Rich.
Sir J. Walmsley.
Mr. Hamilton.
Mr. Sotheron.
Sir T. F. Lewis.
Mr. Cobden.
Mr. Ewart.
Mr. Shafto Adair.
Mr. Stafford.
Mr. Hamilton.

Mr. *C. D. Collet*, again examined.

[Adjourned till Friday, at One.

---

*Veneris*, 16° *die Maii*, 1851.

Present:

Right Hon. T. MILNER GIBSON, in the Chair.

Mr. Cobden.
Mr. Ewart.
Mr. Shafto Adair.
Mr. Stafford.
Mr. C. Fortescue.
Sir J. Walmsley.
Mr. Hamilton.
Mr. Rich.
Mr. Tufnell.

Mr. *S. G. Bucknall* and Mr. *J. Cassell*, examined.

[Adjourned till Tuesday next, at One o'clock.

*Martis*, 20° *die Maii*, 1851.

Present:

Right Hon. T. MILNER GIBSON, in the Chair.

Mr. Ewart.
Mr. Sotheron.
Sir Joshua Walmsley.
Mr. Cobden.
Sir T. F. Lewis.
Mr. Tufnell.
Mr. Rich.
Mr. Hamilton.
Mr. Stafford.

Mr. *Cassell*, again examined.

Mr. *A. Russel* and Mr. *Parkhurst*, examined.

[Adjourned till Friday next, at One.

---

*Veneris*, 23° *die Maii*, 1851.

Present:

Right Hon. T. MILNER GIBSON, in the Chair.

Sir J. Walmsley.
Mr. Shafto Adair.
Mr. Sotheron.
Mr. Rich.
Mr. Hamilton.
Mr. Ewart.
Mr. Tufnell.
Mr. Cobden.
Mr. C. Fortescue.

Mr. *Rowland Hill* and Mr. *William Bokenham*, examined.

[Adjourned till Tuesday next, at One o'clock.

---

*Martis*, 27° *die Maii*, 1851.

Present:

Right Hon. T. MILNER GIBSON, in the Chair.

Mr. C. Fortescue.
Mr. Cobden.
Mr. Rich.
Mr. Stafford.
Mr. G. A. Hamilton.
Mr. Ewart.
Mr. Sotheron.
Sir T. F. Lewis.
Sir J. Walmsley.

Mr. *Morris*, Mr. *Bunting*, and Mr. *F. K. Hunt*, examined.

[Adjourned till Friday, at One o'clock.

*Veneris*, 30° *die Maii*, 1851.

Present:

Right Hon. T. MILNER GIBSON, in the Chair.

Mr. G. A. Hamilton.
Mr. Ewart.
Mr. Cobden.
Mr. Rich.
Sir J. Walmsley.
Mr. Tufnell.

Rev. *Thomas Spenser*, Mr. *Anderson*, Mr. *A. Heywood*, Hon. *Horace Greeley*, and Mr. *H. Watkinson*, examined.

[Adjourned till Tuesday next, at One o'clock.

*Martis*, 3° *die Junii*, 1851.

Present:

Right Hon. T. MILNER GIBSON, in the Chair.

Mr. G. A. Hamilton.
Mr. Shafto Adair.
Mr. Cobden.
Sir J. Walmsley.
Mr. Ewart.
Mr. Rich.
Mr. Tufnell.

Mr. *Henry Cole*, Mr. *Smith*, and Hon. *H. Greeley*, examined.

[Adjourned till Tuesday, 17th, at One o'clock.

*Martis*, 17° *die Junii*, 1851.

Present:

Right Hon. T. MILNER GIBSON, in the Chair.

Mr. Shafto Adair.
Mr. Cobden.
Mr. Rich.

*Veneris*, 20° *die Junii*, 1851.

Present:

Right Hon. T. MILNER GIBSON, in the Chair.

Mr. G. A. Hamilton.
Sir Joshua Walmsley.
Mr. Rich.
Mr. Ewart.
Mr. Shafto Adair.
Mr. Cobden.
Mr. Sotheron.

Mr. *Keogh*, further examined.

Mr. *Rust* and Mr. *Hickson*, examined.

[Adjourned till Wednesday week, 2d July, at One o'clock.

---

*Mercurii*, 2° *die Julii*, 1851.

Present:

Right Hon. T. MILNER GIBSON, in the Chair.

Sir Joshua Walmsley.
Mr. Shafto Adair.
Mr. C. Fortescue.
Mr. Rich.
Mr. Tufnell.
Mr. Cobden.

The Committee deliberate on their course of proceeding.

[Adjourned till Friday week, at half-past Eleven.

---

*Veneris*, 11° *die Julii*, 1851.

Present:

Right Hon. T. MILNER GIBSON, in the Chair.

Mr. Rich.
Mr. Ewart.
Mr. G. A. Hamilton.
Mr. Cobden.
Mr. C. Fortescue.
Mr. Shafto Adair.
Mr. Stafford.
Mr. Sotheron.
Mr. Tufnell.
Sir J. Walmsley.

The Draft Reports prepared by the *Chairman* and by Mr. *Rich* were respectively read a first time, as follows:

 DRAFT

## DRAFT REPORT proposed by the *Chairman.*

"In conformity with the object for which Your Committee was appointed, they have examined witnesses competent to give information upon the state of the law affecting Newspaper Stamps, and the operation of that law upon the Newspaper Press and the public welfare.

"Your Committee have further taken evidence respecting the transmission of newspapers and other printed matter by the Post Office.

"Upon the interpretation which the Board of Inland Revenue put upon the law, and the practice which has been pursued by that department, Your Committee have examined the Solicitor and the Assistant Secretary of the Board. Among the witnesses practically cognizant of the details involved in the publication of newspapers Your Committee have examined the manager of the "Times" and other gentlemen connected with the metropolitan and the provincial press; and upon the policy of imposing a direct tax on the diffusion of a knowledge of current events through newspapers, they have examined several gentlemen who have given attention to the subject.

"It appears to Your Committee that the Board of Inland Revenue have always held that there are three classes of publications liable to the newspaper stamp: 1. Any paper containing public news, without reference to price, size, interval of publication, or to its being published more than once. 2. Any paper printed at less intervals than 26 days, containing only or principally advertisements. 3. Any paper containing remarks on public news printed at less intervals than 26 days, where the price is less than 6 *d.*, or the size less than two sheets.

"With regard to the first class publications Your Committee would remark upon the great difficulty which appears to exist in determining what the taxable article 'news' is, and whether any or how much of it may be contained in an unstamped publication; and therefore they were not surprised to find that the officers of the Board of Inland Revenue were unable to define the character of the intelligence which may legally be published on unstamped paper, or that the practice of the Board had not been uniform as to the kind of publications upon which they had felt themselves bound from time to time to enforce the stamp. In proof of the difficulty of defining the meaning of the term 'news,' Your Committee would point to the evidence of the Solicitor of the Boad of Inland Revenue, who states (Ev. 100–165), that the Queen's Speech is 'news,' and he thinks that any one who printed the Queen's Speech on a piece of unstamped paper would be liable to a penalty of 20 *l.*, but he doubts whether the Chancellor of the Exchequer's speech is news, as it is 'less of a state affair than the Queen's Speech' (Ev. 170); and in the case of the Queen's Speech being printed on unstamped paper, he says (Ev. 100), 'that it is done almost immediately after every speech is delivered, but when we have notice of that, we write and tell the parties they have infringed the law; if we had a copy of it, so that we could bring the offence home to the party, we should prosecute him.' Further, the Board of Inland Revenue, as it appears from the evidence of their Secretary, recognise a difference hard to be understood between public and private news, and draw a distinction unknown to the law between public and class news. Respecting private

news

news, the secretary states (Q. No. 407) that a paper containing nothing but records of proceedings in private families, and calumnious insinuations as to the conduct of individuals, is not liable to the stamp; and as to class news, it is understood that a paper addressed to one particular subject, for instance, architecture, or law, &c., and giving news bearing on that particular subject only, or on persons connected with it, is not considered a newspaper; thus the 'Legal Observer' publishes without a stamp an account of a meeting of lawyers upon any subject, as class news; but if it had published an account of a meeting of clergymen (Q. 469), then the secretary 'would not have had the slightest doubt' as to its liability to the stamp duty.

"It appears that the Board of Inland Revenue have not usually interfered with class publications confined to particular objects, in consequence of the insertion therein of some trifling paragraphs of public news; yet, there are exceptions to this rule, for in the case of an unstamped class monthly publication, called the 'Norwich Reformer,' where only one-sixteenth of the contents came under the description of news, the solicitor to the Board thought it necessary to intimate to the publishers that they were infringing the law.

"On the second class of publications, Your Committee have not much information before them. It appears, however, that the circulation of these papers must be much restricted by the stamp, and the facilities to the public of advertising thereby considerably lessened. This is especially true in regard to the cases of advertising sheets which are given away, where the point at which expenditure and receipts balance each other, and beyond which no circulation can take place without absolute loss, is sooner arrived at where each copy is compelled to bear the stamp than if it were free from that tax.

"As to the third class of publications, which are held by the Board to be liable to the stamp, Your Committee would observe that if it is difficult to make clear the meaning of the term 'news,' the difficulty is greatly increased in attempting to define remarks upon news, and in drawing the distinction between remarks upon news and news itself, a distinction necessary to be made, because the former may, under certain conditions, be published without a stamp, while the latter is always liable to the duty. The object for which the third class of publications was rendered liable to the provisions of the Newspaper Act appears to have been to subject to restrictions small and cheap publications issued at frequent intervals, not considered as newspapers, but merely containing essays on political subjects; the solicitor to the Board of Inland Revenue states (Q. 32) that there has been 'very little practice at all' in reference to this class of publications.

"It appears to your Committee, that with respect to comments on news in cheap publications, the law has been allowed to sleep, and has not for some years past been enforced at all. One witness, extensively engaged in publishing periodicals of various kinds, pointed out the difficulty of keeping within the law about commenting upon events, and it is notorious that a great number of publications issued at intervals of less than 26 days, and at prices less than 6 *d.*, by philanthropic, religious, political, and other societies, are published without a stamp, and contain comments and observations upon public events.

 "It

"It appears to Your Committee that if the law, imposing a stamp on intelligence, and on observations on intelligence, were carried out, nearly all periodical printed matter, and a large portion of occasional printed matter would be subjected to the stamp duty; whilst, if it be understood that the law is not to be fully observed, much unequal competition must continue to arise between different publishers, and the Board of Inland Revenue will continue to be placed in the undesirable position of censors of the press, by having to decide upon what periodicals the law is to be enforced, and in what cases its provisions may be dispensed with.

"The want of uniformity in the practice of the Board, even as to the sort of publications on which they appear to intend to enforce the law, is shown by the Evidence. Amongst many instances that might be cited, the Committee would point to the case of the 'Wakefield Examiner,' a provincial paper, where a prosecution was instituted against, and a penalty inflicted upon the publisher for reprinting separately, on unstamped paper, the report of a trial which had previously appeared in his own stamped newspaper, whilst it is a custom of almost daily occurrence in the metropolis and elsewhere for speeches in Parliament and accounts of public meetings to be issued without stamps in a similar manner. It would appear from the evidence of one of the witnesses (Ev. 896), supported by cases, that the law is differently applied in the provinces and in the metropolis; whether this be so or not, it is proved, at least, that violations of the law less frequently escape the notice of the Board in the country than in London.

"Having regard to the foregoing considerations, and to the concurrence of nearly all the witnesses as to the uncertain application of the Newspaper Stamp Act, Your Committee are of opinion that a thing so undefinable as public news, or observations thereon, is not adapted to be the subject of taxation.

"With regard to the operation of the stamp on the established newspapers, it is of course obvious, that by increasing their cost, it limits the field of their circulation; and, moreover, it has been shown (A. 2755-2756) that the penny stamp on each copy of a newspaper generally raises the price to the public beyond the mere addition of that sum. The effect of the Newspaper Act by restricting the superficial extent of letter-press in newspapers, and affixing an additional stamp on supplements to newspapers, is to make it necessary for the proprietors of the London 'Times,' in order to avoid loss, not only to reject advertisements, but to prevent the circulation of that paper from exceeding certain limits. The manager of the 'Times' states (Ev. 2043), that 'if there were no considerations but that of supplying the public demand for that paper, it would probably double its circulation within two years.'

"Some opinions are expressed that the proprietors of existing newspapers have an interest in the maintenance of the stamp, and would be injured by its abolition. Were these views correct, they could not be considered to furnish a good ground for retaining the stamp if the public interests required its repeal; but it is satisfactory to Your Committee to find no evidence in support of those opinions from many most competent witnesses, and they point to the testimony

of

of the manager of the 'Times,' who states (Ev. 2225), 'as his conviction, that if the stamp duty be taken off, the commercial advantages to the 'Times' would be enormous.' Indeed it is difficult to see how a diminution in the cost of production of newspapers should be injurious to the producers, and Your Committee lean to the conclusion that if the stamp were abolished, that papers of established reputation, and enjoying the public confidence, either would not be affected at all or have their circulation extended.

"It is stated to Your Committee by the editor of a provincial paper (Ev. 1471), that the penny stamp is 'a favourable arrangement for newspapers on the whole;' that he does not 'consider it a tax,' but 'a payment made to the Post-office for services which he does not think could be so efficiently performed in any other way for much more cost.' Other witnesses do not participate in this opinion, nor is it supported by the Post-office authorities. It appears to Your Committee that newspapers do not practically enjoy such favourable terms for transmission by post as a large portion of other printed matter; for whilst newspapers are compelled to stamp every copy of their impression, whether sent by post or not, other publications, up to the weight of two ounces, obtain the same freedom from postage as newspapers, by stamping only so many copies as are actually required to be sent by post. If the newspaper stamp were allowed to be affixed only to such copies of newspapers as go through the post, it might then assume the character of a mere equivalent for postal services; but in those cases, and they are numerous, especially in that of provincial papers where the post is little used, the compulsory stamp upon every copy can be viewed in no other light than that of a tax. In reality, however, the freedom from postage charge is not always accorded to newspapers in return for the newspaper stamp. As an instance of this, in the London district, a circle of three miles round the Post-office, and where the post might be of much use for the distribution of newspapers, a stamped newspaper is charged a penny, if posted in one part of that district to be transmitted to another.

"From the evidence before Your Committee, they consider that the present system of requiring printed matter to be stamped by the Board of Inland Revenue, for the purpose of obtaining a free circulation by post, is open to much objection. Mr. Rowland Hill states (Ev. 1765), that this system is 'unquestionably defective,' and that there is 'a good deal of evasion;' and it is proved to your Committee, that unstamped copies of publications are to a considerable extent carried free, as well as stamped copies. Pointing to Mr. Bokenham's statement (Ev. 1976), 'that from 120,000 to 260,000 newspapers are transmitted daily from the London Post-office,' and that there can be no effectual examination whether each publication is printed on stamped paper or not, without causing great additional expense and delay, it is not difficult to understand why Mr. Bokenham further states (Ev. 1987), 'that the greater portion of the frauds are not detected.'

"If a revenue is to be derived from the postage of newspapers, it would be simpler and more economical that the collection of such revenue should be managed, as in the case of letters, directly by the Post Office, rather than indirectly by another department. Were this

this suggestion adopted, and the present newspaper stamp abolished, Your Committee see no reason to doubt that the Post Office authorities would devise means of regulating the transmission and distribution by post of newspapers, if not of all printed matter, at a small charge not exceeding a penny for each packet, up to a weight equal to that of the largest existing newspaper, without exposing the revenue to the frauds to which the present system unavoidably renders it subject. In passing, it may be right to mention the peculiar use which is sometimes made of the existing privilege of sending papers within the United Kingdom, free from postage charge for ever, in virtue of the original Somerset House stamp. Mr. Parkhurst (Ev. 1677) says, 'We know that newspapers are sent as waste paper very often through the post; there have been cases of very old bundles of papers being sent in that way.'

"On the whole, considering on the one hand the various modes now in use by railways and private agency of distributing newspapers through the country, and on the other, the frauds upon the Post Office from unstamped publications being now unavoidably carried post-free; seeing, in short, that in many cases the stamp is paid where no postal advantages are received, and in other cases the stamp is not paid where postal advantages are obtained, your Committee are of opinion that immediate steps should be taken to place the regulations affecting the transmission of newspapers and other printed matter by post, on a more satisfactory footing.

"In examining witnesses as to the operation of the law on the newspaper press, it is found that an opinion prevails to some small extent, that the maintenance of the stamp has the effect of rendering newspapers more respectable than they would be if free from that restriction. After weighing the reasons for such opinion, your Committee conclude that it does not rest on any good foundation. No deterioration of the newspaper press, but, on the contrary, an improvement followed the reduction of the stamp which took place in 1836; and doubtless the character of newspapers would continue to improve in proportion to the advance in public taste and morals, although the stamp should be entirely abolished. It is stated by one of the witnesses, as an objection to the removal of the stamp, that a new class of journals would spring up, if the stamp were repealed, in the smaller towns and country districts, and that it would be (Ev. 1555) 'a misfortune that there should be local papers of a more petty character than at present exist.' The general bearing of nearly all the other evidence is of a contrary tendency; and the unanimous opinion of those gentlemen who, being persons who had devoted attention to the education and social improvement of the working classes, were specially examined on this branch of the subject, was to the effect that great moral advantages might be expected to follow the establishment of cheap local newspapers.

"Your Committee concur with the proprietor of the 'Liverpool Journal' in thinking that the cheapening the cost of existing provincial papers would extend their circulation and improve their quality; whilst they also believe that, should a new class of small and cheap local papers arise, they would occupy a field hitherto not reached

reached by existing newspapers, and be the vehicles of knowledge to large classes of persons who otherwise would get no newspaper at all. The evidence of Lord Brougham, given when Lord Chancellor, on this branch of the question, is brought under the notice of Your Committee, and in citing the following passage they would at the same time call attention to the whole of that valuable evidence. His Lordship says, 'If a man can have in his cottage, at a cheap rate, accounts of the debates, which they look to with great interest, and which it is their duty as well as their interest to read; the proceedings in courts of justice, which they also are delighted with reading; if in addition to these departments, commonly called the news of the day, we could circulate four pages more, which could all be done for a penny without this pernicious stamp duty, we might give the cottager for one penny a newspaper with wholesome general information, which might be of use to him in various ways, beside giving him all the intelligence of the week. I am quite certain that this would be the effect of repealing the stamp.' 'If instead of newspapers being sold for 6*d.* or 1*s.* they could be sold for a penny, I have no manner of doubt there would immediately follow the greatest possible improvement in the tone and temper of the political information of the people, and therefore of the political character and conduct of the people.' The present extensive sale of penny publications, as shown by the evidence (Ev. 2494 and 2509), abundantly proves the desire among the humbler classes for some kind of reading and mental improvement; but the stamp prevents the penny paper from containing a record of the current events of life, thus depriving the readers of small periodicals, who are for the most part persons living by labour or of limited means, of that most useful knowledge, the news of the day; for which, as is stated by Mr. Abel Heywood, a gentleman extensively engaged in supplying cheap literature, 'as the result of his experience' amongst the class of readers alluded to, there is a greater desire than for any other kind of information. It may be said with truth, that the newspaper stamp prohibits the existence of such newspapers as from their price and character would be suitable to the means and wants of the labouring classes.

"If the newspaper stamp be repealed it appears that 350,000*l.* would be the annual loss to the inland revenue, but a considerable portion of this sum would be restored to the Exchequer by a small postage charge upon such papers as pass through the post.—(Evidence of Mr. Rowland Hill.)

"In conclusion, Your Committee, having been satisfied by evidence of the unfitness of news as a subject for taxation, the inevitable inequality in the application of the Newspaper Stamp Act, the limitation imposed by the stamp on the circulation of the best newspapers, the anomalies and evasions which it occasions in postal arrangements, the impediments which it throws in the way of the diffusion of useful knowledge, its special oppressiveness on the poorer classes in their desire to be acquainted with the occurrences of the day, and its insignificance as a source of revenue, Your Committee recommend the entire repeal of the tax on news, and the adoption of a low postage charge on all printed matter to a certain weight, when the post is used for its transmission and distribution."

 DRAFT

## DRAFT REPORT proposed by Mr. *Rich*.

"YOUR Committee, in obedience to their instructions to inquire into the present state and operation of the law relative to Newspaper Stamps, as well as into the law and regulations relative to the transmission of newspapers and other publications by post, have examined witnesses competent to give information upon both these heads of inquiry.

"Upon the interpretation of the law, and its administration, they have examined the Solicitor and the Assistant Secretary of the Board of Inland Revenue. Upon the transmission of newspapers they have examined the Secretary to the Postmaster-General and the Superintending President of the Inland Office, and two of the principal newspaper agents of London and Manchester. Upon the publication of newspapers, they have examined the Manager of the "Times," the Sub-editor of the "Daily News," and others closely connected with the provincial press; they have also examined various persons generally more or less conversant with the unstamped press, and with educational, temperance and other societies, who entertain strong opinions against the continuance of any tax whatever upon newspapers.

"Before entering on their inquiry, Your Committee think it essential, to a just and comprehensive view of the subject, to compare the general working of the Newspaper Stamp Laws, and the state of public feeling respecting them at present, with that which prevailed prior to the reduction of the duty in 1836 from 4 *d.* to 1 *d.*

"Without going further back than the three years prior to 1836, it abundantly appears that prosecutions for offences against these laws were then exceedingly frequent; and, although very severe penalties and imprisonments were inflicted, that the law was not the less openly set at defiance. This was publicly admitted by the Chancellor of the Exchequer of that day. There was also much general dissatisfaction; frequent motions were made in Parliament; and very numerous petitions from all parts of the kingdom were presented, either for the abolition or reduction of the duty. Meanwhile, the extension of the newspaper press, notwithstanding the vast increase of population and wealth, within the 22 years years since the peace, was scarcely perceptible. On the other hand, since the reduction of duty, prosecutions and penalties have subsided to a mere trifling amount; the circulation of the newspapers in the 15 years which have elapsed, has nearly trebled, and there have been but few hostile petitions. These satisfactory results will be more clearly seen and established by a reference to the following Tables:—

"For OFFENCES against NEWSPAPER STAMP ACTS:

"IMPRISONMENTS.

| | | |
|---|---|---|
| "From March 1834 to Dec. - 1836 | In London, exclusive of Provinces - | 163 |
| "Three years, ending July 1851, in the three Kingdoms - | | 0 |

"PROSECUTIONS.

"PROSECUTIONS.

| | | |
|---|---|---|
| "Three years, ending June | 1836 | 133 |
| ,, - - - ,, - | 1851 | 13 * |

"FINES.

| | | |
|---|---|---|
| "Three years, ending June | 1836 : Fines, highest | £. 620 |
| ,, - - - ,, - | 1851 : Fine, highest | £. 2 |

"PETITIONS.

| | | |
|---|---|---|
| "Year ending June | 1835 | 136 |
| ,, - - | 1836 | 585 |
| "Twelve years - | 1848 | 1 |
| "Year ,, - - | 1849 | 2 |
| ,, - - | 1850 | 14 |
| ,, - - | 1851 | 117 |

"Number of Newspaper Stamps issued in *Great Britain* and *Ireland*.

| | | |
|---|---|---|
| "Year ending March | 1814, at 4 *d.* | 28,788,404 |
| ,, - - - | 1834 ,, | 34,718,922 |
| ,, - - - | 1837, at 1 *d.* and ½ *d.* | 53,897,926 |
| ,, - - - | 1845 ,, | 84,119,770 |
| ,, - - - | 1851 ,, | 91,661,089 |

"There are no means of ascertaining the extent of circulation of the unstamped penny and other cheap publications issued in the form and within the usual periods of newspapers; but all the witnesses who have been examined on the subject attest its enormous and increasing extent, and improved and improving character. Mr. Heywood, a very intelligent publisher and newspaper agent of Manchester, estimated, on data which he submitted to Your Committee, the circulation of these papers in Manchester and its neighbourhood, 18 months ago, at 80,000 a week, and added, 'since then the circulation has in- 2494.
creased very rapidly, and that, with a few specified exceptions, they are most decidedly of a good tendency, and the greatest increase being 2505.
decidedly in the best papers.'

"Bearing this comparative view in mind, Your Committee proceed to report on the present general operation of the law, the inconveniences stated, and the alterations suggested.

"The duty on newspapers is imposed by the Act 6 & 7 Will. 4, c. 76, and is as follows:

"For every sheet or other piece of paper whereon any newspaper shall be printed, 1 *d.*

"A further

* Of these, 6 were stayed.

"A further additional duty of $\frac{1}{2}d.$ and $1d.$ is imposed in case the paper exceeds certain sizes specified in the Act.

"These additional duties are practically, not incurred.

"On supplements not exceeding a certain size, $\frac{1}{2}d.$

"These duties are declared to be payable on—

"1st. Any paper containing public news, intelligence, or occurrences printed in any part of the United Kingdom, to be dispersed and made public.

"2d. Also, any paper printed weekly or oftener, or at intervals not exceeding 26 days, containing only, or principally, advertisements.

"3d. Also, any paper containing any public news, intelligence or occurrence, or any remarks or observations therein, printed for sale, and published periodically, or in parts or numbers, not exceeding 26 days between the publication of any two such papers, parts, or numbers, when any of the said papers, parts, or numbers respectively shall not exceed two sheets of the dimensions specified, or shall be published for sale for a less price than 6*d.*, exclusive of the duty by the Act imposed.

"This last provision is held by the Board of Inland Revenue to apply only to papers containing remarks or observations on public news, intelligence or occurrences.

"The net produce of these duties, in the year 1850, was 350,418*l.*; and, on an average of the years 1848, 1849, and 1850, amounted to 350,545*l.* per annum.

"Some witnesses have complained that the law is not clearly expressed, and that in its interpretation and enforcement a latitude is assumed by the Board of Inland Revenue which exposes newspaper publishers and proprietors to a dangerous uncertainty; but, on the other hand, it has been distinctly stated by the officers of Inland Revenue, that, notwithstanding the subtle distinctions which can be raised with respect to all definitions, they have, under the advice of the Law Officers for the time being of the Crown, and guided by preceding decisions of the law courts, practically found no difficulty in carrying out the law. With the great body of the established newspaper press, there has been hardly even any correspondence; legal proceedings have rarely been resorted to, and then only on comparatively unimportant cases that have arisen from time to time, while the correspondence and discussions with the Board have occurred only with a few individuals who either have sought to obtain the profits of publishing news without the payment of the legal duty, by astutely endeavouring to keep on the very verge of what they consider to be the provisions of the law.

"Your Committee have felt that their instructions scarcely extended to the second class of publications; but with the remaining class they have found a few instances in which the printers of certain papers, published at intervals beyond 26 days dispute the interpreta-

tion

tion given to the law by the Board of Inland Revenue, and one of these cases is now depending before the Court of Exchequer, whose decision will settle the question.

"In the course of this inquiry, some stress has been laid upon a case in which the Board of Inland Revenue is accused of a want of uniformity in its proceedings. In that case, the publisher of a newspaper, the 'Wakefield Examiner,' was visited with a penalty for re-printing, on unstamped paper, a portion of the public intelligence contained in the last number of his newspaper; and it has been asserted by some of the witnesses that such republications occasionally occur on the part of the London newspapers, and that the Board have not prosecuted the parties, as they did in the case of the 'Wakefield Examiner.' In that instance, the penalty imposed was substantially a commutation for the duty on the unstamped copies. In the other cases it is not contended that the infringement of the law was within the knowledge of the Board, and it can scarcely be an imputation upon their proceedings that occasional infringements of the law are committed, but remain undiscovered, or cannot be brought to conviction.

"Stamped newspapers are entitled by law to transmission through the Post-office free of postage; and by a Treasury Minute of 1838, any publication which bears a newspaper stamp is allowed to go free through the Post-office, provided it does not exceed two ounces in weight. The former advantage, which applies strictly to newspapers, is of long standing, and may have been granted as a set-off to the stamp duty. The relative value of this advantage has been maintained by the reductions of charge common both to newspaper stamps and to the carriage of letters.

"If newspapers were subjected to the ordinary rate of postage, they would pay much more than 1 *d.*; and the present duty collected on all the copies, whether sent by the post or not, may, upon the whole, be less than the due charge for postage on the papers actually conveyed by the Post-office.

"Some of the witnesses assert that considerable evasions of the postage charge take place under cover or pretence of stamped newspapers; that letters and unstamped publications and parcels are sent concealed within rolls of stamped newspapers; and that unstamped and foreign newspapers are occasionally passed without being subjected to charge. This is partly admitted by the Post-office autho- 1694.
rities, who attribute much of the evasion to the papers which pass through the Post-office by virtue of the Treasury Minute of 1838; but they deny that there is any systematic fraud, and state their 1748. 1727.
reasons for holding the amount of evasion to be small. 1976. It is clear that in a department transmitting daily from 120,000 to 260,000 papers, and which are despatched within two or three hours after the greater portion of them are received, nothing but an extravagantly large force of examiners could prevent a certain amount of evasion; but it appears advisable to Your Committee that a little more attention should be paid to the examination of papers passing through the Post-office. It appears also worthy of consideration, whether means might

might not be devised for gradually introducing a practice of so folding up separate newspapers as to render the stamp clearly discernible; license being granted to newspaper agents to transmit their papers, as at present, in bulk, on security being given to abide by appointed regulations.

"It has been stated to Your Committee, that if the stamp duty were abolished, a considerable revenue might be derived from charging 1*d.* for every newspaper, exclusive of supplement, transmitted through the Post-office, with an additional 1*d.* for each subsequent re-transmission. Mr. R. Hill was examined at considerable length on this important subject. From a memorandum which he read, it ap-
1823. pears that in May 1850, he estimated the maximum revenue thus to be obtained at 137,500*l.*; but he frankly added, 'I cannot say that I think there is much probability of our ever reaching it.' On further examination he admitted that the Post-office, with all its advantages of establishment and letter deliveries, would be unable to compete with the newspaper agents in the transmission and delivery of newspapers to the great towns and populous districts; he said, 'all they could expect would be the transmission of the old, that is, once-read
1838. papers, and to supply villages and small towns;' thus leaving the
1933. populous, and the profitable to the news-agents, and retaining only the reverse. In order to meet this competition, which, at 1*d.*, he admitted would be hopeless, he stated, that he had endeavoured to devise a plan by which the Post-office might carry and distribute
1909. newspapers at a less price than 1*d.*; but that he found practical difficulties in the way, which rendered it impossible to carry it out; and, although repeatedly urged, he still adhered to this opinion, pointing out that it would be quite open to the public to establish a great
1951. company for the distribution of newspapers.

"There would also, in the event of the adoption of this postage scheme, be thrown on the Post-office the additional delay, labour, and expense incurred for the daily obliteration of the newspaper postage-
2007–8. stamps, which, it is stated, would be considerable.

"Your Committee cannot, therefore, find itself justified in reporting that there would be any surplus revenue worth consideration derivable from this plan of substituting for the present stamp duty a postage charge for all newspapers sent through the Post-office. If such substitution were to be effected, the loss would be probably not less than 300,000*l.* out of the average annual 350,000*l.* now raised.

"This duty is collected at a charge of not more than $1\frac{3}{4}$ per cent.; there is but trifling evasion of payment; very few prosecutions result from it; and, with slight exceptions, there is no dissatisfaction with it expressed, either by the newspaper press or by the public in general; for the 12 years that followed its adoption, there was but one petition presented to Parliament against it. Financially, therefore, this tax appears to be as unobjectionable as any tax can well be.

"It is also to be observed that, while by the reduction of duty in 1836 great public relief was afforded, there was still preserved a small duty which, by the increase of newspapers, now nearly replaces the revenue

revenue then surrendered; but, by the plan proposed, there would be an irrecoverable loss of revenue.

"Some witnesses express strong opinions against the social policy of this tax, viewing it as a bar to the diffusion of useful knowledge and the formation of moral habits amongst the labouring classes. They contend, that were this tax abolished, there would spring up a multitude of 1 *d.* or even ½ *d.* newspapers, full of sound principles and 2366.
attractive intelligence, edited by men of superior intelligence, and 2414.
which would lead on the people to reading and thinking habits. If this were to be the result, Your Committee consider it would be most cheaply purchased at a loss to the revenue of 300,000 *l.*; but they find much reason to pause before they can arrive at so favourable a conclusion. In the first place, they find that the topics which some of these witnesses assert as most attractive, and likely to lead to such beneficial results, are, without specifying them, not those which Your Committee would consider well adapted to improve either the minds or habits of their readers. But without pursuing this subject, Your Committee believe that, generally, the demand, unless strongly checked, governs the supply. In the present healthy state of the periodical press, and of public opinion in respect to it, there are no signs of an obstructed demand. The press seems fully to supply the demand which education creates, and there is much plain good sense in the observation of Mr. Greeley, the publisher of the "New York Tribune," that the schools create a demand for newspapers, rather than that newspapers create a demand for reading.

"More temperate views are entertained by others, who, without speculating on particulars, dwell on the general advantages of competition and cheapness. Your Committee cannot find that the reduction of 3 *d.* on the duty of newspapers in 1836 produced permanently so much as an equivalent reduction in price, nor does their general experience of reductions of duties on other subjects of taxation lead them to believe that the abolition of the present 1 *d.* duty on newspapers would permanently lead to a greater reduction in price than the amount so abolished. Many, if not all, of the present widely circulating and useful unstamped periodicals would undoubtedly insert news in their columns; but this news would, under the most favourable view, necessarily be meagre, and copied (that is pirated), or referable to chance local topics which are soon exhausted; so that these publications would never be able, as newspapers, to sustain any real competition with the great established newspaper press, whether metropolitan or provincial. There may be some reasonable doubt whether this insertion of news would, in the long-run, add either to the circulation or character of the unstamped press. There is far less doubt that the immoral portion of it would profit largely by the stimulus which articles, such as it would not hesitate to insert, would afford to its readers.

"It will be found that the witnesses do not recommend an abolition of the precautions which have long been enforced against the publication of private or public libels in newspapers, by requiring a registration of the names and abodes of the several publishers and proprietors,

proprietors, as well as the guarantee of sureties, to a definite amount, for the payment of fines or costs in the event of conviction. These precautions would evidently become more urgent in the extended field proposed to be opened, and they might, perhaps, be felt by some parties to be more onerous and vexatious than the privilege of publishing (but not transmitting) news, stamp free, was found to be remunerative. All the witnesses conversant with the newspaper press who have advocated the abolition of the stamp duty, have admitted the necessity for some legal protection against piracy; and this, too, might be found more oppressive to the weaker portions of the newspaper press, and more fruitful in misconception, evasion and litigation than the present duty. In either of these cases the same necessity for an indisputable legal definition of news, newspapers, &c., which now constitutes one of the principal objections raised by the witnesses against the duty, would still remain.

"Your Committee also have some grounds for questioning the undoubting assumption of cheapness which is entertained by most of these witnesses, if cheapness be taken as a measure of value received. Two very intelligent gentlemen connected with the London press declared that a leading English daily newspaper was, at its price, and for its contents, (regard being paid to their amount, their rapid conveyance, their variety, and the authentic and often remote and costly sources of its intelligence), cheaper than any of the cheap papers of France, or of the United States. The practical effect, also, of the stamp in lowering the cost of newspapers, by its right of gratuitous re-transmission, is a consideration of great importance. Mr. Smith, the head of a London newspaper agency firm, which
2813. has been established for the last 60 years, and which transmits
2832. about one-seventh of all the London daily papers, states distinctly that the re-transmission of newspapers is carried on to a most enormous extent, so as greatly to reduce the cost of their newspaper to those least able to pay for it. He gives instances in which the cost of the "Times" is thus reduced to 2*d.*, and to even 1*d.*, and yet read
2840. by the last person in the series on the second morning after publication, and he adds, that the number of persons thus receiving the best newspapers at a very cheap rate, is exceedingly numerous, and that the proposed charge of 1*d.* for each re-transmission would, in fact, prevent them, probably, from taking any paper at all, unless it was a weekly paper. In support of the prevalence of this systematic and
2848. cheapening circulation of newspapers, Mr. Smith states his belief, that most of the newspapers published in London ultimately pass through the post; and he rates the average transmission at two or three times. If this be so, then the average cost of the "Times" and other London daily newspapers to those to whom the price is of importance need not be more than 2*d.* The same process of reduction of price, by means of association and of re-transmission through the Post-office, applies to all other papers whatever, whether metropolitan or provincial, that have the privilege, by means of the 1*d.* stamp, of passing free through the Post-office.

"It does not therefore appear to Your Committee that this 1*d.* stamp does act as an impediment to the diffusion of knowledge, but, by by its practical working, becomes rather a vehicle by which the earliest and most authentic intelligence, together with opinions of all shades, is with the utmost regularity disseminated at an equable and extremely low price to every remotest corner of the empire; by which, in fact, the choice of the very best papers, at a very low price, is placed at the command of every one, without respect to distance or locality. This appears to involve the very substance and reality of competition. Great as is the number of associated readers now, their numbers, as speed and facilities of communication spread, will be still more multiplied; and it is worthy of remark that this multiplication of readers is obtained without any, or at the most trifling increase of expense in the production of the article read.

"Your Committee having found that a net revenue exceeding 350,000*l.* a year is raised by the 1*d.* stamp on newspapers, at an exceedingly low rate of collection, and that it is accompanied by a great advantage to the public, and more especially to the poorer classes; that the evil symptoms which characterised the period of the high rate of duty on newspapers have gradually and steadily disappeared after its reduction to 1*d.*; and, finally, that the periodical press, both stamped and unstamped, is steadily and rapidly improving in tone, character, ability, and circulation; that, in fact, it stands almost unquestionably and pre-eminently high, not only within this country, but throughout the world; cannot admit that any sufficient facts have been proved, or sufficiently matured plan proposed by the witnesses that have appeared before them to authorize their recommending the sacrifice of nearly the whole of the revenue thus raised, by changes which might also unsettle a state of things so promising and so beneficial.

"Your Committee believe that the extension of education, and the augmented share and interest taken in public affairs by the great industrial classes of the community, and the growing attention paid by successive administrations to their welfare, have tended, in conjunction with the increase of wealth and population, to this satisfactory progress of the periodical press, and multiplication of its readers. It is to these approved sources, rather than to financial experiments, that Your Committee confidently look to a still greater and more rapid increase and improvement.

"Before closing this Report, Your Committee would refer to a practice which appears for some while to have prevailed, of registering various publications that are not in strictness newspapers, with a view to the transmission of a portion of them through the post stamped, and therefore free, the remaining portion, intended for local circulation, not being stamped. It also appears that prices current, catalogues and similar papers, having no pretensions whatever to the character of newspapers, are registered as such, for the purpose of obtaining stamps on which these matters are printed, also for transmission through the post.

"The publishers of the former description of papers, by printing a portion of the copies without stamps, admit that they are not newspapers; and the fact, as Your Committee understand, is really so; and

and such being the case, they are not by law entitled to the free transmission of the stamped copies through the Post-office. In both instances, the advantage derived from the newspaper stamp appears to be a privilege which is liable to abuse, and requires revision. It appears that the Board of Inland Revenue have no authority to prevent any person from registering a paper as a newspaper, or to refuse stamping blank paper for the person so registering. There are, therefore, no means of preventing this abuse in that department; but the Postmaster-general has, in conjunction with the Treasury, a power under an Act of Parliament of determining whether a paper professing to be a newspaper is really so or not, and therefore in both the cases mentioned it is competent to the Post-office to refuse free transmission to the stamped papers mentioned, and to charge them as letters. Whether it would be desirable to exercise this power, or to enact, that any paper registered as a newspaper should be deemed and taken to be one, whatever might be its contents, and that all its copies should be stamped, may be subject for consideration; but it appears to Your Committee that the present irregularities and evasions cause discontent, and require correction."

Question, "That the Draft Report prepared by the *Chairman* be read a second time, paragraph by paragraph," put. Committee divided:

| Ayes, 6. | Noes, 4. |
|---|---|
| Mr. Shafto Adair. | Mr. Rich. |
| Sir J. Walmsley. | Mr. Sotheron. |
| Mr. G. A. Hamilton. | Mr. Tufnell. |
| Mr. Cobden. | Mr. Stafford. |
| Mr. C. Fortescue. | |
| Mr. Ewart. | |

The Committee proceeded to read the Chairman's Draft Report.

First and second paragraphs read and agreed to.

Paragraph beginning "Upon the interpretation" read, amended, and agreed to.

Motion made (Mr. *Rich*):—"Before entering on their inquiry, Your Committee think it essential, to a just and comprehensive view of the subject, to compare the general working of the Newspaper Stamp Laws, and the state of public feeling respecting them at present, with that which prevailed prior to the reduction of the duty in 1836 from 4*d.* to 1*d.*" Question, "That those words be there inserted," put. Committee divided:

| Ayes, 3. | Noes, 7. |
|---|---|
| Mr. Rich. | Mr. Shafto Adair. |
| Mr. Tufnell. | Mr. Sotheron. |
| Mr. Stafford. | Sir Josh. Walmsley. |
| | Mr. G. A. Hamilton. |
| | Mr. Cobden. |
| | Mr. C. Fortescue. |
| | Mr. Ewart. |

Motion

Motion made (Mr. *G. A. Hamilton*), "The duty on newspapers is imposed by the Act 6 & 7 Will. 4, c. 76, and is as follows:

"For every sheet or other piece of paper whereon any newspaper shall be printed, 1 *d.*

"A further additional duty of ½ *d.* and 1 *d.* is imposed in case the paper exceeds certain sizes specified in the Act.

"These additional duties are, practically, not incurred.

"On supplements not exceeding a certain size, ½ *d.*

"These duties are declared to be payable on—

"1st. Any paper containing public news, intelligence, or occurrences printed in any part of the United Kingdom, to be dispersed and made public.

"2d. Also, any paper printed weekly or oftener, or at intervals not exceeding 26 days, containing only, or principally, advertisements.

"3d. Also, any paper containing any public news, intelligence, or occurrence, or any remarks or observations therein, printed for sale and published periodically, or in parts or numbers, not exceeding 26 days between the publication of any two such papers, parts, or numbers, when any of the said papers, parts, or numbers respectively shall not exceed two sheets of the dimensions specified, or shall be published for sale for a less price than 6 *d.*, exclusive of the duty by the Act imposed."

Question put and agreed to.

Motion made (Mr. *Rich*), "The nèt produce of these duties in the year 1850 was 350,418 *l.*; and, on an average of the years 1848, 1849, and 1850, amounted to 350,545 *l.* per annum." Question put and agreed to.

Paragraph beginning "With regard to," read. Amendments made.

Another amendment proposed (Mr. *Rich*), to leave out the words after "stamp," down to "prosecute him."

[Adjourned till Wednesday next, at half-past Eleven o'clock.

---

*Mercurii*, 16° *die Julii*, 1851.

Present:

Right Hon. T. MILNER GIBSON, in the Chair.

| | |
|---|---|
| Mr. Shafto Adair. | Mr. G. A. Hamilton. |
| Mr. Rich. | Mr. Ewart. |
| Mr. Cobden. | Mr. Sotheron. |
| Sir J. Walmsley. | Mr. Stafford. |
| Mr. Tufnell. | |

Paragraph beginning "With regard to." Amendment proposed by Mr. *Rich*, at the last sitting of the Committee, by leave, withdrawn. Question, "That the paragraph as amended stand part of the Report," put and agreed to.

Paragraphs down to the paragraph beginning "Having regard," read, amended, and agreed to.

Paragraph beginning with "Having regard" read. Question, "That this paragraph stand part of the Report," put and negatived. Paragraph struck out.

Motion made (Mr. *Rich*) and question proposed, "That having stated these instances of irregularities, chiefly alleged by witnesses who have been involved in discussions with the Board of Inland Revenue, or by the Secretary to an Association for the Abolition of Taxes on Knowledge, Your Committee consider it to be their duty to report, that on the other hand it has been distinctly stated by the officers of inland revenue, that notwithstanding the subtle distinctions which can be raised with respect to all definitions, they have, under the advice of the law officers for the time being of the Crown, practically found no difficulty in carrying out the law. With the great body of the established newspaper press there has been hardly ever any correspondence; legal proceedings have rarely been resorted to."

Amendment to the question proposed (Mr. *Shafto Adair*), to leave out all the words after "That," in order to insert the following words: "Your Committee conceive that, inasmuch as offences against the Newspaper Stamp Act are committed in consequence of the uncertainty in the administration of the law, while the punishment, if conviction ensue, is so disproportionate to the offence, that the full penalty neither is nor can be exacted. The Board of Inland Revenue, although exercising its authority with great moderation, is the depositary of a power which is opposed to sound principles of public policy, as being alike arbitrary and inefficient."

Question, "That the words proposed to be left out stand part of the question," put. Committee divided:

Ayes,

| Ayes, 4. | Noes, 5. |
|---|---|
| Mr. Rich. | Mr. Shafto Adair. |
| Mr. Sotheron. | Sir J. Walmsley. |
| Mr. Tufnell. | Mr. Cobden. |
| Mr. Stafford. | Mr. G. A. Hamilton. |
| | Mr. Ewart. |

Words struck out.

Question, "That the proposed words be added," put. Committee divided:

| Ayes, 4. | Noes, 5. |
|---|---|
| Mr. Shafto Adair. | Mr. Rich. |
| Sir J. Walmsley. | Mr. Sotheron. |
| Mr. Cobden. | Mr. G. A. Hamilton. |
| Mr. Ewart. | Mr. Tufnell. |
| | Mr. Stafford. |

Paragraph beginning, "With regard to," read, amended, and agreed to.

Paragraph beginning, "Some opinions," read, amended, and agreed to.

Paragraph beginning, "It is stated," read. Several amendments made.

Another amendment proposed (Mr. *Tufnell*), to leave out the words, "as an instance of this," in order to insert the words, "Your Committee think it right to advert to an anomaly that exists with regard to the transmission of newspapers by post, viz., that." Question, "That the words proposed to be left out stand part of the paragraph," put. Committee divided:

| Ayes, 2. | Noes, 4. |
|---|---|
| Mr. G. A. Hamilton. | Mr. Shafto Adair. |
| Mr. Cobden. | Mr. Sotheron. |
| | Mr. Tufnell. |
| | Mr. Stafford. |

Words struck out.

Question, "That the proposed words be there inserted," put, and agreed to.

Another amendment proposed (Mr. *Tufnell*), to add at end of the paragraph the words, "Your Committee do not see any good reason for this regulation, and would therefore recommend that it be abolished." Question, "That those words be there added," put, and agreed to.

Question, "That the paragraph, as amended, stand part of the Report," put, and agreed to.

 Paragraph

Paragraph beginning, "From the evidence," read. Question, "That this paragraph stand part of the Report," put. Committee divided:

| Ayes, 4. | Noes, 5. |
|---|---|
| Mr. Shafto Adair. | Mr. Rich. |
| Sir J. Walmsley. | Mr. Sotheron. |
| Mr. Cobden. | Mr. G. A. Hamilton. |
| Mr. Ewart. | Mr. Tufnell. |
| | Mr. Stafford. |

Paragraph struck out.

Motion made (Mr. *Rich*), and question proposed, "Your Committee find that considerable evasions of the postage charge take place under cover or pretence of stamped newspapers; that letters and unstamped publications and parcels are sent concealed within rolls of stamped newspapers; and that unstamped and foreign newspapers are occasionally passed without being subjected to charge. This is partly admitted by the Post-office authorities, who attribute much of the evasion to the papers which pass through the Post-office by virtue of the Treasury Minute of 1838. It is clear that in a department transmitting daily from 120,000 to 260,000 papers, and which are despatched within two or three hours after the greater portion of them are received, nothing but an extravagantly large force of examiners could prevent evasion; but it appears advisable to Your Committee that more attention should be paid to the examination of papers passing through the Post-office."

Amendment to the question proposed (Mr. *Sotheron*), to leave out from "It is clear," down to "evasion." Question, "That the words proposed to be left out stand part of the question," put. Committee divided;

| Ayes, 5. | Noes, 4. |
|---|---|
| Mr. Rich. | Mr. Shafto Adair. |
| Mr. Ewart. | Mr. Sotheron. |
| Mr. G. A. Hamilton. | Sir J. Walmsley. |
| Mr. Tufnell. | Mr. Cobden. |
| Mr. Stafford. | |

Another amendment to the question proposed (Mr. *Ewart*), to leave out the words from "evasion" to the end of the question. Question, "That the words proposed to be left out stand part of the question," put and negatived."

Words struck out.

Main question, as amended, put and agreed to.

[Adjourned till Friday next, at Twelve o'clock.

*Veneris*, 18° *die Julii*, 1851.

Present:

Right Hon. T. MILNER GIBSON, in the Chair.

| | |
|---|---|
| Mr. Ewart. | Mr. Rich. |
| Sir J. Walmsley. | Mr. Cobden. |
| Mr. G. A. Hamilton. | Mr. Stafford. |
| Mr. Shafto Adair. | Mr. Sotheron. |
| Mr. Tufnell. | |

Paragraph beginning "If a revenue," read. Amendments made. Question, "That the paragraph stand part of the Report," put. Committee divided:

| Ayes, 4. | Noes, 3. |
|---|---|
| Mr. Shafto Adair. | Mr. Rich. |
| Mr. G. A. Hamilton. | Mr. Sotheron. |
| Mr. Cobden. | Mr. Stafford. |
| Mr. Ewart. | |

Motion made (Mr. *G. A. Hamilton*), "There is however a consideration connected with the additional cost supposed to be caused by the imposition of the stamp on newspapers, which requires a particular notice, viz., the right of gratuitous re-transmission of newspapers through post. Mr. Smith, the head of a London newspaper agency firm, which has been established for the last 60 years, and which transmits about one-seventh of all the London daily papers, states distinctly that the re-transmission of newspapers is carried on to a considerable extent, so as greatly to reduce the cost of their newspaper to those least able to pay for it. He gives instances in which the cost of the "Times" is thus reduced to 2 *d.*, and to even 1 *d.*, and yet read by the last person in the series on the second morning after publication, and he adds, that the number of persons thus receiving the best newspapers at a very cheap rate, is exceedingly numerous, and that the proposed charge of 1 *d.* for each re-transmission would, in fact, prevent them, probably, from taking any paper at all, unless it was a weekly paper." Question put and agreed to.

Paragraphs down to "Your Committee concur," read and agreed to.

Paragraph beginning "Your Committee concur," read. Amendment proposed (Mr. *Rich*), to omit the words from "newspaper at all" down to "the present." Question, "That those words stand part of the paragraph," put and negatived. Words struck out.

Question, "That the paragraph, as amended, stand part of the Report," put and agreed to.

 Motion

Motion made (Mr. *Rich*), and question proposed, "That there have been submitted to Your Committee the legal provisions against the publication of private or public libels in newspapers, by requiring a registration of the names and abodes of the several publishers and proprietors, as well as the guarantee of sureties, to a definite amount, for the payment of fines or costs in the event of conviction. The necessity for these precautions would evidently become more urgent in the extended field proposed to be opened by the abolition of the stamp duties. In this case the same necessity for an indisputable legal definition of news, newspapers, &c., which now constitutes one of the principal objections raised by the witnesses against the duty, would still remain."

Amendment to the question proposed (Mr. *Adair*), to leave out all the words after "That" in order to add the words, "It having appeared to Your Committee that they are precluded by the order of reference from considering the questions of registration of newspapers, of the copyright of intelligence, of advertisement duty, and of the excise duty on paper, they do not report thereon."

Question, "That the words proposed to be left out stand part of the question," put. Committee divided:

| Ayes, 2. | Noes, 5. |
|---|---|
| Mr. Rich. | Mr. Shafto Adair. |
| Mr. Stafford. | Mr. Sotheron. |
| | Mr. G. A. Hamilton. |
| | Mr. Cobden. |
| | Mr. Ewart. |

Words struck out.

Question, "That the proposed words be added," put. Committee divided:

| Aye, 1. | Noes, 6. |
|---|---|
| Mr. Shafto Adair. | Mr. Rich. |
| | Mr. Sotheron. |
| | Mr. G. A. Hamilton. |
| | Mr. Cobden. |
| | Mr. Stafford. |
| | Mr. Ewart. |

Motion made (Mr. *Rich*), "That the question of pirating articles of intelligence by one newspaper from another has been brought under the notice of Your Committee by witnesses conversant with the newspaper press, and favourable to the abolition of the duty. The established newspapers, particularly the London daily press, collect the valuable information which they report to the public at a very great expense, and publish it at a very costly celerity. It has been stated, that if the newspaper duty were abolished, there would be great temptation to the numerous halfpenny and penny publications which would then spring up to pirate the public intelligence collected at so much cost and exertion. It has been proposed that some short privilege of copyright should therefore be conferred." Question put. Committee divided:

Ayes,

| Ayes, 6. | Noes, 3. |
|---|---|
| Mr. Rich. | Mr. Shafto Adair. |
| Mr. Sotheron. | Mr. Cobden. |
| Sir J. Walmsley. | Mr. Ewart. |
| Mr. G. A. Hamilton. | |
| Mr. Tufnell. | |
| Mr. Stafford. | |

Paragraph beginning with "If the newspaper," read. Question, "That this paragraph stand part of the Report," put and negatived. Paragraph struck out.

Paragraph beginning, "In conclusion," read. Amendment proposed, (Mr. *Rich*), to leave out all the words after "In conclusion," in order to add the words:—"Your Committee having found that a net revenue exceeding 350,000 *l.* a year is raised by the penny stamp on newspapers, at an exceedingly low rate of collection, and that it is accompanied by advantage to the public, and more especially to the poorer classes; that the evil symptoms which characterised the period of the high rate of duty on newspapers have gradually and steadily disappeared after its reduction to 1 *d.*; and, finally, that the periodical press, both stamped and unstamped, is steadily and rapidly improving in tone, character, ability and circulation; that, in fact, it stands almost unquestionably and pre-eminently high, not only within this country, but throughout the world; cannot report that any sufficient facts have been proved, or sufficiently matured plan proposed by the witnesses that have appeared before them to authorize their recommending the sacrifice of nearly the whole of the revenue thus raised, by changes which might also unsettle a state of things so promising and so beneficial. Your Committee believe that the extension of education, and the augmented share and interest taken in public affairs by the great industrial classes of the community, and the growing attention paid by successive administrations to their welfare, have tended, in conjunction with the increase of wealth and population, to this satisfactory progress of the periodical press, and multiplication of its readers. It is to these approved sources, rather than to financial experiments, that Your Committee confidently look to a still greater and more rapid increase and improvement."

Question, "That the words proposed to be left out stand part of the paragraph," put. Committee divided:

| Ayes, 4. | Noes, 5. |
|---|---|
| Mr. Shafto Adair. | Mr. Rich. |
| Sir J. Walmsley. | Mr. Sotheron. |
| Mr. Cobden. | Mr. G. A. Hamilton. |
| Mr. Ewart. | Mr. Tufnell. |
| | Mr. Stafford. |

Words struck out.

Question, "That the proposed words be added," put. Committee divided:



Ayes,

| Ayes, 3. | Noes, 6. |
|---|---|
| Mr. Rich. | Mr. Shafto Adair. |
| Mr. Tufnell. | Mr. Sotheron. |
| Mr. Stafford. | Sir J. Walmsley. |
| | Mr. G. A. Hamilton. |
| | Mr. Cobden. |
| | Mr. Ewart. |

Another amendment proposed (Mr. *G. A. Hamilton*), to add the following words: "Your Committee consider it their duty to direct attention to the objections and inconveniences incident to the present system of newspaper stamps, arising from the difficulty of defining and determining the meaning of the term 'news;' to the inequalities which exist in the application of the Newspaper Stamp Act, and the anomalies and evasions that it occasions in postal arrangements; to the unfair competition to which stamped newspapers are exposed with unstamped publications; to the limitation imposed by the stamp upon the circulation of the best newspapers, and to the impediments which it throws in the way of the diffusion of useful knowledge regarding current and recent events among the poorer classes, which species of knowledge relating to subjects which most obviously interest them, call out the intelligence by awakening the curiosity of those classes. How far it may be expedient that this tax should be maintained as a source of revenue, either in its present or in any modified form, Your Committee do not feel themselves called upon to state; other considerations, not within their province, would enter into that question." Question, "That those words be added," put, and agreed to. Words added.

Another amendment proposed (Mr. *Cobden*), to add the following words; "But, apart from fiscal considerations, they do not consider that news is in itself a desirable object of taxation." Question, "That those words be added," put, and agreed to. Words added.

Question, "That the paragraph, as amended, stand part of the Report," put, and agreed to.

Question, "That this be the Report of the Committee," put, and agreed to.

Chairman ordered to report.

EXPENSES

## EXPENSES OF WITNESSES.

| NAME of WITNESS. | PROFESSION or CONDITION. | By what Member of Committee Motion made for Attendance of the Witness. | Date of Arrival. | Date of Discharge. | Total Number of Days in London. | Number of Days under Examination by Committee, or acting specially under their Orders. | Expenses of Journey to London and back. | Expenses in London. | TOTAL Expenses allowed to Witness. |
|---|---|---|---|---|---|---|---|---|---|
| | | | | | | | £. s. d. | £. s. d. | £. s. d. |
| S. G. Bucknall - | - - Editor of a newspaper. | Chairman | 15 May | 16 May | 2 | 1 | 1 12 - | 2 2 - | 3 14 - |
| H. Watkinson - | Ditto - - | Ditto - | 16 May | 30 May | 6 | 1 | 3 13 6 | 6 6 - | 9 19 6 |
| Abel Heywood - | Publisher, &c. | Ditto - | 30 May | 31 May | 2 | 1 | 4 - - | 2 2 - | 6 2 - |
| C. J. Bunting - | Printer - - | Ditto - | 13 May | 14 May | 2 | 1 | 1 1 - | 2 2 - | 3 3 - |
| | | | | | | | TOTAL - - - £. | | 22 18 6 |

LIST

# LIST OF WITNESSES.

# MINUTES OF EVIDENCE.

*Veneris*, 2° *die Maii*, 1851.

MEMBERS PRESENT.

Mr. Ewart.
Mr. Cobden.
Sir J. Walmsley.
Mr. Rich.
Mr. G. A. Hamilton.
Mr. Stafford.
Mr. Sotheron.
Mr. Tufnell.

THE RIGHT HON. THOMAS MILNER GIBSON,
IN THE CHAIR.

*Joseph Timm*, Esq., was called in; and Examined.

*J. Timm*, Esq.

2 May 1851.

1. *Chairman.*] WHAT situation do you hold under the Board of Inland Revenue?—I am Solicitor to the Board of Inland Revenue.

2. Is the control or superintendence in reference to the stamping of newspapers in your department?—Not the control or superintendence exactly; but parties before they can obtain stamps for the printing of a newspaper must come to my office and enter into certain securities against libels, and also make a declaration as to the parties who are the printers, publishers, and proprietors of the paper.

3. The whole of the business connected with the stamping of newspapers is within your knowledge, is it not, from the office which you hold under the Board of Inland Revenue? —The preliminary proceedings, not the actual stamping.

4. Will you be good enough to refer the Committee to the Acts of Parliament that regulate your proceedings?—Yes; the principal Act is the 6 & 7 of Will. 4, c. 76, which imposes the present stamp duty of one penny upon newspapers, and



a halfpenny

*J. Timm*, Esq.

2 May 1851.

a halfpenny upon supplements. The first section of that Act imposes duties upon newspapers, contained in Schedule (A.) annexed to it. In that schedule there are not only the duties, but the definitions of what in law are to be deemed newspapers. The first is, "Any paper containing public news, intelligence, or occurrences printed in any part of the United Kingdom to be dispersed and made public:" "Also any paper printed in any part of the United Kingdom, weekly or oftener, or at intervals not exceeding 26 days, containing only or principally advertisements:" "And also any paper containing any public news, intelligence, or occurrences, or any remarks or observations thereon, printed in any part of the United Kingdom for sale, and published periodically or in parts or numbers, at intervals not exceeding 26 days between the publication of any two such papers, parts, or numbers, where any of the said papers, parts, or numbers respectively shall not exceed two sheets of the dimensions hereinafter specified (exclusive of any cover or blank leaf, or any other leaf upon which any advertisement or other notice shall be printed), or shall be published for sale for a less sum than sixpence, exclusive of the duty by this Act imposed thereon: provided always, that no quantity of paper less than a quantity equal to 21 inches in length and 17 inches in breadth, in whatever way or form the same may be made, or may be divided into leaves, or in whatever way the same may be printed, shall, with reference to any such paper, part, or number as aforesaid, be deemed or taken to be a sheet of paper: and provided also, that any of the several papers hereinbefore described shall be liable to the duties by this Act imposed thereon, in whatever way or form the same may be printed, or folded or divided into leaves, or stitched, and whether the same shall be folded, divided, or stitched, or not." Then there are exemptions: "Any paper called 'Police Gazette, or Hue and Cry,' published in Great Britain by authority of the Secretary of State, or in Ireland by the authority of the Lord Lieutenant; daily accounts, or bills of goods imported and exported, or warrants or certificates for the delivery of goods, and the weekly bills of mortality; and also papers containing any lists of prices current, or of the state of the markets, or any account of the arrival, sailing, or other circumstances relating to merchant ships or vessels, or any other matter wholly of a commercial nature, provided such bills, lists, or accounts do not contain any other matter than what hath been usually comprised therein." The third section directs that the Commissioners

*J. Timm,* Esq.

2 May 1851.

missioners of Stamps and Taxes (now the Commissioners of Inland Revenue), "shall cause a proper die for stamping each such newspaper to be prepared under their directions, and a new or other die to be from time to time prepared, in like manner as they shall think necessary; and the reasonable costs and expenses of preparing such stamps or dies shall be from time to time defrayed by the proprietor of each such newspaper, and paid when and as required by the said Commissioners to such person as the said Commissioners shall appoint to receive the same, before any paper shall be stamped under the directions of such Commissioners for each such newspaper; and that from and after the 31st day of December next after the passing of this Act no newspaper liable to duty under this Act shall be printed upon paper not stamped with such die, containing the title of such newspaper, or some part thereof as aforesaid; and if any newspaper shall be printed on paper stamped otherwise than as aforesaid, the stamp thereon shall be of no avail, and such newspaper shall be deemed to be not duly stamped." Section 4 declares that the newspapers mentioned in the schedule shall be subject to the regulations of this Act; and that it shall be sufficient to describe any such paper as is contained in this schedule by the word "newspaper." Section 5 directs that certain particulars shall be printed on papers that are sold as supplements to the newspapers; that they should contain the word "supplement." Then section 6 enacts, "that no person shall print or publish, or shall cause to be printed or published, any newspaper before there shall be delivered to the Commissioners of Stamps and Taxes, or to the proper authorized officer at the head office for stamps in Westminster, Edinburgh, or Dublin respectively, or to the distributor of stamps or other proper officer appointed by the said Commissioners for the purpose in or for the district within which such newspaper shall be intended to be printed and published, a declaration in writing, containing the several matters and things hereinafter for that purpose specified; that is to say, every such declaration shall set forth the correct title of the newspaper to which the same shall relate, and the true description of the house or building wherein such newspaper is intended to be printed, and also of the house or building wherein such newspaper is intended to be published, by or for or on behalf of the proprietor thereof, and shall also set forth the true name, addition, and place of abode of every person who is intended to be the printer, or to conduct the actual printing of such newspaper, and of



every

*J. Timm,* Esq.

2 May 1851.

every person who is intended to be the publisher thereof, and of every person who shall be a proprietor of such newspaper who shall be resident out of the United Kingdom, and also of every person resident in the United Kingdom who shall be a proprietor of the same, if the number of such last-mentioned persons (exclusive of the printer and publisher) shall not exceed two; and in case such numbers shall exceed two, then of such two persons, being such proprietors resident in the United Kingdom, the amount of whose respective proportional shares in the property, or in the profit or loss of such newspaper, shall not be less than the proportional share of any other proprietor thereof resident in the United Kingdom, exclusive of the printer and publisher; and also where the number of such proprietors resident in the United Kingdom shall exceed two, the amount of the proportional shares or interests of such several proprietors whose names shall be specified in such declaration; and every such declaration shall be made and signed by every person named therein as printer or publisher of the newspaper to which such declaration shall relate, and by such of the said persons named therein as proprietors as shall be resident within the United Kingdom; and a declaration of the like import shall be made, signed, and delivered in like manner whenever and so often as any share, interest, or property soever in any newspaper named in any such declaration shall be assigned, transferred, divided, or changed by act of the parties or by operation of law, so that the respective proportional shares or interests of the persons named in any such declaration as proprietors of such newspaper, or either of them, shall respectively become less than the proportional share or interest of any other proprietor thereof, exclusive of the printer and publisher; and also whenever and so often as any printer, publisher, or proprietor named in any such declaration, or the person conducting the actual printing of the newspaper named in any such declaration, shall be changed or shall change his place of abode, and also whenever and so often as the title of any such newspaper, or the printing-office, or the place of publication thereof, shall be changed, and also whenever in any case, or on any occasion, or for any purpose, the said Commissioners, or any officer of stamp duties authorised in that behalf, shall require such declaration to be made, signed, and delivered, and shall cause notice in writing for that purpose to be served upon any person, or to be left or posted at any place mentioned in the last preceding declaration delivered as aforesaid, as being a printer,

J. Timm, Esq.

2 May 1851.

printer, publisher, or proprietor of such newspaper, or as being the place of printing or publishing any such newspaper respectively; and every such declaration shall be made before any one or more of the said Commissioners, or before any officer of stamp duties or other person appointed by the said Commissioners, either generally or specially in that behalf; and such Commissioners or any one of them, and such officer or other person, are and is hereby severally and respectively authorised to take and receive such declaration as aforesaid; and if any person shall knowingly and wilfully sign and make any such declaration in which shall be inserted or set forth the name, addition, or place of abode of any person as a proprietor, publisher, printer, or conductor of the actual printing of any newspaper to which such declaration shall relate, who shall not be a proprietor, printer, or publisher thereof, or from which shall be omitted the name, addition, or place of abode of any proprietor, publisher, printer, or conductor, of the actual printing of such newspaper, contrary to the true meaning of this Act, or in which any matter or thing by this Act required to be set forth shall be set forth otherwise than according to the truth, or from which any matter or thing required by this Act to be truly set forth shall be entirely omitted, every such offender being convicted thereof shall be deemed guilty of a misdemeanor."

5. Will you just refer the Committee to the Acts of Parliament, and state the points without reading the whole in detail?—The 7th section imposes a penalty of 50 *l.* upon any person who shall print and publish a newspaper before such declaration has been made and delivered. The 8th section directs that the declaration shall be filed, and that certified copies thereof shall be admitted in evidence against the parties who have signed the same in all courts, and on all occasions whatsoever; and that after the production of a newspaper bearing the same title as that specified in the declaration, it shall be evidence against the parties named in that declaration as the printer and publisher of it. Then the 11th section directs that the printers and publishers of a newspaper shall give security for the payment of the advertisement duty, by bond with sufficient sureties, to the satisfaction of the Commissioners of Stamps and Taxes. The 13th section directs that copies of newspapers shall be delivered to the Commissioners of Stamps and Taxes by the printer for the purpose of assessing the advertisement duty, and also for the purpose of being filed as evidence. The 14th section requires the names and additions and places of abode

*J. Timm,* Esq.

2 May 1851.

abode of the printers and publishers, and also the places of printing and publishing, to be printed upon the newspapers. The 15th section enacts that none but the Commissioners of Stamps and Taxes, or their officer, shall supply stamped paper for printing newspapers upon, without having given security that they will not supply any parties who have not previously registered a newspaper at the Stamp Office, and thereby entitled themselves to receive stamps for the newspaper. The 17th section imposes a penalty of 20 *l.* upon every person printing or publishing or selling unstamped newspapers, a penalty of 20 *l.* every copy. There are other clauses, but not at all bearing upon the practice. I may mention that "a printed copy of every pamphlet or paper containing advertisements" is also to be delivered to the Commissioners of Stamps, that they may assess the duty upon the advertisements contained in it. Section 22 authorises justices of the peace, upon information on oath of a suspicion that newspapers are printed without being stamped, to grant a search warrant, and under that warrant if unstamped newspapers are found, the printing engines and machines may be seized, and shall be condemned as forfeited. Section 24 provides that persons who are possessed of printing presses may give notice to the Commissioners that they print certain publications, specifying the title thereof, if there be any doubt about their being newspapers, and then no prosecution shall be instituted against them, nor shall their presses be forfeited for printing these publications without stamps until they have received notice that such publications are newspapers.

6. *Chairman.*] You mean those that have registered themselves, I presume?—The persons who print publications about which they may have some doubt as to whether they are newspapers liable to the stamp duty or not, but who conceive that they are not liable, may give notice to the Commissioners, and send those publications to them, and then they shall not be prosecuted for printing any of such papers without the stamp, nor incur any penalty until the Commissioners have given them notice that any such paper is liable to the duty.

7. Mr. *Cobden.*] Are they all liable to penalties if they do not send a copy of their publication?—Yes; any person in that case who prints a paper liable to stamp duty as a newspaper unstamped, incurs a penalty of 20 *l.* for every copy.

8. He is liable to that penalty for all the copies he has printed previously to the time you make the discovery that he has done so?—Yes, for every copy; but of course no penalty

*J. Timm*, Esq.

2 May 1851.

penalty can be recovered beyond the copies which the Board may have in their possession, and be able to give in evidence.

9. As I understand you, parties are bound to send to the Board a printed copy of every periodical that they may issue, or if they fail to do that, then you hold them responsible for publishing unwittingly a newspaper; but if they do send you a copy, and you do not give them a notice that it is a newspaper, then they may go on, and are not liable for any penalties until the time that you give them notice that it is a newspaper?—Exactly.

10. *Chairman.*] What other Acts are there which you can quote as bearing upon this subject?—There is the Act of the 60 Geo. 3, c. 9, which enacts, that no person shall print or publish a newspaper, until he has entered into a recognizance, if in London, Westminster, Edinburgh, or Dublin, or a bond, if resident elsewhere within the kingdom, with sureties to the satisfaction of the Baron of the Exchequer taking such recognizance, or of the justice of the peace taking such bond, in the sum of 300 *l.* if such newspaper shall be printed in London or within 20 miles thereof, and in the sum of 200 *l.* if such newspaper shall be printed elsewhere in the United Kingdom, conditioned that such printer or publisher shall pay to his Majesty, his heirs and successors, every such fine or penalty as may at any time be imposed upon or adjudged against him by reason of any conviction for printing or publishing any blasphemous or seditious libel. The provisions of that Act were extended by 1 Will. 4, c. 73, to secure the payment of damages and costs to be recovered in actions for libels at the suit of individuals. The first Act was to secure fines on convictions for blasphemous or seditions libels, and the provisions of that Act were extended by 1 Will. 4, c. 73, to secure the damages or costs recovered by private individuals against newspaper proprietors for libels. And the amount of security required was also increased from 300 *l.* in the case of a paper published in London, Westminster, Edinburgh, or Dublin, to 400 *l.*, and from 200 *l.* in the country to 300 *l.*

11. The 60 Geo. 3, c. 9, and its extension by 1 Will. 4, c. 73, only refer to the case of a person about to publish a newspaper?—Yes.

12. He is not required to give any security for any other sort of publication whatsoever, is he?—No.

13. He might libel without any liability or any security having been previously given, if he libelled in a publication not

*J. Timm,* Esq.

2 May 1851.

not a newspaper?—Not without liability, but these securities apply to newspapers only. I believe I have now stated the whole of the law bearing upon this question.

14. Are there no parts of old Acts of Parliament which may be unrepealed, though the main parts of the Acts in which they were repealed are still alive, which affect the newspaper press?—No, they were consolidated by this Act of 6 & 7 Will. 4, except 60 Geo. 3, and 1 Will. 4.

15. Supposing a person printed news upon something not paper, the idea was that he would not be liable to the stamp duty. I have been informed that that was a mistake, for there was in existence some clause in some old Act of Parliament which made it equally illegal to publish news upon linen or silk, or anything of that sort, as upon paper?—Yes. I understood the question to refer to enactments relating exclusively to newspapers. A number of them were repealed by this Act of 6 & 7 Will. 4, c. 76. The provision to which you have referred applies to stamp duties generally. By all the Stamp Acts, from the first imposition of the stamp duty, the duty was imposed upon deeds, writings, and other written and printed instruments, on vellum, parchment, or paper; and by 38 Geo. 3, c. 85, it is enacted, "that the several and respective rates and duties now chargeable on vellum, parchment, and paper, in respect of any matter or thing engrossed, written, or printed thereon, shall be charged, raised, levied, and paid upon every other material of what nature or kind soever on which any of the said matters or things shall from and after the passing of this Act be engrossed, printed, or written; which several and respective rates and duties shall be charged, ascertained, and secured in like manner as the duties now payable on vellum, parchment, and paper are directed to be charged, ascertained, and secured by the laws now in force." By sect. 5, it is enacted, "that all the powers, provisions, rules, regulations, methods, articles, clauses, penalties and forfeitures, and applications of penalties and forfeitures, and all other matters and things which in and by any Act or Acts of Parliament now in force, relating to any of the rates and duties on stamped vellum, parchment, and paper, shall" apply to the like matters written or printed upon any other material.

16. What is the title of the last Act to which you have referred?—I have not got the title. The Act itself is the 38th of Geo. 3, c. 85, s. 4 & 5. That provision is kept in force and applied to the duties imposed by 6 & 7 Will. 4, on newspapers, by the first section of the latter Act, not expressly, but it

J. Timm, Esq.

2 May 1851.

it is enacted that all the powers, provisions, rules and regulations relating to any stamp duties, so far as they are applicable to these duties on newspapers, shall be observed and enforced.

17. You began by giving the Committee the definitions in the schedule of 6 & 7 Will. 4, c. 76, as to what constitutes a newspaper. I think you read three definitions?—Yes.

18. Just read the first of those definitions again?—"Any paper containing public news, intelligence, or other occurrences, printed in any part of the United kingdom, to be dispersed and made public."

19. That has no reference to any interval of publication, or any repetition of publication; but if it be printed once, under that definition, on paper, it ought to be printed on a stamped piece of paper?—That is my opinion, and the practice of the Board has always been in accordance with it; because until the passing of 60 Geo. 3, c. 9, there was no other definition of a newspaper than that. The 60 Geo. 3, which has reference to intervals of publication, was not intended to supersede that enactment, but to make other publications liable to the stamp duty which were not so before, and not to supersede the former enactment.

20. Would it not appear then that that first definition includes the two other definitions?—No, not exactly; the third may be said to include the first, but with some limitation, and that is as to the intervals of publication.

21. The first definition seems to be larger than the two following definitions. The effect of the two subsequent definitions upon the first is not quite plain. If you say that news shall always be printed upon stamped paper, under all circumstances and conditions, which you do in the first, I do not see what the effect of the two subsequent definitions is? —To leave the second one out of the question, because that applies to advertisements only, and to go to the third; the third renders liable publications containing remarks or observations upon news, not news substantively; and to do that they have repeated the words, "containing public news, intelligence, or occurrences, or any remarks or observations thereon." All these three definitions existed in distinct Acts of Parliament before the passing of 6 & 7 Will. 4, which consolidated the provisions of the Acts relating to newspaper stamp duties. From the time of the first imposition of a stamp duty on newspapers down to the passing of 60 Geo. 3, the only definition was the first which I have read to the Committee, nearly in the same words from first to last.

22. Then if I understand you rightly, in no case must

facts,

*J. Timm*, Esq.

2 May 1851.

facts, intelligence, or occurrences be printed upon any material without a stamp?—Yes; that is, public news; anything coming within the description of public news, intelligence, or occurrences.

23. But comments or observations you may publish, under what conditions, without a stamp?—The Act says that they shall be published at intervals exceeding 26 days.

24. Are there any other conditions?—That if published at shorter intervals they shall exceed two sheets of paper, each sheet containing a quantity not less than 21 inches in length and 17 inches in breadth, and that the publication shall be published for sale at a sum not less than 6 *d.*, exclusive of the duty.

25. Is it necessary to comply with those four conditions in order to be entitled to comment and observe without a stamp? —If the publication exceeds two sheets, and be sold for a sum not less than 6 *d.* over and above the duty, then it is not liable, although it may be published within intervals of 26 days. The regulation is this: that if a paper, containing comments or observations upon public news, be published at intervals within 26 days, it shall be liable to stamp duty, unless it exceed two sheets of a certain size, and exceed 6 *d.* in price.

26. Then this provision applies to papers commenting and observing at intervals of less than 26 days only, does not it? —Yes.

27. It allows them to do that without a stamp, provided they comply with three conditions, namely, that they shall be printed on a quantity at least equal to two sheets of paper; that each of those sheets shall be 21 inches in length and 17 inches in breadth; and that the price shall be 6 *d.* and upwards?—Yes; on these conditions they may print at intervals of less than 26 days without being liable to the stamp duty.

28. But if they published at intervals longer than 26 days, what would be the consequence?—Then they would not come within the charge of duty; such a paper not containing news substantively, but comments and observations upon news, would not be liable.

29. If the paper be published at longer intervals than 26 days?—Yes.

30. This is merely to apply to weekly and fortnightly publications?—Yes; no doubt the object was to exclude the monthly magazines by limiting it in this manner, to avoid rendering the usual monthly magazines liable to stamp duty.

31. Has

31. Has it been the practice of the Board of Inland Revenue to act under this interpretation of the law?—Yes. *J. Timm,* Esq.

32. In both cases?—Yes, in both cases; but with regard to the latter there has been very little practice at all upon it, because the publications that have come under the notice of the Board have generally contained public news, and therefore they have come under the first definition of newspapers. Parties have attempted to excuse themselves by stating that their paper is not a newspaper within the third definition; but our reply to that is, "It is a newspaper within the first definition, because it contains public news, intelligence, and occurrences." 2 May 1851.

33. Will you just explain to the Committee, practically, what a man has to do who contemplates the publication of a newspaper?—A party desirous of publishing a newspaper in London must make application at the office of the solicitor of Inland Revenue, and he there receives a printed form of particulars required to be given by him in order that the necessary declaration and recognizance may be filled up. This is the form of the particulars that he is required to give.

[*The same was handed in, and is as follows:*]

No. 5.

PARTICULARS required at the INLAND REVENUE OFFICE, SOMERSET HOUSE, previously to the Printing of any NEWSPAPER, or upon any Change in respect to the same.

---

*Note.*—It is requisite that the particulars be inserted, under each head, in words at length, in a legible hand, and especially as regards names of persons and places, in a clear and distinct character, so as to prevent mistakes in preparing the documents.

Married women and minors are incompetent to be parties to such documents.

---

1.—The correct title of the newspaper, quoted literally as it is to stand in the imprint.

2.—Place of Printing.—No. (if any) of house or office; and the parish in which the house or office is situate, and if a part of any dwelling-house, and whose.

3.—The like as to the place of publishing.

4.—The Christian name and surname, and residence, of every person who is to be a printer of the newspaper, or who is to conduct the actual printing thereof.

5.—The

*J. Timm,* Esq.

2 May 1851.

5.—The Christian name and surname, and residence, of every person who is to be a publisher of the newspaper.

6.—Number of shares into which the newspaper is divided, when the proprietors (exclusive of the printer and publisher) exceed two.

7.—Name of every proprietor resident out of the United Kingdom, with the place of his abode and occupation.

8.—The Christian names, surnames, residences, and occupation of every proprietor resident in the United Kingdom; and where such proprietors (exclusive of the printer and publisher) exceed two, the number of shares held by each.

*Note.*—The declaration required by law must be made by the proprietor, or by both proprietors, if they do not exceed two; and where they exceed that number, it must be made by two of them, whose shares are not less than those held by any other person (exclusive of the printer and publisher); if, therefore, there be more than two of the largest proprietors who hold the same number of shares each, let it be stated which of them it is proposed shall make the declaration.

9.—The Christian names, surnames, residences, and occupations of two responsible householders as sureties for securing the advertisement duty.

*Note.*—The proprietors who make the declaration will be required to join the printers and publishers in the bond to secure the advertisement duties; these sureties are required in addition.

10.—The Christian names, surnames, residences, and occupations of two responsible householders, as sureties against the publication of libels

REFEREES.

11.—The Christian names, surnames, residences, and occupations of two respectable persons, of whom inquiry may be made as to the responsibility of each of the proposed sureties for advertisement duty.

12.—The like as to the sureties against libels.

The next step is, that a printed letter goes out in the name of the solicitor; that printed letter goes to the persons referred to in that paper, as to the responsibility of the sureties, to ascertain whether they are of sufficient responsibility.

[*The same was handed in, and is as follows:*]

Inland Revenue, Somerset House,
London, 185 .

HAVING been referred to you, as to the responsibility of as a surety to the Crown, I beg to state that the bond will be in the penalty of pounds, and to request the

*J. Timm, Esq.*

2 May 1851.

the favour of you to inform me whether Mr. is a householder, and, of your knowledge, possesses sufficient property to render his security good for that amount; and if so, of what his property consists.

I am,
Your very obedient Servant,
*J. Timm,*
Solicitor of Inland Revenue.

On Her Majesty's Service.

If the answers are satisfactory, and it appears to the solicitor that the sureties are sufficiently responsible, a declaration is prepared, of which this is a blank form :

[*The same was handed in, and is as follows :*]

in the of printer , do solemnly and sincerely declare and say, that the printer , publisher , and sole proprietor of a certain newspaper, intituled, " "

And that the said newspaper is intended to be printed at in the parish of in the of and to be published at in the parish of

And do make this solemn declaration, conscientiously believing the same to be true, and in pursuance of an Act passed in the seventh year of the reign of His late Majesty King William the Fourth, intituled, "An Act to reduce the Duties on Newspapers, and to amend the Laws relating to the Duties on Newspapers and Advertisements."

Declared at the , Somerset House, in the city of Westminster, by the this day of 18 , before me,

——, A Commissioner of

A recognizance is also prepared to answer for the damages and costs or fines on conviction for libel, of which this is a copy.

[*The same was handed in, and is as follows :*]

Middlesex } Be it remembered, that on the day
to wit. } of in the year of the reign of our Sovereign Lady VICTORIA, by the grace of God of the United Kingdom of Great Britain and Ireland Queen, Defender of the Faith, and in the year of our Lord one thousand eight hundred and fifty

came before me, one of the Barons of the Exchequer, in England, and acknowledged to be indebted to our said Lady the Queen,

*J. Timm,* Esq.

2 May 1851.

Queen, her heirs, and successors, in the sum of four hundred pounds, to be levied upon their goods and chattels, lands and tenements, for the use of our said Lady the Queen, Her heirs and successors, if default shall be made in the performance of the condition hereunder written.

WHEREAS
is about to become the printer and publisher of a certain newspaper.

Now, the condition of the above written recognizance is such, that if the said do and shall well and truly pay, or cause to be paid, unto Her Majesty, Her heirs or successors, every such fine or penalty as shall or may be imposed upon or adjudged against the said
by reason of any conviction for printing or publishing any blasphemous or seditious libel at any time hereafter; and if the said
his heirs, executors, or administrators, do and shall well and truly pay, or cause to be paid, to the person or persons respectively who shall recover the same, all damages and costs which shall be by such person or persons respectively recovered in any action or actions against the said
by reason of any libel or libels contained or published in any newspaper, then the said recognizance to be void, or else the same to remain in full force and virtue.

Taken and acknowledged before me,

34. Either a public libel or a private libel?—It includes both. A bond is also prepared for securing the duties upon advertisements to be contained in the newspaper, of which this is a copy.

[*The same was handed in, and is as follows:*]

ADVERTISEMENT DUTY BOND.

Dated

KNOW all men by these presents, that we

are held and firmly bound unto our Sovereign Lady Victoria, by the grace of God of the United Kingdom of Great Britain and Ireland Queen, Defender of the Faith, in the sum of
pounds of good and lawful money of Great Britain, to be paid to our said Lady the Queen, Her heirs or successors: To which payment, well and truly to be made, we bind ourselves, and every of us, severally, and any two or more of us jointly, for and in the whole, our and each and any of our heirs, executors, and administrators, and every of them, firmly by these presents. Sealed with our seals. Dated the day of
in the year of our Lord One thousand eight hundred and

Now

Now the condition of this obligation is such, that if the said

*J. Timm, Esq.*

2 May 1851.

heirs, executors, or administrators, shall and do well and truly pay, or cause to be paid, unto the Receiver-general of Inland Revenue, or his deputy or clerk for the time being, at the chief office of Inland Revenue, to the use of Her Majesty, Her heirs and successors, all such sum and sums of money as shall arise or become due and payable to Her Majesty, Her heirs or sucessors, for the duties due, and to become due, on all and every advertisement and advertisements, from time to time inserted in a certain newspaper called

Then this obligation is to be void; or else the same is to remain in full force and virtue.

Signed, sealed, and delivered by the above bounden
in the presence of

Upon all these documents being completed, a certificate goes down from my office to the superintendent of the stamping room stating that the party is entitled to receive stamps for newspapers.

35. And he has as much paper stamped as he likes?—Yes.

36. After completing all those necessary documents?—Yes; after completing all those necessary documents he goes to the receiver-general's, fills up a warrant, pays the duty, and has what quantity of stamps he pleases.

37. What are the powers which the Board of Inland Revenue possesses of enforcing the law, and punishing those who infringe or evade the provisions of the Act?—In the first place, every person who prints or publishes a newspaper before the declaration is made, is liable to a penalty of 50*l.*; secondly, every person who prints a newspaper without a stamp is liable to a penalty of 20*l.* for every copy of the same.

38. Every person who prints any public news, intelligence or occurrences upon a piece of unstamped paper, is liable to a penalty of 20 *l.* for every such piece of paper?—Yes; that is for every copy of the publication; if it extended to two or three sheets he would only be liable to one penalty for one copy.

39. Your mode of proceeding would then be to sue for penalties in the Court of Exchequer; a question would then arise as to whether what was printed on the paper was news or not, and that would go to the jury, would it not?—Yes; a question would then arise whether the publication was a newspaper in fact and in law; and that would be a question which the judge would leave for the jury.

40. Supposing

*J. Timm,* Esq.

2 May 1851.

40. Supposing that you did not sue for penalties in the way mentioned, what other mode of procedure have you to put down an unstamped newspaper?—All printing presses used in the printing of unstamped newspapers are liable to seizure and forfeiture.

41. Would it be at your discretion, or for the Board of Inland Revenue to judge, themselves, whether a given publication was a newspaper, and if the law had been violated to seize the presses?—It would be at our discretion whether we should adopt such a proceeding or not; but ultimately a question would arise which might come before a jury, whether the papers were newspapers or not; because after the seizure was made it would be returned into the Court of Exchequer, and the party might contend then that they were not newspapers, and so try the question in that way.

42. But in the first instance you would have it in your power to seize the printing presses and stop the carrying on of the publication?—Yes; but some person must go before a magistrate and make oath that there is reason to believe that unstamped newspapers are printed at a certain place before he can obtain a search warrant to make that seizure.

43. Can any person go before any magistrate and lay any such information?—No, it must be an officer of inland revenue. The application must be made by an officer of inland revenue for a warrant, and information must be given to the justice, on the oath of one or more credible witnesses, that there is reasonable and probable cause to suspect a person of printing unstamped newspapers.

44. Then upon that a search-warrant would be granted, and the presses would be seized, would they?—Provided that in executing the warrant unstamped newspapers are found. It is enacted that if any such newspaper not duly stamped, and any printing press which shall have been used in printing or publishing a newspaper shall be found, it shall be lawful for the persons named in that warrant to seize them.

45. Then supposing it should afterwards turn out that it was not news in the eye of the law that was printed on those papers, what means of redress would the party have whose printing presses had been so seized?—I think the officer who seized them would be liable to action after the judgment of the Court of Exchequer for the claimant.

46. In a book just published on the press, it appears that the jury in Hetherington's case decided, after there had been a great many fines and seizures, and a great deal of property confiscated, for publishing a certain description of news on papers,

papers, that it was not news; and it did not appear that those parties who had been fined, and had their presses seized beforehand, were compensated?—No, because it was not with respect to the same publication that they were proceeded against. The case alluded to is, the "Poor Man's Guardian:" I remember the case very well. But there were other papers that were decidedly newspapers as much as the "Times" itself. At that time newspapers were published in defiance of the law, daily papers. Then there were others that were not so decidedly newspapers, and that was one of them. Hetherington was prosecuted for publishing two unstamped newspapers. As to one, there could be no question about its being a newspaper; the other was the "Poor Man's Guardian," which contained principally observations upon news, and very little of news itself. They were both included in the same information, and it was more for the purpose of obtaining the opinion of the court upon the "Poor Man's Guardian" than anything else that that was included.

*J. Timm,* Esq.

2 May 1851.

47. During the last Session of Parliament I moved for a return which was made to the House of Commons of the papers registered as newspapers which were published in the metropolis without stamps. The return was made in February 1850; in all probability there may be some difference now; but you will be able to say whether that return gives a pretty nearly accurate account of the papers published in London at this time without a stamp, registered newspapers. (*A paper was handed to the Witness*)?—Yes, I dare say it may be so. It is not within my knowledge or department to know this; but I dare say it may be so. Besides these, there are a number of prices current, published by mercantile people, that are not strictly newspapers. They are entered as newspapers with us; they enter the title, make a declaration, give the security, and obtain the stamps.

48. This return is a return of the papers published in the metropolis, which are registered as newspapers, a portion whereof is published without stamps?—Yes.

49. Would it be competent for those parties, if you sued them for penalties, to plead that the thing was not a newspaper, though they had themselves signed the declarations, and registered it as such?—I think it would.

50. It would still be competent to them, although the publication had been registered as a newspaper, to plead that it was not a newspaper?—Yes, and it would be incumbent upon me to prove that it was a newspaper, independently of their registration

*J. Timm,* Esq.

2 May 1851.

registration. If there were any doubt about the nature of the publication, perhaps the registration of it would be a feature in the case to submit to the jury. Although the party called it a newspaper, yet if its contents were really not public news, intelligence, or occurrences, the mere registering it and stamping it would not make the party liable to penalties for printing unstamped copies of it.

51. In fact a publication is not a newspaper in virtue of its registration, but in virtue of its contents?—Yes, that is the fact.

52. With respect to these papers, which are all within your knowledge, the "Athenæum," the "Architect," "Bent's Literary Advertiser," the "Botanical Gazette," and others of which I have a list, do they, in your opinion, contain any news, public intelligence, or occurrences, or any comments or observations thereon?—It is impossible for me to say that any or all of them may not contain a paragraph or two of matter which may strictly be deemed news; but looking at the whole contents of them, I should say that they do not serve the purpose of newspapers generally.

53. Do they comment and observe upon facts, intelligence, or occurrences?—I dare say they do.

54. If they do why are they not liable to be stamped?—I would say that some of them in strictness possibly might be liable, but they are of that nature that I think it very doubtful whether I should get a jury to come to the conclusion that they were newspapers.

55. What is your test at the Board of Inland Revenue, or mode of ascertaining whether a given publication is a newspaper or not?—Our test is, whether it contains public news, intelligence, or occurrences.

56. Or comments or observations thereon?—Yes, published at intervals not exceeding 26 days. Although the paper might perhaps contain some portion of intelligence or public news, merely a trifling paragraph, or it might contain observations upon public news, yet unless those contents were such as would probably induce a jury to say it was substantially that upon which the duty was intended to be imposed, the Board might not prosecute for penalties.

57. Is there not any clear line or definition within which a man may feel himself secure, when he publishes without a stamp, that he is not liable to these heavy penalties?—The security is, that he may give notice to the Stamp Office, and in that case he will not be liable for any penalties till the Stamp Office in reply have told him that the thing is a newspaper

paper which he is printing, and in that case he may join issue with them if he pleases; he may either discontinue it, or he may contend that it is not a newspaper, and try the point with them. *J. Timm,* Esq. 2 May 1851.

58. But have you found yourself in any great practical difficulties in deciding at the Stamp Office as to what is news and what is not?—None whatever.

59. Several questions have been put in Parliament lately relative to proceedings that are said to have been commenced against the publishers of a "Narrative of Current Events," edited by Dickens; can you explain to the Committee what the ground of those proceedings is, and what the nature of them?—Yes, I can explain the point to the Committee. A special case has been stated, and the point is this: the contents of that paper are undoubtedly those of a newspaper, and Mr. Dickens, I think, will not dispute that; and the only question is whether, not being published within intervals of 26 days, it is liable to stamp duty. It is not with reference to its contents at all, but merely to the periods of its publication that the point is raised.

60. I thought, as you explained the law, it was clear that any paper or material upon which was printed any news, facts, or occurrences must be stamped?—Yes.

61. It had no reference to the interval?—That is our interpretation of the law, but Mr. Dickens disputes it.

62. That has been your universal practice?—Yes; and that is the point now to be determined, whether the third of these definitions supersedes the first.

63. Supposing it should be determined in Dickens's case, that inasmuch as it is published at a certain interval of 26 days, he can publish without a stamp, would not your past proceedings have been illegal?—No, I do not know that we have taken any in such a case; I do not think we have prosecuted in any case a monthly publication.

64. Have you not intimated an intention to do so, so as to cause persons to discontinue such publications?—I have no doubt we have; it is our practice in all cases, when we observe a paper containing public news, at whatever intervals it may be published, to caution the parties.

65. But supposing in Dickens's case, that the jury should decide that this publication of Dickens's is not a newspaper, would not those parties have some reason to complain of the uncertainty of the law, if they have been induced to give up publishing papers upon the ground that they were liable to the stamp duty?—I am not aware whether any parties have

 been

*J. Timm,* Esq.

2 May 1851.

been induced to give up their publications in consequence of that.

66. Was not there a case of the kind at Norwich; the case of the "Norwich Reformer"?—That did not come immediately before me, I think, but I am not aware whether it was a monthly publication or not; if it was the party was written to, without reference to its being a monthly publication, but as containing public news. He was cautioned against a repetition of news in his paper.

67. Can you give the Committee any more distinct definition of the class of publications which are entitled to the privilege of stamping only a portion of their impressions, and publishing another portion unstamped for local circulation?—I do not look upon it as any privilege at all. The Board have no power of preventing it. The party who comes and enters the title of a newspaper, and makes a declaration as to who are the printers and publishers, is entitled to stamps as a matter of course, and upon those stamps he can print what he pleases; he can print news upon one part, and that which is not news upon another, or he may print a novel upon the other, and we have nothing to do with that, nor can we prevent it. We have no control as to the use the party makes of the stamps when he obtains them.

68. It is your duty to prevent anything in the shape of news or comments, or observations thereon, being printed on unstamped paper, in fairness to those who stamp all the copies of their publications, is it not?—It is.

69. Do you make it a rule to look to it yourself, or do you act upon information. Inasmuch as every person who obtain stamps must send one copy of the publication to you, is it your habit to see that there is no unfair competition going on, parties publishing news upon unstamped paper competing with those who stamp all the copies of their impression?—No, it is not my province to do so; it does not come before me, the copy of the publication goes to the registrar of newspapers; but he receives only a stamped copy, and probably may know nothing about the unstamped one; they send a stamped copy to him, and he might not know that any part of it was published without stamps.

70. Mr. *Cobden.*] I understood you to say that prices current were excepted in that Act of 6 & 7 Will. 4, as not being liable to the newspaper stamp?—Papers containing matters wholly of a commercial nature are exempted from the duty, and prices current, I think, by name.

71. Prices current, strictly such, and confined exclu-

clusively

*J. Timm,* Esq.

2 May 1851.

sively to the intelligence connected with business of a particular firm, are not newspapers?—They are not.

72. You deliver stamps for the purpose of publishing prices current, notwithstanding that the Act specifically states, that prices current are not newspapers?—Yes; but a person might publish a newspaper under the title of "Prices Current."

73. I hold in my hand a copy of several "Savory and Son's Prices Current," bearing a newspaper stamp; has that ever come under your observation?—Not particularly. I have no doubt that the title has been entered as a newspaper, and security given in the usual way.

74. Then, seeing this little pamphlet containing pictures of tea-urns, salt-cellars, teapots, and dish covers, with a stamp upon it, and being strictly prices current, you would not consider that it comes within the scope of your duty to say that this ought not to be published as a newspaper?—Not at all.

75. This publication goes through the post free of expense, does it not?—That rests with the Postmaster-general. I presume it does, and that is the object of the party putting the stamp upon it.

76. This pamphlet of 64 pages, containing all these pictures, of tea-urns and salt-cellars, and which will weigh more than an ounce, goes through the post for one penny, because it has had a stamp put on it by you at the Inland Revenue Office, under the false designation of a newspaper?—No, I beg your pardon, the stamp is impressed upon the paper before it is printed.

77. This stamp is given by you at the Inland Revenue Office; you know of the existence of this pamphlet which is thus stamped, after it has been published; you know that bearing this stamp, this pamphlet of 64 pages, weighing more than an ounce, and which would be charged 4*d.* if it had not your stamp upon it, goes through the post for a stamp of one penny; you knowing that this stamp has been obtained by a person declaring that this is a newspaper, though the Act of 6 & 7 Will. 4 says that prices current are not newspapers; knowing that this has been done contrary to the Act, and that a postage of 3*d.* each time is evaded, you do not think it necessary to interfere?—No, and for this reason; we never think it necessary to interfere with any use whatever that the parties may make of newspaper stamps; we manufacture and sell stamps, and the party who buys them is at liberty to print anything he pleases upon them. It may be a question afterwards

*J. Timm,* Esq.

2 May 1851.

afterwards, of what use it may be to print it upon stamps; but whether he can legally send it by post or not is no business whatever of the Inland Revenue Department; that is solely the business of the Post-office. The stamp will not authorize the party to send anything through the post-office that is not a newspaper.

78. Still as I understand, you describe a price current not to be a newspaper?—Not liable to the newspaper stamp duty.

79. Yet you see that publication with a newspaper stamp affixed by yourself upon it, and you think it is not your duty to interfere to prevent it?—Certainly not; we cannot refuse to enter any title that a party may please to adopt as the title of a newspaper.

80. I am speaking of a case after the fact has come to your knowledge that the stamp is used for the purpose of stamping a price current; do not you think it the duty of the Board to interfere to prevent that going on contrary to the provisions of the Act?—It is not in our power to prevent it.

81. Is it a satisfactory state of things, that you should be parties to an infraction of the law in a certain sense?—I do not consider that we are parties to any infraction of the law; we are manufacturers and sellers of stamps, and have no control whatever over the use of them.

82. You are aware that the stamp gives the right of transmission through the post-office as a newspaper?—I believe it does not *per se;* it does not.

83. Practically it does, does it not?—But the Board of Inland Revenue have nothing to do with that; that is entirely the business of the Post-office. I believe the law does not allow that.

84. You are aware, are you not, that that stamp is obtained to procure transmission through the post at one penny?—I have no doubt of it.

85. Mr. *G. A. Hamilton.*] Do you consider the paper shown to you to be a price current?—I think it is a catalogue of the goods to be sold by Savory & Sons.

86. Mr. *Rich.*] You consider it your duty to ascertain that papers containing news are stamped?—Yes.

87. You confine your duty to making all papers publishing news pay a stamp duty?—Yes.

88. *Chairman.*] As your duty is to see that no news is printed upon paper or other material without a stamp, how do you define the word "News;" what is news, in the opinion of the Stamp-office?—I suppose it is a matter of notoriety what

what news is: an account of the transactions of the present times. *J. Timm, Esq.* 2 May 1851.

89. There is a paper published, unstamped, called, the "Legal Observer," which gives a systematic record of the proceedings in our courts of justice; is that news?—Perhaps it might strictly be termed "news." But that paper is looked upon rather as a reporter of cases decided by the courts, and to be referred to as authorities.

90. There are various journals devoted to particular subjects, such as scientific purposes and religious purposes, and each giving an account of the meetings relative to the subjects to which they relate, and speeches at those meetings; do you consider those to contain news?—These are what may be termed class publications, and strictly their contents are news.

91. Do not those matters when all brought together form a newspaper. Supposing that there is a meeting reported in the "Evangelical Christendom," relative to some public matter; or in the "Labourer's Friend;" or in the "Lancet," of a meeting upon some surgical question, and the speeches of the medical men reported, would you not call that news?—I should.

92. Do not you allow those sort of proceedings to be published systematically in those publications that you laid before the House of Commons without a stamp?—I am sure I do not know; I do not know particularly.

93. Is it not the fact that every one of those publications systematically contains such matters as I have mentioned; you having laid a return before the House of Commons, stating that those publications were published without a stamp with your knowledge?—Some of those are certainly not liable to the duty.

94. Will you select one that is not liable, out of the 53 registered newspapers, a return of which you laid before the House of Commons, as being published without stamps?—I do not think there is one in the whole list that I could get a jury to say was a newspaper published unstamped.

95. Why do you suppose so. Would not they have to decide upon facts, and not upon law, whether a paper contained a certain thing or not?—Yes; but they would not be influenced by a mere paragraph or a few slight observations.

96. Would you undertake to say that a man could, with security to himself, publish the matter that is contained in any one of these papers without a stamp?—I should like to have

*J. Timm*, Esq.

2 May 1851.

have the paper before me, if the Committee will allow me to have it in my hand. There are very few that I have ever seen. (*The Return being handed to the Witness.*) That is a return by the registrar of newspapers, not by me.

97. I will take "Punch." Do you consider that "Punch" does not comment or observe upon public news?—In his way, undoubtedly. But I think if I were to attempt to prosecute that paper for being a newspaper unstamped I should be laughed out of court. His only object is to make a pun or a piece of witticism, or something of that kind; not for the purpose of giving news. It is rather assumed in those cases, I think, that everybody is aware of the news or other matter which he puns or jests upon.

98. With regard to publishing upon a separate paper the contents of a newspaper without a stamp, supposing a person extracts parts of a newspaper, and publishes them upon an unstamped paper, would that render him liable to a penalty of 20 *l.* for every copy?—I think it would; an isolated paper, containing news that had appeared in a newspaper.

99. Mr. *Rich.*] Without reference to what it contained?—No. It must be news; but it would not be the less liable to duty by reason of its having previously appeared in a stamped newspaper.

100. *Chairman.*] If anybody printed the Queen's Speech upon a piece of unstamped paper, would he be liable to a penalty of 20 *l.*?—I think he would. It is done almost immediately after every Speech is delivered; and when we have notice of that, we write and tell the parties that they have infringed the law. If we had a copy of it, so that we could bring the offence home to the party, we should probably prosecute him.

101. Mr. *Stafford.*] You never have prosecuted, have you?—I am not sure.

102. Mr. *Cobden.*] Would you prosecute a party for publishing the Queen's Speech, with the hope of getting a jury to convict?—I think, under the direction of the judge, they would.

103. I understood you to say, in answer to the Honourable Chairman's question regarding the "Legal Observer," that you looked upon that as a special publication for giving reports, and that therefore you did not treat that as an ordinary newspaper. Can you call to mind the circumstance of one of my constituents in Yorkshire, the proprietor and publisher of the "West Riding Examiner," at Wakefield, who some time ago republished from his own paper 2,000 copies

*J. Timm, Esq.*

*2 May 1851.*

copies of the report of a trial which was interesting to certain parties, and are you aware that that party had notice of an action for penalties amounting to 40,000 *l.*?—I remember the case very well. But it is a mistake to suppose that he had notice of an action for penalties amounting to 40,000 *l.*, or anything like that.

104. It was intimated that he was liable to that amount, was it not?—It was intimated to him that he had incurred penalties, but not to that amount; and not only that, but a prosecution was instituted against him to recover penalties for printing the paper without a stamp; and the Board mitigated the penalties to 10 *l.*, which the party paid.

105. I understand you to say that you have allowed the "Legal Observer," published in London, to continue to give reports of proceedings in the courts of law without a stamp, and that you do not molest the parties, but that in the case of the proprietor of the "West Riding Examiner," for reprinting one report you threatened him with a prosecution, and you compelled him, under intimidation, to pay you 10 *l.*?—Yes.

106. Will you explain upon what principle the Board of Inland Revenue acts when it allows a constant and weekly violation of the law by the "Legal Observer," but visits with penalties one example in the case of the "West Riding Examiner"?—In the case that you have mentioned the information was very interesting to a large class of people in that neighbourhood. The sole object of that was "news," nothing else, and very interesting news, so much so that the party printed 2,000 copies, and it was complained of by a newspaper proprietor, in that neighbourhood, and I think he had just ground for complaining, because it anticipated the publication of that news in his paper. With regard to penalties, the party stated that 2,000 copies had been printed, the penny stamp duty would amount to a little above 8 *l.*, and therefore the penalty that was inflicted was but a trifle more than the duty.

107. In the case of the "Legal Observer," it is recognised as a standard authority for the reports of proceedings in our courts of law, is it not?—Yes.

108. Do not you think that parties interested in a trial, for instance, if it were a trial concerning a railroad, would be disposed to buy a copy of that "Legal Observer" in order to obtain a good report, and if so would not the "Legal Observer" be serving the same purpose precisely that the "West Riding Examiner" served by reprinting the report I have

J. Timm, Esq.

2 May 1851.

have referred to?—It might do so; but I believe that is not the general object of the publication.

109. I understood you to say that you never prosecuted parties if they sent you a copy of their publication, unless you had previously given them notice that they must stop their proceedings?—Yes.

110. Did you give any notice to the party in this case to stop that publication in the West Riding?—He never gave the notice required by the Act of Parliament.

111. He did not furnish you with a copy of that sheet which he reprinted, but you had a copy of his paper, had you not?—Yes.

112. Was not that a very venial offence, the reprinting an article which had previously appeared on stamped paper as compared with a systematic violation of the law by a newspaper published every week in London?—It was a venial offence, and I think it was treated in a very lenient manner, but as to a systematic evasion of the law, I am not aware of any such case.

113. Did you not say that the "Legal Observer" was a newspaper?—No, I do not think that I should get a court and jury to say that it was.

114. I ask you for your opinion?—It certainly comes within the strict definition of a newspaper contained in the Act of Parliament.

115. When you have defined the law to the Inland Revenue Board and proceed against parties, you are the sole judges as to what amount of penalties you will sue for, as in the case of the "West Riding Examiner," you may claim 40,000 *l.* or take 10 *l.*, is that not so?—Not exactly so; we could not have claimed 40,000 *l.*; we had not evidence that the party had published that number of copies.

116. It was assumed in the correspondence that 2,000 copies had been printed, was it not?—The party himself stated that he had printed that number when called upon; but we should not make use of that evidence against him; that was with a view to assessing the duty upon him.

117. When you took 10 *l.* as a compromise from that publisher, what did you consider your claim was; what amount of penalties could you have sued for?—We then had sent up 90 copies, so that we could have prosecuted him for 20 *l.* for each copy.

118. That would be 1,800 *l.*?—Yes.

119. You had the power to prosecute him for 1,800 *l.*, and you accepted 10 *l.* by way of compromise?—Yes.

120. Is

J. Timm, Esq.

2 May 1851.

120. Is not that a very formidable power which your department exercises, especially upon small country publishers?—The power may be formidable, but I think that the exercise of it cannot be complained of.

121. Is it not a very arbitrary power, when it appears that you accepted 10 *l.* as a composition for 1,800 *l.*, and you had legal grounds for pursuing the party for that sum?—Yes. The Legislature has vested that power in the Board to compromise all cases, either on payment of a portion of the penalties, or without payment of any penalty at all.

122. And to interpret the law which up to this time has not been settled by a court of law?—We have acted as we must always act, according as we are advised by the Attorney and Solicitor-general, in cases of doubt or difficulty. We had been advised by them on this very point years ago.

123. I understood you to say in your definition of a newspaper, that it is a publication of public news, intelligence, or occurrences, to be dispersed or made public, and without reference to the intervals of time at which it is published?—It has no reference to that.

124. It may be published fortnightly, or published at intervals of two months, but still it is a newspaper?—Yes.

125. Do you consider that it is your duty, or the duty of any one at the Inland Revenue Board, to see that that law is enforced and fairly observed, or do you trust to persons volunteering information to you before you attempt to enforce the law?—All our distributors have instructions to forward to the Board any paper that may come to their knowledge, and that appears in their judgment to be liable to the newspaper stamp duty, and then such papers are judged of at the Board.

126. Do you consider that it is your own duty, for instance, if you see a publication which is flagrantly violating the law, to lay an information?—Yes, I should consider it my business to write to the party officially.

127. You would consider that to be the duty of Mr. John Wood, and of every one connected with the Inland Revenue Board?—I should.

128. Do you consider the "Annual Register" to come within the scope of the law?—The "Annual Register," I think, is a bound book.

129. It is a volume, is it not?—Yes; it has never been considered that bound books are newspapers. Publications to be liable as newspapers should be published in the form in which a newspaper usually is.

130. The

*J. Timm,* Esq.

2 May 1851.

130. The "Annual Register" is published in boards, is it not?—Yes.

131. Then adding a pasteboard cover to a publication destroys its character as a newspaper, does it?—In a publication of that nature we must judge of it taking all the circumstances together, whether it is a newspaper or not.

132. Having regard to your first definition, will you say whether you consider the "Annual Register," which is wholly made up of public news, occurrences, and intelligence, ceases to be a newspaper by having a pasteboard cover put to it?—I should say that a bound book would not be considered a newspaper.

133. Will you be good enough to answer my question specifically; it is not a bound book in the ordinary acceptation of the word; what I ask you is this, do you consider that putting a pasteboard cover upon a publication destroys its character as a newspaper?—No; I would not say but that the "Times" would be just as much a newspaper to-morrow morning with a pasteboard back as it is now.

134. Then why is the "Annual Register," which is wholly made up of public news, events, and occurrences, not a newspaper after your previous definition of what a newspaper is?—I should think that a great part of the "Annual Register" has long since ceased to be news.

135. I understood you to say at the outset, that a newspaper did not at all depend for its character upon the intervals at which it was published?—No; but the contents of it must be news, an account of recent transactions.

136. Is not the "Annual Register" full of occurrences and events?—Not recent; they have ceased to be news.

137. At what time does a publication cease to be a newspaper?—There is no interval of time of publication at which a paper shall not be deemed a newspaper, if it contains news; if your meaning is, when events or occurrences cease to be news, that I cannot say.

138. Does not the whole question depend as to whether a publication be a newspaper or not according to your position now, upon the intervals at which it is published?—No.

139. I understood you to say that the "Annual Register" is not a newspaper, because the events recorded there are of so old a date, that they cease to be news?—Yes; it is a matter of history then.

140. Then tell me what is the lapse of time necessary to destroy the character of a newspaper, and to give it the character of history?—There is no defined time.

141. Then

*J. Timm*, Esq.

2 May 1851.

141. Then how do you apply the law?—The question is, whether the matter of the publication is of recent occurrence; but I cannot say whether it should be a thing that has happened this week or last, or within the last month; I cannot define that; it is impossible that I can define news, any further than that it is an account of recent transactions.

142. If you are called upon to enforce the law, as you have laid it down to the Committee yourself, by what principle are you guided?—This: whether a publication really does injury to the fair traders; whether they would have reason to complain if a certain publication were allowed to go on; whether the proprietor of a stamped newspaper would have any fair and reasonable ground of complaint against us if we allowed it.

143. You are aware that the newspaper stamp has been laid on for the purposes of revenue?—Yes.

144. You are, as an officer connected with the Revenue Board, bound to protect the revenue?—Yes.

145. It is not, is it, to protect one class of publishers against others, that you enforce the law, but it is to protect the public revenue?—Yes; but in doing that we must endeavour not to strain the cord too tight, and carry the thing too far, otherwise it would become oppressive to the public, and therefore some discretion must be exercised.

146. With regard to monthly magazines, such as the "New Monthly Magazine," which contains a department called the "Chronicle of Events of the Month," do you consider that a newspaper?—Magazines have from the time that the newspaper stamp duty has been imposed, obtained a character different in some respects from that of a newspaper, because although they contain news in one or two articles, yet generally they are filled with other matter than is common to newspapers. When the duty was first imposed on newspapers, a different duty was also imposed upon pamphlets; and monthly magazines and things of that kind paid the pamphlet duty of so much a sheet upon one copy. That pamphlet duty was repealed some years ago, and it would not have been right, nor should we have been allowed, to turn round and say that a publication which up to that time had never been considered a newspaper, but as a pamphlet liable to the pamphlet duty, should upon the repeal of that duty be subject to the newspaper duty.

147. I am not speaking of comments now; pamphlets are comments?—But a pamphlet such as I speak of always contained news.

148. I am

*J. Timm,* Esq.

2 May 1851.

148. I am speaking of a magazine which contains a chronicle of events for the month; do you consider that to come under the definition of a newspaper?—It never has, from the time of the newspaper stamp duty being imposed, been considered as a newspaper.

149. If the decision on Monday in court should be, that "Dickens's Household Narrative," published monthly, is a newspaper, will not that decision also carry with it and include the large monthly publications, such as the "New Monthly Magazine?—No, their contents are totally different from Dickens's paper.

150. Mr. *Rich.*] In carrying out the law, do not you rather consider what is the general character of the newspaper, than any particular paragraph contained in it?—Exactly so.

151. "The Annual Register" you look upon as an historical record?—I do.

152. Not as a work containing news?—Not as a newspaper.

153. The chronicle in the "Monthly Magazine," you would regard as a chronicle of past events, rather than as a publication of news, would you not?—Certainly.

154. Mr. *Cobden.*] Is not the "Times" newspaper one of the most perfect historical records in existence?—Yes.

155. Yet you compel it to be stamped?—Yes, because it is news, full of news; it is the very thing upon which the legislature has imposed the duty, without any doubt whatever.

156. To go back again to the question, as to what course you pursue, in order to punish infractions of the law, you say that it is your duty, and the duty of every one connected with the Revenue Board, to see that the law is enforced?—Yes.

157. Suppose you see an advertisement in the "Times" newspaper, to this purport: "Just published, by Ridgway and Sons, the Speech of the Right honourable the Chancellor of the Exchequer, on proposing his Budget last Thursday in the House of Commons, price One Shilling;" would you think that it was your duty to see that that publication was stamped?—No.

158. But legally it ought to be stamped, you say?—No, I do not know that I said that.

159. Am I to understand you to say that the proprietor of the "West Riding Examiner" was liable to 1,800 *l.* penalty for reprinting a report of a trial, and that Ridgeway is not liable to any penalty for reprinting a report of the Chancellor of the Exchequer's speech?—If he repeated the whole of the debate

debate in the Commons upon the subject, I should say that it was news, and ought to be stamped as a newspaper, but as to printing the speech of the Chancellor of the Exchequer in the form of a pamphlet afterwards, I should not consider that that was a newspaper.

*J. Timm,* Esq.

2 May 1851.

160. *Chairman.*] Probably you recollect the case of the "Plymouth Journal;" the Queen's Speech having arrived at Plymouth too late to be inserted in the paper, in order to accommodate his customers, the publisher printed the speech upon a separate piece of paper, and sent it round to his subscribers?—I do not recollect that case; but it has frequently happened.

161. In that case a letter was received, asking him why he should not be prosecuted, and threatening to pursue him for a penalty of 20 *l.* for every copy; that was a strong measure, was it not?—No, I should like to see the letter; I should almost doubt whether it contained any threat to sue him for a penalty.

162. With regard to slips from newspapers, is it not a very common practice in London to publish separate parts of a newspaper upon unstamped paper?—I am not aware that it is.

163. If you were aware of it would you feel it your duty to interfere in such cases?—I should.

164. If it were brought before the Board?—Yes, provided the matter so printed were news.

165. If it were part of the newspaper, for instance, the Queen's Speech?—The Queen's Speech, I should say, was news.

166. Take the letter of Lord John Russell to the Bishop of Durham, which appeared first in the newspaper; and supposing that a person had taken it out, and printed it on a separate piece of paper, dispersed it, and made it public; would he be liable to a penalty of 20 *l.* for every such copy?—No; I should not hold that to be news at all.

167. What is the distinction you draw between the letter of the Minister upon a public subject, and the Queen's Speech?—The letter of the Minister, in the first place, is not a public document.

168. If I extracted, for instance, the account of a trial, or a meeting, or a speech, from the "Times," and printed it upon a piece of unstamped paper, and made it public, would you proceed against me, or not?—I should notice it if it were news. I should not proceed against you merely because it formed a part of the previous publication in the "Times."

169. Supposing

*J. Timm,* Esq.

2 May 1851.

169. Supposing there were speeches delivered at a meeting that had taken place in this town, and a report appeared in the "Times" newspaper, and I extracted that report from the "Times" newspaper, and printed it upon unstamped paper, and circulated it separately, would you proceed against me?—I should certainly notice it, as an infraction of the law.

170. Are you aware that such proceedings are very common in London?—No, I am not.

171. Mr. *Tufnell.*] You stated, as I understood you, that you considered that the Chancellor of the Exchequer's speech would not require a stamp, but that the Queen's Speech would; how do you draw the distinction between the two speeches?—The Queen's Speech is more of a state affair than that of the Chancellor of the Exchequer.

172. Mr. *Cobden.*] Do not you think that there is a great deal more interest taken in the Chancellor of the Exchequer's financial statement than in the Queen's Speech?—There may be. But, after all, the object of our noticing these things is not for the sake of the prosecution of a party for penalties, nor should we have prosecuted in all cases, but it is a matter of caution to the party; and unless we noticed the slightest infraction, as we might think, that comes to our knowledge, the thing proceeds, until ultimately it becomes a newspaper decidedly; and then if we prosecuted the party, he would say, "Why did not you tell me this before?"

173. How do you reconcile that statement with the course you pursued with my constituent in the West Riding of Yorkshire, from whom you extorted 10 *l.*?—In that case it was undoubtedly news of a very interesting nature that was published without stamps; 2,000 copies were printed; the duty upon those amounted, at 1 *d.*, to upwards of 8 *l.*, and he was let off for 10 *l.*; and he was complained of by a newspaper proprietor in that neighbourhood.

174. Sir *J. Walmsley.*] I apprehend that you are guided in your proceedings against parties for any infractions of the law rather by what a jury would say, than by your own discretion and judgment in the case?—That is the case; although when there is any infraction of the law, and we observe public news printed on unstamped paper, the party is written to and cautioned.

175. Mr. *Rich.*] Your first consideration is, has the law been broken?—Exactly.

176. And the second consideration is, can the law be enforced?—Yes; or whether it would be right to enforce it under the circumstances.

177. *Chairman.*]

J. Timm, Esq.

2 May 1851.

177. *Chairman.*] You have the Act of Parliament for your guide; I do not understand that those who have the charge of the public revenue are always considering what juries would think; but they are guided by the advice of the Attorney and Solicitor General, the law officers of the Crown, as to what is the proper construction of the Act of Parliament, are they not?—Yes; but they must have some reference as to what juries may think upon it; because, after all, they are ultimately to decide.

178. By the law?—It is a question of law and fact together, therefore they decide both under the direction of the judge. In the case that the honourable Chairman mentioned, there is no doubt that that "Poor Man's Guardian" contained comments and observations upon news, and it also contained news; but inasmuch as there was at the same time a paper which was as much a newspaper as the "Times" itself, Lord Lyndhurst, who tried the case, held up the paper to the jury, and said, "Gentlemen, with regard to this paper you can have no doubt." Holding up the "Poor Man's Guardian," he said, "Gentlemen, it is for you to say whether this is a newspaper; it appears to me to be a very meagre affair." It no doubt did contain comments and observations upon news, and it also contained a few slight articles of news, yet, left to them as it was by the judge, the jury found it to be not a newspaper.

179. Have you had no applications from the proprietors of newspapers, who are now under the necessity of stamping every copy that they publish, to be allowed the privilege that these 53 registered newspapers enjoy, of only stamping that portion which goes by post?—Yes.

180. Why have you not been able to grant those applications?—Because the law prevents the Board from doing so. They are undoubtedly newspapers; no question about it. As I have observed, it is no privilege: that which you have alluded to as a privilege is nothing that we can prevent.

181. You rather implied, did you not, that you did not interfere when there was no complaint from the proprietors of other newspapers?—No, I was misunderstood in that respect.

182. The proprietors of the other newspapers who stamp all those impressions, are applying to the Stamp Office for the privilege, which is not granted; and therefore they may be said to be complaining of the privilege which is enjoyed by the 53?—But there is a wide distinction between their publications and the publications of the applicants for this privilege

*J. Timm,* Esq.

2 May 1851.

privilege as it is termed. The papers of these applicants are clearly newspapers, without any doubt at all; and I think there can be no doubt that most, if not all, of those which are published one part stamped and the other unstamped, are not newspapers.

183. It seems that you can sometimes decide, and sometimes you cannot so readily decide what a newspaper is? —Yes; I should have no difficulty in deciding that the "Times" newspaper of this day is a newspaper, liable to stamp duty; some are so decidedly newspapers that nobody can entertain a doubt about it.

184. What should you say to that (*The "Assurance Record" being handed to the Witness*). Just read the first article. Is that comments or observations upon public intelligence?—The first paragraph is not news.

185. Is it comments or observations thereon?—Not upon news.

186. What is the title of it?—"Benefit Societies."

187. You may say what you please about benefit societies upon unstamped paper, may you not?—No; there may be news bout them as well as anything else, but this is not news.

188. What is the next?—It is an observation upon benefit societies generally, as to whether they are advantageous or not; but it is not news.

189. What is the next article?—"The Revenue."

190. Are comments and observations upon the revenue news?—I should say that that article was neither news, nor comments or observations upon news.

191. Not upon the revenue?—No.

192. Just read a little of it?—"The country remains in uncertainty about the financial arrangements for the ensuing year; it would therefore not be unprofitable if we attempt to define what can and ought to be done by the Chancellor of the Exchequer to lighten the burdens of taxation." Now if there be any news in that, it is in the first line and a half. Then they go on: "The late Sir Robert Peel justly declared that the taxing of the commodities which support life had reached its highest limit." I should say that that was not news, nor any observations upon news. I should look at it generally.

193. If a man may write an article upon the public revenue and the budget of the year, giving his views as to what ought to be done, and what can be done, is not that something very like commenting and observing upon public intelligence; and what the "Times" does in its leading article.

*J. Timm, Esq.*

2 May 1851.

article. I do not see what distinction you can draw?—The whole of the difficulty that is attempted to be raised, is raised only by those who are desirous of sailing as near to the wind as possible.

194. If the thing be of such a peculiar character, that no two men can be found to agree upon it at all, does not it become rather a questionable matter for a tax. One could understand taxing a horse or a gig, but as you do not seem to be able to agree as to what news is, neither juries, nor Attorney or Solicitor General, is it not rather a questionable matter for a tax?—No; the tax has existed a century and a half and upwards, and it seems to have been taken at the time it was imposed as a matter of notoriety what was a newspaper, and there has been no difficulty until of late years, and then it has been raised and felt solely by parties whose desire is to evade the law; with those who publish things that are really newspapers, there is neither doubt nor difficulty.

195. You recollect when the stamp duty was reduced, do not you?—Yes.

196. Can you call to mind the number of people that were imprisoned at one time for printing news on unstamped paper?—I cannot say the number. Upon the whole, I believe there were 40 or 50 people.

197. Were not the prosecutions very frequent?—Yes.

198. Is it not the fact that the impossibility of enforcing the duty at that time was one of the principal reasons alleged for reducing it?—Yes; the impossibility was caused by the want of a more stringent law, and especially by the want of power to search.

199. Was not Hetherington's case in itself a proof how difficult the taxation of news was, or anything that was printed in the nature of comments upon news about that time?—If that publication of Hetherington's, the "Poor Man's Guardian," had been submitted alone to the court and jury they would have held it to be a newspaper; but because they had two papers before them, and one was decidedly a newspaper (and there were papers published in those days without any stamp, as much newspapers as the "Times" itself), the jury comparing the two together, and having regard to the observation which fell from the Lord Chief Baron, that one of them was a meagre affair, let the defendant off the penalty in respect of that one. But I think the decision of the jury in that case was influenced more by a desire to relieve the party from an additional penalty than from any opinion entertained about the publication being within the Act.



200. Mr.

*J. Timm,* Esq.

2 May 1851.

200. Mr. *Rich.*] Have you had many prosecutions with regard to violations of the stamp laws?—Not many that have gone on to any length of proceeding. Writs have been issued, but they always have been for slight infringements of the law.

201. Speaking from your own legal experience, has there been greater difficulty found in carrying out the law with regard to the stamps tax upon newspapers than in carrying out the law with regard to exciseable matters or customs?—No, I should say not; I should say that there is no difficulty experienced in the department of inland revenue in collecting what is fairly the duty upon newspapers.

202. *Chairman.*] Does not the experience of the past show that the endeavour to enforce the law by prosecutions has rather operated as a check upon the Stamp Office, showing that the best way to keep the stamp at all is to allow an extensive violation of the law to go on with impunity?—I do not consider that an extensive violation of the law does go on.

203. Do not you consider that a considerable violation does go on?—No, I cannot call it a violation of the law, publishing a paper that I think a court and jury would not hold to be a newspaper.

204. Are there not many publications now issued into a face of day without a stamp, to the proprietors of which the have written, cautioning them that they are liable you penalty?—I dare say there may be; but it does not follow that because I have cautioned a party against continuing to insert news, that I have prosecuted him because he continues that publication. If he goes on to a certain length, until I think that the paper has become such a one as a court would hold to be a newspaper, I should submit it to the Board for prosecution.

205. Are there not cases in which you have pointed out to parties that the publication of certain matter without a stamp rendered them liable to a prosecution, and yet they have still gone on and no steps have been taken?—I am not aware of that.

206. You do not know that it is not so?—No; it does not follow that because I should caution a party against inserting matter which may be news in his paper, and he continues to do so, that I should prosecute him for a penalty.

207. Those letters do not mean that you will prosecute after all, do they?—They do if I say that I will; if he then joins issue with me upon it, I should go on.

208. What

*J. Timm,* Esq.

2 May 1851.

208. What has been the cause of the delay in the proceedings against the proprietors of the "Narrative of Current Events;" when did you write your first letter?—More than a twelvemonth ago.

209. Since that they have gone on publishing the same matter in the same form without a stamp, have they not?—They have, but there is a prosecution pending.

210. What has been the cause of the delay?—It was agreed to submit the question to the court in a mode to avoid expense as much as possible; that the facts should be stated in a special case for the opinion of the court and not for a trial by jury; but the delay occurred through the disagreement of counsel in the settlement of that case. Now if it had not ultimately been settled, I should have tried it in a prosecution hostilely; and in order to compel the parties to come to some terms, I actually issued a writ, and commenced a hostile prosecution against Messrs. Bradbury & Evans, to try the case before a jury, and then counsel agreed, and a case was stated, and it stands for argument on Monday next. There has been no delay on the part of the Crown that could be avoided.

211. Mr. *Cobden.*] What is the point that you consider to be at issue in the trial to come on next Monday?—The question is, whether a paper, which from its contents would be a newspaper, if published at intervals not exceeding 26 days, is liable to stamp duty when published at intervals beyond that limit. It is a question of law.

212. *Chairman.*] You have no doubt yourself of the law; the Attorney and Solicitor General have advised you that it is a newspaper?—We were advised before the last Act of Parliament that the definition of a newspaper contained in 60 Geo. 3 did not supersede the more general one in the former Acts; I think it was Sir James Scarlett and Sir Edward Sugden (I am not certain) who advised that a paper was liable to duty although it was published at intervals exceeding 26 days; and in a prosecution at the period before alluded to against Carpenter, who was prosecuted for publishing a series of letters, political letters; one, a letter to Sir Robert Peel, and another to somebody else, but all containing news; those were not parts or numbers, we could not connect one with another; and there the question was, whether the papers, not being portions of a periodical or parts or numbers, were liable to duty. Lord Lyndhurst intimated that a paper might be a newspaper although not within the definition contained in 60 Geo. 3.

213. Mr. *Cobden.*] Supposing the court should rule that in

*J. Timm*, Esq.

2 May 1851.

in the case that has been referred to the publication is a newspaper, although published at intervals of a month, how would you deal with a publication coming out bi-monthly?—Supposing that at the time when it was published it contained the news of the day, I should say that it was a newspaper, without reference to its being periodical or otherwise.

214. And without reference to its bulk?—No, I have not said that; it would depend upon what the contents were; if the whole contents of it were news, I should say that it was liable.

215. If the whole contents were news, and if the news were brought up to the latest period at which it could be collected for publication, would you consider the work to be a newspaper, no matter what its bulk might be?—That must depend upon the character of the publication.

216. I have given you the character; a work comprised of foreign news, events, and occurrences brought up to the latest period at which it could be collected for publication; would you consider that a newspaper, whatever its bulk might be, and whatever period of time it might cover in its narrative of events?—I should perhaps not think that that was a case in which to insist on the liability to duty, although the publication might contain news.

217. Will you give the Committee a definition of the law, according to your interpretation of it; and assuming that the court shall rule that you are right in saying when a publication ceases to be a newspaper; you say you are going for damages because a work is published monthly with news; the publishers say, "We are not liable to pay the tax." You say its being published at a month's interval makes no difference. Will you inform the Committee whether there is any limit in your mind to that definition?—My opinion is that the paper is a newspaper without reference to its being published at any intervals whatever.

218. And without reference to its bulk?—If the bulk consisted wholly of news I should say then, without reference to its bulk.

219. Will you tell me whether, by a strict interpretation of the law, you can say that the "Annual Register" is not a newspaper?—It certainly is not in my opinion.

220. Mr. *Rich.*] You consider it in the light of a history of the past year, do you not?—Yes.

221. Mr. *Cobden.*] I understand you to say, that you consider a publication to be a newspaper, if it contains news and occurrences, no matter what its size may be, or what the

*J. Timm*, Esq.

2 May 1851.

the time may be over which its narrative ranges: am I right?—No; I do not think that you are.

222. Will you define then the bulk to which you go in your definition of a newspaper: have you any limit?—No. The fact is, you want me to give you a definition which it is impossible to give. You want me so closely to define it, as to say whether a single line makes a paper liable to the stamp duty or not.

223. You are aware that you have suppressed some papers which were published monthly, under the belief that they were exempted from the newspaper stamp, because they were published at so long an interval. I will mention the case of Mr. Bucknell of Stroud, who published a paper, of which he sold 1,700 copies monthly, and that paper was dropped. It was called the "Stroud Free Press." There was another paper, called the "Norwich Reformers' Gazette"; that was published monthly, under the belief that as it was at so long an interval it was not a newspaper. You threatened the publisher with a prosecution, and he being in a small way of business and in humble circumstances, he discontinued the paper immediately. There was one or two Welsh papers, were published in Welsh, and those papers were discontinued n the same way. A mere letter from you frightened those poor people into submission, and they dropped their papers; saying that they had acted under the belief that the newspaper was not a newspaper, because published monthly, They had purchased type, had made arrangements for reporting, and advertised their newspaper, and it was stopped, because it was still a newspaper by your interpretation of the law, although published monthly. What guarantee will the public have that they will not be stopped in the same way from publishing works bi-monthly or tri-monthly, unless you define the time at which they may publish them?—There is no time at all; I say that the single publication of a paper containing news is a newspaper.

224. Mr. *Ewart*.] Then if a history contains news, which is brought up to a certain date, it becomes a newspaper?—If published in numbers, and the history goes on from day to day, otherwise you might publish a History of England and bring it down to the opening of the Exhibition.

225. Mr. *Cobden*.] You say published from day to day; the Committee have brought you to this point, that you will not allow a paper to be published from month to month; I want to know whether you will allow a paper to be published bi-monthly?—

*J. Timm,* Esq.

2 May 1851.

bi-monthly?—No; if it is a newspaper, it ought not to be published at all without a stamp on each copy.

226. If it is a tri-monthly record of news published every three months, and brought up to the latest time, you would compel it to be stamped still?—Yes, if one paper were published which I thought a newspaper, I should not wait to see if any further papers were published, whether perodically, or at any intervals whatever.

227. Then if Mr. Dickens should determine to publish a six-months narrative of public events, should that be stamped the same as a monthly publication?—Very likely not, because the greater part of that publication would be filled with matter that was not news, but matter of history.

228. Will you tell me when you cease to regard a publication as news, and then commence to view it as a history?—We do not clearly understand each other upon this point; you have reference to the intervals of publication, and you say that I hold that a paper published monthly or bi-monthly, would be a newspaper if it contains news, but I take it that your question really is, when do occurrences cease to be news, and that I cannot define.

229. How are the public to know what they can publish without stamps?—They cannot publish a paper containing news without a stamp, that is all I can say.

230. Do you mean to say that they can publish at no time the events of the past year, or the events of the past six months, or the past month, without a stamp?—No, I do not mean that; when they are published as a record, as a matter of history, that is not, I think, a newspaper subject to the newspaper stamp duty.

231. Is not the "Narrative of Public Events," published by Dickens, an historical narrative, when compared with the daily record of the "Times" newspaper?—It may be, but looking at Dickens's newspaper, no one can entertain a doubt that its contents are such as are usually contained in all newspapers. There is no doubt about the contents. If Dickens's paper were published daily or weekly, no one would doubt that it was a newspaper; and it is not the less so because it is published monthly.

232. If I understand you correctly, Mr. Dickens will be liable to the same interference from you if he publishes the "Narrative of Public Events" bi-monthly, as if it were published monthly?—Yes, if it contain news.

233. I am supposing a work of the same character altogether published once in two months; will you say specifically, that it

*J. Timm,* Esq.

2 May 1851.

it is your view of the case that that would be liable to a stamp?—If the contents were events as recent as those contained in his monthly publication, I should hold it to be so.

234. Understand me always that I put it as a publication carried out, only merely extended, upon precisely the same principle as the monthly publication; you say that if carried on and published bi-monthly, and brought up to the latest hour, you would still consider it liable to a stamp?—Yes, if the character of the contents were the same as at present.

235. If he brought this publication out tri-monthly, always retaining the same character in the work, and publishing it up to the latest hour at which it could be brought out, would that be liable to a stamp?—Now you are stating a hypothetical case, not likely to be carried out practically; I cannot imagine that he would publish such a publication tri-monthly.

236. Supposing this publication to come out every three months, precisely the same in character, would it be liable to a stamp?—I think it would be published in such a form in that case, that it would not be deemed a newspaper.

237. I am assuming the same character of work entirely? —His present publication is a broad sheet not stitched or bound, but if he brought it out as you speak of, it would no doubt be a book.

238. I am assuming that he brings it out in precisely the same form, but intended to be bound into a volume, in wrappers or without wrappers at all?—It is a difficult question to answer, unless I had the supposed publication before me.

239. I understand you to say that you are clear as to the law for a month; that there is no doubt that a monthly publication of news must be stamped?—I do not apply myself to a periodical publication at all.

240. You are quite clear that Dickens's "Household Narrative," published monthly, is liable to a stamp, are you?—Yes, that is my opinion; but the point stands for the decision of the Court of Exchequer.

241. And you have admitted that if the same work were published bi-monthly, and retained the same character, then it would also be liable to a stamp?—It would depend upon the form and character of it. It cannot be published bi-monthly and maintain the same character.

242. Am I to understand you to say that bulk makes any difference in the character of a publication?—Bulk and form together might. I should say that I could not insist upon a book in this form and size (*pointing to a book*) being stamped

*J. Timm,* Esq.

2 May 1851.

stamped as a newspaper; it would be ridiculous to say that that was a newspaper.

243. If Mr. Dickens published his "Household Narrative" in a more extended and minute form of news, and put it in the shape of Tait's "Magazine," with a buff cover, would you still consider it as a newspaper?—No, I think that it would assume the character of a magazine.

244. Then do you say that if Dickens's "Narrative of Public Events" were published without a buff cover, like Tait's "Magazine," being a more perfect record of facts than now, more minute, more detailed, and consequently more valuable as a newspaper, it would not be liable to a stamp?—I think if it were published monthly, and the whole body of it were of the same character as at present, it would still be liable to a stamp duty in whatever form it might be.

245. Whatever the size and whatever the cover?—The cover can make no difference.

246. When you move on to two months instead of one month, do you then interpret the law with the same conditions?—We have never had such a case.

247. I will assume that you have these bi-monthly publications: will you inform the Committee when a book ceases to be a newspaper?—I cannot tell you.

248. Mr. *Rich.*] In all questions of law, have you not found it very difficult to define precisely the matter at issue? —Certainly.

249. And that the definition is generally made out by experience from proceedings before the courts?—It is so. And in all revenue matters, if it is to depend upon so nice a definition as the honourable Member for the West Riding would suppose ought to exist, it would be impossible to collect any revenue at all.

250. With regard to newspapers, do you not find that every publication, by so much as it recedes from being a daily publication, recedes from the character of a newspaper, and that a weekly newspaper is less of a newspaper than a daily one?—Yes.

251. So that a publication, if it came out fortnightly, would bear less of the character of a newspaper, and so as the distance increased, it would recede more from the character of a newspaper?—Yes; because its contents become more and more other than those of news, and are matters of history. Bi-monthly publications, containing a narrative of all the occurrences of the bi-monthly period, must contain a quantity

quantity of matter which would be deemed rather stale as news. *J. Timm, Esq.*

2 May 1851.

252. If a weekly newspaper were published in the same manner, and with the same topics, and the same method of recording events as a daily newspaper, would it not cease to be remunerative?—Undoubtedly; that is my opinion.

253. If conducted in the same way it would more and more fall off if it became a fortnightly or a monthly one?—Yes.

254. In that point of view, you conceive that were Mr. Dickens to publish at the end of every two or three months, a paper similar to that which he publishes now at the end of a month, he must necessarily, in order to obtain a sale, so modify its character?—Yes, he would modify its character by making it less of a newspaper.

255. If Mr. Dickens were now to establish his right to publish his newspaper monthly, would it not be competent for him to combine with some other persons who might also bring out what they would call a monthly newspaper, and then publish them in succession on the first week, the second week, the third week, and the fourth week of every month, whereby they would in fact have a weekly newspaper, and avoid paying the stamp duty?—Certainly that plan might be adopted, and unless we could prove that those publications were one and the same, the newspaper stamp duty would be evaded altogether.

256. Mr. *Cobden*.] You stated in answer to a question just put to you, that a newspaper receded from the character of a newspaper according to the longer interval at which it was published; I presume you do not wish to imply that that is a rule which applies to all periodical publications; I have in my hand a list of some twenty or thirty weekly publications which are not newspapers you say, but in the case of Dickens's "Household Narrative," published monthly, you say that is a newspaper; how is that consistent with your answer that a publication becomes less of a newspaper in proportion to the longer interval at which it appears?—The publications to which you allude, do not generally contain news.

257. Then it does not follow that a publication should be more of a newspaper because it is published weekly?—Yes, if it purports to give the occurrences; the further you recede from them the less they have the character of news.

258. *Chairman*.] You state that a publication may have some news in it, and be allowed to be published without a stamp?—

*J. Timm,* Esq.

2 May 1851.

stamp?—I will not say that they would be allowed to be published; it is one thing allowing to be published, and another to refrain from prosecuting that party for the penalty.

259. It is virtually allowing it if you do not interfere, is it not?—We caution parties.

260. Suppose you caution them and they still go on, is that not allowing them afterwards?—I think there is some distinction.

261. You state that the large publications of high price and large size, and so forth, may comment without a stamp at intervals of less than two months?—Yes, if they exceed two sheets, and are sold for more than sixpence.

262. Small ones under sixpence, and small in size, are not allowed to comment without a stamp?—That is the law.

263. You stated that the Queen's speech was news, did you not?—Yes.

264. Then comments upon the Queen's speech must be comments upon news?—Yes.

265. Look at the leading article of that publication (*handing a paper to the Witness*), and say whether it comments upon news?—This is not a comment upon any particular Queen's speech, it would serve for all Queen's speeches, and all King's speeches, it is so general.

266. Just read the first passage, and the title of it?—"The Queen's speech. A sneering philosopher once said that language was given to man in order to enable him to conçeal his thoughts, and whatever truth that opinion may have in relation to affairs in general, there is very little doubt but that it is peculiarly applicable to Royal speeches in general, and to the speech for 1851 in particular."

267. Is not that a case of comment upon news, below the price at which parties are entitled to comment without a stamp?—It is so as far as that goes.

268. Is it not the fact that the law is extensively violated; can you deny that?—I cannot hold such trifling things as these, whatever number there may be, as extensive violations of the law; they are very slight infringements indeed.

*Martis*, 6° *die Maii*, 1851.

MEMBERS PRESENT.

Mr. Cobden.
Mr. Rich.
Mr. Ewart.
Mr. G. A. Hamilton.
Mr. Chichester Fortescue.
Mr. Shafto Adair.
Sir T. F. Lewis.
Mr. Sotheron.
Sir J. Walmsley.

THE RIGHT HON. THOMAS MILNER GIBSON,
IN THE CHAIR.

---

*Thomas Keogh*, Esq., called in; and Examined.

*T. Keogh*, Esq.

6 May 1851.

269. *Chairman.*] WHAT office do you hold at the Board of Inland Revenue?—I hold the office of Assistant Secretary for Inland Revenue.

270. Is it a part of your duties to have brought under your notice the newspaper stamps?—All the business, the secretarial business, relating to newspapers or stamps; I attend the Board and transact all the business that passes at the Board with them relating to that description of business, as well as many others.

271. Then you are cognizant of the proceedings that take place when parties propose to establish a newspaper?—I am not cognizant of the proposal; the sending in of the particulars, the names of the proprietors, and publishers, and printers; that is all transacted in the solicitor's office. When a person desires to set up a newspaper he is told to go to the solicitor's office, where a printed form is provided, stating everything he has to do in the matter; he has to state the names of the proprietors, publishers, and the printers, the sureties for the advertisement duty, and sureties against libels. He then sets down those particulars in a printed form, and inquiries are made by the solicitor without any distinct order of the Board on the subject, except under a general order, as to the sufficiency of the persons proposed as sureties; and if he finds them sufficient he always submits the inquiries to the Board, and if they approve of them they are accepted, and the qualification is completed.

272. I

*T. Keogh,* Esq.

6 May 1851.

272. I have frequently seen letters addressed to persons connected with the press, bearing your signature?—Yes; every letter from the Board upon the subject is signed by me.

273. You write on the part of the Board, do you not?—Yes.

274. You are aware, I suppose, of the views which are taken by the Board as to the law relating to newspaper stamps?—Yes.

275. And you are aware of the practice that prevails under that law?—Yes.

276. How many places are there in the United Kingdom where papers are stamped?—London and Manchester for England, and Edinburgh and Dublin.

277. What papers are stamped in London?—There are not only all the London newspapers, but a great many that are published in the country; and persons find it more advantageous to deal with paper-makers or paper agents in the vicinity of London, even for the supply of distant parts of the country, than with paper-makers in their own neighbourhood.

278. Supposing a newspaper, for instance, published at Norwich, would the publisher be obliged to send the paper to London to be stamped?—They do not send the paper to London; they deal with a paper-maker or paper agent, the former having his manufactory in the vicinity of London, and the latter his place of business in London, and he provides the stamps for them, and transmits them to them.

279. But otherwise, if there were no paper-makers or agents that it suited their purpose to deal with near London, they must send the paper from the country to London, must they not?—If there were no such thing as a paper-maker or agent, but that is not the case; there are most eminent paper-makers in the vicinity of London.

280. Does not that give an advantage to the paper-manufacturer near the place of stamping, over the paper-manufacturer at a distance?—I should think it does. There is great competition amongst paper-manufacturers and paper agents; they send their travellers about to all the newspaper proprietors, and offer them terms which perhaps are something under those at which they had been previously supplied. For instance, the proprietors of some newspapers that are published in Glasgow do not deal with the manufacturers of paper at Edinburgh, of whom there are several very eminent ones; Mr. Cowan amongst the number; but they

*T. Keogh,* Esq.

6 May 1851.

they deal with a person at Manchester, and he supplies them from Manchester, instead of people at Glasgow or Edinburgh.

281. All the paper that is printed in Glasgow has to be sent from Manchester to Glasgow, when there are paper-manufacturers close to Glasgow where it might be purchased in the first instance?—Yes, all the paper ordered from Manchester for the newspapers to which I have referred.

282. Sir *T. F. Lewis.*] What I understood you to say was, that they bought paper manufactured in the neighbourhood of Manchester, and printed it in Edinburgh and Glasgow; not made in Scotland?—I will explain. What I meant to say was this, that several newspaper publishers at Glasgow find it their interest to deal with the paper-makers at Manchester, and to have their stamps transmitted from Manchester, where they are impressed, to Glasgow, instead of dealing with a person at Glasgow, who would only have to send the paper to Edinburgh, to be stamped there.

283. *Chairman.*] Have you received any complaints at the Board of Inland Revenue of the inconvenience arising from there being only this limited number of stamping places in the United Kingdom?—We have.

284. Can you lay before the Committee the nature of those complaints, or the letters that conveyed them?—Yes; I have no objection. The one I principally recollect, and which was pressed most urgently upon the Board, was from a person at Glasgow. He proposed a variety of schemes. One was, that the stamp should be impressed in a mill, instead of at the stamping establishment belonging to the revenue; and another, that if that could not be done, a special stamping establishment should be formed at Glasgow, within a very short distance of Edinburgh, as the Committee know. Originally, some years ago, perhaps 15 years ago, there was but one place for stamping. London was the only place; and then the papers in the north of England, and some of the papers in Scotland, pressed very hard to have an establishment at Edinburgh. That was conceded, and very shortly after that it was thought that the north of England should have a place where they might have their papers stamped without sending to London, and so Manchester was established.

285. Would not the necessity of sending so far for stamped paper cause it to be necessary for a newspaper publisher to keep a larger stock of stamped paper by him than he would have to keep if, when any sudden necessity arose,

T. Keogh, Esq.

6 May 1851.

arose, he could apply on the spot for a further supply of stamped paper?—No doubt it does require a newspaper proprietor to be provided against emergencies, by having a larger stock on hand. But it was conceived, when the duty was reduced from 4 *d.* to 1 *d.*, that that would not be a very great evil or hardship upon the newspaper proprietors.

286. Sir *T. F. Lewis.*] Does a proprietor pay duty as soon as he receives the stamps?—Before he receives the stamps.

287. Mr. *Rich.*] Do not railways and electric telegraphs obviate a good deal of that inconvenience?—Yes, certainly.

288. *Chairman.*] Will you state more fully what were the grounds of complaint to which I alluded just now?—The ground of complaint was, that it was a hardship (if you allude to the case at Glasgow) for persons at Glasgow to be obliged to send the paper to Edinburgh. The gentleman himself who made this complaint is a paper-maker; and his object, as it appeared to me, was to get for himself the supply of newspapers that he does not now supply, notwithstanding his propinquity to the parties. Several, as I have before said, of the Glasgow newspaper proprietors, choose to get their paper from Manchester, or the larger portion of it.

289. Surely it is a disadvantage to the paper manufacturers who live at a distance from a stamping place to be deprived of their fair share of the market for the supply of paper?—They may esteem it so, no doubt; but I should think that the person who requires the paper is the best judge of the place at which he ought to get it for his own advantage.

290. Will not it be always for his advantage to get it from a paper manufacturer nearer the Stamp Office, because it will have the least distance to travel?—I should suppose not; I should suppose that the people who now deal with paper manufacturers at Manchester get their paper upon cheaper terms than they could get it from a person at Glasgow; otherwise they would have no motive in dealing with a Manchester manufacturer.

291. How is the practice in the case of the south of England?—The south is supplied from London, of course.

292. Why should not the paper be stamped where there is a stamp office or a collection of excise?—In the first instance, you should have a stamping establishment and a supervision. There are certain checks upon stamping which are necessary, and which do exist at Manchester and at Edinburgh

Edinburgh just as much as in London, and you could not confide a parcel of dies to any ordinary person to impress on any quantity of paper, without having the strictest check over the number that he impresses.

*T. Keogh,* Esq.

6 May 1851.

293. You collect the excise duties in various parts of the United Kingdom, do not you?—Yes, and so we have a distributor of stamps in every county in England, and sometimes two in one county. His office, if a stamping establishment were to be introduced, would be the place at which the stamping would be carried on, but it would be a very great expense.

294. I have received a communication from Glasgow, from which I will read this passage: "There are now in Glasgow and neighbourhood about 20 newspaper proprietors, who are compelled to get their paper stamped either in London, Manchester, or Edinburgh. About two years ago 16 news proprietors of Glasgow forwarded a petition to the Board of Inland Revenue, praying that they might have their paper stamped on the spot, and pointing out the great inconvenience and expense in transmitting their paper even to and from Edinburgh, the transit being 92 miles; and although this petition pointed out to the Board how this stamping could be done wherever there was a collection of excise, with all its extra officers attached, who could discharge the duty required without a farthing of expense to the revenue, still the Board was immovable"?—I have not any precise recollection, in the vast mass of business of different descriptions that passes through my hands, of that; that is to say, of any petition from the whole body of newspaper proprietors at Glasgow, the 16 mentioned. The only application of which I have a distinct recollection is from the person I mentioned before, who is a paper-maker, and who seemed to have in view his own advantage.

295. Will you make a note to supply the Committee with that memorial, and the reply?—Yes.

296. Is it for the prevention of fraud that you consider it necessary to confine the stamping to those particular places?—That is one of the reasons; another reason is the expense that would be incurred to the revenue by having separate stamping establishments all over the country.

297. Would there be any necessity for an addition to the establishment if the duty of stamping were added to the other duties of the excise?—Most certainly; for instance, we have detached from the head office, I think, four stampers at Manchester, with a supervisor, and I think five at Edinburgh

*T. Keogh*, Esq.

6 May 1851.

burgh, with a supervisor placed there to control them; and no stamp is impressed except under a warrant, which acknowledges, by the receiver-general, or some other receiving officer, the payment of the duty, and authorizes the stamping of the number mentioned in the warrant. That goes into the hands of the stamping officers, and it would be a high offence if those persons impressed a single stamp without having such a warrant, or impressed a stamp more or less than the number mentioned in the warrant.

298. Are you of opinion that this convenience could not be extended to newspaper proprietors of stamping in various parts of the United Kingdom, in addition to the places where they now stamp, without the danger of fraud and of increased expense to the country?—I think such a concession could be made to them without the danger of fraud, if the expense were incurred; but there would be a great increase of expense.

299. Mr. *S. Adair.*] Can you state what the expense of the separate establishments at Edinburgh and Manchester amounts to?—About 500 *l.* at year at Manchester.

300. And probably the same at Edinburgh?—It is something less at Edinburgh.

301. Mr. *Rich.*] Practically you find that the newspaper publisher at Glasgow prefers sending to Manchester, a greater distance, to having his paper stamped at Edinburgh, which is nearer?—I know he does so, and I assume that it is for his own advantage that he does so.

302. Mr. *Ewart.*] Is it the cheapness which determines his preference?—That I cannot know; I only infer from the circumstance of his choosing to do so, that there is a sufficient motive.

303. Mr. *Cobden.*] Do you think that there would be a great risk of fraud if the exciseman in the neighbourhood where newspapers were printed were allowed to affix the stamps to the paper on the spot?—I think it might possibly be done under certain checks; it would necessarily repose a new trust in the exciseman, but he should do it as I have described, under warrants, which are his sole authority for the act of stamping; you could not entrust to an exciseman and put into his hands dies to impress any quantity of paper without any check; you must have some check over him that he impresses only the quantity for which the revenue has been paid.

304. You remember probably the time when there was an excise duty upon printed cottons?—Yes; but I am not sufficiently

sufficiently informed upon matters of excise to give the Committee much information; I have a general recollection that there was such a thing as a duty.

T. Keogh, Esq.

6 May 1851.

305. Probably you are aware that when that duty existed the excisemen visited every printing place in the kingdom, and affixed the stamp at the end of the piece of cotton?—Yes, that I believe was one of the many precautions or securities; the stamping was only an ingredient for the security of the revenue from fraud, which was partly secured by many other means; but the stamp in the case of a newspaper is the only thing that denotes the payment of the duty.

306. Are you aware that the stamp affixed to cottons was very similar indeed in form to the stamp impressed on newspapers?—No.

307. That was the case, and it was subject to no check excepting that which is exercised over the excisemen in taking the duty on paper or soap, or any other article liable to excise duty?—I apprehend that that is quite a different matter; the exciseman visits a soap manufactory, and ascertains the exact quantity which has been manufactured, or is in certain process of manufacture, and from time to time he makes a report, and that is supervised by another officer, a supervisor, who ascertains as far, I believe, as very close checks can do, that no fraud is committed by the manufacturer; all this I say from general impression merely.

308. Are you aware that in the case of cotton goods one of the arguments why the duty should be abolished was, that great frauds were supposed to exist?—I believe there is scarcely any branch of the excise revenue in which they do not exist.

309. Do you consider that it is necessary that the printers of newspapers should obtain the supply of their papers from three central sources, to prevent the frauds that would arise if you entrusted an exciseman in the vicinity of each newspaper with the stamps?—The stamp which is imposed upon a newspaper is in common with all other stamp duties, the forgery of which would be a transportable offence; now I apprehend that in the cases you mention, where the excise, for its own security, in addition to every other, choose to impress a stamp, as they do now, upon paper, and upon other things, that stamp is not considered of the important character of a stamp duty, which is secured by the highest punishment that the law awards for any forgery, or imitation, or other offence.

310. Am I to understand that the reason why you restrict the

T. Keogh, Esq.

6 May 1851.

the stamping of newspapers to three places, London, Edinburgh, and Manchester is, that you would be afraid of frauds if you entrusted the dies to the local excisemen?—Pardon me; that is not the reason. As I have said before, the original sole place of stamping newspapers was the place where every other stamp is impressed, that is, at the head office in London. In consequence of the representations that were made from Edinburgh and from the north of England, the Board consented to establish exactly the same kind of stamp-office as is at the head office for newspapers at Edinburgh, and upon subsequent representations they made a similar concession to Manchester; but they have never considered it necessary, nor thought of such a thing, as establishing a variety of stamp-offices all over the kingdom for impressing newspaper stamps. We never had such a proposition before us as the introduction of stamp-offices all over the kingdom for newspapers; therefore I cannot say that any such reason as was referred to prevailed in the minds of the Board.

311. What I wish to draw you attention, and that of the Board, to, is this, that in all other cases where any article is liable to duty, the exciseman visits the manufactory in which the article is produced, and there levies the tax; but in the case of newspapers you require the publisher of a newspaper to send the paper sometimes a hundred miles, in order to have the Government stamp affixed to it; and I ask whether the reason why the printing business of a newspaper is subjected to that great inconvenience, delay, and loss, be in order to protect the revenue from the frauds that you apprehend if you entrusted excisemen to levy the tax on the premises, as was done in the case of cotton prints, and in the case of printed papers for furniture?—The answer I should give to that question is this, that the revenue of the excise is collected under totally different regulations from those under which the stamp revenue is received; and there is not the slightest analogy in any one particular between the mode in which the duties under the excise department are charged and collected, and those under which the stamp revenue is collected; there is no such thing as visitation.

312. Was it with the view to prevent fraud that you have not entertained the idea of levying this duty on the premises and at the establishments of the parties?—To that I should answer that it was not with any idea of preventing fraud, because the idea of the thing never occurred, and was never debated,

*T. Keogh,* Esq.

6 May 1851

debated, of putting the stamp duties upon the same terms as the excise duties, which are collected by visitations of the premises of the manufacturers by the excise officers, to ascertain what quantity of goods liable to duty, exciseable articles, they make. All that is quite foreign from the Stamp Office, which has nothing to do but to impress the stamp upon the paper after it is paid for, and deliver it to the parties.

313. You have stated that the idea has never been entertained by you to stamp newspapers on the premises where they are printed, but you have had complaints and remonstrances on the inconvenience of sending newspapers to be stamped for 50 miles, have you not?—With regard to complaints of not permitting the stamps to be impressed at the place where the newspapers were printed, there was never such a suggestion as that. It has been proposed to put the stamp on where the paper was made, but never where it was printed; that would be in the private establishment of each newspaper proprietor.

314. The Glasgow memorialists who complained of the trouble and expense of sending the paper to Edinburgh would be satisfied if they had the papers stamped at the manufacturers at Glasgow, would they not?—I suppose they would.

315. You have never entertained the subject at the Inland Revenue Board of the inconvenience and loss that newspaper printers are subjected to, owing to the necessity of having their paper stamped from a distance?—We never have, further than to the extent I have mentioned, that we consented to furnish Scotland with the stamps from Edinburgh, and also portions of the north of England from Manchester.

316. Mr. *Ewart.*] You can lay the memorials on these subjects before the Committee, can you not?—I shall be glad to do so.

317. Mr. *Cobden.*] You stated, did you not, that the publishers of newspapers in the west and south of England generally obtained their paper from London?—Yes.

318. The publishers of papers in the north of England will get their paper from Manchester?—Yes.

319. That would include the publishers in North Wales, I presume?—It would.

320. Take a Carnarvon newspaper, the publisher would obtain the raw material from Manchester, would he not?—Yes, he might; but it is a very extraordinary thing that there

*T. Keogh,* Esq.

6 May 1851.

there are proprietors of newspapers in the neighbourhood of Manchester who obtain their paper from London.

321. Suppose a person publishing a newspaper in Kent, in the neighbourhood of Maidstone, and there is a paper manufactory in his neighbourhood, the paper manufacturer I presume sends his paper for sale to London as a rule?—Yes; but that is not the way in which the thing really occurs. There are a great many agents in London of paper manufacturers, who supply all the newspaper proprietors that they can get the supply of, direct from London, upon terms agreed on between them. The transaction occurs in this way between the newspaper proprietor and the agent: he writes to Venables & Company, or some other great agent, that he wants on such a day so many reams of paper. This agent comes to the office, pays the duty upon it, and states the newspaper for which the stamp is wanted, and the stamps are impressed and delivered back to him, and he forwards them to the newspaper proprietor; so that it is a transaction in fact not directly between the paper manufacturer and the newspaper proprietor, but between a great agent in London for the sale of the paper, who pays for the stamps and has them impressed, and sends them back with his charge for the paper and the stamps, to his constituent.

322. There are no paper manufactures carried on in London, are there?—There are some very near; one I know is carried on by a very eminent man, Mr. Dickenson.

323. In Hertfordshire?—Yes.

324. You necessarily require pure water for the manufacture of paper, do not you?—I do not know.

325. Notoriously the paper sold in London is manufactured in a very scattered way all over the midland and southern counties, is it not?—Yes.

326. And that paper comes up to London to be stamped; but what I wish to ask you is this: suppose a publisher of a newspaper at Maidstone, and that there is a manufacturer of paper close to Maidstone, would it not be a very natural transaction for that publisher to find the means of supplying himself with paper from his own neighbour, who might, if he required credit, be more disposed to give it than a person at a distance; and would he not, by getting his paper from him, not only have this facility, but save all the expense of the carriage to London, and the commission you spoke of, of Mr. Venables, or any wholesale house?—To be able to judge of that, I should know the terms on which he deals with his agent; I apprehend that in all those cases where there

*T. Keogh,* Esq.

6 May 1851

there is agency to a large extent, as in the supply of paper to a newspaper, the persons who deal with the manufacturers are the agents; that a newspaper proprietor rarely has any transaction directly with the manufacturer; and that the agent so accommodates his terms to the newspaper proprietor, as makes it quite as cheap to the person, the consumer, the newspaper proprietor, as if he dealt directly with the manufacturer for the small quantity of paper that he would require.

327. Is it an advantage to a person requiring paper at the Land's End that that paper must of necessity travel up to London and back again; assuming that the paper be made in Cornwall, is it any advantage that the Cornish publisher should of necessity have to pay the expense of transmitting the paper to London and back?—Clearly no advantage, if he did so; but that is not the course of things: a person in Cornwall when he wants paper writes up to such persons as I have described, Messrs. Venables & Co., and those men deal with the paper manufacturers for immense quantities of paper; not in driblets; and I apprehend that few great manufacturers would deal with a newspaper proprietor for the small quantity that he requires; it must necessarily be done by some great paper agent; those persons deal for immense quantities, and a newspaper proprietor writes to them to say that he wants so much paper by such a day, and those persons send the paper, having it in store of all sizes, to Somerset-house; they have that paper stamped, and send it to the man in Cornwall; there is no such thing as the transmission of paper from Cornwall to London and back again.

328. Is that the way in which the London newspaper proprietors obtain their paper?—I believe so.

329. Does the "Times" do so?—I understand that the consumption of the "Times" is so large that they deal with more than one person. I have understood that a large portion of the supply of that paper is sent from a house in Lancashire, having an establishment in Manchester.

330. Sir *J. Walmsley.*] Do you speak from your own knowledge when you say that newspaper proprietors do not deal with manufacturers?—I say my impression is formed from the business transacted at our office; the persons who send in for the stamps are, generally speaking, not the newspaper proprietors, but agents.

331. That is your impression?—Yes; I know that the greatest quantity of newspapers are taken out by agents; there

*T. Keogh,* Esq.

6 May 1851.

there may be instances to the contrary, but we refuse stamps to nobody authorized to receive them, who puts in the paper; my impression is, that all the country newspapers are supplied by agents.

332. The question of the honourable Member for the West Riding had reference specially to the London press?—No, it related to the proprietor of a paper at Cornwall, who, he supposed, was under the necessity of sending up his paper from Cornwall in the first instance, and then having it back stamped; I understood the general tenor of his inquiry to be with regard to country newspapers.

333. His subsequent inquiry of you was as to the London press; I understood you to say that the London press did not deal with the paper manufacturers directly, but through particular agents; then I asked you whether you knew that as a certainty?—My impression with regard to the course of the honourable Member's examination was, that he was desirous to ascertain whether, there being only an establishment in London, and an establishment at Manchester, for stamping the country newspapers, the proprietors were subjected to any hardship by the necessity of procuring their stamps at a considerable distance from their place of residence, either from London or Manchester.

334. *Chairman.*] I think you have admitted that confining the stamping to London, Edinburgh, and Manchester, has a tendency to give a sort of partial monopoly to the paper manufacturers in the immediate vicinity of those places; an advantage in the trade?—It would apparently have that tendency, but for the circumstances that I have mentioned; that, notwithstanding there is a stamping establishment in the vicinity of the newspaper, many newspaper proprietors find it advantageous to deal with persons at a distance.

335. A particular person?—No, I say that in Glasgow there are several.

336. Mr. *Rich.*] You stated, did you not, that there were newspapers in the neighbourhood of Manchester that were supplied with paper from London?—Yes; this constantly occurs: A newspaper proprietor in the north of England enters into the qualifications, and writes to us to send a die for his newspaper to Manchester. We send it to Manchester, and after it has been there for, perhaps, six months, and he has received his supply there, he writes to us to send it to London, and he is supplied from London for the next six months, or perhaps 12 months. He then again requests to have it sent back to Manchester; and all that is, as I believe,

T. Keogh, Esq.

6 May 1851.

believe, the result of the applications of the travellers of papermakers or agents, who propose to those persons terms somewhat cheaper than the terms on which they are at present supplied, and induce them to have their stamps from London or Manchester according to those terms. So that it is, in fact, altogether a transaction between the paper agent and the newspaper proprietor; it depends upon which agent underbids the other.

337. It has been stated that frauds were committed in regard to stamping printed cottons and calicoes, in the way in which it was formerly carried on?—The honourable Member for the West Riding said that.

338. Are you aware that any frauds have taken place in the issuing of stamps for newspapers under the mode adopted now by the Stamp Office?—No.

339. Do you think it probable, if the mode adopted formerly with regard to calicoes, were applied to newspapers, that frauds would ensue?—I think the thing impracticable altogether.

340. You have stated that the newspapers published in the neighbourhood of Manchester are in the habit of getting their stamped paper from London; has that practice increased, or is it on the decrease?—I am not prepared to say, but I was struck by the oddity of the circumstance that a newspaper published somewhere in the north of England, within a short distance, or a much shorter distance than between London and the place in question, should choose to get its supplies from London.

341. Do you fancy that it is the remains of the old connection that may have subsisted between that newspaper and London previously to the concession that was made to Manchester, or is it a transaction that has grown up since? —I think it occurs in the way that I have already attempted to describe; that some of these newspapers first get their supply from Manchester, and that goes on for a certain time, and then they suddenly call upon us to send the die to London, where they intend to have their future supplies; and that goes on for a time, and then the London agent is underbid by some man near Manchester, and they have the die sent back to Manchester.

342. It has been stated that delay and loss accrue to the proprietors of newspapers from having to get their paper stamped at a distance. From your experience at the Board of Inland Revenue, can you state whether you are aware that there is any amount of delay and loss accruing, taking into

*T. Keogh,* Esq.

6 May 1851.

into consideration the present facilities of communication? —There have been occasions, certainly, from the neglect of the parties themselves, and not from any want of facility in the transmission, upon which they have published a certain number of their copies upon unstamped paper, from the failure of the supply; but that has been from their own neglect in ordering a supply of paper three or four days before the day of publication, and the necessary delay intervening to prevent the supply at the time required; that does occur.

343. *Chairman.*] Have you not had applications made by parties to be allowed, in a case of sudden emergency, to print upon unstamped paper, they agreeing to pay the stamp duty afterwards, so as not to disappoint their customers?—We have had applications of that nature; and where the transaction is one that occurs for the first time, we always pass it over on payment of the duties.

344. Would you grant it beforehand?—No; the Board would consider that they sanctioned a violation of the law if they said beforehand, "You may print on unstamped paper;" but when the thing has actually occurred, we accept the duties if it be the first transgression of the kind upon the part of a particular person; but if it be the second or the third, we should probably prosecute him for a small penalty.

345. When a person prints a newspaper upon unstamped paper because if he does not supply his customers with the news it would be of no use at all, with the *bonâ fide* intention of paying the duties, but from the inconvenience of sending all the way to London he cannot get stamped paper in time, and he did it a second or a third time, you say you would prosecute him?—We can be no judges of his desire or intention, except so far as he declares it.

346. Supposing he said he had done it, and offered to pay the duty?—Yes, he may say that, but it depends upon himself to state what number of copies he has printed without stamps; and that is a thing that we should not like to take from a newspaper proprietor who was in the habit of printing without stamps.

347. Will you be good enough to lay before the Committee any applications that you may have received upon that point, where parties have printed upon unstamped paper, and have offered to pay the duty?—Yes: they generally make the application after they have printed, but the instances in which they make application beforehand, stating that

that they are about to print a certain portion of their impressions without stamps, are rare. *T. Keogh*, Esq.

348. Mr. *Rich.*] You stated that the expense of collecting the duty would be greatly increased by instituting other centres for issuing stamps?—Certainly it would. 6 May 1851.

349. Can you state to the Committee what is the average cost of raising the stamp duty at present on newspapers?—There being no place except Manchester where there is any charge in respect of the distribution of stamps, the only expense at London and at Edinburgh is the salaries of the stampers and the machinery. I may mention perhaps that we have at present a plan in contemplation for reducing the expense of manual stamping.

350. *Chairman.*] Who appoints the stampers? — The Treasury.

351. What do they receive per annum?—There are three classes; one 75 *l.*, another at 90 *l.*, and a third 100 *l.*; but those are not confined to newspaper stamps; they stamp every description of paper and parchment.

352. Mr. *Cobden.*] As I understand it, you allow on one occasion parties to print in a case of emergency unstamped paper?—We pass over the transgression; we never allow them to print; we never previously sanction their doing so.

353. You pass it over, do you not?—Yes; after it is done we do not inflict any penalties upon persons who have violated the law in that respect.

354. You stated, did you not, that it is the fault of the parties themselves if they are under the necessity of repeating that offence?—Yes; it is their fault in the first instance, as well as in any subsequent one.

355. When you say it is their fault, I suppose you mean that they are bound to keep a larger stock of stamped paper on hand, to be able to meet all such emergencies without having recourse to unstamped paper?—What I mean is this: they know their circulation, they know the number of copies they issue on each day of publication, and they ought to make such arrangements as to have a sufficient number of stamps for that publication the day before, or by a certain number of days before it occurs.

356. We were speaking of an unexpected emergency, arising from some important news which the public had a great desire to see; those are extraordinary emergencies for which you would say the parties were to blame if they did not provide themselves?—That is the very case in which we pass

*T. Keogh,* Esq.

6 May 1851.

pass over the infringement of the law by printing on unstamped paper.

357. Once, as I understood you?—Once we do it it any case, under any circumstances; but if an extraordinary emergency occurred, requiring an additional number (observe, not the whole number, but an additional number above the ordinary supply), then we should pass it over, whether it cccurred once, or twice, or three times.

358. *Chairman.*] Taking the duty?—Yes. If the quantity printed exceeded the ordinary quantity, under some circumstances of emergency, then we should pass it over on the payment of the duty without penalties.

359. They are obliged, in order to supply the public with news, from the circumstance of your keeping these stamping places confined to London, Edinburgh, and Manchester, occasionally to print news on unstamped paper?—I do not know that that is the reason; I am not sure that the same circumstances would not occur if the stamping establishment were in their immediate vicinity; it occurs in London with the London newspapers.

360. Mr. *Cobden.*] In such a case as that what check have you against fraud, if you allow them to print on unstamped paper in cases of emergency?—I must repeat that we do not allow them to print on unstamped paper in cases of emergency; we pass over the offence without inflicting penalties, upon the printer and publisher making an affidavit of the number of unstamped copies that have been published.

361. *Chairman.*] If they know beforehand that you always pass it over, it is practically allowing them to do it, is it not?—I do not know that.

362. If the whole newspaper press is aware beforehand that the habit of the Board is to pass over cases of that kind, is it not virtually an allowance of the practice?—I am not sure that they know it; I apprehend that the parties do not know anything but what occurs in their own particular case.

363. Mr. *Rich.*] Cases occur sometimes in which you exact penalties, do they not?—Yes.

364. Sir *J. Walmsley.*] Are the arrangements between the Board and the newspaper proprietors for the stamps always direct between the two, or is there an intermediate party in many cases?—There are agents, as I said before; I believe all the country newspapers are supplied by agents, whether by agents in London, or by agents in Manchester, or by agents in Edinburgh.

365. Do not the paper makers themselves frequently supply

supply the newspaper proprietors with stamps?—I believe not, except in London. *T. Keogh,* Esq. 6 May 1851.

366. You do not know of any such case in Manchester, for instance?—There is a great paper manufacturer of the name of Wrigley, who supplies, I believe, most of the newspapers in the north of England.

367. With paper?—Yes.

368. And with stamps?—Yes; he never sends them but stamped paper.

369. In such cases as those in which Mr. Wrigley supplies a newspaper proprietor with stamps in the country, is there any direct communication between you and such newspaper proprietor?—Certainly not; that house comes to the Stamp-office at Manchester, and puts in a warrant, as I have said, which is signed by the distributor as having received so much duty for so many penny stamps, and that warrant is sent down to the supervisor who is perfectly independent of the distributor, and is a check upon him; he delivers it with the paper, and receives the paper into the stamping-room, distributes it among the stampers to be impressed, and when that is done he delivers it back to the paper manufacturer.

370. In a case where a newspaper proprietor has issued his publication upon unstamped paper in a case of emergency, you would not apply to the party who supplied him with the paper, but to the newspaper proprietor directly?—Yes, certainly, he would be the person who committed the offence.

371. Sir *T. F. Lewis.*] Is the course pursued with respect to the stamping of newspapers the same as that which is pursued with respect to the stamping of deeds, and bills, and documents of that kind?—Precisely.

372. In the one case do not you stamp them and keep them in stock?—No.

373. Do not you keep stamped parchments ready?—All the country is supplied through distributors of stamps, who hold stocks of all descriptions of stamps.

374. With respect to newspapers is not the course different in this respect, that the persons who wish to have stamps for newspapers bring the paper themselves to the office where it is stamped for them, it being their paper in the first instance?—Yes.

375. Then if I understand you rightly there is this essential distinction between the two, that you never have a stock of newspaper stamps though you keep stocks of all other descriptions

*T. Keogh,* Esq.

6 May 1851.

descriptions of stamps?—I should say that we only supply stamps on paper of our own to our distributors in the country, but the public in London send in all their own paper and parchment, and every other thing requiring a stamp, to be stamped, just as the newspaper proprietors or their agents do.

376. Then the stock is for the country supply only?—Yes.

377. *Chairman.*] At what rate can you stamp newspapers?—Each man stamps 8,000 stamps a day.

378. Eight thousand sheets?—Yes; sometimes a great deal more.

379. How many stampers are employed?—We have got about 40 upon newspapers.

380. In London?—Yes.

381. Sir *T. F. Lewis.*] Are they persons employed on newspapers only?—Only; it is done in a long room, divided from the other portion of the stamping department, because it is a different operation.

382. Is it by separate machinery?—It is by hand; the stamp is impressed by hand, which is done almost as rapidly as by any machinery.

383. The stamps upon deeds and upon bills are affixed by presses?—Yes.

384. Mr. *Rich.*] Would there be any practical objections to printing stamps for newspapers as stamps for deeds are prepared, and supplying the stamp distributors in the country with them, and allowing them to send them to the newspapers?—It would be impossible to provide paper of all the sizes that are required. Every newspaper has its own sized paper, which differs essentially from the paper of another, and we never could supply the varieties of paperfor each.

385. Would it be impossible to devise means by which stamps could be attached to newspapers?—By labels?

386. Yes.—Such a thing is possible, but I confess that I never heard of such a proposal.

387. With regard to the instances which you have stated as having occurred, of newspaper proprietors publishing more papers than they had stamps in hand for, and where they have come to you with an explanation offering to pay the duty, you stated that instances had occurred in London, did you not?—Yes.

388. And also at Manchester?—I cannot pretend to say at the moment; I know that instances have occurred in London, and I dare say also at Manchester.

389. You

389. You can, perhaps, furnish the instances in which they may have occurred at Manchester and Edinburgh since the concession of stamp offices to these places?—Yes, I am sure they have occurred at Edinburgh, and I am sure they have occurred in London. *T. Keogh, Esq.* 6 May 1851.

390. Mr. *S. Adair.*] You stated that there were 40 stampers engaged in this manual operation of stamping, and that their salaries varied from 70 *l.* to 95 *l.*, did you not?—They vary from 75 *l.* to 100 *l.*; 75 *l.*, 90 *l.* and 100 *l.*

391. Suppose you take 80 *l.* as the average, probably the lower class would be the largest employed?—Yes.

392. Might not a considerable saving be effected by the application of steam power to such a process?—We have tried everything with newspaper stamps; we had plates formerly, by which the stamps were impressed by machinery, but we found, after some experience, that stamping by hand was the most rapid process; if any gentleman were to look at the stamping-room, and see the process of stamping by hand, and the rapidity with which it is executed, he would be surprised; it is nearly as fast as machinery; stamps are impressed upon postage envelopes by steam machinery, and it is not much more rapidly performed than the stamping by hand upon newspapers.

393. Then, in this particular instance, manual labour is cheaper than machinery?—I will not say cheaper, but we find it more convenient for the supply of newspaper stamps than printing by plates.

394. Sir *J. Walmsley.*] What notice is required when a party wants paper stamped?—I believe that if they pass in a warrant to-day, in the morning, for a not very great quantity of stamps, they will have them by the evening.

395. Are notices required?—No notice; there is nothing to do but to pay the duty and put in the warrant, which is a document which states the stamps that the party requires; the party fills it up with the amount of the duty, and hands it into the receiver-general's office; the receiver-general receives the duty and acknowledges it at the bottom of the warrant, and then that is carried by a shoot into the comptroller-general's office, and the comptroller-general's clerk examines the warrant, sees that the amount is right, and charges the receiver-general with the amount paid; he signs it, and from thence it is shot down into the stamping-room, and it is their business in that room to receive from an outer room the paper marked by the person who has passed this warrant. It is received into the stamping-room, and

*T. Keogh*, Esq.

6 May 1851.

and under the authority of that warrant the stamps are impressed.

396. Then no stamps are issued but those that are paid for?—Certainly not.

397. Is no credit given?—None whatever; no stamp can be impressed without the previous payment of the duty.

398. Then, for what reason do newspaper proprietors give sureties for newspapers' stamps?—That is as to the duties upon advertisements printed in their newspapers.

399. *Chairman.*] Supposing a person has more stamps than he wants, do you make him any return if he brings you back the stamps?—Yes, if they are spoiled; for instance, if a newspaper becomes defunct, having on hand a certain supply of stamps, or if it changes in size.

400. Supposing that he prints a greater number of impressions than he sells, do you return the stamp duty to him?—No, we do not allow for printed paper. I believe that the newspaper proprietors know very exactly the number of copies they require, I have frequently sent to a newspaper office for a copy of the newspaper of the preceding day, having lost a copy, which I wanted for a particular purpose, and I could not get it. I have done that several times.

401. You hold at the Board that it is your duty to prevent the printing of any public news, intelligence, or occurrences on unstamped paper, do not you?—We hold that any paper containing public news, intelligence, or occurrences, is a newspaper, and subject to the stamp duty.

402. That is, that if there be printed on a piece of paper any public news, intelligence, or occurrences, and there be no stamp on that paper, the party dispersing it and making it public would be liable to a penalty of 20 *l.*?—Certainly.

403. Mr. *Ewart.*] And on other material, as well as paper, it would be the same, would it not?—I have heard that, as a subtlety, advanced and discussed; but certainly the law only imposes a duty on any newspaper or paper containing news, intelligence, or occurrences; therefore, if such a thing as the printing of a newspaper were to occur on a piece of cotton, I do not think the law would comprehend that.

404. It is required that any person who wishes to be entitled to print public news, intelligence, or occurrences upon stamped paper must enter into securities that he will not libel anybody?—Yes.

405. Supposing a person publishes a newspaper for the purpose

*T. Keogh,* Esq.

6 May 1851.

purpose of descanting upon private character, and not for the purpose of giving public news, intelligence, or occurrences, but what might be called private news, intelligence, or occurrences regarding the proceedings of private families, would he be required to enter into any security that he would not libel anybody ?—No, the law only requires that the publishers of newspapers shall enter into security with regard to libels.

406. Those who mean to print public news, intelligence or occurrences upon paper ?—Yes.

407. There was a paper published called "Sam Sly," and that paper contained nothing but records of proceedings in private families and calumnious insinuations as to the conduct of individuals, mentioning them by name, their residences, and so forth ; that was not liable to stamp duty, was it ?—I should say not from your description. I have no recollection of it ; but if it only contained the matter that you describe it was not liable to stamp duty.

408. And therefore no security was required from the party publishing such a paper that he would not libel anybody ?—No.

409. Though his sole business was to report to the public the affairs of private families and of private individuals ?—Yes. The law with regard to security has relation solely to newspapers.

410. Mr. *Ewart.*] Your news is restricted to public news, is not it ?—Yes, intelligence or occurrences.

411. Mr. *G. A. Hamilton.*] Has that difference between public and private news ever been brought to issue ?—I am not aware that it has, or that any such question has been raised ; the consequences in the case which the Honourable Chairman has described of a publication containing defamatory matter upon private individuals, are, that if the party injured were desirous of obtaining compensation by law, he would have to prove the publication by the common law course, and the only advantage of registration of every newspaper is, that it affords an easy means of proving the fact of publication.

412. *Chairman.*] In the case of a party who had given security that he would not libel any one, there would be funds forthcoming to pay the damages, would there not ? —Yes ; in the case that the Honourable Chairman has described, the printing of the publication could not be proved by registration ; that applies to newspapers only, and the fact of publication should be proved according to com-

 mon

*T. Keogh,* Esq.

6 May 1851.

mon law. In the case of a libel in a newspaper, the security might be enforced for the recovery of the damages.

413. An application was made, was it not, to the Stamp-office in the case of the paper called "Sam Sly," as to whether it was liable to stamp duty, and you decided that it was not?—If I did I thought so.

414. Mr. *G. A. Hamilton.*] I understand you to say, that you did not conceive it was desirable to bring the point to issue by prosecution; whether in point of fact a publication of that nature, professing to enter into private transactions, and giving those transactions to the public, did not come under the legal definition of a newspaper?—We never attempted to try such a question.

415. If I printed on a piece of paper to-morrow the fact that this Committee sat to-day, and you were examined before it, and I were to disperse that piece of paper and other copies of it, should I be liable to a penalty of 20 *l.* for each transaction?—I think that would be public news and intelligence; I think that the reports of transactions of all the Committees of Parliament, railway committees, and election committees, and so on, are all public news.

416. Then for each copy, if I understand you rightly, that I dispersed and made public, whether I gave them away or sold them, I should be liable to a penalty of 20 *l.*?—I think so.

417. Sir *T. F. Lewis.*] Is it required that a newspaper should be published periodically, or would a single publication be enough?—We hold that a single publication, containing public news, is substantively a newspaper, and requires no repetition of it.

418. *Chairman.*] Supposing I printed on a piece of paper an untruth, and that this Committee had not sat, with a view to deception, and I printed a falsehood in fact, would that make me liable?—That could hardly be news; that is a negation of a particular occurrence.

419. Mr. *Ewart.*] Does news necessarily involve truth; may not anything *pro tanto* be news?—I apprehend that the word "news" in its ordinary signification, means an account of some recent occurrence or circumstance published or communicated to persons by whom it was previously unknown.

420. Sir *J. Walmsley.*] Suppose a history of England, brought down to the present day, and published, would that be news in your acceptation of the term?—In the first place, the thing on which the duty is imposed is a newspaper,

*T. Keogh,* Esq.

6 May 1851.

paper, which is a familiar term, and is familiarly understood, or a paper containing public news, intelligence, or occurrences; now I do not consider that, to a common apprehension, a book is a paper, and, therefore, a history printed in the form of a book, and giving a consecutive account of public events for a certain period, is not a thing which falls at all within the scope of the term.

421. *Chairman.*] With regard to respectability of parties, it has been urged that the stamping of newspapers is some security for their respectability?—I think so decidedly.

422. If a party may publish a libellous paper, provided he does not put public news in it, what security is there for the respectability of the paper that you require a stamp in other cases?—What I should say upon that subject is this, that the policy of the original Act imposing a restriction upon newspapers in respect to registration, by which the parties may be known at once, and the publication proved by a statutory mode instead of by common law, and the imposition of the necessity of giving security, were intended for this purpose, that the public might have the facility of knowing with whom they had to deal; and there can be little doubt that the responsibility thus created on the part of publishers of newspapers has the effect of repressing the insertion of libels in those papers. The persons who set up newspapers are, generally speaking, responsible and respectable parties. There are of course no such means of knowing or reaching persons engaged in the publication of papers not being newspapers, nor is there any such security in their respectability

423. But a paper like "Sam Sly" was the very sort of paper, if I understand you rightly, that it was intended to guard against?—Not at all; the intention of the 38th of George the Third was to prevent the publication of blasphemous and seditious libels in newspapers; that was the Act that first imposed any restriction upon the press in the way of registration; then comes the 60th of George the Third, one of the six Acts which first created a security; and it obliged all the printers of newspapers to give security for any fine that might be awarded against them for the publication of similar libels; then comes the Act of Lord Abinger, which extended the security to private libels, which had never existed before; there was no security from the year 1798, the time of the passing of the 38th of George the Third, down to the passing of Lord Abinger's Act against private libels; the security from 1798 to 1820, the 60th of

*T. Keogh,* Esq.

6 May 1851.

of George the Third, related only to libels against the public interest, to blasphemous and seditious libels, and Lord Abinger's Act first extended that security to libels against individuals.

424. Mr. *Ewart.*] That was to prevent a public paper being made a vehicle for private calumny?—There was no remedy previously except against the publisher. Any person aggrieved by the publication of any defamatory matter had to bring an action or prosecution, but that was against the proprietor or publisher of the paper. After Lord Abinger's Act he had this additional security, that if the proprietor was unable to pay damages, he had two sureties to resort to, as far as the amount of the security goes.

425. Mr. *S. Adair.*] I observe in Mr. Timm's evidence, that the form of a printer and publisher's libel bond is put in: it appears that by this bond they are bound to answer for the damages in costs or fines on conviction for libel: in the case of a party prosecuting a newspaper publisher and obtaining damages, would he apply in the first instance to be reimbursed from such funds as were in the hands of the Commissioners?—We have no funds. I apprehend that the effect of the bond would be this, that if they could not recover their damages from the principal, they would be at liberty to put this bond in force so far as it went as against the sureties. The plaintiff in an action who recovered damages against the printer of a newspaper for libel, would, if he failed in recovering the amount from that person, be at liberty to come to the Commissioners and ask them to be allowed to put the bond in suit against the sureties.

426. Then would not the Commissioners to that extent be responsible for recovering and paying over the amount of the damages to the plaintiff in such action?—Not at all; they would merely give the party the privilege of suing upon the bond.

427. Mr. *Ewart.*] You stated, did you not, that a book could not be a newspaper?—I think it is not.

428. Supposing "The Times" were printed in the shape of a book every morning, would the mere shape make a difference in the spirit of the publication?—I am not prepared to say. Every newspaper is printed upon a sheet or piece of paper. Those are the terms of the Act of Parliament, "Any newspaper or paper." "For every sheet of paper or piece of paper on which the same shall be published."

429. *Chairman.*] Surely a paper giving a record of the transactions

*T. Keogh*, Esq.

6 May 1851.

transactions of private families, or private individuals gives intelligence, does it not?—It does, but not public news, intelligence, or occurrences; the word "public," I apprehend, over-rides the three substantives, public news, public intelligence, or public occurrences.

430. What is a public occurrence?—The opening of the Exhibition the other day, and the opening of Parliament.

431. Suppose an accident happens on a railway, is that a public occurrence?—That is not a private accident; not an accident to an individual; but an accident upon a great public institution, such as a railway, would I conceive be a public occurrence.

432. Mr. *Ewart*.] If a paper were published containing an account of a private accident it would not be so?—No.

433. *Chairman*.] There would be no security for its respectability, or that it would not libel individual character; and a paper that confined itself to those private transactions, might be unstamped and published with impunity? —Yes; the law does not subject them to the duty chargeable upon newspapers, nor to any restrictions respecting newspapers.

434. What security does the newspaper stamp afford the public against periodical publications of a libellous character?—The newspaper stamp does not afford the public any security, whether in the case of a newspaper or not, but the restrictions regarding newspapers, the necessity of registration, and the necessity of giving a bond to secure the public in the case of damages, in an action for libel, does afford security; registration gives them the means of getting at the parties, and the means of producing a copy of the declaration made to the Stamp Office, stating that A. B. and C. D. are the printers and publishers of that paper, which is conclusive evidence upon that point. These securities to the public do not exist in the instance of a publication not being a newspaper.

435. Mr. *C. Fortescue*.] You stated, did you not, that the object of Lord Abinger's Act was to extend the protection from public libels to private libels?—Yes. Supposing the proprietor of a newspaper attacked a person's character in some private relation, and he brought an action against him for damages, in the event of the jury awarding him damages, if he failed to recover them from the proprietor he could resort to the bond which he gave at the Stamp Office, and get those damages from his sureties, as far as the bond went.

 436. Then

*T. Keogh,* Esq.

6 May 1851.

436. Then news, or pretended news, in a newspaper, about a private party, would be addressed to the public as public news, would it not?—I do not say that an attack upon the character of an individual, in a newspaper, is public news, intelligence, or occurrences; but I say that if it was published in a newspaper, the facility of reaching the person who had published that slander would be much greater than in the case of a paper not registered, and also the facility of recovering your damages; and that affords the public very great security in the case of a newspaper, which does not exist in the case of publications not liable to newspaper duty.

437. Mr. *Rich.*] With regard to libels upon individuals, it has been stated that a publication that contained attacks upon individuals, and nothing else, without any public news whatever, would not have much circulation; do you apprehend that such would be the case?—I should think not. There have been such newspapers set up in London, not recently, but there were, some years ago, papers set up for the express purpose of extorting money by aspersions of private character.

438. If they contained news, would not that add very much to their circulation?—Undoubtedly; all of them did; they never expected to have an extensive circulation of a parcel of stories about individuals that the public knew nothing of, and therefore it was necessary to mix public intelligence to obtain any considerable circulation.

439. Are you prepared to say that it is not true that those publications do contain some portions of public news? —I say that the publications to which I refer, as having existed some years ago, the main design of which apparently, as everybody believed, was to extort money by defamation of individuals, did contain public news, and were registered as newspapers, and contained a considerable number of advertisements. I do not believe that they would have attempted to circulate those slanders if there had been nothing else in them. The public is not interested in hearing that E. G., of Bermondsey, did so and so in his private life; I apprehend that no considerable circulation could be obtained for a vehicle of private slander, unless it were mixed with public news.

440. Mr. *Rich.*] So soon as they contain so much of news as gives them a circulation, it becomes a question then at the Stamp Office whether they do not contain sufficient news to justify the sending them before a jury, for publishing without a stamp?—Yes; if one of those papers, all

T. Keogh, Esq.

6 May 1851.

all of which are watched in some degree as far as we are able, began to insert public news, we should warn the party that by doing so he rendered himself subject to the laws relating to newspapers, and if he persisted in it we should prosecute him.

441. And thereby you compel him to cease the publication or to take out a stamp?—Yes; to register and stamp the paper.

442. Then having registered, he becomes more accessible to prosecution by the individuals whom he has libelled?—Yes; and he gives a security which would be available to them.

443. Whereby the stamp becomes a protection to individual character?—That is one way of stating it; but it is the liability, as a newspaper, which becomes the protection.

444. Mr. *G. A. Hamilton.*] You do not consider that the fact of a newspaper containing intelligence which is sought for by the public, and bought by them, and distributed amongst them, is sufficient to constitute public intelligence, unless it relates exclusively to matters of public concern?—I do not say unless it contains exclusively matters of public concern. Every newspaper contains a variety of matter that has no public concern, as accidents to individuals, and various other things of no public interest, but it contains at the same time political and public matters.

445. The schedule states, that "Any paper containing public news, intelligence, or occurrences, printed in any part of the United Kingdom, to be dispersed and made public," constitutes a newspaper. The case I would wish to put, is that of a paper containing remarks upon private families, which remarks are sought for by the public, the paper being bought by them, and which is dispersed and made public; and I ask whether that would not constitute public news?—The only reason which the honourable Member seems to assign for such matter being liable to be regarded as public news is, that the public buys it, but that I should think would not constitute it public news.

446. Take "The Court Circular," which may relate to private transactions or to persons of public character; do you consider that the publication of that kind of intelligence constitutes a newspaper in the sense of the Act of Parliament?—I should say that the announcements relating to the Court, the journeys of the Queen, or other matters of that description, would constitute public news.

447. So that a newspaper containing that kind of news,

 such

*T. Keogh,* Esq.

6 May 1851.

such as the movements of the Court, would have to be stamped, and would be subject to prosecution unless it were stamped, whilst a paper containing remarks that may be of a scandalous nature, with reference to private families, does not require a stamp?—The case of a paper containing merely an account of the movements of the Court, and nothing else, is a case that I can hardly suppose; no such case exists; I believe that "The Court Journal," or "The Court Circular," which does announce the movements of the Court, contains every other kind of news. But to answer the question more completely, I should say that a paper such as has been described, containing nothing else than paragraphs relating to private characters of individuals, would in no sense be a newspaper, nor would that matter be public news, intelligence, or occurrences.

448. *Chairman.*] A return was laid before Parliament with respect to which Mr. Timm was examined; you must be cognizant of that return of 53 registered newspapers published in London last year without stamps?—I think not without stamps, but partly so.

449. A portion of them?—Yes, as we understood.

450. Those 53 registered newspapers the Board held not to be newspapers, otherwise you could not have made a return to Parliament of their being published without a stamp, if you do not hold them not to be newspapers?—If any of those papers were, in our judgment, newspapers, in fact, we should have prosecuted the parties for the penalties for printing a portion of them without stamps.

451. There were 53 registered newspapers at your office that you held not to be newspapers, were there not?—There were 53 papers registered as newspapers which are not so.

452. Why are they not newspapers?—Because they do not contain, as we conceive, that matter upon which the newspaper duty is imposed; they do not contain either public news, intelligence, or occurrences, or remarks or observations thereon, if they are published within 26 days.

453. The "Legal Observer" is one of those registered newspapers; do you mean to say that the "Legal Observer," which gives a systematic record of the proceedings in our public courts of justice, does not give public news or intelligence?—I am really not aware of the contents of the "Legal Observer."

454. A copy of it is sent to you every time it is published, is it not?—I apprehend it is; but unless my particular attention

*T. Keogh,* Esq.

6 May 1851.

attention was drawn to that I should not see it; I confess that I have never seen the "Legal Observer." Is it a weekly or monthly publication?

455-6. It is a weekly publication. It is called the "Legal Observer, Digest, and Journal of Jurisprudence," and the contents are "Legal measures before Parliament; annual certificate duty; notices of new books; papal aggression; Manchester Law Association; conveyancing reform; selections from correspondence; suggested improvement in arbitrations; candidates who passed the examination, Hilary Term, 1851; Orders of the House of Commons, as to public petitions; notes of the week; law reform; Parliamentary Returns; postscript; sittings of the right honourable the master of the rolls, at the Rolls, and at the judicial committee, after Hilary Term, 1851; proceedings in Parliament relating to the law; Private Bills; certificate duty repeal; law appointment; recent decisions in the superior courts; and short notes of cases"? —What is the date of that publication?

457. This is February the 15th, 1851?—What is the date of the return?

458. That was February the 15th, 1850; it is the same publication; I have no doubt that the number we have here is just the same as you returned?—Of course there is an alteration every week in the matter which a paper contains; but whether at the time the return was made it contained all these elements which you have mentioned, I am not aware.

459. Upon what principle do you undertake to make a return to the House of Commons of this publication as one that is entitled to publish a portion of its impressions without a stamp, when its contents seem to be entirely public news, intelligence, and occurrences?—Does the return say "entitled to publish without a stamp"?

460. It says, "A return of papers published in the metropolis, and registered as newspapers, a portion whereof is published without stamps;" therefore it was within your knowledge that a portion of this "Legal Observer" was published without stamps?—I must have been so informed.

461. Upon what principle is it that it is published without a stamp?—I really cannot undertake to say without referring to the publications anterior to the date of that return. I should say, that if that paper does contain matter of the description you mention, it would be subject to the newspaper duty; and therefore without referring to the publications,

T. Keogh, Esq.

6 May 1851.

publications that took place prior to or at the date of that return, I cannot explain why it is stated that it is one of those published without a stamp, and which it would be implied that the parties were entitled so to publish.

462. Mr. *Rich.*] Do you not make a distinction with regard to the subject matter, whether it is treated as news, or with a view to literary, scientific, or legal instruction?—It has been held that a paper addressed to one particular subject, for instance, architecture and building, and which only inserts in its paper something bearing upon that particular subject, is not to be considered a newspaper within the contemplation of that expression.

463. For instance, a paper the heads of which have been just read to you; those heads may be so treated as to conduce to instruction in legal matters, that being the main object, and the circumstances and facts which they relate become incidents to that object, do not they?—Yes; that is just the principle I have stated with regard to publications on building or architecture; the "Builder," for instance.

464. *Chairman.*] In the "Legal Observer," an article is headed "Papal Aggression. The address to the Queen, and the petitions to Parliament, which were presented last week, were signed by upwards of 6,000 attorneys, solicitors, and proctors, praying for the adoption of such measures as will effectually prevent the papal bull from being in any manner recognized or acted upon, and guarding against, and effectually resisting all attempts directly or indirectly to re-establish the papal powers within these realms. In the 'Legal Observer' of the 7th December the petition is fully set forth, with a report of the speeches made and resolutions passed at the meeting in the Hall of the Incorporated Law Society"?—Yes; the connexion of that with this paper is because it is a petition from the Law Society.

465. Is it "public news, intelligence, or occurrences"?—I think it is.

466. Then is it fair to allow that to be published without a stamp, if you insist upon newspapers which give public news, intelligence, or occurrences, publishing all their impressions with a stamp?—It would not be fair, certainly, in us to do so, if, upon consideration of the contents of that paper or any other, we were of opinion that we could maintain a prosecution against the parties for printing newspapers without stamps.

467. Are not you bound to believe that the courts and the juries of the country will act upon the law laid down in the

T. Keogh, Esq.

6 May 1851.

the statutes?—If we ourselves believed that it was a case which fell within the liability imposed upon newspapers, we should prosecute for the penalty.

468. Why does not it fall within the statute if it is "public news, intelligence, or occurrences"?—As far as that goes, it appears to me to be "public news, intelligence, or occurrences;" and if at the time that the return was made the paper contained articles of a similar description, I should say that we then made an erroneous return; I cannot say how that is, without looking to the paper anterior to the date of that return.

469. Sir *T. F. Lewis.*] If instead of being an account of a meeting of persons strictly connected with the law, it had been an account of a meeting, say of clergymen, should you have entertained any doubt then?—Not the slightest.

470. The distinction that you take in this instance is, that being connected with the law, it more nearly comes within your rule, although it does not strictly come within your rule?—I think that is the nearest approach to the rule I have described, with regard to a paper established for a particular object.

471. Mr. *Cobden.*] Will you take that paper in your hand (*the "Town" being handed to the Witness.*) That is a weekly publication, published at a penny, upon very fair paper, and with woodcuts fairly executed, of a very demoralizing character. The number that you have in your hand has for its frontispiece a large woodcut called "a scene in a brothel." You will perceive that the greater portion of the contents of that weekly publication, at a penny, is news and intelligence relating to the practices and scenes in public brothels, and similar places; and I ask you whether you think the penny stamp upon a newspaper, which prohibits the publication of a penny newspaper, is not calculated to give a monopoly to that class of publications which are not stamped, and therefore can be brought out at a much cheaper rate than any newspapers can?—I apprehend that it would be as easy to publish a moral publication as one of this description, for a penny.

472. But do not you think that if a newspaper could be published at a penny, upon as good paper as that, and as large, that newspapers would be likely to compete in the market against such libidinous trash as that which is allowed to be published without a stamp?—I would not say "allow." We cannot prevent their being published without a stamp.

473. What, in your opinion, would be the effect of the competition

T. Keogh, Esq.

6 May 1851.

competition of a newspaper at the same price as this?—I confess that I have not reflected very much upon the subject, but there are some cosiderations which lie upon the surface that have occurred to me since I was summoned here as a witness, and that would be very obvious to any one. It is supposed that noxious publications of this description would be expelled from the field altogether, if papers containing "public intelligence, news, and occurrences," intermixed with essays on moral or scientific subjects, or other instructive or agreeable matter, were to be their competitors. That is certainly a benevolent theory, but I am afraid it is not sustained by the facts which are notorious: for instance, I know that in London there are two or three weekly newspapers, written with the greatest ability, containing excellent summaries of public news, and criticisms upon new books and new inventions, matters of considerable interest, and all got up with very great ability. Those publications I know have a circulation that is comparatively small to that of a paper which contains little else but a collection of all the police reports, murders, and atrocities of every kind, and is read both in the country and in London. The circulation of that paper is five times as large as that of the best Sunday newspaper to which I have alluded.

474. You are now comparing publications which are non-political, not newspapers, with others which are?—No; I am comparing newspaper with newspaper; newspapers printed for the same price, all containing public intelligence, and containing the other matters which I have alluded to.

475. Are the Committee to understand you to say that the newspapers which are of an immoral character have a preference in the market?—I do not say of an immoral character, but containing information principally of the description that I have alluded to; reports of trials for all sorts of criminal offences; reports of the police-offices, and so on; that is the great material of the publication that I have referred to, and it seems to be much more interesting to the class of persons by whom it is read, than those of a better description, and sold for the same price.

476. *Chairman.*] At what prices were those respective newspapers published?—Sixpence.

477. They would circulate not exactly amongst the working classes?—The one to which I have alluded does reach the working classes, and I believe scarcely any other.

478. Mr. *Cobden.*] Are the Committee to understand you to

T. Keogh, Esq.

6 May 1851.

to express an opinion that if newspapers could be put in competition with such a publication as that which is before you, that they would not be likely to divert the minds of the reading public from such works?—I only infer that from the facts that I have just stated, namely, the preference given to a newspaper that contains little else than matter such as I have described, instead of papers that contain a great variety of matter written with literary excellence of a high degree, and containing all manner of intelligence of much interest. If moral and instructive publications could successfully compete with or entirely supersede papers of this description they can do it now. They may be published on the same terms. In giving to the former the right to publish news without a stamp, you would give it to this kind of publication also.

479. You are aware that at present no one in England can purchase a newspaper for a penny?—I believe not.

480. But you can buy that paper before you, containing such matter as you see in it, for a penny?—Yes.

481. Do you think that the newspaper stamp does really contribute to preserve the purity of the press, when such a publication as that before you is allowed to go untaxed, and those of an unobjectionable character are taxed?—The law does not allow it, but it has not prohibited the publishing a paper of this kind without a stamp. I presume the Honourable Member's notion is that the stamp duty should be imposed upon this paper.

482. No; I am desirous to have your opinion upon the matter: I understood you to say that you regarded the penny stamp as a safeguard to the character of our periodical press?—I say that I regard the registration and the duty, combined together, as securing a press of a high description, such as exists in this country, and perhaps exists in no other.

483. Is any registration necessary for the paper before you?—No.

484. In what way does the Newspaper Stamp Act protect the public against infamous publications such as the one before you?—The Newspaper Stamp Act has nothing to do with them.

485. I understood you to say just now that the character of our periodical press was improved by the newspaper stamp?—Not by the newspaper stamp; I could not have meant to say that; what I mean to say is, that the character of our newspaper press is considerably preserved, I think, by registration, which is required as to newspapers, by the facility

*T. Keogh*, Esq.

6 May 1851.

facility it affords of getting to the parties, and which the public would not otherwise enjoy, by the persons being known characters; the stamp is a mere incident to that, but it is the registration which is most serviceable to the public; the stamp is a mere matter of revenue.

486. You do not think it is necessary that there should be a registration for all periodical publications?—Hitherto there has been none but with regard to newspapers.

487. You do not think it necessary that there should be any registration for the purpose of improving the character of such publications as the one before you?—I do not pronounce any opinion upon that; it may be desirable to have registration, by means of which the author of such a publication as that could be got at.

488. As the matter stands at present these vile publications are not in any way prevented, nor is there any kind of surveillance exercised over them under the Newspaper Stamp Act?—Certainly not; the Newspaper Stamp Act has nothing to do with them; that is rather a matter for the Home Department, as being *contra bonos mores*: if in fact there be anything in this paper which amounts to an offence against the law.

489. Therefore the Newspaper Stamp Act does nothing to protect the public from infamous publications, such as the one before you?—Certainly not; no more than against obscene books, or any other publications which the Newspaper Stamp Act has no relation to.

490. When you say that the newspaper stamp tends to maintain the character of the press, you mean that portion of the press that is stamped?—I set out by stating that it is the registration which I think is useful to the public; the duty is only useful to the revenue; by means of the registration the public can reach the publisher of any matter that affects them injuriously, and it as well enables the Government to reach a person who publishes anything against the public peace.

491. That registration could exist, could it not, without a newspaper stamp at all?—It has nothing to do with the stamp; the registration and the security are for purposes unconnected with the stamp.

492. Sir *J. Walmsley*.] Has not the charge of 1 *d.* stamp upon the better class of newspapers, and the non-charge upon publications of a worse description, a tendency to increase the sale of those of the lower class?—It is difficult to form an opinion upon that.

493. Is

T. Keogh, Esq.

6 May 1851.

493. Is it not a protection to the worst class of publications, and an encouragement to their sale and circulation over those which are of a better description?—I do not see that, for the reasons which I have already assigned.

494. Sir *T. F. Lewis.*] You stated, did you not, that these publications were not newspapers?—Yes; they are periodical publications without news; they might as well be songs.

495. Mr. *G. A. Hamilton.*] Suppose a man with 1*d.* in his pocket desirous of obtaining news, and there are two papers, one costing 2*d.*, a good paper, and the other such as the one before you, costing only 1*d.*, he would buy the 1*d.* one would he not?—That depends upon what he wants.

496. Mr. *Rich.*] You stated, did you not, that the newspapers which are published stamp-duty free beat the better character of papers which are equally published free?—I said that in turning the thing over in my mind I could not help observing the circumstance, that a particular paper has larger circulation than another. I say that as between two newspapers which are sold for the same price.

497. Have you had any experience of unstamped publications not being newspapers?—They never came under my notice at all; except this one, I do not think I ever saw one.

498. Sir *T. F. Lewis.*] Have you any knowledge of the extent of the circulation of the paper before you?—We can have no knowledge whatever.

499. *Chairman.*] There is another definition of newspaper, which I will read from the Act: "Any paper printed in any part of the United Kingdom weekly, or oftener, or at intervals not exceeding 26 days, containing only or principally advertisements"?—That is a newspaper, and declared to be a newspaper.

500. Is it not the fact that that law is violated?—I apprehend not. We have a great number of these advertising publications which are registered, and pay the duty, I believe, with perfect regularity. I never heard of an instance of one being published without a stamp.

501. Mr. *Ewart.*] Must not everything which tends to produce competition, such as the freer circulation of news, with regard to such immoral publications as the one you have just seen, tend *pro tanto* to diminish the influence of such immoral publications?—That, I think, is almost a truism. There is no doubt that if other publications of an opposite

*T. Keogh, Esq.*

6 May 1851.

opposite character occupy the field, they may tend to expel them altogether, or to counteract their ill effects.

502. I asked whether the freer circulation of news, if news could come into competition with immorality in the way suggested, would not *pro tanto* tend to diminish the influence of such publications?—Undoubtedly it would tend to do so; but that it would have the effect of superseding and driving out of the field all of the publications of that kind, I very much doubt, for the reasons I have before mentioned.

503. My question was *pro tanto*?—Of course.

504. *Chairman.*] With regard to the other branch of the question, namely, commenting and observing upon news, a person may comment and observe upon news at intervals exceeding 26 days, without a stamp; but if he comments and observes upon news at intervals of less than 26 days, the price must be above 6 *d.*, or at least 6 *d.*, and the size of the publication must be two sheets, of certain dimensions, must they not?—Yes.

505. With regard to the 53 class publications, are not many of those less in price than 6 *d.*, smaller in size than the size set forth, and also published at intervals of less than 26 days?—Yes; but do they comment upon public news?

506. Are they not of that small size that they are disentitled to comment upon public news at intervals of less than 26 days?—Yes: I should say that if they commented upon public news they would be, within the period of 26 days, subject to the newspaper duty.

507. What is the meaning of saying that a person may comment upon public news if the publication be of a certain size, but that he may not comment upon public news if it be less than certain dimensions?—That involves a history of the objects with which the Act, the 60th of George the Third, was passed. That Act was passed for the purpose of subjecting to restrictions publications that were then not considered newspapers, but merely containing essays upon political subjects, such, I believe, as "Cobbett's Register," and the "Black Dwarf," and other publications of that description which were arising, and had an extensive circulation at that time, and were not subject to the laws relating to newspapers. Then, for the purpose of reaching those papers, they fixed the price, namely, not exceeding 6 *d.*, and the intervals of publication within 26 days; and if the price was above 6 *d.*, and if the intervals of publication

T. Keogh, Esq.

6 May 1851.

tion were beyond 26 days, they did not consider that the necessity of the case required that they should be brought within the limits of the law as to newspapers.

508. It was considered that if they were dear and large they might be permitted to comment upon public affairs, but if cheap and small they might not?—That was the meaning of it, I believe; I presume that was the meaning; I can only infer it from the nature of the enactment.

509. Many of those cheap and small ones which are not allowed to comment upon public affairs do so without a stamp, do they not?—I am not aware that they do.

510. Would you conceive that comments upon the public revenue of the country, the financial statement of the year, the Queen's speech, or the speeches of Members in either House of Parliament, were such a kind of commenting as the small and cheap publications are not permitted by law to indulge in?—It would be a species of commenting which would subject them to the newspaper duty.

511. If I were to show you many of those small and cheap publications which do so comment, you would call that a violation of the law, would you not?—I certainly should.

512. What is the meaning of saying that a person shall not comment upon public affairs unless in a publication of certain dimensions?—It is impossible for me to explain to the Committee the object of a law that was framed in the year 1820, before I had any connexion with the revenue, and which was in fact the act of the Statesmen of the day. I can only infer their intentions from what they have done, and, as I said before, I believe the object was to bring within the range of the newspaper laws publications that were sold for a price less than 6*d.*, and published at intervals short of 26 days.

513. And of small size?—Yes; those papers they desired to bring within the range of the laws that related to newspapers.

514. Does the Board of Inland Revenue consider it their duty to enforce those conditions of high price and large size?—We look to the law as it stands, and if we consider that it is infringed we endeavour to enforce it, but we first of all always give warning to the parties and tell them the position in which they stand, and if they resist we of course prosecute them.

515. "Punch" is under 6*d.*?—That is a very peculiar publication. "Punch" refers to public events to make them

 the

*T. Keogh,* Esq. 6 May 1851.

the vehicle or the subject of some jest or humorous sally, and the point of the sally would be lost if the event were not previously known; it gives no news.

516. My question referred to the comments?—The comments I consider to be not serious comments nor anything more than a joke, which it would be ridiculous to notice, I should say.

517. Mr. *S. Adair.*] Then probably the discretion of the Board in instituting a prosecution would be governed by their estimate of the opinion that the jury were likely to form of the publication?—Certainly.

518. *Chairman.*] I should have thought that the object of the Statesmen of 1820 was to prevent persons in small publications, and sold at a low price, from turning public institutions into ridicule, and treating with contempt the laws and public arrangements. Was not the Act rather directed against publications which commented without spirit upon public matters?—I apprehend that the intention of the framers of the Act of the 60th of George the 3d was to bring within the range of the newspaper laws, and therefore to make amenable to the law the publishers of prints in which public transactions were seriously discussed, but not in the manner in which "Punch" or any paper of a mere jocular character refers to public events.

519. Would you not say, that in such a paper, for instance, as the "Christian Spectator," or the "Church Missionary Magazine," public matters were seriously discussed?—Yes.

520. They are published unstamped, and the price and size I believe are both within the limited conditions?—I confess that I never heard of the papers before.

521. You made a return of them?—Will you allow me to look at it (*The same was handed to the Witness*). The way in which I made the return was this: I called upon the registrar of newspapers, the officer with whom all these papers are deposited upon the day of publication, to state what newspapers he knew were published partly without stamps, and according to the information he gave me, the return was made. On looking at it again, I perceive that it is, in fact, the return of the registrar of newspapers, and signed by him; not a return of mine; I was aware that such a return had been made, but as to my going through each of these papers to see whether they contained matters of intelligence or observations upon public concerns, I never did.

522. Those papers have generally printed upon them, "stamped"

"stamped" so much, and "unstamped" so much; so that, inasmuch as one copy of each is sent to the Board of Inland Revenue with that information affixed to it, you must be perfectly aware that there is a portion of the impression unstamped?—The officer must be aware of that with whom it is lodged, and I suppose if he thought that by printing a portion without stamps the law had been transgressed, he would bring it under the notice of the Board. The Committee do not suppose for a moment that the Board can look over every newspaper that is printed in the country and deposited in our office from time to time; that is the duty of the particular officer with whom they are lodged, and he would, if he considered that the paper was not entitled to publish a portion without stamps, bring it under the notice of the Board.

*T. Keogh,* Esq.

6 May 1851.

523. Mr. *Cobden.*] Anybody may register anything that comes to your office as a newspaper?—A person coming to register a paper as a newspaper says, "I intend to publish a newspaper with a certain title;" and if he makes a declaration and enters into a bond relating to a newspaper under that title, it is no business of ours to inquire whether it is a newspaper or not; we have no power of making any such inquiry.

524. You are aware that a great number of publications go through the post, owing to your having given a newspaper stamp to them, which would not go through for less than 4 *d.* if it were not for your stamp?—I know that papers that are not really newspapers do pass through the post-office under a penny stamp, but whether they would cost more if put in as letters and charged the ordinary postage, I cannot say.

525. I hold in my hand a catalogue of Savory's, the silversmith, consisting of 64 pages, and stamped as a newspaper, which goes through the post for a penny?—The Post-office has the power to allow free transmission to any paper registered and stamped as a newspaper, but it does not follow that, because this catalogue or any other paper is stamped with a newspaper stamp, it is entitled to free transmission through the Post-office; practically it does go; that is a matter for the Post-office itself, and I believe that the policy on which it has proceeded in allowing papers, not in point of law newspapers, to pass under the penny newspaper stamp, is, that it is a matter, not of the difference between the penny stamp and the postage which would be payable on the thing transmitted, but it is a matter

T. Keogh, Esq.

6 May 1851.

between the newspaper stamp and nothing, for the paper never would be published at all if it had not that privilege.

526. Do you think that prices current would not be published if they had to pay the postage stamp?—I do not think that they would be published to the extent they now are.

527. Mr. *Ewart.*] You strain the law for the purpose of giving that facility?—The Post-office authorities, with the concurrence of the Lords of the Treasury, may determine whether any paper professing to be a newspaper, and stamped as such, is really so, and can pass through the post-office. I believe the view of the matter on which they have proceeded is this: they say, "if this circular or this price current were to be treated by us as not a newspaper, and refused transmission, the revenue would never get anything at all; therefore it is not a question with us as to the difference between the penny newspaper stamp and the postage that would be payable upon them, but it is a question between the penny newspaper stamp and nothing at all to the revenue."

528. Mr. *Cobden.*] Do you suppose that merchants would not transmit their prices current, or tradesmen send out their catalogues, if they could not send them by post for a penny?—Not to the extent that they now do, if they had to pay postage upon them every time they were put into the post-office; for instance, some person in London may send a price current to his corresponding agent in Manchester, stamped with a newspaper stamp, and the agent in Manchester may put it into the post again, and direct it to a person in Bristol, and so it may go all round the country under that stamp during seven days; and if he had to pay 1 *d.* or 2 *d.* every time it was put into the post, it would not obtain the extensive circulation that it now does.

529. Mr. *Rich.*] Or he might resort to other means of transmitting it?—Yes.

530. Mr. *Cobden.*] Might not the same argument be used, then, to warrant your sending large books by the post at 1 *d.*?—I was only endeavouring to assign some reason for the liberal policy which has been pursued by the Post-office in this matter. If the Post-office were required to carry heavy books under 1*d.* stamp, of course they would change their policy. It is in their discretionary power to decide whether any paper shall be admitted to the privileges of a newspaper or not, and if they found that persons attempted to pass under 1*d.* stamp a heavy book, which would add

add accumulatively, if they came in numbers, great weight to their post-bags, of course they would refuse it. But it is in respect to small publications, such as a price-current, which does not seriously add to their expense of transmission, that they think it right to give to the public a benefit which it would not otherwise receive.

*T. Keogh,* Esq.

6 May 1851.

531. Do you know any instance in which the Post Office has refused to transmit any publication that has once been stamped as a newspaper?—I am not aware; that would not come at all within my knowledge.

532. Mr. *Ewart.*] This power is not given to the Post Office by statute law, is it?—Yes, it is.

533. *Chairman.*] You are conducting now a case against a "Narrative of Current Events"?—Yes, it was to have come on yesterday, but it is postponed till Wednesday.

534. Several monthly publications, I believe, have received intimations from the Stamp Office that they contained matters that render them liable to the newspaper stamp; is the decision on the "Narrative of Current Events" case to govern that class of cases?—Certainly; we did not think it right to institute a whole crusade of prosecutions at the same time against several parties, and we selected, I think, a respectable antagonist to contest the matter with, and, of course, the decision in that case will settle the question, whether we have viewed the law rightly or otherwise.

535. Then the decision in that case of Dickens's publication, will render all the monthlies that contain news liable to the stamp?—Yes.

536. Such as "Tait's Magazine"?—There, I think, we forget the terms in which the duties are imposed; as I said before, the duties are imposed upon "any newspaper," a word which has a signification understood by everybody, or upon "any paper containing public news, intelligence, or occurrences;" now I do not consider that a magazine, a large book, a considerable book, at all events a pamphlet at least, is a paper, or would fall within, to ordinary apprehension, what would be considered a newspaper, and it neverhas been.

537. Mr. Timm stated that if a person printed the Queen's speech upon a piece of paper without a stamp, he would be liable to a penalty of 20 *l.* for every copy, and he said that it was news beyond question: supposing I were to extract from the "Times" the financial statement of the Chancellor of the Exchequer, and to print it upon a separate piece of paper, and distribute it without a stamp, would that come under the same head as the Queen's speech?—I confess that at

*T. Keogh,* Esq.

5 May 1851.

at the moment I do not see any material difference between them; the one is information of a public nature as well as the other, which the public is interested and deeply concerned in.

538. Is it not an unfair thing upon the regular newspapers that parts of a newspaper should be printed on unstamped paper, perhaps the most interesting part to the public, and dispersed without paying a duty; the newspaper is obliged to pay duty for inserting such things?—Yes, it is unfair upon the regular newspapers, but it depends upon the form in which it is published; supposing an extract from the "Times" newspaper were to be introduced into an essay upon any particular subject.

539. Supposing one morning, when the public were anxious to read the speech of the Chancellor of the Exchequer upon the budget, I were to cause it to be printed upon unstamped paper, for I might get an early edition of the "Times," and copy it out, and print it on unstamped paper, and circulate it, should I not be liable to a penalty?—Yes, if it were published in the form and within the limits that apply to a newspaper; I do not see any distinction between a speech delivered in Parliament by the Chancellor of the Exchequer, or any other person, and published in a separate form on a piece of paper, and the Queen's Speech.

540. Then how is it that you allow those separate speeches to be published separately on separate pieces of paper, which is frequently the case, without stamps?—When you say we allow it, I should observe that if a case comes under our notice, and we consider it to be a transgression of the law, we should notice it; but we are not ubiquitous, and instances such as you allude to, in which the law has been literally, though perhaps unconciously overstepped, may happen without our knowledge.

541. Is it not your duty to protect the regular newspapers published, all those impressed with stamps, and to take care that they are not exposed to unfair competition, and that parties do not publish either the whole or a portion of their contents without a stamp?—Most undoubtedly it is, and as far as we have the power to do so we do.

542. If a person printed the Chancellor of the Exchequer's speech upon a separate piece of paper, unstamped, might not a person buy that speech in preference to buying the newspaper, the one being unstamped and the other stamped, and would not that be unfair competition?—I think it would be.

543. Then

543. Then, if that be so, why is it allowed?—I say that it is not allowed when it comes under observation. *T. Keogh, Esq.* 6 May 1851.

544. Whose business is it to see that the law is complied with. You say to the newspaper publishers, "You shall stamp all your impressions, every copy." I ask whose business is it to see that other parties do not publish the same matter without a stamp?—I should not say that it was the business of any particular person; but such a circumstance, if it occurred, would very soon be brought to our notice, by somebody aggrieved. If an unstamped paper were published in London we should very soon hear of it from some stamped newspaper: we cannot have our eyes everywhere, but somebody would be aggrieved, and it would be greatly to their interest to communicate the circumstance to us. We have no police, and we have no observers of every thing all over the country that would bring such a thing to our notice.

545. Have you not the distributors of stamps and your officers, with their eyes open, and cannot they see in the shop windows unstamped news?—Undoubtedly; and if it came under the observation of a particular officer it would be his duty to communicate it. But I mean to say, with regard to a paper published in London by some bookseller, which he does not conceive to be a newspaper, such as the speech of the Chancellor of the Exchequer, it might happen that that would never come under our notice, and that we should never see it.

546. You say that in the case of the Queen's Speech there could be no doubt?—It might happen that we might never see such a publication.

547. You would interfere if you did see it, would you not?—I am not sure; perhaps we should, and perhaps we should not. In instances of single transgressions of this kind in determining on a prosecution the Board are influenced by the particular circumstances of the case.

548. Have you not received a memorial complaining of the privileges enjoyed by 53 registered newspapers from other newspaper proprietors, asking that the same privileges should be given to them?—Certainly; that is, we have received a request from newspaper proprietors, whose papers are undoubtedly newspapers, to be put on the footing of papers that are not newspapers at all.

549. That is the matter in dispute?—That is how we view it.

550. You are now contending before the Court of Exchequer,

*T. Keogh,* Esq.

6 May 1851.

chequer, are you not, that many of those very publications to which I refer are newspapers, and have been all along?—No, there is no such question. Not one of the papers mentioned in that list is the same as the paper that we are now prosecuting in the Court of Exchequer. We say that the paper published by Mr. Dickens contains "public news, intelligence, or occurrences," and falls within the first definition in the Newspaper Act of a newspaper, and that its periods of publication are wholly immaterial. Then we say, if we can establish that fact, we will bring in the monthly newspapers, containing "public news, intelligence, or occurrences," and make them liable to the duty, in the same way as we contend that Mr. Dickens's is. But the papers that you refer to do not contain either "public news, intelligence, or occurrences, or any comments thereon," as we think.

551. I have been informed that in the memorial presented to the Board of Inland Revenue, the memorialists set forth particular cases in which those publications do enjoy the privilege of not stamping all their copies, and that they point out the actual "public news, intelligence, or occurrences" contained in them, and the "comments thereon," the precise matter that was complained of that was published unstamped, and therefore came into unfair competition with them?—I do not recollect any other memorial to the Board on the subject than one referring to "Punch," and to two or three other publications, all of which we considered not to contain any such matter as subjects them to the duty upon newspapers.

552. Will you lay before this Committee any complaints or memorials that you may have received from any newspaper proprietors, complaining that an unfair competition is allowed by the Board of Inland Revenue?—I will do so.

553. Mr. *Cobden.*] You have stated that there is a trial coming on on Wednesday concerning "Dickens's Household Narrative." Supposing that the Court rules, and the jury determine, as you expect, that that is a newspaper, then all the monthly publications of the same kind, such as the "Freeholder," will require to be stamped, will they not?—Yes.

554. With reference to a publication that contains nothing but reports of proceedings in the House of Commons, do you consider that news?—It depends upon the form in which it is published.

555. For instance, "Hansard's Debates" published in weekly

T. Keogh, Esq.

6 May 1851.

weekly numbers?—It is undoubtedly news; but whether it is a newspaper I do not know, unless I knew what the form is.

556. Do you consider that the character of a newspaper is altered by an alteration of the form of publication?—I think it is. I think that a book, for instance, the "Annual Register" which contains news down to the latest period of the year to which it refers, is not a newspaper, and that no one would think of calling it one.

557. Confining yourself to "Hansard's Debates," is that not published in the same form weekly that "Dickens's Household Narrative" is monthly, in the octavo form?—I do not know. The only form in which I see "Hansard's Debates" is in a bound volume.

558. Mr. *Rich.*] Would you not rather judge of it as a subject conducive to history, than as diffusive of news?—Yes. It is a printed record of the occurrences in a particular place, and is I believe published by order of The House.

---

## *Veneris*, 9° *die Maii*, 1851.

MEMBERS PRESENT.

| | |
|---|---|
| Sir J. Walmsley. | Mr. Sotheron. |
| Mr. Ewart. | Mr. G. A. Hamilton. |
| Mr. Tufnell. | Mr. Rich. |
| Mr. Chichester Fortescue. | Mr. Cobden. |
| Mr. Stafford. | |

THE RIGHT HON. THOMAS MILNER GIBSON,

IN THE CHAIR.

---

Mr. *Michael James Whitty*, called in; and Examined.

Mr. *M. J. Whitty.*

9 May 1851.

559. Sir *J. Walmsley.*] YOU reside at Liverpool, do you not?—I do.

560. Are you connected with the press?—I am. I am editor, proprietor, and conductor of the "Liverpool Journal," and publisher also.

561. How long have you been so?—Since 1844.

562. You

Mr. *M. J. Whitty.*

9 May 1851.

562. You were previously in London, were you not?—I was several years before on the press.

563. In the year 1829?—Yes. I then left it to go down to conduct a journal for another party.

564. What had been your occupation in London?—I was connected with the press, more immediately with literature. I was the editor of several periodicals, and I contributed to them nearly all.

565. After you went to Liverpool, how long did you remain on the journal which you have mentioned?—Until 1833. I then became the chief of police, and remained in it till 1844. I resigned then from ill-health.

566. You have not only had much experience as a pressman, but as a policeman and chief constable of Liverpool?—Yes, I presume so.

567. I presume you have turned your attention to the effect of the newspaper stamp duty, have not you?—Yes, very much.

568. What is the result of your consideration of that subject; is the penny stamp favourable, or the contrary?—Most decidedly unfavourable.

569. You say that, after you have had considerable experience, do you not?—A great deal of experience. I have given a great deal of attention to the press in other places.

570. Of what kind of experience do you speak?—I will give the Committee, in illustration, my own experience. I published a cheap paper; but I published first the usual priced paper. I then published a low-priced paper, and I now publish a high-priced paper again.

571. Then you have found, have you, that high-priced paper answers your purpose best?—Yes, it answered my purpose better; but it did not answer the public purpose so well.

572. It was worse for the public, was it?—Decidedly. It reduced the number of purchasers, and it made them pay 50 per cent. more for their paper, while it prevented the same number from taking the paper.

573. Am I correct in inferring that if good newspapers were cheap, there would be more buyers and more readers?—I should say twenty-fold or thirty-fold.

574. What are your reasons for saying so?—I published a high-priced newspaper till 1846, and the circulation that it attained then was about 2,700 on the average. A cheap newspaper, at 3 *d.*, was started in the town by a person of no capital, and immediately it reduced my circulation to 1,800.

575. What

Mr. *M. J. Whitty.*

9 May 1851.

575. What did you do to obviate that?—I published a newspaper at 3*d.* also, and the effect was that within a month I killed the cheap one; and all the others, except one, followed my example, and published at 3*d.* or 3½ *d.*

576. Your sale decreased very materially, you say? —Considerably. But when the price was reduced they all doubled their circulation; and I increased mine from 1,800 to 8,000 on the average, to 10,000; and it would have been considerably more had I had machinery to have printed.

577. Then did this circulation pay?—It paid me very well, but it was ruining the others.

578. But you did not continue to sell your newspaper at a low price, did you?—No. They complained very much that I was ruining the profession, and I did not like to live in enmity with them. I was not at all indisposed to receive a larger income myself, and so I increased the price of the paper at first to 3½ *d.*, and subsequently to 4½ *d.*

579. In what way was it ruining your contemporaries?—The profits on the circulation were very small at 3 *d.*, and they did not increase their advertisements; but my circulation being large, my profits were pretty equal to what they had been before; and I added 50 per cent. to my advertisements in consequence of the great increase of the circulation.

580. Did you think that you should obtain a monopoly by the increase of the price?—The effect of the high price was to give the newspaper a monopoly; it gives one newspaper in every town a monopoly, similar to what the "Times" has in London; it has exactly the same effect.

581. Has it given you that monopoly?—It gave it to me partially then, and I endeavoured to keep it.

582. What did you raise your price to?—To 4½ *d.* from 3 *d.*; first to 3 ½ *d.*, and then to 4 ½ *d.*

583. What was the quality of the cheap newspaper, as compared with the other; was it equal to it?—I should say it was better; that the cheap one was by far the best. The moment that we reduced the prices every one increased his literary staff; I increased mine very considerably; and I have no hesitation in saying that that movement improved very much the character of the ability employed on the Liverpool papers.

584. Then the addition of 1 ½ *d.* made a great difference in the circulation of the Liverpool papers?—Considerable; it threw down all the others to what they were before; and it reduced mine 2,000 or more per week.

585. Among what class of persons?—Among all classes; for when the papers were cheap, the rich took in two or three papers,

Mr. *M. J. Whitty.*

9 May 1851.

papers, while the poor took in one; and a great number, when it was raised, gave up their subscriptions altogether, and the circulation now is not more than it was seven years ago.

586. It advanced the circulation of the good papers, did not it?—Yes, it advanced the circulation of mine, which I consider the best, of course.

587. Are there any immoral or improper papers published in Liverpool?—Not in Liverpool.

588. Are there in other places about Liverpool; in Manchester, for instance?—No, I do not think there is an improper paper published in the provinces anywhere whatever; not that I know of; there are several in London, and there have been always.

589. Do you think that those improper papers are read by the working and poorer classes?—Yes, very extensively, for the want of better.

590. Can you give the Committee any illustration of that opinion?—Yes; the Committee will recollect the time of the unstamped newspapers, and there were a great number of them, Hetherington's and others; before that there were an immense quantity of penny papers and twopenny papers of a very obscene and improper character published; but the appearance of the unstamped newspapers killed them off in dozens.

591. Then their publication did good?—A great deal of good, because though bad themselves they displaced what was a great deal worse.

592. In what way was that effected?—They presented that which was more desirable to the reader, and which the reader preferred. The reduction of the stamp duty led to the publication of newspapers at 3*d.*

593. Can you name any of those papers?—At the present time there are threepenny papers published in London, and I believe there is one very disreputable paper published, but that I have never seen. There are several threepenny papers, "Lloyd's," "News of the World," and several others.

594. Have they a large circulation?—An immense circulation; they must have an immense circulation to pay, because they get no advertisements, and they depend upon the profits entirely for sale; I have seen them all.

595. You can speak as to their character, can you not?—Yes; the character is not bad, but it is not good, and they are not conducted with any kind of literary ability, not much at all events, nor with very proper feeling.

596. You think them better than the old unstamped papers, do you not?—Infinitely better.

597. Though

597. Though very bad, still you say that the people read them?—Yes, simply because they have nothing better that is accessible. I can give the Committee a very curious fact in reference to that. Previous to the reduction of the price of newspapers in Liverpool to 3 *d.*, in 1847 there came into Liverpool about 20,000 of those threepenny papers weekly, and the moment that we reduced our prices, and sold at the same price, of course we had a decided preference, and the result was that we nearly annihilated that trade; but the trade immediately revived on going up in our prices again, and is now almost as flourishing as ever it was.

598. Then you are of opinion that if newspapers were sold at low prices there would be few or no bad publications issued?—Yes, very few indeed. That is my decided opinion after all the reflection that I have given to the subject, and the exercise of the experience that I have had.

599. Can you state to the Committee some grounds for that assertion?—One is the illustration that I have just given of the effect produced in Liverpool; the other two illustrations are, first, the unstamped publications driving out the obscene trash, and the threepenny papers, which indeed have nearly annihilated all that kind of publications.

600. You fancy that a purer taste has been created?—Yes, the appetite grows by what it feeds upon; in fact, newspapers are the only things that people will ever read, and that they desire to read; for instance, the working people now can read them only through the public-houses or coffee-houses. In Liverpool we have no coffee-houses, and they must go to the public-houses, and they get them when they are very old.

601. Does it follow that the taste for good papers is the most prevalent?—Unquestionably; we find that good is always preferred by the multitude; in a theatre, for instance, and even the speeches delivered in Parliament reported in newspapers, and in literature of every description their taste is natural; in other and the more educated ranks of course the taste is to a great extent artificial—conventional; it may be bad or it may be good; but the taste of the people I apprehend is always correct.

602. Some doubts have been entertained as to the effects of cheapness on the quality; you seem to think that it would do good?—Immense; I should say decidedly that in our own case it improved our paper very considerably; besides, the very fact of addressing a larger number would have a great influence upon the writer, as it would have in the same way on an orator; he would exert himself more, and feel more sympathy; that was the case I know always with myself.

603. Do

Mr. *M. J. Whitty.*

9 May 1851.

603. Do you think that the cheapness of these papers, supposing the penny stamp taken off, would improve the working classes in intelligence, and fit them for higher positions?—Decidedly; it is the only knowledge indeed which they will appreciate, that which is contained in newspapers; they address themselves much more to politics than to science or literature.

604. You think then that newspapers are the vehicles through which the working classes obtain their information chiefly?—All the information they get is through that means and conversation, all of which originates in the newspapers.

605. Was your paper a scientific one?—No, it contained nothing but news and politics; I gave them as much of that as I could.

606. What were your politics?—Liberal.

607. And those politics I suppose are what the producing classes generally, as a body, adopt?—Yes, decidedly, nine out of 10; you might go to 99 out of 100.

608. Did you ever receive any compliments relative to your own paper from the authorities?—My paper was complimented by the Attorney-general in 1848, when there was great agitation, and when he was prosecuting prisoners; I would adduce that as a curious instance of what I presume would be the beneficial effect of cheap newspapers; at that time my paper was cheap; I had an immense circulation, sometimes as many as 18,000 a week very frequently, as much as my machinery would print; and although I was myself denounced by name by some of the discontented individuals at that time, yet the working classes never forsook the paper; they always supported it; and I flattered myself that it produced a very beneficial effect upon them.

609. In your opinion, a cheap press is essential to the maintenance of good and sound political opinions?—Yes, a cheap press is essential to everything good.

610. You speak of cheap papers: to what price do you suppose it would be possible to reduce papers?—If the stamp were taken off newspapers, and the duty off advertisements, you would, the same as in America, be able to sell papers at a penny.

611. Would they be of inferior quality?—No, I should say very superior quality. In the first place, a very large circulation would be necessary to pay, and a large circulation could not be obtained without the exercise of great abilities in the paper. We find that the case in America; although there is no stamp duty, and a multitude of daily papers, for they

are

are very numerous, and the circulation is very large indeed, they are very good papers. Mr. *M. J. Whitty.*

9 May 1851.

612. You think that cheap penny papers would pay a great deal better to the proprietors than the present high priced papers?—Infinitely. It would destroy the monopoly of any individual paper, but it would make every other paper better; those that did not pay, and even I should say, not half pay, it would either set them aside, or make them pay. There would not be 50,000 *l.* a year made by any daily paper; but other papers would not lose several thousands a year as they do now.

613. Do you know anything of publishing papers in America?—Yes, I have paid attention to it, as I have been connected as agent and correspondent with American papers.

614. Can you give the Committee any information as to the character of the papers published in America?—They are, speaking generally, much better printed than ours. For instance, we could not print them at all here on the kind of paper that they do; their paper is very good, and their type is legible; they are easily read. Newspapers after being read, of course, are worth nothing; any kind of paper that is readable is quite sufficient. Their paper is excellent to the eye, and their type is really beautiful, and they print in a manner like which we cannot print at all.

615. As to the ability employed, can you give any opinion?—I believe the whole available talent of America is engaged on the newspaper press. I believe there are now six editors of newspapers who are members of the House of Representatives, and four in the Senate. I have seen all that stated in a most respectable newspaper published in Philadelphia.

616. You spoke of the talent employed upon the American papers, but an opinion of an opposite nature prevails in this country?—Yes, but it is quite a mistake; it arises in this way; they are not conducted like the "Times" newspaper or the "Daily News," and for this reason, there is no metropolis. In America every large town is a metropolis to the district immediately around it, the same as Liverpool and Manchester are, and the consequence is that they have not that fulness of reports that you have in the London papers; for instance, their Parliamentary proceedings are printed only in the papers published in Washington, the same as in London here. In New York, New Orleans, St. Louis, Boston, and other places, they are generally satisfied with the Parliamentary intelligence that they receive at present by means of the electric telegraph; they receive intelligence by despatches

Mr. *M. J. Whitty.*

9 May 1851.

despatches from their correspondents as we do in Liverpool at present. The Friday's proceedings in Parliament we only get through the electric telegraph, and we never hear any more of it. The debates in Parliament are read by very few, and as the Committee may see in the daily papers in London, to meet the desire of the public to know what is done in Parliament, they give a summary every morning, very brief but exceedingly correct, of what is done in Parliament; but in the places that I have referred to, the news appertaining to themselves is published very fully, and for that reason a very small paper suffices, because the local news is not of a nature to extend very largely; the foreign news is very copious, and is collected at an immense expense.

617. As to the amount of capital employed, have you any idea of that as compared with the amount of capital employed in this country?—I cannot speak exactly to that; I only presume that it must be very large; I know that in this country to publish cheap papers would require about four times the capital that is required to publish a paper at present; but in America, so far as expenses go, for one of them, the "New York Herald," a paper which is not in the best repute in America, but which still is conducted with very much spirit and at great expense, the expense is greater than that that is resorted to by the London "Times," and all the papers are so; their correspondence is much more extensive than ours; they have the whole world round them, besides all that we have. If you look at the "Delta" and other papers published in New Orleans, you would see every day news which had been obtained and which must have been obtained at an immense expense from all the districts in South America and California, and they anticipate a great part of our news; that is done by dispatches. The electric telegraph does not extend at present into South America; it is confined almost exclusively to the Union.

618. You are aware that the London daily papers incur an immense expense for news; if sold cheap could they afford that expense?—Yes, and much more, as the Committee will see. For instance, supposing that they have a profit of a penny on a paper, or twopence or threepence on a paper, and they only sell 2,000, that will not be equal to a profit of a halfpenny on a paper of which they sell 20,000. The "New York Sun" circulates 50,000; and the "Herald" about 20,000.

619. A penny or twopenny paper then would be as profitable in your opinion as the London "Times"?—No, I do not apprehend that; I do not think that if the stamp duty were taken off any

Mr. *M. J. Whitty.*

9 May 1851.

any paper would ever produce the income of the "Times;" and the "Times" would not do it after that was done, but all the other papers would have a great deal more income.

620. The penny stamp operates to create a monopoly, does it not?—Decidedly; you have only one leading paper in every town; in fact that may be illustrated like the "Fat Pigeon" in Paley, there is only a very fat one and all the lean ones contribute to it.

621. What would be the effect of the abolition of the stamp and advertisement duties?—To equalise a great deal the circulation of newspapers, and to give a decided preference to the best one; in fact it would have the best possible effect to society generally in this way; at present, from the high price of the paper, families read but one, but if sold at a penny they would read three or four; the consequence would be that their minds would be perplexed and corrected, but reading from one newspaper only they think through that paper.

622. Is it your opinion that if the penny stamp, the advertisement duty, and the duty on paper were removed, you would have newspapers published in this country at a penny, and be as well conducted as the London "Times"?—Yes, I am certain that they would be as well conducted as they possibly could be. I would publish one myself instantly, and I dare say I should do it a great deal better than I do now, because there would be a greater effort required to succeed. Now, when you get into a position you get into a groove, and go on very comfortably.

623. Are you of opinion that it would be as profitable to you to publish at a penny with the advantages you would obtain as it is at the present moment?—No. As far as I am concerned I should like things to remain where they are, but I would not at all for that reason repudiate my former opinions. I would be quite content, for the good of others, to take my chance, and I would do what I could to succeed. I am at present satisfied; but I do not know that taking off the duty would at all leave me where I am. I should doubt it very much.

624. A change, as far as you are concerned, would be prejudicial to you?—I do not think it would render me any service whatever; my apprehension is that it would do me an injury.

625. But only because you have a large circulation, and publish as many papers as you can anticipate?—There is a good circulation now, and I do not think that I can increase it at all by any efforts I can make; but, in the other case, if

Mr. *M. J. Whitty.*

9 May 1851.

if I succeeded, the profits might be larger, but the chances are that they would not, and that my income would not be increased by it. The taking off of the stamp would cause a total revolution in the whole press of the country.

626. I understood you to say that there would be no more monopoly in large towns that there is now; that there would not be so many papers, but the circulation of one or two would be much larger?—No, there would be no monopoly whatever; there are only a certain number of readers in a certain district, and when you have supplied them you have supplied all. If I publish a penny paper and my next door neighbour does the same, and they are both good, three out of four will take the two papers, and I do not think there will be a monopoly similar to what there is now. There is now a paper in Liverpool, printing perhaps 1,300 or 1,400, and one printing 8,000. The other day the "Times" was printing 80,000. I do not mention this as any disparagement to the "Times" at all; but it is a fact that the accounts given in some of the other papers were better than in the "Times," but they did not increase their circulation a single copy.

627. How many papers are published in Liverpool?—Nine or ten; three papers on the Saturday, one on Friday, one on Thursday, one on Wednesday, two on Tuesday, and one on Monday, with two commercial papers.

628. If a reduction of the duties that have been spoken of were made, would there be an increased number of papers in your opinion, or would the number decrease?—There would be a great increase in this way; there would be as many weekly papers published as at present, and there would be bi-weekly and tri-weekly papers in addition to them. We have no daily papers in the country; a great number of those papers which now publish weekly would then publish daily papers.

629. Mr. *Ewart.*] Do you mean that the number of the different papers will increase, or that the number of the copies will increase?—The number of both would increase; there would be an immensely larger consumption of papers.

630. Sir *J. Walmsley.*] It is apprehended that if the stamps were removed, the country would be inundated with cheap papers; is that your opinion?—I do think that they would be more numerous, but that they would be still limited, from the necessity of having a very large circulation to pay.

631. Would the fact of their requiring a much larger capital have any injurious influence?—It would make it more difficult.

Mr. *M. J. Whitty.*

9 May 1851.

difficult. A newspaper now is started very often by an individual, or a party having a peculiar object to attain; it does not cost much, but then you could not commence a newspaper certainly under 10,000 *l.* The machinery alone to print 20,000 in four hours would cost at least 5,000 *l.*; and to conduct the paper would at all events take 5,000 *l.* more. In New York I believe the establishments there have cost, for buildings alone, something like 20,000 *l.* for a penny paper.

632. Do the papers published in Liverpool, or in the country, require a great deal of capital now?—Comparatively little; they can commence and get credit from the papermakers, and they get credit for type, and any kind of press will do. When I commenced first, for a small circulation, I borrowed and made use of another person's machine; it had only one cylinder, and that could not meet my circulation, and I was obliged to go to the expense of 1,000 *l.* for machinery, containing two cylinders, to print anything like the number, and that was totally inadequate; it was similar to the one that was used in the "Times" office, made by Middleton, and that cannot always meet the increased demand, even that one.

633. Do papermakers, or the persons who supply paper to the local press, at any time find stamps?—Constantly; in fact almost constantly they give credit for stamps. When I commenced I had just barely sufficient capital, and unfortunately I entered into partnership. I left the management to my partner, and he went into debt to a papermaker for the sum of 3,000 *l.* or 4,000 *l.*, which I had to pay.

634. Then capital is frequently found by papermakers, as they furnish not only paper, giving credit for it, but they supply the stamps also?—They supply the whole.

635. If the stamp duty and the other duties were reduced, you would then do a greater trade with those men, would you not?—No; paper would then be much more easily found, but still a larger capital considerably would be required for the machinery. The machinery alone will cost 5,000 *l.* or 6,000 *l.* to commence a cheap paper, which is a very important fact to observe, that an immense circulation requires immense machinery; when I say immense, it is complicated machinery, and that is very expensive.

636. You have had a great deal of experience generally in London, in Liverpool, in the provinces, and in Ireland, and you have given the Committee some information with regard to the American press; what, in your opinion, would be the effect of a cheap press?—The best possible effect. In the first place, diffusing the most desirable and most necessary of all knowledge

Mr. *M. J. Whitty.*

9 May 1851.

knowledge for men to know; in the next, making that knowledge cheap, it would also make it good, and increase the desire for it, and the necessity for a large circulation would command inevitably the necessary amount of talent and enterprise.

637. Can you state anything as to the effects of cheap papers in America?—I should say that I have no doubt that to that is attributable the very extensive information which the people of America possess. It is acknowledged by all who go there, and was admitted, I think, in Parliament, by Mr. Labouchere, that they were much better informed than our countrymen. It is, I know, the universal opinion, as I see by the written accounts of those who have visited the country, that they are the most intelligent people in the world, and I impute the whole of that to the cheap newspaper press. In other places, where education is quite as much diffused, the people are not so well informed.

638. You stated, in the former part of your evidence, that when you reduced your newspaper to 3*d.* you drove out of circulation some 20,000 copies of a low description of papers that were distributed?—It nearly annihilated that trade.

639. Do you speak positively upon that, from your own experience and knowledge, or is it a mere idea of yours?—I speak positively, on my own information. It appertained to me to make the inquiry; first, before I reduced my paper to 3*d.*, to ascertain what the circulation of those papers was, and next what it was that affected the other papers when we advanced the price, and I found that it was the sudden influx of those papers again. I will give a curious illustration of that. In Liverpool we keep printing as we sell, and when we have important local news to publish, the circulation increases very considerably, to as much as 10,000 in a day; and the moment that the London news or general news becomes not interesting locally we drop down very considerably, and people buy those threepenny papers.

640. Mr. *Ewart.*] From your experience of America, inasmuch as questions are discussed and sifted, and errors more likely to be exposed by so large a press, do you conceive that the press of America has conduced to the preservation of good order?—Most assuredly.

641. The mischiefs which are allowed to be collected, afterwards to explode in other countries, are freely considered there beforehand, expanded and exposed?—Yes. For instance, there is one paper talking in one way, and another paper talking in another way, as you find it in London; and it is a very curious

Mr. *M. J. Whitty.*

9 May 1851.

curious illustration of the appetite of the people for what is good and correct, that the whole of London could not support even one "Satirist;" it is dead.

642. Do you think that the freedom of the press in America acts as a kind of safety valve for public opinion?—Yes, quite so.

643. You have stated that the stamp duty, and the advertisement duty, operate to create a monopoly?—Yes, certainly.

644. What is the effect of the advertisement duty in a commercial town like Liverpool?—Most injurious.

645. Have you ever compared the advertisements inserted in American newspapers with those inserted in English newspapers?—I could not avoid doing so. I have a St. Louis paper, where there is a population of only 44,000; it is a paper larger than the "Times," printed with smaller type than the "Times," and it is, all but four columns, filled with advertisements. In Liverpool, I know that advertisers hesitate very much to advertise in consequence of the high price of the advertisements; and a reduction of the advertisement duty would operate precisely as the taking off of the stamp, it would reduce the advertisements so low that advertisements would become general, and tradesmen and others would make themselves better known.

646. Do not you consider that a duty like that operates like a stoppage on a public highway, or like anything which impedes free communications between the public with regard to their mutual wants?—No doubt it does. You can get no advertisement into a Liverpool newspaper under 3 *s.* 6 *d.*, consisting of only three lines. A tradesman's advertisements will cost 14 *s.* or 15 *s.*

647. Have you ever observed the great advantage which in the agricultural districts of America is enjoyed by the agriculturists who wish to advertise the articles which they have to sell, as compared with English agriculturists?—In every respect they have an immense advantage over the English press. The American people have an immense advantage in that kind of press in respect to trade and commerce, and it is infinitely better conducted than ours. Some years ago I was induced to publish in Liverpool a daily commercial paper, without a stamp; it was then very badly done, and I was dissatisfied with it, and I wanted to see how it was done in other papers, and the American paper was a model at once, it was so much superior, as they always are.

648. My question referred to agriculturists; it struck me that the American producer had a great advantage over the British

Mr. *M. J. Whitty.*

9 May 1851.

British producer, in consequence of the facilities he enjoyed for advertising?—Yes, it is an immense advantage.

649. Have you not stated that in the case of provincial papers they have become more extended in circulation as they became more local in the nature of their intelligence?—Quite so, and I adduce my own experience. The foreign news I never let exceed a column; the Parliamentary news of the week I always confine to at least a column and a half; all the remainder of the paper is local.

650. From your experience, should you say that extreme facility of communication with respect to their local wants and interests, when given, as in America, to people in a district, has had a good effect upon their character, by enabling them to know what they are about, and what is doing around them?—Yes, and it elevates them in their own estimation. In this country the shadow of London is very much upon the provinces; they deem nothing good that is not London, and they look to London for everything. But in America it is not so, each town being a district within itself; each is a capital, and they have no presiding influence whatever.

651. Do not you think that it is very desirable to encourage that diffusion of the press, which is created by greater facilities being afforded in the provinces, instead of concentrating it all in one place?—Quite so.

652. Where do you obtain your newspaper stamps from?—From Manchester; it is the only provincial place, I think, in England, where there is a newspaper stamp office.

653. Do you ever vary the place; on what depends your selection of the place where you get your stamps?—Proximity. Stamps cost a great deal, something like 9 *l.* a thousand; they cost me something like 100 *l.* a week, and at that rate I could not keep a large stock. If we run low and have an increased demand we can have them down from Manchester in an hour by sending a message up by the electric telegraph, and down they come. I have often printed, when my capital was less than at present, on other people's stamps, having none of own issued, nominally increasing the circulation, but not giving any advantage to my own.

654. It does not always depend upon proximity, does it? The Committee have been told that some of the newspaper proprietors living near Glasgow procure their stamps from Manchester?—They may do so, but their circulation must be very small; if you have a large circulation you must have a stamping office near you.

655. Sir *J. Walmsley.*] Would there be any advantage in having

Mr. *M. J. Whitty.*

9 May 1851.

having an increased number of stamp offices; for instance, one at Liverpool?—Yes, very great.

656. Mr. *Ewart.*] Have any memorials ever been presented to the Inland Revenue Board to increase the number of places for obtaining stamps?—No, I think not; the newspaper people are satisfied; they think that they have a monopoly, and they wish to keep it; but they are quite mistaken, for it is their ruin.

657. What facilities and advantages would a stamp-office at Liverpool give to you?—Then you would have paper stamped immediately, and you could buy your paper where you liked. When we get it stamped in Manchester we get it from Messrs. Wrigley; they produce the paper, and very good and excellent men they are; but if I wanted paper I could get it from Wales. I could buy it in Wales cheaper, but the expense of conveying it to Manchester and back again would make it dearer than buying it from Messrs. Wrigley, whose office is opposite the stamp-office in Manchester.

658. If you bought the paper where you pleased, and could get it stamped in Liverpool, you would be able to publish your paper on better terms, would you not?—Yes, no doubt; because we could buy the paper anywhere, and could get it in larger quantities, and have it by us.

659. Have you made any estimate of your losses in that respect?—No.

660. Mr. *Cobden.*] You have stated that you have had an opportunity of giving a good deal of attention to the character and quality of the American press?—Yes; I have never been in America.

661. But you have been in connexion with the American press?—Yes.

662. And you have had a great variety of American newspapers pass through your hands?—Yes; I was so much interested in it, that I paid a very large sum for an account and history of all the principal papers in America, and I published it in Liverpool some years ago.

663. You alluded just now to the "Satirist" paper; do you remember ever to have known a paper in America of that same character as the "Satirist" that is not characterised by coarseness, vulgarity, or rudeness in argument, or virulent personalities, but being of an obscene character?—No; I have heard that there is one now, published in Boston, of that description, something similar to a paper the Committee may have heard of, which is not published in Dublin at present; but amongst the circulating papers I have never seen one of that description.

 The

Mr. *M. J. Whitty.*

9 May 1851.

The lowest paper I have ever seen is the "New York Herald," and that went not further than many of our own papers; obscenity I never saw in it at all.

664. You have not seen it in any paper that has passed through your hands?—Never.

665. Sir Charles Lyell, in his second visit to the United States, volume the second, page 41, says, "Newspapers for a penny or twopence are bought freely by the passengers (at the railway stations), and having purchased them at random wherever we went in the Northern, Middle, Southern, and Western States, I came to the conclusion that the press of the United States is quite as respectable, in a moral point of view, as our own. In the present crisis the greater number of prints condemn the war party, expose their motives, and do justice to the equitable offers of the English ministry in regard to Oregon. A large portion of almost every paper is devoted to literary extracts, to novels, tales, travels, and often more serious works. Some of them are specially devoted to particular religious sects, and nearly all this class are against war. There are also some 'Temperance,' and in the north 'Anti-slavery papers.'" Does your experience of the American press induce you to affirm that opinion given by Sir Charles Lyell?—Quite so; I have always endeavoured to defend the American press, from my knowledge of it, and I recollect extracting that very point as a confirmation of my own opinion. In this country I know that an opinion prevails extensively adverse to the respectability of the American press, but it is an entirely wrong one.

666. You think in regard to moral character that the American press is equal to our own?—Quite so.

667. As regards price, taking quantity for quantity, would you consider that the price in America is about one-third of our own?—Yes, less than one-third.

668. Do you consider that the American people obtain, for one-third of the cost that the English people pay, mental aliment of the same quality?—Yes, they do.

669. And you would consider that to be an inestimable advantage to any community having a free constitutional government; would you not?—Yes. I would add, what I omitted before, that their newspapers are full of advertisements; and there is no reading so interesting, locally, as local advertisements; it is at once useful, and it induces people to read probably what is better matter; but advertisements are amongst the most desirable reading.

670. Do you think that if we were free in England from the taxes on knowledge, as they are popularly called, that we should have

Mr. *M. J. Whitty.*

9 May 1851.

have as cheap a press and as good a press in England as they have in America?—Quite, and a much better one than we have now; for instance, newspaper editors of many of our provincial newspapers are generally supplied with what they call leading articles from London. I have received circulars from London, stating that they will supply leading articles for 15 *s.*; they are of no value, and a great many of our provincial newspapers are supplied with this kind of stuff written in London. Where they have a local editor they hardly ever pay him more than 150 *l.* a year, and I need not tell the Committee that no man, with proper qualifications, would be content with that sum. In fact, provincial papers are not well conducted generally, except in a few places, such as Liverpool, Manchester, and other large towns. In Edinburgh the papers are as well conducted as at any place in the world, and they are so in Dublin. Perhaps on the whole, the Irish newspaper press, which 20 years ago was very degraded, is now the best conducted press in the world.

671. Mr. *Rich.*] To what do you attribute that?—To the fact of a great number of well educated men editing the papers.

672. You just now stated that you considered the English press to be below the American press; how do you reconcile that with your statement that such a great improvement has taken place in consequence of well educated men acting as editors?—I spoke of Ireland.

673. Mr. *Cobden.*] You have expressed your opinion that the newspaper press of America is equal in character to our stamped press?—Quite so.

674. What opinion have you been led to form, having been the chief of the Liverpool police, and having also been engaged as a newspaper proprietor, of the character of our unstamped periodical literature?—That it is very bad.

675. The weekly unstamped press you consider very bad?—There is not much of it at present, but it was infamous; it is not quite so bad now; there are parts very bad still, but the quantity of it produced is greatly diminished, which I attribute much to the threepenny stamped papers.

676. You speak now of Liverpool, do not you?—No, of London; we have nothing of that kind in Liverpool whatever, nor in our provinces; they all come from London.

677. You are decidedly of opinion that if the competition of newspapers, that is, periodical publications, containing news, were let in on the same terms upon the unstamped periodical press of this country, that it would completely change the character

Mr. *M. J. Whitty.*

9 May 1851.

character of it?—It would annihilate what you call now the unstamped press, I am satisfied.

678. You think that there would be no cheap periodical publications which would not contain a large proportion of news? —None.

679. You think that news would be a substitute for the present trashy tales, novels, and often obscene anecdotes and jokes which fill up the unstamped press?—Quite so; I have no doubt that you would have, instead of horrible tales of imagination, real tales from the police office, which are about the most instructive reading in the world.

680. Mr. *Rich.*] You have stated, have you not, with regard to unstamped papers, that you consider they have an evil tendency and are of a loose character?—Very; I do not allude to literary papers, such as the "Athenæum," but the trash.

681. You think that the majority of those papers which are published are of bad character?—Yes; there is a great deal of unobjectionable matter published in numbers at one penny, such as novels, standard works, and so on, but those I do not include.

682. But upon the whole those loose publications of immoral tendency have a large preponderance?—Yes; the majority of them.

683. In fact they beat the others, do not they?—They did, decidedly. I stated before that the immoral and obscene trash has disappeared to a great extent. There is a great deal of bad politics and bad principles published at 1 *d.* at present. I have observed that these things happily disappear very rapidly, all the immoral ones; these go on to a certain time, and die out as the "Satirist" did. There is a publication now in London, by a person well known; he published several very obscene things; he is a very clever man, but he perverts his intellect unfortunately for himself, and I am afraid for others; he has tried several newspapers, and several low publications, by all of which he lost. And I believe that another also has been a bankrupt once or twice, and on his oath he declared that none of his publications ever paid.

684. The trade in cheap and immoral publications does not appear to be lucrative?—Not at all, and the works are comparatively very few now. When I come to London I generally make a search for things of that kind, as a matter of curiosity; but the number has been greatly diminished of late, which I attribute altogether to the threepenny stamped papers.

685. Do not you think it possible that if those immoral papers

Mr. *M. J. Whitty.*

9 May 1851.

papers had the advantage of publishing news more or less distorted, to suit the tastes of those whom they address, by means of a stamp, they would greatly increase their circulation?—Not at all; if they had a stamp upon them they would not sell at all; they are published now on the chances of obtaining a large circulation. A publication obtaining a certain degree of notoriety, the world for the moment is attracted by the notoriety, and it is a gratification of curiosity to see those things, but when that is satisfied they drop and die.

686. Say then that there were no newspaper stamps, and that they were enabled in addition to their ribaldry, which they now publish, to add news, would not that greatly tend to increase their circulation?—Not at all; for instance, there is a mechanical reason, which I will mention, and it is of very great consequence; there must be the quantity as well as quality; and the publisher of a large circulation can give a large quantity better.

687. He is sure to beat a man who does not compete with him on both points, is he not?—Yes.

688. Are you aware that a London weekly paper, which has the largest circulation, is one not so much addressed to the reason of its readers as to an appetite exciting horror found in extracts from some of the most frightful police reports?—I have just stated that I consider police reports the most instructive and most desirable reading in the world; those who give police reports as matters of fact, instruct every one; it is the result of no distorted imagination; it is true; the matter and business of the life around you.

689. Do you consider the "Weekly Dispatch" a most instructive paper?—I consider police reports a most instructive thing; and I consider the "Weekly Dispatch" one of the ablest papers published in the world.

690. And also tending to moral results?—I do not say anything about that; I do not think that society is in any danger of being injured effectually by those things. The tendency may be bad, and there are many things in the "Weekly Dispatch" which I entirely disapprove of, such as obtruding religious notions into politics; but at the same time it is a most admirably conducted newspaper apart from that.

691. With regard to the American press, you say that on the whole the tone of the American press is higher than that of the English press?—I do not say higher; I think that the tone of the English press is unimpeachable altogether; not higher, but it is as high.

692. From your experience of the English press, should you not

Mr. *M. J. Whitty.*

9 May 1851.

not say that almost yearly the education and the tone of mind of the gentlemen who contribute to the press are rising in this country?—I am afraid not.

693. For what reason?—I have known for a fact that a great number of gentlemen who were connected with the press, and who were perfectly capable of imparting dignity and ability to it, have obtained, in consequence of the great demand for such people, situations, and have gone from the press.

694. Without depreciating the American press, are you not aware that a great number more deaths from assassination and duels result from calumnious attacks in the American press than in England?—I never heard of one.

695. Have you not heard of editors being shot?—Yes, and in England too.

696. Not lately?—Yes; there are quarrels arising out of newspaper reports constantly.

697. Do you mean quarrels attended with loss of life?—Yes: the Committee will recollect the "Beacon," published in Glasgow; and there was the loss of life of a very worthy man, Sir Alexander Boswell.

698. That was 20 years ago, was not it?—Yes, and more.

699. In those 20 years, speaking cursorily, should you not say that there have been, from like causes, 20 times the amount of life lost in America?—Not from newspapers, I should say; and even if done, I do not see anything in that; society is very different there, and our notions of duelling are very different now to what they were 25 years ago. In America they are not in the same state; besides, it is a very rude and very dispersed population, and I should say that if they did not stand more upon personal honour there, it would not be so well for them.

700. Mr. *Ewart.*] Is it not a much newer population, and also a much more mingled population?—Yes; and if they do not stand upon their personal dignity and honour there, society would degrade itself immediately.

701. Is it not a progressing people; are they not marching upon the desert, as it were; and in that state of circumstances society must be necessarily unformed, and therefore they are bound to protect themselves?—Yes; I have heard of a number of duels between editors, and so on; but those I have put down as mere *facetiæ*. I have not for some time seen any account of a death, or of a duel resulting from newspapers. I have seen plenty of reported fighting, and I believe one or two duels did take place from discussions in their Parliament.

702. Do

Mr. *M. J. Whitty.*

9 May 1851.

702. Do you think that the press is the cause of duels, or that the cause was antecedent to the existence of the press?—Yes; and I believe that if the press were not as free as it is they would be more frequent.

703. Mr. *C. Fortescue.*] You stated that the American press was equal to the English press morally; is it equal, in your opinion, intellectually?—Yes, I think it is. I will state what a newspaper editor in the "Philadelphia Intelligencer," a paper of old standing, said, in reply to the "Times;" he stated, "If they are inferior, it merely argues that the intellect of the country is inferior, for all the available intellect of the country is engaged upon the press."

704. Are all the American papers equal, intellectually, in a literary point of view, to the "Times," or the "Morning Chronicle?—Yes; the "New York Courier and Inquirer" is just as well edited. I should also observe, that in reading editorial articles in other places it is just like reading national poetry; we seldom sympathize with that which did not belong to our own country.

705. Mr. *Ewart.*] Do you happen to know whether the Americans have not entered the book market very much in Europe, and now are great purchasers of books, for the sake of establishing libraries in America?—That was stated in the "Spectator" some time ago; they made the discovery in noticing the life of a gentleman just dead. It appeared that though they had not a British Museum, they had more books, but more diffused; that every place had its own sufficient library. All the works of any value in Europe are republished there, and it is creditable to them that they always select the best; Macaulay's history, for instance. I think I have a copy of it, in two volumes, which I bought at 2 *s.* 6 *d.*

706. With regard to the police reports, do you mean that a diffusion and knowledge of facts, though they may be sometimes perverted, are on the whole conducive to truth, and therefore desirable?—Yes; it puts people on their guard. Many individuals involve themselves in difficulties from an ignorance of the facts, which they might have learnt had they read the previous police reports. You find humanity there precisely in its proper character; you find every one, from the nobleman to the thief, all in the police court, and all speaking their own opinions.

707. Sir *J. Walmsley.*] You meant to say, humanity in its real character, rather than its proper one?—I substituted the one for the other.

708. Mr. *Stafford.*] You stated that you thought the "Weekly

Mr. *M. J. Whitty.*

9 May 1851.

"Weekly Dispatch" was one of the most admirably conducted papers?—Yes. In the first place, in editing, it is admirably done; the condensations are done carefully, and by able men, that strikes me obviously; and in addition to that, the writing, however faulty, is good.

709. And able?—Yes; it is intellectually so. I do not say good in principle, that I omit.

710. Mr. *C. Fortescue.*] But it is bad, morally?—I did not say that. A man may have very good morals, but very perverse religious notions.

711. *Chairman.*] You were merely speaking of the mode in which that paper, as a whole, is conducted; as a person having experience in that branch of business, both in the literary department, and in all the mechanical departments of a paper?—Yes. And beyond that paper, in my estimation, the best conducted and the best edited paper in the world is the "Spectator;" it is far before the "Dispatch" in everything.

712. Mr. *Sotheron.*] I understood you to say that you thought the taste of the multitude was always towards a good paper?—Yes.

713. Having now had many years experience, do you deliberately adhere to that opinion?—Yes, decidedly; I have not the shade of a shadow of a doubt of it.

714. Mr. *Cobden.*] Then you think that the prevailing taste of mankind is a good taste?—Yes, quite so.

715. Not only with regard to contents of papers, but as to all other matters?—Everything.

716. You would apply the same principle to the newspaper press, as to every other matter; you would open the widest field possible for competition of caterers to the public wants?—Yes.

717. You think that the public themselves would always in the end choose the best?—As you enlarge the sphere of criticism, you always improve in everything. These are no peculiar notions of mine. It was one of the most deliberate articles that Dr. Johnson ever wrote, in which he states that the only judges of poetry were the people.

718. Mr. *Sotheron.*] By a good paper, do you mean an ably written paper, or good morally?—Good literature and good morals are identical, I should say.

719. Therefore you exclude from your understanding of good papers, papers that are of decidedly bad principles morally?—Yes, and inferiorly conducted.

720. *Chairman.*] I presume you give your opinion that the public will gravitate towards the best paper, on the same principle

ciple that in the end they prefer the best actor, or the best orator, or the best of anything else?—Yes.

Mr. *M. J. Whitty.*

9 May 1851.

721. There is no inherent disposition in the human mind to prefer bad to good?—No; and even if you collect the bad together, the bad will always applaud what is good.

722. Taking the duty on the newspaper stamps and the advertisement duty together, if they were put into one sum, would you say that that was a considerable fiscal burden upon the press?—Quite so; it is not on the press so much as on the public. I should say, if you polled the newspaper proprietors through England, nine out of ten would be disposed to keep them just as they are.

723. Can you state whether the imposition of the advertisement duty only when you advertise in a newspaper or in a periodical, and not when you advertise in other ways, is calculated to make a very direct attack upon the press, and to deprive it of a very legitimate advantage, that of advertising? —Yes; it affects the public more than the newspapers.

724. My question had reference to the effect upon the press?—It limits the press; but the press, like other people, must be content with an average profit; some get more; but take off those impediments, and then you enlarge the field of competition very much, and you have a better article.

725. Inasmuch as the laws say to an advertiser, "If you advertise in a newspaper you shall pay a tax of 1*s.* 6*d.*, but if you advertise on a wall, or in a railway carriage, or upon a van in the streets, you shall pay nothing," is not that calculated to deprive the newspaper press of a fair share of advertising profits which they would otherwise obtain?—Of course, if they were compelled to stamp the placards on the walls, the newspaper would have a great preference.

726. If all advertisements were taxed, that would be but doing justice to the newspaper press?—Quite so; but I own that it would be much more desirable not to tax them at all.

727. But if advertisements were taxed at all, you would prefer that they should be all taxed?—Quite so.

728. Mr. *Ewart.*] Are you aware of another disadvantage that the newspaper press labours under with respect to advertisements, namely, that by the Act an advertisement put at the end of a book ought to pay the advertisement duty, but that it does not, whereas the newspaper press is obliged to pay it?—Yes, the advertisement duty is paid on magazines I know, but in books I think not.

729. Are you aware that that is the fact?—I was not aware of

Mr. *M. J. Whitty.*

9 May 1851.

of the fact, but I believe now you mention it that it is so; I know that magazines pay it.

730. *Chairman.*] Have you had any experience of the practice of the Board of Inland Revenue in reference to the stamping of publications; whether they are enabled to do it fairly and o stamp all news?—That I have only been able to pay general attention to; I never had anything to do with it except to pay my duty.

731. Have you never had any communications from the Board?—I had perhaps a very strange one; the 14th fell upon a Sunday, and I omitted to pay my duty till Monday; and they would not take it, but on writing to the Board they immediately took the money; it appears I should have paid it the day before, on the Saturday. I had another communication; there was a dispute as to which paper had the largest circulation, and as I was convinced that I had, I wanted them to publish that, but they refused to do so. I wanted them then to give me a return of my own stamps, and that they also refused, which was I think very proper.

732. Sir *J. Walmsley.*] Have you occasionally published papers without a stamp?—Never; and thereby we suffer a very serious loss; for instance, when the machine goes very fast, take the "Times" newspaper for instance, they are obliged to use very strong paper in order to come out; we who do not do that, when the machinery goes very fast, spoil a number of stamps, sometimes as many as 300 or 400, and then we pay 300 or 400 pence to the revenue in addition to the duty, and it is all lost; they will not make any allowance to us for spoiled stamps.

733. Mr. *Cobden.*] You say that the machines travel very fast in printing the London papers, and that therefore they are obliged to have thick paper; do they use the same kind of machinery in New York that they do in London?—I have already stated that we could not print at all as the newspaper press of America prints. Their paper is very good paper to the eye, but very thin; but then their types are excellent, I always thought; practically they do not, what they call, "wet" their paper; we are obliged to wet it before it goes through the machine, but how they print it I never could learn.

Mr. *Collet Dobson Collet,* called in; and Examined

Mr. *C. D. Collet.*

734. *Chairman.*] WILL you state to the Committee what means you have had of becoming acquainted with the operation

Mr. C. D. Collet.

9 May 1851.

tion of stamps upon newspapers?—I have been secretary for the last two years to a society, the special object of which has been to get rid of all the taxes on knowledge, and particularly the newspaper stamps; and some of the members of that society were members of a society, or at least were in some way or other concerned in the agitation for getting the stamps reduced in the year 1836. Mr. Francis Place was the treasurer of the committee then, I think, and he is the treasurer also of our association, and one or two of the persons who were prosecuted for printing unstamped papers before are members of our association. Mr. Hetherington was a member of the Newspaper Stamp Abolition Committee.

735. Since there was a reduction of the stamp to a penny, nevertheless, there has been a society always asking for a total repeal; and, as I understand you, it has never been regarded as a settled question?—It has never been regarded as a settled question by any part of the working classes who take any interest in politics or in newspapers; but there has not been any committee for this purpose till within the last two years; it commenced on the 7th of March 1849.

736. Since you have been secretary to the society you have turned your attention a good deal to the subject, have you not?—I have turned my attention to every part connected with newspapers, and have endeavoured to obtain all the information that I possibly could from every part of the country.

737. Will you state what conclusions you have come to with regard to the mode in which the law is administered by the Board of Inland Revenue, and also with regard to the effects of the stamp upon the newspaper press; first of all with regard to the mode in which the law is administered as to the stamping of news?—The result of my inquiries has been that we are living under a disguised censorship of the press. I use the word advisedly; and I find that generally where there is an avowed censorship of the press, there are no taxes on knowledge; no stamp duty, and generally no paper duty. From the time when the stamp duty was first imposed in the reign of Queen Anne, the number of newspapers has been very much diminished by the stamp. For instance, Steele's Spectator was nearly if not quite ruined by it; and from that time to this the amount of revenue has never been so large as to be a serious subject of consideration. The meaning of the word "newspaper," the taxable article called news, has changed from time to time. Now when the tax was first laid on, essays, which nobody now would call news, or even comments upon public events, were liable to the tax; and the "Spectator" was

 nothing

Mr. *C. D. Collet.*

9 May 1851.

nothing but a series of essays which had very little indeed to do with politics or with news; and yet that paper was stamped. I have seen the stamp on one of the old copies that were printed at that time. Then about the time of the Reform Bill; the stamp having been raised from a halfpenny and a penny to 4*d.*, and the demand for cheap publications and for political news having become very great, a number of persons supplied it contrary to law; and prosecutions were instituted without succeeding in putting down the publications. In the year 1836, Mr. Spring Rice, who was then Chancellor of the Exchequer, brought in a Bill to diminish the stamp from 4*d.*, (or more correctly speaking, from 3¼*d.*, for there was a discount of 20 per cent.), to a penny; and he stated that it then amounted to about 445,000*l.* In 1831 he said it amounted to 483,000*l.*; that was the highest amount it had ever reached. That has now been diminished to one penny, and in the last year the gross amount of revenue was 356,964 *l.* 17 *s.* 2 *d.* Lord Monteagle in his speech states, that the revenue was falling off that was derived from newspapers; and he says, "This diminutiou did not arise from any falling off in the education of the people, or their anxiety for political information. On the contrary, the changes of the last few years had greatly added to the desire for political information and discussion, and every man would have expected that the revenue yielded by newspapers would have increased. It was this tax that prevented the increase. The appetite of the people did not remain without food, but it was supplied, contrary to law, by unstamped newspapers. Here, as in every other case, a duty raised above the legitimate amount led to successful smuggling, in order to supply the public demands without contributing to the public revenue." He then goes on to say, that "the total number of stamps taken in the United Kingdom was 36,000,000. On one occasion the officers of the stamp department seized, on the Thursday, an incomplete publication of newspapers to be given to the public on the Saturday, amounting to 40,000 sheets. This gave for a weekly paper 2,000,000 of sheets per annum, being equal to one-eighteenth of the stamped press, and this was only a single instance." Then he states "that it was his fate to read much of the unstamped press; indeed some persons were kind enough frequently to send him packages of unstamped papers, with a view to prove to him the extent at which it had arrived; and this he could say, that according as it had augmented in circulation it had improved in quality. Since the first appearance of unstamped publications to the present moment, their character

Mr. *C. D. Collet*

9 May 1851.

character had gradually altered, the reason of which was to be found in the fact of a wide circulation. A publication of limited circulation would be found to be supported by a particular class for which it was prepared, by exciting their passions and flattering their prejudices; but if they came to a largely circulated paper they found it must suit itself to the taste of the people." Then he goes on to say, "that it was much better to communicate knowledge to the people through the medium of the stamped press, which was responsible to the country and the King, than to trust to the construction that might be put on all public proceedings by those men who were not recognised by the law, and whose illegal publications were largely circulated because easily obtained." I believe I may say on the part of our association, that we consider the whole of that speech to be very excellent, excepting the last passage; we do not understand in what way the existence of the stamp makes the press responsible to the country or to the sovereign for its conduct.

738. Are you of opinion that the penny stamp has, to a great extent, the same effect in driving the poorer classes to the unstamped press that the higher rate of stamp used to have?—It has the same effect, but to a limited amount; that is to say, those persons who can afford 3 *d.*, or who can afford to read the threepenny paper, to hire it, will of course not be driven to penny literature. But there can be no doubt that the penny stamp does prevent the penny newspapers altogether. In order to meet the demand of one penny from the Government, you are obliged not only to add that penny to your price, but another penny more, to meet the reduction in the sale; and the consequence is that the class of readers is altogether changed. Then it requires a very considerable capital to bring out a good penny paper. If you bring out a bad penny paper, of course the circulation is small; but if you, on the contrary, bring out a good one, you have a very considerable outlay to make, and you cannot afford to pay the stamp out of the penny, and of course you cannot even afford to pay it out of 2 *d.* You must raise the price, and the consequence is that that sort of newspaper which the people would purchase ceases to exist; and the vacuum is supplied partly by very indifferent unstamped newspapers, and partly by half-stamped newspapers that contain very little news, and partly by cheap novels and trash.

739. You stated that the meaning of the word "newspaper" had altered from time to time; that there had been a different meaning attached to that term by the authorities; have you

 reason

Mr. *C. D. Collet.*

9 May 1851.

reason to believe that at present the meaning is clear or definite that is attached to a newspaper?—At present I think there is no definite meaning whatever attached to it by the Stamp Office. About the time of the unstamped papers, from 1832 to 1836, there was a very definite meaning attached to it. Any paper at that time that was issued oftener than once a month was put down, if it contained a very small quantity of news. One paper was called the "Harlequin," and devoted entirely to theatrical reports; and that paper was put down, because it was said to contain news.

740. Did it only give an account of theatrical subjects?—I think it gave reports and critiques on the play; but it was entirely and purely theatrical.

741. And it was held to be a newspaper?—Yes, and was put down. Now at the present time, any paper that confines its news to class news is not held to be a newspaper, unless that class news have some special relation to politics. For instance, there is a paper called the "Musical World," that gives musical news; and there is the "Legal Observer," that gives legal news; and the "Builder," gives building news.

742. How do you show that when this particular sort of news has reference to what you call politics, that it then becomes a newspaper?—The "Norwich Reformer" was the organ of the Parliamentary Reform Association in Norwich, and that contained a column, called "Record of Progress;" I think it is about the smallest quantity of news that any unstamped newspaper does contain, and the editor received a letter from the Stamp Office, stating that there was a column in his paper, called "Record of Progress," which could appear only legally on stamped paper, and where, therefore he must cease to publish; and he afterwards omitted it.

743. The greater portion of his publication was not for the purpose of giving news?—The greater portion of the publication was a series of comments upon the subject of Parliamentary reform and freehold land societies.

744. Mr. *Cobden.*] Was it published weekly or monthly?—Monthly, at the price of a penny.

745. *Chairman.*] Because the publisher had one column of news, although the rest of his paper was confined to those particular subjects, he was interfered with by the Stamp Office?—Yes.

746. Sir *J. Walmsley.*] Do you know of your own knowledge that it was on account of that particular portion of news being published?—I have a letter from the editor stating that, and

Mr. *C. D. Collet.*

9 May 1851.

and he has also sent to me printed copies of the correspondence between himself and the Stamp Office, which I will read, if the Committee please. " Inland Revenue, Somerset House, 7th March 1850. Gentlemen, The attention of this Board having been directed to some articles of public news contained in Nos. 1 and 2 of your publication, the ' Reformer,' under the head of the ' Record of Progress,' of a character that cannot lawfully be published in any but a stamped newspaper, I have been desired to acquaint you with the circumstance, and to caution you against any future insertion of like matter. I am, gentlemen, your obedient servant, J. Timm, Solicitor of Inland Revenue." Then he replies : " Norwich, 12th March. Sir, I have received your intimation that the intelligence given in the ' Reformer,' under the heading ' Record of Progress,' cannot be lawfully inserted in any but a stamped newspaper. I should feel greatly obliged if you would inform me on what ground the ' Gentleman's Magazine,' ' United Service Magazine,' ' Tait's Edinburgh Magazine,' ' Christian Observer,' ' People's Journal,' with others that might be mentioned (including unstamped copies of the ' Freeholder,' ' Athenæum,' &c.). are permitted to furnish similar information : also, why the organs of societies of a literary, philanthropic, and scientific character are allowed to contain details of their respective operations, whilst that privilege is denied to the journal of a political association. Thanking you for your caution, and soliciting information upon these points, I remain, Sir, your obedient servant, The Editor of the Reformer." This is the reply : " Inland Revenue, Somerset House, 13th March 1850. Gentlemen, I am this morning in receipt of a letter without signature, but purporting to come from the ' Editor of the Reformer' ; and as it is written in reference to mine of the 7th instant, addressed to you, I reply to it as proceeding from you. The publications to which allusion is made are not before me, either officially or otherwise ; I know therefore nothing of their contents. But assuming them to be unstamped papers, and to contain matter which they ought not to publish, it is not for me to offer any explanation upon the subject, nor can the circumstances justify irregularities in others. I may, however, remark, as I am aware that the subject has been under notice, in reference more particularly to learned societies, that articles, although relating to the transactions of such societies, and therefore savouring of public news and intelligence, yet as partaking of the character of a review, are not looked upon as matters to be objected to in unstamped publications. So also

Mr. C. D. Collet.

9 May 1851.

also with regard to dramatic performances, and such like. I am, gentlemen, your obedient servant, J. Timm, Solicitor of Inland Revenue."

747. You stated, did you not, that a paper which had nothing but accounts of dramatic performances in it, had been put down?—That was before 1836; before the change in the law.

748. But the definition of the word "newspaper" was the same before as after, was not it?—Yes; but the practice of the Board has been very different, and in order to keep the stamp on and to avoid the unpleasantness of prosecutions and making martyrs, they have allowed a very wide and gradually increasing deviation from the letter of the law.

749. You say that we are living under what you call a disguised censorship, because this paper is singled out and made subject to a rule that does not seem to be applied to other similar publications containing news?—Yes; I say that we are living under a censorship, because the amount of news or the political comment that we are allowed to write depends entirely upon the pleasure of the officer at the Stamp Office, and not upon the law of the land.

750. Mr. *Rich.*] Is there no appeal from the decision of the Board of Inland Revenue?—Yes, but the law is so much more stringent than the practice, that there is practically no appeal.

751. Then you are living more easily than under law, are you not?—No; the law is made more stringent than any jury is likely to keep it; in fact it is made more stringent than it can be enforced; and the Board of Inland Revenue exercises a sort of dispensing power to parties to break the law.

752. If they thought that the Inland Revenue Board were too severe in the administration of the law, would they not have the power to appeal to a jury?—Yes; but then as the law would be clearly against them they would not like the chance; and parties possessing capital will not expend it under such a liability; no person of capital will invest it in a newspaper with the intention to run the risk of prosecution.

753. If those people have confessedly transgressed the law, they take the consequences?—Yes.

754. Mr. *C. Fortescue.*] You think that the Stamp Office has a dangerous discretion as to whom they shall pick out for prosecution and whom not?—Yes.

755. There being many papers that they might prosecute with success?—Yes, and I think it a mischievous one; not because it injures any particular paper, but because a vast deal of

Mr. *C. D. Collet.* 9 May 1851.

of useful information is prevented which would exist if the law would permit it.

756. You spoke of censorship. If the Board of Inland Revenue used that discretionary power to interfere with a paper which they disapproved of, that would then amount to censorship, would it not?—I do not think that the Board use their power in that way.

757. Mr. *Rich.*] You speak of the law being definite; are you aware of any public body entrusted with the carrying out the law who are not obliged constantly to exercise their judgment as to when and how they shall prosecute?—I am not able to answer that question.

758. *Chairman.*] You say that in the case of the "Norwich Reformer," this intimation was received. Have you any other instances of a similar kind to offer to the Committee?—I have instances of a contrary kind, rather than of a similar kind. Mr. Timm, in his letter, says, "The publications to which allusion is made are not before me, either officially or otherwise, I know therefore nothing of their contents." Now there is a clause in the Newspaper Act by which every publisher of a paper containing advertisements is bound to send a copy of the publication to Somerset House, and even if it do not contain advertisements; if you send a paper to Somerset House, and it contains matter liable to prosecution, you are free from all penalties till the Stamp Office give you notice that you are infringing the law; the consequence is that, practically, all publications are sent to the Stamp Office directly. I therefore assume, according to the 19th clause, that it is the business of some officer at the Stamp Office to ascertain whether they infringe the law, or not. But Mr. Timm says, "These publications are not before me, either officially or otherwise." I thought it would be a good thing to put some of those publications before him officially, with the view of obliging him to carry out the law, and accordingly I got a friend to write this letter: "To the Commissioners of Inland Revenue. Gentlemen,—By the Act 6 & 7 Will. 4, c. 76, it is enacted that no one, under severe penalties, shall publish a newspaper on paper not duly stamped; and in the schedule, at the end of the Act, a newspaper is defined to be 'any paper containing public news, intelligence, or occurrences, printed in any part of the United Kingdom, to be dispersed and made public.' And again, 'any paper containing any public news, intelligence, or occurrences, or any remarks or observations thereon,' 'at intervals not exceeding 26 days.' I beg to call your attention to the fact, that a newspaper registered at Somerset House, and

Mr. *C. D. Collet.*

9 May 1851.

and entitled 'Punch,' and printed by William Bradbury, of No. 13, Upper Woburn-place, in the parish of St. Pancras, and Frederick Mullett Evans, of No. 7, Church-row, Stoke Newington, both in the county of Middlesex, printers, at their office in Lombard-street, in the precinct of Whitefriars, in the city of London, and published by them at No. 85, Fleet-street, in the parish of St. Bride's, in the city of London, is in the habit of circulating unstamped, the country edition alone being stamped. That 'Punch' is as much a newspaper as the 'Times,' or the 'Morning Chronicle,' will appear on examining three or four numbers. Almost every number contains 'public news, intelligence, or occurrences,' to say nothing of 'remarks or observations thereon.' It even ventures to report public meetings and debates in Parliament. In laying this information before your Board, I think it sufficient to specify the following articles in the enclosed number of 'Punch,' which was published as aforesaid on Saturday, the 16th of February 1850: 'Mr. Punch on Church and State Education,' 'Louis Napoleon, spare that Tree,' 'Punch's Parliamentary Hodge-podge,' 'The Credit of an Emperor,' 'Affairs of Hungary,' 'Our Colonel's Experience,' 'Mr. Horsman's Anatomy,' 'Our Foreign Feuds,' 'Wit and Wisdom in the House of Lords,' 'The worst of Taxes,' 'A Minister is Infallible,' 'Nothing like Grog.' Should the Board imagine that this number of 'Punch' is an exception to the general rule, I am prepared to show that the reverse is the truth, and that the violation of the law on the part of that paper is wilful and systematic, and that justice to the rest of the press requires that it should be prosecuted. Hoping that you will no longer permit this gross infringement of the law, I remain, gentlemen, your most obedient humble servant. (signed) *William Gellen.*" He received no reply, and he wrote to know whether they had taken any notice of his information; and this is the reply of the Board of Inland Revenue: "Sir,—Having laid before the Board your letter of the —— instant, I am directed to state that they do not think it necessary or desirable to enter into any discussion with you on the subject therein referred to, in which you appear to have no personal concern. I am, sir, your obedient servant, *Thomas Keogh.*" About the same time the fol-following letter was also sent to them: "To the Honourable the Commissioners of Inland Revenue. Gentlemen,—Understanding that you are about to commence proceedings against the 'Norwich Reformer' for infringement of the Newspaper Stamp Act, I beg to call your attention to a paragraph in the enclosed paper, the 'Reasoner,' headed, 'Taxes on Knowledge—Deputation

putation

Mr. C. D. Collet.

9 May 1851.

putation to Lord John Russell,' which is clearly contrary to the letter of the same Act. I trouble you with this information, as there might be some show of reason for complaint, were the one periodical punished for that which the other was suffered to do with impunity. I am, gentlemen, your obedient humble servant, *John Hincks*." To which the Commissioners sent a polite reply: "Sir,—Having laid before the Board your letter of the 8th instant in regard to the publication called the 'Reasoner,' containing an article which subjects it to stamp duty as a newspaper, and renders the publisher liable to prosecution as much as the publisher of the 'Reformer,' against whom you understand proceedings are about to be taken, I am directed to acquaint you that the Board have no present intention of prosecuting the publisher of the paper called the 'Reformer,' printed in Norwich, although the publisher has certainly been cautioned against the insertion of matter which would constitute the publication of a newspaper." The editor of the 'Reasoner' was not cautioned, though decidedly his paper contained an account of a deputation of our own society to Lord John Russell. Here is another intimation that was sent by another person, who was a brother of a friend of mine. "J. Timm, esq.: Sir,—May I beg to call your attention to the 'Democratic Review;' here is a paper which not only gives a thorough epitome of the 'current news,' but does it in a manner that panders to the depraved taste for abuse of the Government and all respectable individuals, while it holds up for admiration the anarchists of France, and the parties who were the leaders of the chartist outbreak of April 1848, which, but for the way it was met by the greater part of the community, might have led to serious consequences, and which advocates muskets as valuable assistants to moral agitation. As I suppose that you cannot be aware of its publication, or, while other papers of more moderate principles, such as the 'Norwich Reformer,' are forbidden to give anything that can be construed as news, this would not be allowed to set such rules at defiance, I enclose a few pages to show the nature of it. I am, sir, your obedient servant, *W. C. Lomax*. *P. S.*—It is edited by Julian Harney, and published by Watson, 3, Queen's Head Passage, Paternoster-row." The reply is as follows: "Sir,—I beg to acknowledge the receipt of your letter of the 1st instant, enclosing portions of a publication entitled the 'Democratic Review.'" I should state, that the "Reasoner," is a weekly publication, and therefore had less right to insert news than the "Norwich Reformer," if there be any difference between them.

759. Was

Mr. *C. D. Collet.*

9 May 1851.

759. Was the "Democratic Review" a weekly publication?—No, it was monthly, and it contained more news, I think, than the "Norwich Reformer;" at any rate, quite as much.

760. Mr. *Rich.*] Do you look upon "Punch" as being as much a newspaper as the "Times"?—I used the word "newspaper" then according to law; it always contains comments and very frequently news, and as "Punch" is a weekly paper, it has no right whatever to make comments.

761. In your opinion "Punch" is as much a newspaper as the "Times"?—Yes, using the word newspaper in a legal sense, and not in a popular sense.

762. Mr. *Sotheron.*] Have you considered the distinction which is sometimes drawn with regard to "Punch" not being a newspaper?—Here is a number of "Punch," published May the 10th, 1851; it was only published last Wednesday, and it contains an article called "What I remarked at the Exhibition;" that is a sort of commentary. Then "Punch's own Report of the Opening of the Exhibition;" that is decidedly a record of facts. It gives the whole account, for instance, of the Chinese; it gives an account of the Marquis of Westminster walking backwards, and an incident between the Duke of Wellington and the Marquis of Anglesey.

763. Mr. *Tufnell.*] But that is given as a sort of quiz upon the whole affair, is it not?—No, it is an article.

764. Mr. *Rich.*] In your opinion it is as much a newspaper as the "Times"?—Yes, decidedly. Here is a piece of news which I believe very few persons would be aware of if it were not for "Punch;" namely, the article called "Scouring a Sovereign;" and there is a picture of the operation that was performed on the statue of George the Third. Now it is perfectly true that that scouring has taken place, and I do not believe that one person out of 20,000 would know it if it were not for "Punch" mentioning it.

765. Do you think that that is public news in the sense of a newspaper?—Certainly.

766. Mr. *Sotheron.*] Why do you think that they would not have been aware of what you have just referred to, unless it had been inserted in "Punch"?—I have not seen it, and I should not have known it if I had not passed by the statue.

767. Mr. *Rich.*] Do you think if that sovereign were alive, and you had been told that he had washed his face, that that would be public news?—Not in the sense of its being new; people would suppose that the sovereign washed his face, but they would not suppose that anybody would be so stupid as to wash the face of a statue.

768. Sir

Mr. *C. D. Collet.*

9 May 1851.

768. Sir *J. Walmsley.*] You do not speak of the fact itself, but of the paper giving information of that fact being news?—Yes. There is another reason why I think that "Punch" ought to be considered a newspaper; instead of being a mere jest, it is very often a serious matter. I will only mention one instance, of a man who was on his trial for sedition: he was accused of having stated that he thought Lord John Russell ought to be assassinated; that he had five sons, and he would disown every one of them who was not willing to assassinate Lord John Russell. Those words were sworn to by a witness who I believe to have been utterly unworthy of credit, and the man was convicted, as I believe, on false evidence. Now about the time of the trial, or before, "Punch" contained a picture of that man and his five children, each smaller than the other, standing in a line behind him, like Professor Risley, or any other acrobat, with a dagger in each hand, all going to murder Lord John Russell. Now I think that that has a tendency to prejudice a jury. There is a general opinion that the statements in "Punch" are correct, and I believe they are generally correct.

769. Mr. *Rich.*] Would not that be more an offence against the law than an article of news?—I think it is news; it is telling everybody that such and a transaction took place, and it happens that the transaction is not true.

770. *Chairman.*] If "Punch" is not a newspaper, which seems to be the understanding from what you state, it is not required to give any securities that it will not libel anybody?—Yes, "Punch" is obliged to give security, because it is registered as a newspaper.

771. He is not obliged; he chooses to do so, because he wishes to have the advantages of a newspaper?—Exactly so.

772. It would not be obliged because of its contents?—That is a question I cannot answer.

773. If it is not a newspaper it would not be obliged to give security that it would not libel anybody?—Certainly not.

774. Mr. *C. Fortescue.*] Does not "Punch" comment sometimes on public and political events in a way and with the view to establish his own opinion?—No doubt of it. He generally makes a dead set at anything political, sometimes even personal, which he dislikes, such as Smithfield Market, which he has attacked, and, I believe, the strictures of "Punch" had a great effect in destroying Mr. Buckingham's British and Foreign Institute.

775. It is more as commenting upon news than as giving news

Mr. *C. D. Collet.*

9 May 1851.

news that "Punch" would be considered a newspaper?—Yes; the comments I think would make it clearly a newspaper.

776. *Chairman.*] Can you state any other violations of the law that you consider are going on?—I should speak of the faults of the Board of Inland Revenue under six heads. I should say, first, that they defraud (speaking technically) the Post Office revenue, by giving to publications a false certificate of their being newspapers. Then I should say, secondly, that they favour a number of registered newspapers at the expense of the rest, by allowing them to circulate a part of their impression without a stamp, thus encouraging unfair competition. They neglect to enforce the law in London. They enforce the law severely in the country. They make statements in writing at variance with each other and the facts, and they succumb to any publisher who defies them. In the first place (speaking technically), I say they defraud the Post Office revenue by giving to publications a certificate of their being newspapers. The Post Office Act allows petitions and addresses to Her Majesty, petitions to Parliament, and newspapers to be sent by post, but it is not compulsory on the part of the Postmaster-general to send you any newspaper by post. The words are these: "Be it enacted, that although newspapers may be sent by the post, and thereupon are subject to the rate of postage set forth in the above table, it shall not be compulsory to send them by post." Then it is stated that the Postmaster-general may examine, detain, and open all newspapers for several purposes, in order to see whether they are duly stamped. Now the Stamp Office allow a number of papers to register as newspapers generally for the sake of going through the Post Office; and they allow them, under the pretence of their not being newspapers, to circulate their country edition unstamped.

777. And the same publications are sometimes newspapers and sometimes not?—Yes; the Newspaper Stamp Abolition Committee sent a memorial to the Postmaster-general, complaining that in this way the Post Office revenue was defrauded. The reply of the Post Office was, "General Post Office, December 9, 1850. Sir,—The Postmaster-general has had before him the memorial which was transmitted by you on the 13th ultimo, and I have it in command to inform you that his Lordship has no power to judge of or determine the questions therein named." If that is to be taken as true, I apprehend that the matter must rest with the Stamp Office; and it is therefore they who are responsible for admitting those newspapers

Mr. *C. D. Collet.* 9 May 1851.

papers to free postage, to which they can only be legally entitled by stamping every one of their copies.

778. Mr. *Rich.*] You say the Board of Inland Revenue allow persons to defraud the Post Office by a false certificate; are you aware that the persons taking out those certificates make oaths that they are going to publish newspapers?—Yes.

779. How then can they be false certificates?—When I say that, I consider that the stamp is a certificate that the paper is a newspaper.

780. That is, it may be a certificate obtained under false pretences, but not a false certificate?—That is what I mean; but I consider that it is the business of the Board of Inland Revenue, as every person who registers a newspaper has to send a copy of his newspaper into the Stamp Office when it is published, to ascertain whether it is a newspaper or not.

781. Are you aware of any part of the Act by which they are required to investigate whether they are newspapers that will be published?—No; I presume simply that if a man registers his paper as a newspaper the law considers that it is a newspaper.

782. Therefore the Board of Inland Revenue could not refuse to give him his certificate on his oath?—No; they could not refuse to give him as many stamps as he wanted, and I think they ought to prosecute him if he published any portion without a stamp.

783. You say that they give a false certificate, and therefore defraud the Post Office revenue?—I consider that the giving a stamp to a party, and allowing him to publish the rest of his impression unstamped, is tantamount to giving him a false certificate to the Postmaster-general.

784. *Chairman.*] They cannot consider his paper to be a newspaper at the Stamp Office if they see a portion of his impression circulated without a stamp?—That is my opinion.

785. Mr. *Rich.*] Can you point out any part of the Act in which they are required to ascertain whether it is a newspaper or not for which the stamp is required?—Certainly not; but I think the Act clearly obliges them to enforce the stamp upon every person who registers his paper as a newspaper; and the Stamp Office themselves have taken a double view of the question.

786. Your complaint is against the Board of Inland Revenue giving a certificate, whereby the Post Office suffer a loss?—Yes.

787. Now the papers which are circulated in London would not involve a loss upon the Post Office. I take you to mean

Mr. *C. D. Collet.*

9 May 1851.

mean that they grant certificates by which papers not being newspapers take advantage of the Post Office to travel free of expense?—Yes, free of expense; that is to say, 1 *d.*, where the natural price would be 2 *d.* or 4 *d.*

788. If the Board of Inland Revenue have no power or authority to ascertain whether a paper as to which an affidavit is made as a newspaper be one or not, I do not see how they can be guilty of granting false certificates for defrauding the Post Office revenue?—I consider that they are bound to exact a stamp from every copy. When the law was changed, Lord Monteagle said that he was entitled to a stamp in return for free postage. Now, as the old law only allowed newspapers to go by post, as, indeed, it was the custom for some papers that were not newspapers to put two or three lines which they called politics into their stamped edition for the sake of going by post, the postage of letters then being as high as 8 *d.*, I consider that this privilege is given to the newspaper press in return for the obligation to stamp every copy, and that if a man publishes something which is not a newspaper he has no right to this special privilege unless he takes with it the special burden of paying a penny for every copy.

789. Mr. *Sotheron.*] In what way could the Board of Inland Revenue prevent this fraud?—By obliging every registered newspaper to conform to the law and to stamp every copy.

790. In what manner could they ascertain that, or how could they set about it?—It would not be difficult to find out whether copies were published without a stamp. Here are a number of publications which do not contain news, and which go free by post, and on every one of them is written two prices. Here is "Willis's Price Current, price 2 *d.*; stamped, 3 *d.*" "Botanical Gazette, price 6 *d.*; stamped, 7 *d.*"

791. Do you mean to say that you think the Board of Inland Revenue ought not to allow of any newspaper circulating under these two heads of stamped and unstamped?—Yes, certainly.

792. And with regard to all those that are registered, and of course supplied with stamps, the Board of Inland Revenue ought to compel them to stamp the whole of their impression?—Just so.

793. Mr. *Rich.*] For instance, Savory publishes an account of the prices of his silver articles, and he has paid a stamp duty on these prices, and he sends them by post?—Yes.

794. Would you prosecute Savory for publishing a price current?—As he registers his price current as a newspaper, I would fine him 20 *l.* for every copy he published without.

795. Do

Mr. *C. D. Collet.*

9 May 1851.

795. Do you think if you produced his price current before a jury that they would say it was a newspaper?—I think, very likely not. I think if the law cannot bear the decision of the jury, and if the law officers will not enforce it, it ought to be altered.

796. Is not the constitutional way of working out a law putting it before a jury?—It is not in the power of anybody to do it, except the Board of Inland Revenue. A clause in the Act forbids any person to inform or prosecute except the Board of Inland Revenue.

797. You think that the Board would exercise a sound discretion if they prosecuted Savory for publishing a paper containing the price of his silver articles?—I think they ought to prosecute everybody who breaks the law. In plain English, I think the law ought to be enforced or repealed; and if the parties who have to enforce it think the law a bad one, if they choose to act upon their opinion instead of upon the law, they ought to say that it should be altered.

798. I do not think you can accuse the Board of Inland Revenue of neglect; you say, I think, rather that the law ought to be altered; the Board are to carry out the law, not to suggest alterations in the law?—I think they should do one or the other.

799. You are of opinion that their neglect consists in not prosecuting Savory for publishing a newspaper?—Yes.

800. *Chairman.*] Savory, according to your explanation, enjoys a greater privilege than any newspaper?—Yes, he does.

801. A newspaper would have to stamp all its copies if it had the privilege of going free by post?—Every one.

802. Whereas Savory goes free by post, and only stamps those that go by post?—Yes; I believe the intention of the Legislature in granting free postage to newspapers was, that while they subjected them to a certain restraint and prevented those who were considered unqualified persons from publishing newspapers, yet they desired that such news as was permitted should be very freely circulated because it was news. I consider that the privilege was granted partly to disseminate widely that news which was permitted to be published, and therefore for anybody who does not publish news to take advantage of the privilege granted only to those who do publish news is contrary to the original intention of the Legislature; and it becomes still more unjust because the party who publishes news is liable also to this burden, that he must stamp every copy, so that those parties for whom the privilege was not intended obtain it contrary to law and contrary to the intention of the Legislature

Mr. C. D. Collet.

9 May 1851.

lature without that special burden which the Legislature intended should accompany it.

803. Mr. *Ewart.*] I understand you, in short, to say, that the Board of Inland Revenue does two things; it gives a preference to some persons and not to others, and it is accessory to fraud upon the Post Office?—Yes.

804. Mr. *Sotheron.*] You state this, not as wishing that an alteration of the law should be made to prevent those persons from enjoying this privilege, but as wishing to get rid of stamps from all newspapers?—I wish to get rid of stamps from all newspapers, and to submit to the Post Office the whole management of the postage of all publications. I do not see myself that a publication which contains news should be treated differently from one that does not.

805. Mr. *Rich.*] You would not allow a price current to be sent otherwise than through the Post Office?—Yes, in any way you liked, if the law was altered.

806. Mr. *Ewart.*] It is your object to show the inconsistency and injustice of the present system?—Yes.

807. *Chairman.*] Have you anything further to add as to the first of the complaints that you have mentioned?—No. I may say that I believe the real truth is that the Board of Inland Revenue simply wish to obtain the duty from what are popularly termed newspapers; and generally speaking they wish to make the law as little a burden as possible; but occasionally they go out of their way in a most unaccountable manner.

808. Mr. *Sotheron.*] In truth, your objection is not to the mode of administering the law, but to the law itself?—Yes. The second fault is a part of the first, that they favour a number of registered newspapers at the expense of the rest, by allowing them to circulate a part of their impression without a stamp, thus encouraging unfair competition. But a great number of those actually contain that news which the law declares ought not to be contained at all.

809. *Chairman.*] With regard to unfair competition, can you show in what way it operates; or do you know of instances where other newspapers have complained of the privilege enjoyed by some?—Yes; the proprietors of the "Coventry Herald," the "Leader," and the "Caledonian Mercury," demanded to have the same privilege which was granted to the other registered newspapers, of circulating a part of their impression without a stamp; and they were told that it could not be granted to them. I should say that some of those papers contain a very considerable amount of news, and that the

Mr. *C. D. Collet.*

9 May 1851.

the amount of news depends upon the boldness of the editor, or rather, his opinion of what the Commissioners will allow. Some persons put in a very small quantity of news, and others put a very large quantity; there is the greatest difference in the world between them. I recollect seeing in a Catholic paper, called the "Catholic Vindicator," "We cannot put news in this paper, and you ought to help us to get rid of the taxes on knowledge." There is another Catholic paper, called the "Lamp," which contains a very large amount of news.

810. What is the reason that they gave to those gentlemen, the proprietors of The "Leader" and the "Caledonian Mercury"?—They said that there was no analogy whatever between those papers and the papers in question.

811. Yet you say that the papers that they referred to as enjoying the privilege, did contain news?—Some of them did contain news, but not news in the opinion of the Board of Inland Revenue.

812. Mr. *Rich.*] It is a question in fact how near they can go to the wind?—Just so. The next complaint is, that they neglect to enforce the law in London. There are several instances of that; the most remarkable are the "Household Narrative," which has at last been prosecuted; but it has been allowed to go on for a year before the prosecution came on.

813. You are aware that proceedings were taken as long ago as that?—Yes; an information was sent by a friend of mine against the "Household Narrative," and I believe on that information, or some other, sent at the same time, proceedings have been taken.

814. Consequently you can scarcely say that it has been allowed to go on?—If it was an understanding that any newspaper might be allowed to go on a year after the proceedings were taken against it, it would be a very great encouragement.

815. But those are proceedings in law over which the Board has no control?—I do not see how that can be; the law permits the Stamp Office to go before a magistrate, and to take or seize all the presses of newspaper proprietors; and as the "Household Narrative" was a registered newspaper, there could be no doubt that they had the power to do that, and of deciding the question in a very summary manner, though of course I do not blame them for not doing that; yet the fact that such is the law deters people from trying the question.

816. You are aware that this is a question of great difficulty, and one upon which the judges have taken time to consider. Is it not consistent with a temperate exercise of authority to proceed

 ceed

Mr. *C. D. Collet.* — 9 May 1851.

ceed slowly, and to take an issue upon such a matter deliberately, it being a matter which will have an influence upon many other similar publications, than hastily to shut up a publication which, if the decision be against the Commissioners, would again be opened?—That would be true, certainly; it would be commendable that they should act in that way if they acted so to everybody; but in the case of the "Norwich Reformer," which was a monthly publication, and which, instead of containing nothing but news, contained a very small column, they frightened the editor out of it altogether; and in the case of a paper in the country, they have put the paper altogether down. Now here is a letter, written to the "Wrexham Advertiser" from the Board. "Inland Revenue, Somerset House, London, 27 February 1850. Sir,—I have laid before the Board your letter of the 22d instant, relative to the publication of the 'Wrexham Advertiser.' In reply I am directed to state that any paper containing public news, intelligence, or occurrences is subject to the duty and qualifications prescribed for newspapers, whatever be the intervals of publication. The Board will pass over the past papers if such matter be carefully excluded from the future numbers." Then a similar letter was sent to Mr. Bucknall, of Stroud; his publication was a monthly, and he published 1,700; and they put that down.

817. Mr. *Rich.*] What was the date of that?—I think about a year ago.

818. Was it prior or subsequent to the proceedings with regard to Mr. Dickens?—Prior; and the case I have just read was on the 27th of February, which was prior to the proceedings against Mr. Dickens.

819. Sir *J. Walmsley.*] Many of those persons, I presume, give up publishing papers rather from the fear of coming into collision with the Board of Inland Revenue than because they think they are in the wrong?—They are frightened by the Board of Inland Revenue, because the law is so very stringent that if it were put in force it would ruin any man, no matter what his property would be; and that is one of the great faults of the law; that instead of giving a reasonable punishment it enacts total ruin, and then allows the Board a dispensing power as to how much of that ruin shall be consummated. The consequence is, that no man with any property at all will run the risk of legal collision with the Board. The case of Bradbury & Evans is the first that has come to a trial since the law has been changed.

820. Mr. *C. Fortescue.*] Is it not your opinion that it would be very difficult to administer the present law with perfect

Mr. *C. D. Collet.*

9 May 1851.

fect fairness between the parties?—If the law as it stands were administered, there would be such a tumult of indignation from every portion of the public that the law must be repealed.

821. You think that it is very difficult, do you not, to define what constitutes news either with regard to the quality of the production or the intervals at which it is published?—I apprehend that the difficulty chiefly arises from this fact, that news is so necessary a thing that nobody likes to say that we shall have none of it; the Legislature has declared that we shall have no news without a stamp, and consequently everybody exerts himself to make out that there is no such thing as news.

822. Do not you think that it is difficult to administer such a law with perfect fairness between different parties?—It is impossible to administer such a law.

823. Mr. *Rich.*] You are aware that the law has been administered nearly a century now, are you not?—The law, as it now stands, has only been administered since 1836.

824. I mean the law, subject to various modifications?—Previous to 1836 it was the practice to allow any publications that were monthly. I believe it was not the law, but it was the practice. But a century ago there was not the same demand for news that there is now. I believe the number of persons who could read at that time was only to be numbered by thousands under a million, the consequence was that the law was inoperative as regarded them.

825. Mr. *Ewart.*] As far as you can trace it back does the administration of the law appear to have been uncertain?—I think not. When the law was first enacted, which was in the year 1712, every periodical paper was liable to a stamp, and a great many were put down.

826. Was not that a very extraordinary interpretation of the word "news"?—It would not at all consort with our definition of the word "news." There is an article in the "Spectator" previous to the day of the Stamp Act coming on. The writer says, "This is the day on which many eminent authors will probably publish their last words. I am afraid that few of our weekly historians (who are men that above all others, delight in war) will be able to subsist under the weight of a stamp, and an approaching peace. A sheet of blank paper, that must have this *imprimatur* clapped upon it before it is qualified to communicate anything to the public, will make its way in the world but very heavily."

827. You said just now, that at the beginning of this



century

Mr. *C. D. Collet.*

9 May 1851.

century a monthly publication containing news was not considered a newspaper?—No; about the time of the Reform Bill.

828. Is that not another inconsistency in the interpretration of the law?—Yes.

829. Strictly according to law, it would have been a newspaper?—Yes, I believe it would.

830. Sir *J. Walmsley.*] You have been asked whether it would not be better to take time for due consideration before making an alteration of the law than to do it suddenly. How long has your association been in existence?—It commenced its existence on the 7th of March 1849.

831. Was there an association of the same kind in existence before for the same purpose?—Before the change of the law there was.

832. What steps have your association taken to obtain a change of the law?—We have taken the steps of petitioning Parliament and circulating information through the country, and lately, of drawing the attention of the Board of Inland Revenue to the inconsistencies of the law, that is to say, demanding that they should prosecute every party whom we considered guilty of breaking the law. Next, we sent them, so lately as last December, a memorial, in which we mentioned 20 or 30 publications that we considered illegal; one of these was a series of pamphlets on the Roman-catholic question, which series of pamphlets has been continued, and has contained all the debates in Parliament, and all the news upon that question; but no notice whatever has been taken of it by the Board of Inland Revenue, nor did we receive any reply to our memorial.

833. What steps have been taken by the Board in consequence of your exertions?—The prosecution of Dickens's "Household Narrative," I believe, was commenced in consequence of our exertions; and a letter was written to the "Freeholder," in consequence, I have no doubt, of the information that was sent at my suggestion. I have not got the first letter, nor the letter that was then sent in reply; but when John Cassel, the proprietor of the "Freeholder," said that his paper was a monthly publication, and therefore ought not to be prosecuted, or rather he got Mr. Scholefield to say so for him, the reply was as follows: "Sir, I have laid before the Board of Inland Revenue your letter of the 21st instant relative to a communication made by this department to the publisher of a paper called the 'Freeholder;' in reply, I am directed to inform you that the Board hold that a paper containing public

Mr. *C. D. Collet.* 9 May 1851.

public news, intelligence, or occurrence is a newspaper, without reference to the intervals of its publication, and they are so advised by the law officers of the Crown. the 'Freeholder' is registered at this office as a newspaper, an appropriate stamp is provided for it, and stamps are issued to the publisher as for a newspaper, which he would not be entitled to receive if it were not registered. A portion of each publication is printed on stamps, and another portion without stamps, to which latter proceeding the Board object, considering that both in respect of its registration and its contents it is subject to the newspaper duty. With regard to this paper having been singled out for a peculiar application of the law, I am to observe that such a notion is entirely without foundation, and that the same rule will be observed with regard to any similar publication which shall come under the Board's notice. I have the honour to be, sir, your obedient servant, *Thomas Keogh.*"

834. *Chairman.*] If I correctly understand that letter, he says that it is liable to a stamp in virtue of its registration?—Yes.

835. Therefore it would appear from that letter that every registered newspaper must stamp all its impression?—It would appear so from that letter. But that is one of the points on which I say that the Board of Inland Revenue contradict their own statements. In reply to Mr. Thomas Allan and Mr. Charles Bray, who requested permission to publish without a stamp, the reply is this: "Sir, I have laid before the Board your memorial, in which you observe that, according to a return made to the House of Commons, certain registered newspapers are permitted to stamp only a portion of their impression, and requesting that that privilege be extended to all registered newspapers. In reply, I am directed to inform you that you are mistaken in supposing that any permission is granted by this Board in the cases referred to, or any other. The papers you allude to are not newspapers, though registered as such, and the publishers could not be prosecuted for printing a portion or the whole of their copies without stamps, to which penalties the publisher of a newspaper, properly so called, would be subject." I may add that there is one paper, called the "Ratepayer," a monthly paper, which, as I am informed by the manager of it, has been compelled to register as a newspaper; but at the same time he was not compelled to stamp every copy. The Board, as he informed me, stated that he must send a stamped copy for the advertisement duty, because it was a newspaper; but he added that they did not oblige him to stamp more copies than he liked. He did not wish

Mr. *C. D. Collet.*

9 May 1851.

wish a stamp at all, but they made him stamp his paper. I speak that on the information of the manager of the paper, not of my own knowledge.

836. Sir *J. Walmsley.*] With reference to the "Freeholder," is that still published?—Yes, it is.

837. And under the same form?—Yes, stamped and unstamped.

838. And containing the same description of news?—Yes, exactly. The proprietor sets the Board at defiance.

---

## *Martis,* 13° *die Maii,* 1851.

MEMBERS PRESENT.

| | |
|---|---|
| Mr. Rich. | Mr. G. A. Hamilton. |
| Mr. Shafto Adair. | Mr. Ewart. |
| Mr. Chichester Fortescue. | Sir Joshua Walmsley. |
| Mr. Cobden. | Mr. Stafford. |
| Mr. Sotheron. | Sir T. F. Lewis. |

THE RIGHT HON. THOMAS MILNER GIBSON,
IN THE CHAIR.

---

Mr. *Collet Dobson Collet,* called in; and further Examined.

Mr. *C. D. Collet.*

13 May 1851.

839. *Chairman.*] IN the last part of your examination the other day, you stated, with reference to a letter that had been received from Mr. Keogh, that the statement contained in it did not correspond with the statement contained in a previous letter of Mr. Keogh; that is, that in the one case he stated that a paper was a newspaper, and liable to a stamp, in virtue of its registration, and in another letter he stated that it was liable to a stamp only in virtue of its contents?—Yes; that when the "Freeholder" declared that it was not a newspaper, Mr. Keogh writes to say, "You are a newspaper in virtue of your registration and your contents;" and when on the part of three newspapers, the "Leader," the "Coventry Herald," and the "Caledonian Mercury," a demand is made to be allowed the same privilege as was granted to 51 registered newspapers, the reply is this: "The 51 registered newspapers are not newspapers at all." I consider those two replies to be contradictory

Mr. *C. D. Collet.*

13 May 1851.

contradictory of each other, and the last reply is contradictory to the fact. A great many of those 51 newspapers, and the others which have been favoured since the time that that return was made, are newspapers according to my view of the law, and that view is exactly the same which is laid down in writing by the Board of Inland Revenue. And that is part of what I did not finish in my last examination, namely, the fact that the law is not observed in London. Now, I have already mentioned the "Freeholder," which contains every month news and comments upon news, and I have mentioned the "Ratepayer," which contains news and comments, which has been obliged to stamp, but has been allowed to stamp only a very small number of copies, till in the month of April it comes out, I believe, as a weekly paper, and stamps every number at the raised price of 4½ *d.* instead of 3 *d.*; I presume, as I took care that several persons should address the Board of Inland Revenue on the subject, that it has been interfered with in consequence of those representations, though I do not know that it has been.

840. With regard to those contradictory letters, was it your wish to convey to the Committee that people find a difficulty in ascertaining from the Board of Inland Revenue clearly when they would be liable to a stamp, and when they would not?—I think there is very great difficulty indeed in ascertaining; each publisher forms his own opinion of what the Board of Inland Revenue considers to be the law, and acts accordingly. Some publishers construe the law rather strictly, and restrict themselves in consequence; other publishers construe the law very liberally, and they find that they are not interfered with, and I should say they violate it very extensively.

841. Do you wish the Committee to understand that people complain that it is a great evil when heavy penalties may be inflicted, and conditions of various kinds attach to the publication of certain matter without a stamp, that they should not be able to ascertain where the line is drawn, so that they might be secure in their proceedings against those penalties?—It is certainly a great evil, but it is rather an evil to the public; I do not find that the press generally, with the exception of the operatives' political press, complain; I should say that the publishers do not complain; they have, by long accustoming themselves to this law, raised up a sort of monopoly of a peculiar sort. I might say that there are three sorts of monopoly: first, the monopoly of the regular stamped press, which gives whatever it likes; secondly, the monopoly of the partially stamped press which gives a very little news, just as much as it

Mr. *C. D. Collet.*

13 May 1851.

it likes, and which would have to recast itself if it were allowed to give more, because the public would demand news if the law allowed it; and then there is the altogether unstamped, which is also a separate field, so that any change in the law would recast the whole of the press; and every publisher who makes a profit on his publication would rather continue to do so than run the risk of a change, which he does not see might be for his advantage. It is the public only that are injured; the publishers very seldom complain unless they receive letters from the Board of Inland Revenue; then they begin to be very much astonished and annoyed, and think themselves very much ill-used.

842. Has not the uncertainty of the definition as to what a newspaper is, and what might be the proceedings of the Board of Inland revenue in reference to any particular publication, a tendency to prevent men of capital from embarking in cheap publications containing a kind of news?—It makes anything like a good newspaper for the working classes at a small price utterly impossible, or anything approaching to a good newspaper, because no man will risk his capital in the present state of the law. If he gives an atom more news than the Inland Revenue Board choose to approve of, they have the power of ruining him, although that power has never been exercised; but if it were exercised, it would change the character of his publication, and he would have to look to another quarter to sell it in. The consequence is, that the supplying of news and political information to the people is left to those who have no capital, or very little indeed. I might say also that it is almost impossible that any political publication, under the present law, should be very good in its quality. As there is no capital, it is impossible that an author should be paid, and the whole is the product either of some very enthusiastic man, who has more zeal than discretion, or of some speculator, who merely tries to sell; and then the probability is that he pirates a large paper that comes out with a stamp. There are many threepenny papers, for instance, that exist almost entirely by taking the news from the daily papers; their leading articles are not worth speaking of.

843. On a former day you used the word "censorship;" do not you think that it is rather the indirect result of giving the Board of Inland Revenue a voice in these matters, that it does to a certain degree favour perhaps some particular papers unfairly and discourage others, than from any intention to establish a censorship at Somerset House?—I do not think that there is any intention at all on the part of the Board of Inland

Mr. *C. D. Collet.*

13 May 1851.

Inland Revenue to trouble themselves as to what the politics or utility of a paper may be; they simply, as it seems to me, consider that a good newspaper is a taxable article; but if it is a bad one, they consider that it is not a taxable article, and they leave it alone; the consequence is, of course, that only an indifferent or imperfect newspaper is allowed.

844. Mr. *Ewart.*] You do not mean that they take a political view, but a fiscal view of the case?—Purely fiscal.

845. *Chairman.*] And that, incidentally to that, they do produce in a certain way the same results as are effected by censorship; is that what you mean?—I should say that they are worse results. If they would prosecute a paper because they thought it was obnoxious to the Government, there would be some remedy against it; but instead of doing that, if the paper is small in circulation and badly conducted, they will let it drop; and if it is a good newspaper it cannot be commenced, because it requires capital, and a capitalist will not venture his capital with the chance of being interfered with.

846. Mr. *Rich.*] Why should he be more interfered with than if the paper was published at 5 *d.*?—I did not say that he would be.

847. You stated, did you not, that the bad papers, meaning papers of small circulation, failed, and that those bad papers were those upon which the Stamp Office put their hands; and that the good papers, meaning those of large circulation, were those which they did not regard?—No. I say that the Stamp Office would put down any good newspaper that came out without a stamp, but they will allow anything that is imperfect to be circulated.

848. What do you mean by good?—I mean well conducted as to talent, and containing a large amount of anything that would come into competition with the stamped press.

849. You mean containing news?—Yes.

850. And not paying the stamp duty?—Yes.

851. Do you complain of the Board of Inland Revenue for exacting the stamp duty upon such a paper?—No; the only complaint which I make, individually, against the Board of Inland Revenue is that they do not carry out the law. I complain more of the law.

852. I do not understand why the law should not be equally carried out against a paper that has a small circulation, if it contains news, as any other?—Nor do I; but the Board of Inland Revenue do, and they do not attack those papers.

853. Can you give instances of papers of small circulation, containing news, that have been put down; and of papers

having

Mr. *C. D. Collet.*

13 May 1851.

having a large circulation, containing news, and not paying the stamp duty, that have not been put down?—I did not say that a paper with a large circulation was put down, I should say that if a good newspaper were to be produced, it would be put down; and that no good newspaper can be produced, because capitalists will not venture their capital so long as they can be interfered with; but I could refer to a great number of small publications that publish news, contrary to law, and which are not interfered with.

854. You mean, I presume, that capitalists will not embark in an illegal proceeding?—They will not embark in anything which the Board of Inland Revenue would consider illegal, but they would embark in an illegal speculation if the Board of Inland Revenue did not interfere.

855. Would not the publication of a paper containing news, and not paying the stamp duty, be illegal?—Yes; here is the "Legal Observer," a weekly publication containing news; I dare say capital is employed in it; it appears to be a well-conducted publication, and contains news.

856. That is, in your opinion, it contains news?—That would be for the opinion of the Committee; I have brought here three monthly parts, so that it might be quite clear; here is the first article.

857. Sir *T. F. Lewis.*] Is there any news in it except what is connected with legal proceedings?—Yes; there are several articles I think on the Papal Aggression.

858. Mr. *Rich.*] Has it not been stated by the witnesses from the Inland Revenue Department that their object is to discover whether the circulation of news is the object, or whether it is referred to only as instruction in class subjects; and that when of the latter class they do not consider it news?—Then when the class subject is political in the country, it is put down, as for instance the "Norwich Reformer," which was a class paper; it belonged chiefly to things connected with the Freehold Land movement, and the Parliamentary Reform movement; there is a small column of news indeed on that subject, and they are told by the Board of Inland Revenue that they must give it up.

859. Do you call politics a class subject?—I think that politics are as much a class subject as law.

860. You think that politics have no more reference to news than questions of jurisprudence?—I think they go in the same category, as coming under the old phrase, matters in Church and State. Here is the "Legal Observer" (*producing the same*); the contents are for Saturday, February 1st, 1851. "The

Mr. *C. D. Collet.*

13 May 1851.

"The Divorce Commission; Ecclesiastical Courts and Judicial Committee; Repeal of the Certificate Tax; Reasons in Support of the Measure; Notices of New Books; Dart's Law of Vendors and Purchasers; the Common Law Commission; Examination of Parties; Incorporated Law Society; Annual Report of the Council; Fire Insurance; Legal Chronology; Michaelmas Term 1849, to Michaelmas Term 1850; Notes of the Week; Lectures at Lincoln's Inn; Report of the Common Law Commissioners; Revenue Prosecutions; Result of the Examination of Attorneys; Practice in Chancery; Production of Probates, &c.; Postscript; Common Law Sittings; Common Pleas; Exchequer of Pleas; Common Law Cause Lists; Exchequer of Pleas; Law Students' Debating Society; Recent Decisions in the Superior Courts, and Short Notes of Cases; Analytical Digest of Cases reported in all the Courts."

861. *Chairman.*] You stated, did you not, that a paper which merely gave an account of theatricals, called the "Harlequin," was interfered with by the Board of Inland Revenue?—Yes, before the stamp duty was lowered to 1 *d.*

862. Mr. *Ewart.*] You mean to say that the law is uncertain, and that a great discretionary power is vested in the Board of Inland Revenue; and that that uncertainty and that discretionary power act as a check to the free publication of newspapers?—Yes.

863. People will not invest their capital where there is uncertainty?—No, they will not; if the Committee will look over the whole of the "Legal Observer," they will find that the reports of cases in the law courts occur every week. Such cases, when reported in a newspaper, are considered as news; and, if published separately, they are prohibited, as in the case of the "Wakefield Examiner."

864. *Chairman.*] You have stated that slips, or parts of a newspaper, printed on a separate paper, are sometimes prohibited in the country, but allowed in London?—Yes, I say they are prohibited in the country, but allowed in London, without exception.

865. Will you give the Committee some instances to illustrate that statement?—"In July 1850 a trial in the Consistory Court of Richmond, for alleged slander, was reprinted from the 'Wakefield and West Riding Examiner,' to order of the defendant in the suit. The publisher never dreamt that the solicitor to the Board of Inland Revenue would manufacture 'an evasion of the newspaper stamp duty' out of the re-issue of matter which had already contributed to the revenues of the

Mr. *C. D. Collet.* — 13 May 1851.

the State. Some person represented the affair to Somerset House in such a way as to elicit the following communication: 'Inland Revenue, Somerset House, 9th August 1850. Sir,— I have to acquaint you that the attention of the Commissioners of this Board has been called to an evasion of the newspaper stamp duty by you, in having printed and published a paper, purporting to be an account of the trial of an action, 'Miss Fernandes *v.* Horner the Elder,' upon unstamped paper. Some copies of the paper in question are now before me, for each copy of which you have clearly rendered yourself liable to the penalty of 20 *l.* I give you this intimation in order that you may, if you think proper, offer any explanation of the case for the consideration of the Commissioners of this Board why a prosecution should not be commenced against you for the recovery of such penalties. I am, sir, your obedient servant, *J. Timm*, Solicitor of Inland Revenue. Mr. Samuel Greenwood.' In reply, Mr. Samuel Greenwood, the publisher, judging, from inexperience in such matters, minute particulars unnecessary, simply stated than an order had been given by a person for some copies of the trial referred to, and executed in the ordinary course of business. This led to the annexed demand for a more circumstantial history of the transaction: 'Inland Revenue, Somerset House, London, 15 August 1850. Sir,—The Commissioners of this Board have had under their consideration your letter of the 10th instant with reference to the subject of my letter to you of the 9th instant, and before they decide upon the steps to be taken against you, they require to be furnished with a statutory declaration, to be made by you and some other competent person in your establishment, of the number of copies of the paper referred to which were printed upon unstamped paper, which declaration I have to request that you will transmit to me without delay. With respect to that portion of your statement wherein you allege that 'a person ordered some copies to be struck off for his own use,' and that you 'simply executed his order,' I may observe, that I am in possession of about 100 copies, which were purchased at your own shop, besides others which had been publicly sold in Wakefield. I am, sir, your obedient servant, *J. Timm.* Solicitor of Inland Revenue, Mr. Samuel Greenwood.' The required declaration, of which we subjoin the substance, was accordingly made before a Master in Chancery." He makes a declaration of the number that he sold, namely, 2,000, and then he goes on to state, that "along with this document were enclosed reprints similar to the one in question, occurring so long ago as 1835, and so recently as a month

Mr. *C. D. Collet.*

13 May 1851.

a month subsequent to the republication of the Horner and Fernandes case, for the purpose of convincing the Stamp authorities that the custom was both of old date and general amongst the owners and representatives of newspaper property. Mr. Beaumont, the editor of the 'Examiner,' addressed a letter to the Board at the same time, exposing the injustice of singling out one journal for what might be alleged in a greater or less degree against the newspaper press of the United Kingdom. These united arguments had the effect of inducing the Commissioners to forego their extravagant claim of 20*l.* per copy for the modest sum of 10*l.*" Then he says he wrote to them, requesting them to remit the fine altogether, and he has this reply: "Sir, I beg to acquaint you that your further letter in this case having been submitted to the Commissioners of this revenue, they decline altering the order made therein; if, therefore, the mitigated penalties of 10*l.* be not paid within a week from this time, the proceedings will be continued to recover the full penalties and costs without further notice. I delayed answering your letter till I had submitted the case again to the Board. The small penalty which the Board has imposed is little more than sufficient to cover the amount payable on the number of copies printed."

866. Is there any distinction there attempted to be drawn between the publication of that one trial on a piece of unstamped paper and the publication of trials on unstamped paper as they appear in the "Legal Observer"?—I heard that distinction made in this room, when I heard Mr. Keogh's evidence; he said that the reports in the "Legal Observer" were reports of cases, and that the reports in a newspaper were reports of great interest to the public.

867. Sir *T. F. Lewis.*] Does copyright to this extent apply to publications in a newspaper. Suppose an article appeared in the "Morning Chronicle," of foreign news, which might have put the proprietors to very considerable expense to obtain, would a Liverpool paper be entitled to copy it in the evening and publish it, and could that be done without an infringement of the copyright?—I believe there is no copyright at present whatever in news.

868. Suppose that the "Morning Chronicle," or any other paper, goes to the expense of employing very able and clever men to report the debates which occur in Parliament, if the local press were very extensively disseminated through the different towns in the country, would each local newspaper publisher be entitled to reprint from either one of those papers the

Mr. C. D. Collet.

13 May 1851.

the whole of those debates, although he should be at no expense at all, without an infringement of the copyright?—I am afraid that, under the present law, he would, and I think that the law ought to be altered in that respect, and that protection might very easily be given to all newspaper property of that sort. I think some protection might easily be given; some copyright even in news, though a very limited one; but at this moment the weekly papers steal the whole of their debates from the daily papers, and I apprehend that the daily papers would not, as regards the debates, be more injured by the country press than they now are by the London weekly press.

869. Still, if I understand you rightly, there would be the power of injuring those newspaper proprietors who originally incurred the expense of collecting the materials by a republication of that which they had published, as rapidly as the railways would convey the intelligence, and that without any let or hindrance?—I do not think that it would be very greatly increased; the evil exists now, and I think calls for a remedy already.

870. Are you of opinion that it is possible, if newspaper stamps were altogether abolished, to permit the circulation of the London papers by post free of cost?—No.

871. Then would not this be the probable effect, that if the cost of transmitting a newspaper were to be paid by the person who received it, and if the republication of the news contained in such papers by the local press was entirely unchecked, would it not of necessity lead to a most extensive contraction of the sale of the London papers in the country which would spring from the cheapness with which their news could be copied and retailed in the country, to persons who would purchase their papers of the nearest re-publisher?—I do not think it would, because those persons who will purchase a daily paper desire their news to be new; and no country paper could compete for novelty with a London paper. A London paper now reaches Birmingham, for instance, not through the intervention of the post, by 10 o'clock in the morning, and a country paper would be obliged to wait at any rate till the arrival of the paper, before it could begin to steal the news. Now I think that those persons who will now, and would then, pay the price of the "Times" or the "Morning Chronicle," would be willing to do so still, for the sake of getting priority of news.

872. How soon do you think the debates which would leave London in the "Times" in the morning could be republished at

at Leeds?—I have no experience to enable me to answer that question. Mr. C. D. Collet. 13 May 1851.

873. *Chairman.*] You stated that in the case of publishing one trial on a slip of paper at Wakefield, a correspondence took place between the Board of Inland Revenue and the publisher, and you were going to point out that this same practice is notoriously permitted in London; can you give the Committee an instance of its being allowed in London?—I can give several slips. Here is one that I had published myself. A deputation from our association waited on the Premier last year. The account was published in the "Daily News," and I ordered 1,000 copies of it, and they made no scruple whatever about letting me have them. (*The same was handed in.*)

874. That was precisely the same case as the Wakefield case, was it not?—Yes.

875. Mr. *Rich.*] Was it distributed by post to their subscribers, or was it circulated by you?—It was distributed by me.

876. Then it was scarcely the same as the case at Wakefield?—Yes; it was not sold to the subscribers.

877. It was circulated by the newspaper proprietor, was it not?—No; he sold 2,000 copies to one man who was connected with the trial.

878. Was this sold to you in the same way?—Yes, it was sold to me. I being the secretary of the deputation, conveyed the account of it to the "Daily News," and I received from them 1,000 copies, for which I paid the price of the paper and the printing.

879. Which copies were circulated by you, with a view to forward the object you had in view, and which had not reference to news?—It is news.

880. *Chairman.*] Can you give the Committee any other instances?—Yes. There is a paper called the "English Churchman," which is in the habit of publishing slips, that is to say, reprinting articles; and some of them contain news, and some of them do not. But here is one, called the "Premier's Letter and the Pope's Bull; a Plain and Friendly Warning to the People of England, by One of Themselves." Then it begins to give an account of Lord John Russell's conduct on the Papal Aggression. It begins with a preamble, and then puts in Lord John Russell's letter. Then it gives a history of that letter, in which it says that the Queen sent for Lord John, and stamping her foot, said, "My Lord, am I or the Pope to rule in my kingdom?"

881. Is the paper that that was taken from a stamped paper?—Yes.

882. Then

Mr. C. D. Collet.

13 May 1851.

882. Then it had paid the duty once as news?—Yes.

883. Then it is published again on unstamped paper?—Yes.

884. And you mean to point out to the Committee that the individual was guilty of precisely the same act as the editor of the "Wakefield Examiner" was, and for which he was fined?—Yes.

885. And you state that the Board of Inland Revenue does not enforce the law as against those publishers in London in the same way that it does as against the publishers in the country?—Yes. It does not enforce the law at all.

886. Mr. *Rich.*] Was this a reprint from a newspaper in the same form as the other was a reprint from the "Wakefield Examiner"?—Yes.

887. Sir *T. F. Lewis.*] What interval of time had elapsed between one publication and the other?—I cannot say exactly; I should think about a fortnight, or perhaps only a week.

888. Was it the same in the other case that you alluded to?—Yes; of course it must follow close upon the publication, or the type would be broken up.

889. Mr. *Rich.*] Are you aware, with regard to the "Wakefield Examiner," that they had not stamps enough?—No. The "Wakefield Examiner" published a separate account. It is a common practice whenever there is a particular part of a newspaper that is interesting to certain parties, for them to go to the printer, and say, "I want such a portion of your paper; strike me off that portion; I will pay you what you charge." They then charge for the printing and for the paper, and very little more. That part was published by itself.

890. Is that circulated through the post?—In any way that the person who buys them chooses. It cannot be passed through the post unless you pay the postage.

891. Would the "Times" do that, for instance?—The "Times" is not much in the habit of doing so. I am not aware of any instance, excepting in the present week; and here is an account (*producing the same*) of the Great Exhibition. On one side there is a reprint of the plan and a description published on the 1st and 2d of May, and on the other side "The opening of the Great Exhibition, May the 1st, 1851." It begins with a long description; it goes on with the address of the Commissioners to Her Majesty; after that comes the Queen's speech, which I presume is news as much at the opening of the Crystal Palace as at the opening of the Palace

Mr. C. D. Collet.

13 May 1851.

Palace at Westminster; and then there is the Archbishop of Canterbury's prayer. Now, as there is an Act which specially exempts forms of prayer, published by authority, from the stamp duty on newspapers, it follows that a public form of prayer must be considered as news; this is not a copy published by authority, and therefore ought to be stamped. It goes on with a complete account, ending with an official account of the ceremonial. Then afterwards there is another article, called "London on the opening Day," published at the "Times" office by the "Times" printer, and there is no stamp on that.

892. *Chairman.*] Do you conceive that they are liable to a penalty of 20*l.* on every copy that was issued?—Yes, I think there is no doubt of it.

893. Mr. *Cobden.*] What price was that sold for?—Price 3*d.* I have some other instances of illegal papers. Here is Charles Dickens's "Household Words," which contains, I will not say news, but it contains comments and observations on news, and I have brought a half-year's numbers in order to show that.

894. *Chairman.*] Are you enabled to lay before the Committee the correspondence that took place between the publisher of the "Plymouth Journal" and the Board of Inland Revenue with respect to publishing the Queen's Speech on unstamped paper?—I am aware that the Queen's Speech was spoken on Thursday in London, and the "Plymouth Journal" came out on the same day; consequently, the Queen's Speech was too late for their paper; and not wishing to deprive their readers of the advantage of having a copy of the Queen's Speech, and not wishing, of course, to publish a fresh edition of their paper, to content those who had already a full copy, they published a copy of the Queen's Speech only, which I have seen, and sent it round to all the subscribers on unstamped paper.

895. Mr. *Ewart.*] Was any notice taken of that by the Board of Inland Revenue?—Yes; they sent them word that they were liable to a penalty of 20 *l.* for each copy, and on promising not to do it again, they were, as usual, let off.

896. Mr. *Cobden.*] You stated, did you not, that the Board of Inland Revenue applies the law differently in the provinces, as compared with the metropolis?—Yes.

897. Do you mean to say that they do that systematically? —I should rather say that they have a system in the provinces and that they have no system in London. I presume that a distributor of stamps in the provinces keeps a sharp look-out

 against

Mr. *C. D. Collet.*

13 May 1851.

against anybody who breaks the law; I do not know that it is so, but I presume that it is so; whereas in London nobody keeps any look-out as to the law being broken.

898. Do you then consider that the reprinting of a speech delivered in Parliament, and published by Ridgway, is news, and liable to a stamp?—I consider it so, becouse it is certainly, as far as I can see, so laid down in the Act of Parliament. I may mention that Gilbert has published all the debates on the Papal Aggression Bill, and all the news bearing upon what is called the Papal Aggression, and I believe he has never been interfered with by the Board of Inland Revenue, though I have myself sent an information against a portion of that series, as also against the slip I have mentioned in the "English Churchman."

899. *Chairman.*] Is it within your knowledge that when a publication was issued relating to the repeal of the Corn Laws, it began unstamped, but was interfered with by the Board of Inland Revenue, who compelled it to be stamped?—No; I believe the Board are much less strict in London now than they were at that time.

900. Mr. *Ewart.*] Do you think that they find it impossible to carry into effect the law in its full strictness in London?—I should be sorry to have to give any reason for their conduct, because it does not seem to me to be guided by any distinct principle. I rather suppose that they get as much revenue now as they have usually done; and as they know that they cannot put down every infringement of the law, they shut their eyes as much as possible.

901. Mr. *Rich.*] You are aware that they are carrying on a prosecution at present with regard to an infringement of the law, by the London press, are you not?—I am aware of their carrying on a prosecution against Dickens, for the publication of his "Household Narrative;" but I do not consider that that prosecution can altogether be considered *boná fide.* It may be so in the intention of the Commissioners; but if you look at the facts, it will appear that it is not so. In the first place, there is only one point to be tried, whereas there are two points of law involved in the case. The "Household Narrative" is a registered newspaper; and if the Board of Inland Revenue wishes to test the whole state of the law, they ought to have demanded a verdict on the ground of its being a registered newspaper. That would have given an opportunity for the Court of Exchequer to have decided whether the registration of a newspaper, that was not a newspaper, was legal or illegal. Then there is another point. There is a great fuss made by the Board

Mr. *C. D. Collet.*

13 May 1851.

Board of Inland Revenue as to the law about every publisher being registered. Now, there is no publisher registered to the "Household Narrative" and "Household Words." Here it is: "Household Words, a weekly journal conducted by Charles Dickens; London, office, 16, Wellington-street, North." There is no publisher's name to be found; there is the printer's name.

902. You consider that because the Board of Inland Revenue do not include all the possible offences that might be collected together with regard to such a publication, that the bringing to issue a very doubtful and important point is immaterial?—I think that if they had been in earnest they would have brought before the court all those points which have been in discussion during the last year.

903. Do you think those points are of more importance than the point which is now before the judges?—It is difficult to say which of the two is most important; I think that both are very important.

904. *Chairman.*] The point immediately at issue with regard to the "Narrative of Current Events" is, that as it is published at longer intervals than 26 days between each publication it is not liable to be stamped, the publishers holding that that third definition of what constitutes a newspaper contradicts the previous definitions?—That is the point.

905. Supposing it should be decided that the "Narrative of Current Events," as it is published at longer intervals than 26 days, is not liable to a stamp, that would in fact be deciding that the definition of a newspaper must be taken from the third of those clauses in the Schedule in which newspapers are described?—I imagine that the first clause would be entirely nullified.

906. Then supposing that were so, would not the effect of deciding that the "Narrative of Current Events" was not liable to a stamp be, that the "Spectator" was not liable to a stamp; the "Spectator," although it is published at more distant intervals than 26 days, yet, nevertheless, as the price is above 6 *d.*, and probably the size is above the size specified, is excepted from that law?—I think the "Spectator" would then become legal, if of sufficient size; but it is not I believe so large as the size required by law. If the third definition is to be taken to the exclusion of the first, it would be understood that the taxable article called a newspaper is simply a paper not very large, and not so dear as 6 *d.*, and that the tax is to be paid simply by the cheap and small articles, and not by the large ones.



907. That

Mr. *C. D. Collet.*

13 May 1851.

907. That would be deciding that if a paper be above 6*d.* in price, and above two sheets in size, then it would escape the tax altogether?—Yes.

908. Would not that be making out the newspaper stamp to be for the very purpose of taxing merely cheap publications, and leaving the dearer ones untouched?—I think there is no doubt of it; but I was going to say, that if the Board of Inland Revenue had wished to try the case thoroughly they should also have proceeded against the other publications of the same publishers. Bradbury & Evans are very extensive publishers of publications, which, however excellent (I admit that very readily), are very questionable as to their legality. They publish, for instance, four registered newspapers, of which they stamp only a portion of their impression, namely, "Punch," the "Lady's Companion," the "Household Narrative," and the "Household Words," the "Household Narrative," I believe, is the least valuable of the four; at any rate not so valuable as "Punch," and I believe not so valuable as the "Household Words." And it is a very convenient thing, and I think they are justified in protecting their property by putting forward the least valuable part for attack. The "Household Words" contain very frequently comments upon news. In the first article of the last half year is "The Doom of English Wills." Here is the account of some person; I believe it is a real person, though the name is given as a *nom de guerre*; and he visits the cathedral close of some town not named, I believe a real town, and he finds the wills in a very bad condition, and that article is continued. There is "The Doom of English Wills," Cathedrals Nos. 1, 2, and 3, and I think No. 4. Here is an article meant to throw into ridicule a proposal to give a testimonial to the Duke of Cambridge, and as it would be manifestly illegal, in an unstamped publication, to attack His Royal Highness, they attack "H. R. H. (His Rolling Hulk) the hippopotamus," and they go through the whole conduct of the Duke of Cambridge, implying that in every respect he exactly resembles the hippopotamus, and they call him so instead of the Duke of Cambridge. Then his presiding at dinners is laughed at, under the shape of the milkman who supplies the hippopotamus subscribing to the testimonial. Then there is an article on the water question, and stating the different merits of the different water companies. Then here is an article called "The Martyrs of Chancery," and in the "Legal Observer" there is a reply to that. They complained that a person of Dickens's high character should so disgrace his position as to write what the "Legal

Mr. *C. D. Collet.*

13 May 1851.

"Legal Observer" considers a very unfair article on the "Martyrs of Chancery." I take it that that is a commenting on public news and matters in church and state. If the Committee will look through "Household Words," they will find that those articles occur very frequently. There is a paper called "Ten Minutes with Her Majesty," and it gives an account of the opening of Parliament in the present year; and then there is a clause from the Queen's Speech, which of course is news; and it is stated in what tone of voice the Queen read it; and in the very last number but one there is an account of the state of the protective force of London, to show that there is no necessity for people being afraid of any outbreak at the Exhibition. Then, besides that, there are other papers which are contrary to the law, one called the "Mirror of the Time," which is constantly containing political articles. Its chief object is to attack the Exhibition; and there is an article called "Romanism as it was and ever will be." There is an article called "The Tablet and its Doctrines," which is a quotation of some political articles from the "Tablet," and it is political; contains news, and comments upon news, in every number; the price is 2 *d.*

909. Sir *T. F. Lewis.*] Is it published in London?—Yes, every week. Here are three illegal papers (*producing the same*), which refer to the Exhibition, and which owe their origin to it. Here is one called the "Expositor," price 4 *d.*, stamped 5 *d.*; and it contains all the correspondence about the British Guiana affair in the Exhibition, and it contains an article entitled "Where are the Exhibitors?" It contains an account of the "Royal Opening of the Exhibition," and two or three other articles on the same subject. It also contains what may be called an official account, namely, the Address to Her Majesty, the Queen's Speech, and the Archbishop's Prayer, all that being published without a stamp.

910. *Chairman.*] Can you state generally to the Committee how many papers, in round numbers, you could produce unstamped that illegally publish news, intelligence, or occurrences, or remarks, or observations thereon?—I am quite sure I could produce 40; I think I could produce 50.

911. Mr. *Rich.*] That is according to your interpretation of news?—Yes, according to my interpretation of the law.

912. Sir *J. Walmsley.*] The "Expositor" is a paper which is partly stamped and partly unstamped, is it not?—Yes, and it has no business to contain news.

913. Mr. *Rich.*] You consider "Punch" as much a newspaper as the "Times," do you not?—I consider that in a legal

 point

Mr. *C. D. Collet.*

13 May 1851.

point of view it is as much a newspaper as the "Times," and if it is a newspaper at all, I do not think the law recognises degrees.

914. *Chairman.*] Can you give the Committee any other instances of the illegality which you think is practised?—Here is a paper (*producing the same*) called the "Red Republican," which contains political articles every week. Here is another article on the same subject as that which I quoted in the "Household Words" about the allowance to the Duke of Cambridge, and it is headed "Royal Paupers and Plunderers," and it goes on with the characteristics of the Duke of Cambridge and the Royal Family. That has not been interfered with.

915. Sir *J. Walmsley.*] That is not of the same class as the "Expositor?"—No, but it is a totally unstamped paper. Then here is an unstamped paper (*producing the same*) which only reached two numbers; it is really too absurd to read it to the Committee; and I produce it to show that we are protected from this, not by the law, which does not interfere with it, but by the unwillingness of the people to buy it.

916. Mr. *Rich.*] Do not you think that a prosecution would tend very much to increase the circulation of a newspaper of that description?—I have not the least doubt of it; I have no doubt whatever if this paper were prosecuted that hundreds of people would purchase it so long as the prosecution continued, but no longer.

917. Does not it therefore strike you that the Board of Inland Revenue exercise a wise discretion in not prosecuting such a paper?—I think it shows that it would be much better that the law should leave us alone. The Board of Inland Revenue cannot protect us by prosecution; and they know that it would not be a protection for them to prosecute. But I think we might have a protection in allowing competition to better writers.

918. Did you hear the evidence of Mr. Whitty?—I heard the latter portion it.

919. Did you hear him state that many mischievous publications arose from time to time; that they had a certain circulation, and then fell off from want of support and notice?—I am perfectly aware of it; I do not contend that the Board of Inland Revenue ought to prosecute this paper because it is bad, but I contend that they ought to prosecute it because it is unstamped.

920. Would not a prosecution by the Board of Inland Revenue for being unstamped equally act as an advertisement for the paper?—Undoubtedly; but if the law cannot be put

in

Mr. *C. D. Collet.*

13 May 1851.

in force, or the Government officers will not put it in force, or a jury will not give a verdict, then I say the law is bad.

921. And when such a paper was left to itself, you heard it stated that the thing died away?—Yes, the paper died away; but there is a demand for something better, which is kept out of existence.

922. Are you aware of the existence of a great many cheap publications, which have a very good tendency?—I am aware of the existence of a great many cheap publications which have, on the whole, a good tendency; I have paid some attention to them; I bought up all that were published at one particular time, and I found that they all suffered in their character, from inability to write news and comments, upon the news of the day; I believe that none but persons of the highest genius are able to write a periodical publication which shall be instructive, and which the people shall like, unless they are allowed a liberty to comment upon what is fresh; and I believe that it is because that stimulus of novelty is denied to the people that the class publications, such as the cheap novels, are so much sold in this country.

923. You recollect the publication of the "Penny Magazine," do you not?—Yes, but that contained very little news; it was supposed to contain none; and that did not reach the classes for whom it was originally intended. I believe that the working classes considered themselves insulted by the "Penny Magazine," because they were told to take it instead of the unstamped papers.

924. Can you state that it did not circulate to a very great extent amongst the lower classes, small artisans and servants, and persons of that description?—I cannot say exactly where its circulation was, but I can say that there was a very large number of operatives who demanded something else, and who not only wanted something else, but felt themselves oppressed because the "Penny Magazine" was allowed to circulate and the penny papers were not allowed to circulate.

925. You are aware of the circulation of "Chambers' Journal," are you not?—Yes, I am aware that it is considerable; but Mr. Chambers himself would be better able to carry on the publication if he could put news into it undisguisedly.

926. *Chairman.*] You mean, do you not, to convey to the Committee that the operatives would prefer to purchase a cheap newspaper to any other kind of cheap periodical publication?—They certainly would.

927. And the extent of these publications merely shows

 that

Mr. C. D. Collet. — 13 May 1851.

that there is an appetite for some sort of publication at a low price, and that there is an attempt made to meet the want, but not a successful attempt, because the papers are not allowed to contain news?—Just so. I may add, also, that finding they are unable to have cheap newspapers, many of the working classes will club together to take newspapers even when they do not altogether approve of them, for they feel it necessary to have something of the kind. I know that many persons took in the "Northern Star" because it was the only newspaper that gave accounts of the Chartist meetings, and yet those very persons very much disapproved of the paper itself, of a great deal that appeared in it, and of the conduct of its proprietor; but finding that it was the only paper which would record the movements of the working classes, they found it necessary to take that paper in. But I am quite convinced that a good paper, a moderate paper, would have a much better chance of circulation than any of the merely violent publications.

928. Mr. *Ewart.*] And if there were no stamp duty, you consider that there would be a great number of papers devoted to giving news to the working classes, do you not?—Yes, certainly; a great number. And it would be a very safe speculation.

929. And you think, do you not, that it would have a good effect upon those classes?—Yes, a very good effect.

930. Mr. *Cobden.*] The association to which you belong seek to obtain the abolition of these taxes on newspapers. What do they propose to substitute for the stamp; do they wish the stamp to be only affixed when the papers go through the post?—I should suggest, in the first place, the separation of the stamping of newspapers from the Stamp Office, and on this ground: I find that in the Post Office, being an important public department, having for its object the managing of the communications throughout the country, and having at the same time to collect the revenue, it collects the revenue by making the revenue a secondary object. Their business is to carry the letters; their second business is to make a revenue, and yet they succeed in the latter object. I find, on the contrary, that the Stamp Office (if you give up the idea of censorship, as I believe the present Government disclaim that aide) consider their business to be simply to get a revenue; whereas the law gives them the management of the diffusion of knowledge; and this is with so little effect to both, that the dissemination of knowledge is very much abridged, and the amount of revenue is very small; only 220,000*l.*, I believe, is estimated at the Stamp Office to be the net revenue of the

Stamp

Mr. C. D. Collet.

13 May 1851.

Stamp Office from the stamps on newspapers. I would propose, in the first place, that the management of the newspaper postage should be left entirely to the Post Office. In the second place, I would suggest, but without any definite certainty of its being the best way, that newspapers should be sent in a stamped envelope. On the present system of stamping newspapers, by letting the stamp remain inside, it is quite possible to defraud the Post Office; and I believe that the Post Office is defrauded. I heard the other day that a person who had "Punch" sent to him for a year, had never paid the postage at the Post Office. I do not know that to be true; but I do know that the other day I took a large packet of Californian newspapers, and I put them in this envelope (*producing the same*) into the Post Office at Northampton, and they arrived at my lodgings. I addressed them to myself, and emboldened by this experiment, I addressed some papers to the Honourable Chairman, which contained, not newspapers, but simply some political papers. There was not a single newspaper in the whole. I also addressed one to the Honourable Member for the West Riding of Yorkshire, which I believe came to hand; it contained nothing but unstamped newspapers.

931. *Chairman.*] Is this what you addressed to me (*handing a cover to the Witness*)?—Yes.

932. Do you see any charge upon that?—No, there is none.

933. Nothing was paid for it?—Certainly nothing was paid by me.

934. Mr. *Cobden.*] Did you send these papers to me (*handing the same to the Witness*)?—Yes.

935. Mr. *Ewart.*] Did you send these papers to me (*handing the same to the Witness*)?—Yes.

936. *Chairman.*] For those various publications neither the stamp nor the postage was paid?—Neither one nor the other. Those documents which I sent to the Honourable Chairman are not newspapers at all; they are a lot of all subjects; the rules of a political society.

937. Then although the Act of Parliament intended merely to give the privilege of going free to newspapers, the practice between the Post Office and the Stamp Office is this; that almost anything that looks like a publication is allowed to go free?—Anything in a long cover open at the sides, but only so little open that you cannot see it, is, I imagine, safe to go through the Post Office; the officials have no time to look at everything.

938. If they were to examine them they would charge the full

Mr. *C. D. Collet.*

13 May 1851.

full postage, would not they?—Yes, if they took that trouble; but it would cost more money than the postage would come to.

939. With regard to the penny publications that are not newspapers, and that are unstamped, do they avail themselves of this chance of not being charged postage, as a rule?—I do not think it is done as the rule, but I think it is done as the exception.

940. The small unstamped publications have no postal privileges, have they?—None. What I propose is, that if they choose to purchase a stamped envelope, which of course would contain the stamp on the outside, they should be admitted to postal privileges.

941. Mr. *Cobden.*] All that you propose is that a stamp should be obliterated each time that a publication passes through the post, the same as in the case of letter stamps?—Yes.

942. Is it your opinion that at present the same newspaper passes through the Post Office repeatedly?—No doubt of it. Some time ago, not being able to take in a daily paper by myself, I, with others, took in the "Express," and "Daily News;" and as there is no free postage in the London district, my friend in London was obliged to send it to another friend of mine at Deptford; then that friend sent it from Deptford to me at Clapton; that making two journeys undertaken for one to convey it to me. Then I sent it to a friend in Cumberland; then it came back from Cumberland to another friend, either at Nottingham or in London; so that it had four or five postages instead of one; and if I could have bought a newspaper without a stamp, it would have served my purpose a great deal better.

943. Mr. *Rich.*] The news was rather stale at the end of the journey, was not it?—Certainly it was.

944. You are aware, are you not, that after a week certain papers are liable to pay for the weight?—That is the law; but in order to ascertain that, it would be necessary that some post-office authority should examine every paper that he came to.

945. Sir *J. Walmsley.*] Is it not the fact that a large number of newspapers, instead of being sent through the post, are sent by railway trains to different parts of the country?—Yes, so as to be had, the "Times" for instance, in Manchester or Birmingham, at 10 o'clock in the morning.

946. If that is so, would not that defeat the object which you had in view when you proposed a stamped envelope?—I do not propose a stamped envelope on every paper; what I proposed

Mr. *C. D. Collet.*

13 May 1851.

posed was, that anybody should be allowed to put a stamped envelope on any paper.

947. I understood you to be providing a remedy against the frauds that are practised; but you would not have a very large number of newspapers stamped if they were sent by railway trains in large masses, would you?—Doubtless the Post Office would not obtain that benefit; I apprehend that if the Post Office were allowed to manage its own revenue for itself, instead of the Stamp Office having anything to do with it, they would be able to afford to the public such accommodation in the matter of conveying cheap newspapers, that looking at the number of the papers which are now not allowed to go by the post at all, they would make as much revenue as they do now.

948. Then I apprehend that your remedy would not apply to those papers sent in the way which I have described?—No; those papers want nothing but to be liberated from the postage charge of 1 *d.*, which they pay without getting any postage in return.

949. Mr. *Cobden.*] The Post Office authorities have no motive for offering temptations to people to send letters by post, but every newspaper must pay the stamp which is required by the Board of Inland Revenue?—Just so.

950. Is it your opinion that a very great increase in the number of newspapers going through the post would take place if the compulsion were taken off?—I do not feel very certain upon that subject, because I have ascertained that the Post Office have no statistics on the question; I apprehend that every person who took in a twopenny paper might be willing to send it by the post for a penny; he would certainly be willing to send it by the post for a halfpenny. I think that if the Post Office were to devote its attention to that subject, and were unfettered by the Stamp Office, they would be able to create a new transmission of all printed papers by the post; but in order to effect that, it would be necessary for them to have a new system, because there would be so many papers going that unless they were sent by separate machinery they would impede the letters; I think the Post Office would want two establishments, or two divisions of its establishment.

951. *Chairman.*] You have had some means of ascertaining the feelings of the working classes upon this question. Will you state to the Committee whether you believe that there is a desire amongst the artisans and mechanics, and the various branches of the industrious classes, to get rid of the stamp on newspapers?—No doubt such is their desire. I may mention that

Mr. C. D. Collet.

13 May 1851.

that we held a meeting on the subject not long ago at St. Martin's Hall, which was attended by as many people as the hall would hold, and some hundreds were unable to obtain admission; and out of 1,400 people who were in the hall, 800 signed a petition for the removal of the penny stamp and all the other taxes on knowledge.

952. Do you believe they feel it to be a grievance that there should be a law which imposes a duty only when news is conveyed in a cheap form?—I have no doubt that they do desire that, and that they regard the stamp on newspapers as something in the light of a personal enemy; that the stamp is personified by them.

953. Sir *T. F. Lewis.*] In what sense do you mean that it is personified?—I mean to say that there is such a hatred against the penny stamp, that they feel as if the stamp itself were a person. It is not considered merely as an institution that it is desirable to get rid of, but that feeling is so strong that it is actually as I have described.

954. Mr. *Rich.*] In your intercourse with those people, with regard to taking off the stamp, at what price have you led them to believe that they would get their newspaper?—They would get it at all prices, from a halfpenny up to fourpence or fivepence.

955. Do you refer to the ordinary papers that they have now?—I do not believe that such a paper as the "Times" would be at all cheaper then than it is now, excepting by the mere reduction of a penny.

956. But as regards ordinary papers that would be read by the public, have you formed any opinion at what price they would be sold?—They would be sold at all prices, I think; for instance, such a paper as the "Times" or the "Daily News" would think it worth their while to publish two or three editions of their paper, containing each less matter than the previous edition. They do at this time publish a third edition of the "Daily News," and a third edition of the "Express" in the afternoon; and I think it would be worth their while to publish penny and twopenny "Daily News" in the evening.

957. Have you formed any calculation of what the expenses are of keeping up the type and the whole of an establishment, and of obtaining the information that it would be requisite to obtain, to constitute a paper such as would give news that would be acceptable to the world?—I have not gone into those calculations, because it is impossible definitely to calculate the number of readers. The great point in all cheap publications is

Mr. *C. D. Collet.*

13 May 1851.

is to have such a number of purchasers as that a very small profit on each copy may repay the fixed outlay upon the whole; and a most excellent paper might be made, provided there was a sufficient circulation of it, if only the tenth part of a farthing were gained on each copy. The question practically is one of circulation.

958. You are aware, are you not, that some of the London daily newspapers, notwithstanding that they sold at 3 *d.*, found it a losing speculation?—I think it is very probable that 3 *d.* would be a losing speculation. Then it must be remembered that they were obliged to compete with the present stamped press.

959. They themselves were stamped, were they not?—Yes.

960. Sir *T. F. Lewis.*] Can you say what portion of the expense of such a newspaper as the "Times" is covered by what they receive for advertisements?—I cannot; I am not connected with the press myself.

961. Can you give any guess; do you suppose a half or a third?—I should say that the "Times" lives by its advertisements. I have heard it said that the "Times" would find it more profitable if it could sell only one copy instead of its whole number; and I believe it to be true that when it has a supplement the fewer it sells the better it is for the paper.

962. Mr. *Rich.*] How does that argument agree with your opinion that a greater circulation conduces to the prosperity of a newspaper?—A greater circulation conduces to the prosperity of a newspaper if there is a small profit on the floating expenses; that is to say, on the striking off of a paper, for each copy. But in the case I allude to, the "Times" when it has a supplement pays I believe on each copy, for the striking off of the paper, and the stamp duty, more than the price which the paper brings in; at any rate, that is the supposition.

963. Then, setting aside the advertisements, the "Times" would, in your opinion, be a losing concern as at present conducted?—No doubt it would.

964. Sir *T. F. Lewis.*] In some of your answers you alluded to the "Times" as a paper so costly that it prevents people taking it in; can you tell the Committee what sized octavo pamphlet or volume the letter-press of the "Times" would make if printed in the form and the type, say of the "Edinburgh Review"?—I cannot say.

965. Mr. *Ewart.*] You were asked about the advertisement duty; has that been a subject very much complained of, as well as the stamp duty?—The advertisement duty is, I believe, a very

Mr. *C. D. Collet.*

13 May 1851.

a very great injury to a newspaper, and I believe every newspaper proprietor, excepting the "Times," considers that his property is injured by it, the amount of the advertisements in America is said to be ten millions annually; whilst the amount of advertisements in the United Kingdom is not much more than two millions annually.

966. Do you mean in number?—Yes; and all sorts of methods are adopted to evade the duty.

967. According to the Act of Parliament which regulates the duty on advertisements, are not advertisements published at the ends of books liable to the duty, as well as advertisements in a newspaper, and yet do they not escape?—The law requires that advertisements in newspapers, and in any literary works, should pay the duty; so that advertisements in any book ought to pay; but the advertisement duty, in point of fact, is levied only on periodicals; in a book you are allowed to break the law.

968. Books ought to come under the law, but in practice they do not come under the operation of it?—No; which leaves room for the observation that newspapers are particularly singled out by Government for that oppressive taxation.

969. Probably it would not be possible to make all the advertisements in books come under the operation of the law, though they come strictly under the words of the law?—There would be no difficulty, I apprehend, because as every book is registered at Stationers' Hall, and they send a copy of every book to the British Museum, means might be taken to ascertain whether those advertisements existed.

970. What then is the reason that those who have to carry out the law do not put it into execution?—Probably they think it too much trouble; they may think that the trouble and expense would be greater than the amount that would be brought into the revenue.

971. But nevertheless it is a flagrant injustice upon newspapers, and it is also an open violation of the law?—Yes, no doubt. I may mention that among the different methods of evading the advertisement duty, a favourite one is to advertise in railway carriages and omnibuses. There is a society called the Omnibus Advertising Company; and for a certain sum you may advertise in a great many omnibuses, and keep your advertisements up, according to what you pay, for a certain length of time. Then here is the proprietor of "Lloyd's Weekly Newspaper," who has a very clever way of advertising; it is a perennial way of advertising; for every penny that comes into his possession he stamps with a machine, "Lloyd's Weekly

Mr. *C. D. Collet.*

13 May 1851.

Weekly Newspaper" on one side, and on the other "Purchase Number One of Lloyd's last Penny Publication." That (*producing the same*) is a current coin that has come to me in the regular course of business.

972. *Chairman.*] Do you know anything of a small publication called the "Family Herald"?—Yes.

973. Have you heard what the circulation of that paper is? —I have heard that it amounts to 147,000 a week.

974. It is published at a penny, is it not?—Yes.

975. That paper is not recognised as a newspaper?—It is not a newspaper in the popular sense of the word, but it contains news.

976. But if a little publication like that can command a circulation of 147,000 a week, does not that show that there is a great desire amongst the working classes to buy cheap periodical publications?—There can be no doubt that they desire it; but I do not think the "Family Herald" circulates exclusively amongst the working classes; I think it circulates amongst all classes.

977. Do you see any reason why a newspaper should not be published at the same rate as that penny publication, provided there were no stamp and advertisement duty?—I think a paper of that size containing news might certainly have a very large circulation, but I think it would perhaps not be as large; but it would be more expensive to bring out a newspaper of that size than such a paper as I may say the "Family Herald" is.

978. Mr. *Rich.*] Could such a paper as that described by the Honourable Chairman be published at a penny?—I think it could be published.

979. *Chairman.*] Is it considered by the working classes, as far as you have collected their opinions, consistent with the desire that is professed to extend education, that there should at the same time be maintained a system of taxation which prevents the diffusion of knowledge?—No; they decidedly consider that the Government cannot be supposed really to care about education so long as they leave a tax which prohibits self-education.

980. Do you think that the dissemination of such knowledge as a newspaper circulates would have a tendency to promote the spread of education?—No doubt of it; in the first place, in the agricultural districts there are many persons who, though they learn to read when they are children, have nothing to read when they grow up, and the faculty of reading becomes altogether lost.

981. Mr.

Mr. C. D. Collet.

13 May 1851.

981. Mr. *Ewart.*] You would present to the minds of men who desire instruction that which was more likely to attract their attention than anything else?—Yes. I believe that after you leave school, with the exception of some small number of persons, there is no method of instruction so available as that of a newspaper. I will not say that there is no other so effective, or so good, for those who are inclined to avail themselves of it, but the generality of persons are too much occupied in life to receive instruction through any other source.

982. You think that newspapers would form a kind of current coin of instruction, circulating throughout the country?—Yes.

983. Although it might be liable to various objections?—I do not think it would be liable to any objections.

984. Although there might be abuses, yet nevertheless such a means of instruction would have a very beneficial effect, would it not?—Yes. I consider that the abuses of the press, and the habit of violent writing, are to a certain extent useful, because the parties for whom it is written gradually get accustomed to see the folly of it. I have known that such has been the effect on persons who commenced life in politics, amongst the working classes, by thinking ill of everybody above them, and supposing the Government to consist of nothing but scoundrels. If the writers are persons of talent and observation they gradually see the absurdity of their notions, and by dint of writing nonsense they write themselves out of it, and the people who read their writings make the same progress at the same time.

985. Sir *T. F. Lewis.*] Looking at the stamp as a payment for the conveyance of a newspaper by post, if the free circulation of newspapers by post were taken away from the public would they not be losers to a very great extent?—I do not think that the circulation is free when we pay a penny for it. If the Post Office said, We will no longer carry newspapers at a penny, no doubt the present readers of newspapers in the country would be very much damaged by it. I do not see that there could be any harm from a penny being paid, simply when the service was rendered.

986. Suppose the question before the Committee was, whether the present amount of revenue could be raised as a postage duty instead of a duty upon newspapers, that of course would impose a somewhat larger cost upon the transmission of so heavy a packet as the "Times," or any other large newspaper; and if the cost of transporting newspapers at the ordinary rate of postage, according to weight, was put upon a

newspaper

Mr. *C. D. Collet.*

13 May 1851.

newspaper, would not such a payment be a very severe check upon the dispersion of knowledge, and would it not necessarily lead to the multiplying of the local press by giving a premium upon the republication of that which had appeared in the London papers?—There is no doubt that if you were to charge a newspaper by a letter rate, the newspapers would cease to go by post altogether; but I apprehend that the Post Office would find some way of carrying all printed papers at such a rate as should both meet the convenience of the people and the demands of the revenue. I may give as an instance, that in the Sandwich Islands, where they have not the advantages that we have, the King of the Sandwich Islands has lately issued an order, by which newspapers going from the Sandwich Islands to California shall be admitted at a rate of postage which is a very cheap one; two cents upon newspapers, I think it is, and three cents upon pamphlets, whereas the letter rate is ten cents for the same distance.

987. In that case does the King of the Sandwich Islands provide the cost of transport?—He allows a certain portion of the postage to go to the captains of ships; the rest, I imagine, goes to the revenue.

988. If the expense of transporting newspapers is not charged upon the newspapers themselves, must it not follow that the charge of conveying them must fall upon some other portion of the revenue, by a tax upon some other persons who derive no benefit from the newspapers?—I never supposed that anybody should pay the charge of conveying newspapers except the newspapers themselves. I proposed, not that they should go free, but that they should go in a stamped envelope.

989. And whatever the weight, it should be simply a penny? —No, I would leave that to the Post Office. I believe that the Post Office, if it directed its attention to the question, would be able to solve the difficulty; I cannot solve the difficulty for them, because I have not the statistics, and nobody but the Post Office can get them; I have applied to the Post Office through a Member of Parliament for the statistics, and they informed him that they did not possess them.

990. Would not the inevitable effect be most essentially to reduce the amount of the circulation of the most prominent London papers, and to multiply to a very great extent publication of the local papers in large market towns, and that by the republication of news which appeared in the London press?—I have no doubt that the number of local papers would be very greatly increased, but I do not believe that

Mr. *C. D. Collet.*

13 May 1851.

that the circulation of the London papers would be diminished; I believe that a new demand would rise up; I believe that the advantage of circulating London papers throughout the country, though a great one, is overrated. There are many persons in the country who are utterly unable to understand a London paper.

991. Do you think that the leading articles of the "Times" are above the understanding of country readers?—Not of those who do read them; but I suppose they are quite above the understanding of agricultural labourers.

992. Mr. *Ewart.*] Would not a man be much more likely to be attracted by reading that which came home to his business and bosom than by things that were of a more abstract nature?—Certainly; I do not think that agricultural labourers would care about what was in the "Times."

993. If you attracted the attention of an agricultural labourer by something within his own practical knowledge, he would be much more likely to learn, would he not, through that instrumentality than through a leading article of the "Times"?—Yes.

994. And so with regard to the manufacturing districts, do not you think that by means of local papers containing local intelligence they would be much more likely to acquire information?—I think that in the manufacturing districts they do take an interest in general politics, and that the leading articles in the "Times" would be as well appreciated in the manufacturing districts as in London; but not so in the agricultural districts.

995. Sir *T. F. Lewis.*] Do you think that the articles that appear in a country town paper are at all better adapted to the understandings of the working classes or the artisans than those which appear in the London papers?—I do not know that they are; but then the country papers in England are not addressed to the working classes. The lowest price of any paper in the provinces is 2½*d.*; the common price is from 4*d.* to 5*d.* A country paper is the same price as a London paper; and I consider that there is no press for the working classes in this country.

996. If those papers are addressed to a particular class of the community, are they better adapted to that class than the London papers?—I do not know that they are; but the parties who read the country papers now also take in the London papers; the only peculiarity of a country paper is its local news.

997. Sir *J. Walmsley.*] Can you inform the Committee what

Mr. *C. D. Collet.*

13 May 1851.

what are the chief elements of profit to which the newspaper proprietors look?—I believe that the advertisements are the chief sources of profit; I know that all the newspaper proprietors regard the advertisement duty as the greatest oppression which they have to suffer.

998. In the second place, is not the circulation a considerable element?—Yes, that is the next; the profit on the circulation.

999. Would not a reduction in the price of newspapers add to their circulation greatly?—Of course it would.

1000. And an increase of their circulation would also greatly increase the advertisements, would it not?—Yes, if there were no advertisement duty.

1001. Would a reduction in the price enable the proprietors of newspapers to pay more for the literary talent employed?—Undoubtedly.

1002. Would they not, by paying more liberally, obtain higher literary talent?—Yes. I was told by one of the managers of the "Weekly Dispatch" that when the law was altered, and the postage reduced to a penny, they had to recast their management; a paper arose at 3 *d.*, which contained all the news of the week, and in order to compete with that paper they were obliged to engage writers of eminence, who wrote articles which no other paper could produce; and having done so, their paper is now in as firm a position as it was before.

1003. You are of opinion, are you not, that a reduction in the price would tend to an improvement of the quality of a newspaper?—Decidedly, a reduction would tend to the improvement of the quality of the small papers; I do not say that it would improve the quality of the very highest-priced London papers, because perhaps they already spend as much money as could be spent.

1004. Sir *T. F. Lewis.*] Would it not very much tend to degrade the quality of the London newspapers if their circulation were diminished?—I do not believe the circulation would be diminished; I believe there is a demand in England for such a paper, for instance, as the "Times;" that would continue. The circulation is I believe only 35,000, and I think there would be always that number sold.

1005. Mr. *Rich.*] You stated, did you not, that the quality of the London press and of the provincial press was rather above the apprehension of the labouring classes?—No; I said that the style of the leading articles in the London papers was beyond the intelligence of the agricultural classes.



1006. You

Mr. *C. D. Collet.*

13 May 1851.

1006. You also made the same remark with regard to provincial papers, did you not?—No, I did not say that.

1007. Then a paper to obtain a circulation amongst those classes, must be of a lower tone than the "Times"?—No, I do not think that; they must relate to affairs which those classes would understand, but they might be treated in a much higher tone. I believe that the highest genius might be employed in addressing those classes.

1008. Have you given your attention to the subjects with which, in your opinion, such papers should be conversant?—I have not paid much attention to that, and I have not the means of knowing; I do not live among those persons; and the only way to find it out, is either to live among them and find out what their habits of thought are, or to be allowed to print a paper, and see what they take in and like.

1009. Your opinion of the circulation of the press among the lower orders is not founded upon any deep consideration of the subject, is it?—I say that the press is not allowed to circulate among them.

1010. You said that there were certain topics, such as the leading articles in the London journals, which would not be adapted to the comprehensions of the lower orders; I asked you what subjects you thought would be adapted, and you said that you had not given your attention to that subject?—No, I have not.

1011. Therefore your notion with regard to the circulation of papers among the lower orders is formed, not upon a very accurate knowledge, but rather upon assumption?—I know that they will buy a paper, if it is within their means, and I they will not buy it if it is out of their means.

1012. From what course of observation amongst the lower classes have you been led to believe that they very much desire to obtain those papers?—I have not said that in the agricultural districts they do; I spoke of the towns. In London, for instance, and in manufacturing towns, they very much desire those papers. I did not say that the leading articles of the "Times" are above the comprehension of the working classes in the towns, but they are above the comprehension of the working classes in the agricultural districts. I may say, that the other day I had a letter from an editor at Spalding, who said that if he could come out without a stamp all the agricultural labourers would take in his paper. I should say that I have arrived at that conclusion, by the fact that in America, where there is no restriction upon the press, a newspaper is the first thing that is set up in every new place.

1013. Mr.

Mr. *C. D. Collet.*

13 May 1851.

1013. Mr. *Ewart.*] And that is so in all the provinces?—Yes, everywhere.

1014. Mr. *Rich.*] Those papers have a great number of advertisements in them, have they not?—Yes, they have.

1015. *Chairman.*] Would two or three columns containing descriptions of ladies' dresses at a drawing-room or some ball be most interesting intelligence for a working man?—I should think not.

1016. He would rather read something useful to him, would he not?—Yes; the last trial for poaching, I should say, would be the most interesting thing to an agricultural labourer; or news of the shipping interests, telling where the different emigrants were gone. I take it that every rural paper would contain, as a matter of course, that news which was most interesting to the persons who lived in that district.

1017. Sir *J. Walmsley.*] When you state that the American papers contained a great many advertisements, you are aware, are you not, that those advertisements are in proportion to the circulation?—Certainly. Advertisements in any paper would be in proportion to the circulation.

1018. Mr. *Ewart.*] You stated that the advertisements were a grievance to the public generally, as well as to the newspaper proprietors?—Yes. The advertisement duty no doubt is a great grievance to the public, but it is not so much as a tax on knowledge as that their trade and business is interfered with. When we consider that the population of the United States is about the same as the population of Great Britain, and that the number of advertisements is about five to one, we may see what a great hindrance to trade must be caused by the advertisement duty.

1019. Mr. *S. Adair.*] I observe amongst the papers handed in that there are some expressing very decided views on points of social economy, and on politics, such as the "Christian Socialist," and the "Red Republican;" are you of opinion that those papers are undertaken simply as a matter of business, and with a view to the profit of the parties setting them up?—Neither the one nor the other. I believe the "Christian Socialist" is chiefly managed by clergymen of England who have spent a great deal of money to carry out schemes of association among the working classes. The "Red Republican" is edited by a man who I believe is very sincere in his opinions. Both of those papers I should say are not speculations, but they are the sincere convictions of the proprietors. The proprietors of the "Christian Socialist" can afford, I dare say, to carry on the paper at a small loss. The editor of the "Red

Mr. C. D. Collet.

13 May 1851.

"Red Republican" is a poor man I believe, and he must sell, or he must give it up. I do not suppose that either paper is got up as a mere speculation.

1020. Then, in fact, the "Christian Socialist" is adapted to be the organ of a particular set of opinions, even at a loss to the proprietors?—Yes. It is the organ of the opinions of a small number of Socialist clergymen of the Church of England.

1021. Have you any means of furnishing the Committee with the number of papers of that description, bearing on political and social subjects, which are published without stamps?—I can give the Committee the names; there are about seven or eight: the "Christian Socialist," the "Reasoner," the "People," and the "Friend of the People." I do not recollect any more at this moment There are not a great many, but all of them are the advocates of opinions. They are not merely made to sell. I wish to hand in one paper, showing the effect of political agitation upon the number of newspapers.

[*The same was handed in, and is as follows:*]

| Year. | Number of Stamps Issued to Newspapers in Great Britain. | Remarkable Events. |
|---|---|---|
| 1814 - | 26,308,003 | Peace of Paris. |
| 1815 - | 24,385,508 | Battle of Waterloo. |
| 1816 - | 22,050,354 | Treaty of Vienna. |
| 1819 - | 23,048,449 | |
| | Including Ireland. | |
| 1819 - | 25,831,352 | |
| 1820 - | 29,387,843 | Trial of Queen Caroline. |
| 1821 - | 27,793,223 | |
| 1824 - | 28,938,908 | Catholic Question. |
| 1825 - | 30,451,176 | |
| 1826 - | 30,453,566 | Commercial Distress. |
| 1827 - | 31,205,116 | Ministry of Mr. Canning. |
| 1828 - | 32,585,481 | Election of Mr. O'Connell for Clare. |
| 1829 - | 32,989,884 | Catholic Emancipation. |
| 1830 - | 34,540,496 | Charles X. dethroned in Paris. |
| 1831 - | 37,713,068 | Reform Bill Agitation. |
| 1833 - | 35,056,793 | Unstamped newspapers circulated abundantly. |
| 1834 - | 34,748,922 | |
| 1835 - | 35,823,859 | Return of the Melbourne Ministry. |
| 1836 - | 39,423,200 | Newspaper Stamp reduced to 1 *d.*, September 15th. |

Mr. *C. D. Collet.*

13 May 1851.

| Year. | Number of Stamps Issued to Newspapers in Great Britain. | Remarkable Events. |
|---|---|---|
| 1837 - | 53,897,926 | Cessation of unstamped Newspapers. |
| 1838 - | 53,680,880 | |
| 1839 - | 58,981,078 | Chartist Agitation. |
| 1840 - | 60,618,308 | |
| 1841 - | 60,759,392 | The Whig and Tory parties equally balanced in the House of Commons. |
| 1842 - | 62,651,342 | Anti-Corn Law League and Chartist Agitations. |
| 1843 - | 65,074,219 | |
| 1844 - | 69,054,067 | |
| 1845 - | 78,586,650 | Anti-Corn Law Bazaar. |
| 1846 - | 83,074,638 | Repeal of the Corn Laws. |
| 1847 - | 82,380,875 | Irish Famine. |
| 1848 - | 86,465,684 | European Revolution. |
| 1849 - | 84,069,472 | |
| 1850 - | 85,671,566 | |

That from the foregoing analysis it appears that the circulation of newspapers fell at the peace, but was raised to an amount equal to that of the most exciting year of the war by the trial of Queen Caroline: that it then fell, but was still further increased by the agitation of the Catholic Question; that a leap of three millions took place owing to the excitement of the Reform Bill, after which the prevalence of unstamped publications reduced it nearly to its former level. That the reduction of the stamp duty caused a start in one year of 14,000,000; that the Chartist agitation of 1839 added 5,000,000; while the great League year, 1845, witnessed an increase of 9,500,000, to which the following year added 5,000,000 more. That while in the year 1847, there was a diminution of nearly a million, the excitement caused by the state of affairs on the Continent in 1848, added 3,000,000 to the number reached in 1846.

This statement I think shows that the natural vent for any political excitement in this country is the newspaper press.

## Mr. *Thomas Hogg*, called in; and Examined.

Mr. *T. Hogg.*

1022. *Chairman.*] YOU have been connected with mechanics' institutions, have you not?—Yes, for the last nine years; since January 1842.

1023. In what capacity?—I have been chiefly as secretary; I was nearly a year secretary to an institution in Leeds; for the last two years and a half I have been secretary to the union of institutions in Lancashire and Cheshire and for about four years

Mr. *T. Hogg.*

13 May 1851.

years I was secretary to the Liverpool Institution; the remaining part of the time, I was assistant secretary to the same establishment.

1024. How many institutions are there in Lancashire, Cheshire, and Yorkshire?—In Lancashire and Cheshire, I should think that there are, including small and great, about 100; and in Yorkshire, from the most recent information, I think there are about 150.

1025. Are you secretary to the union of 100 mechanics' institutes in Lancashire and Cheshire?—The hundred are not included in the union.

1026. How many are included in the union?—At present only 30 or 40; the others have declined to join for different reasons.

1027. Sir *J. Walmsley.*] Did you succeed Dr. Hodgson? —Yes.

1028. He is now principal of the Chorlton High School at Manchester, is he not?—Yes.

1029. *Chairman.*] How many of these institutions have news-rooms?—Nearly the whole of them; the great exception is that at Liverpool; it is now chiefly a very large day-school. The question of having a news-room has been repeatedly proposed in it, and has been usually set aside in consequence of the building being in an unsuitable locality; it was not placed in a position where it was likely that people would come to read newspapers, being away from their places of business.

1030. Do you find that the news-room is an attractive department in many of these mechanics' institutions?—Many of them are most attractive. In some of the small towns there is no other good room in the place.

1031. Are they generally well supplied with papers?—In all large towns they are, but in the small towns there is the greatest difficulty in getting a good supply. They have to beg from all the friends of the institution to give them a secondhand copy of the "Times," a secondhand copy of this paper and the others; their own funds being too low to buy them at cost price, and at first hand.

1032. Then what are the chief difficulties which those institutes have to contend with?—The first great difficulty is the want of sufficient funds. As they are adapted to the working classes, the subscriptions are fixed at a very low sum, and as the working classes have not taken much interest in them, the funds are consequently very small, that is one chief difficulty; but the greatest one, perhaps, is the want of interest

Mr. *T. Hogg.*

13 May 1851.

terest on the part of the working classes, though the institutions bear their name, and were established by them.

1033. It would appear that taking into account the present price of newspapers, and the funds of these institutions, the supply of newspapers is but small?—It is very small as applied to the country institutions.

1034. Do you think that if the price of newspapers were low, and the supply large, the working classes would attend those mechanics' institutes in greater number?—Certainly; for at present there are many of them who prefer to go to a public-house, where they can have a sight of the paper, and where there are not so many demands for it. I believe that if the supply were larger at mechanics' institutes, so that they could get hold of a paper, and the subscription proportionally low, they would go there from preference.

1035. Do you think that the news department is an attractive department, and that if it were better supplied, the effect would be to cause those mechanics' institutes to be better supported than they now are by the working classes?—Certainly; the working classes I believe would attend in larger numbers than at present; they do not take much interest in the scientific and literary subjects that are treated of in the lectures. Of course they feel much more strongly interested in the leading questions of the day, and they go to the newspapers for their information.

1036. Then they go to a public-house where they can find a newspaper perhaps more at hand than it would be at a mechanics' institute?—Yes, and there is another attraction there that there is not in a mechanics' institute, they can talk and discuss the subjects of the day, which is not allowable in a public news-room.

1037. Are there any collateral advantages that would follow from inducing the working classes to attend the news-rooms of these institutions?—I think there are many. If a working man is brought within the sphere of an educational institution, no matter whether he comes for the news-room or the library, he is likely to go on in a course of usefulness. If he comes merely to read the newspaper, he knows that there are classes going on in the same building for certain objects; he may feel the want of some knowledge, and he knows that he can attend these classes without any extra charge; he finds lectures being delivered, and he, as a member of the institution, can attend them. There is usually a very good library attached, open to him also; and by bringing a working man to the news-room to read the newspapers, there is every probability that he will avail

Mr. *T. Hogg.*

13 May 1851.

avail himself of the other advantages of the establishment, which, in an educational point of view, are very great.

1038. Mr. *S. Adair.*] In any of the mechanics' institutes of which you spoke, is any provision made for supplying cheap refreshments in the shape of coffee or tea for the parties frequenting the news-rooms, they being members?—I am not aware of any at present. It has been talked of repeatedly; and in one or two cases it was tried, but it was not found to succeed.

1039. Have you not heard that in some of the regiments of the Guards such reading-rooms are provided, which have had the best effect in keeping the men from the canteen?—Yes, I have heard of that. I heard it discussed among the directors of institutions; and one great difficulty was how the refreshments were to be provided, and the arrangements for selling them. In many of them there is no one living on the premises, and it was thought that it was better to avoid it.

1040. *Chairman.*] Have the news-rooms in those mechanics' institutes been very much objected to by the general supporters of such institutes, on political grounds?—Yes, in almost every case. When it was proposed to introduce them they were objected to chiefly by the wealthier classes, who assisted in founding the institutions. They thought that they would be used for mere party and political purposes; that the news-rooms would take only certain papers which upheld the views of a certain party, and it was strongly objected to in many places; in fact, in one or two instances, it caused the loss of some of the wealthier supporters of the institutions.

1041. When news-rooms were established in connexion with the mechanics' institutes, it caused the loss of some of the wealthier supporters?—In one or two cases; but I have known several instances where those gentlemen who withdrew on that ground, afterwards, by watching the results of introducing the newspapers, and finding that they were beneficial rather than otherwise, have come back and supported the institution more liberally than they had done before.

1042. Mr. *Cobden.*] In the origin of mechanics' institutes, news-rooms, I think, were never contemplated as part of those institutions?—No.

1043. As I understand you, they were added to the mechanics' institutes to attract and to induce the working people to come and join them?—Yes, afterwards.

1044. They are now held to be the greatest attraction to the working classes, connected with those institutions, are they not?—Yes, in many towns. Of course, in some towns, where the

the institution is large, as in Manchester and one or two other places, there are other departments equally attractive; but as a whole the news-room is most attractive.

1045. The objection taken to them by some of the larger and most influential supporters was, that they feared that the introduction of newspapers would introduce party politics?—Yes.

1046. Practically, do not you find that in a news-room, where you admit papers of all politics, politics in a party view of the case cease to exist, which altogether gets rid of that objection?—Yes, where the directors of the institution have always taken care that all parties were represented, and that there should be a fairly-balanced supply of newspapers, that no one might say, you are giving a greater number of papers for one particular side of the question. And they have acted with the greatest prudence and delicacy in that respect.

1047. *Chairman.*] The present price of newspapers renders it rather difficult, does not it, considering the low funds of those institutions?—Yes, it is exceedingly difficult, because the question is raised principally with the London papers. With regard to the "Times," there can be no doubt that every news-room that wishes to be so, must take a copy of the "Times," but when it comes to the others it raises a difficulty, and these London newspapers are always the most expensive to country institutions.

1048. Mr. *Rich.*] Do not you make arrangements by which you obtain them at half-price?—Then you must wait a day. The directors wish to have the papers laid upon the news-room table as soon as in any other place.

1049. Sir *J. Walmsley.*] How many mechanics' institutions within your knowledge are there in which newspapers are introduced?—I cannot answer that question as applied to the whole country. I should say that in Lancashire and Cheshire, out of the 100 there are at least nine-tenths of them.

1050. Are newspapers introduced into the mechanics' institution at Liverpool?—No, for the reason that I stated. The question was raised several times, and it was objected to because the institution was not in a good part of the town for a news-room.

1051. Is it recently only that newspapers have been introduced into mechanics' institutions?—It dates back for perhaps 12 or 15 years.

1052. *Chairman.*] Do you know of any instance in which the results of introducing newspapers into mechanics' institutions

Mr. *T. Hogg.*

13 May 1851.

tions have not been satisfactory?—No, I do not; on the contrary, they have been found to be extremely beneficial.

1053. Mr. *Rich.*] Do you find the practice increasing?—Yes. In fact no institution now considers itself complete unless it has a news-room.

1054. Sir *J. Walmsley.*] Do you think newspapers a good source of information for the members of mechanics' institutions?—For certain subjects they are. It is essential for a man now to keep up with the news of the day, and if he is given that at a mechanics' institution, I think it is a legitimate department.

1055. What portions of a newspaper do you think are of the most service to mechanics' institutions; what portion would the members select for reading?—I should say that the London daily papers are the most useful; that is to say, if they were taken away, their loss would be most severely felt. Then the newspapers of the town or the district where the institution is situated may be said to come next.

1056. My question rather had reference to this: what portion of the information contained in any particular paper would the mechanics themselves direct their attention to more especially?—Chiefly, when Parliament is sitting, to the debates in the two Houses, and to events going on on the Continent and in other parts of the world.

1057. It has been stated in evidence that the police reports are very much sought after?—I have not seen much reading of police reports.

1058. Do you find much preference given to the stamped over the unstamped publications in mechanics' institutions?—There is this difference, that the unstamped publications being purely literary, containing many tales and romances, are read by the junior part of the members, while the newspapers, with the news of the day, are read by the older members. "Chambers' Journal" and "Eliza Cook's Journal," and periodicals of that stamp, are read by the younger part of those who attend.

1059. *Chairman.*] Can you mention any of the economical plans which such institutions are obliged to adopt in consequence of the expense of the papers?—In several cases they have to purchase after the day has expired, because the funds are so low. In one or two instances they have to make a distinction between two news-rooms; they have two, one charging a higher fee, and another charging a lower fee; the working classes usually go into the one with the lower fee, and the wealthier members into the other; and of course the papers

papers in the second room are usually a day behind those in the first, and that causes a great deal of jealousy and bad feeling between the two classes, and has done much harm to the institutions; but they have been obliged to do it in consequence of the expense of the news-rooms.

1060. I noticed in a report some time ago that was printed and published, an allusion to a report from the union of mechanics institutions in Lancashire and Cheshire, as to the effect of newspaper stamps and other taxes on knowledge; have you recently passed any resolutions, or made public any opinion as to the effect of those taxes upon the prosperity of these institutions?—In a committee of the union we passed a resolution to petition the House of Commons; the resolutions were embodied in that petition, and applied to the taxes on knowledge generally, the advertisement duty, and the duty on paper, as well as the stamps on newspapers.

1061. The petition prayed for the repeal of the whole three, did it not?—Yes, because the whole three directly interfered with the prosperity of the institutions, by increasing the expense under those three heads; the expenditure of the institutions is very heavy in all three, and it is much heavier in the advertisement duty, proportionally, than in any other public establishment.

1062. Do you think that if newspapers were made cheaper by the abolition of the stamp, the supply of the news-rooms could be so greatly increased as to cause a great accession of members, and as a necessary consequence increase both the power of such institutions to assist in the education of the people, and the number of persons brought under their beneficial influence?—I decidedly am convinced that that would be the result.

1063. Mr. *Rich.*] Do you find any practical inconvenience now from the price of the newspapers?—The practical inconvenience is, that in such institutions their supply is so very limited, that they can scarcely provide enough for those who come.

1064. Do the members complain of there not being sufficient newspapers for their perusal?—Yes, constantly; if you go into some of the institutions in Manchester, for instance, about half-past two, when the London papers come in, there will be five or six people waiting to seize on the paper when it is put down, and they will crowd round each other and read it.

1065. Do they read them themselves, or do they occasionally read them out to the others?—They are not allowed to read them out.

1066. Sir

Mr. *T. Hogg.*

13 May 1851.

1066. Sir *J. Walmsley.*] Could you furnish the Committee with the names of the 90 out of the 100 mechanics' institutions that have adopted the principle of news-rooms ?—Yes, I could hand in a list of even more than 90, if it applied to Yorkshire.

1067. Mr. *S. Adair.*] You spoke of the news-rooms being frequented by the working classes ; I presume there is a large number of subscribers who are not strictly included in that term, such as young men in retail houses of business, clerks, and others ?—Yes ; I have already said that the great difficulty which these institutions have to encounter, is the want of adequate support on the part of the working classes ; though a portion of them do come to the news-rooms, yet generally speaking the working classes do not form the majority of the members ; they consist of the class that has just been mentioned, namely, young men in offices, and others engaged in retail establishments, and the like.

1068. Then do you suppose that two or three individuals of the working classes club together to purchase a newspaper to read at their own homes, or do they go to public-houses ?—I think in the towns they rather go to places of resort ; in the country I know that they do club together, but that is in places where there is no proper news-room that they can go to.

1069. Sir *J. Walmsley.*] By introducing news-rooms into each of the mechanics' institutes in the country, would that, in your opinion, have a tendency to take the mechanics from more solid pursuits than newspaper reading ?—I think not ; I rather think that it would take them from worse pursuits, and lift them up rather than bring them down.

1070. You have had some experience of the Mechanics' Institute at Liverpool ; you know that a great many mechanics attend there in the evening, who are instructed in various pursuits connected with their professions. Now, if there were a news-room in that mechanics' institute, do not you think it would have a tendency to take them from the school in which they were receiving instruction in connexion with their profession, into the news-room ?—No ; those young men who come to the evening classes are there so decidedly in earnest, and feel so much the value of their instruction, that no inducement would persuade them to prefer the news-room to their classes.

1071. Then I apprehend that it is those who are least in earnest whom you desire to attract by newspapers ?—Yes, those who are getting newspapers at rather questionable places at present, or spending their time in loitering about.

1072. Not

Mr. *T. Hogg.*

13 May 1851.

1072. Not the others?—No; the others, I think, may be left to take care of themselves.

1073. Mr. *S. Adair.*] Speaking practically, may there not be some disinclination or disability on the part of a working man to engage after his hours of severe labour in any new and prolonged course of study, such as attending scientific lectures? —Yes; that objection has been repeatedly urged. The working classes have repeatedly urged it themselves, that after a hard day's work they are more disposed for amusement, and, as has been observed by a lecturer, "after working at wheels all day they ought not to be made to study wheels at night."

1074. Sir *J. Walmsley.*] Your experience goes to this, that mechanics' institutes, as pure mechanics' institutes, have been failures?—Decidedly.

1075. And you are obliged to make them more attractive to induce young persons to become members?—Yes.

1076. Mr. *Cobden.*] Do you know whether in the majority of cases these mechanics' institutes get their London daily papers through the post, or by the ordinary conveyance?—In every case where there is a news agent in the town they receive them through him, and he, of course, gets them down by rail.

1077. Not through the post?—No.

1078. In that case does he generally charge any additional price for the papers?—Yes. The London papers in Liverpool are charged 6*d.* each, the additional penny being charged by the news agent; that is, if they are bought in single numbers, and if a full year's payment is made of course there is a proportionate charge.

1079. Then the mechanics' institutes in Lancashire and Yorkshire pay a stamp upon the newspapers, and they pay for the carriage in addition?—Exactly; but then in many instances they sell the papers after a time, and then they are sent through the post.

1080. Practically, the penny stamp upon the London morning newspapers is paid by the mechanics' institutes in Lancashire and Yorkshire without their receiving the postage service in return, and which it was calculated would be given for it? —Yes, that is the case.

1081. The papers being brought by railway?—Yes.

1082. Have you ever seen it calculated what the saving would be upon the newspapers, if the taxes called the taxes on knowledge were removed?—I have not seen it calculated with respect to newspapers alone. I have gone into calculations

regarding

Mr. *T. Hogg.*

13 May 1851.

regarding all the three taxes; that is, the tax on paper, and on advertisements and the newspaper stamp, and I find that in Lancashire and Cheshire it amounted, the taxes alone, to three per cent. upon the entire income; that, in fact, it was a tax upon those institutions, the greater part of which have incomes under 150 *l.* a year, and they are taxed an amount equal to the Income-tax in the duty on the advertisements, on the paper, and on the newspapers.

1083. They are generally not in a very flourishing condition as regards their funds, are they?—No. It is very seldom that they can conclude a year with a balance in hand.

1084. Then it would be a great relief to those societies if those taxes were removed, would it not?—Yes; not only in taking away the sum which they now expend, but it would enable them to expand the institution to such an extent as to bring a vast number of new members, and increase its sphere of usefulness in that way.

1085. They might either save their money to pay off any debts that they might have on their buildings, or increase the attractions to their readers, and so add to the number of their members?—Yes. The disposition, I think, would be to increase the attractions of the institution. Unless it be those that have buildings, there are very few of them that have debts; and then the mortgage on the building is often just equivalent to the rent.

1086. Mr. *Rich.*] Is the proportion of artisans who attend those mechanics' institutions increasing or decreasing?—In some places it is increasing, but generally, I should say, decreasing.

1087. To what do you attribute that?—There is a great deal of prejudice on the part of the working classes against the institutions; they seem to think that, though nominally they belong to them, they are neither adapted to them nor are they managed by them. And again, there is not that disposition to strong, continuous, severe study on the part of the working classes which there is on the part of many young men engaged in offices and other places.

1088. Has the introduction of newspapers tended to increase the attendance of artisans, or not?—In some places it may; in the country places I have no doubt that it has done so to a great extent.

1089. Is that a recent introduction?—It is perhaps of 12 or 15 years standing.

1090. Is the encouragement from the higher classes of manufacturers and persons in that position decreasing or not in in the districts with which you are acquainted ?—That I should say is decreasing, and the reason is this, that they have given assistance to the institution to start it, and have put it in a fair way of being self-supporting, and as they derive little or no benefit from it themselves, they think that now it should be put on that self-supporting basis. The class of honorary members is generally decreasing; that is, of those who pay but receive no benefit.

Mr. *T. Hogg.*

13 May 1851.

1091. There is an indirect advantage resulting from the better conduct and more improved minds of those who attend, is there not ?—Yes; but I have known one or two instances where the very fact of the master of a large establishment supporting an institution, and encouraging his hands to attend, roused a feeling of jealousy on their part, that he had some sinister object in view.

1092. With regard to the penny that is charged on the newspaper, that includes the delivery, does it not ?—No; if you buy a paper in Liverpool or Manchester, you pay 6 *d.* for it.

1093. But with regard to those newspapers which come to the institution with which you are connected, are you obliged to send for them to the newspaper office, or does the agent send them to you ?—The agent sends them usually.

1094. Mr. *S. Adair.*] There must be a great profit obtained by the newspaper agents on the mere transmission of the papers ?—Yes.

1095. Mr. *Cobden.*] You stated, did you not, that the union of mechanics' institutes, of which you are the secretary, petitioned for the removal of these taxes on knowledge ?—Yes; the central committee petitioned; at the last annual meeting held in Chester, there were forms of the petition given, and there were delegates present from many institutions, and they all decided that when they went back they would induce their directors to do the same; at a previous meeting at Preston, a formal resolution was passed, requesting the different institutions to take the same step.

*Veneris*, 16° *die Maii*, 1851.

MEMBERS PRESENT.

Sir J. Walmsley.
Mr. Shafto Adair.
Mr. G. A. Hamilton.
Mr. Cobden.
Mr. Chichester Fortescue.
Mr. Ewart.
Mr. Rich.
Mr. Tufnell.
Mr. Stafford.

THE RIGHT HON. THOMAS MILNER GIBSON,
IN THE CHAIR.

Mr. *Samuel George Bucknall*, called in; and Examined.

Mr. *S. G. Bucknall.*

16 May 1851.

1096. *Chairman.*] WHERE do you reside?—At Stroud, in Gloucestershire.

1097. What is your profession or calling?—A Printer and Publisher.

1098. You have been engaged in publishing newspapers?—Yes.

1099. What newspapers?—I have been engaged in publishing the "Stroud Observer," and the "Stroud Free Press." The "Stroud Observer" was considered a newspaper by the Board of Inland Revenue, and in consequence of such consideration I was obliged to suspend the publication, greatly to my own loss.

1100. At what price did you publish the "Stroud Observer"?—One penny.

1101. What was the interval between each publication?—About a month. It was published something like the fourth Thursday, or the fourth Friday, in each month, but not always on the fourth; the time being varied as the county court was held.

1102. Did the interval exceed 26 days?—In every case.

1103. Did the "Stroud Observer" contain news?—Our customers were of a different opinion to the Board of Inland Revenue, and how to decide between the two I cannot tell. I have copies of two of the numbers here, which I will lay before the Committee (*producing the same*); only three were published.

1104. Sir *J. Walmsley.*] Your constituents did not consider it

Mr. *S. G. Bucknall.*

16 May 1851.

it news, did they?—They grumbled a great deal at its want of news.

1105. *Chairman.*] When you brought out the "Stroud Observer" it obtained a considerable circulation, did it not? —For a small thing like that I was very well satisfied with the circulation; that, and the advertisements, made it a profitable speculation.

1106. What was the communication that you received from the Board of Inland Revenue?—A letter, stating that the Board had had before them the "Stroud Observer."

1107. What was the date of that?—I had two communications from the Board. The "Stroud Observer" was published first of all in August 1848; and before publishing it I sent up a prospectus to the Board of Inland Revenue, and received a reply, telling me that the Acts of George the Third were repealed, and that the present law was 6 & 7 Will. 4, c. 76, and that the publication of news was prohibited by that Act, under any circumstances, on unstamped paper. After I had published the first number I received a letter from the Stamp Office, stating that they had before them copies of the "Stroud Observer," and inquiring why I should not be prosecuted for penalties incurred thereby. In reply, I threw myself entirely on the indulgence of the Board. I heard nothing more of it till after the publication of the third number; then I received a second letter, couched in very similar terms to the first, and in my reply I threw myself again on the indulgence of the Board, but submitted whether I was liable to the penalties attached to the publication of unstamped news. The only answer I received was, that the Board had my reply before them, and that they had directed a prosecution to be commenced against me. My reply was very short. I merely stated that I had a communication of such a date before me, and that the "Stroud Observer" would not again be published. They then wrote to me, stating that the Board had forborne the prosecution.

1108. Have you had any personal communication with the Board?—Yes, I have; I called at Somerset House and saw Mr. Keogh, and had a good deal of conversation with him.

1109. When was this?—After the receipt of the second communication from the Board; some time, I should say, about the end of October or the beginning of November 1848.

1110. When you believed, in fact, that there was a prosecution pending against you?—Yes, certainly; after they had told me that a prosecution had been ordered against me.

 1111. You

Mr. *S. G. Bucknall.*

16 May 1851.

1111. You then came to London and saw Mr. Keogh?—Yes.

1112. What passed on that occasion?—Mr. Keogh said that the Board must enforce the law, and I represented to him the hardship of enforcing it upon me, whilst other publications, containing news equally with the "Stroud Observer," were allowed to continue their issue uninterrupted, and I asked him what course I was to pursue; and, as nearly as I recollect, his reply was that I could hardly expect him to instruct me. Then I said, "Sir, will you be kind enough to tell me wherein I have offended?" He took up the "Stroud Observer" that he had before him, and pointed to different articles therein, containing different pieces of intelligence.

1113. Did he point to any one in particular?—The Parliamentary Reports was one thing, some news of some occurrence was another; and when he pointed to the Parliamentary Reports, I said, "Pardon me, the Parliamentary Reports cannot be news, or how is it that Mr. Hansard is allowed to publish the Reports of the Debates in twopenny sheets, certainly at very frequent intervals, and unstamped?" That question was not answered; but he pointed to others, some intelligence and occurrences. I said, "The 'Athenæum,' the other day, published the latest reports from the North Pole, which was copied as news by every one of the daily press, and by all the country press; and the 'Athenæum' is issued to a greater extent without a stamp." And in every instance wherein he pointed out news as being published in the "Stroud Observer," I answered him by referring to other publications which appeared to me to give information of a similar character, and which were unstamped. Mr. Keogh made me no reply to this; but when I asked him what I had better do, he said, "You had better go home, write to the Board, and make out your case as well as you can, which you appear to me to be very well able to do, and then I will take the instructions of the Board upon it." I left him with the impression, from his having said that I was very well able to make out a case for the Board, that no further proceedings would be taken: but I had another letter from the Board, from Mr. Keogh, as secretary, stating that a prosecution was in force, and that a writ had been issued. Those were his words.

1114. For what amount?—I do not know; I never received the writ, and I replied by return of post, stating that the "Stroud Observer" would not be again published. They wrote again to me stating that the Board had forborne the prosecution.

*Mr. S. G. Bucknall.*

16 May 1851.

prosecution. I was not then in a position to have defended myself in a court of law, otherwise I certainly considered that the "Stroud Observer" was not liable to the stamp duty, for two reasons; first, that there was nothing there which could be legally considered news; and secondly, that the size of the sheet, especially as it was at first published, was within the limits prescribed by the Act of Parliament as the dimensions of a sheet of newspaper, which were to be 17 inches by 21, exclusive of the margin; if it is less than that it may possibly be a piece of paper, but it is not a sheet of paper. The Act specially provides, "that no quantity of paper less than a quantity equal to 21 inches in length and 17 inches in breadth, in whatever way or form the same may be made or may be divided into leaves, or in whatever way the same may be printed, shall with reference to any such paper, part, or number as aforesaid, be deemed or taken to be a sheet of paper." But the only question which then would have remained would have been, whether if it was not a sheet of paper it was a piece of paper. What the courts of law might hold to be a piece of paper I cannot tell; but certain it was that I could not have defended myself, and consequently I was obliged to give it up.

1115. Why could you not have defended yourself; what was your reason for holding back?—I had not the means to go before the Court of Exchequer.

1116. You considered that it would be a very expensive undertaking, did you not?—Yes; for even if I had succeeded I should lose my own costs, as I have understood, though I have no positive warrant for saying so, that the Crown neither gives nor takes costs, and even if I had succeeded it would have been a very expensive undertaking; and as the Board would have been at no loss for money, whilst I should have been without any means at all, I could not go to law with the Board of Inland Revenue.

1117. Upon your promising to give the paper up altogether the prosecution was discontinued, was it not?—Yes.

1118. Do you conceive that you suffered any pecuniary loss?—Most unquestionably. As the printer and publisher of the "Stroud Observer," I was earning what to me was a considerable remuneration, and a very important proportion of my income was what I should have received from the "Stroud Observer." The time I was able to give to it would not have interfered with my ordinary calling as a then assistant to my father in his shop. My direct earnings would have been somewhere about 120*l.* a year, beside the income from the

Mr. *S. G. Bucknall.*

16 May 1851.

Mr. Keogh were that Hansard published the Parliamentary Debates, and that the "Athenæum" gave an account of some proceedings at the North Pole?—Yes, and the law reports: there were other things that passed between us, but I forget what they were now. I distinctly remember that with regard to every item which he pointed out in the "Stroud Observer," I answered by pointing out paragraphs of a similar character as contained in some of the best publications of the day, which were unstamped, and which I could hardly suppose were issued without the knowledge of the Board.

1141. Does it not strike you that a newspaper might contain a variety of articles, each of which might be found separately in other papers, but each separate paper, containing such an article only as conducive to its class subject, might not be considered as publishing news, whereas a paper containing all of them together would constitute a newspaper?—I cannot see any justification for such a distinction in the Act.

1142. You mentioned your pecuniary loss: you are aware that that loss was the loss of a gain made by what the authorities considered an illegal transaction?—If it was an illegal transaction, why were not other publishers treated in like monner? At the time, I thought it was illegal, or so far illegal as being without the permission of the Board; since then, I have learned that the Board treated me very differently to the manner in which other similar publishers were treated.

1143. You find now that you have complied with the law that you do not make that profit which you did when you were transgressing it?—Yes, exactly; and I find that other publishers have been allowed to continue equally infringing the law, but who are not interfered with by the Board.

1144. You stated that the revenue lost much by the advertisement duty that was paid upon your paper; is the advertisement duty as large upon your present paper?—No, I believe not; I have not gone to the trouble to compare them, but I do not think there is much difference.

1145. There being not much difference, the Government loses not much on the advertisement duty, and gains by the stamp?—But it is impossible to continue the "Stroud Free Press," as it is carried on at a loss. I think no more argument can be drawn from that than as though I, out of my private resources, contributed an equal sum to the advertisement duty for the "Stroud Observer" to the revenue; for that is pretty nearly, in fact, the case.

1146. Do you think it possible that the advertisements which did appear in the "Stroud Observer" might, on the cessation of

Mr. *S. G. Bucknall.*

16 May 1851.

of its publication, have found their way into other papers that were stamped?—Of this I am sure, that a great many persons advertised in the "Stroud Observer" who would not have gone to the expense of doing it anywhere else; and for this reason, that the circulation of the "Stroud Observer" was at least eightfold, within the district of its circulation, that of the best circulated newspaper near. No paper is circulated in the borough of Stroud of a number equal to one-eighth of that of the number of the "Stroud Observer."

1147. Mr. *Stafford.*] Are all the other newspapers distinguished by party politics?—There are no other newspapers in Stroud. The "Stroud Observer" was deemed a newspaper by the Board of Inland Revenue, and stopped. Since then I have commenced the "Stroud Free Press," but there is no other newspaper. The largest circulated newspapers in the borough of Stroud are, the "Gloucester Journal" and the "Gloucester Chronicle."

1148. Of what politics are they?—The "Gloucester Journal" is a Liberal paper, and the "Gloucester Chronicle" is a Conservative paper. I have had it upon very good authority, that the circulation of the "Gloucester Journal," within the district covered by the "Stroud Observer" was not more than 200.

1149. What is the circulation of the other Gloucester paper?—About one half.

1150. One hundred?—Yes; I cannot speak with exactness as to the circulation of the "Gloucester Chronicle" in Stroud. I am not possessed of the particulars from the same authority as I am with the particulars with respect to the "Gloucester Journal." I believe that the aggregate circulation of the Chronicle is not more than one half of that of the Journal; and I should think that the proportion in Stroud would be less than half, because the Journal is more extensively read, and the politics of the Chronicle are in disfavour in the neighbourhood of Stroud.

1151. *Chairman.*] You have reason to believe that the circulation of the "Stroud Observer," before it was put down by the Board of Inland Revenue, was a growing circulation, and would have increased considerably above what it then was?—Certainly, the circulation of the third number was some hundreds above that of the second.

1152. Have you reason to believe that there was a wish amongst the people of that district to have a cheap local organ similar to the "Stroud Observer;" and was a desire expressed by the public of that neighbourhood to have a cheap local organ

Mr. S. G. *Bucknall.*

16 May 1851.

organ like the "Stroud Observer"?—Certainly. I had several representations from many persons who wanted to know why I did not go on with the "Stroud Observer." I was told that it was a useful periodical, that it would bring local matters before the inhabitants, inform them as to what was doing, and in many respects fulfil the mission of a newspaper; and, of course, my reply was that I could not; I was prohibited by the Board of Inland Revenue from going on with it; and I circulated a notice to that effect pretty generally throughout the neighbourhood.

1153. Sir *J. Walmsley.*] You stated that the greater proportion of your readers of the "Stroud Observer" were of the poorer classes; how is the void now produced by your giving up that paper supplied, as regards them; have they any means of obtaining that information which you supplied to them?—I am not aware of any.

1154. Do they read the other papers now?—I am not aware of any increase in the circulation of the other papers in consequence.

1155. Then, in your opinion, the loss of that paper was a very great injury to the working classes?—I think so.

1156. Mr. *Tufnell.*] You think that the dropping of that paper was a great loss to the working classes about Stroud?—The representations that I had from some of the most thinking of the working classes certainly led me to that conclusion.

1157. Mr. *Cobden.*] Did you not say that "Hansard's Parliamentary Debates" are sold in twopenny sheets?—I believe they are.

1158. Do you mean that you can buy a sheet, if you wish, of any particular debate?—I have not had occasion to buy any lately; but I recollect that five years ago I bought several numbers of Hansard's Debates at twopence a sheet.

1159. *Chairman.*] Not at the printer's office, did you?—I believe so; certainly the impression upon my mind is so. I was at one time a bookseller's collector, in the employ of Messrs. Hamilton, of Paternoster-row, and it was for them, or I certainly am very much mistaken if I did not, buy the reports of Hansard's Debates at twopence a number.

1160. Mr. *S. Adair.*] Not made up in the same shape in which they are furnished to the public?—They were folded in sheets like that, without any wrapper (*describing the same*).

1161. Mr. *Cobden.*] Is there a considerable circulation of unstamped periodical papers in Stroud?—That is a question I certainly cannot answer with satisfaction in the affirmative; we circulate a great number of such publications as the "Working

Mr. *S. G. Bucknall.*

16 May 1851.

"Working Man's Friend," and some few other periodicals, such as Chambers's Journal, and so on; but altogether our circulation of those was not more than 150 a week.

1162. Are there any other booksellers who sell unstamped publications of another character?—We formerly supplied another bookseller in the town who does a good deal of the business, and I think his sale was about 100 of these unstamped publications; certainly if I put down the weekly circulation of unstamped publications in the neighbourhood of Stroud at 300, I think I should be beyond the mark.

1163. You stated that the reason why you did not try the question with the Board of Inland Revenue as to the legality of your publication was, that you were not in circumstances to bear the costs?—Exactly.

1164. Had you been in more affluent circumstances should you have contested the point?—Most assuredly I should if I had had then the same information as to the permission granted by the Board to similar publishers.

1165. You stated that the Board have not enforced the law in the same spirit against other publications; do you allude to the "Freeholder" and "Household Narrative of Public Events"?—They may be instances; not those that I have now before me; I speak more particularly of Scottish publications; here is one, the "Dunfermline Journal" (*producing the same*).

1166. *Chairman.*] Is this permitted to be unstamped?—Yes, unstamped and stamped; that is one published unstamped; that is a monthly publication that is published in Dunfermline, where I am told there are several other similar publications.

1167. Mr. *Cobden.*] You are aware probably that a similar communication to that which was sent to you, was sent from the Board of Inland Revenue to the publisher of the "Freeholder," a monthly publication?—I have heard so.

1168. Are you aware that that publication is still continued notwithstanding?—Certainly it is.

1169. Do you think that if you had been in such a position as the publisher of the "Freeholder" is, and had disregarded the threat of the Board of Inland Revenue as the publisher of that work has, that you would have been allowed to continue your publication till the present time?—I think I should.

1170. Mr. *Stafford.*] Why cannot you do so now?—Even now I have not means to go to law with the Board.

1171. You stated that if you had known as much as you do now, you would have contested the case?—I wish to express myself

Mr. *S. G. Bucknall.*

16 May 1851.

myself in this way, that if I had had the means and the same information that I have now, I should most assuredly have done so.

1172. Mr. *Cobden.*] Your work was suppressed in 1848, was it not?—Exactly.

1173. From that time to this, nearly three years, other richer publishers have been allowed to go on pulishing precisely the same kind of work which was suppressed in your case, have they not?—Yes, they have.

1174. In those cases the parties interested are richer people than yourself, are they not?—Yes.

1175. Do you consider that it was on account of your want of means to withstand the threat of the Board, you have been deprived of the profits of your publication for nearly three years?—I think so; and that under the circumstances I was treated with the grossest injustice.

1176. *Chairman.*] You set your loss at 120 *l.* a year, do you not?—Most certainly at that, and most probably at a great deal more; but that without any speculation.

1177. Mr. *Rich.*] When you say that publications precisely the same as yours were allowed to be published, upon what knowledge do you make that assertion?—I say works of a very similar character; and I think in the eye of the law of precisely the same character.

1178. Mr. *Cobden.*] You are aware that precisely the same letter was sent to the publisher of the "Freeholder," that was sent to yourself, are you not?—I have never seen a copy of the letter.

1179. You are aware that they had notice given them that they were infringing the law by the publication of the "Freeholder"?—Yes.

1180. That was the notice that was given to you, was it not?—Not exactly a notice that I was infringing the law. First of all an inquiry was made by the Board why I should not be prosecuted for penalties incurred.

1181. That was upon the assumption that you were infringing the law, was it not?—Yes.

1182. You are aware that there is a trial now pending against the publishers of "Dickens's Household Narrative," are you not?—Yes.

1183. That is to decide precisely the case which the Board decided in your case without a trial; to decide the legality of publishing a monthly periodical containing news?—Yes, it is; I have never had any doubts myself as to the legality of the publication of the "Household Narrative," for it always appeared

*Mr. S. G. Bucknall.*

16 May 1851.

peared to me illegal; that is, if its contents are considered to be news. The definition in the Act is very vague, and it certainly appeared to me to be such that a court could not convict upon it. I have always understood "news" to mean fresh intelligence which had not been published before; and as the whole of that intelligence has in the main appeared in other newspapers, I cannot consider that it is news, in the legal definition of the word.

1184. May it not be useful to you as a bookseller and publisher, to know that the definition of news is, that if you print the Queen's Speech on a piece of paper, extracted from the "Times," you are liable to penalties; or are you aware of that?—I am aware that the Board have prosecuted persons for doing so; but I am not aware that it has ever been decided in the Court of Exchequer that so doing is publishing news. I am not aware that they have prosecuted persons who have had means to defend themselves in a court. There is the question.

1185. Then practically you think that the effect of the law as it stands is this, that a threat of the Board of Inland Revenue to a small publisher in the country with humble means, would have the effect of inducing him to abandon his publication; but in the case of a rich publisher in London, he risks the consequences, and goes on publishing with impunity?—Undoubtedly.

1186. That is the result of your experience?—I consider that in the operation of the Act, and its administration by the Board, it is obvious that however conscious a poor man may be of the legality of his own proceedings, he cannot afford to risk a trial in the Court of Exchequer, especially against the Crown, when he would not recover his own costs. I should have had no fear whatever of the result of a trial in the Court of Exchequer, in the matter of the "Stroud Observer," if I had had the means to go there, and to have prosecuted it with the utmost rigour.

1187. *Chairman.*] Have you had any communications from the Board of Inland Revenue in reference to your present publication, the "Stroud Free Press." Yes, on the 15th of April I sent up a single unstamped copy of the "Stroud Free Press" to the Board of Inland Revenue, inquiring if I was liable to any penalty, and whether the Board would enforce it. The reply that I had runs thus: "Inland Revenue, Somerset House, London, 23rd April 1851.—Sir, With reference to your letter of the 15th instant, inquiring whether you are liable to any penalty for publishing the 'Stroud Free Press' without a stamp, I am directed to observe, that the Board are surprised

Mr. *S. G. Bucknall.*

16 May 1851.

surprised at the inquiry, and they do not believe that you can be ignorant that the printing and publishing of a newspaper, without stamps, subjects you to penalties. I am to add, that the Board have ordered a prosecution to be commenced against you." This letter reached me on the 24th of April, and on the same day I received a note from Mr. Brisley, the stamp distributor at Stroud, running thus: "Sir, I am requested to procure two or three unstamped copies of the 'Stroud Free Press,' published by you, for the purpose of transmission to the Stamp Office. If you publish in time for post to-night, please to let me have them in time for the same post; but, if not, supply me with the number required in the morning. I am, Sir, your most obedient servant, *J. P. Brisley.* Stroud, April 24th, 1851. Mr. Samuel George Bucknall, publisher of the 'Stroud Free Press.'" In answer to that note I saw Mr. Brisley, and told him that, on the 15th of April, I had sent up this unstamped copy; that besides that, no unstamped copy had been published, and that we had never sold a single copy. Mr. Brisley afterwards told me that he stated my reply to the Board, adding that he sincerely believed it to be true, as he had, after diligent inquiry, been unable to hear of any issue of unstamped copies. I may add, that about that time we had several applications for unstamped copies of the "Free Press," all of which were refused. I expected to hear nothing more of the matter after Mr. Brisley's reply; but on the 30th of April, a week afterwards, I was served with a writ, at the suit of her Majesty's Attorney-general, for 100 *l.*

1188. What for?—I do not know what for; I have not the slightest idea.

1189. You state that you sent an unstamped copy to the Board of Inland Revenue, with the view of ascertaining whether that publication could be circulated with a stamp?—Yes, whether I could circulate the "Stroud Free Press" precisely in the same way as the "Dunfermline Journal" was circulated, and this is the correspondence in consequence (*producing the same*).

1190. You have been served with a writ for 100*l.*, and that matter is now pending?—Yes; here is the writ that I was served with on the 30th of April last (*handing in the same*). I have had no correspondence with the Board which states that they forbear the prosecution.

1191. Sir *J. Walmsley.*] You stated, did you not, that the only copy you issued was the one that you sent to the Stamp Office for the purpose of ascertaining their opinion upon it?—Exactly. I wished to know what I had done, and on the

1st

1st of May, that was the following day, I wrote to Mr. Timm, the solicitor to the Board of Inland Revenue, in these terms: "Sir, I was yesterday served with a writ for 100*l.* at the suit of the Attorney-general, and Mr. Hawkins, the agent here, informs me you are the solicitor in the matter. Will you allow me to inquire what conduct on my part has led to this proceeding, as I am wholly unconscious of any act whereby I have incurred penalties to that amount. The only explanation that occurs to me is, that on the 15th instant I sent an unstamped copy of the 'Stroud Free Press' to the Board of Inland Revenue, inquiring if I was liable to any penalty for issuing it; beyond this, no unstamped copy has to my knowledge ever left my printing office. I cannot conceive that by this one act I have rendered myself liable to a penalty of 100*l.*, and, therefore, beg to be excused the liberty I am now taking. I am, Sir, your most obedient servant, *S. Geo. Bucknall.* Stroud, 1st May 1851." To that I received from Mr. Timm this letter, dated, "Inland Revenue, Somerset House, 3d May 1851.—Sir, I am at a loss to account for the contents of your letter to me of the 1st instant, particularly with reference to the letter of the Board to you of the 23d ultimo, wherein it is stated, 'that the Board have ordered a prosecution to be commenced against you,' for issuing the unstamped copy of the 'Stroud Free Press,' on the 28th March last, whereby you have incurred a penalty of 20*l.* If you are disposed to address a memorial to the Board, praying them to suspend the proceedings against you, and will forward such memorial to me, I will take the instructions of the Board upon it: you say that the copy sent to the Board was the only unstamped one printed; it remains to be explained why that was so printed. I am, Sir, your obedient servant, *J. Timm,* Solicitor of Inland Revenue."

1192. Mr. *Rich.*] Do not you think that that letter explains what you said was inexplicable?—No, I do not, because I can hardly suppose that if I allowed judgment to go by default, that a penalty for judgment allowed to go by default would be five times the amount of the penalty incurred.

1193. That would be for non-appearance. It attaches not to the Board of Inland Revenue, but to the Court of Exchequer?—I never had an idea that when I was served with a writ for penalties, if I allowed judgment to go by default as to those penalties and costs, that I should be subject to a penalty of 100*l.* for doing so.

1194. Mr. *G. A. Hamilton.*] The penalty is for contempt of court?—True; but I know such is not the practice in the

county

Mr. *S. G. Bucknall.*

16 May 1851.

county courts: there all the contempt of court is that you allow judgment to go by default. I have known instances repeatedly; and it is only for contempt in disobeying the instructions of the court as to the demand sought to be recovered, or the orders as to payment, or the judgments, that I have ever heard of any penalty or imprisonment attaching. I never dreamt of such a thing as that, because I allowed judgment to go by default, I was to be subject to a penalty of 100*l.* for not appearing to contest the case.

1195. Sir *J. Walmsley.*] What were your reasons for sending up an unstamped copy to the Board?—Because, as well as the "Rugby Advertiser" and the "Dunfermline Journal," I learnt that there were other newspapers published; and, especially, in Dunfermline, the people are very well supplied with unstamped news. There are, I believe, four papers in that town, certainly three, and I believe others within a very short distance of the town, that appear each of them at an interval of a month; but then appearing in alternate weeks, the public get an unstamped newspaper pretty nearly every week: and I thought if that was allowed to such an extent in Scotland, when I can see no difference in the provisions of the Act in causing the law to differ in Scotland and in England, I thought that surely, upon a proper representation, I should be able to get a similar privilege granted to me. I was perfectly aware that to ask the Board to give me permission to publish the "Stroud Free Press," when they could not know what the contents would be, would be folly. I learnt that the "Alloa Advertiser" printed a number similarly as I had done, and sent that number to them, and that permission was granted to publish that particular number; and permission having been granted to print that particular number, the publishers have gone on printing similar numbers ever since, and still continue to do so.

1196. Were you aware that it was the practice of the Board not to take any proceedings until they had given notice?—I wished to get their opinion as to the "Free Press," and I certainly never dreamt that they would commence a prosecution against me because I asked their opinion upon a matter which had not gone before the public.

1197. You had no notice whatever from the Board before the issue of that number?—Only the letter that I have read; and after that letter those proceedings took place between myself and Mr. Brisley, which he says were represented to the Board with his confident belief that my assertions were true; and nothing took place in the interval between that letter of

Mr.

Mr. Brisley and the receipt of this writ from the agent of the Board in Stroud.

Mr. *S. G. Bucknall.*

16 May 1851.

1198. *Chairman.*] Have you anything more that you wish to state to the Committee in reference to your own case, how far your business has been interfered with by the Board of Inland Revenue?—I should wish to call the particular attention of the Committee to the different practice that has been carried out by the Board, and to the hard treatment I have had at their hands, and to their positive permission of those publications in Scotland and in England which are published with their knowledge, inasmuch as the advertisement duty upon each number is paid, as it was in the "Stroud Observer;" 1 *s.* 6 *d.* is paid upon each, just the same as I paid. That is another of them, the "Dunfermline News" (*the same being handed in*). It is true that the publishers of those Scotch papers tell me that they consider themselves prohibited from saying anything about general news, but I find they do.

1199. What do you mean by "general news"?—Foreign intelligence, such as Californian, Australian, or English news.

1200. To what sort of news are they obliged to confine themselves?—They tell me that they consider themselves confined to local news, and on that account I wrote up to the Board some time ago, telling them that I had before me a list of certain monthly publications, and this is the reply of the Board: "Inland Revenue, Somerset House, London, 9th March 1850.—Sir, The Board have had before them your letter of the 4th instant, stating that you had before you a list of certain monthly publications which are issued, you understand, by their permission without stamps, and requesting to be informed under what limitations you may print similar periodicals. In reply I am directed to acquaint you that you are mistaken in supposing that the Board grant any permission of the kind referred to." I would submit to the Committee that this statement by the Board is directly at variance with the information that I have respecting the "Alloa Advertiser;" I was told that with regard to one number of that newspaper, a permission was granted by the Board. It is true that I had that statement only on the authority of a correspondent in Dunfermline; but I should apprehend that the exact facts of the case might be learnt from the Board of Inland Revenue. "If the publications in question are not liable to the newspaper stamp the printers need no permission from this Board; but whether they be so or not, the Board are unable to say, without knowing what papers are referred to." I then wrote to the Board,

Mr. *S. G. Bucknall.*

16 May 1851.

Board, telling them that the paper contained local news, adopting the words of my informant in Dunfermline, and had this answer: "Inland Revenue, Somerset House, London, 16th March 1850.—Sir, I have laid before the Board your letter of the 11th instant. In reply I am directed to inform you that local news cannot be published without the newspaper stamps I am, Sir, your obedient servant, *Thomas Keogh.*" I had previously called the attention of the Board to the fact of papers being published in Scotland, and of their permission being granted, as alleged by my Dunfermline correspondent, and this is the answer: "Inland Revenue, Somerset House, London, 3d January 1851.—Sir, With reference to your letter of the 26th ultimo, I am directed to observe, that when you speak of papers in Scotland being permitted to publish in the way mentioned, you are under a misconception, as the Board grant no permission in these or any other cases. If the law permits the publication without stamps, the Board have no power to interfere with it; but if it does not, it is their duty to enforce the law. I may add, that the Board cannot judge whether or not the paper alluded to by you is liable to the stamp duty on newspapers until they have seen it." I should have laid before the Board the exact facts of the case, as far as they came to my knowledge, but I could not do so without a breach of confidence with my Dunfermline correspondent, who being one of the publishers, might have been brought into trouble with the Board of Inland Revenue; so that I considered in that case I was prevented from making my own case good with the Board under those circumstances; and especially as I had no guarantee that there would be any even practice between us; that the Board might after all not choose to suppress my correspondent whilst they permitted other publishers, or that they would permit me; and even if they permitted me, that they would not suppress my contemporaries.

1201. Mr. *S. Adair.*] Did that declaration that you have last read induce you to think that you were perfectly safe in transmitting your unstamped copy of the "Free Press" for the inspection of the Board?—Certainly it did. I thought that in sending a single copy unstamped I was doing nothing whatever to transgress the law.

1202. Sir *J. Walmsley.*] What was the date of that letter?—The 3d of January.

1203. What was the date of the first number of the "Free Press"?—It was first published in November. This correspondence took place with the Board in consequence of the heavy loss at which the "Stroud Free Press" was being carried

carried on; and if I could now publish it without a stamp immediately, instead of it being carried on at a heavy loss, it would yield a good profit, a profit sufficient not only to pay the cost of printing, but of editorial management of a superior order to that which it now has.

1204. *Chairman.*] Where do you obtain your stamped paper?—Our stationer sends it to us; he, I believe, goes as our agent to the Stamp Office.

1205. You obtain your paper at an increased cost in consequence of having it to buy through an agent, do you not?—Yes; we have to pay him a commission upon the stamping. He will not send his cart down to the Stamp Office with our paper, and bring it back stamped, without our paying him for it, and also for the attendance of his clerk; so that the very fact of stamping it causes an increase in the price beyond the cost of the stamp.

1206. Mr. *S. Adair.*] Are there paper mills from which you could furnish yourself more readily with paper, within reach of Stroud, supposing that there were the means of stamping in Stroud?—Yes.

1207. Are there any paper mills in the immediate neighbourhood of Stroud?—Not now in the immediate neighbourhood; there are some 10 or 12 miles off.

1208. So that the expense of supplying yourself, if you could get the paper stamped in Stroud, would be considerably diminished?—Yes, but I cannot say that it would be a material feature; it would amount to, perhaps, a few shillings on an impression.

1209. Mr. *Rich.*] You would equally have to pay for getting it stamped at Stroud, would you not?—But we should be able to do it ourselves instead of employing an agent in London and paying for the stamps, and consequently do it much cheaper; it would be very much less than paying an agent to run all over London.

1210. Are you aware that there are newspaper establishments in large towns, such as Manchester, where the stamps may be impressed, which are in the habit of getting their stamped paper from London as a more cheap means of supply?—I am not; I should hardly have thought it, for I know that we can buy our paper now quite as cheaply in Manchester as in London, if not a little cheaper; and we have now under consideration the offer of a paper maker in Lancashire to supply us with paper.

1211. It is equally open to you to get it from London, Manchester, or any other place?—Yes, because we have nothing

Mr. *S. G. Bucknall.*

16 May 1851.

thing to do with the stamping; if we buy paper we should stipulate with the seller that he should send it to us stamped.

1212. *Chairman.*] Do you wish to express to the Committee any opinion as to the general effect of the stamp in preventing the diffusion of knowledge amongst the people?—I think it is very serious; in the first place, the intentions of the Acts which are consolidated in the 6 & 7 Will. 4, c. 76, I believe were to provide against any efforts to bring into contempt the established institutions of the country, and the operation of this Act is precisely the reverse; and I apprehend that even now, however large my broad sheet, were I to go into the Court of Exchequer and contend that every item contained in it was false, I should be in a very good position, and that the Board would be unable to enforce any penalty at all; I should consider that the element of news was truth, and if instead of truth I filled the paper with falsehood, I should be perfectly safe. And certain it is that I may write any article bringing into contempt all those established institutions which constitute the safety of England, and still be perfectly free from any fines or forfeitures under this Act. The operation of this, again, I believe to be that the people to a considerable extent lose the power of reading, because they do not particularly care for any of those very useful miscellanies published by Chambers and other publishers.

1213. Mr. *Rich.*] How do you then account for their very extensive circulation?—They are circulated extensively, but not amongst the lowest class of the people.

1214. Do you think that the lowest class of the people read newspapers?—A much lower class than those who read these periodicals. We have sold a considerable number of "Chambers's Journals," and "Chambers's Miscellaneous Papers for the People," and we find, in our experience in the shop, that the class of persons who buy them are the better educated and thinking order of operatives, children who go to school, or young men who have just left school, and so on: but we find that upon an important trial, or when anything very particular has taken place, the demand for newspapers is increased, and even persons who never purchase a well-written periodical will buy a newspaper. The newspapers again are purchased for reading in public-houses, where I know that those cheap miscellanies and useful publications never get by any chance, consequently I am justified in supposing that newspapers will be read by a class of people very much lower and less educated, with very much more blunted moral feelings than those who read useful publications; in other words, that the newspaper is the

*Mr. S. G. Bucknall.*

16 May 1851.

the only means you have of educating a very large proportion of the people, which proportion constitutes, or, at all events contains, those classes that are at present the most dangerous to the best interests of society and good order. The "Stroud Observer" was just the thing, if it had been well carried out, that would have suited them. It told them something about what was going on; it was true, in perhaps a very crude, ill-digested, and unfinished shape, but still it was that general miscellany of news, advertisements, and business which they would read, and that was proved by my circulating it to that large number, as compared with other things. I therefore contend, and I think I should be supported in that opinion by almost every one in Stroud, that with the "Stroud Observer" I reached a large number of people who could not be reached by any other publication, or, at all events, by no publication of a different character.

1215. Sir *J. Walmsley.*] And you reached them for good, to improve their understandings and their morals?—Certainly, I think so: what unstamped publications they have are, generally speaking, rather of a demoralizing class than otherwise; large numbers of them are novels, such as "Dick Turpin," "Jack Sheppard," the "Highwayman," and the "Black Pirate;" all those, the foulest filth of the printing press, are read by those persons eagerly, and they encourage a love of adventure which may be natural, but which certainly, I think, ought not to be encouraged beyond very restricted limits; and it presents to them acts of daring and heroism which, however morally wrong, they cannot but view in their uneducated state with admiration; and consequently to their education such reading as they get is bad instead of good. The "Stroud Observer," or any publication of that class (I speak only of the operation of this Act), which could say without this Act what it cannot say with it, must do good; because it would, by the very truthfulness of its narrative of what was doing, tend to elevate them in their condition, which would enable them to judge how far things were progressing for their own good; and these very publications are prohibited; and it is the circumstance of their containing these important and useful things that prohibits their publication.

1216. The result of your experience and observations is, that a reduction in the price of newspapers would tend to drive out those immoral publications from circulation?—Certainly.

1217. Can you give the Committee any instances that have come under your observation?—It is difficult to allege particular

Mr. *S. G. Bucknall.*

16 May 1851.

ticular instances, and especially to say where they have happened. I think that the good will always drive out the bad, and that if you referred back 10 or 12 years you would find that the penny scurrilous publications, for instance, the "Penny Satirist" and "Cleave's London Gazette," circulated to a large number; and that inasmuch as they have been driven out of circulaton, it has been by a better class. The "Family Herald" of the present day, unquestionably, is of a superior character to the other; and no matter by what means, whether by news or otherwise, you drive out immoral publications, you do it by giving them something better; and I contend that the most effectual way of doing it is by supplying them with news. News is what we all care about, almost beyond anything else.

1218. Referring to your own place of residence, Stroud, are there many of these immoral publications sold there?—I cannot answer that question with any degree of accuracy, because we endeavour ourselves, as booksellers, as much as possible to discountenance them. We never take any orders for them unless we are paid beforehand. We refuse to take any orders for their regular supply; and if a person comes and orders a single number, we tell him that we will not sell it; that he must order half a dozen. We interpose as many barriers as possible, and others do the same; still there are channels through which they are circulated, and those are below my own observation. I know there is one man in particular who gets his living almost entirely by the sale of such and similar publications, and I know that in many towns there are men that do just the same thing; and I must suppose that the sale is very large, or it could not support them.

1219. Are you able to speak as to the effects of the large circulation that the "Stroud Observer" at one time had upon those immoral publications?—I cannot, because, as I have said before, the channels were completely out of my sight.

1220. You have no doubt that it had a great effect upon them?—No; and I have no doubt that it would have had a much greater effect.

1221. Mr. *Rich.*] You stated, did you not, that the good will always drive out the bad in matters of publication?—I think so, generally speaking; that is the result of our experience as booksellers.

1222. Do you find also, with reference to cheap unstamped publications, that the good drives out the bad?—So far as it operates.

1223. In the earlier part of your evidence you stated I think rather,

rather, that publications such as "Jack Sheppard," and works of that sort, and exciting accounts of perilous achievements and evil deeds, were more read than good unstamped publications?—They are more read by the class who are not reached by those good ones. There are classes that you cannot reach, unless you go to them with something which is the nearest thing to what they want. Had we perfectly true accounts of Jack Sheppard, and well-written novels of that class, I am perfectly ready to admit that they might be read by those very same individuals.

1224. At present those rather of an evil tendency are more acceptable than those of a moral character?—Yes, I think they have rather an evil tendency; nothing that has a good tendency rivals with them, and those persons do not care for the useful miscellanies upon different subjects; what they must have is that narrative of adventures and occurrences that a newspaper gives, and then it is that a newspaper supplies truthful accounts, and that its operation is to drive out those things, because it gives a healthy turn to the very same spirit which is most objectionable when taken into another course.

1225. Do you not think that the editors and publishers of those papers which you state to be of a pernicious tendency would be glad to make use of the vehicle of public news also, to give their publications a still wider circulation?—You will see that immediately they do so they are furnishing an antidote, and this antidote is prohibited by the action of the Stamp Act. I am perfectly willing to admit, because I know it to be the case, that persons might wish to bring our institutions into disrepute, and they might avail themselves of the permission to publish news, as it were to cover the pill that they are endeavouring to force down their readers, the effect of which we wish to avoid; and I think the experience we have had of newspapers shows that, generally speaking, they have done good. If the Committee were to look at the "Weekly Dispatch" 20 years ago, its general character was very much worse than it is now; then it was a so-called radical, almost a blasphemous, scurrilous, and contemptible paper, but with an enormous circulation. Now other papers have so much improved, that the "Weekly Dispatch" has been compelled, in its own defence, very materially to change its tone. Ministers and other persons, for whose opinion in such matters I have very much respect, say that the "Weekly Dispatch" of the present day is exceedingly different from the "Weekly Dispatch" of 1831. Therefore I think that in the competition to which it has been exposed lately the good has driven out the bad; or why has the character of the "Weekly Dispatch" so much improved?



1226. From

Mr. *S. G. Bucknall.*

16 May 1851.

1226. From your own experience should you say that the tone of the press of the country generally is improving or not? —I can only give an opinion; I should certainly say that it was.

1227. From the instance you have given of the "Weekly Dispatch," you would be inclined to think, would you not, the improvement general?—Yes; as regards the "Weekly Dispatch," I do not remember a great deal of what it was 20 years ago, yet all the accounts that I have had of it have represented it to me as the very prince of scurrility and blasphemy; it certainly is nothing like so bad now.

1228. You are aware that the publication of stamped newspapers has been gradually but steadily progressing each year? —I believe so.

1229. Mr. *Tufnell.*] And their character improving?—Certainly; I would beg to represent to the Committee that whilst there are those large classes of the people that cannot be reached in any other way than through newspapers, the best way of ensuring excellence among newspapers is, by open and free competition. A newspaper cannot afford, when there is an unlimited competition, especially of that which is good in character, to give bad or untruthful accounts, for directly that a newspaper is lagging behind its contemporaries in intelligence, it goes down in public estimation, and the operation of the Stamp Act limits the market, and prevents newspapers being published, for the difficulty now with the publisher is immense to publish a newspaper. I had not an idea till I began to publish the "Stroud Free Press," of the labour necessary to counteract the legal restrictions upon publishers.

1230. Mr. *Rich.*] You stated that the widely circulated and well-established newspapers will beat the weaker and less well-established newspapers, and drive them out?—No, I have been misunderstood. I admit that a well-conducted newspaper will drive out a badly-conducted newspaper; but it does not follow that therefore a well-established newspaper will drive out a new one; I do not think it will. If there is room for it in the field, a new newspaper will get established just in the same way as the old; but it is by a keen competition of industry and of intelligence.

1231. You are aware of the immense expense in establishing a newspaper, such as you describe, independently of anything connected with the stamp duties; such as its correspondence, its plant, and its editors?—Those are features which are not affected by the stamp, but then they remain the same with the stamp and without it; and with the stamp your field is very much

Mr. *S. G. Bucknall.*

16 May 1851.

much restricted to what it would be otherwise. Here is the "Stroud Free Press," for instance, and that very slightly altered, and without a stamp, I should sell at 1 *d.*; and I am confident that the difference in character between that and the "Stroud Observer" would justify me in estimating the sale at from 2,500 to 3,000 every publication.

1232. Do you take into your calculation that if the stamps were taken off you would then have many competitors, and you would not have that monopoly of circulation which you now have by running the risk of incurring penalties?—I do not know that; I have just observed that the expenses of establishing a newspaper in other respects are not affected, consequently it would still require capital, energy, and intelligence to establish a newspaper then as now.

1233. Therefore those would be impediments to that wide increase of newspapers which you anticipated?—I do not quite understand the question.

1234. You said that if the stamp duty were taken off, there would be an immense increase in the number of newspapers?—I think there would be an immense increase in the number of newspapers, certainly; and it would give rise altogether to a different class of newspapers. We should have small newspapers published at a lower price, and more within the reach of the poorer classes.

1235. You just now stated that the impediment resulting from the want of capital would prevent such a multiplication of newspapers?—I think that the impediments I have mentioned would prevent the field being so occupied as to deprive us of the circulation. I think I should be justified in estimating the circulation of the "Stroud Free Press," if sold at 1 *d.*, and if published very nearly of the same size, at 2,500 to 3,000 a week, at 2,000 numbers, even if two or three others started in Stroud.

1236. You are aware, are you not, that when the stamp duty was taken off in 1836, some of the London newspapers were published at 3 *d.*?—Yes; and there are some newspapers now published at 3 *d.*

1237. Do you know whether those papers are profitable concerns?—I think they must be.

1238. Do you think, if they were profitable concerns, that those other proprietors who published at 3 *d.* would have raised their prices to 4 *d.* and 5 *d.*?—Many are still continued at 3 *d.*; some have raised their price.

1239. What London newspapers are published at 3 *d.*?—"Lloyd's Weekly Newspaper" is one.

1240. My

Mr. *S. G. Bucknall.*

16 May 1851.

1240. My question referred to the London daily papers?—I do not speak of them. I was not aware that any of these were published at 3 *d.* The "Daily News" was published at 3 *d.*, and the "Express" is now sold at 3 *d.*

1241. Are you aware that the "Morning Chronicle" was also published at a reduced price?—Yes, at 4 *d.*

1242. And both of those daily papers found it necessary to raise their price to 5 *d.*?—I would venture to represent to the Committee that that increase of price was altogether a separate matter from the protection of newspapers. When those newspapers raised their price, I believe it will be found, upon inquiry, that they changed proprietors; that the new proprietors wished to occupy a different field; and if inquiry were made, I think the "Daily News" would be found to have paid at 3 *d.*; and the "Express" still pays. And certain it is that "Lloyd's Weekly Newspaper," the "News of the World," and several of those threepenny papers, go on, and have an immense circulation.

1243. Are you aware that the cost of publishing a London daily newspaper is so great that hardly one of them can be called a profitable concern, independently of advertisements?—It would almost be the same thing for a landowner to speak of the profits of his estate independently of his rents.

1244. You look upon the advertisements as the profit of the newspaper?—Certainly they are. The "Stroud Observer" would have paid without its advertisements, but that would have been with such an immense circulation that I could never have hoped to obtain. The chief receipts of the "Stroud Free Press" are from the advertisements; and if the Committee will allow me, I will explain that a little as to the proportionate cost of it. To produce a newspaper, the first thing of course is, the editor and literary materials; the second, the cost of composition, as printers term it, that is, the arranging of types in the necessary order for printing: those expenses are fixed, and are unaffected by any sale. The third is the expense of paper, stamps, and printing, which is dependent only upon the quantity actually printed. Now, if I can but obtain sufficient advertisements to cover the editorial cost and cost of composition in the first instance, however small a fraction the price of the paper leaves me after paying the charge of paper, stamps, and printing, I am working it at a good profit. Now the expenses of the morning papers we know to be enormous; far more in proportion than for any weekly paper, because they have to go first for the information, which the others afterwards obtain almost free of cost; and

Mr. *S. G. Bucknall.*

16 May 1851.

and that enormous expense would be far too great, or at least would be so great, that if you were to have a halfpenny each copy profit upon the newspapers when printed, you would require an enormous circulation, far more than they ever can have, before you would have covered the original cost of the literary production. But when you take advertisements into consideration, those advertisements not only meet the literary cost, but yield a profit besides.

1245. Sir *J. Walmsley.*] Are you aware that there are papers published and given away, containing merely advertisements?—Yes, I am; and I should do the same with the "Stroud Free Press," were I not prohibited by the Stamp Act.

1246. Do you believe that those papers pay the proprietors?—Yes; I believe that now, if the last section but one in this schedule were omitted, I should be able to make the "Stroud Free Press" far less a loss than it is. I should wish to do the same as is done in Scotland to some extent; that is to say, to take the outside of those two pages as they are here upon the "Free Press"; I should put all my advertisements upon those two pages, and fill it up with literary extracts, correspondence, and other things, which would not come under the denomination of news; and then I would print it and give it away.

1247. You stated, did you not, that you thought there had been an increase of late years of pernicious publications?—I do not know enough of them to answer that question with satisfaction; I know that it is enormous. I do not know whether the Committee have seen a pamphlet which was published a little time ago, entitled "The Power of the Press," and of which a good deal was reprinted by Dr. Campbell, when he published the "British Banner," and which contained most startling statements as to the extent and influence of those scurrilous and baneful publications. Taking the whole issues of all the Tract Societies, Bible Societies, and Missionary Societies, they do not constitute anything like a third of the number of those publications, which are more readable with the lower classes, because many of the publications of those societies are dry theological disquisitions, which people, generally speaking, do not care for.

1248. Have you any doubt that those pernicious publications are increased from the difficulty of buying a higher priced paper?—Not the slightest doubt.

1249. And that that is greatly enhanced by the stamp duty?—Unquestionably the operation of the Stamp Act is in that way; I have not the slightest doubt of it. I speak, perhaps, with some degree of confidence from being connected for many

Mr. *S. G. Bucknall.*

16 May 1851.

many years with the book trade, and having a considerable knowledge of how my customers are affected by those things.

1250. By a reduction of the taxes upon knowledge, do you believe that the general tone of the press would be greatly improved?—Exactly; and that the general condition of society would be improved likewise.

1251. Would it increase the demand for literary men?—I think that is unquestionable; that follows as a natural consequence. If I were able, if the "Stroud Free Press" were a paying publication instead of the contrary, I should directly be able, on the part of the conductors, to employ men of high literary ability; but instead of that, we are obliged to be content with what we can get.

1252. Consequently you would be able to remunerate them better?—Yes.

1253. Then literary men have a direct interest in this question?—Yes.

1254. Mr. *Tufnell.*] You stated, did you not, that you considered the character of the stamped newspapers had improved, and that they had very much increased during the last few years; and that the number of the unstamped publications had very much increased, while they were of a lower character?—No, I am not aware of having said that. I believe that the tone of society, generally speaking, has improved in the last 20, 30, or 50 years, and that the press, as the reflex of that character, has improved likewise; but I believe it would have improved in a tenfold greater progression had it not been for those restrictions which operate only banefully upon the people, generally speaking.

1255. You stated in a former part of your evidence that the character of the stamped newspaper press, and you instanced the "Weekly Dispatch," had very much improved within the last 20 years. At the same time you stated just now, in answer to the Honourable Member for Bolton, that the number of the unstamped publications of an improper tendency had rather increased?—I am not aware that they have increased, because I am not aware of what their number was in former years. I only know that their present issues are enormous, and that millions, I believe, are issued monthly of those things that we should like to see put down by a better class of publications.

1256. *Chairman.*] By the competition of cheap newspapers?—Exactly.

1257. Mr. *C. Fortescue.*] You think that a very cheap newspaper press would rival those publications in interest?—Yes.

1258. And

*Mr. S. G. Bucknall.*

16 May 1851.

1258. And you think that the exclusion of newspapers prevents you from rivalling those publications in point of amusement and interest?—Yes.

1259. And that a cheap newspaper press would reach the class which no other species of publication now reaches?—Exactly. I also believe that it would not rival the others in iniquity.

1260. Mr. *Stafford.*] What means have you of ascertaining the number of those publications?—We can ascertain that to some extent from the quantities that we see; the different news agents and different booksellers will frequently know within a very near guess as to the quantities consumed by other agents.

1261. *Chairman.*] You referred to a pamphlet just now, what was the name of it?—"The Power of the Press."

1262. By whom was it written?—I do not know the author's name; I believe it was not given. I own that it is difficult exactly to state what the circulation is of any publication, because a definite answer could only be given by the proprietors from their own books, and no one else can tell exactly the business they are doing; still a very shrewd opinion may be obtained, and we can tell very nearly; as regards very many of them we can tell exactly; the proprietors will say what they are, and they have no hesitation in doing so; when we see cartloads leaving at a time we know that it must be enormous, if we are wrong as to a few thousands. If you go into Salisbury-square on a Sunday morning and see the numbers that leave that place, and look again into Holywell-street, and in some places near Paternoster-row, it only requires a person to go and stand there and see the persons leaving the publisher's office with immense loads.

1263. Mr. *Stafford.*] Where are those offered for sale; at the railway stations?—Very little; if you go into some of what we call the back slums, and different places both in London and in the provincial towns, you will see very often shops open on the Sunday morning. Those are out of the general reach of observation; and unless you go there and positively watch the sale, it is impossible that you can have any idea of the amount of moral depravity of these things.

1264. Mr. *C. Fortescue.*] There are always shops of that description in every country town, are there not?—Pretty nearly so.

1265. Mr. *Rich.*] Are those publications so very immoral?—Many of them. Some time ago there was a review of the different classes of publications, serials, in the "Daily News,"

Mr. *S. G. Bucknall.*

16 May 1851.

News," and it took them in batches; batch one, batch two, and so on, considering "Chambers' Miscellanies" in one batch, and the "Parlour Library" and other publications in another; and then it came to those that it represented as the foulest filth of all literary matter. Robbery was represented as merely a skilful sleight of hand, murder as nothing else but heroism, and seduction and prostitution as being anything else but blameable.

1266. Are not those rather exceptions?—Exceptions to the rule of general publications they may be, but I say that those publications are circulated to a very great extent, and those are circulated amongst the classes that we cannot reach by a beneficial circulation in any other way.

1267. Mr. *C. Fortescue.*] Many of those that are not obscene are full of stories of excitement, tales of horror and of crime?—Yes; the obscene publications are perhaps the very worst of all, but several of the others are little better.

1268. Very much of the class of the play bills of the low theatres?—Yes.

1269. Mr. *Tufnell.*] Are those improper publications generally issued on Sunday morning?—A very large sale takes place on Sunday morning.

1270. Mr. *Rich.*] You speak this from hearsay, rather than from actual knowledge?—I have seen it to some extent. I have not dealt in those publications, and so far my evidence may be worthless; but next to having dealt in them, I have been connected with the book trade, and have seen a good deal of it.

Mr. *John Cassell,* called in; and Examined.

Mr. *J. Cassell.*

1271. *Chairman.*] YOU are engaged extensively in literary matters, and in publishing works of different kinds, are you not?—Yes.

1272. Have you been engaged in publishing periodicals?—I have.

1273. Are you the publisher of a periodical called "The Freeholder"?—I am.

1274. Is that a monthly publication?—Yes.

1275. Have you received any communication from the Board of Inland Revenue, with regard to that publication?—Yes. I received several communications at the period, or soon after I started "The Freeholder," to the effect that I was subjecting myself to very heavy penalties; and a correspondence took place between Mr. Keogh, of the Board of Inland

Inland Revenue, and myself, which resulted in no further notice being taken of my proceedings. I have continued to publish "The Freeholder" up to the present time as an unstamped publication, and have also availed myself, like many others, of the penny stamp for the facilities of transmission through the post.

Mr. *J. Cassell.*

16 May 1851.

1276. You publish a portion of your impressions without stamps, do you not?—Yes, the greater portion.

1277. Have you received any permission from the Board of Inland Revenue, as the result of that correspondence, to publish a proportion of your impression without stamps?—No, I received no permission; but as no further steps were taken with respect to me, I presumed that I was at liberty to continue, and I determined to continue till steps were taken; for I conceived that I was singled out from a number of others who were pursuing the same course. I will state the reason which led to the starting of "The Freeholder" as an unstamped publication. There were a number of monthlies in the field. Almost every religious and philanthropic movement had its monthly organ, which not only gave leading articles upon that movement, but also reported its proceedings and progress. There was the temperance movement, which had various organs; the Ragged School Union had its monthly organ; and the Free Church of Scotland had its organ, both an unstamped edition which they sold through a bookseller, and a stamped edition which they sent through the post. I also saw that various publications that they published in the shape of magazines were to all intents and purposes monthly newspapers. Take, for example, "Tait's Magazine" and its Political Register, the "Eclectic Review," and its Events of the Month. I thought that a great movement, which I believed was calculated to advance the social well-being of the working classes, was as much entitled to its monthly organ as the temperance movement, the Ragged School Union, or any other movement. I therefore started "The Freeholder" as the organ of the freehold land movement; and when I received Mr. Keogh's communication I thought it was very inconsistent, when a number of publications were in existence, and had been in existence for years, that immediately a publication of this nature, the organ of a movement like this, which might be viewed as having a political tendency, should be pounced upon; and I made up my mind that I would not submit till the case was fairly tried; and the opinion that I formed was, that the Board of Inland Revenue had a power which I thought the Act did not entrust them with. There was

Mr. *J. Cassell.*

16 May 1851.

was "The Builder," and that to all intents and purposes is not only a monthly but a weekly newspaper. It reports progress of all matters connected with building, and it is news to all intents and purposes. There is "The Athenæum," and in fact I could point out 40 or 50 publications, and those I mentioned to Mr. Keogh. I asked him what constituted a newspaper: Is a monthly? I was keeping entirely to that. Is a monthly periodical? All the publishers had the impression that they could bring out a publication monthly and chronicle events, and not come under the Stamp Act. Mr. Charles Dickens was under the same impression; and I asked what constituted a newspaper; if it was its external form, then I would alter "The Freeholder" and put it into the shape of a magazine. The only reply which I obtained was, that the very fact of a paper being registered as a newspaper constituted it a newspaper. I immediately replied that if Mr. Keogh (and no doubt he very frequently did) purchased "Punch" as he might be coming into town, he would find that he was purchasing an unstamped periodical; but by reference he would find that that periodical was registered as a newspaper, and that the mere fact of a publication being registered for the purpose of transmission through the post did not constitute it a newspaper, for the Board of Inland Revenue gives every facility to people in trade. For instance, Messrs. Benetfinck Jones & Chapman are large ironmongers, and issue a pamphlet and catalogue of their prices, and deliver them unstamped, and avail themselves of the penny stamp for the purpose of transmitting their trade catalogue through the post.

1278. Have you got the corrrespondence with you that took place?—I have not.

1279. As far as you know, the Board has not altered the opinion that it gave you, that your publication ought to be stamped; all that you know is, that they have not gone into a court of law with you?—That is all.

1280. Mr. *Rich.*] Your publication is stamped partly, is it not?—Yes.

1281. Sir *J. Walmsley.*] Have you altered your paper since the communication that you had with the solicitor of the Board of Inland Revenue, as respects news, or any other matter?—Not in the least.

1282. You continue to publish it as you did at first?—Yes.

1283. Do you suppose that you were permitted to continue to publish it in consequence of the action which is pending against the proprietor of the "Household Narrative" being undecided,

Mr. *J. Cassell.*

16 May 1851.

undecided, or from any other cause?—Yes. Of course the impression that I had formed was this, that the Board of Inland Revenue were determined to settle the question of monthly publications, and that they had selected the "Household Narrative" to test the question by.

1284. Do you consider their threat against you in abeyance until that matter is decided?—Yes, I suppose so.

1285. *Chairman.*] I presume that if they were to sue you for all the penalties which you have incurred from the beginning, the amount would be very large by this time, if you are liable to a penalty of 20*l.* for every one?—It would.

1286. Mr. *Rich.*] There is some limit as to time, is there not?—I do not know as to their power.

1287. Would they by law be enabled to prosecute you for a contravention of the law by the publication of a paper years ago?—If it were decided that in this paper there was that which constituted it a newspaper, and that it came under the provision of the Act, then they could prosecute me for every newspaper that I had issued.

1288. Practically speaking, would you be under the least apprehension of that?—I do not know, no notice having been given.

1289. Was the notice to you prior to the correspondence with regard to the publication of the "Household Narrative"?—Yes; I believe that the correspondence took place between the Board of Inland Revenue and myself previously to any steps being taken with the "Household Narrative." I instanced the "Household Narrative of Current Events," as showing the general impression which prevailed. I thought it would be at once inferred that an individual like Charles Dickens would not go recklessly to break the law; and I was labouring under the same impression.

1290. In fact, the whole question hinges on this trial, does it not?—Yes.

1291. Sir *J. Walmsley.*] You have not a doubt that "The Freeholder" contains news?—It contains all the news regarding the Freehold Land Movement; and it being a monthly publication, we conceive that we can comment, if necessary, upon the events of the month.

1292. It contains comments also upon news, does not it?—Yes.

1293. Then the reason why you continue to publish it is, that other papers of a similar character are allowed to be published?—Yes, in immense numbers.

1294. *Chairman.*] Supposing it is decided in the case of the

Mr. *J. Cassell.*

16 May 1851.

the "Narrative of Current Events" that that publication ought to be stamped, what will your position be then?—A question will then arise with the publishers of monthly periodicals, whether we shall discontinue, or feeling that one is singled out from the others, and that the only motive why it should be singled out was, because rather of its political character; and I suppose it may be shown that the Freehold Land Movement is not in one respect a political movement and organ representing religious bodies being allowed to exist, whether we should, for the purpose of seeing that that law shall be impartially enforced, continue.

1295. If it is decided that the "Narrative of Current Events" ought to be stamped, all monthlies will have to be stamped, will they not?—Yes; but the difficulty will be as to drawing a distinction between what is an ordinary periodical and what constitutes a newspaper. I have in my hand a copy of "The Working Man's Friend;" it is a very difficult matter to come strictly within the Act when commenting upon events. For instance, the working-classes throughout the kingdom take a very deep interest in a subject like the Great Exhibition; and in my little "Working Man's Friend," we give articles upon the Exhibition, and we cannot help commenting upon what has taken place. If a number, for instance, was coming out on the opening of the Exhibition, we should have an article on "The opening of the Exhibition," and the influence that it exercised.

1296. That would be a violation of the law, would it not?—Yes; but the question is as to where the line is to be drawn.

1297. Mr. *Rich.*] On those occasions a discretion must be exercised by the proper authorities as to the carrying out of the law, must there not?—Yes.

1298. *Chairman.*] You do not feel very comfortable whenever now and then you get a reminder from the Board, that you should give some reason why you should not be prosecuted; you would rather have some rule by which you knew what you might do, and might not do; would not that be far more satisfactory to the trade?—Yes; we feel in a very peculiar position in reference to this question. I may just state that I am an extensive publisher, but not like many others; I entered more into the publishing trade for the purpose of issuing a series of publications which I believed were calculated to advance the moral and social well-being of the working classes. Now, I have a religious magazine; I call it the "Pathway" (*producing the same*), and one of the most interesting

interesting portions of this magazine is what would at once constitute it a newspaper; "a retrospect of the month;" we take a retrospect of those events which are interesting to the class of readers, everything that has taken place at home and abroad; any striking event, such as the death of Dr. Chalmers, or the death of Dr. Pye Smith, or any great man; we bring those in the retrospect of the month, and of course by the construction given by Mr. Keogh, we ought not to publish such a retrospect.

Mr. *J. Cassell.*

16 May 1851.

1299. Mr. *Tufnell.*] When the decision shall have been given in the case now pending, the law will, in your opinion, be then no longer doubtful; if it is decided that the "Narrative of Current Events" should be stamped, you will have no doubt that your publication will be liable to a stamp?—No, as far as this; I say the difficulty that I shall have to determine with respect to "The Working Man's Friend" is this: there is a subject in which they take a deep interest, and that is, the abolition of capital punishment. There happened to be an execution in a previous week, and two or three cases had recently occurred, and we inserted an article upon circumstantial evidence; now, to carry out the letter of the law, we ought not to have inserted that article.

1300. *Chairman.*] That is something more than the letter of the law; it says that you must not comment and observe upon occurrences and facts, and so on, at a less price than 6 *d.*, and in a smaller size than two sheets, without being stamped; what is the price of that?—This is only 1 *d.*

1301. Then the cheapness, and the size of it, at once bring it within the stamp law for commenting upon an execution which has recently taken place; you consider it a violation of the law to comment upon any public event, do you not?—If taken in the strict manner there laid down; there is scarcely a publication in existence which would not be obliged to leave out some of the most important articles if that construction is to be put upon the magazines that I am speaking of.

1302. Then your business, as an extensive publisher of that description of works, of a moral character, for the working classes, could not be carried on if this Stamp Act were to be enforced?—If it were to be enforced according to the version that is given in the exact words of the Act, it would very materially interfere with my business and the immense capital that I have invested in this publishing trade.

1303. Mr. *Rich.*] A blind and rigid carrying out of the letter of almost any fiscal law would be impossible, at least very difficult, would it not?—I do not know.



1304. Would

Mr. *J. Cassell.*

16 May 1851.

1304. Would it be practicable to carry out the present Stamp Act literally and with the extreme rigour of the law?—It would be very difficult.

1305. Mr. *Ewart.*] You state that the law at present is very uncertain?—Yes.

1306. And if made more uncertain by being made more severe, it would become very oppressive, would it not?—Yes, it would become very oppressive, not only to capitalists, but it would arrest, in my decided opinion, the moral and social progress of the people. Almost every movement is dependent upon the press for the advancement of its principles. There is one movement in which I take a very deep interest; that is the temperance movement. We have been the means of spreading our principles almost entirely, with the exception of the advocacy of working men, through the medium of the press. We have a small number of periodicals, which may be termed newspapers, which are allowed to be in existence; of these we have stamped copies, but they are merely to send to the newspapers or to send abroad, or for the supply of subscribers in the country; while the great bulk of them are bought for a penny, unstamped. This is one of them, a temperance publication (*producing the same*), full of what we call temperance news, and everything connected with the temperance movement, and this must cease to exist if the decision is given against the "Household Narrative."

1307. Mr. *Rich.*] You are aware of the distinction between class subjects and subjects of general news, with regard to papers that are published?—Yes. Then we have not had that laid down except as the exercise of a discretionary power on the part of the Board of Inland Revenue, who are allowed to be the arbiters in those questions.

1308. You stated that "The Builder" was one of those; that it published news, but at the same time it might be considered as a class newspaper?—Yes, the same as "The Athenæum" or "The Literary Gazette."

1309. In these class distinctions, do not you think that there might be some whose subjects might so nearly approach to politics as to bring them within the definition of a newspaper?—For my part I cannot understand what constitutes a newspaper. This gives public news; news affecting a certain movement; it is a class publication of course; but I should consider it a very dangerous power for any man to be entrusted with, the definition of what constitutes a newspaper.

1310. But that power would be under the correction of public opinion, and its exercise would be tested by trials before

Mr. *J. Cassell.*

16 May 1851.

before juries?—Yes; but then it would make the Act of Parliament of no avail, because it would be gradually widening the breach, which has been the case as it is. There are a number of magazines giving comments upon the events of the month, and also giving all the events of the month.

1311. The interpretation of the Act of Parliament would be considerably explained and enforced by decisions in the courts of law?—Yes.

1312. Mr. *Ewart.*] With respect to such publications as "The Working Man's Friend" and others which advocate certain principles that you deem beneficial to the working classes, such as temperance and self-instruction; the chief mode of making those principles prevail is by connecting them with passing events, and so giving them a practical application; and you think that you are prevented by the existing law, or you are impeded in doing so?—Yes.

1313. You consider that the illustration of such principles by facts is an essential ingredient in the promulgation of those principles?—It is almost everything to our success. I take this "Working Man's Friend" for instance; it is almost entirely a literary work, on which I expend considerable sums; it is published at 1 *d.*, but the getting up of each number would be somewhere, with editor and writers, about 10 *l.* for each number. Now if I could introduce into this magazine a more extended account of what is doing in the world, if I could make half of it literary and half of it news, I feel convinced that my circulation would be more than double with the working classes. There is such a thirst for current events that it gives a freshness to it; in fact it is almost like sauce.

1314. Sir *J. Walmsley.*] You have stated that in the event of the action going against the "Household Narrative," the temperance advocates would be put down also?—We should be under considerable apprehension in publishing 1 *d.* periodicals. An individual would feel himself very uneasy about it, and you may depend upon it that in soliciting an opinion from the Board of Inland Revenue, that opinion is sure to be against you.

1315. Will you inform the Committee whether you do not know that similar publications to yours, local publications, have already been put down by the Board of Inland Revenue? —I have had my attention drawn to the fact by the public press, containing an account of "The Norwich Reformer," and also "The Wakefield and West Riding Examiner."

1316. My question had immediate reference to particular

 papers

Mr. *J. Cassell.*

16 May 1851.

referred, that there is a vast amount of demoralizing and impure trash issued from the weekly press, which finds customers somewhere?—Yes.

1325. Are these publications evanescent; do you consider that they generally have a large circulation, or does each number not attain a large circulation?—You will find that in the cheap literature a great improvement is taking place; they may have a large circulation, and there are several in existence. I took an interest in ascertaining what progress the most demoralizing publications made. There was one called "The Town," another "The Paul Pry," and another called "Peeping Tom." All those publications, I believe, seem to have passed away. For a time they had a very large circulation I know, but the intelligence of the public was such, and in our factories the moral tone is such, that a man known to take in such a publication as "The Town" or "Peeping Tom" would, to a very great extent, lose caste with his more intelligent fellow men, and he must take it in on the sly, just to gratify a morbid appetite. Then there are a class of publications which if you look into you will see the contrast; take what is called the "London Journal," and you will find a very great improvement taking place; such periodicals keeping pace, as it were, with the improved morals of the people.

1326. Mr. *Ewart.*] Then you infer that if the greatest liberty were allowed to the publication of these small papers, they would effectually counteract the influence of the more immoral publications?—I believe if you would give us freedom not only from the penny stamp, but likewise from the paper duty, that desirable object would be effected; for I am just feeling the effect of the restrictive law now with my "Working Man's Friend." The profit of the office, so to speak, is sadly interfered with through the advance that has taken place in the price of paper. The consumption of paper is greater for each individual in America, that is for the purposes of literature, than in England; and they have no penny stamp, nor any paper duty; consequently they are now coming into our market, purchasing up the raw material, and they ship it at Hull, and they ship it at Liverpool, and at several other of our ports. The consequence is that many sorts have gone up 30 and 40 per cent., and a general rise of a halfpenny per lb. has taken place upon the price of the paper. I know that in one publication alone there was only an advance of 6 *d.* a ream, and that made a difference of 500 *l.* a year to that one publication.

1327. Mr. *Rich.*] Would you state from your own great experience

Mr. *J. Cassell.*

16 May 1851.

experience that there has been in the present state of affairs a vast improvement both in the stamped and unstamped periodical publications?—Yes.

1328. If the decision with respect to the "Household Narrative" be favourable to Mr. Dickens, it would have a very beneficial effect, would it not?—As far as monthly publications are concerned it would.

1329. It would set all those questions at rest which are now in a state of uncertainty?—Yes, as far as monthly publications are concerned.

1330. Mr. *Tufnell.*] Have you had much opportunity of ascertaining the character and the supply of unstamped publications that are circulated in the metropolis?—Yes, as good an opportunity as most persons of looking into the character of the different publications, of knowing the circulation, and also of understanding what is the public taste.

1331. *Chairman.*] Do you publish any weekly publications? —Yes.

1332. Is "The Working Man's Friend" a weekly publication?—Yes.

1333. Then the decision upon the "Narrative of Current Events" will not decide the case of "The Working Man's Friend," as to whether it ought to be allowed to comment or observe upon facts or occurrences. "The Working Man's Friend" contains comments and observations upon passing events, does it not?—We found an article upon anything; just as I was saying of the Great Exhibition, or anything whereby we can give an article to forward those views which we consider have a tendency to promote morality.

1334. As the Act states "that any person who comments or observes upon facts at more frequent intervals than 26 days between each publication, and at a price less than 6*d.*, or of a size less than two sheets," which that is, "is liable to a stamp;" whichever way the question as to the "Narative of Current Events" be decided, it would still leave your "Working Man's Friend" a questionable publication, would it not? —I should go under this impression, that if the Board of Inland Revenue thought proper at any time to prosecute me, taking the literal wording of the Act, they could do so; but I should go on still as I do at present, under the impression that they would not trouble their heads about me.

1335. You carry on your business in the hope that they will not enforce the law?—Yes.

1336. Mr. *Tufnell.*] You would think that the law would not be put in force?—Yes. I should think that, with a number

Mr. *J. Cassell.*

16 May 1851.

number of my neighbours, we were all sailing in the same boat together; if that law should be strictly enforced it would be mine and my neighbours' destruction.

1337. Mr. *Rich.*] Or if attempted to be enforced there would always be aa appeal to a jury, would there not?—There would be in that respect; but I do not know how far the powers go with reference to the penny stamp. I know the power with respect to advertisements; that the Board of Inland Revenue have very great power, and they would not give you the chance of going to a jury. I am just bringing out a publication now, and I may come into collision with the Board of Inland Revenue with respect to advertisement duty. It happened to me with regard to my paper in this way, that being connected also with a weekly journal, I found it inconvenient, and I agreed with two persons to collect the advertisements, and they were to pay the advertisement duty, but they neglected to do so. I was not aware of it; and one day, without any previous notice, I was arrested. I do not know whether their powers extend to the penny stamp, but I was arrested, and had to find bail upon the spot.

1338. *Chairman.*] They would have the power to seize your presses, and to suspend your business, and, if I understand rightly, you would then be left to seek your own redress, as against them, for an improper proceeding?—Yes; then I say that a man, unless he is a very strong man—any small man, though he might have justice on his side, if they placed him in such a position, would be ruined.

1339. If they were to stamp "The Working Man's Friend," what would be the effect upon the publication itself, if you carried it on as a stamped publication?—That is a question which has often forced itself upon me; here I have a very large sheet. As I say, I pay 10 *l.* each for each number for literary matter; you may ask, why not make this sheet into a newspaper, it would make a very good newspaper, and publish it at 2 *d.*, and pay 10 *l.* for collecting news? why, for this reason: to create facilities for cheap publications, you must allow a considerable discount to a bookseller, upwards of 40 per cent.; for instance, this is published at 8 *d.* per dozen, and 13 are a dozen; I reckon it 2 *l.* 10 *s.* a thousand, and if I published this as a newspaper, I must find every week about 208 *l.* capital; look at the capital that I should have to find, with a circulation of 50,000, to pay for the penny stamps, and upon that I should have no profit whatever, and no interest for my capital; neither could I allow a bookseller any profit; for, from paying me the extra 1 *d.*, the profit must come out of the

first

Mr. *J. Cassell.*

16 May 1851.

first 1 *d.*, and not upon the 2 *d.*; I could not publish this sheet under 2½ *d.*; I must have a halfpenny to give a profit upon the 1 *d.* paid, to pay the interest upon the capital.

1340. Mr. *Rich.*] A halfpenny would be a large profit, would it not?—We have full 40 per cent. This is a penny publication, and 1,000 fetch 4 *l.* 3 *s.* 4 *d.*, and all I get for those is 2 *l.* 10 *s.* per thousand.

1341. Mr. *Ewart.*] According to that, the existing law is a premium upon the dearer publication, is it not?—It is with the penny stamp; you have no opportunity of doing anything unless it is in a dear publication, that is, to serve any particular cause.

1342. *Chairman.*] You say that the circulation of that paper is 50,000?—Yes.

1343. Fifty thousand weekly?—Yes.

1344. You would be obliged to raise the price to 2½ *d.* if the law were enforced, and you were obliged to stamp, would you not?—Yes.

1345. What would your circulation probably be then; how many would you sell at 2½ *d.*?—I should sell very few.

1346. In fact, it would kill the publication to stamp it, would it not?—Yes, and if I published it at 1½ *d.* The Messrs. Chambers started their "Miscellany," a penny publication, and it attained a circulation of 80,000 weekly, which they gave up.

1347. Stamping your paper would destroy it?—Yes.

1348. In fact, it lives through the neglect of the law, does it not?—Yes; we make it entirely now as a literary publication.

[Attendance of witness required for the following Session]

*Martis,* 20° *die Maii,* 1851.

MEMBERS PRESENT.

Mr. Ewart.
Mr. Rich.
Mr. Sotheron.
Mr. Stafford.
Sir J. Walmsley.
Mr. Tufnell.
Mr. G. A. Hamilton.
Mr. Cobden.
Sir T. F. Lewis.

THE RIGHT HON. T. MILNER GIBSON IN THE CHAIR.

Mr. *John Cassell* called in; and further Examined.

Mr. *J. Cassell.*

20 May 1851.

1349. *Chairman.*] WHEN the Committee adjourned on Friday, you were stating that to a considerable extent the law was allowed to sleep as regarded commenting and observing upon facts, and that in consequence of this neglect a publication like the "Working Man's Friend," carried on as you carry it on, is allowed to exist?—Yes.

1350. Is it your habit every week to comment and observe upon the interesting public events of the day?—In connexion with the "Working Man's Friend," we take up, as I have before stated, any question that we may consider connected with the social well-being of the working classes, or those questions with which we are known to be identified—as I instanced, the Great Exhibition. We should take notice in some form or other of what had transpired during the past week, and throw it into the form of a letter; or if it was upon any other great question, such as the abolition of capital punishment.

1351. It is the fact that you do comment upon such kind of public events, and if you were precluded from doing that, according to the Act of Parliament, a publication like the "Working Man's Friend" could not be carried on successfully, could it?—No.

1352. Mr. *Rich.*] You stated, I think, that it was not so much because it was interesting to your readers, as that it was conducive to the object that you have in view?—Yes; of course, if we cannot make our publication interesting to our readers, it must limit the publication. As an instance, one week we left out an article on the Exhibition; we were anxious to make room for other articles.

1353. If

Mr. *J. Cassell.*

20 May 1851.

1353. If I understand you rightly, you mean interesting to your readers, but within the class subjects of your paper?—Yes.

1354. Mr. *Sotheron.*] What was the result in that case you were about to mention?—That week we received a number of letters from publishers in the country, stating that if we left out those articles on the Exhibition which had taken up the events of the week, and were interesting to the working classes, the circulation would be greatly affected.

1355. *Chairman.*] It has been stated that the stamping of news is considered no burthen by many in consequence of the postal privilege being afforded, so that a stamped paper may be carried free by post. Do you consider that that arrangement is a great benefit to the public, and that it affords all the convenience of a post office to publications?—Certainly the transmission of papers through the Post Office to some individuals is a great convenience, but to the public at large I think it is not such a convenience as people imagine; because we know that in any part of the kingdom we can obtain a daily paper on the day of publication, and the obtaining that paper is not to be attributable to the convenience of the Post Office, but to the railways. But for obtaining that paper on the day of publication I have not only to pay 1 *d.* stamp,—which, taking the argument of the convenience of the Post Office, is levied for the facilities afforded by the Post Office, and which I do not use with respect to that paper,—but I have also to pay an extra 1 *d.*; they charge me 6 *d.* for that paper on the day of publication. They put on that extra 1 *d.* for the special carriage of that newspaper, for its delivery; consequently, to a very great extent, with the daily press, the public do not avail themselves of the facilities afforded by the Post Office.

1356. Do you avail yourself of the privilege of free transmission in any way in the circulation of the "Working Man's Friend," or can it be of any use to you?—We avail ourselves of the Post Office, not to subscribers, but merely to the press. We supply the public through the trade. We do not avail ourselves of the Post Office in the least; but the "Working Man's Friend" is stamped, and we avail ourselves of the penny stamp, because if we, like all other publishers, send it without a penny stamp, we should pay twopence; we therefore send a single copy to each of the newspapers for review. We send about a hundred to the newspapers.

1357. Out of the 50,000 that you mentioned?—Yes; and sometimes more.

1358. You stamp a few out of the whole number, for the purpose

Mr. *J. Cassell.*

20 May 1851.

purpose of sending those few by the post, do you not?—Yes.

1359. And you distribute the remaining portion by private means?—Yes, by carriers. We send off immense bales late on Saturday nights; our parcels go off, and are delivered the next morning.

1360. If the authorities were to tell you that you were to stamp your whole 50,000, and that in return for that they would give you the benefit of any of those 50,000 going free by post, you would not consider that much of a boon to your publication, nor to the public, would you?—I should consider it my destruction.

1361. Do you consider that the removal of the stamp, and charging 1 *d.* only for the paper transmitted by post, would seriously affect the revenue?—I believe in the first instance it might affect the revenue, but ultimately it would prove a benefit. I consider that the abolition of the penny stamp would be the means of creating a number of new papers; and not only so, but be the means of greatly extending the circulation of those already in existence. Consequently, imagining that if the 1 *d.* stamp were repealed, we should still have the facilities of the Post Office, the same as with the American newspapers, and the newspapers published in the Channel Islands; for they have no 1 *d.* stamp; still they have the use of the Post Office by affixing a Queen's head; but they have not the power of reposting. I consider that there would be a great posting of newspapers; not merely by five or six individuals, as is the case now, subscribing for one newspaper, but by those five or six individually taking in a newspaper; and we know, especially with the humbler classes, their desire, if any event takes place in their respective neighbourhoods, to be informed of it; and when families are grown up, and are very much spread, their desire to transmit a paper to their friends and relatives. As it is now, the Post Office is made use of, not for the circulation of a paper direct to an individual, but a paper may be circulating till it is almost worn out, through making use of the penny stamp. Generally, by the transmission of a paper direct to one individual, without the power of reposting, and looking to the great increase that would take place in the circulation of newspapers, I believe that an equal number, if not a greater number, would be transmitted by post, and pay the penny postage.

1362. Mr. *Tufnell.*] Did you intend to say that the abolition of the penny stamp would increase the sale of this paper, the "Working Man's Friend"?—No; but the abolition of the

the penny stamp would increase the circulation greatly of the "Working Man's Friend," for this reason; we should then alter the character of the "Working Man's Friend." Instead of commenting upon a subject or a passing event, we should alter its dimensions and its appearance, and make it in part a literary paper, and in part a newspaper; because even the dimensions of it now would admit of its forming a very good newspaper, even as a daily paper.

1363. You take care now, do you not, that the news inserted in it is not such as to bring you under the operation of the Stamp Act?—If the Act were strictly interpreted now, we might be interfered with, and not only our paper, but almost every periodical that is published. I take up Dickens's "Household Words;" they do not give it as if it were news, but they take up an event and comment upon it, and give all the particulars relating to that event, embodying it in an article. We do not say that an accident took place in the city, just giving the bare particulars of it, but we might, if we saw that it would be of importance to the public, say that houses should be so constructed as to prevent those accidents, and we should found an article upon such an event; but by the strict interpretation of the Act, I think that we are not permitted to make those comments. If the penny stamp were removed, we should then give it, and give a freshness to our periodical, and insert the news of the day, because we know, especially among the working classes, the anxiety they manifest to be made acquainted with current events.

1364. Mr. *Rich.*] How do you show that the revenue would derive a benefit by the abolition of the stamp duty on newspapers?—Of course I am reasoning not in connexion with my periodical alone, but I imagine we should not only have weekly newspapers, but we should have daily papers; and that too, not only in London (looking at the facilities of the electric telegraph), but also in our country towns at a great distance. I am not only the publisher of a periodical, but I am the proprietor of a newspaper, which is a class newspaper; and almost every week we have letters to this effect, "Please to discontinue my paper; our club is broken up." Five working men will each be subscribing their penny a week to take in the paper; two of that number perhaps, or three, may be agricultural labourers, and remove, and the consequence is, that those remaining cannot afford it; they close their club, and they cannot continue the paper any longer; to those five individuals, there is just one postage, but if each of those persons could have the newspaper for a penny, which might be

Mr. *J. Cassell.*

20 May 1851.

be supplied to them if it were not for the penny stamp, this paper might be delivered to them independently of the Post Office. It may be a local paper, and this local paper would be greatly circulated by post. After a man had read his weekly paper, his Lancashire paper, perhaps he has a son in London, and some remarkable event has taken place, a wedding, or an accident of local interest which he wishes to communicate to his son; and I know by my own experience, that anything relating to Lancashire that is striking I am always anxious to see, and my friends are always anxious to communicate; so there would be that desire to transmit that intelligence by paying an extra penny.

1365. What proportion of your paper now in circulation pays the penny stamp in comparison with those numbers which go by other means?—As to the "Working Man's Friend," I circulate scarcely any by post, except now and then to send to a local newspaper.

1366. If in a mercantile point of view it is now so advantageous to you to send almost the whole of your impressions by private means, why should not the same causes operate upon all other newspapers if the stamp were abolished?—They would to a very great extent, but it is very different, particularly as the intelligence there may constitute news. We know that in villages they like having the news immediately. To one portion of the population the Post Office would be a great convenience, while to another portion it would be none at all.

1367. In the earlier part of your evidence you stated that by means of railways newspapers can now be conveyed to almost every part of the country more quickly than through the Post Office?—Yes, according to the present arrangements of the Post Office; but there are a great number of persons, it is true, whose cases the town facilities do not meet; for instance, for that class of persons there are the evening editions, which are transmitted and delivered the next morning through the Post Office. Of course, we make use of the railways on account of the earlier delivery.

1368. Would not these same evening papers be transmitted in a mass by means of the railways to the great towns, instead of being sent by post, each paying a penny?—I believe to the great towns they would.

1369. How then would the revenue be benefited by taking off the penny stamp?—By the great increase that would take place by the papers going through the post; they would so augment from transmission to individuals, the greater number

of

Mr. *J. Cassell.*

20 May 1851.

of persons taking in newspapers, that there would be an immense increase of transmission by the railways, and there would gradually spring up such a circulation through the Post Office, that the revenue ultimately would not be affected.

1370. Mr. *Ewart.*] That would be because they would have the freshest news under the change proposed?—No; I am just looking at it in this way: there would be a great tendency on the part of the people to receive a paper, and after reading it, though it is only a penny paper, to fold it up and send it to their friends. There would be a great number of persons in what I may call a scattered population, and there would not be the convenience of sending to them or to the different places three or four papers, and they would avail themselves of the Post Office for that purpose; for instance, I may say, with regard to a publication which I bring out, the Temperance publication, we have a great number of what I call scattered subscribers, and though the price is merely a penny, they pay twopence for it, to have the convenience of the post.

1371. Which they would do under the change proposed, and why do they not do it now?—I will endeavour to show the Committee that I could publish a newspaper, my "Working Man's Friend," at 2*d.*; and if I could create such great numbers of direct subscribers, it would pay me. I should have no discount, no reductions to take place, not selling them through the trade, and we should get a greater number of subscribers who would pay their 2*s.*, a greater number than at the present time; but under existing circumstances, we could not get such a number of subscribers as would induce us to publish a cheap newspaper. Take the threepenny newspapers; they have to send three-fourths of them through the trade, and about one-fourth to independent subscribers. Take my newspaper; I say I have 1,000 subscribers, and I get 4*l.* 3*s.* 4*d.* more profit upon that 1,000 subscribers than if I sent them through the trade.

1372. Then if the stamp were abolished, more would be sent through the post in consequence of the increase in the number of subscribers?—Yes, from the great augmentation of single subscribers.

1373. Mr. *Rich.*] Setting aside the question of cheapness or dearness, I do not see how it could be more beneficial to you and to newspaper publishers, or to the receivers of the newspapers, that their papers should be transmitted at 1 *d.* a piece through the Post Office, than if they were sent by railway?—I speak of a portion of the population in some parts. If there were only half a dozen subscribers in a district, an

 extra

Mr. *J. Cassell.* 20 May 1851.

facilities for the delivery of papers, but we know that persons all over the kingdom prefer a direct delivery. But the Committee must bear in mind that there is a strong feeling on the part of newsvendors against the publishers availing themselves of the opportunity of sending their papers direct from their offices to their subscribers; they look at it as robbing the trade.

1386. Mr. *Sotheron.*] With regard to your own papers, if your plan were adopted what alteration would take place, do you think, as to their delivery. At present you send them down in large masses to the considerable towns, where they are distributed by private hands, do you not?—That is more particularly the case with the daily papers, not the weeklies.

1387. What alteration would take place, do you think, in that respect; under the new system suggested, do you think that those newspapers would be sent down, individually stamped, by post, or would they be sent down in a mass and distributed in the different localities?—I believe to a great extent they would be sent down in a mass.

1388. By railroad, and not through the post?—Yes, they would be sent by the post if the Post Office would meet the necessity in the morning; supposing the Post Office met the requirements of the public, so that they had the receiving and transmitting by the first train. The reason why the public avail themselves of the railway is this—that they can get them sent earlier by railway than through the post. The paper for Manchester goes through the Post Office and does not leave London before 10 o'clock in the morning, but if it were to go by railway it would leave London at half-past six o'clock.

1389. Is it not the fact, that in the answers you have given to the questions put to you, you contemplated some alteration of the Post Office arrangements, by which they would give greater facilities for delivering the early papers?—Yes; I have always supposed that the Chancellor of the Exchequer, keeping an eye to the revenue, would compete with private enterprise.

1390. Therefore it would be hardly fair to make a comparison between the existing state of things and the state of things which you contemplate if your plan were carried into execution?—We can scarcely estimate that; it is scarcely possible for a person who is only acquainted with the existing state of things to estimate the change.

1391. As matters at present stand, the great increase which you contemplate in the revenue of the Post Office would be from the papers not being reposted, but from fresh papers

Mr. *J. Cassell.*

20 May 1851.

papers being put into the post; that is the principal element from which you think that the Post Office, as matters now stand, would receive an increase of revenue?—Yes, and from the great increase of individual purchasers of newspapers; now there are four or five individuals to one newspaper, but each individual would then become the purchaser of a newspaper.

1392. Supposing your plan were fully carried out, as you contemplate it, there would be an additional gain to the Post Office, you expecting if greater facilities were afforded, from the greater number of individual papers that would be sent by post?—Yes, especially if they competed with the railways as to time; if we had an early post, as great a number would go direct through the Post Office as by railway; the public gives a preference to that which brings them the earliest news.

1393. Sir *J. Walmsley.*] Have you formed any estimate of the mercantile difference between the cost of sending a thousand newspapers from London to Liverpool by railway, and then distributing them to the readers, and by paying a penny stamp or a penny postage, sending them direct?—No; but I must say that there would be a gain on the part of the publishers; where there was a large circulation, and having their own delivery, they could deliver cheaper than they could send by paying the penny stamp.

1394. You send them by railway, and you have then to employ agents to distribute them in the different parts of a own, by which much time is lost; have you formed any estimate as to what would be the difference between that cost and sending them through the post?—No, I have not.

1395. Mr. *Cobden.*] Practically, I believe, when a great number of newspapers are sent, the London morning papers for instance, to Liverpool or Manchester by railway, they are not for the purpose of being distributed from house to house by the person receiving them in Liverpool or Manchester, but the great bulk of them are for the reading-rooms, and a considerable portion I believe are sold there to individuals who call at the shop for them?—Yes; no doubt there are great numbers in Manchester who are regular subscribers to newsvendors, and those regular subscribers, for the privilege of having their papers on the day of publication, have to pay an extra penny. We know that if we had an unstamped press, something like the "Working Man's Friend," it would not be a delivery from house to house. Those persons who wish to become regular subscribers, the greater number of them, would receive

Mr. *J. Cassell.*

20 May 1851.

receive the paper direct through the post; but the cheap press publishers would have their parcels, and the public would not pay them for delivery, but go to the shop; and the same person estimates the number he can get through of the "Working Man's Friend," and he takes those, and those are not delivered singly to the subscribers at the subscribers' houses; the people go to the shops and purchase them.

1396. You, who are so well acquainted with Manchester, know that there is a person, a Mr. Lewis, in Market-street, who, if you resided there, would supply you with the "Times" newspaper at about two or three o'clock on the afternoon of each day of its publication: what price would you pay for that?—Sixpence.

1397. Delivered at your own house?—Yes.

1398. In that case you pay the penny stamp and a penny extra, do you not?—Yes; that is paid to cover the cost of carriage and delivery. If I put my name down with Mr. Lewis, and say, "Order me this paper through the post," I should only pay 5 *d.*; but if I say, "Deliver it to me on the day of publication," if Mr. Lewis delivers it, I must pay the penny stamp, and also pay him a penny for the extra delivery.

1399. Then it appears to me that your answer to the Honourable Member for Bolton would be, that private enterprise cannot compete with the Post Office in delivering newspapers to single individuals at their homes?—That is if the Post Office will only render the facilities.

1400. If the Post Office made arrangements by which they could have more frequent deliveries, they would be enabled to supersede altogether the private dealers, as they would not charge the 1 *d.* for delivery?—Yes, as far as this; there are a great number of persons desirous of having the papers delivered at their houses.

1401. Do not you think that if Mr. Rowland Hill had the management of the postage upon newspapers in the same way as he has the postage upon letters, he would make the same arrangements to compete with private traders in the delivery of newspapers in the country, that he has in London in the more frequent delivery of letters by the penny post, with his present organization of postmen travelling to and fro, and deliver them cheaper than the private trader could, and quicker? —I should say so, having his army of deliverers at his command; whereas with newspapers alone, they would have to go out and travel over the same district merely to deliver to subscribers.

1402. Mr. *Rich.*] You say that they now charge a penny at

at Manchester for the delivery of a London newspaper on the same day by private hand?—Yes. Mr. *J. Cassell.*

1403. That is a delivery not to a very large class of persons, is it?—It is a delivery more to the inns and some of the leading firms and the reading-rooms, and they have all to pay 6 *d.* 20 May 1851.

1404. Therefore the private distributor of this small number of newspapers in Manchester can compete, and does compete, with the Post Office, inasmuch as he distributes his paper for 1 *d.*; he does not charge 2 *d.*, because the 2 *d.* is made up of the 1 *d.* charged upon the newspaper and the 1 *d.* which the distributor charges?—Yes; but then the individual subscribers in Manchester most likely have their papers delivered by newsmen, and why they prefer them through newsmen is, because their papers are transmitted at half-past six in the morning; whereas, if they got them through the Post Office, they would not only pay the postage, but from that postage a revenue would be derived; they now avail themselves of the newsvendors.

1405. If they can distribute a few papers for 1 *d.*, supposing that the whole of the newspapers in Manchester were distributed by them, they might have such an organization as would enable them to distribute them at much less probably than 1 *d.*, might they not?—Yes; but they would not deliver them; for instance, a publisher would not deliver to any one.

1406. My question referred to London newspapers coming from London in a mass to Manchester?—Yes; if they went in a mass to Manchester, and if you had those papers delivered at your own house, you would have to pay for the delivery; it is a very different matter in a publication; unless it is a high-priced publication, you must go to the publisher's shop and purchase it, and you take the chance whether you can get a copy; you must put your name down as a regular subscriber to depend upon that. A person is fearful lest he should not see the news, and instead of running the chance of not getting his paper, he would become a direct subscriber.

1407. If the stamp duty were taken off, might not a company be organized at Manchester for the distribution of all the London newspapers, and be able to distribute them at a much lower price than a penny?—No; I do not think any company could; it would be entirely a matter with individuals.

1408. You find that individuals can now do it separately on a small scale for a penny?—Yes; we are talking about a small scale, but the circulation of daily papers by rail is enormous.

 1409. It

Mr. *J. Cassell.*

20 May 1851.

1409. It is small in comparison with the number that arrive by post, is it not?—I should say not in towns like Manchester.

1410. Sir *J. Walmsley.*] Your previous answers have had reference to the transmission of papers from London to Manchester by post, those papers that are sent off early, the morning papers?—Yes.

1411. Now apply your mind to those that are sent out in the evening; evening papers or cheaper publications that would be sent out of an evening, they would be delivered, I apprehend, as regularly and as cheaply by nine o'clock in the morning at each of the large towns as far as Edinburgh, Glasgow, Liverpool, and Birmingham, and more promptly and with greater certainty than by any other means, would they not?—Yes, where all circumstances are equal; take, for instance, the evening papers; there are very few persons in the country who receive those through newsmen, I mean local newsmen; they go direct to the subscribers, and are delivered by post, because there is no advantage in getting them through newsmen.

1412. For such papers as you have spoken of, cheap publications such as the "Working Man's Friend," would you propose to send those papers by post through the country?—If we had daily news in we should have a very large circulation through the Post Office, because people are anxious to see the news, and they would get it the next morning.

1413. Then instead of sending 50,000 or 60,000 away as you do now by railway, you would send the greater proportion by post, would you not?—Yes, I should send a great number, not the greater proportion. No doubt I should, as an individual, render every facility for creating as great a circulation as possible, more especially in the large towns. There is no doubt that, containing news, of our late editions the greater number would go by post.

1414. Mr. *Rich.*] You would send them in a way most profitable to yourself and most convenient to the readers, would you not?—Certainly.

1415. *Chairman.*] The competition among newspapers if the stamps were removed would be greatly increased, would it not?—No doubt of it.

1416. Do you contemplate a penny daily newspaper?—Yes.

1417. Are there many people employed earning wages in the production of a newspaper?—A great number; more so than in any kind of literary production.

1418. Then the more you limit the number of newspapers that

that are produced, the more you limit the employment of labour in producing them?—Certainly.

Mr. *J. Cassell.*

20 May 1851.

1419. Have you formed any estimate as to the number of persons or families that might be supported in producing a penny daily paper?—I have not gone into a calculation as to the number of individuals upon a daily paper, but there are a great number of compositors that have to be employed. I have not estimated the number, but I should say that it would take about 20 compositors; that is, as a cheap newspaper; I am speaking as if the penny stamp were removed; of course with existing papers the staff is very large indeed.

1420. Mr. *Rich.*] As a prudent man, if the stamp duty were taken off to-morrow, you would go into a very careful estimate of what would be your outgoings in conducting a penny newspaper before you entered into the speculation, would you not?—Yes.

1421. You now talk with tolerable certainty of the circulation of penny newspapers; have you made any estimate upon the subject?—Yes, I have estimated the circulation of penny newspapers at 50,000 daily. I presume by putting the question the Honourable Member is keeping in view the removal of the penny stamp. Looking upon it as a labour question, it is beyond all conception the great increase that would be given to the employment of the people. In the first place, there would be an enormous increase in the consumption of paper, and we know that in the production of paper there is a greater amount of labour employed than in any other article. I take up my publication, and the fabric upon which it is printed derives its value more from the labour employed upon it than the cost of the material; and after the production of the paper we have the compositors, and of course, if we had three papers where we now have one, there would be a great increase to the employment of compositors.

1422. *Chairman.*] Would there not be a greatly increased demand for the services of literary men; would not good writers and men of talent be more in request, and be able more readily to find employment and remuneration for their services than they do now?—I believe that if we were to have cheap daily papers, they would become partly newspapers and partly literary; of course each proprietor would make his paper as attractive as possible, by employing first-rate talent in the production, whether of fiction or narrative, or any other kind of literary production, similar to the American and French papers.

1423. Mr. *Ewart.*] A higher description of talent would be

Mr. *J. Cassell.*

20 May 1851.

be employed upon the unstamped press, would it not?—Yes; now we simply employ writers for the leading article, a political article.

1424. *Chairman.*] Do you suppose that there is a feeling on the part of the proprietors of the established newspapers, that the stamp affords them a kind of protection from increased competition?—If I may speak as an individual, I should expect that if the penny stamp were removed, the paper of which I am now the proprietor would be seriously affected; I have no doubt about it.

1425. Your established newspaper?—Yes; that is, the high-priced paper, for which I get 5*d.* a copy. I consider there would be a complete revolution in the newspaper press of this kingdom.

1426. Mr. *Ewart.*] Do not you consider that the general result of repealing the penny stamp, and charging postage for reposting a newspaper, would be to increase the circulation of local newspapers?—Decidedly to increase the circulation of local newspapers, and also to create a new class of news papers, though at the same time the old newspapers would endeavour to meet the altered circumstances in which they would be placed.

1427. Do you think that the increase of local newspapers would be an advantage to the different districts in the country in which they were established?—I should say decidedly so.

1428. You think, do you not, that local information is of great consequence?—Yes; we in London, unless we have a class newspaper, stand no chance in competing with the local newspapers.

1429. You have adverted to agricultural labourers, and to the papers they take in; what newspapers generally circulate among them?—Speaking of agricultural labourers, I should say that there is a very small minority who do see a newspaper; there is an intelligent class amongst them who are anxious to see a newspaper, of whom I have many subscribers to my paper, that form themselves into clubs.

1430. Do you consider that if the penny stamp were abolished, you would be enabled to publish newspapers on equal terms with the publishers of American newspapers?—No, not merely by the removal of the penny stamp.

1431. What other alteration, in your opinion, would be required?—The great source of support to the American newspapers is their advertisements; consequently, if the penny stamp were removed, and the advertisement duty continued, we

Mr. *J. Cassell.*

20 May 1851.

we should still have great difficulties to contend against. I take up an American newspaper, and in some of them there are upwards of 1,000 advertisements; if they only get 2*s.* on the advertisements, they have their 100*l.*, independently of the circulation; but if the circulation only paid their expenses, and their advertisements were profit, there is a splendid property. The difficulties we have to contend with by the regulations as to advertisement duties are great impediments. I bring out a publication in connexion with the Great Exhibition, with the view of affording facilities for persons obtaining lodgings; there are a great number of what may be termed advertisements of people who can provide apartments or furnished houses. We charge them 2*s.* 6*d.* for the insertion of their advertisements in that paper, and 1*s.* 6*d.* we have to pay as advertisement duty; we only obtain therefore 1*s.* But it is not that alone. I was anxious to increase the number of insertions, but after the appearance of that publication I was prevented from so doing, and if I were to add now to that publication any fresh matter, every insertion would be charged fresh duty. I was anxious to affix a date for which any lodging was taken, so that a person in the country, by glancing at it, could see that that lodging was taken from such a date to such a date, but the advertisement duty prevents my doing so. If I were to put a date this week to any impression that I worked off of that publication, the whole of those insertions would be charged fresh advertisement duty.

1432. You mean that what might be considered as an appendix to a former advertisement, would be deemed a new advertisement?—Yes; if any addition took place by the insertion of another advertisement, or the insertion of any fresh matter, it would be considered a new edition of that publication, and consequently the whole would be charged with a new advertisement duty.

1433. For instance, supposing you had inserted an adverment about a railway, and subsequently you thought proper to add to that advertisement by stating that steam-boats were connected with that railway, you would have to pay a new advertisement duty?—Yes.

1434. Although it had reference to the old advertisement? —Yes. We are allowed 24 hours with the weekly newspaper on Friday, and on the Saturday we may put in other advertisements by heading them "Additional Advertisements;" but if we were to bring out the paper on the following Monday we could not do that; consequently the circulation of that publication is greatly impeded, and also my profits

Mr. *J. Cassell.*

20 May 1851.

profits very much interfered with. If I could have gone on adding to that publication, and charging one advertisement duty, I might have been going on bringing out each week sufficient to meet the demands of the public, and making these alterations in the dates.

1435. Sir *J. Walmsley.*] If you could carry out your own views, you would have a continuous advertisement in your publication ?—Yes; but I should have to charge only for one insertion. As far as the convenience of the public and the advertisers is concerned, I may be only disposing of 30 of these each week; it would be too much to charge those people 2*s.* 6*d.* each week for the appearance of their advertisements; but whereas, if it were one distinct publication, it would be a very great convenience.

1436. Would not that greatly depend upon the amount of your circulation, whether it was too much or too little ?—Yes; but I brought out a publication like this in connexion with the Exhibition, and if I could have fixed the dates for which any lodging was taken, it would have been a great convenience.

1437. Do not you think that charging people 1*s.* 6*d.* for advertising in newspapers has the effect of destroying the public revenue in various ways, and also of preventing a knowledge of wants on the part of the community, by obstructing the interchange of communications from time to time ?—Yes; and I was anticipating that that might have been elicited in connexion with this question of cheap newspapers. It entirely prevents a certain class of advertisements from appearing; it is only by such as costly books and by property sales by auction that really afford an opportunity of advertising and for paying the duty; consequently we are deprived of the means of availing ourselves of that class of advertisements whereby people could afford to pay 2*s.* or 2*s.* 6*d.*, where they will not pay 4*s.* or 5*s.*

1438. Mr. *Ewart.*] Do you not refer to a most numerous class, and also a class which has suffered most from their wants not being communicated ?—Yes; as to bringing this out with advertisements, we are compelled to affix a stamp to it, and make it a stamped publication, because it is a newspaper, through filling it with advertisements. It is very frequently brought forward about the American newspapers being published at a penny, and it is attributed entirely to there being no penny stamp; now, I say that there being no penny stamp has a great deal to do with it, but the having no advertisement duty also is another great reason.

1439. Mr.

Mr. *J. Cassell.*

20 May 1851.

1439. Mr. *Rich.*] You have referred to the great benefit that would result from the circulation of penny newspapers; would you have the kindness to put in an estimate of what you conceive would be the expense of conducting one with profit?—My answer to such a question is, that I feel convinced that I could establish a penny newspaper containing news, and I could satisfy any member of the Committee that I could do so; but I feel objections to giving an estimate as to the way in which I should work it out, and placing it upon a public record.

1440. Mr. *Stafford.*] You would not like, perhaps, to mention even the size of it?—Yes, I have no objection to mention that; I would take this—(*producing a paper*)—this is a sheet of double crown, and I could bring that out.

1441. Sir *T. F. Lewis.*] In obtaining news for a paper of this description, should you feel at liberty to copy without restraint that which was collected as news by the late London papers, such as the "Morning Chronicle" or the "Times"? —If I brought my paper out as an evening paper, I might follow the practice of other papers; it is the custom now with all the evening papers to take from the morning papers the news of the previous day, but they employ reporters for taking all the events of the day; for instance, in the police courts of that day, and also in the law courts.

1442. But they would be at liberty, you say, to copy the reports of proceedings in the law courts and the police courts, if given the following day?—Yes.

1443. Would not that be quite soon enough for the supply of such a class of readers as you refer to?—No.

1444. Would they require an account on the immediate day of what passes in the London police courts?—Of course, an individual possessed of greater spirit and enterprise would have an advantage over his competitors if he supplied earlier news than is supplied by other papers containing intelligence.

1445. Would that, in point of fact, give him an advantage; for instance, in the case of the gold dust robbery, if he gave an account of it on the day it was published in the "Times," would that be any advantage, as compared with the publication of the same fact on the following day?—Very great; the last would not meet the necessity of the case.

1446. With reference to the debates in Parliament, is it not very expensive to the proprietors of those newspapers to employ the class of reporters which they do employ, to report the speeches in the manner in which they are reported? —Yes.

1447. Would

Mr. *J. Cassell.*

20 May 1851.

1447. Would it be fair to take advantage of the whole of that expense, and the whole of that labour, and permit it to be republished, as it would probably be, in every market town in the country, without incurring any expense whatever?—Of course, it is what is done now, and of course by taking the news, they lose the advantage of early publication. The weekly papers take from the daily papers all their Parliamentary intelligence, but on Saturday morning, when they have to bring out their Saturday editions, these weekly papers must have their own reporters in the gallery of the House, because, having to come out at the same time with the morning papers, they cannot avail themselves of the news contained in the morning papers.

1448. Not immediately, but by the rapidity of communication that exists now, would not very many of those papers be enabled to publish in the evening that which the "Times" had published in the morning?—Yes, they do so now.

1449. And that, you think, is no infringement of copyright, and not an unfair proceeding towards the "Times," or the "Morning Chronicle," or the "Morning Herald," as the case may be?—I look upon it as not taking news; it is not like availing ourselves of a literary production, and it is not considered so.

1450. In what does the difference consist; if all the expense is to be incurred by one party, and a large portion of the profit to be taken by another, without consent, in what sense does that differ from the copyright of a work?—I suppose it is considered as news, and it loses its value the next day, that the value is destroyed as far as the paper that published that news goes, and I have all the advantage of having that news by bringing it out on the same evening; it is not the course that I pursue myself, nor in making my calculations have I ever contemplated it.

1451. Have you any doubt that it is the course that would necessarily be pursued if all papers were published without stamps, and the cost of transporting the papers by post from one place to another was charged upon those who paid for the newspapers brought from a distance?—It would not. But take Manchester for instance; a paper adopting that course, if a daily paper, would not get a standing, and that paper which furnished the earliest news would have an advantage over all of them; and to obtain that in the case of a morning paper brought out in Manchester, they would have their reporter in the House of Commons, just to take a summary of what had transpired, and to communicate it by telegraph, so that the people

Mr. *J. Cassell.*

20 May 1851.

people of Manchester would have the previous night's debate by breakfast time next morning; consequently, those papers that came out with an evening edition would have to wait till the London papers brought down the intelligence, which is done now, and of that all the newspapers throughout the kingdom avail themselves.

1452. Amongst the newspaper reporters who sit in the gallery of the House of Commons, are there any who are employed for any newspaper published out of London?—I should think not, except it is to furnish what is called the London Correspondent's Letter.

1453. Then all the accounts of the debates in Parliament that are furnished by country newspapers, are now republications from a text supplied at the cost and by the labour employed upon the London newspapers, are they not?—Yes.

1454. Suppose a case, that every London newspaper that was sent into the country were to pay, for the cost of its transport, a postage similar to the letter postage, is it not evident that that would greatly increase the charge upon the London newspapers to the country purchasers?—If the Post Office charged by weight, I should say that very few would go by post.

1455. Suppose then that the London newspapers were to circulate at the present cost with a stamp?—Yes.

1456. And that the country newspapers would be published without the cost of a stamp?—The same as the London papers, except for going through the post.

1457. Then every person who bought a London paper in Manchester would buy it at the same price as he does now?—Yes; but there are so many considerations. It would take rather a lengthened explanation to show that even the fivepenny papers, with a penny stamp, would be published for 4*d.* under the altered circumstances.

1458. But not transported to Manchester for 4*d.*?—Yes; that was the question that was put to me on Friday last. If a newspaper is published in the morning, and the same newspaper is published in the evening, the circulation of the sixpenny edition over the threepenny would be four or five to one.

1459. On account of the earliness of the news?—Yes, and the country papers could not get any greater advantage from pursuing such a course than they have at the present time. We know in London that the evening papers stand scarcely any chance from the early intelligence which is furnished by the

Mr. *J. Cassell.* 20 May 1851.

the morning newspapers, such is the anxiety on the part of the public to get the earliest news. And there is the great advantage of the "Times" in having their foreign correspondents, and giving the earliest intelligence; people do not scruple to pay a trifle extra for getting it.

1460. Do you think that that is the sole reason; is not the mode of conducting the morning papers very much superior to that of the evening papers, and is not the news supplied, and are not the articles written, very much superior in the morning papers?—Because such are the whole arrangements throughout the kingdom, and I may say the world, that the most important intelligence arrives in the morning. The evening papers cannot furnish the Parliamentary debates from their own collecting, because they take place in the evening after they have published. The arrival of intelligence is generally at three and four o'clock in the morning by the mail trains, or by the electric telegraph. The only intelligence that comes to the evening papers is what takes a place of not more than a column. The great events arrive early in the morning.

1461. Are the Committee to understand you to say that you think there would be no unfairness and no disadvantage to those London papers that go to the expense of acquiring news, and of reporting the debates, if a postage rate were imposed upon them, suffering any persons in the country to publish and sell newspapers without the imposition of a penny stamp or any tax for transport; in short, would it not be an imposition of a duty upon one with liberty to republish by another, matter that he could sell without the imposition of any duty at all?—There would be no greater disadvantage to the London morning newspapers, under such a change, than at present exists. They would be placed at no greater disadvantage than under the present circumstances.

1462. And the way in which you explain that is, that the rapidity with which the news could be supplied by post would be so great an advantage, that the time taken up in reprinting and republishing would be more than to compensate for the payment of the stamp?—Yes, it would be more than to compensate for the payment of the stamp, or the transmission by rail. If a daily paper had a great consumption in any particular part, they would send down a large bale by railway, and there would be an early delivery before any provincial newspaper could get their news up in type; and if that local paper wanted to compete with the "Times," it must go to the same expense as the London morning newspapers do in obtaining their intelligence.

1463. Mr.

Mr. *J. Cassell.* 20 May 1851.

1463. Mr. *G. A. Hamilton.*] Is that the general impression of those who are connected with the London papers?—I do not know. My impression is, that many of the newspaper proprietors might imagine that the removal of the penny stamp would affect their interests.

1464. Sir *T. F. Lewis.*] Have you any acquaintance with Ireland?—A little.

1465. Can you explain to the Committee at all what effect the alteration that is at present under consideration with respect to the removal of the stamp and charging a postage rate would have in Ireland?—No.

Mr. *Alexander Russel*, called in; and Examined.

Mr. *A. Russel.*

1466. Mr. *Rich.*] YOU are the proprietor of an Edinburgh paper?—No; editor of the "Scotsman."

1467. It has a large circulation?—Yes, the largest in Edinburgh, I think, but cannot be quite sure.

1468. You have had considerable experience of the newspaper press?—Yes, I have been editor of the "Scotsman" for some years, and have been editor of three other papers.

1469. How long have you had experience of the newspaper press?—Twelve or 13 years.

1470. Have you turned your mind to the effect of the penny stamp on newspapers?—Yes, to some extent; but taking mostly the facts within my own cognizance as to how it would affect ourselves, the Scotch papers.

1471. What is your opinion of the effect of the penny stamp on the newspaper press?—I think it a favourable arrangement for the newspapers on the whole. I do not consider it a tax at all, but a payment made to the Post Office for services which I do not think we could get so efficiently performed in any other way for much more cost.

1472. Do you find that there are many unstamped newspapers published in Edinburgh?—There are none in Edinburgh.

1473. Nor in Scotland?—Not that I am aware of; there may be one occasionally spring up for a week or two in Glasgow, but I have not heard of any for some years.

1474. Do you find that any particular advantage accrues to Edinburgh from having a stamping department established there?—It is very convenient for us of course, and the Newcastle papers have to send to Edinburgh for their stamps, I think.

Mr. *A. Russel.*

20 May 1851.

1475. Do you consider that it gives you an advantage over Glasgow?—It is a very small advantage over Glasgow, the communication is so rapid and cheap; and most of the stationers and paper makers, who supply the stamps to the newspapers, have their head-quarters in Edinburgh.

1476. Are all the Edinburgh newspapers supplied by the stamping department for Edinburgh?—So far as I am aware.

1477. You do not know that any of them obtain the stamped paper from Manchester or London, do you?—No.

1478. Do you look upon the penny stamp as a convenience to the press, or as a tax upon knowledge?—I consider that it is not a tax at all, and that the only effect it has upon knowledge is to spread and improve it.

1479. Do you think it prevents an increased publication of newspapers, and a more widely extended circulation?—It would be difficult to say. I think that the removal of the stamp, and the substitution of a postal rate, which I suppose is the only alternative, might have the effect of raising some papers in districts that have not them now; if you make the papers of a district where a man lives a penny cheaper, which would be the case if you are to have only the penny postage on the papers, or, if you follow the letter rate, 4 *d.* or 6 *d.* cheaper, than the papers published in London or Edinburgh, of course it will encourage small local papers.

1480. From your experience of the press, should you say that since you became acquainted with it, the general tone of the newspaper press has been rising or falling?—It has been rising very much, especially since the Reform Bill; people became more political; there was more discussional writing in the papers after that, and the reporting and every other department has very much improved in Scotland.

1481. There is an unstamped press circulating in the form of newspapers, without coming within the strict definition of a newspaper, is there not?—Yes, such as "Chambers' Journal." That is a portion of the press that has been born within these 20 years. I think "Chambers' Journal" began about 1830, and it was the first, except one that only lived a short time.

1482. Are there many unstamped publications, for instance, periodicals of an evil tendency, published in Edinburgh?—I am not aware of one in all Scotland; I cannot speak positively as to Glasgow, but if there had been I think I should have heard of it.

1483. To what do you attribute so creditable a fact?—I do not know; the people are pretty intelligent, and fond of politics rather than scandal.

1484. *Chairman.*]

Mr. *A. Russel.*

20 May 1851.

1484. *Chairman.*] You are the editor of the "Scotsman"?—Yes.

1485. Are you the proprietor?—No.

1486. You have no interest in the paper?—No; but I may mention that Mr. Ritchie, who is the proprietor, and who understands the business department of a paper much better, and has been connected with newspapers longer than I have, is of the same opinion as I am as to the effect of the stamp; that that is a favourable arrangement for the press.

1487. You stated that the removal of the stamp would cause newspapers to spring up in districts where they do not now exist?—I think the tendency would be to cause a crop of small local papers, by the fact of the papers of the town where a man lives being cheaper to him than the papers of London or Edinburgh.

1488. Is not a man entitled to have his local paper for less than a man who has had a paper brought to him some hundreds of miles?—Yes; he is entitled in one sense, of course, the same as you might say that a man is entitled to have a letter through the post cheaper on the other side of the street than at John o'Groat's.

1489. Do you conceive that the public is bound to carry your paper to a town, so that when it gets there it shall stand exactly on the same footing as a paper that is published in the town?—I say that, on the whole, it is better both for the public and the press.

1490. Is it just?—It is best; as near justice as you can come, on the whole.

1491. Sir *T. F. Lewis.*] If anybody chooses to give you a paper as cheap as you can buy it in the neighbourhood, would it be just to deprive you of that benefit?—Certainly not.

1492. *Chairman.*] You stated that the removal of the stamp would cause a crop of papers to spring up in districts where they are now not published; then you complained, as I understood you, that when the "Scotsman" was carried into those districts a freight upon the "Scotsman" would have to be paid, so that it would cost the people there, perhaps, a little more on account of its freight than a paper published in the district?—Yes, that is what I mean to say.

1493. Do not you think that that is a reasonable arrangement; why should the public undertake to bear the freight of the "Scotsman" to a place where those local papers had sprung up, in order that it might stand there on the same footing with them?—It is not the public; it is the reader of the

 paper

Mr. *A. Russel.*

20 May 1851.

paper that bears it; it is not laid on the revenue; the man who gets the paper pays for it.

1494. Mr. *Rich.*] You look upon it as being analogous to the low rate of the penny postage?—Yes, and much cheaper.

1495. Sir *T. F. Lewis.*] Would not the charge of a postage upon the paper be a great check to the dispersion of knowledge throughout the country; would it not confine the demand to local papers, and take away the benefit which a man now enjoys of buying a paper published in any part of the kingdom, and paying nothing whatever for the cost of carriage?—Precisely so. At present, a Caithness man, living in London, gets a Caithness paper, and the Caithness people get the London papers, and the Edinburgh papers, and so on, and the different districts are thus, as it were, *carded* through each other, to the mutual benefit of all; but if you make the paper of a district always cheaper than the paper which is to be carried by some means of conveyance, you separate the country into sections as to that department of information, and it would have a tendency to the promotion of local prejudices, and to the narrowing and embittering of political and all manner of discussions.

1496. Do not you consider that it must be a great advantage to the inhabitants of the counties of Donegal, Antrim, and Sligo, to obtain all that is published, or any portion of what is published by the London newspaper press, without any charge whatever for the transport of the newspaper from London to those counties?—I think it an immense advantage that they should get it at the postal rate of a penny for what is on the average three ounces weight, while a letter pays a penny for half an ounce.

1497. If persons in those counties had to depend upon such papers as were likely to be published in their own neighbourhoods, would not that tend to increase prejudices, and prevent the general spread of national feeling through one part of the country and another?—Very greatly; it would operate that way very powerfully.

1498. *Chairman.*] Supposing the stamp taken off, and you paid no more than the price of the stamp for the freight of the "Scotsman" into the districts into which you sent it, the readers would still get it at the same price as they do now, would they not?—Yes, of course they would.

1499. Why do you suppose that the circulation of the "Scotsman" would not be so large if they got it at the same price as they do now?—But I do not suppose that the price would be the same.

1500. Why

Mr. *A. Russel.*

20 May 1851.

1500. Why not?—Because, according to Mr. Hill, it would not remunerate the Post Office.

1501. What is the "Scotsman" published at?—Fourpence halfpenny; the price of all the Scotch ones.

1502. Supposing the stamp were taken off, at least it could be brought out for 3 ½ *d.*?—Yes, it could be brought out for 3½ *d.* in Edinburgh.

1503. And it could be sold 100 miles from Edinburgh as it is now, for 4 ½ *d.*, if the postage were a penny, could it not?—Yes.

1504. Then why should you suppose that, if the price remained the same, the circulation of the "Scotsman" would not be as large under the new state of circumstances as before?—I never supposed so; I can see no harm in that system if you like to tax the Post Office revenue for the carriage of newspapers. I supposed that one of two things must be done; either that, if all newspapers are not to go through the post free, you would treat them as letters, and the postage of my newspaper would be 6 *d.*; or ——

1505. I ask you this simple question, whether you would be still able, if the postage were a penny, to deliver the "Scotsman" in those distant districts at the same price as that at which it is now delivered?—Yes, of course.

1506. Then what is your reason for supposing that the circulation would be less if the price remained the same?—I never supposed that the circulation would be less if the price remained the same. I think my circulation would be increased.

1507. You stated, did you not, that the country districts would be liable to take up prejudiced notions, and so on, from the effect of the charge of a postage upon the papers from a distance; but if they are sold at the same price why should that be so?—But I have answered no questions upon the supposition that they were to be the same price.

1508. Then it was under the idea that the postage was to be 6 *d.*, or something of that sort?—Even a penny would have the effect of localizing papers. I think the effect, of such a plan as seems proposed, for instance, upon a paper such as my own, would be to increase the circulation; the papers that would be killed off would be the less remunerative papers in large towns. I believe a number of London ones would be killed off, the smaller ones. The great papers in the large towns, such as Liverpool, would go on and be better, but the smaller ones would be killed off, and then a crop of petty papers would spring up; but the papers that are remunerative just now have too good a hold upon the market to suffer.

 1509. Do

Mr. *A. Russel.*

20 May 1851.

1509. Do you recollect the period when the stamp was reduced?—No; it was just a little before my experience began.

1510. Was that a most beneficial thing?—Yes; it was the repeal of a heavy tax, and the substitution of a postage rate.

1511. Sir *T. F. Lewis.*] Was not the penny stamp limited to papers of a smaller size at the beginning of this century than it is now?—All the country newspapers enlarged greatly after 1834, and improved in every way. They used to have no other editor perhaps than the schoolmaster in the town, who wrote something for them. Now they have editors, sub-editors sometimes, and reporters.

1512. *Chairman.*] Do you think it would be a fair arrangement if the whole of the impressions of a publication containing news should be stamped, in order to pay the expense of carrying a portion of them by the post?—Yes.

1513. Supposing no portion goes by post, do you think it would be fair then to make those parties pay the stamps?—No; I speak of it as a postal rate.

1514. Is it your opinion that only that portion of an impression should be stamped that does go by post?—I do not think that by any system of that sort you would get so near justice and convenience as by the present system.

1515. There are 53 registered newspapers in London, according to a Parliamentary Return, that are permitted to stamp only those copies that they choose for the purpose of being sent by post; would you think that a bad arrangement to extend to the whole newspaper press?—I do not see that you can do that without raising the postage. I may state that Mr. Rowland Hill in an official document last year showed that at the rate of a penny the Post Office at present loses upwards of 30,000 *l.* a year by the carriage of newspapers, crediting the Post Office with the whole return of 350,000 *l.* for the stamps; if only those sent through the post are to pay the stamp, then there must be a large reduction from that 350,000*l.*, and you must either increase the rate on the papers that you send, or you must commit a greater injustice than some people think attaches to the present system; you must take it out of the revenue, and carry newspapers through the post at the expense not only of those whose newspapers do not go through the post, but of those who receive no newspapers at all.

1516. Will you be good enough to explain as to what you mean by saying that the present system is a favourable arrangement for newspapers; what per-centage is this penny

upon

Mr. *A. Russel.*

20 May 1851.

upon the price of the "Scotsman," in order to entitle it to the privilege of being sent by post?—It is a penny out of 4½*d.*; it is about 27 per cent.

1517. Do you consider it right that you should be taxed 27 per cent. upon every publication you issue, in order that you may have the privilege of sending as many as you please by post?—I consider that we do it cheaper that way than we could in any other way.

1518. Do you consider it right that you should be taxed 27 per cent. upon every publication, in order that you may have the privilege of sending as many as you please by post? —I think it is right, because it is the cheapest way we can do it.

1519. What per-centage is a penny upon a penny paper? —It is 100 per cent.

1520. Do you think that another man should be taxed 100 per cent. upon the price of his publication, to have no greater privilege than you enjoy?—It is difficult to answer that; it is something like asking whether a letter full of nonsense should pay a penny, when a letter on important business pays no more; it is the quality of the article.

1521. Will you explain how it can be right or fair that one man should pay 100 per cent. upon his publication, to have no greater privilege than you enjoy for 27 per cent.?—You cannot charge carriage by anything but weight; not by quality.

1522. But the man who sells at a penny gives less weight than you do?—Then I do not see that there is any objection to his paying less, except as to the matter of convenience or practicability.

1523. Would you propose that there should be a proportionate amount of stamp duty according to the value of the publication, in order that they should all get the same return for their money?—What I propose is, that things should remain as they are.

1524. Would it be just to say to a man who issues a penny publication, "I will tax you 100 per cent., and give you no greater privilege than I give to another man, who is only taxed 27 per cent."?—It is perfectly just, if it is not absolutely necessary; a man carrying goods can only charge by the weight.

1525. It is not a question of weight; the Post Office carries so much weight for such and such a payment?—I do not look upon it as a tax that can be made *ad valorem*.

1526. The stamp is not affixed upon the paper according to the

Mr. *A. Russel.*

29 May 1851.

the weight; it is affixed upon the paper if it only weighs a grain, while we know that the "Times," which weighs nearly a quarter of a pound, pays no more?—It is rudely adjusted to weight, for you cannot go above a certain size.

1527. Have you ever read the Newspaper Stamp Act?—Long ago I did; not lately.

1528. There is not anything said there about weight?—It comes to the same thing. There is a restriction of the surface; you cannot print upon a sheet beyond a certain size.

1529. Any sheet that has news upon it, has to pay a penny if it only weighs a grain, just the same as the "Times"?—Yes, but the "Times" cannot go above a certain size in its sheet.

1530. Mr. *Rich.*] Are you aware, with regard to postage, that some letters weigh more than others, have contents infinitely more valuable than others, and go distances 50 times greater than others, and yet they all pay a uniform price?—Yes; it is just the same principle; you cannot come nearer to equity.

1531. You do not see your way clear to the adoption of an *ad valorem* duty upon newspapers, or an *ad valorem* duty upon letters?—No.

1532. *Chairman.*] Supposing a man says, "I make no use of the post at all; mine is a penny publication, and I do not propose to ask for the services of the post; will you permit me to put news in my paper, and publish it without being liable to penalties under the Stamp Act?" Would you consider it fair to grant that gentleman's request; and if not, why not?—I should think it quite unreasonable; you can have no system at all that you will not detect some inequalities in.

1533. Do you think it would be unreasonable to grant his request?—Yes, quite so; you must have some system to which you must adhere; you cannot deal with each individual case.

1534. Though the small unstamped publications make no use of the post, have they any privileges granted to them?—Of course they have not.

1535. They must pay by weight, must they not?—There is an anomaly in the case of the "Athenæum" and others, which can stamp a portion of their impression; but that is defensible, I presume, because it does not cause an increase of the machinery of the Post Office, while bringing an addition to the revenue.

1536. Mr. *Rich.*] You were asked whether it would be fair that an unstamped paper, which published news, should be called upon to pay 1 *d.*; you are aware that newspapers containing

containing news pay the 1 *d.* as a contribution to the revenue? —Yes.

1537. Therefore, does it not strike you that if an unstamped newspaper were allowed to circulate without paying anything, there would thereby be an undue advantage given over the public newspapers which do pay the duty?—Of course it would.

1538. Mr. *Cobden.*] I understood you to say that you considered the stamping of newspapers to be the best mode of levying the postage tax upon them?—Yes.

1539. I hold in my hand a copy of Savory and Son's "Price Current," containing engravings of tea urns, and salt cellars, and watches, and clocks, containing about 32 pages, and weighing upwards of an ounce, which would be charged 4 *d.* if it went by post in the ordinary way, but by having a newspaper stamp affixed to the corner it goes through the post for 1 *d.*; do you approve of that arrangement?—I say it is an anomaly that I cannot defend. I suppose the Post Office can do it at a gain, having their machinery ready at any rate; and these publications not being so many as to cause any increase of machinery, they get a little money by it. It is not defensible on principle. I think it is an anomaly altogether.

1540. Do you approve of this as a part of your plan of levying the postage in the shape of a stamp?—No, I do not.

1541. Would you allow, under your plan for carrying out a system of paying the postage by stamps, those publications to go for 1 *d.*?—I think I should be inclined to say that that is a matter for the Post Office; if they can carry them without an increase of cost, I do not see that any parties are injured by their going. They do not come into competition with newspapers.

1542. Speaking of it only as a postage question, you are aware that there are 50 or 60 publications in London which publish a part of their impressions on stamped and a part on unstamped paper, and that the stamped impressions go through the post for 1 *d.*; do you approve of that plan?—No; I say it is an anomaly. It seems to me to be an excrescence on the system altogether. I was not aware that it existed till lately.

1543. Do you not think that it would be better that Mr. Rowland Hill, at the Post Office, should have the settling of the postage upon everything that passed through the Post Office, rather than allowing the Stamp Office to affix the stamp upon a "price current" like this?—I have great faith in Mr. Rowland Hill; but he has not produced any system yet that would

Mr. *A. Russel.*

20 May 1851.

would accomplish that. All that he has said upon the subject is, that at a penny the thing does not pay; taking all the papers together, he says the Post Office loses 30,000 *l.* a year already.

1544. But that loss must be increased by sending such publications as this for a penny instead of fourpence, must it not?—I could suppose that it might not, because they have the clerks there already: if these publications increased so much as to cause an increase of the Post Office machinery, that would be another thing.

1545. You are aware that, practically, the Post Office has no voice in the matter, as it is the custom to carry everything by post that bears this stamp, conformably to the Act of Parliament relating to newspapers?—Yes.

1546. Do you approve of that plan by which the regulation of the postage is taken out of the hands of the Postmaster-general, and placed in those of the Board of Inland Revenue?—No; I think it would be better entirely in the hands of the Post Office.

1547. Besides viewing this as a fiscal question, you have some objections, have you not, of rather a moral character, to the removal of the stamp; did you not say that you thought that if the stamp were removed, there would be a number of unstamped publications of inferior quality springing up?—Yes, local publications; all papers would then be unstamped, in one sense.

1548. And you think that would give rise to the growth of newspapers of an inferior quality?—Yes; in the thinner districts you would have papers where you have not them now, and the most struggling papers in the larger towns would be killed off owing to them. I think that the leading papers, like the London leading papers, or the leading papers in Edinburgh or Glasgow, might be better off than before.

1549. Do not you think that in those smaller localities people are very much interested in having details of their own local news?—Yes, and they have them; each county has a paper publishing local news.

1550. Published in the county town?—Yes.

1551. But you would object, would you not, to the smaller towns having their papers?—No, I do not.

1552. You object, do you not, to the removal of the stamp, because it would give rise to the growth of an inferior kind of newspapers in the smaller towns?—That would be one effect.

1553. And that is one reason why you are opposed to the removal of the stamp?—Yes.

1554. You

Mr. *A. Russel.*

20 May 1851.

1554. You stated that the leading papers would still be published in the large towns, and that your own paper would probably rather gain than lose by the removal of the stamp; as those papers would continue to be published in the county towns, and as the people in the smaller towns would still have the choice of buying the newspapers from the county towns, or of buying the paper in the small towns, do you see any objection to leaving them a free choice between the two?—I do not know if that would be a good argument in favour of legislating towards that particular end; but I think it is good in favour of an existing system, which can be shown to be fair and beneficial as a whole.

1555. You do not see any moral objection to people in the small towns having the option of buying their little local papers, or of buying a superior paper from the county town?—I do not think that you should prevent it by an express law; but I think it would be a misfortune that there should be local papers of a more petty character than at present exist.

1556. You stated, did you not, that you were opposed to the removal of the stamp, because it prevented the growth of those smaller papers?—Yes, that was one reason.

1557. But do not you think that the people in the smaller towns might be safely left to discriminate between the paper that came from the county town and that which was published in their own locality?—They have a moral right to discriminate, undoubtedly.

1558. But would they not be likely to prefer the paper that suited them best, if they had a free choice?—If the penny has so much weight in this matter as is said, a penny would make the difference, and instead of buying the paper, say, at Cupar Fife, they would start one at Dunfermline or Kirkcaldy, because you could not have any paper but that of the town where you reside without paying a penny or twopence more for it.

1559. Assuming that they would still have a paper for a penny from Cupar Fife to Kirkcaldy, as they now have, and that they would have it by post for a penny, they would stand in the same position as they do now, would they not?—Except that the local paper would be cheaper, which comes to the same thing as making the other dearer.

1560. You said, did you not, that you would not impose a tax to prevent a local publisher from publishing a paper?—I do not think it would be fair to legislate directly for that; but if you have had a system existing which I think is fair and beneficial,

Mr. *A. Russel.* — 20 May 1851.

beneficial, I hold there would be nothing wrong in taking into consideration that matter.

1561. If you consider that the present system has a beneficial tendency as it now exists, why would you not pass a law to ensure that good result which you seem to recognize in it?—I think the less that the Legislature meddles with those matters the better; trying to legislate to get people into a certain course of reading is one of those things that are better left alone.

1562. Do not you find generally that people like to have the details of their own local news that is interesting to them?—Yes, they all have them; these county papers have a correspondent in each little village for the local news.

1563. If a small town published its own papers, do you not think that it would give greater details of local news?—Of course it would, and that is what I think would be a portion of the misfortune; it would tend to local and personal gossip.

1564. You stated that in order to procure local news you employ a correspondent to supply local news in each locality?—Yes, anything that is really worth mentioning.

1565. You give anything that is worth recording?—Yes.

1566. In this case you are the judge of what is worth recording, and yours is the only newspaper; but I assume a case in which there is a local paper, and that the public in those small towns wanted a paper giving a greater amount of local news than you can give; would it not be an advantage to those parties to be allowed to have a full knowledge of what was going on?—I think that it would be a disadvantage that local news and local subjects should be more fully dealt with than at present, as they would be then; it is rather overdone now, and it would be regrettable that papers should become more petty in their range and tone.

1567. Do you carry out that principle with regard to the Edinburgh papers. The Edinburgh papers may be regarded as local papers in competition with the London papers. Is it a disadvantage to have such details in your Edinburgh papers to a much greater extent than the "Times" can furnish them?—Of course not; I speak of the extent of the details, keeping this in view, that these little local papers that we are speaking of could not go beyond the immediate district; you could not carry the paper further without a postage in some shape or another.

1568. You have spoken of Kirkcaldy; do you think that the same argument which you applied to your own case, in comparing Edinburgh to London, would hold good when you are

Mr. *A. Russel.*

20 May 1851.

are speaking of Kirkcaldy in comparison with Edinburgh?—No; I think there are matters fit to be discussed, and which can be discussed with benefit, occurring in the capital; whereas as to matters in Kirkcaldy, I should say generally that anything that is not of sufficient moment to carry up to Cupar had better be left alone.

1569. You think if there is any local news in Kirkcaldy, beyond what the Cupar paper can profitably print, that that is news which it is not desirable that the Kirkcaldy people should have to read?—I would say, on the whole, yes.

1570. You would say that the capacity of the Cupar paper should be a criterion of the amount of local news that should be given to the public at Kirkcaldy?—I do not say that it should be a criterion; I am speaking of the fact.

1571. Kirkcaldy is a manufacturing town of linens, is it not?—Yes.

1572. With a considerable amount of commerce and manufactures?—Yes; there are about 10,000 inhabitants.

1573. Do not you think that the people of Kirkcaldy would be better judges of what local news they would like to read than the people at Cupar?—If they are, they can set up a paper; unless it is to circulate solely in the town, there is no tax upon it.

1574. Then, according to the theory which you lay down, it appears that you think it would be undesirable that the law should be changed to that state of things in which a town like Kirkcaldy should have a newspaper giving greater details than they now get from the Cupar paper?—I think it would be an incidental misfortune of such a change as I am supposing, namely, the removal of a uniform stamp and the substitution of a postal rate. I think incidentally that would occur.

1575. Do you think that would be the opinion of the people of Kirkcaldy, this town of 10,000 inhabitants?—I cannot speak of their opinion.

1576. Do you think that if the taxes on knowledge were removed, so that a newspaper could be published as cheaply here as it is in America, and that in consequence Kirkcaldy had its daily paper, it would be a disadvantage as compared with the present state of things, when they get a paper once a week?—I cannot answer that. I look upon it as an impossibility. You cannot have papers as cheaply as in America by merely taking off the penny. In America also the carriage of newspapers is more heavily charged than here. They pay 1½*d.* there for any distance within 100 miles, something more for greater distances, and that for only one posting.

1577. Assuming

Mr. *A. Russel.*

20 May 1851.

1577. Assuming it to be true what the Committee have in evidence before them from very competent persons, that if the taxes on knowledge were removed we could print newspapers here cheaper than they can in America, and assuming that in consequence Kirkcaldy had a daily paper, as every town of 10,000 inhabitants has in America, would you consider that a disadvantage?—It is difficult for me to answer that; I cannot imagine it; I cannot assume it as a possible fact.

1578. Cannot you assume that to be possible here which is a matter of universal occurrence in America?—If the Hon. Member means that by taking off the stamp such a thing could be done here, I cannot assume it; there are so many differences between this country and America—which I will state if you will allow me—that I cannot assume it as a fact.

1579. Would you have the same difficulty in assuming that weekly papers would spring up in Kirkcaldy, in consequence of the removal of these taxes on knowledge?—I should think that more likely.

1580. Assuming that, would you consider it a disadvantage?—I think on the whole, and in a majority of cases, it would be incidentally a disadvantage that such should be the effect, as I think it would, of removing the uniform stamp.

1581. Assuming that such a newspaper existed, would it not be a proof that the people of Kirkcaldy found it useful and desirable?—I do not know that you can assume that everything that exists is useful and desirable.

1582. I ask you whether, if such a paper were started in Kirkcaldy, it would not be a proof that the people of Kirkcaldy considered it useful and desirable?—It would be a proof that the people who bought the paper thought so.

1583. I ask you whether you think that the people of Kirkcaldy, or somebody at Cupar, ought to be the judge whether they should have this newspaper or not?—I think that the people at Kirkcaldy are the best judges; and already the Kirkcaldy people are as much at liberty to supply the people in Cupar, as Cupar is to supply Kirkcaldy.

1584. Mr. *Rich.*] Do you think that the penny stamp prevents the people of Kirkcaldy from having a newspaper if they want one?—If the paper is to circulate solely in Kirkcaldy, the stamp does tend to prevent it; but it is difficult to suppose a paper existing solely in Kirkcaldy. If it is to go beyond it, the stamp, I say, would tend to encourage such a paper. But it is difficult to deal with that question, as I do not see how they mean to carry the paper after the stamp is off.

1585. You are aware of the constant communication between

Mr. *A. Russel.* 20 May 1851.

between Kirkcaldy and Cupar Fife, are you not?—Yes, it is constant.

1586. Practically, Cupar and Kirkcaldy touch one another, do they not?—There are six or seven trains a day.

1587. A paper published at Cupar is almost a paper published at Kirkcaldy, is it not?—Yes; and Edinburgh is within 10 miles.

1588. Mr. *Cobden.*] Is not Kirkcaldy a sea-port?—Yes, a small sea-port.

1589. Cupar is an inland town, is it not?—Yes.

1590. Are not the interests very different between a sea-port town and an inland town?—They may be.

1591. What are the manufactures carried on at Cupar?—The same as at Kirkcaldy, linen, but much smaller; but Kirkcaldy can set up a paper and supply Cupar if it chooses to try.

1592. Mr. *Rich.*] More copies of the paper published at Cupar are taken in at Kirkcaldy than at Cupar, are there not?—I was once the editor, and I think they are pretty equal, the reason being that Kirkcaldy is within 10 miles of Edinburgh.

1593. With regard to the multiplication of papers, there must be a limit to the number of towns and places that would possess a newspaper?—Yes.

1594. And that limit is not solely confined to the number of inhabitants, but to the news that those inhabitants would require?—Of course.

1595. Whether it should be merely local news or provincial news, district news or domestic, or foreign news?—Yes.

1596. You stated, with regard to American newspapers, the tax upon conveyance; are you acquainted with the amount?—It is three cents within 100 miles, and more beyond; or it was very lately.

1597. And increasing with the distance?—Yes.

1598. While that tax existed, would it not necessarily operate in favour of local papers?—Yes, it tends to localize the press.

1599. Admitting the benefit of local papers, you consider the metropolitan papers a greater advantage still for the circulation of sound intelligence, do you not?—Of course.

1600. Sir *J. Walmsley.*] You stated that levying the penny stamp had a favourable effect upon the press. I presume you meant by that, that the public received an equivalent by having the newspapers carried free of postage?—Precisely.

1601. That was all you meant by that answer?—Yes.

1602. You did not mean to say that a reduction of the penny

Mr. *A. Russel.*

20 May 1851.

penny stamp would not be better for the newspaper press?—Better, in what respect?

1603. I presume you are of opinion that a reduction of the duty would produce more competition?—Yes, it would in one sense. I think I stated before that it would kill off the weak large-town papers, but that it would improve the stronger large-town papers, and cause a crop of papers to spring up in the thinner districts; but I am speaking pretty much at random, so long as I do not know what plan for the carriage of newspapers you propose to substitute.

1604. Do you think competition desirable in newspapers?—Of course.

1605. As desirable as it is in everything else?—Yes.

1606. Would a reduction of the penny stamp and competition increase the number of the papers published?—I am doubtful whether it would increase them on the whole; it might kill off one class and increase another.

1607. Would the number be doubled or trebled?—I cannot tell. You must tell me how, if the stamp were taken off, you are to carry them. What are they to be carried at?

1608. I apprehend that means would be found to carry the papers?—Yes; but I must know at what cost they would be carried.

1609. You are of opinion that a reduction of the stamp and competition would necessarily increase the number of papers published, are you not?—I am not very sure that the whole number would be increased, for the reason that I stated before.

1610. Would it be a means of furnishing to the masses of the people more knowledge?—The papers of a district would be cheaper, and other papers, I infer, would be practically dearer.

1611. Would it increase the number of readers if the price were materially reduced?—If the price of all were materially reduced it would increase the number of readers; but I may state as an opinion gathered from trials made in Scotland, that I am afraid that the calculation of 1 *d.*, up or down, causing much difference, is an over estimate. We have had several of our country papers, some of the best of them, trying to go on at 3 *d.*, and some at 4 *d.*; and they had only to compete with papers 50 per cent. dearer. All the old papers that tried it have had to come back to the old prices; and all the new ones that tried it have died off. Although they were selling 2 *d.* cheaper, and 1 ½ *d.* cheaper, they could not get a circulation. I think on the whole they had to lower their quality.

1612. Do

Mr. *A. Russel.*

20 May 1851.

1612. Do you think it is desirable to increase the number of newspaper readers?—It depends upon the quality of the newspapers a good deal; I should like to see it very much.

1613. In your opinion, what is the best mode of educating the masses as regards their reading?—I should say that reading good newspapers is a very good mode after you can get them to read, and it is a great loss in this country that there are so few people who can read, that is, who can read with pleasure, read without toil.

1614. Do you not think that cheapness would be the means of enabling them to read?—No; you must begin by enabling them to read; I do not think they would learn to read out of newspapers.

1615. When they could read, do not you think that that is the best means of teaching them, and that a reduction of the price would be the means of inducing them to read more generally?—Decidedly; I have said nothing against a reduction of price; I have only said that this stamp is not a tax, or an addition to the price.

1616. You would apply the same rule to the newspaper press that you would to any other operation in business or trade, would you not?—Quite the same rule.

1617. And you would extend free trade to the newspaper press as to anything else?—Decidedly, unless so far as there might be a question of revenue or of compensating services concerned.

Mr. *Rodie Parkhurst* called in; and Examined.

Mr. *R. Parkhurst.*

1618. *Chairman.*] WHAT are you?—A Senior Clerk in the secretary's office of the Post Office.

1619. Can you inform the Committee what the regulations are at the Post Office in reference to the transmission of newspapers by post?—Publications which are *bonâ fide* newspapers, and which are legally liable to be stamped, are sent free of postage within the United Kingdom, without reference to weight. Publications which are not *bonâ fide* newspapers, and are not legally liable to stamp-duty, are allowed the newspaper privileges, if stamped, and not exceeding two ounces in weight.

1620. Under what authority is that?—Under the authority of a Treasury Minute, and by Act of Parliament also.

1621. Will you produce the Treasury Minute?—I have a copy, which I will read: "Copy of Treasury Minute, dated 28th November 1838. 21,355. Read a letter from the Post-

 master-general,

Mr. *R.* *Parkhurst.*

20 May 1851.

master-general, dated 9th October last, respecting the postage chargeable on a publication, entitled the 'Scottish Jurist.' 19,954. Read also a letter from the Postmaster-general, dated 18th September last, transmitting a French publication which is not entitled to newspaper privileges. 19,466. Read also a further letter from the same, dated 10th September last, on the subject of the conveyance by post of the 'Essex Journal.' 21,796. Read also a letter from the same, dated 16th October last, on the subject of allowing a French publication, entitled 'La France Musicale,' to pass free of postage, with an enclosure. 24,341. Read also a letter from the same, dated 19th instant, respecting the circulation by post of a publication, entitled 'The Musical World.' My Lords have before them the several stamped papers transmitted by the Postmaster-general in the above-mentioned letters, in which his Lordship requests the decision of this Board how far such stamped papers should be permitted to pass as newspapers, free of postage. It appears that these papers, though stamped as newspapers, are not, according to law, newspapers, and consequently need not have been stamped; but that the proprietors have caused them to be stamped for the purpose, probably, of obtaining the facility of passing them free of postage. My Lords consider that all publications which are in the construction of the law newspapers, and are compelled to be stamped, are in equity entitled to the privilege of passing free of postage; but with respect to publications which, like these now under consideration, are not properly newspapers or necessarily stamped, they are of opinion that they are not in equity entitled to the privilege, and that my Lords must take into consideration the convenience of the public service, and the other circumstances of the case. My Lords are desirous of affording every fair facility which may not be inconsistent with the proper dispatch of the mails; and in this view they consider that a limit of weight may be properly applied, and adverting to the average weight of a large newspaper, they are of opinion that the limit may be properly fixed at two ounces. They are pleased, therefore, to direct that for the future, in all cases where applications are made for the transmission of any stamped publication through the Post Office free of postage, if it shall appear that such publication is legally a newspaper, and compelled to be stamped, such paper shall pass postage free, whatever may be its weight; and that when such publication may not appear to be strictly a newspaper, still it should be permitted the indulgence, in case the weight shall not exceed two ounces."

1622. Mr.

Mr. *R. Parkhurst.*

20 May 1851.

1622. Mr. *Ewart.*] What is the date of that?—November 1838.

1623. *Chairman.*] Every stamped publication that does not exceed two ounces in weight goes free, does it not?—Yes, that is practically the result.

1624. You have never raised the question at all at the Post Office as to whether any particular publication is a newspaper and liable to the newspaper stamp, but you merely just ascertain or judge it to be stamped, weigh it, and if it is under two ounces, so stamped it goes free?—Yes; the permission of the Postmaster-general must first be obtained in each case.

1625. The permission of the Postmaster-general depends upon two of those conditions stated in the Treasury Minute being complied with, does it not?—Yes.

1626. He does not exercise a discretion as to whether it is a newspaper or not?—No.

1627. Mr. *Ewart.*] He cannot refuse if it comes within the definition, can he?—No, it is more a form.

1628. Mr. *Rich.*] He might refuse if he found the conditions infringed, might he not?—Certainly.

1629. *Chairman.*] What is the Act of Parliament under which the Treasury thought themselves authorized to issue that Minute?—I cannot state the Act. They have a power, under the Penny Postage Act of the 10th of August 1840, to determine the question of transmission of newspapers by post; that was subsequent to that Minute.

1630. Could they put a postage upon newspapers now if they pleased?—Not upon newspapers originating and delivered within the United Kingdom.

1631. In fact, newspapers are not entitled by law to free postage, are they?—They are, if sent under the regulations established by the Act I have quoted.

1632. They are entitled to free postage, with the consent of the Treasury?—They are entitled to go free of postage if sent in conformity with the Act.

1633. The Treasury could at their discretion, to-morrow if they pleased, put a postage charge upon every newspaper, could they not?—I believe not.

1634. What other regulations have you in reference to the transmission of publications by post, besides what you have referred the Committee to, as regards newspapers?—I am not aware of any others. Those are the general regulations under which newspapers are sent.

1635. Supposing that a person wants to send a publication by

Mr. *R. Parkhurst.*

20 May 1851.

by post, what has he to do in order to obtain the Postmaster-general's consent previously?—He merely states that he is about publishing a work, and he applies to have it sent as a newspaper, under the newspaper privilege.

1636. Does he enter into any security that he will affix a stamp?—None whatever.

1637. He merely says that he shall stamp those that he sends by post?—Yes, and he applies that they may be allowed to pass under the newspaper privilege.

1638. Then the Post Office takes no kind of security from him that he will go previously to the Stamp Office and put a stamp on?—Certainly not.

1639. Supposing he does not put a stamp on, what would be the effect?—Then it would be charged as a letter.

1640. Supposing you do not find it out?—That would be the fault of the machinery of the Post Office.

1641. Mr. *Rich.*] If you did find it out should you suspend his privilege?—It would be charged as a letter.

1642. Have there been any instances of people sending papers unstamped who had the privilege of sending them stamped, and who, on being detected, have been deprived of their privilege in future?—Not that I am aware of.

1643. Have there been many instances of attempts at fraud?—I think not now; formerly there were.

1644. *Chairman.*] A Member of the Committee received by post, without any charge, several publications that were neither newspapers nor have any stamp on them; one was a parcel of Californian newspapers, that never had had a newspaper stamp put upon them, and paid no postage. That must have arisen, I presume, from the actual impossibility, in the time that is allowed between posting a newspaper and its transmission by the mail, of its undergoing any investigation by opening it?—Quite so; it is impossible to examine all.

1645. In point of fact, it is a mere hap-hazard concern. If a man is disposed to be dishonest, all that he has to do is to say beforehand that he is going to put a stamp on; you take no further notice, but continue to post them, though they may not be stamped?—Many might escape, but they would not go as a matter of course. Probably the bulk would be found out. The principal examination should take place at the delivering office, not at the dispatching office; it is impossible completely to examine them at the dispatching office. We have between 100,000 and 200,000 newspapers to sort and dispatch in about two hours to different parts. At the delivering offices they would be examined. Still many escape.

1646. Unless

Mr. *R. Parkhurst.*

20 May 1851.

1646. Unless you were to open a newspaper you could not tell whether it had a stamp or not?—No; as in almost every instance the stamp is so placed as to come in the inner side when the paper is folded.

1647. Would not the necessity of opening and examining them all cause a great addition to the expense of the Post Office establishment, and make it impossible that the public could have that quick transmission which they now enjoy?—Yes.

1648. What precautions do they take at the places of delivery?—They have more time to examine them at the delivering offices in the country than we have in London, where the number posted is too great to admit of more than a cursory examination.

1649. Do you suppose practically that they do open the newspapers?—My real opinion, is that, generally speaking, they do not.

1650. In point of fact, there is no security under the present system that the parties go to the Stamp Office for a postal frank?—I fear not.

1651. Such a system surely must render the revenue liable to very considerable fraud?—There is an evasion, no doubt; it is exposed to it, certainly, but whether it be so or not, I do not know.

1652. Supposing there was anything visible to the eye on the outside on every newspaper, in the shape of a stamp, would not detection then be far more easy than when it is wrapped up on the inside?—Undoubtedly.

1653. Mr. *Cobden.*] Do you know whether it was contemplated by the Minute of the Lords of the Treasury that the same newspaper should pass through the post repeatedly for the same stamp?—I cannot say.

1654. Practically, you are aware that a newspaper does go through the post repeatedly?—Yes, it is admitted, and it is perfectly well known.

1655. It would be impossible to prevent it, would it not, as the stamp is inside, and it cannot be obliterated after going once through the post, as it is folded up on the inside of the paper?—Yes.

1656. Therefore, whatever the directions of the Lords of the Treasury were, you could not practically carry out the instructions to the effect that a newspaper should only go through the post once without payment?—Not without a vast accession of force.

1657. Is it known at the Post Office to what extent the



postage

Mr. *R. Parkhurst.*

20 May 1851.

postage is evaded by folding up papers that are not strictly newspapers and sending them by post?—I should say not.

1658. For instance, take that bundle of pamphlets and old papers in your hand (*the same being handed to the Witness*); that has been posted and transmitted to the Chairman of this Committee without any charge; many members of this Committee have received similar packages, posted at the same time, no stamp being affixed to any of them; I myself saw the other day a large bundle of Californian newspapers which was put into the post office at Northampton as an experiment, and addressed to a party in London; it arrived without a farthing of charge, though it was a very heavy bundle of newspapers. Is it known at the Post Office that practically this evasion of postage goes on?—It is known that papers are so posted, and that those errors occur occasionally; this is a glaring error apparently.

1659. You have no means of correcting it so long as the stamp which franks the paper is folded up in the interior?—No, unless the force was increased to an enormous extent. The expenditure would be immense.

1660. Would that not necessarily delay the delivery?—Yes; I should say a perfect examination would.

1661. You stated that when the papers became dispersed, they were more likely to be examined in country places than in town in the hurry of transmitting them; but the papers that arrive in London from the country, I presume, are not liable to be examined?—We have not the time in London.

1662. You have no time in the morning to examine the papers in London that come from the country, any more than in the evening to examine the papers sent off?—None.

1663. Would not the same argument apply to most of the important country post offices, such as Manchester, Liverpool, or Glasgow; are there not a crowd of merchants' clerks waiting at the post offices for the moment the newspapers are ready for delivery, and are not they pressed as much for time there as you are in London?—In the larger towns, probably the same argument holds good.

1664. Practically, there is no time for examining the newspapers?—I think not; in the larger towns it is probably the same as in London; the margin of time is very small.

1665. Suppose that in a small village, where the postmaster has not much to do, and there is no great hurry in applying for newspapers, he takes the trouble to examine one, unfolds it, and finds that there is no stamp, that it is a foreign paper,

Mr. *H. Parkhurst.*

20 May 1851.

paper, what does he do with it?—He charges it with postage, and it is his duty to do so.

1666. Is it charged by weight to the party?—Yes.

1667. And that party probably refuses it?—Yes, probably he does.

1668. And no penalty attaches to the party to whom it is addressed?—None whatever.

1669. You cannot reach the party who posted it?—No.

1670. Therefore, if you detect an attempt at fraud, you have no means of tracing it home to the party who committed the act, and no means of punishing it?—No.

1671. Suppose you carry a paper to a village down in Devonshire, and there you find that you have been carrying a paper that has not paid the stamp duty, the postmaster there, having detected it, makes a charge, which the party refuses to pay, and says he knows nothing about it, does the postmaster return it?—Yes, to the Dead Letter Office. If the unstamped paper be legally liable to stamp duty, it is sent to the Commissioners of Inland Revenue.

1672. You carry it over the journey a second time, and then what becomes of it?—It is destroyed, if not legally liable to stamp duty.

1673. Therefore the detection of fraud in such a case does not at all lead to the prevention of it?—No.

1674. *Chairman.*] Is there no limit of time at all that prevents a paper being constantly carried in virtue of the old stamp: is it carried for ever?—Yes, within the United Kingdom.

1675. Supposing I had a quantity of old newspapers that I did not know what to do with, and I kept directing them to the Honourable Member for the West Riding, and he kept directing them back to me, you would carry them for us all our lives, would you not?—Yes, and we know it is done.

1676. Mr. *Rich.*] Are you sure that the daily papers can be transmitted during the whole of a year?—Yes.

1677. There is no limit to the time?—No. We believe that newspapers have been sent as waste paper through the post. There are cases of very old bundles of papers having been sent in that way, apparently.

1678. *Chairman.*] In fact, if I were to send a bundle of papers as large as a diving-bell, you must carry it for me?—I believe so; there are certain dimensions that apply to letters generally, but which do not, I think, affect newspapers.

1679. What are the dimensions of the bulk?—Two feet in length.



1680. What

Mr. *R. Parkhurst.*

20 May 1851.

1680. What is the width?—I think two feet.

1681. Sir *J. Walmsley.*] Can you inform the Committee whether a newspaper sent by the post, regular in all other respects, would be surcharged for a name written on the outside?—Yes, it would; but newspapers are allowed to go with writing upon them if you put a penny stamp outside.

1682. The mere name would make that paper liable to a surcharge, would it not?—Yes, the name of the party sending.

1683. Would that rule apply if it were printed?—Yes, unless it came from a newsvendor.

1684. Is the name of the publisher allowed to be printed outside?—Yes.

1685. Mr. *Ewart.*] If any particular article is marked in a newspaper, it is liable to be charged, is it not?—Yes. But you may send newspapers containing writing, provided you pre-pay them with a penny stamp.

1686. Have you time to examine whether a mark is put upon a particular article in a newspaper?—The time would not allow of a strict examination.

---

*Veneris,* 23° *die Maii,* 1851.

MEMBERS PRESENT.

| | |
|---|---|
| Mr. Tufnell. | Mr. Ewart. |
| Mr. Shafto Adair. | Sir J. Walmsley. |
| Mr. Cobden. | Mr. Rich. |
| Mr. Sotheron. | Mr. C. Fortescue. |
| Mr. G. A. Hamilton. | |

THE RIGHT HON. T. MILNER GIBSON IN THE CHAIR.

---

*Rowland Hill,* Esq., called in; and Examined.

*R. Hill,* Esq.

23 May 1851.

1687. *Chairman.*] WHAT office do you hold in the Post-office?—That of Secretary to the Postmaster-general.

1688. You are aware of the existing arrangements at the Post-office in reference to the transmission of newspapers by post, are you not?—Yes.

1689. Can you state generally what are the existing arrangements there?—Every newspaper has, as the Committee are aware,

aware, a right to free transmission through the post; but of course it is necessary to take some steps to determine whether any publication is or is not a newspaper; and with that view a return is made weekly from the Stamp-office to the Postmaster-general of all newly-registered papers, when a copy of each is obtained, and it is submitted to the Postmaster-general to say whether it is to be considered a newspaper or not; and according to the decision of the Postmaster-general, it passes through the post free, or is excluded. I should add, however, that by a Treasury Minute dated in 1838, any publication which bears a newspaper stamp is allowed to go free through the Post-office, provided it does not exceed two ounces in weight; the limitation of weight not applying to papers that are strictly newspapers.

*R. Hill*, Esq.

23 May 1851.

1690. That Minute would appear to render any inquiry on the part of the Postmaster-general, as to whether a publication was or not a newspaper, unnecessary?—It would render it unnecessary, provided the publication is under two ounces.

1691. But nevertheless, if I understand you correctly, there is a sort of inquiry made in consequence of this return from the Stamp-office, and previously to the Postmaster-general giving his consent to this publication being carried according to the Minute?—Yes; at the same time I should explain, that meanwhile the privilege of free transmission through the post is not withheld. If a paper finds its way into the Post-office, and has all the appearance of a newspaper, and bears a stamp, then it would be passed, but immediate inquiry would be made with reference to the future. I should add, that information is transmitted of the decision of the Postmaster-general to the three Metropolitan offices, and if the paper be a provincial paper, to the post-office of the town in which it is published.

1692. Then there is a sort of newspaper privilege of going free granted to those publications if they be stamped and under the weight of two ounces; how does that privilege practically work which is granted to this class of publications that are not newspapers?—I am afraid that it is one cause of evasion. The regulations respecting newspapers are very much evaded, and probably the admission of portions of an impression may tend to promote that evasion. If a document is strictly a newspaper, as the Committee are aware, the whole impression must be stamped. But there are certain papers which are not, perhaps, strictly newspapers, which still have the privilege of passing through the post, so far as they may bear a newspaper stamp, unstamped copies being of course deprived of that privilege.

1693. You

*R. Hill*, Esq.

23 May 1851.

1693. You stated that there is great room for evasion; what kind of evasion do you refer to?—There are various kinds of evasion arising out of the whole arrangement; one is, that parties write in newspapers; another is, that sometimes an old newspaper is employed to enclose something which is not privileged to pass through the post, as a letter, for instance, or some article of dress; and again, I may mention that the fact of certain papers, such as the "Athenæum" and "Punch," being partially stamped, no doubt leads to unstamped copies being passed through the Post-office without detection.

1694. If I were to purchase, for instance, an unstamped copy of "Punch" at the office, and put it into the post, the probability is that it would go just the same, free from charge, as if I purchased a stamped copy?—There would be the chance of detection, and that is all.

1695. Mr. *S. Adair.*] Does detection very soon follow such a transmission?—I am afraid not invariably.

1696. Mr. *Tufnell.*] You do not insist upon the stamp being outside, do you?—No.

1697. Would it not be a good thing to have a regulation of that sort?—If there were such a regulation, unquestionably it would tend to check evasion; but there would be great difficulty in enforcing such a regulation.

1698. For what reason?—Because in printing a paper the stamp does not always fall on the first page.

1699. It could be so folded, could it not, that it would appear on the outside?—No doubt it would be possible.

1700. Would there be any difficulty in it?—None, if the public would take the necessary care; but we always find that there is great difficulty in enforcing regulations of that kind.

1701. Suppose a paper were not transmitted unless it were folded in that way, so that the stamp was on the outside, would not that ensure its being done?—No doubt it is possible, but it would lead to a great deal of complaint.

1702. Mr. *Cobden.*] You stated just now that newspapers were frequently made use of as a means for evading the postage, by enclosing articles of dress or unstamped publications inside of them?—Yes, various enclosures which are not entitled to the privilege.

1703. Suppose that you had an arrangement or regulation, by which it was necessary that the public should put a stamp outside of a newspaper, in the way suggested by the Honourable Member, that would not prevent frauds being committed by enclosing things in the interior, would it?—No, it would

*R. Hill*, Esq.

23 May 1851.

would not prevent one class of fraud, but it would prevent the other class of fraud, which consists in sending papers that bear no stamp at all.

1704. Would it not rather facilitate the other class of frauds, as the clerks at the Post-office would cease to be influenced by the main motive which now induces them to examine a newspaper at all to see if it is stamped?—I do not think they are much influenced by motives of that kind. They have instructions to examine in certain cases, and if the time admits of such an examination it is made; but there is no effective examination, it must be admitted.

1705. Would it be possible, under any circumstances, to establish a rule by which newspapers should be generally examined on being passed through the post?—It would be attended with a good deal of labour and expense. Of course we could do it, with a sufficient strength of clerks and others for the purpose.

1706. Could you do it within the same time as at present?—Unquestionably, with a sufficient amount of strength; but it would require a very large addition to our force.

1707. *Chairman.*] Perhaps the expense incurred would be great, in proportion to the revenue secured by the operation, would it not?—I think it would.

1708. Mr. *Tufnell.*] A newspaper to be passed through the Post-office must have a wrapper, and be open at the two ends?—Yes.

1709. Would there be any real difficulty in ascertaining whether there was any article of dress inside, or any waste paper?—No difficulty, if we had a sufficient force to do it; but I apprehend that the cost of that force would not be counterbalanced by the saving to the revenue.

1710. Would not an experienced clerk know immediately, in a rough way, whether that paper was really a *bonâ fide* paper, or whether it contained any concealed article?—Not without examination; without opening it. If there were any very large article enclosed, of course it would be detected without any careful examination; but you could not detect the enclosure of a letter without a careful examination.

1711. Mr. *Ewart.*] Are not several papers often wrapped up together?—It frequently happens that many papers are put under the same cover.

1712. *Chairman.*] Supposing that a person were to buy an unstamped copy of "Punch," and posted it, and you were to discover that it was an unstamped copy, you can enforce no penalty, and take no steps or proceedings against the party,

on

R. Hill, Esq. on the ground that he had attempted to defraud the postal revenue, can you?—We could make him pay the letter postage of the packet, if we could discover who sent it, but the difficulty is to discover who sends it.

23 May 1851.

1713. Mr. *Tufnell.*] Would it not practically operate as a check if it was perfectly well known that that paper, if posted without a stamp, would not be forwarded?—If it were certain that the paper would be stopped in the post, there would be very little attempt at evasion. It is the great chance of evasion passing undetected that leads to the present state of things.

1714. *Chairman.*] The only risk which a person runs is just the loss of the paper, is it not?—That is the real penalty in nine cases out of ten.

1715. Mr. *Cobden.*] Does not that operate to check the activity of your postmasters and clerks in detecting fraud, seeing that it can lead to no correction or punishment of the party who has attempted to evade the law?—I do not know that it does. The real state of the case is this: the public of course desire to have the letters and newspapers forwarded with as little delay as possible; the Postmaster-general, on the other hand, desires also to have the service performed at as small an expense as possible; and in the attempt to reconcile the two desires, the less important duties are apt to be neglected.

1716. It was stated by a former witness from the Post-office, that the detections of those frauds generally took place in the country post-offices, where they have more time to examine newspapers than they have, owing to the rapid circulation in the London Post-office. Supposing the detection of a newspaper sent unstamped to take place in a country post-office, the process is to charge, is it not, postage according to the weight, to the person to whom the newspaper is delivered?—Yes.

1717. And then the party invariably refuses to pay the postage, does he not?—Almost always.

1718. The local postmaster is then bound to return that newspaper to the London Post-office, is he not?—To the Dead Letter-office.

1719. Seeing then that the only result of the detection of this fraud in a country post-office must be that the Post-office would be charged with the duty of carrying that newspaper back again to the London Dead Letter-office to be burnt or destroyed, would not that operate as a deterring motive, and make an intelligent man not care much about detecting fraud at

*R. Hill*, Esq.

23 May 1851.

at all?—I do not think that the postmasters in the country know what is the result; they have performed their duty when they have presented the newspaper to the party to whom it is addressed and demanded the postage, and on his refusal to pay the postage they send it up to the Dead Letter-office, but they have no means of knowing what is done with the newspaper when it reaches the Dead Letter-office.

1720. Every intelligent postmaster must know, that if a newspaper comes without any signature attached inside or outside, that the Post-office authorities in London cannot know who dropped that into the Post-office?—No doubt they must arrive at that conclusion if they consider the question; but I do not think that, in point of fact, they are much influenced by these considerations. They have a routine duty to perform; some of the more intelligent postmasters, perhaps, consider those matters and are influenced by them, but I should expect they form a very small minority.

1721. *Chairman.*] In case a discovery is made, the consequence in point of fact is, that the newspaper that has been carried unstamped, the Post-office is compelled to carry back again?—Yes, but it is not much expense.

1722. Mr. *Tufnell.*] Do not you think, if it was publicly known that it was useless to put an unstamped publication into the Post-office, because it would not be forwarded, that that would be a much greater check against such a practice than any penalty whatever?—Certainly.

1723. *Chairman.*] Do you conceive that the injury to the revenue is the principal evil resulting from this system of evasion?—No, I do not think it is; I think the principal evil is, that it begets a habit of fraud and trickery on the part of the public.

1724. Mr. *Cobden.*] It relaxes the moral sentiment of the public, does it not?—Unquestionably. I think that the loss to the revenue by it is not great; and that though there is a large absolute number of evasions, the proportionate number is small. I do not think there is any very large proportion of newspapers that would be stopped, even with the most rigid examination.

1725. *Chairman.*] That is as far as you know?—Yes.

1726. If there be no effectual examination, you can hardly say at any particular time what proportion of unstamped newspapers there is amongst a large lot of newspapers?—Yes; we have the means of determining the proportion with tolerable accuracy, because, in the London office for instance, there are a good many examined every night; a sufficient number

*R. Hill*, Esq.

23 May 1851.

number to determine with some degree of accuracy the ratio of the evasions which are attempted.

1727. Do you take a sample out of a heap?—Yes; no doubt the men select the most suspicious looking of the newspapers, and the proportion of evasions detected is perhaps larger than that which would apply to the whole bulk.

1728. Mr. *Tufnell.*] Is not the great mass of the papers sent through the London Post-office into the country posted by newspaper agents?—I can scarcely speak to that question; but Mr. Bokenham, the gentleman at the head of the Inland Department, could speak to it.

1729. It is easy enough is it not to distinguish a newspaper which is sent by a newspaper agent from one that is transmitted by a private individual?—Yes.

1730. They have generally their names printed?—Yes, and they are made up in a different way.

1731. Those frauds, that you say take place, are not perpetrated by newspaper agents, but by private individuals?—They are chiefly perpetrated by private individuals, but I have seen attempts made by agents, in transmitting their accounts for instance, and in transmitting placards to be put up as advertisements of their papers, and so on.

1732. Mr. *Ewart.*] Is it not likely that the improper transmission of newspapers will increase, because, on the one hand, the wants of society will require a greater circulation of newspapers, and on the other hand, the time that can be allowed at the Post-office for examination will be so short, that they will not be able to detect attempts at evasion?—There is a constant increase in the desire for quicker transmission, but the Committee will see that with a sufficient force we could examine any number of papers.

1733. You must not only have a sufficient force, but an increasing force?—Yes, it must increase in proportion to the whole number, and in the indirect ratio of the time in which the work is done.

1734. Mr. *Tufnell.*] But merely to see that the stamp is on the outside, would that take much additional force?—No, very little.

1735. Mr. *S. Adair.*] Will you inform the Committee how many clerks are generally detached for this unprofitable examination?—I cannot say.

1736. Mr. *Cobden.*] The Committee have received, I believe all of them, a bundle of large tracts, and similar publications, which were sent through the post, addressed to them, and which came without the payment of any postage;

a witness

a witness who has been examined posted a bundle of Californian newspapers at Northampton, and they arrived at his address in London without any postage; in the face of these facts that have come within the knowledge of the Committee, of packets of papers being sent without postage, can you say that there is any plan in contemplation at the Post-office by which that system of evasion is to be prevented?—I am not aware of any; the question has been considered more than once, but the result at which we have arrived has generally been this, that the cost of an efficient scrutiny would be so large, that it would be unwise to incur it.

1737. Do you carry many newspapers through the Post-office for newsvendors?—A great many.

1738. They are folded up in sheets, are they not?—They come in various ways, some folded and addressed to individuals, and a great many put in large bundles, addressed to an agent, for distribution in a town.

1739. An Honourable Member has suggested that the stamp should be put on the outside of the newspaper when it is folded, in order that it may be seen that it is a stamped publication; would it be practicable, in the case of bundles of newspapers sent to newspaper agents, to exhibit the stamps of all the papers in a bundle on the outside?—No; it would not be practicable that all the stamps should be at top, of course, but they might with care arrange them so, that on lifting the ends of the papers in succession, it might be seen that the stamp was there; but, as I said before, we find great difficulty in enforcing regulations of that kind.

1740. Sir *J. Walmsley.*] Would not the difficulty be well met by putting one stamp of a sufficient value on the outside cover containing the whole?—That is assuming that a different system of charging existed.

1741. Mr. *Ewart.*] If you obliged the public to fold up the papers with the stamps outside, that would not prevent them from putting a great number of unstamped papers inside, so that a great number might circulate under colour of the outside stamped papers?—There would be no mode of preventing such an evasion, except that which we now take to a certain extent, namely, that of opening the papers.

1742. *Chairman.*] Taking a large paper like the "Times," with two sheets, if an individual wanted to send it to another, would he not find it a troublesome operation to fold up a great piece of paper like that so that the stamp should present itself on the outside?—I am afraid we should find it extremely difficult to enforce the rule.

1743. Mr.

R. Hill, Esq. — 23 May 1851.

1743. Mr. *Tufnell.*] Is not the stamp invariably put in the corner of the sheet?—I believe it is invariably struck in one corner of the sheet.

1744. Then what difficulty would there be in folding it so that it should appear on the outside?—It would require care, and we find it very difficult to induce care on the part of the public.

1745. Mr. *Ewart.*] Taking several sheets of the "Times," supplement and all, a man turns over the paper in different directions; perhaps the paper is turned inside out, and he has to search for the corner where the stamp is; would not that be a difficult operation?—It would require some little care, unquestionably; I do not think it would be difficult; the difficulty I contemplate is the difficulty we should have in enforcing the regulation. We should have endless complaints, I am afraid, if such a regulation were attempted.

1746. Mr. *Rich.*] Have the authorities at the Post-office had no plan under consideration by which they might obviate these consequences?—I am not aware that it has ever been ull y considered.

1747. You have been aware of the existence of these frauds? Yes, well aware of the existence of fraud to some amount.

1748. Does it exist to any great extent?—I have no doubt that every day many documents pass through the office which ought not to be allowed to pass free; I do not think that the proportion is large. We send off now from the London office, on the average, about 150,000 newspapers every day, and I am inclined to think that the proportion of those which go in breach of the law is small, but I have no exact information as to what it is.

1749. The difficulty does not appear to be so much with newspapers as with unstamped papers, or the circulars of tradesmen?—Yes, I think the chief difficulty is with that class of papers which is partly stamped and partly unstamped.

1750. Mr. *Ewart.*] What limit is there to the bulk of papers which you carry through the Post-office in one parcel? —There is no limit, that I am aware of, to the number of papers, each bearing a stamp, put together. It is well known that the size of a newspaper which passes under a single stamp is limited.

1751. If a man sent a considerable number of papers together, and you did not open them at the Post-office, the outside one being stamped, there is no particular limit to the number?—I am not aware that there is any limit; we have bundles weighing 10 or 20 pounds.

1752. *Chairman.*]

R. Hill, Esq.

23 May 1851.

1752. *Chairman.*] With regard to those publications which are partly stamped, and which are not newspapers in one view of the question, they go through the post, do they not, under a Treasury Minute, which says that anything that is stamped, and under two ounces, though it be not a newspaper, still shall pass as though it were a newspaper; but in the case of those that are newspapers, and where there is no limit as to weight, how do you decide whether they are newspapers or not?—By an examination of a specimen. I presume that the Stamp-office would refuse to apply the stamp to a sheet exceeding certain dimensions.

1753. But I might get a large number of sheets stamped?—Unquestionably.

1754. There is no limit as to the weight of a newspaper, is there?—None at all.

1755. Then supposing a parcel above two ounces is sent, with the intention that it shall go free, because it is a newspaper, how do you decide whether it is a newspaper?—If any doubt arose it would be referred to the solicitor of the department to report upon it. In point of fact, there is rarely any doubt as to whether a document is a newspaper or not.

1756. Mr. *Rich.*] Practically, your difficulty is not so much with newspapers, properly so called, as with the class of publications which are not newspapers at all?—There would be a difficulty, probably, if a paper, not clearly a newspaper, exceeded two ounces in weight. So long as it is under two ounces we do not care whether it be a newspaper or not. If it has a newspaper stamp it goes free.

1757. It has been stated that in the case of papers, for instance "prices current," or unstamped newspapers, passing through the Post-office not stamped, and the person to whom they are addressed being required to pay for their weight, he has the option to refuse to receive the paper, so that, practically, there is very little redress; but with regard to newspapers, properly so called, you could come upon the publisher of the newspaper, could you not, for a contravention of the law in sending a newspaper that was not stamped?—If any one were to print a newspaper on an unstamped sheet, the Board of Inland Revenue could deal with that case, but we cannot deal with the publisher as the party who sends it.

1758. Taking the newspapers generally, there is no great danger of the revenue suffering?—That is a case which the Board of Inland Revenue would deal with.

1759. If those newspapers, properly so called, were sent in contravention of the Act, the Board of Inland Revenue



would

R. *Hill*, Esq.

23 May 1851.

would know whom to proceed against for penalties?—I presume they would.

1760. But with regard to the class of publications like circulars, their transmission through the post improperly could not be made an offence against the persons from whom those circulars originated?—Not unless they gave their addresses, which, of course, they would not do.

1761. You could not prove that they were the parties who put the papers into the post?—The law gives to the Post office great facilities in convictions of that kind; it is assumed that a letter is sent by the party whose signature it bears, and it would rest with him to prove that he did not send it.

1762. If Savory & Son's circulars were sent through the Post-office, and many of them were not stamped, and it was discovered by the Post-office that they were not stamped, there would be no remedy against Savory, would there?—Certainly not, unless they bore his manuscript signature.

1763. Unless you could prove that they were put into the Post-office by them, and by their directions?—Certainly not.

1764. With regard to a newspaper, properly so called, if it was found in the office unstamped, the remedy would be directly against the publisher of such a newspaper, would it not?—I presume it would, but it would rest with the Board of Inland Revenue; we should refuse to pass it.

1765. *Chairman*.] Would you say that the arrangements you have described are defective?—Unquestionably they are defective.

1766. Do you think they are defective to some considerable extent, and, without overstating it at all, that the system of making the newspaper stamp the evidence of a right to go free by post is not an arrangement which you consider satisfactory?—As I have stated, there is a good deal of evasion, and I need not add that any law which is extensively evaded does not work well.

1767. Mr. *Tufnell*.] There is a limit to the size of the sheet to which the Stamp-office will affix a stamp, is there not?—Yes, I believe so, either to the size of the sheet or the superficial extent of the print upon it; I am not certain which.

1768. Do you know what the weight is?—There is no limit, I believe to the weight.

1769. They might stamp a paper of any thickness, provided it did not exceed a certain size?—A certain superficial extent.

1770. Mr.

1770. Mr. *Cobden.*] You stated that newspapers in any quantity or any bulk might go through the Post-office in one parcel?—Yes. *R. Hill,* Esq.

23 May 1851.

1771. May they be of any date, or is there any restriction as to the age of the papers?—None as to the age, so far as the transmission through the inland post is concerned. You cannot send a paper more than a week old through any foreign or colonial post.

1772. So far as the United Kingdom is concerned, you may send newspapers of any date, in any quantity, of any weight, and in any bulk, through the Post-office without charge?—Yes.

1773. Consequently, if a person in London had an accumulation of old newspapers, and had a friend living in a remote parish in the country in want of waste paper, they might be sent through the post free of charge?—Yes.

1774. And if, after that friend had done with those papers, he packed them up again and sent them to somebody else, the same papers and the same stamps would go through again?—Yes.

1775. And they might be transmitted 50 or 100 times?—Yes, they might be; but one can hardly conceive of a motive for doing that.

1776. There is no obstacle in the regulations at the Post-office?—None whatever.

1777. Was it always contemplated, when the newspaper stamp gave the franking privilege to newspapers, that that should be a frank, or that it should be for once only?—I cannot speak to that point; the Legislature has not provided any restriction.

1778. In all other cases, when you perform the service of carrying a letter or packet through the Post-office, you do not allow that letter or packet to have the same privilege again of carriage without a fresh payment?—Certainly not. Even in the case of redirected letters, where a letter is sent to one town, and the party to whom it is addressed is gone to another town, and the letter follows him thither, it has an additional charge upon it.

1779. Excepting in the case of newspapers, you never carry the same thing twice without a double charge?—No, certainly not.

1780. Has this part of the question ever come under your consideration, with a view to making a regulation in case an alteration took place in the newspaper stamp?—Yes; it is a question that has been considered in the Post-office more than

R. Hill, Esq. than once, whether, under the present arrangement, measures should not be adopted for preventing newspapers from passing twice through the post.

23 May 1851.

1781. That has been the subject of deliberation, has it?—Yes.

1782. You feel that it is an anomaly that ought, if possible, to be put an end to?—We consider it an abuse of the privilege, but which, I believe, is within the letter of the law, and therefore an alteration of the law would be required to prevent it.

1783. When you speak of the abuse of the privilege, have you reference to the carriage of the same newspaper twice for the same charge, or to carrying an old newspaper of very old date?—To the carriage of any newspaper more than once.

1784. Has it ever been a matter of consideration how you could provide against this abuse?—Yes, it has.

1785. You have no plan at present that you contemplate bringing into practical operation?—No; all plans have been rejected on the ground that the trouble and expense of applying them would be greater than the advantage gained would justify.

1786. In order to carry out any plan of preventing parties sending the same newspaper twice through the post, it would be necessary, would it not, to have the means of obliterating the stamp which has once passed through the post?—Unquestionably, and in that way arises the trouble.

1787. In the case of letters and packages which contain Queen's heads stamped on the covers, you obliterate them with ink, and they therefore cannot pass through a second time?—That is so.

1788. To carry out the same principle in the case of newspapers, it would be necessary to have the stamp always on the outside, would it not?—Certainly.

1789. You apprehend that there would be a difficulty in enforcing any such restriction, and that the public would not conform to your rule of putting the stamp outside?—That was one difficulty; another was, that it would throw upon the office the trouble of obliterating the stamp.

1790. Mr. *Tufnell.*] How do you know that the public would not conform to your regulation?—We know by experience that there is great difficulty in controlling the public.

1791. Mr. *Sotheron.*] Is there more difficulty with the newspapers than with the letters, or only the same?—We have not attempted to oblige them to place the stamp on the outside of newspapers.

1792. Mr.

1792. Mr. *Tufnell.*] When the penny stamp was first put on letters, used it not to be the practice to put it on any part of the cover?—No; in the first instance we requested that it might be placed in a particular part, and that request has been very generally attended to, and that does certainly hold out some encouragement to hope that the public would be induced to observe other regulations.

1793. *Chairman*]. It would be competent for the Treasury, in the present state of the law, if they thought fit, to make any regulations for the carriage of newspapers, or other papers, that circumstances might require. A newspaper is not absolutely entitled by law, is it, to pass free from charge through the Post-office?—I think it is entitled by the Act; but the Treasury has great powers granted to it by the Legislature, and I see no reason to doubt that they would be empowered to make the alteration which you contemplate; but I cannot speak decidedly upon that point.

1794. Supposing that the newspaper stamp were abolished, there would have to be a postage charge substituted for that on newspapers, I presume?—I presume that the public would expect to have their newspapers carried at a lower rate than that charged on letters; but if there were no such provision, of course we should charge the letter rates.

1795. You would have to carry them, you think, according to the public wishes, for a lower charge than letters?—Unquestionably.

1796. What charge should you say?—That is rather a question for the Legislature than for myself. The obvious arrangement would be to charge a penny as a postage rate, in lieu of the penny stamp imposed at the Stamp-office.

1797. Mr. *Ewart.*] A penny per half-ounce?—No; that would be subjecting newspapers to the same rates as the letters. I was assuming that a privilege would be continued to newspapers.

1798. Mr. *Cobden.*] You have a case in point, in foreign newspapers that comehere; the American newspapers come here for a penny, do they not?—I think we charge a penny, and I think the Americans charge a penny; but the rates upon foreign newspapers are so very anomalous that I cannot bear them in recollection.

1799. The Belgian newspapers come here for a halfpenny, do they not?—Many of the newspapers come free.

1800. A Brussels newspaper pays a halfpenny, but the American papers pay a penny, and that penny is marked on the cover. You would not have any difficulty in adopting the same

*R. Hill*, Esq.

23 May 1851.

same plan with reference to the internal postage of newspapers, would you?—I should very much object to any plan which allowed a paper to be sent without prepayment.

1801. You would have a penny stamp upon the cover?—The obvious plan is to have our present postage stamp put on the outside.

1802. *Chairman.*] You would place all the newspapers, in fact, upon the same footing as the "Athenæum" and "Punch," and such publications; that is to say, instead of using newspaper stamps for the purpose of sending through the post, those who wished to send through the post should send them by affixing a penny stamp, such as that which is now put on letters?—Yes, the same arrangements, except that the postage stamp would be substituted for the newspaper stamp.

1803. Then, in a pecuniary point of view, all the newspaper press would be put into the same position as the "Athenæum" and "Punch," and such papers, now are?—With the exception that I should advise that a stamp should be required every time that a paper passes through the post.

1804. That would be common to all, would it not?—Yes.

1805. Would you restrict the privilege of going for less than the letter postage to newspapers, or would you extend it to all printed publications, within certain limits?—The fairer principle probably would be to extend it to all printed matter; but we should be much afraid of increased evasion if that were done. I should consider it inexpedient in the first instance to extend such a privilege to all printed matter.

1806. You would like to try it first, would you not?—I should like to try it in a limited form, and gradually extend it, if it should appear from experience that it was safe to extend it.

1807. Mr. *Cobden.*] In case the law with respect to newspaper stamps were altered, the postage for newspapers would then become entirely a Post-office regulation, would it not?—I presume it would.

1808. You would have to deal with newspapers and other printed matter in the same way that you now deal with books and packets, and it would be left for you to make such regulations at the Post-office as you thought most conducive to the public interests and the revenue?—It would rest with us to advise the Treasury upon the subject. The authority rests with the Treasury.

1809. Would it not be more likely that the service of the Post-office would be carried out with most advantage to the public if the fixing of the postage and the regulations regarding

*R. Hill*, Esq.

23 May 1851.

ing it were left entirely in the hands of the Post-office, rather than allowing the franking privilege to be affixed to publications at the Stamp-office?—I do not think that practically there would be any difference. Now, if any inconvenience arose in consequence of the present privilege, it would be of course open to the Postmaster-general to advise the Treasury upon the subject.

1810. I have in my hand a catalogue of Messrs. Savory & Company, containing 64 pages, which would weigh more than an ounce; it contains drawings of tea-urns and wine-coolers, and other things, and it goes through the post with a postage stamp as a newspaper, for a penny, and it may go any number of times for a penny, may it not?—Yes.

1811. If you had the regulation at the Post-office of the postage of all printed matter, you would allow publications of that kind to be considered as newspapers, even though they were not strictly such, would you not?—I think, in the first instance, the better way would be to take the present list of newspapers, and of all publications which enjoy the privilege, and continue the privilege to them in a modified form, requiring the use of a postage stamp, rather than an alteration of the newspaper stamp.

1812. Mr. *Rich*.] If this system of newspaper stamps which has been suggested to you were adopted, do you not apprehend that the London publishers would send the great bulk of their papers to the principal towns by means of the railways, independently of the Post-office?—I have little doubt they would.

1813. Would there not, therefore, be a great loss to the revenue?—No doubt the change would involve a great loss to the revenue.

1814. Practically, then, the putting the London newspapers upon the same footing as the "Athenæum" and the other class of papers, would be very nearly an abolition of the stamp duty?—Not of all, but of a large proportion.

1815. If the distribution of the London daily newspapers in London was duty free, and if the great bulk of the London newspapers which are sent to the principal towns were sent by railway conveyance, independently of the Post-office, would not that lead practically almost to an abolition of the stamp duty?—There would be still a considerable set-off in the shape of postage; we should not lose all the newspapers, but I think we should lose a very considerable proportion of them.

1816. You would lose, speaking roughly, two-thirds of your

*R. Hill*, Esq.

23 May 1851.

your duty, would you not?—I prepared some time ago an estimate, which I can put in, if the Committee desire it.

1817. With regard to the plan proposed to you of exposing the stamp on newspapers, and requiring that they shall be folded so that the stamp shall be visible, if such plan could be made practicable, would not the fact of newspapers being charged which were folded up so carelessly as not to have the stamp visible, tend very soon to make all people fold them so carefully as that the mark would be visible?—No doubt, if you could enforce the regulation.

1818. If a person were reminded every morning that the regulation was not observed, by having to pay for his newspaper, instead of getting it duty free, that would induce him, would it not, to require his correspondent so to fold his newspaper as not to expose him to a charge?—I am afraid that the first inference would be that the Post-office had lost it or stolen it.

1819. Before the introduction of the penny postage, I apprehend that a great number of newspapers were sent by friends as conventional tokens, in substitution for letters, thereby saving the postage?—There was a considerable amount of evasion unquestionably.

1820. Since then have you not found that this method of circulating has decreased considerably?—I think it may be inferred *à fortiori* that it must have decreased; I cannot speak to that as an ascertained fact.

1821. With regard to the continued circulation of newspapers, which has been referred to, should you think that it exists to a very large extent?—I think it does.

1822. To the encumbrance of the business of the Post-office?—No, I cannot say that we are embarrassed by it.

1823. Do you think, if a penny stamp were affixed to newspapers, and they were circulated in that manner, that they would produce any material revenue?—I have an estimate here, dated the 9th of May 1850, which I will read: "Memorandum as to the number of newspapers passing through the Post-office.—No record is kept of the number of newspapers passing through the Post-office, but it may be estimated with tolerable accuracy thus: In 1838, the number of newspaper penny stamps being 53½ millions, the number of newspapers passed through the Post-office was ascertained to be 44½ millions. In 1849 the number of newspaper penny stamps was 79 millions, consequently the number of newspapers passed through the Post-office (assuming the proportion to be the same as in 1838) was 65½ millions. In this

*R. Hill*, Esq.

23 May 1851.

this estimate a newspaper is counted every time it passes through the office. Any estimate of the number of newspapers which would pass through the Post-office, if a postage charge of one penny were substituted for the stamp duty, must, I think, be viewed as very questionable; on the one hand, the number of newspapers published would be largely increased; but on the other, a much smaller proportion than at present would be sent through the Post-office. Taking all circumstances into account, and assuming the limitation of weight to be such that a present newspaper and its supplement would be counted as two, I am inclined to think that half the present number, or 33 millions, would be a high estimate. Thirty-three millions of newspapers, at 1*d.* each, would amount to about 137,500 *l.*" This, it will be observed, I view as the maximum estimate; I cannot say that I think there is much probability of our reaching it.

1824. *Chairman.*] If it were possible to ascertain the proportion of "Athenæums" and "Punches," out of the whole number published of the "Athenæum" and "Punch," that goes through the post, would not that furnish the Committee with something like a clue, because would not those parties who now stamp for postage continue to do so?—I think it would be a fair criterion to ascertain the proportion of "Athenæums" that are stamped. That, I presume, might be learned from the publisher, but the number actually sent through the Post-office we could not give.

1825. Assuming that those that were stamped were stamped for the purpose of passing through the post, they would give you pretty nearly the proportion, would they not?—It would afford you the means of calculating with some degree of accuracy.

1826. Mr. *Rich.*] Commercially speaking, it would be much more advantageous, would it not, to send an immense quantity of newspapers, such as are published daily in London, to Manchester or Liverpool, than to send down a small number of "Athenæums," or such weekly papers?—The demand for an early sight of the morning papers in the large towns is such, that many are sent by other means than through the Post-office.

1827. Mr. *Cobden.*] They are now sent?—Yes.

1828. You were asked whether, in case the stamp were removed, the great bulk of the London papers would not be sent to the principal towns by other means of conveyance than by post, and you said that they would; that is practically the case now, is it not?—Yes, it is practically the case with

*R. Hill*, Esq.

23 May 1851.

with the morning papers supplied to the large towns; they go by the early trains.

1829. The evening papers go by post still, do they not?—Yes; I think that the larger portion of the evening papers go by post, and a large number of the morning papers go by post also, having been read first at the coffee-houses, and such places.

1830. Mr. *Rich.*] If those newspapers are now sent at a certain cost to Manchester and other large towns by railway, when they could be sent through the Post-office for nothing, is not that an indication of how many more would be sent when there would be a charge for the transmission by the Post-office?—No doubt, as I have stated, there would be a much larger proportion sent by other means.

1831. Practically, the London newsvendors now forego the privilege of sending their papers for nothing by the evening mail or by the morning mail; and they prefer sending them at their own expense, or at the expense of the readers, by railway?—To a great extent that is the case.

1832. Mr. *Cobden.*] It is one class only, as I understand, who now do not avail themselves of the Post-office; that is, the newsvendors who send their packages to their agents in the large towns for distribution to individuals, and for the news-rooms and other public places?—To a great extent those papers are sent by railway; but we have a considerable number of packages and bundles of such papers through the Post-office.

1833. Are you acquainted with any instance of an individual sending a single paper by any other conveyance than the post?—I think not.

1834. In case of a change in the system, do you think that the same class of people who now send their papers by railway and by private conveyance would still continue to do so?—Unquestionably, and the class would be increased.

1835. The number of papers sent would be increased, would they not?—Yes.

1836. Would not individuals who bought newspapers in London for their own reading, or coffee-houses that had a few papers to dispose of at the close of the day, continue to send their papers through the post?—Yes.

1837. Would not the number of individual newspaper readers be very much increased if the papers were cheapened, owing to the abolition of the stamp?—No doubt they would be increased; but we can conceive a reduction in the price so great as that the temptation to transmit a paper to be read a second time should be greatly weakened, if not destroyed.

1838. Would

*R. Hill,* Esq.

23 May 1851.

1838. Would that be so in the case of a newspaper published in London being sent by a Londoner to a friend living in the country, who would have no opportunity of seeing a London paper, however cheap it might be, unless it was transmitted to him?—I think we should transmit papers to the villages and to small places which are, perhaps, not reached so readily by any other means as by the Post-office. We should supply those places with new papers, and carry the old papers, I mean those that have been read before, even to the large towns. I think that that would be pretty nearly the extent of the circulation through the post under the contemplated change.

1839. Mr. *Rich.*] Are not those papers which are now read by persons in town, and sent to their friends, frequently sent by newsmen themselves. For instance, a person reads a paper in the morning, and returns it to the newsman at the end of one, two, or three hours, and that newsman then transmits it either to a friend of this person, or to some other customer of his own?—Yes, I believe that is done also.

1840. And might not London newspapers, by private organization and arrangements, be sent to all the great towns, and distributed in those towns, at a less expense than a penny?—There is no doubt that it may be done at a less expense than a penny; but I do not see how individuals could avail themselves of that organization; the newsagents would, but I think not private individuals.

1841. Might not a company be formed for transmitting newspapers to different towns, and would not that company be enabled to transmit them at a less price than a penny, or less than a halfpenny each?—To towns, I think, they would.

1842. Mr. *S. Adair.*] Are you aware of the charges that are made by newsagents in Liverpool for the newspapers transmitted to them by railway?—No.

1843. The Committee have it in evidence that the London papers in Liverpool are charged 6 *d.* each, an additional penny being charged by the news agent for delivery; that is to say, the newsagent charges for two services, namely, for the newspaper stamp, and for the conveyance by railway, the party only receiving one service. Will you inform the Committee whether you do not think it probable that if the newspaper stamp were removed, and a postage stamp were simply necessary to transmit the paper through the post, the additional cheapness of that transmission would not induce parties to order their agents in London or in Liverpool to transmit their papers to them direct by post?—It appears to me, that instead of there being greater cheapness, there would be greater expense.

1844. On

*R. Hill,* Esq.

23 May 1851.

1844. On the transmission by post?—Yes; at present, there is no expense at all in transmission by post.

1845. The newspaper agents charge 6*d.*, that is to say, an additional penny, to the parties to whom they distribute their newspapers received by railway?—Yes.

1846. If there were no charge for the newspaper stamp, would there not then be the saving of a penny on the transmission by post?—No; if the cost of transmission by the railway and the delivery by the newsagent is a penny, as I understood your statement, and the cost of transmission and delivery by the Post-office were a penny, the two arrangements would be upon an exact equality.

1847. But in the one case the newsagent charges a penny, which is for the newspaper stamp representing an equivalent postage stamp, and an additional penny for I presume the proportion of the expense incurred in the transmission of the newspapers by railway?—If the newspaper stamp were abolished, which I presume is the state of things contemplated, of course the newsagent would not include the newspaper stamp in his charge; the two means of distribution would be upon an equality, I think.

1848. Mr. *Ewart.*] You would take a penny, as it were, from each side of the equation?—Yes.

1849. Mr. *S. Adair.*] In the first instance we presume the paper to be charged 5*d.* in consequence of the addition of the newspaper stamp; and the agent, on receiving this paper in Liverpool, charges an additional penny for the presumed proportion of the cost of transmission by railway?—Yes.

1850. If from the newspaper costing 5*d.* the stamp were removed, reducing it to 4*d.*, and a postage stamp placed upon it as an equivalent for the transmission, which would make it 5*d.*, would not parties in Liverpool then apply for the transmission of their newspapers, to be delivered to them for the sum of 5*d.*?—I think that would make no difference; the comparative cost would still remain as it is now.

1851. Mr. *Ewart.*] Would it not be more convenient to receive a paper direct through the post, than that it should go by railway, and then be re-distributed by another person, who must take charge of it at Liverpool on the part of the agent; supposing each to cost a penny, is it not probable that the simple operation of putting it into the Post-office would be preferred?—That would of course depend upon the comparative excellence of the means employed by the Post-office and by the newsagent; the cost would be the same in each case.

1852. Mr. *Cobden.*] Would the carrying of newspapers be

profitable

*R. Hill,* Esq.

23 May 1851.

profitable to the Post-office at the present rates, provided you were left to adopt your own regulations as to the transmission of newspapers without the intervention of the Board of Inland Revenue?—In one sense it would be profitable, and in another it would not. If we were to charge against the newspapers a share of the fixed expenses of the establishment; then it is very questionable whether it would be profitable; but if you consider, as we probably should, that the expenses of the establishment are incurred in respect of the letters, and only calculate the additional expense which would be thrown upon us for the transmission of newspapers, then I think we should find them profitable.

1853. Having an immense organization at the Post-office, with a certain amount of fixed charges, with a large amount of postmen necessarily travelling over the whole of the kingdom, you would find it profitable to carry newspapers for a penny, in addition to the letter carrying, would you?—Yes.

1854. Therefore, if the newspaper stamp were abolished, and you were to be left to regulate the postage at the Post-office, you would deem it profitable to carry newspapers at a penny each?—Yes, certainly we should; what I mean is, that the carrying of newspapers would not increase our expenses to the extent of a penny each.

1855. *Chairman.*] If the newspapers were removed altogether, you would not be able to make anything like a corresponding reduction of your expenses?—Certainly not.

1856. Mr. *Cobden.*] You were examined just now upon the subject of the distribution of newspapers in Liverpool; you are aware, that if a person takes a London morning newspaper in Liverpool, he pays to the newsagent there 6*d.* for it?—So I hear.

1857. That is, the party who pays the penny stamp, which would cover the postage of the newspaper, pays a penny to the newsvendor for delivering it to him at his house?—Yes.

1858. Seeing that it would be profitable to you to carry newspapers for a penny, supposing the regulation were left in your own hands, and you saw that newspapers were sold in Liverpool for 6*d.*, in fact, that you had a competitor in the market, who, by delivering newspapers earlier than you could do through the post, superseded you in the market, would it not be a matter for consideration, whether you could not adopt a mode such as you have in London for expediting the transmission of newspapers, and would you not contrive to send down newspapers by the morning mail?—It would be our duty undoubtedly to consider that question.

1859. In

R. Hill, Esq.

23 May 1851.

1859. In that case, if you could send a morning mail with the newspapers as early as they are now sent to the news-agents, the Post-office, having already an organization of letter-carriers in Liverpool, would be able to deliver these newspapers from house to house along with the letters, cheaper than they could be delivered by the news agents, who send out messengers expressly with them?—I cannot say that we could do it more cheaply; I am afraid we should not do it more cheaply.

1860. Did you not say that it was profitable to carry newspapers for a penny?—Yes.

1861. You understand, do you not, that the newsvendor finds it necessary to charge a penny for the stamp, and a penny for the delivery?—I learn that he does charge the penny; whether it is necessary, is another question.

1862. Do not you think that competition would bring that, as it does every other charge, down to the lowest possible sum?—No doubt, but looking at the comparatively expensive manner in which the Post-office department is managed, I am afraid that the competitors would beat us in point of expense.

1863. You stated, did you not, that it was profitable to carry newspapers for a penny?—Yes; reckoning it in the way that I pointed out, I do consider it profitable.

1864. Supposing you have customers at Liverpool willing to take the newspapers of you for a penny postage, in preference to paying a newsvendor 2*d.*, would it not be to your benefit to send a morning mail in order to deliver those newspapers in Liverpool?—I think it is very likely it would; but I understood your question to be, which would do the work most cheaply, the Post-office or the competitor; I suppose that the competitor would employ boys to deliver his newspapers, and he would deliver them probably unaddressed, which would simplify the means of delivery very much.

1865. You would deliver them for a penny, whereas they now cost the public 2*d.*?—No; the cost to the public in respect of transmission and delivery is 1*d.*; the penny stamp that is imposed upon them has nothing to do, I submit, with the cost of conveyance or delivery.

1866. In the case supposed, there would be no newspaper stamp?—Certainly not; I think that you cannot reckon the stamp as any portion of the payment for the transmission of the newspapers to Liverpool at present.

1867. Mr. *Sotheron.*] If you entered into competition, do not you suppose that a private competitor would distribute the

*R. Hill*, Esq.

23 May 1851.

the newspapers for less than a penny?—I think he would if we drove him down in price.

1868. Is not that the ground upon which you are of opinion, that in a direct competition between the Post office and a private individual, the Post-office would get the best of it?—I do not expect that the Post-office would get the best of it, but the worst of it in the large towns.

1869. If then the Post-office charge one penny, you would expect that a private competitor would charge three farthings or less?—I think they would either charge less or do the work more rapidly than we should in the towns, but we should have the advantage in the villages.

1870. Mr. *S. Adair*.] In the estimate which you have handed in, of the number of newspapers passing through the Post-office, have you calculated for each newspaper separately, and the number of times it passes, or have you taken separate newspapers and the number of parcels of newspapers?—We count every paper separately every time it goes through.

1871. *Chairman*.] Can you form any estimate of the addition to the expenses of the Post-office that is caused by carrying newspapers?—No, I have not attempted it; it would require much consideration.

1872. My question had reference to the additional labour it causes. Suppose, for instance, the newspapers were removed altogether from you, how much could you reduce your expenses?—Very little indeed.

1873. Then, in point of fact, the carrying of newspapers is all into pocket, or a great portion of it into pocket, if you are obliged in any case to carry on this large expenditure?—The greater part of it would be profit, reckoned in that way, I think.

1874. Is not that a fair way to reckon it, if you must in any case carry on a certain expenditure?—Yes, I think it is.

1875. Mr. *Rich*.] In reply to the Honourable Member for the West Riding, you stated that the carrying of newspapers at present was only profitable if you cast out of the consideration the expenses of the establishment?—That is my opinion, that it only is profitable on the assumption that you must maintain the establishment, and must pay for the transmission of the mails, whether you have the newspapers or not. We have a large machinery, and the additional expense required to manage the newspapers, as well as the letters, is in my opinion small.

1876. *Chairman*.] If I understand the sort of substitute that might be proposed for the newspaper stamp it is this,

to

R. Hill, Esq. — 23 May 1851.

to place all newspapers on the footing on which the "Athenæum" and some others now are; namely, to charge a penny each parcel sent through the Post-office?—Yes.

1877. To be paid by attaching a postage stamp outside, or by using stamped wrappers?—Yes. The latter was the mode originally proposed by Mr. Charles Knight for franking newspapers many years ago.

1878. This stamp would be obliterated each time the newspaper passed through the Post-office?—Certainly.

1879. So that it would carry the paper only once?—Yes.

1880. Papers posted in a town to be delivered in the same town are now subject to the extra charge of one penny?—Yes.

1881. Would you continue that extra charge, or extend this suggested arrangement to them?—I would place all upon an equality.

1882. The prepayment of this stamp would be compulsory in all cases?—It would be very important to make it so.

1883. So that parties could not send a newspaper even upon a double payment after its receipt?—No; I should very strongly advise that you give no such option.

1884. With regard to limitation as to weight, what limit would you place to the weight which you would allow to be carried in this way?—That is a question which I am not prepared to answer. I can give the Committee some information as to the actual weights of certain of the larger newspapers, which perhaps might assist them.

1885. Would you consider the weight of the "Times" and its supplement, as the maximum weight that you would carry for a penny postage stamp, would be too large?—I am not prepared to answer that question. I find that the heaviest paper sent through the Post-office for a single stamp is the "Weekly Dispatch," and that its weight is about three ounces and three quarters.

1886. Your plan would be, would it not, that there should be a limit of weight, and that all above that weight should be charged proportionately?—Unquestionably there must be a limit.

1887. The precise limit that you would fix you are not now prepared to state?—No; the weight of the "Times," without the supplement, is about two ounces and three quarters.

1887*. The "Dispatch." would require a limit of four ounces?—Yes; but that would be very high.

1888. Mr. *Sotheron.*] Would you have any limit to the bulk?—No; I would make it entirely a limit of weight; that would

would be easily ascertained, the other would be a work of time. *R. Hill*, Esq. 23 May 1851.

1889. *Chairman.*] You would allow different papers to pass under one postage stamp, if the whole did not exceed the limit of weight, would you not?—I see no objection to that; I think it would rather facilitate our proceedings.

1890. So that in the case of papers that were considerably less in weight than the "Times" and its supplement, several of them might be sent in virtue of one postage stamp?—The simplest arrangement unquestionably would be to regard the weight only of the packet.

1891. Without regarding the number of distinct publications?—Yes.

1892. Would you impose any other condition upon publications so transmitted, either as to the mode in which they should be folded, or anything of that sort, to guard against evasion?—I think we should require that a list should be made of the publications authorized to pass through the Post-office at those rates, and therefore some mode must be devised of regulating the admission to the list if the newspaper stamp were abolished. It appears to me that the better course would be to admit all publications to that list, upon condition of their paying a moderate fee, in order to prevent frivolous applications; and then, in addition to that, I think it would be necessary that there should be a small annual payment, with a proportionally higher rate of payment for shorter periods, so as to enable us to keep the list within manageable limits, by clearing it, from time to time, of publications which had ceased. If you require a periodical payment in advance, then of course, in the absence of such payment, the name of a publication would be struck off the list.

1893. In the folding up of any publication, do you propose any mode by which its identity could be established if required?—I think it should be folded so as to expose the title, or that the title should be printed or written upon the wrapper.

1894. The great danger you apprehend is this, that if you grant a postal privilege, that is, a less rate of postage than the letter postage to packets, they may contain, in point of fact, letters and things that the privilege was not intended to apply to, and you would, to a certain extent, be still exposed to some of those evasions to which you are now exposed under the newspaper stamp system, namely, that a packet that professes to be a newspaper, or a publication entitled to the postal privilege, is in reality something else?—Certainly, I am afraid that

*R. Hill*, Esq.

23 May 1851.

that the evasions, in the absence of the limitations I have endeavoured to describe, would be greatly increased.

1895. To some extent there would be a set-off, because now you may carry a packet that is not even stamped, and nothing stamped inside of it, that never has paid any duty, but still goes free; at least, under this system you would secure the postage stamp, and you would be the better by the postage stamp, because at present you may carry packages that never paid?—Yes; we should be secure against packages going through the office without any payment at all.

1896. You would secure a penny on everything?—Yes.

1897. Even if it did not happen to be a publication entitled to go through the post?—Yes.

1898. At present you may carry things that have paid nothing at all?—Certainly.

1899. Mr. *Rich.*] Would not those precautions against fraud be quite as difficult of execution as the precautions suggested by the Honourable Member for Devonport with regard to stamping a newspaper, and requiring that the part stamped should be visible?—No, I think not, because the title of a publication may be printed in every page; indeed it is generally printed in every page.

1900. Still it must be folded up so that the title may be visible on the outside, must it not?—Yes, but there is only one stamp on the paper, and there are generally several titles, or rather the title is several times repeated. I would admit of the title being printed on the wrapper or written upon it, the object being to enable us readily to discover what the document is, or rather what it purports to be.

1901. There would be the same difficulty in detecting, as the Honourable Chairman has stated, would there not, many things being sent which had not paid the stamp?—There would be the same difficulty, unquestionably, as to the detection of inclosures, but, as the Honourable Chairman pointed out, we should be secure of our penny.

1902. At the same time, while you secured that penny there would be a loss to the revenue of all the newspapers that did not pass through the post?—Yes, I have said before that I cannot expect that under any arrangements Government could avoid a considerable loss of revenue.

1903. Mr. *S. Adair.*] I presume that stamped wrappers are a part of your plan?—Stamped wrappers were recommended many years ago, when the same question was under consideration.

1904. I presume that the object of using them would be with

R. *Hill*, Esq.

23 May 1851.

with reference rather to the weight of the parcels that were transmitted through the post, than as representing so many individual franks?—I think it would be a convenient mode of applying a postage stamp, and, as a paper requires a wrapper, it might be struck upon the wrapper. It would save the trouble of applying a loose stamp; that is the object.

1905. Inasmuch as the newspapers are of considerable weight, might it not be a fair concession to newspaper publishers to allow of the transmission of one aggregate weight contained in a wrapper. Take, for instance, the "Weekly Dispatch;" you stated that it averaged about three ounces and three quarters; four of these would average 15 ounces. Supposing they could enclose four copies in a 15-ounce wrapper, might not that be advantageous as well to the public as to the parties concerned in the publication?—I should recommend that the charge have reference simply to the weight of the packet, the total weight of it, not to the number of papers included therein. It would be difficult for us to levy a rate which had reference to the number of papers enclosed, but comparatively easy to weigh the whole packet.

1906. Reference being had to the weight of papers enclosed in a wrapper, would not a great deal of fraud, likely to result from enclosures, be obviated?—I am afraid not, because the Committee appear to contemplate a low rate of charge, a rate very much lower than that levied upon letters; therefore, though any enclosure would still pay something, inasmuch as it would pay a much lower rate than if sent properly, the temptation would remain. Suppose the limit should be placed even at two ounces, which is the present limit to documents that are not newspapers, the postage charge upon a letter or any unprivileged packet would be 4*d.* if it exceeded an ounce at all; and therefore, if you carried a two-ounce packet for a penny, you have a temptation to the extent of 3*d.* to evade the rate.

1907. But the security would be in case of uniformity of charge as between letters and newspapers?—Any privilege involves evasion.

1908. *Chairman.*] The precautions which you have mentioned were with a view to lessen the amount of the risk?—Yes.

1909. Have you endeavoured to devise any plan by which the Post-office might be enabled to distribute newspapers on lower terms than a penny?—I have turned my attention to that point, and at one time I thought they might be carried on lower terms than a penny, and still with a profit; I endeavoured

*R. Hill*, Esq.

23 May 1851.

voured to devise a mode similar to that which the newsvendors adopt of sending newspapers unaddressed, which would of course save trouble to the newsvendors, and would save the trouble at the Post-office of the assortment; but I am afraid that there are practical difficulties in the way which render it impossible to carry out such a plan; as yet I have not been able to overcome the difficulties.

1910. Could you state rather more in detail the nature of your plan?—The plan I contemplated was this: that we should take the newspapers, provided that they were supplied to us in large numbers, unaddressed, except for the several towns; one for Liverpool, one for Manchester, one for Birmingham, and so on; and that we should then deliver them according to lists of the parties with their addresses, which should be supplied to us by the newsvendors, and which should be open to alteration only at certain periods; say once a quarter; that was the plan I had in view, and there is no doubt that such an arrangement would save great trouble in the London office; but I am afraid that it would even increase the trouble in the provincial offices, from which they would be delivered.

1911. How would that be?—In this way: if we had to deal with one newsman only, then even in the delivering office trouble would be saved; but we should have perhaps 50 bundles of those newspapers sent for each town by as many London agents; some would be sending first editions of the "Times," and some second editions, and so on, and it would not do to mix all the copies of the "Times" together, and distribute them to the letter-carriers, simply taking care that each had the proper number, and so with the other papers, which was what I had in view. The letter-carriers must be enabled to deliver at each house, not only a copy of the "Times" or "Chronicle," as the list may indicate, but the particular edition of the "Times" or "Chronicle" intended for that house on the particular day. Thus the matter would become so complicated that no advantage, I fear, would result.

1912. But if you could carry out that plan, you think that you could distribute the papers at a less charge than a penny; at how much less than a penny do you think?—I was in hopes that we might distribute them at a halfpenny, if we could have completed a plan in the simple form in which it presented itself to my mind at first.

1913. The plan is so far under consideration, and, perhaps, these difficulties may be got over?—I cannot hold out any expectation

expectation of that; I think I have considered it sufficiently to see that those difficulties are all but insuperable; of course, it would be absurd to say that it is impossible to overcome them.

1914. Mr. *S. Adair.*] With respect to the delivery of letters, have you any scale of maximum weight which the letter deliverers are compelled to carry round. For instance, the weight of their letter-bags would be considerably increased in the case of distributing newspapers; have you any limit?—No; of course, if it should so happen that any letter-carrier had a larger burden than he could manage conveniently, some assistance would be given to him; but I never heard of such a case.

1915. It appears from the average you have given, that 40 copies of the "Times" would weigh 7 lbs.; that would be a considerable addition, would it not, to a man's labour, having to carry that weight over his beat at the pace at which he is compelled to travel?—Forty copies without the supplements would weigh something about that; the weight that I gave was of the "Times" without the supplement; but if any letter-carrier had a greater weight than he could manage, assistance would be afforded him. We are not afraid of being overworked; the more work we get, the more profit we obtain.

1916. With respect to deliveries by country postmen, they have to travel great distances with very heavy weights, have they not?—Yes; the greatest burdens are the large Blue Books. Except by an occasional heavy Blue Book, I do not know that there is much danger of the country postman being over-burdened.

1917. Does the Scottish department of the Post-office come under your supervision?—Under the general supervision of the Postmaster-general.

1918. There is a postman who travels from Gortlich, in Inverness-shire, to Fort Augustus; the weight he has to carry is considerable, and though not excessive for a foot post, it would be much increased if he had to distribute newspapers on the line, would it not?—You will please to bear in mind that newspapers are now distributed, and that the apprehension is, not that the number sent through the post would be increased, but so much decreased that we should lose a good deal of revenue.

1919. Mr. *Ewart.*] You would not have more to carry in such a district as the one that has been mentioned, under the altered system, I apprehend?—I fear that we should carry very many less.

 1920. *Chairman.*]

*R. Hill*, Esq.

23 May 1851.

1920. *Chairman.*] With respect to the difficulties you have mentioned, of carrying out a cheap mode of delivering papers, a newsvendor would send to the Post-office, would he not, a file of the "Times," a file of the "Chronicle," and a file of any other paper, to be delivered in particular towns?—Yes.

1921. With a list with each?—Yes.

1922. Then the Post-office would despatch to Manchester a file of the "Times," and a file of the "Chronicle," with the respective lists?—Yes.

1923. Then the distributors of the letters would distribute them according to the lists; where is the difficulty?—There is no difficulty if we had to deal with one newsvendor only; but many of them would do precisely the same thing, and each letter-carrier would have to deliver three or four copies of the "Times" for one newsvendor, and three or four copies for a second newsvendor, and three or four for a third; and some of those copies would be first editions, some second, and some third editions; it would not do that he should mix them all together. Then with reference to some house at which a copy of the "Times" must be delivered, the letter-carrier must leave the particular edition that the newsvendor sent, and this consideration complicates the machinery so much, that I think it would be better to have the newspapers addressed and assorted in the usual manner.

1924. You mean that by the same post there would be several editions of the same paper going?—Yes.

1925. And that the distributor of those papers would have nothing to show him whether the party to whom he was to distribute the "Times" was to have the first edition, or the second, or the third edition?—Certainly, that is the difficulty.

1926. Might not it be provided for by saying that only the first edition could be allowed to be distributed in this way, and that if it was a second edition of a paper, or a third edition of a paper, then, in that case, the newsagent must post it with a postage stamp in the ordinary way?—That would greatly diminish the utility of the arrangement; if you restrict a newsvendor so that he cannot send the latest edition that is published up to the moment, of course you very greatly diminish the utility of the plan.

1927. But, as a general rule, I presume that the first edition is the one that people generally get?—That depends very much upon the hour of publication; papers that go out by the evening mails, I suppose, would consist very much of the later editions of the day; then the evening papers publish, some of them,

them, a succession of editions; the "Sun," for instance, publishes two or three editions at night, and great efforts are made to include the latest edition in the despatch of the evening. *R. Hill*, Esq. 23 May 1851.

1928. It would not be possible to have separate files of the editions, would it?—It would complicate the matter too much; that is what I tried to arrange, but I found it was becoming so exceedingly complicated that I gave it up.

1929. With regard to this question of different editions, is that the only difficulty that you have to overcome?—That is the main difficulty, I think.

1930. But for that difficulty, the plan might be carried out, might it not?—I am not prepared to speak so decidedly as that; I do not at present see any other serious difficulty than that of the variety of editions.

1931. Mr. *Rich.*] After all the precautions which have been suggested, would you not have to drop the carrying of newspapers into the hands of a private company or private newsvendors?—I was endeavouring to devise a plan to enable us, at a profit, to carry newspapers at a lower rate than a penny, to retain the custom which I fear we shall lose if we charge so much as a penny; and I at present have failed in accomplishing the object which I had in view.

1932. You feel that at a penny you could not compete with private conveyance, and that at a reduced rate you would be obliged to have restrictions and precautions, which would equally deprive you of the advantage of cheapness?—At a penny we should still carry newspapers to villages, and the old newspapers, those that have been read, to the towns; but I do not think that we should supply towns with fresh papers; and it was in order to secure that part of the custom that I endeavoured to devise the arrangement to which the Honourable Chairman refers. I have talked the matter over with some of the practical officers, and, among others, with Mr. Bokenham, and he pointed out the difficulty that stopped me.

1933. Practically you would be left with the less populous districts, and the more onerous distribution, while the more profitable part of the business would fall into the hands of certain newsvendors, or a company of newsvendors?—I am afraid it would be so.

1934. Sir *J. Walmsley.*] In provincial towns, do you suppose that it would make it necessary to increase your staff of postmen very materially, if you had a considerable number more letters to deliver, or would they be able to deliver more letters than they do now in their rounds?—Any very large increase

R. *Hill*, Esq. — 23 May 1851.

increase of letters would unquestionably require some increase of staff in all the larger provincial towns; but it would not require a proportionate increase of staff; if we double the number of letters, we need not have twice as many letter-carriers.

1935. You are of opinion that a great many more newspapers than those which go by post now might be delivered by the local letter-carriers without any material increase in the staff?—Without any very material increase.

1936. Such being the case, will you state to the Committee where the difficulty is in your competing with the newsvendors, seeing that you have already the letter-carriers upon the spot to deliver the newspapers; could they not deliver a greater number of papers than they now do?—The difficulty consists partly in the circumstance which I pointed out; besides, for the purpose of delivering letters, we require men, whereas the delivery of newspapers is in the large towns managed almost entirely, I believe, by boys; and it would probably be considered unsafe to entrust boys with the delivery of letters. That is one reason. Another reason is, I have mentioned, that the Government always works more expensively than a private individual; and the third is, that our times of delivery are fixed with reference to the letters, whereas the newspapers are, to a very great extent, sent by the early trains, which are not mail trains. If we were to despatch newspapers by those same trains, then we should require something like a special delivery of newspapers, and we should lose the advantage which you have pointed out, of mixing the newspapers up with the letters.

1937. Mr. *Ewart*.] In that case you might employ boys, if the delivery solely consisted of newspapers, might you not? —If the delivery solely consisted of newspapers, probably we might employ boys; but the Government does not work so cheaply as a private individual does.

1938. Mr. *Rich*.] But they would be boys in addition to your staff of men, would they not?—Yes.

1939. Sir *J. Walmsley*.] Seeing that you can deliver a much larger number of papers than you do now, and seeing that the men must go their various rounds, I do not see how your expenses would be increased, provided you had a much larger number of letters to deliver?—I have not stated that our expenses would be materially increased, by the increase of newspapers, if they fell in with the ordinary delivery of the letters. But the Committee will bear in mind that the morning mails start generally about 10 o'clock, whereas the

*R. Hill*, Esq.

23 May 1851.

the morning newspapers for the large towns are despatched generally by the first train, perhaps at six and seven o'clock; therefore the train carrying the newspapers has the start of us by three hours. Then again, on the arrival of the mail bags, the letters have to be assorted, and the newspapers would have to wait that assortment, which occupies generally another hour. Therefore I think the Committee will see, that unless we resort to some special means for the delivery of the newspapers, a newsagent would beat us in time; and if we did resort to special means, then we should lose the advantage that has been described of employing our staff, which is formed chiefly with a view to the delivery of letters, also for the delivery of newspapers.

1940. In almost all the large towns in the kingdom you have mid-day and afternoon deliveries as well as morning deliveries, have you not?—Yes, we have.

1941. Then could not your newspapers that come by the early mails from London be delivered in the afternoon by the letter-carriers at the same time that they deliver the letters? —Yes; I am supposing that they would be delivered at that time, but that would be some hours after the newspapers would be delivered by the newsvendors, and they would beat us in time, unless we, like them, had a special organization for the purpose.

1942. No doubt your attention has been well directed to this subject; but I apprehend that in the large towns this would be the case, that the postmen would be able to deliver papers generally more promptly in every part of the town than any small newsvendors could do, from the number of your staff? —I think not. I think that the boys of the newsagents would start very much earlier than our letter-carriers could start, because they would not be embarrassed with the assortment of any letters, and with the securities which we are obliged to take with reference to letters. For instance, if there is postage to be collected on the letters, an account of that postage must be taken; there is a good deal which necessarily delays the despatch of the letter-carriers, which would not delay the despatch of the boys employed by a newsagent; therefore, even if the parcel of newspapers were carried by our mail train, I am afraid that the newsagent would get the start of us in the delivery. But he would not wait for the mail train; he would get his parcel by the earliest train after the hour of publication; and if we are to attempt any competition in large towns, I think that then we must totally alter our system. I think it would be necessary that we should have, as

*R. Hill*, Esq.

23 May 1851.

as it were, newspaper mails by those early trains, and that we should employ persons, either men or boys (and perhaps there would be no objection to employ boys), for the special delivery of newspapers. I think we should be driven upon such means as those if we attempted to enter into competition with the newsvendors in the large towns. In the smaller places, where the organization for the delivery of newspapers is less perfect, or perhaps does not exist at all, we may employ our letter-carriers, and add the newspapers to the ordinary business of the Post-office, as we now do, and retain the postage.

1943. You are aware, I apprehend, that at present there is very little competition between newsvendors and the Post-office authorities, as regards the delivery of newspapers in various towns, save those papers which are delivered in large masses at the news-rooms, and various places of that description; that is to say, the newsvendors do not undertake to deliver newspapers singly to persons to any great extent?—I was not aware of that fact. I certainly have assumed that the newsagents distribute a considerable number of newspapers at the houses in the larger provincial towns; if I am mistaken as to the fact, of course then much that I have said falls to the ground. But I certainly was strongly impressed with the opinion that the distribution of newspapers in the larger provincial towns is effected very largely by the newsagents, even to the houses of private individuals.

1944. Mr. *Rich.*] Since the large towns and London would not avail themselves of the penny stamp, generally speaking, to convey their newspapers, and the smaller towns in remote districts would, practically the result of the plan proposed would be, that the newspapers would, in London particularly, and also in the large towns, be cheaper than in the small towns and in the country?—No doubt they would, but that is the case with everything else; everything almost is cheaper in the larger towns than in the country; everything that has to bear the cost of carriage; it is not peculiar to newspapers.

1945. One great element of the reform introduced by you in the postage was, that there should be one uniform rate throughout?—Yes; it was proposed with a view to simplification, but the principle has been carried to an extent that I did not contemplate, and did not recommend.

1946. In London, for the daily papers, there would be a gain of nearly a penny, would there not?—I presume there would, fully a penny.

1947. And in Manchester, Liverpool, and the large towns, probably a gain to the extent of a halfpenny?—The mode of

circulation

circulation, which has been mentioned, at Liverpool, of an additional charge of a penny for the transmission and delivery of newspapers by newsagents, seems to me to disturb one's calculations very much; if that system is at all general, then I do not to the same extent fear the competition. I have supposed that it was done without an extra charge; if it is a general thing for the newsagents to charge an additional penny in the towns, then, inasmuch as we propose to charge a penny, we should be upon an equality as regards the cost of the distribution.

1948. Do you not conceive that if the penny stamp were taken off, there would be so many more sent to those large towns, that there the distributors would be able to distribute them, at a profit, at a lower rate than a penny?—I imagine that it must be so; we know that there are many penny publications, for instance, there was the "Penny Magazine," a work of a very extensive circulation, that was delivered at the houses, and I believe without any additional charge; and therefore the means must exist for an exceedingly cheap distribution in the provincial towns.

1949. Sir *J. Walmsley.*] Then the same rule would apply to the Post-office that would apply to newsvendors; if they got a profit by the increase, the Post-office also would get an increase at the same time, would it not?—No doubt; I have in my estimate spoken of that as a cause of increase, only that unfortunately it is counteracted by more active causes of decrease.

1950. Mr. *Rich.*] It would be counteracted by the competition you have alluded to in your evidence?—It would be counteracted by the fact that the distribution through the Post-office now costs the public nothing, and then it would cost a penny.

1951. Mr. *S. Adair.*] Are the Committee to infer, from what you have stated of the complicated machinery that would be necessary in case you entered into competition with newspaper distributors of unaddressed papers, that a most advantageous change, on the whole, for the revenue would be for the Post-office to take charge of the distribution of addressed newspapers at a differential postage somewhat less, or at least less, than the charge on the postage of letters?—I think so; of course, if the Legislature should determine on abolishing the newspaper stamp, it would become the duty of the Post-office to consider whether they could not retain their share of the delivery of newspapers, even in the large towns; but I must own that I do not see at present the means of accomplishing it

*R. Hill*, Esq.

23 May 1851.

it. I need not point out to the Committee that the Post-office has no monopoly of the distribution of newspapers; it would be quite open to the public to establish a company for the distribution of newspapers.

1952. *Chairman.*] You would try hard not to lose them?—Certainly, I should wish to keep the custom if we could.

1953. Mr. *S. Adair.*] Have you a reasonable expectation that by reducing the cost of postage on newspapers you might retain any portion of the business?—We might retain a considerable portion even at a penny.

1954. Mr. *Rich.*] There is a wide difference between maintaining your ground by carrying letters according to your present mode against any company that might be organized, and carrying and distributing newspapers?—Yes, because letters must be addressed, and you must have the trouble of assorting them, to say nothing of the monopoly, which, however, does not stand for much.

1955. Mr. *Cobden.*] At present the money paid to the revenue for the newspaper stamps all goes into the account of the inland revenue?—Yes.

1956. So that the Post-office, in your annual accounts, does not take credit for the portion of the postage which comes under the head of newspaper stamps?—Certainly not.

1957. Do you think, if an alteration were made by which you yourself would be at the Post-office authorized to regulate the postage of newspapers, that you could carry out a plan by which the Post-office would probably receive 130,000 *l.* a year as postage on newspapers?—I have put that down as the maximum estimate; I cannot say that I think we should get so large a sum.

1958. Then would you put down that as the sum that you possibly might receive?—Yes.

1959. Have you taken into account the probable great increase in the number of newspapers that would be published if the price were as low as it is in America?—Yes, I have.

1960. You have contemplated that there would be an increased number of newspapers sent to individuals arising out of that increased circulation?—Yes.

1961. Have you abandoned altogether in despair the idea of competing with newsvendors in sending the great bulk of the papers to the large towns?—No, I have not altogether abandoned it, but I do not see much hope of succeeding.

1962. You would apply yourself probably to that question with more earnestness, provided the regulation of the postage of newspapers were thrown entirely into your hands?—Yes.

1963. It

*R. Hill*, Esq.

23 May 1851.

1963. It would be your endeavour, if possible, and if you could see a profit resulting from it, to sweep the whole of the newspapers into the Post-office for transmission?—Certainly, it would be quite fair to attempt it; seeing that we enjoy no monopoly, it would be fair to get all the custom we could.

1964. Mr. *Sotheron.*] Have you not already indicated a mode by which you could enter into this competition with some chance of success, by having a special delivery of newspapers?—That would be one mode which it would be our duty very carefully to consider, as holding out at least a prospect of being able to accomplish the work in large towns at a less rate than a penny.

1965. In any plan that you have been devising for the transmission of newspapers with a stamp, you have not contemplated carrying them for less than a penny?—No.

1966. Supposing you fixed the rate at a penny, and that it was necessary to increase your establishment in large towns so as to have a special delivery of newspapers to meet the early editions, do you think then that a penny would remunerate you?—I can scarcely say; that would depend entirely upon the number we should have to deliver at the same time.

1967. Supposing that the result of such a special delivery should be, that you did obtain for the Post-office the carriage and the delivery of the early editions of newspapers, and that in fact you drove out private competition from the market, do not you think then that a penny per paper would remunerate you?—I believe that a penny per paper would remunerate us under any circumstances, but if we attempted to beat down competition, we should be obliged, in the large towns where we delivered a great many, to deliver them for less than a penny.

1968. Mr. *Cobden.*] Would you be able to receive any probable increase in the number of newspapers at the Post-office, and transmit them profitably for a penny?—Yes, I think so.

1969. In that case, if there was a very considerable increase in the number of newspapers, that would be pretty nearly clear profit for any beyond the present number, and would not add to your fixed charges?—In a very slight degree.

1970. Your carriers would carry a greater weight than they now carry?—There are few letter carriers that would not bear a large increase of burden.

1971. You stated, did you not, that you contemplated some increase of labour in case you had to obliterate each stamp on the

*R. Hill,* Esq. — 23 May 1851.

the envelopes of the newspapers?—Certainly, there would be that in addition to the present labour.

1972. Can you give any idea of the number of stamps that a clerk obliterates in a given time?—Mr. Bokenham can state that to the Committee. It may be proper to add, that throughout these suggestions I have had in view the distribution of newspapers in the United Kingdom only; and that before they could be reduced to practice, it would be necessary carefully to reconsider them, and, perhaps, to modify them to some extent.

Mr. *William Bokenham* called in; and Examined.

Mr. *W. Bokenham.*

1973. *Chairman.*] WHAT office do you hold?—That of Superintending President of the Inland Office.

1974. The transmission of newspapers comes under your immediate supervision, does it not?—Yes, to all parts of the world.

1975. Have you any estimate of the number of newspapers, on an average, that are transmitted from the London Post-office to different parts of the kingdom?—Mr. Hill has given, I think, about the best estimate that could be made; therefore I did not prepare one.

1976. How many are transmitted daily?—The numbers vary daily from 120,000 to 260,000.

1977. Are any effectual steps taken at the Post-office to examine a sufficient proportion of those newspapers, in order to ascertain whether the newspaper stamp has been affixed to them?—No, it is not done effectually, but newspapers are occasionally examined; for instance, within the last three months we charged about 5,000 copies of one publication, with a picture inside which did not bear the supplement stamp; a separate engraving.

1978. There was a stamp deficient?—Yes.

1979. They ought to have been stamped?—Yes.

1980. You stopped 5,000 copies?—We charged about 5,000 copies, and forwarded them.

1981. Did the parties pay the postage upon them?—Not many; a great many did, but not one in six, and they gave us a vast deal of trouble in complaining of the charge.

1982. You had some reason, had you not, for suspecting that particular publication?—No, it was discovered in the ordinary way; we found one paper without the stamp, and then we looked at the whole.

1983. And

Mr. *W. Bokenham.*

23 May 1851.

1983. And you found that the whole 5,000 were in the same condition?—Yes.

1984. At the country post-offices, do the postmasters, not the letter-carriers, take any steps to examine whether the papers are properly stamped?—Occasionally they do; I very frequently see papers that have been charged in the country offices.

1985. Supposing anything like an effectual examination were made to ascertain whether the newspaper stamps were properly affixed, would that be the cause of considerable expense and probable delay in the transmission of the mails?—Undoubtedly, if it was done effectually.

1986. Can you give the Committee any other examples (besides the one you have mentioned of the 5,000) of attempts to send newspapers through the post without a stamp?—Yes; we occasionally find different publications wrapped up in pieces of newspaper, so as to give them the appearance of a newspaper. They send by post books, and things of that kind, as newspapers.

1987. Mr. *Rich.*] Is there any systematic fraud going on?—Not to a large extent; it is individual attempts.

1988. They are more casual than systematic, are they not?—Yes.

1989. Mr. *Ewart.*] Do you detect the greater proportion of them?—No.

1990. *Chairman.*] Do not you consider that the arrangement by which the newspaper stamps are obtained at the Post-office, for the purpose of passing free of postage, a defective arrangement as regards the postal revenue?—Yes, undoubtedly; because in many instances the stamp is paid, and the paper is never sent by the post, and therefore the penny is paid to no purpose if you consider the stamp as actual postage.

1991. In many cases the stamp is paid where no postal advantage is asked for, and in other cases the stamp is not paid where postal advantages are obtained?—That is the case occasionally.

1992. The stamp is paid when they do not go by post, and it is not paid when they do go by post?—If a newspaper were not stamped we should stop it, and send it to the Commissioners of Inland Revenue at once.

1993. From the defects of the system, if I understand you rightly, the result is this, that in consequence of the difficulty of guarding against those evasions, the effect is that papers that have not paid what is called the postage, namely, the newspaper stamp duty, are carried free?—Very few indeed.

1994. But

Mr. *W.* *Bokenham.*

23 May 1851.

1994. But publications?—Yes, publications, and the supplements of newspapers occasionally. I remember an instance; some years ago, the "Illustrated News" by some accident printed one of their large engravings on unstamped paper; those are the cases that arise more particularly.

1995. Somebody sent that to me, (*a paper being handed to the Witness*), and it came free by post; what should you call that?—I should not call it a newspaper; this has been mistaken for a newspaper; there is no doubt about it; things of this kind do occur.

1996. It would appear that the existing system does not afford a security that the parties who avail themselves of the post really pay the postage?—Perhaps not, but I myself think this, that it would cost us more to detect these abuses than the revenue is now defrauded.

1997. Mr. *Cobden.*] If you detect a fraud upon the revenue by opening a newspaper and finding it unstamped, have you any means of punishing the party who attempts the fraud, by tracing the paper to him?—If it is a newspaper, we send it at once to the Commissioners of Inland Revenue to deal with; and if it is a publication of the kind that has been shown to me, and not a newspaper, we treat it as an unpaid letter.

1998. How do you manage in those cases where newspapers are published partly stamped and partly unstamped, as in the case of the "Athenæum" or "Punch;" you are aware that there are 50 or 60 papers printed partly on stamped and partly on unstamped paper?—Yes; those are not, strictly speaking, newspapers; but in those cases, where a paper is stamped, we send it forward as a newspaper; where there is no stamp, if we find it, we treat it as an unpaid letter.

1999. And charge postage according to the weight?—Yes.

2000. But that paper is universally refused, is it not?—Yes, as a general rule it is.

2001. You have no means of tracing the party who posted it?—None whatever.

2002. Mr. *Rich.*] With regard to newspapers, purely and clearly newspapers, the redress rests with the Board of Inland Revenue, does it not?—Yes.

2003. Mr. *Cobden.*] You think that it is your duty, in case a newspaper is detected in the Post-office without a stamp, to transmit it to the Inland Revenue Board?—Yes; I think there is a Treasury order upon the subject.

2004. Sir *J. Walmsley.*] Can you say how many persons are employed in the Post-office to examine newspapers?—There is no person employed specially for that.

2005. Are

Mr. *W. Bokenham.*

23 May 1851.

2005. Are there persons partially employed in that duty?—Yes, all the sorters; if they happen to suspect anything, as a matter of course they either open the newspaper or hand it over to some one to be opened. If a newspaper is seen nicely sealed up, they open it, expecting to find writing in it, or they think it would not be so sealed, and perhaps in three cases out of six they are right.

2006. Would great facilities be given to the despatch of newspapers provided a wrapper with a penny stamp upon it were substituted instead of the present mode?—Does the Honourable Member mean if we had the same number of newspapers as at present?

2007. Yes.—No, certainly not. The newspapers having a penny postage stamp upon them, supposing we had the same number as now, would materially increase our business; all those stamps would have to be defaced.

2008. Would it not take less time to deface those stamps than it would to examine whether they were newspapers or not?—No, so few are examined.

2009. Mr. *Cobden.*] You acknowledge that there is great evasion of the postage under the present system, do you not?—No, my impression is otherwise. I think that people do evade the postage by sending things in newspapers, but not to an extent that would cover the expense of examining all the newspapers.

2010. *Chairman.*] It is difficult for you to say to what extent it is carried on, is it not?—Yes.

2011. Mr. *Cobden.*] You would have no other means of altogether preventing that fraud than by examining all the papers?—Certainly not.

2012. It would be much more expensive and troublesome, would it not, to examine all the papers, than to efface the postage stamps that were put on the outside of the newspapers?—Certainly it would.

2013. You have heard Mr. Hill's evidence, have you not?—Only a part of it.

2014. *Chairman.*] Would you open a copy of "Punch," to see whether it was a stamped edition or an unstamped edition?—Yes, "Punch" more particularly than any other, knowing that so many of them are sold without a stamp; the "Athenæum" is also more frequently looked at than most other newspapers.

2015. Mr. *Rich.*] The labour undergone in searching for casual frauds is not equal to the labour that would be incurred by effacing the stamps on all the papers sent through the Post-office?—Certainly not.

*Martis*, 27° *die Maii*, 1851.

MEMBERS PRESENT.

Mr. Ewart.
Mr. Rich.
Mr. Stafford.
Mr. Chichester Fortescue.
Mr. Sotheron.
Mr. Cobden.
Mr. G. A. Hamilton.
Sir T. F. Lewis.
Sir J. Walmsley.

THE RIGHT HON. THOMAS MILNER GIBSON IN THE CHAIR.

Mr. *Mowbray Morris*, called in; and Examined.

Mr. *M. Morris.*

27 May 1851.

2016. *Chairman.*] YOU are connected with the "Times" newspaper, are you not?—Yes, I am the Manager of it.

2017. When you say "manager," will you describe the duties you perform?—I am charged with the general superintendence of the paper.

2018. The financial arrangements of the paper would come under your charge, would they not?—Yes.

2019. What amount per annum is charged upon the "Times" for penny stamps; for instance, what amount was charged last year?—For penny stamps there were paid last year 50,000 *l.*, for 12,000,000 of stamps.

2020. Does that include the halfpenny stamps upon supplements?—No.

2021. How much altogether last year was paid for stamps? —£. 66,666 were paid for stamps.

2022. That must be a considerable increase to the cost of the production of the "Times" newspaper, is it not?—Of course; but as regards the penny stamp, it is all paid by the readers; the public.

2023. By the public, in the shape of an additional charge upon the papers?—Yes.

2024. What is your opinion as to the effect of removing the stamp; would it leave the existing press in the same relative condition to one another in which they now stand?—I think it might have the effect perhaps of destroying some altogether.

2025. But if you made a diminution in the cost of the production

Mr. *M. Morris.*

27 May 1851.

duction common to all, why should the position of any one be rendered worse comparatively?—Because I think that those who have not much hold upon the public, and have not a large circulation, would have raised up against them rivals who would destroy them. I think upon those which have a hold upon the public it would probably have no effect, or a beneficial one.

2026. You think that papers of an established reputation, that enjoy the public confidence, would either not be affected by it, or, if so, would have their circulation extended?—Yes.

2027. And the only papers that you think would be injured by an increased rivalry would be those which do not enjoy the public confidence?—That is my opinion.

2028. You say that the proprietors of the "Times" paid 66,000*l.* during the last year for stamps altogether; how much of that was paid for stamps on the supplements?—£. 16,666 odd, for halfpenny supplements; but that is not the whole amount. Sometimes the "Times" publishes double supplements, upon which the stamp is a penny, because the surface of the letterpress exceeds the amount regulated by the statute.

2029. Then, they could not print the "Times" newspaper upon one sheet of a larger surface than is prescribed in the Act of Parliament?—No; we are only just within the limit.

2030. No person by law is entitled to print upon any sized sheet he pleases, but only upon the sheet specified?—It depends not upon the sheet, but the surface of letterpress; you may have as large a margin as you please; I am not aware that the statute affixes any limit to the size of a paper, but only to the surface of letterpress which covers it.

2031. It would be in consequence of the surface of letterpress being limited that you would be obliged to have a penny stamp, would it not?—If, for instance, when you opened the paper there were seven columns instead of six on one side of the "Times" paper, it would have to pay a 1½*d.* stamp instead of 1*d.*; if the surface of letterpress exceeded what it now contains, it would have to pay an additional stamp, according to the statute of William the Fourth; the statute specifies the square inches; the surface of letterpress is limited to 1,530 square inches, and for that surface you pay a penny stamp; if you exceed that, and do not exceed 2,295, you pay 1½*d.*; and if you go beyond 2,295 square inches you pay 2*d.*

2032-3. Mr. *Ewart.*] That change was made by Lord Monteagle, was it not?—Yes, when Mr. Spring Rice.

2034. *Chairman.*] What is the effect of the stamp upon the supplement

Mr. *M. Morris.*

27 May 1851.

supplement of the "Times" on the general interests of the paper?—Certainly to limit its circulation.

2035. Do you mean to say that it causes the circulation to be a loss?—Yes, beyond a certain sum; the supplement consists of advertisements, which have a fixed value; it is the same on one paper as on 100,000. The sum paid for paper and printing, and so on, fluctuates, and is increased with the circulation. Of course there is a certain point at which the two sums balance each other. Suppose that the value of the advertisements in the supplement was 200*l.*, you would know that you could publish as many papers as would cost 200 *l.* to manufacture in paper, stamps, and printing, and if you go beyond that you publish at a loss; that is of course obvious.

2036. Mr. *Rich.*] On the other hand the extent of the circulation attracts advertisements, does it not?—Clearly.

2037. *Chairman.*] The greater the circulation the greater the loss?—The greater the loss, beyond a certain limit.

2038. Mr. *Cobden.*] Do you not mean that the profit is less?—No; the greater the absolute loss from a circulation beyond the point at which the expenditure and receipts balance each other.

2039. Including the advertisements, you do not speak of an absolute loss, do you, but of a comparative gain?—No; of an absolute loss.

2040. *Chairman.*] Do not you mean this; that when you have a supplement, as far as that supplement is concerned, if you only printed one copy of it your gain would be the greatest?—Yes.

2041. And for every copy that you sell you diminish your gain, and when you pass a certain line it becomes an absolute loss?—Just so; that is to say, when the expenditure exceeds the value of the advertisements.

2042. Mr. *Rich.*] Does it ever occur that the cost of publishing a supplement in all its branches, exceeds the amount that you have received for the advertisements contained in the supplement?—Whenever a double supplement is published it always does, and we have now exactly reached the limit at which a single supplement can be published without loss. This day the cost and the value of the advertisements published in the supplement of the "Times," exactly balance each other, the circulation of the "Times" now being nearly 39,000.

2043. *Chairman.*] You are compelled to take care that your circulation is to a certain degree kept within bounds, or the loss would be considerable, would it not?—Yes; I have no doubt in the world that if there were no considerations beyond

beyond a mere desire to circulate the paper, it could be made to double itself within a couple of years.

2044. You say that the stamp upon the supplement has the effect of limiting the circulation of the paper, and making it impossible without great loss to the proprietors to extend its circulation so as to meet the demands of the public ?—Yes, exactly.

2045. Mr. *Stafford.*] Can you check the circulation of the paper ?—Yes, by certain management; you cannot do it directly; you can indirectly. The paper is of no value the next day; if you do not supply it within a certain time nobody wants it, so that you can practically limit it as much as you please.

2046. Mr. *Rich.*] Is there a point at which the circulation of the "Times" could arrive when it would become a losing concern ?—I have just stated that a balance is just struck this day; that is to say, that the value of the advertisements in the supplement exactly covers the expenditure.

2047. My question rather had reference to the whole publication of the "Times" ?—That is a question of management from day to day. Sometimes there is no supplement published, and then the gains are balanced against the losses when a double one is published.

2048. It was stated by a witness that the advertisements were looked upon as the great support of a widely circulated paper, and more especially of the "Times" ?—Yes, that is true, with certain explanations which I have given.

2049. Mr. *Sotheron.*] That which you have been stating relates to the supplements, does it not ?—Yes.

2050. *Chairman.*] Do you mean that the losses upon the supplement destroy the profit upon the paper ?—Exactly; they would do so.

2051. Then it would be a beneficial thing both for the proprietors of the "Times" and for the public if that stamp on the supplement were removed, would it not ?—Yes, I think that the stamp is extremely unjust. The Committee will observe that the supplement consists solely of advertisements, each of which is taxed.

2052. Mr. *Ewart.*] It is unjust on the public as well as on the paper, is it not ?—Yes, because it limits the advertisements. The average amount of advertisements kept out of the "Times" daily is from 20 to 30 columns at this season of the year.

2053. Mr. *Rich.*] Even if the halfpenny were limited, according to the statement which you have made, the circulation of the supplement might reach an amount which again would render it unprofitable ?—It is possible, but it is not likely.

Mr. *M. Morris.*

27 May 1851.

2054. You could not state what would be the amount of circulation at which it must arrive again to become profitable, the halfpenny being limited?—No, but it could easily be calculated, taking 39,000; it is a rule-of-three sum.

2055. Mr. *Cobden.*] Have you not stated that in your opinion the stamp tends to keep alive the weaker newspapers that have not the confidence of the public now?—I would not state that directly, but only by way of inference. I think that the stamp protects them from a certain amount of rivalry; that the number of rivals they would have to contend with would be greater if it were removed.

2056. I understand you to say that you contemplated, as one of the effects of a removal of the stamp, the destruction of some of the weaker papers which had not the confidence of the public?—I think it possible.

2057. To that extent then you think that the stamp has the effect of keeping those papers in existence?—I think it is very likely.

2058. Does not it operate then to protect an inferior commodity, and deprive the public of the choice of a better article?—To that extent it would; but you must balance your evils.

2059. It has the effect, on the other hand, of limiting the circulation of those papers, the "Times" included, which enjoy the confidence of the public. Did you not say that you yourelves discouraged an increase of the circulation of the "Times"?—Rather.

2060. And you are driven to that by the operation of the stamp, are you not?—On the supplement, not the stamp on the paper.

2061. You never sell the supplement without the paper, do you?—We never sell the paper without the supplement.

2062. Practically, the effect of the stamp on the supplement is, to induce you to discourage the circulation both of the paper and of the supplement?—Yes.

2063. The result of your statement appears to be, that the stamp on the one hand keeps alive an inferior article, and on the other checks the production, and consequently the circulation, of a superior commodity?—The stamp on the supplement checks the circulation of a superior commodity.

2064. It has the practical effect of limiting the circulation of both, has it not?—No. The stamp on the supplement limits the circulation.

2065. Practically, I understood you to say that the stamp upon the supplement checks both the sale of the supplement and

Mr. *M. Morris.*

27 May 1851.

and of the paper?—Of course it does, because the paper is never sold without the supplement.

2066. Am I not correct in saying that the result of your evidence is, that the stamp upon the newspaper tends to keep alive an inferior article, and to check the circulation of a paper which has, to the largest extent, the confidence of the public?—If such an inference is to be drawn; I do not draw it myself.

2067. Did you not say that the proprietors discouraged the sale of the "Times" paper?—Yes, to a certain extent.

2068. And that they did so because the stamp upon the supplement which is given with the paper renders it a loss to circulate beyond a certain number?—Yes.

2069. Then do you not draw the inference that the effect is to restrict the circulation of a paper which enjoys the confidence of the public, and has the largest circulation?—That is the effect of the stamp on the supplement.

2070. But it has the effect of limiting the sale of the paper, has it not?—The stamp on the supplement has; it is quite possible to have a uniform stamp of a fixed denomination without reference to size; the supplement is just as much a part of the paper as page No. 6; you have no more right to stamp it than a particular page.

2071. What was the object of limiting the superficial extent of the paper when Lord Monteagle's Stamp Act was passed?—I fancy that it had some reference to postage; I can only tell from a reference to the debates; I have always understood that to have been the case.

2072. Mr. *Rich.*] You stated that the "Times" paid last year some 66,000 *l.* for stamp duty?—Yes.

2073. And that that is a charge upon the public?—That portion of it which was paid for penny stamps.

2074. In saying that do you cast out of consideration that the public undertakes to carry the papers and deliver them for that?—I did not take that fact into consideration: no doubt it is a drawback.

2075. To that extent therefore there is service rendered for the money paid, is there not?—Yes.

2076. Are you acquainted with the method in which the papers are transmitted to the great towns?—Yes.

2077. Is it done chiefly by post?—The "Times" very little by post.

2078. Are you aware at what additional price the morning papers which are transmitted by the mail are sold in the great towns?—The "Times," when sent express by the early trains,

Mr. *M. Morris.*

27 May 1851.

trains, is charged a small additional price. That increase was made about two years ago.

2079. *Chairman.*] Have you any calculations bearing upon that statement that you made with regard to the effect of the stamp upon the supplement?—Yes; for instance, in the case of the supplement that was published yesterday, the cost of that was 269 *l.*, and the gross value of the advertisements in it was exactly the same.

2080. Mr. *Sotheron.*] Does that cost which you have now mentioned solely consist of the cost of the paper, the ink, and the printers' time?—What may be called the material charges; no literary charges can be said to enter into the supplement, although of course the supplement would, strictly, be chargeable with a portion of the cost of management of the publishing and advertisement offices. I have not taken that into consideration; if I were to do so the supplement would be certainly published at a considerable loss; I have merely taken the material charges, and the taxes paid to the Government, and balanced them against the gross receipts.

2081. *Chairman.*] How much taxation altogether does that single supplement pay to the Government?—In direct charges to the Government, the supplement of the paper of yesterday paid 152 *l.*; and the "Times" and the supplement together paid 395 *l.*

2082. In mere Government taxes?—Yes; that is to say, stamps, excise duty on the paper, and advertisement duty.

2083. Mr. *Ewart.*] Will you give the Committee the distinctive charges?—Yes. The value of the stamps was 243 *l.*, in round numbers; the excise duty on the paper was 64 *l.*, and the advertisement duty 88 *l.*

2084. *Chairman.*] Can you state to the Committee, taking the value of the thing produced, what is the per-centage of taxation levied upon it?—I cannot say. The circulation being 39,000, and the total cost being 395 *l.*, the calculation is easily made.

2085. Mr. *Rich.*] Supposing a reduction of the stamp duty took place, what reduction of price do you think could be made in the publishing price of the "Times," or any other daily paper?—If the whole of the stamp duty were taken off?

2086. Yes.—I should conceive it to be the duty of every paper to take off exactly the amount of the stamp.

2087. Do you conceive it practicable to publish and maintain at a profit a newspaper at a penny?—I do; but not a newspaper that the people of England are accustomed to.

2088. Not a newspaper containing news, and articles written with

Mr. *M. Morris.*

27 May 1851.

with a sufficient degree of talent?—No; I feel sure that it is not possible.

2089. Mr. *Ewart.*] Would there not be a greater number of local newspapers?—That is a question which involves a consideration of the postage. I think that if you took off the stamps from newspapers, and did not allow them to pass through the post free, the effect might be to limit the circulation of papers within the neighbourhood of publication in a great measure. I do not think it would have that effect upon the "Times," judging from what we know. Almost all the papers are sent by railway.

2090. *Chairman.*] You pay in stamps on the "Times" (if it is to be considered as a payment for the postage) for a privilege which you do not enjoy?—Yes, that is the fact.

2091. Mr. *Cobden.*] Did you not say that the removal of the stamp would tend to limit the circulation of newspapers to their own localities?—Not the removal of the stamp, but the charge for postage; consequently if you take off the stamp, and leave the papers to pay according to weight, it seems to follow that the circulation would be confined to the immediate neighbourhood of publication.

2092. Assuming that the penny stamp was removed, and that a newspaper would be allowed to go through the post for a penny, as it does now, by affixing a penny stamp on the envelope, would that, in your opinion, tend to restrict the circulation of a newspaper?—Very slightly, if you allowed that.

2093. The paper would be published at a penny less; therefore the addition of the postage would still enable readers at a distance to obtain it at the same price?—Yes, to some extent; but it must not be forgotten that many persons take the "Times" with a view to post it in the evening to their friends: all those persons would have to pay the penny.

2094. Is it your opinion that a penny newspaper would not succeed in England, on account of the expense of bringing it out, the large machinery, and the necessity for large capital being employed on account of the expense of collecting the necessary news?—I could not separate the one from the other; the whole expenses of producing a good newspaper render it impossible to work it at that price.

2095. Has your attention been drawn to those publications in America which are brought out daily at a penny?—Yes.

2096. Mr. *Ewart.*] Do not you think that provincial papers, which merely repeat the news they receive from the metropolis, and confine themselves otherwise to local intelligence,

Mr. *M. Morris.*

27 May 1851.

gence, might publish at a much lower rate?—Yes; I think if a newspaper be published on the principle of copying everything and paying for nothing, it might be published at a penny.

2097. Mr. *Cobden.*] The "New York Sun," for instance, is a penny paper?—Yes.

2098. Has your attention been directed to the improvements in machinery for printing that paper which have taken place within the last few months?—Yes.

2099. There is a machine exhibiting at the printing office of the "Sun," at New York, called the Mammoth Machine; are you aware what number they print per hour?—I am not quite sure; but about a year or a year and a half ago I investigated the respective merits of that machine and the one which is now in use for printing the "Times," and I conceive the latter to be very far superior, so far as mechanical advantages go, and that the English have the advantage.

2100. My question referred to a machine that has been in use in the office of the "New York Sun" for the last three months?—Then I have not known of that.

2101. It is stated in one of the columns of that paper that they have a press, which is exhibited to every one who chooses to go, which throws off 25,000 copies in an hour; have you not heard of that?—Yes; an American called the other day upon me, who said that he had a machine to turn out 30,000 copies in an hour; but when I examined him, I found that that was not true; and I do not believe a paper of the size of the "Times" could be printed at the rate of 25,000 copies an hour, without an expense so enormous that it could not pay.

2102. Have you reason to believe that the statement in the "New York Sun" is untrue, that they produce 25,000 copies an hour?—Yes, I do not believe it.

2103. What number is printed of the "Times" in an hour?—They can print 12,000; they do generally print 10,000.

2104. A witness has been examined from Liverpool, Mr. Whitty, of the "Liverpool Journal," and he gave it as his opinion that the machinery used in America for printing their newspapers is superior to that of the English press, and that they print on a kind of thin paper which could not be printed on in England by our machines at all. Have you ever been led to observe any superiority in their machinery?—No, I have not; I have compared them. I wish the Committee to understand that I am not an engineer, and therefore I speak perhaps more with reference to the way in which I am advised by a person who does understand it than of my own knowledge;

Mr. *M. Morris.*

27 May 1851.

ledge; but I am quite satisfied myself that there is no machinery in America at all equal to Applegath's machine, of which a specimen may be seen in the Exhibition.

2105. *Chairman.*] Is there anything in the mode of stamping the paper which would prevent the application of improved machinery for throwing off a great number of papers in a short time?—Nothing whatever that I am aware of; the paper might be stamped at the same time that it is printed.

2106. Mr. *Rich.*] With regard to the printing machinery used in New York, it has been stated that it is better than the machinery used for the "Times." You are, I presume, naturally on the look-out for all improvements made in machinery, are you not?—Yes, certainly; I state my own opinion to the Committee, that Applegath's machinery, which is now in use at the "Times" office, is superior to anything in use in any part of the world.

2107. It is so obviously to the interest of the "Times" proprietary to print cheaply, that they would naturally seek for and adopt any improved machinery?—Yes; the object is not so much to print cheaply, but as fast as possible.

2108. You stated that you did not think a paper could be maintained at a penny; do you think that it could be maintained at 2*d.*?—No. The question is put, I conceive, on the supposition that the stamp will be taken off.

2109. Yes. At what price should you say a paper could be maintained?—That is a difficult question to answer.

2110. A newspaper that would stand a chance of competing with the papers in circulation generally throughout the country now?—I think that perhaps the Committee had better examine the manager of the "Daily News" upon that; he can tell you of his own knowledge. The "Daily News" was started at 3*d.* I am quite sure no good paper would pay at 2*d.*

2111. In the transmission of a twopenny paper to any place distant from where it was printed, if the stamp were taken off it would be necessary to affix a penny stamp, which would raise it to 3*d.*?—Yes.

2112. Mr. *Ewart.*] Are not the provincial newspapers generally sold at a lower price than the metropolitan newspapers?—The provincial newspapers are almost all published either twice a week or once a week, so that they are able to copy from the others.

2113. If the provincial newspapers copy from the others, they can probably publish more cheaply?—Yes.

2114. Mr. *Rich.*] Have you been led to compare the matter

Mr. *M. Morris.*

27 May 1851.

matter published in the American newspapers with that which is published in the English papers?—Yes, frequently.

2115. What is your opinion of their comparative merits?—I think our newspapers are far superior, and that the worst of ours are better than the best of theirs; speaking of the general tone of the papers, the influence they are likely to exercise upon those who read them, and the information they can give to those who want it.

2116. And you would consider their character in all respects as inferior to that of the English press?—In all respects.

2117. Mr. *Cobden.*] Do you say that taking such a paper as the "Journal of Commerce," or the "Courier and Enquirer," of New York, you would put these papers, in point of talent and tone, below the lowest of our weekly newspapers?—No, not the lowest of our weekly papers; I spoke of the daily press.

2118. Would you put them lower than the "Morning Post" or the "Morning Herald"?—Certainly.

2119. In point of style or the solidity of their views, or how do you compare them?—First of all I would compare their leading articles; and I would say they are more scurrilous and less true; you will find in them more absolutely false assertions.

2120. Are you speaking with a knowledge of the papers I have cited?—Yes, the "New York Courier and Enquirer;" that paper I particularly allude to.

2121. *Chairman.*] Upon particular occasions, when there is anything very interesting to the public, you are obliged to add very largely to the circulation of the "Times," are you not?—Yes.

2122. At the opening of the Exhibition, for instance?—Yes, there were 52,000 printed, and the publication was stopped only because no more could be printed; because there was no supplement on that day.

2123. Why was it stopped?—Because we could not print any more; the day was not long enough.

2124. Did you not print an account of the opening of the Exhibition upon a separate paper?—Yes, afterwards; a copy of what had before appeared.

2125. Are you aware that that ought to have been stamped?—My own opinion was that it ought not to have been stamped; and I sent a copy to the Stamp Office.

2126. And yet it was merely an account of the opening of the Exhibition, which you extracted from the "Times," and printed

Mr. *M. Morris.*

27 May 1851.

printed upon unstamped paper?—Yes, which had been previously published.

2127. Did the Board of Inland Revenue inform you that it was according to law?—The Board of Inland Revenue made no remark upon the subject.

2128. You have had no intimation from them?—None whatever. I took the opinion of the legal advisers of the paper; I am also a lawyer myself, and I am of opinion that it did not require a stamp.

2129. It has been stated in evidence before the Committee, that the editor of a local paper called the "Wakefield Examiner" published a trial which had previously appeared in his own paper, on a separate piece of unstamped paper, and was threatened with a prosecution; would there be any distinction between printing an account of the opening of the Exhibition on unstamped paper, and printing the account of a trial on unstamped paper?—I think I must protect myself from answering that question.

2130. Does not it appear to you strange that this gentleman in the country should have been threatened with a prosecution, and forced to pay money by way of compromising the matter, for publishing on a piece of unstamped paper the account of a trial which had previously appeared in his stamped paper?—My answer might possibly involve a censure upon the Board of Inland Revenue.

2131. Mr. *Rich.*] You would require to have all the circumstances of that case before you on both sides?—Yes; and I am not here to pronounce censures upon any portion of Her Majesty's Government.

2132. *Chairman.*] Are you in the habit of printing matter from time to time upon unstamped paper which has previously appeared in your stamped paper?—We never did such a thing before.

2133. Mr. *Rich.*] The Queen's Speech is printed and published almost immediately it is delivered in the House of Parliament, without a stamp, is it not?—I rather think it is.

2134. *Chairman.*] Where do you procure your paper from upon which you print the "Times;" do you procure it from various parts of the country?—Yes; there are now two manufacturers who make it.

2135. Do they supply the paper to you stamped?—No; that is the difficulty we have. It is sent first to the Stamp Office, and thence brought to Printing-house Square, at the expense of the proprietors.

2136. First of all, you must purchase that paper, send it

to

Mr. *M. Morris.*

27 May 1851.

to the Stamp Office to be stamped, and then it has to be carried back again to the "Times" office?—Yes; in the way I have explained.

2137. The cost of those transactions is equivalent to a small addition to the stamp duty, is it not?—No. Goods are usually delivered free to the purchaser; the paper is delivered free at the Stamp Office, and the only charge is the expense of bringing it from the Stamp Office to Blackfriars, an expense of 200*l.* or 300*l.* a year.

2138. The price for the paper is greater in consequence of that amount of freight having to be added to it, is it not?—I do not think so.

2139. Does it cost nothing to bring the paper from various parts of England to London, and then to send it to the Stamp Office?—It must be sent to the person who wants it, in any event; that enters into the ordinary charges of manufacture.

2140. Mr. *Rich.*] That is 500*l.* upon 66,000*l.*?—Yes, added to that.

2141. A very considerable loss was predicted to established newspapers when the stamp duty was reduced in former times, was there not?—I have heard so.

2142. Was not the effect of that reduction to confer considerable advantage upon the established papers?—Yes; upon these which had a hold upon public opinion.

2143. You shared in the increased advantages which were given to the rest of the press, to the full extent, did you not?—Yes; we shared in the increased advantages to this extent; that as the article could after the reduction of the stamp duty be produced at a less cost to the public, a greater number of purchasers naturally arose; that is all.

2144. The increased rivalry that was predicted, and so much feared, had not the effect of depriving you of the advantages arising from the reduction in the cost of production?—No; but I have heard it said that some papers ceased after that. I cannot speak of my own knowledge; I know nothing of newspapers, excepting within the last four years.

2145. At that time there were great prophecies of the establishment of cheap newspapers throughout the kingdom, were there not?—I think there were.

2146. *Chairman.*] You say that the reduction in the price would only be to the amount of the stamp; would it not answer the purpose, if were there no stamp, of the "Times" to publish an evening or afternoon edition at a cheaper rate?—Probably the Committee know that the "Times" is published three

three times a week under the name of the "Evening Mail," without the advertisements, for circulation in the country.

Mr. *M. Morris.*

27 May 1851.

2147. You gave an opinion upon the American press, and you stated that the leading articles of the American press were inferior to those in the English press?—I think so.

2148. Would you apply the same remark to the leading articles of the French press?—No; quite the reverse.

2149. Do you consider the leading articles of the French press superior to ours?—I would say superior; but perhaps, in point of delicacy, I could hardly answer that.

2150. What is your opinion of the leading articles of the French press?—I think very highly of them.

2151. Are they written in a philosophical and unprejudiced tone?—I can hardly say unprejudiced. They show the highest literary talent and much reflection; but I cannot call them unprejudiced, because the French press always advocates, at least each particular paper advocates, some particular view. The spirit of faction is stronger.

2152. Mr. *Cobden.*] Is not the tone of the leading articles in the French press more courteous than in those of the English press towards public men?—Yes, a portion of it.

2153. Have you had an opportunity of forming a similar opinion of the press of Spain or of Germany?—Of the German press I have.

2154. Has it not struck you that there is greater courtesy shown towards individuals?—No, especially considering that they write with fetters; the German press write with a perpetual fear of the censor.

2155. *Chairman.*] Although in the United States it would appear that you think that the leading articles of the unstamped press are inferior to ours, yet with regard to the press in France you do not make the same remark, there being no stamp?—Excuse me: I think when there was no stamp in France everything with regard to newspapers was inferior; he inferiority was immediately apparent.

2156. You think that the stamp does improve the character of the papers?—I do.

2157. Do you think that if you were to increase it, it would improve them still more?—There is a certain point at which I think it might.

2158. Could you keep on stamping them up to a state of perfection?—No; that is a *reductio ad absurdum.*

2159. There must be some line, you think: what is your reason for supposing that the removal of the stamp has had a prejudicial effect upon the press in France; can you state any facts?—

Mr. *M. Morris.*

27 May 1851.

facts?—It is very difficult to say whether it was the removal of the stamp or the shock which society received at the time of the revolution. I judge of the number of papers that appeared immediately after the revolution of February 1848, and I think that the tone of the established papers was deteriorated almost immediately. I think the reason of that was that they had to write down to the level of their readers, because a number of persons had started up their rivals who were to catch the ears of a certain class of readers; and rather than be thrown out of the market and lose their subscribers, the old papers wrote down to the level of those people.

2160. Do not you think that the great anxiety of the public, at a period like that, to obtain intelligence and to get articles upon public affairs, would cause an immense addition to the number of sheets issued?—Of that there can be no doubt; whenever the demand is increased the supply will be.

2161. Do not you believe, even in this country, at a time of great public excitement, that the Board of Inland Revenue, acting under the 6 & 7 of William the Fourth, would have to succumb to the anxiety of the public for a constant supply of intelligence?—Not in England, I think; I think we respect the law too much.

2162. Are you aware that previous to the reduction of the stamp the number of unstamped publications, though the times were not full of excitement, was very great?—Yes; just in the same way as previously to the reduction of the customs there were many more smugglers. Now you have just hit the happy medium, and raised the revenue without prohibiting the article.

2163. Would you levy stamps on newspapers in reference to the principle upon which the old Acts were passed, namely, as a matter of public policy, with a view to restrain the press, or as a mere fiscal consideration?—I think they should be maintained for revenue: that is the chief point.

2164. Then supposing fiscal considerations put on one side, you would not, for the sake of any public advantage, think it right to stamp the press *per se*?—If there had never been a stamp upon newspapers, I would not stamp them now; that is, if you did not require the revenue; but setting aside fiscal considerations, as there has been a stamp many years, since the 10th of Anne, I think it not advisable to take it off.

2165. As to the supplements, you would take it off them, would you not?—Merely for the reason that it has the effect of restricting the circulation of a good article, which cannot be the object of anybody.

2166. Mr.

Mr. M. Morris.

27 May 1851.

2166. Mr. *Rich.*] You would take that off as a nominal tax?—I think it is a heavy burthen, which ought not to be imposed on any ground whatever.

2167. In giving your opinion as to the superiority of the French press generally, as compared with ours, do you speak of it as to literary or political works?—I think that their views on politics are not worth anything; I allude to their literary merit; they are fine philosophical essays, and theoretical arguments.

2168. You refer more to their political than to their literary merits, do you not?—I refer to their literary, not their political merits.

2169. Are you aware of the prices of the French journals?—Yes, I think I know the prices; but they have changed so frequently lately, that I cannot state at this moment.

2170. They are higher than the American press, are they not?—Yes, considerably.

2171. Are you aware of the charges for transmission in France?—I cannot state positively; I have always been under the impression that they were the same as here; that the stamped papers went through the post free; I have received them myself.

2172. With regard to the goodness of a French newspaper, and its price, you do not attach an importance to the stamp itself, as keeping up the tone of the newspaper; but you hold that a cheap newspaper cannot at the same time be a good newspaper?—I think so.

2173. Mr. *Cobden.*] You stated, did you not, that when the stamp was taken off the French press at the time of the revolution, its quality deteriorated?—I think so.

2174. Was not that at the time of a revolutionary crisis, when in any country the press would become more vehement and more virulent?—A bad press would; but I think in the crisis of a country that a good press might be the saving of it.

2175. Have you looked back to the pages of the "Times" newspaper during the crisis of the Reform Bill?—Yes.

2176. Was not much of the writing that then appeared rather stronger and somewhat coarser than that which is now written?—Yes.

2177. Would not the same argument serve in mitigation of the character of the French press during the revolutionary excitement?—Certainly.

2178. Therefore though the stamp was suddenly taken off at the time of a revolutionary crisis, the fact that the press

 deteriorated

Mr. *M. Morris.*

27 May 1851.

deteriorated under those circumstances cannot be traced so much to the removal of the tax as to the existence of the revolution?—I do not draw that inference. I do not find that the language of the "Times," or papers generally, at the time of the Reform Bill was worse than it was before the Reform Bill or immediately afterwards. But I find that the language of all the newspapers at that time, on all subjects, was very different to what it is now. I think there was only that additional vehemence and additional vigour of expression which are inseparable from discussions upon matters of great and immediate interest.

2179. You consider that the tone of the press was altogether inferior in point of courtesy previously to the Reform Bill era, as compared with what it is now?—Yes.

2180. Was not the stamp 4*d.* on each sheet?—Yes.

2181. Do you consider that the reduction of the 4*d.* to 1*d.* has been followed by an improvement in the tone of the newspaper press?—I admit the fact.

2182. Did you not state also that the removal of the penny stamp would have the effect of deteriorating it?—Yes, I think so.

2183. You admit taking off three-fourths of the duty has been followed by a great improvement in the tone of the press?—Not as a consequence.

2184. But taking off three-fourths of the ta x has be e followed by a great improvement in its tone; you admit that?—If my answer is to be taken down, it must be taken down in my language and not in yours. I admit that since the reduction of the stamp the tone of the English press has improved.

2185. You admit that the tone of the English press has improved since the reduction of the stamp from 4*d.* to 1*d.*?—Yes, with reference solely to time.

2186. I understood you to state it as your opinion that the removal of the remaining penny would be followed by a deterioration in the tone of the press?—The press generally; I believe so.

2187. Is that an argument which you would apply to any other commodity; take for instance the corn laws; would you not consider that going step by step in the process of reduction, until the public were supplied with a better article, would be an encouragement to go on in further reduction?—Provided you treat the two things as cause and effect, which I deny.

2188. You assume as a consequence, do not you, that great deterioration would be caused by the removal of the penny stamp?—I anticipate some deterioration.

2189. And

Mr. *M. Morris.*

27 May 1851.

2189. And yet the reduction from 4 *d.* to 1 *d.* on newspapers has been followed by a totally different result?—Yes.

2190. Then I ask you whether, in dealing with any other article but a newspaper stamp, it would not be considered as a sound reason why you should continue in a course which has been followed by such a salutary result?—That is an inference which you may draw; it is a matter of opinion.

2191. You stated that you did not advocate the retention of the stamp as being to the established newspapers a matter of interest?—Yes; I think the reduction of the stamp would have no effect, for instance, upon the "Times," except perhaps to increase its circulation.

2192. No injurious effect?—Certainly not.

2193. I gather from your evidence that the only reason why you would retain the tax is, because you think it has a tendency to keep the character and tone of the press superior to what it would be without the stamp?—Yes; but that is not the only ground; the chief ground upon which I advocate the retention of the stamp duty is, that you raise a considerable revenue without imposing any sensible burden.

2194. Did you not state that you considered the penny stamp to be exactly the right stamp upon the press?—Yes, with reference to postage.

2195. It raises a revenue without limiting the supply?—No, it does limit the supply; it does not limit the supply of a good article, but it limits the miscellaneous supply.

2196. Will you state by what process you consider that the penny stamp tends to improve the tone of the press?—Yes, the stamp duty, as the Committee are aware, is paid in advance, and it is therefore necessary that persons should have some capital to pay it; I think that is some small protection to the public; that persons who have capital and some stake in society, something to lose, should have these papers in their hands; I think that is one thing, though it is not of very great importance; then I think a more important consideration is, that if there were no stamp you would have a very vast increase in the number of papers; and you would have different kinds of papers published, papers advocating perhaps opinions not quite so advantageous to society as are advocated now by the press.

2197. But do you consider that it is for the interest of the public that any branch of industry such as that of producing newspapers for the public, should be limited to a few hands and be in the hands of parties who are great capitalists, rather than

Mr. *M. Morris.*

27 May 1851.

than the pursuit being thrown open to the competition of parties with more moderate capitals?—Yes.

2198. You think it is an advantage to confine the newspaper press as much as possible in the hands of a few persons with large capitals?—Yes; but I would have it understood that I do not think it necessary persons should have very large capitals; some capital is necessary; a man without money, credit, or character cannot now set up a newspaper as he might if there were no stamp, and as they did do in Paris after the revolution.

2199. Do you consider that it is sound policy to legislate for the purpose of restricting the production of newspapers to a particular class of persons, being large capitalists?—I cannot answer that question directly, except by reference to a previous answer which I gave to the Honourable Chairman, when I stated that if the thing were *res integra*, if there had never been a stamp on newspapers, I should not advocate the imposition of one; and therefore I should, in answering this question, perhaps say no to the first part. I should not advocate any legislation on the matter if there had been none; but there having been legislation on the matter, and the stamp having existed for a long time, I do not recommend its being taken off; I wish it to be let alone.

2200. Do you consider that the character of the press is improved by being in the hands of large capitalists, because those large capitalists are themselves of a superior character; or is it because the public are confined to a higher priced article, and therefore the common people have not an opportunity of buying newspapers at all?—If the question of the Honourable Member infers that the common people do not read newspapers, I think he is mistaken; I think the common people do read the best newspapers now; I think that the "Times," for instance, is in the hands of large numbers of the common people.

2201. Assuming that the stamp were taken off the press, and that the "Times" newspaper were produced at a penny less, would not the common people have a better opportunity of buying the "Times," in preference to those inferior papers which you fear would spring up?—Yes; but I should be sorry that they should have the choice; I think it is a pity, if you can give a man wholesome food, to give him the chance of having unwholesome too.

2202. Would you carry out that principle in other matters, that the producers of articles should be themselves the judges of

Mr. *M. Morris.*

27 May 1851.

of how many competitors there should be in the market to supply the public?—As a principle, of course not.

2203. You would not apply that principle to the producers of corn?—No.

2204. Would you consider that an exception should only be made in favour of the producers of newspapers?—Not newspapers, but in regard to the press generally: I think there is a great difference between interests which are solely material and those which are moral and social as well.

2205. Do you think that the people at large, if they had a free choice amongst a great number of competitors who would supply them with news, would not exercise the same wise discrimination which they do now, in preferring a good to a bad paper?—No, I do not think they would.

2206. By what process have they arrived at the preference which they have now for the "Times"?—The other papers, in point of tone, are perhaps as good, only perhaps the "Times" has got the ear of the market; and there is a prestige attached to its name, and they take it in preference to the "Chronicle" or other daily papers, though those papers are just as good. That is a question that I cannot be expected to speak to. I think if it came to be a question in the trades unions and those meetings between the "Times" and some paper which advocated violent doctrines, and which pandered to the feelings of persons who were perhaps often excited, I think they would choose the latter.

2207. Is it your opinion that those doctrines ought not to be discussed and canvassed in the public prints?—Not in the way in which they would be discussed and canvassed; it is not merely the discussion, but the manner of the discussion.

2208. It appears to me that your doctrine is one which would warrant a censorship?—Censorship does exist in this country.

2209. In what form does censorship exist?—Blasphemy and sedition, any offence against religion, are punishable.

2210. That is an offence against the common law?—Yes.

2211. Did you not state that you advocated the retention of the stamp in order to prevent the mass of the people discussing doctrines that you think dangerous?—No, I would not prevent the mass of the people from discussing; I would not care at all what was discussed by word of mouth, or what was said; but if those things were written in leading articles, I think they would do very great injury.

2212. But would you not have the antidote as well as the bane if you had free competition?—Yes, if you could be

 sure

Mr. *M. Morris.*

27 May 1851.

sure that a man would not be poisoned before he got the antidote.

2213. Is it, therefore, proper to restrict the circulation of newspapers, because you fear that certain doctrines might reach certain parties who might not have the opposition papers put into their hands; and might you not leave it to the sagacity of people, to their own self-interest and love of truth, to find out what was sound?—I have very little opinion of the sagacity of uneducated people.

2214. Mr. *Ewart.*] Do not you think that when questions are discussed in print, they are much more likely to be maturely considered than when brought before a popular assembly. Is not the very fact of circulation amongst the public, and the time which elapses, favourable to mature deliberation, more so than when precipitate counsels are suddenly adopted in a public assembly?—Yes; provided the leaders and managers of those papers that you speak of were such as you would wish them to be. It is only my opinion; it is mere speculation; but I think that the press would fall into the hands of persons who would not maturely consider what they wrote, and who would be incapable of maturely considering the questions that they would discuss.

2215. Do not you consider that we possess an immense advantage in discussing, by means of the press, any question of importance, in comparison with the mode in which such questions were brought before the people in Athens, or the Forum in Rome?—The Committee must always remember this, that any fool or incendiary can manage to get his opinions read, provided only he can get some editor to employ him. Unless a man has a certain degree of talent he would not be listened to in a public assembly, and I mean to say that the character of the speech would be infinitely better than the character of the leading article in a bad newspaper.

2216. Do not you consider that the tone of the newspapers in this country has very much improved of late years?—Yes; because the tone of society has very much improved.

2217. Has there not been a great improvement in the manners, tastes, and feelings of the nation?—Yes.

2218. May not this change in national manners, tastes, and feelings have had, rather than the stamp duty, a considerable influence in causing the improvement in the tone of newspapers?—That is my opinion; I do not think that the stamp duty has anything to do with it; I think as it stands the stamp duty is some protection, in the way in which I have explained it.

2219. *Chairman.*]

Mr. *M. Morris.*

27 May 1851.

2219. *Chairman.*] You mentioned that there was a censorship in England; will you explain what you meant?—I mean that though the police do not come and break up the printing presses, and take away the papers, yet the common law of England, and some portions of the statute law, act as a practical censorship of the press, to all the extent that is required for the protection of society.

2220. Mr. *Rich.*] While you admit the improvement that has taken place in the press generally since the reduction of duty in 1836, I gather from your answer to the Honourable Member for Dumfries, that you consider that improvement to have been contemporaneous rather than consequential?—Yes, I do not think there is any cause and effect at all. I think it has partly arisen from the improved tone of society; I think that the tone of society and the tone of the press act and re-act upon each other in this country.

2221. With reference to papers established by persons without capital, are you aware that some London weekly papers, and others, have begun without other capital than a great stock of scurrility and calumny, by which they have gained a temporary circulation?—Yes, like the "Satirist," and the "Age," they have acted upon the fears of persons who knew that their characters would not bear scrutiny.

2222. And some of them having obtained a circulation by these means, have gradually as they gained capital in money, abated their scurrility, and become more respectable papers?—That I cannot say. I do not know the point at which the "Satirist," or the "Age," became respectable. The scurrility of the "John Bull," when Hook first wrote it in person, was carried out by its extreme cleverness, his wit.

2223. *Chairman.*] Sometimes the stamp is represented, as it has been to-day, merely as a fair postage charge?—Yes.

2224. In order to be entitled to send the "Times" by post, you are obliged to stamp every copy that you publish, but the "Athenæum," and other papers of that class, are allowed to go by post, and only to stamp such particular copies as they send by post, and not to stamp their whole impression; do you think it reasonable that a different rule should be applied to you from that which is applied to the "Athenæum" and "Punch," in reference to postage?—It does not seem so; I never considered the question, and I never heard the arguments that could be advanced in favour of that view. There may be some good reason for it. I have never considered the matter, but I do not see the justice of the distinction at this moment.

2225. The effect is that, as far as postal considerations enter into

Mr. *M. Morris.*

27 May 1851.

into the question, a regular newspaper is in a worse condition than a class publication ?—That seems to be the inference from what you have just now said. In order that my opinions may not be thought to be dictated by interest, I beg to state my conviction, that if you take off the stamp duty the commercial advantages to the "Times" will be very great.

2226. Whatever was done with the stamp on the paper itself, you think that the stamp on the supplement decidedly ought to come off?—Yes, I enter my protest against that.

2227. Mr. *Cobden.*] You have just stated that you believed that the commercial advantages to the "Times" would be enormous if the stamp duty came off; that would arise from the large increase in the circulatiou of the "Times," would it not ?—Yes.

2228. You stated that it would be possible for the "Times" to double its circulation ?—Yes.

2229. That circulation of course could only arise out of the increased demand and consumption on the part of the public? —Yes.

2230. And there must be as many persons again, supposing that supposition to prove true, who would become subscribers to the "Times"?—Yes.

2231. Would not that of itself be an answer to much of the objection that you have urged as to the danger that the removal of the stamp would lead to the consumption of an inferior article?—No; the inference is erroneous, because you do not take into consideration the question of the supplement; if you take off the stamp on the newspaper you cannot keep it on the supplement; so that the profit, no longer diminished by that burden, would increase with the circulation in direct proportion.

2232. Practically the effect would be, that you would supply double the quantity of what you consider to be a good article to the public as compared with what is now consumed by them? —I think that as regards the "Times," it is exceedingly probable; it is of course a mere speculation on my part; I state that as my conviction.

2233. The increase to the circulation of your paper would be probably twice as much as the whole circulation of all the other daily papers, excepting the "Times," now amounts to; I take it that they do not circulate 20,000?—I do not think they do.

2234. Would not it, according to your view of the superiority of the "Times" paper, be a great advantage to the public that that great increase in the circulation of this useful vehicle

vehicle of general news should take place?—It can hardly be expected that I should say "Yes," and I cannot say "No." Mr. *M. Morris.* 27 May 1851.

2235. You expressed a fear that the removal of the stamp would lead the public to patronize inferior papers; and that you did not like the temptation to be put before them, lest they should accept things of an inferior kind?—Yes.

2236. You have now stated that the removal of the stamp would increase your circulation probably to double its present amount; is that not so far an answer to your apprehensions of the consequences that would result from a removal of the stamp?—I did not say that a removal of the stamp would increase our circulation to double its present amount. I stated some time ago that I thought it possible, provided all restraints were taken off our circulation, and I alluded particularly to the burden laid upon us by the stamp on the supplement, that the "Times" might be increased in circulation nearly double; but I supposed then that the penny stamp is kept on. When I made that remark I stated it solely with reference to taking off the halfpenny stamp on the supplement, and I stated afterwards, as I state now, that I think the removal of the stamps altogether would be of great advantage to the "Times;" but I did not intend those two remarks to be put together.

2237. Mr. *Rich.*] You have stated that the effect of taking off the stamp duty in France was, for a time at least, to deteriorate the tone of the French press, by compelling, or rather tempting the different newspapers to write down to the level of the lower tone which was assumed by the competitors that then sprung up?—Yes; not quite to the level, but it tended to depress them, and made the tone somewhat inferior.

2238. That is an evil which might also occur in this country, might it not?—Yes, I think so, with those who were within the range of the temptation. But I wish to observe that, in reply to all these questions respecting the moral and political effect of the stamp duty, I have been not so much giving evidence of facts as stating my own individual opinions upon points which are open to controversy.

Mr. *Christopher James Bunting*, called in; and Examined.

2239. *Chairman.*] YOU have been connected with the newspaper press in Norwich, have you not?—Yes; with the "Norwich Reformer." Mr. *C. J. Bunting.*

2240. What

Mr. *C. J. Bunting.*

27 May 1851.

2240. What was that paper?—It was the organ of the Norwich Reform Association; it was an unstamped paper.

2241. You stamped a portion of your impression for the post, did you not?—No; no impressions were stamped.

2242. Did you make no use of the post?—Very little.

2243. Had you any communication with the Board of Inland Revenue in reference to that paper?—Yes, informing us that the insertion of news was prohibited, and stating that we should be subject to penalties if we continued inserting a slip of news. About one-sixteenth of the paper was devoted to the proceedings of reform associations, anti-state-church associations, freehold franchise societies, and other associaions connected with political movements.

2244. How often was its publication brought out?—Monthly.

2245. What were the remaining fifteen-sixteenths of the paper devoted to?—One page advertisements, and the other pages articles written by individuals in the town, and extracts from other journals.

2246. Original essays?—Yes, and extracts from other journals, but not of a character to be called news.

2247. Did the Board of Inland Revenue write to you in reference to this sixteenth part?—Yes; it was called the "Record of Progress." The Board named the part that was objected to.

2248. It was only published once a month, was it?—No.

2249. What was the nature of the correspondence which you had with the Board of Inland Revenue?—I wrote to the secretary of the Board, asking why the "Reformer" was prevented from publishing its "Record of Progress," when other journals were allowed to publish intelligence, and referring to the "Freeholder," the "Household Narrative of Current Events," the "Athenæum," "Punch" and other journals. The answer which I received was to the effect that those papers were not before the secretary in his official capacity; but I could get no direct answer to the question as to why the "Reformer" was interfered with, when the other journals were allowed to continue inserting intelligence.

2250. Have you a copy of the "Reformer" with you?—Yes; that is the "Record of Progress." (*The same being handed in.*)

2251. Were you obliged to discontinue its publication in consequence of the interference of the Board of Inland Revenue?—I believe that the interference had an effect upon the sale;

Mr. *C. J. Bunting.*

27 May 1851.

sale; I will not say strictly that it was the cause of its being discontinued.

2252. The omission of this sixteenth part of the paper, the "Record of Progress," rendered the publication less attractive, did it not?—The "Reformer" was the organ of an association, and it was felt a hardship that it should not be allowed to report its operations; and it was useless to continue it as the organ of the association when that privilege was not allowed.

2253. And it had then to be given up?—It was given up. There was an expectation of another journal coming out in London, and it was thought that the interference of the Board of Inland Revenue had an effect upon the sale; it was intended only for local circulation, and a very slight difference of sale had an effect upon it.

2254. You had no idea, when you were publishing this paper, that you were violating the law?—Not at all. We were publishing at the same time the "Temperance Visitor," giving information of temperance meetings, which I should imagine was quite as contrary to law as inserting political intelligence. We had no intimation respecting the "Temperance Visitor," although it contained as much news, or nearly so, as the "Reformer" did.

2255. Mr. *Rich.*] You thought that the publication of news was not violating the law?—I was not aware that it was in monthly periodicals.

2256. Are you not aware that newspapers pay stamp duty? —Yes.

2257. You admit that this was news that you published?—Yes, the 16th part.

2258. Did you find that that 16th part increased your circulation, or did it fall off when that part was not published?—Yes, it fell off slightly; I do not lay any particular stress upon that; there was a slight difference.

2259. *Chairman.*] Did the Board of Inland Revenue pretend to sue you for any penalties?—No.

2260. Mr. *Rich.*] Did your paper pay?—A circulation of 1,000 monthly would have paid, but it fell to about 700 or 800.

2261. In fact, you suffered very little injury?—We suffered very little injury from the interference of the Board.

2262. And the Board told you, did they not, when you remonstrated with them with regard to other papers, that the cases of those papers were under consideration?—No; that they were not before the secretary in his official capacity. I suppose

Mr. *C. J. Bunting.*

27 May 1851.

suppose his attention had not been called to them, as it appears to have been in the case of the "Reformer." A great deal of ill feeling is caused in country districts by certain individuals being suspected as informers.

2263. *Chairman.*] Did he not tell you, to guide you, that what you inserted might savour of news, but that you must not give news?—No.

2264. Did he say that you might very nearly give news, but not quite, without a stamp?—No.

2265. Have you the letter?—Yes.

2266. Will you read it if you please?—"The publications to which allusion is made are not before me either officially or otherwise; I know therefore nothing of their contents; but assuming them to be unstamped papers, and to contain matter which they ought not to publish, it is not for me to offer any explanation upon the subject, nor can the circumstance justify irregularities in others. I may however remark, as I am aware that the subject has been under notice, in reference more particularly to learned societies, that articles, although relating to the transactions of such societies, and therefore savouring of public news and intelligence, yet as partaking of the character of a review, are not looked upon as matters to be objected to in unstamped publications; so also with regard to dramatic performances, and such like."

2267. What is meant by the words "such like"?—It is not for me to explain.

2268. Did you obtain any information that was of any use to you from that letter?—No.

2269. What do you understand from being told that you are at liberty to insert what savours of news without being stamped, although you must not publish news?—I should imagine that the "Reformer" might have contained an article alluding to certain events, but must not contain a record of those events; it might allude to them.

2270. But you might give a record, according to that letter, of theatrical entertainments, although not of meetings of the Reform Association?—Yes.

2271. Did you understand that by law there was any distinction between a record of theatrical entertainments and a record of the meetings of the Reform Association?—Certainly not.

2272. Did you ask for any explanation of the terms "such like"?—No, I did not.

2273. What is the opinion of you and your friends in Norwich as to the policy of attempting to interfere with the publication

cation of these newspapers; is it calculated to do any good?—Certainly not. Mr. *C. J. Bunting.*

27 May 1851.

2274. Mr. *Rich.*] Do you think it is fair towards other unstamped newspapers which do not publish news, that some should be permitted to publish news, being still unstamped, and thereby increase their circulation to the detriment of those others?—I admit it is not.

2275. Mr. *Cobden.*] What is the feeling of the working class generally now in Norwich upon the subject of the stamp upon newspapers?—They are decidedly desirous of its abolition.

2276. It is unpopular, is it?—Yes.

2277. What is the popular idea with regard to the stamp on newspapers; do people generally think that it is kept on for the purpose of raising a revenue, or to prevent them obtaining cheap publications?—They think it is for both purposes, and that feeling was increased by the interference with the "Reformer." The "Reformer" was known to be conducted by a working man, and the interference with it was felt to be a peculiar hardship.

2278. I presume that the stamp itself is unpopular among the working classes, is it not?—Decidedly.

2279. *Chairman.*] Do you think it is calculated to promote the views that are said to be entertained by the Parliament of the country, that education should be afforded to the working classes, if this restriction upon the press is continued?—Decidedly not. The professed efforts of the Government to forward education are laughed at by a great portion of the working classes, on account of their retaining the stamps on newspapers, and other taxes upon knowledge.

2280. And they look at the professions that are made upon the subject of education with suspicion, do they not?—Yes, whilst the newspaper stamp is retained, and the other taxes upon knowledge (as they are called). I believe the newspaper stamp is particularly obnoxious.

2281. Mr. *Rich.*] How can you send a newspaper without a stamp?—They seem to have the impression that postal arrangements might be made which would not be regarded as a tax upon knowledge, but simply as a charge for transit.

2282. You would not require the Government to carry it for nothing, would you?—No.

2283. Could you send it by private hands for less than a penny?—In a large quantity you might.

2284. But with a circulation that a provincial paper would have, such as persons read in the scattered districts in and around

Mr. *C. J. Bunting.*

27 May 1851.

around Norwich, might it not cost you more than a penny to circulate?—Those copies which were sent round Norwich certainly did not cost a penny.

2285. Those that were sent to villages and the districts around?—Yes.

2286. They did not cost a penny?—No.

2287. At all events, they cost something, did they not?—Yes; 30 or 40 copies might be sent by the carrier for sixpence.

2288. The advantage of sending by post for a penny is certainly so much taken off from what you consider to be a tax upon knowledge, is it not?—Not much.

2289. *Chairman.*] You never made any use of the post, did you?—Very rarely.

2290. It is of no use to you?—But little.

2291. Therefore it is of no use to speak to you of postal advantages?—Not so far as the "Reformer" was concerned.

2292. Mr. *Cobden.*] Do you think that periodicals containing news are more likely to lead working people to habits of reading than those periodicals which are unstamped, and therefore prevented from inserting news, such as the "Working Man's Friend," or "Chambers' Journal"?—I believe that the desire for reading on the part of the working classes is principally for intelligence, for the events of the day; I believe that is the leading inducement for them to read.

2293. Mr. *Rich.*] A desire for what you call essentially news?—Yes.

2294. Mr. *Cobden.*] That is just the very kind of reading which is rendered almost inaccessible to them by the penny stamp, is it not?—Yes.

2295. In Norwich is there much of the unstamped London trash sold?—There is some.

2296. Did you find that in your little publication it was necessary to give a good deal of local news to tempt the people to read the paper?—I will not say that it was necessary to give a good deal of local news to tempt them; it was necessary, in accordance with the object of the publication of the "Reformer," as the organ of an association.

2297. It professed to give a good deal of local news?—It professed to give the movements of that association.

2298. Do you find generally now, that working people in a locality like Norwich take more interest in the news of the immediate district than they do in news from a distance?—Not more interest.

2299. Are they interested in Parliamentary proceedings, for example?—

Mr. *C. J. Bunting.*

27 May 1851.

example?—Yes. And from what I have seen of the intelligence of families connected with the working classes, where a newspaper is regularly taken, and comparing them with those to whom newspapers are strange, I am led to think that it is advantageous to facilitate the communication of intelligence as much as possible; the advantage is greatly in favour of the former. My acquaintance with the working classes has led me to that conclusion.

2300. Mr. *G. A. Hamilton.*] Do you mean local newspapers?—I mean newspapers generally. I took families where I had the means of knowing that newspapers were regularly taken in and read, and I have compared them with families where they did not take them in, and I was struck with the value of the newspaper as an educational agent.

2301. Mr. *Rich.*] Are not the minds of those people prepared by other means to enjoy the contents of a newspaper?—The parties who do not take in a newspaper may be inferior in education to the other parties, but you find a difference in their intelligence.

2302. But the people must begin by taking in a newspaper?—Of course.

2303. And beginning, they must have some previous education or instruction to make them desire a newspaper?—Take two parties equal in educational advantages, or means of acquiring information, let one have a newspaper regularly and the other be a stranger to it, and you will find the advantage on the side of intelligence decidedly in favour of the newspaper reader.

2304. If the other party took in "Chambers' Journal," might he not derive as much improvement from that as the person who read news?—I think not. I think, on the part of the working men, it is desirable that they should be acquainted with the leading facts of the day, and that that is much more useful to them in the end than such matter as is contained in Chambers' and other journals. It is necessarily more practical and attractive, and I think more useful.

2305. The information is more useful?—Yes.

2306. Mr. *Ewart.*] They are more likely to seek knowledge by that path than from "Chambers' Journal," it being more attractive to them?—Yes.

2307. Should you say that a family that took in a paper, and that had not done so before, was improved by the reading of it?—Yes.

2308. Mr. *J. A. Hamilton.*] Does not that depend upon the

Mr. *C. J. Bunting.*

27 May 1851.

the character of the newspaper taken in?—Of course it does; I should imagine that the majority of our local newspapers are of a character that is not objectionable by any means.

2309. Mr. *Ewart.*] You think they are more likely to do good than harm?—Decidedly so; I think one proof of the desire of the working classes for intelligence is shown in the sale of the reports of certain events, such as murders, and other matters that it is perhaps not desirable should be reported in the way they are; I have been struck with the large sale of these papers, and I think that the operation of the newspaper stamp offers a premium upon their circulation.

2310. *Chairman.*] You have observed, have you not, the great differences of opinion which have prevailed as to the mode in which the people should be educated on religious grounds, and that persons cannot agree as to the forms of religion that should be taught in particular schools?—Yes.

2311. And that that stands in the way very much of any general system of diffusing knowledge through the country?—Yes.

2312. Probably there would not be the same difficulty in coming to an agreement upon the question of removing the obstacles to the diffusion of knowledge?—Decidedly not.

2313. You do not find that on religious grounds there is any disposition amongst the people to disagree as to the propriety of removing those obstacles?—No.

2314. Though there may be as to the mode in which knowledge should be given?—Yes.

Mr. *Frederick Knight Hunt*, called in; and Examined.

Mr. *F. K. Hunt.*

2315. *Chairman.*] YOU are connected with the "Daily News," are you not?—Yes.

2316. What office do you hold on that paper?—I am Sub-editor of the "Daily News;"—the editor of the news portion of the paper;—the details of the paper.

2317. The general management and position of that paper are of course within your knowledge?—Yes.

2318. Have you an account of the amount of stamp duty that you paid last year on papers and supplements?—I have not. A knowledge of that falls within the province of the manager of the paper; I have only to do with the news of the journal, the reports, and the reception and arrangement of news. In fact, I am the working editor of the paper, apart from its opinions. I have nothing to do with the number of stamps issued.

2319. Do

Mr. *F. K. Hunt.*

27 May 1851.

2319. Do you conceive that the "Daily News" would be benefited by the repeal of the stamp upon newspapers?—I have taken some trouble to examine the progress of different newspapers, with a view to a book, the "Fourth Estate," which I printed some time ago, and I am of opinion that the best papers would thrive by the removal of the stamp; that is to say, that the "Times," the "Daily News," and other morning papers that are conducted with talent, would thrive if the stamp were removed, provided that on the removal of the stamp they were protected in the property they publish; that is to say, in the possession of important news. At present the chief morning papers, which are in the hands of about four sets of proprietors, pay for all the important intelligence that is distributed over these kingdoms. Four sets of proprietors out of the six morning papers pay for the Indian mail; they pay also for reports of the law courts, and they give the most elaborate account of the Parliamentary proceedings; and all the special reports they pay for ought to be regarded as their property. If you give the newspaper proprietors some 12 hours' copyright in that which they pay for, I think they would then thrive by the removal of the penny stamp, and that all the papers might then be reduced in price; say the "Times," be sold for 3½ *d.* or 3 *d.*, and the "Daily News" certainly for 3 *d.* I should say. But if you were to take off the stamp to-morrow without giving any copyright in important special news, (the Indian mail, for instance, which perhaps might cost 80 *l.* or 100 *l.*,) the effect would be to reduce the character of the newspapers; because men would not give 80 *l.* or 100 *l.* for an Indian mail, unless they could have a property in it for a certain number of hours.

2320. You are exposed to piracy now, are you not?—Yes, we are exposed to piracy to a very large extent; but if you take off the stamp, (judging by the character of the cheap productions of the present day,—the penny papers,—who pay nothing for authorship, and who pay nothing for reporters, and whose papers are made up almost entirely from other journals,) you will lay the morning papers open to a larger amount of piracy than at present; and the proprietors, in self-defence, must cease to give you so complete a newspaper as they now offer.

2321. Sir *T. F. Lewis.*] Would it be possible to devise any scheme of effectual protection in the nature of copyright newspapers. You have suggested the idea that it should be penal to republish, during a certain number of hours, that which appeared in the "Daily News" or "Times"; would it be possible

Mr. *F. K. Hunt.*

27 May 1851.

possible to prevent persons from taking the substance of the news and, as it were, recompounding it, and putting it in somewhat different phraseology, condensing it a little, and putting it forth as if it were their own?—I think it would. Say that the Indian mail is brought by steam to Trieste, and sent through Austria, Prussia, and Belgium, to Calais, and then brought over by a steamer (kept waiting for the message with her steam up at a large expense) to Dover, and thence by electric telegraph to London, as is the practice of the morning papers at present. It is not possible that a penny newspaper could go to such expenses for such news, and no change in the verbiage of the telegraphic dispatch could so conceal the piracy as to protect the party guilty of it. The overland mail comes by telegraph, *viâ* Trieste, perhaps 12 or 24, or 36 hours before letters from India are delivered.

2322. Are the Committee to conclude that your opinion is that there would be sufficient protection if persons were prevented from pirating intelligence, and giving the debates in Parliament equally for a certain time?—Any paper might give the debates in Parliament; they are things at home. They could send a reporter into the gallery to write them a summary containing quite as much as the general public would care to read; that is not the class of news that requires anything like a law against piracy, but copies of such as the Indian mail; such news as the earliest intelligence by six or eight hours of some convulsion in some town in Europe to which a set of proprietors have sent a correspondent should be protected. At present you have in London, papers which, for the extent of their intelligence and the character of it, are certainly unequalled; they have grown up to their present position under a great many difficulties, though they are now subject to piracy. But the only persons in a condition to pirate are persons who have stamped newspapers, and who are restrained, to a large extent, by considerations of honesty and character. But as to piracy with the penny unstamped publications, which are issued in large numbers in some parts of London, the case is widely different. Such men, when they get a press, will print anything they can take hold of. They pay no authorship. It may happen that an article from the "Times" is quoted all over the country; to the "Times" it now matters not; if an article is taken and quoted the "Times" may regard it as a compliment; but if the "Times" had to run in competition with a three halfpenny journal, it would be another matter. The "Times" in order to supply its 38,000 subscribers must issue its first copies at half-past four in the morning

Mr. *F. K. Hunt.*

27 May 1851.

morning to get the trains for the north; if a man in London got one copy and took the articles and reprinted them, he would be running into competition with the "Times," without incurring one-tenth part of the expenses paid by that journal.

2323. Mr. *G. A. Hamilton.*] How could you prevent piracy with regard to news when the events had occurred abroad?—In any alteration of the law relative to the press,—if you took off the stamp,—you should, as at present, require persons issuing newspapers to give security against libels and defamation, and make them in addition give security that they would pay the damages in any action that might be brought against them for piracy, and the thing would be complete. With regard to the "Daily News," we have had one or two notable instances in which, partly by money and partly by the exercise of diligence and energy, we have got news to London before other papers; such successes are essential to a paper, as helping to establish its character; but these same things have been taken, as the law stands at present, by other papers, without any chance of redress.

2324. Sir *T. F. Lewis.*] On the same day?—Yes. From the London papers at present we are liable to piracy; if you make free trade in newspapers you must have a law which shall give a property in a piece of exclusive news for a certain number of honrs, and which would enable the owner of that news to proceed against any person who stole it.

2325. Mr. *G. A. Hamilton.*] How is it possible with reference to an event which has occurred, for instance in Germany, that you could devise any plan by which the copyright of that intelligence could be secured?—I will endeavour to explain. You have, say, on the 26th of May intelligence which shall appear in the "Daily News," in its intelligence from India of a given date, the 29th of April; we know it is impossible for steam to bring it in the time, it can only come by the electric telegraph, and that is only to be accomplished by elaborate arrangements and agencies, which are most costly. If the "Times," or the "Daily News," or the four papers now paying these expenses, bring a piece of important Indian news to London, say of a battle, or some other great event, they take it by the ordinary mail packet to Malta, and send it to Trieste by steam, and through Austria, Prussia, and Belgium, to Ostend or Calais; they keep a boat waiting to bring it across to Dover; it reaches London in the middle of the night, say three in the morning, it comes to the offices of these four papers, it is printed by them, say at half-past four, in

Mr. *F. K. Hunt.*

27 May 1851.

in order to go by railway to supply their customers at Manchester, Birmingham, and Liverpool, and if this was pirated they would be enabled, under a law such as I suggest, to go into a court of law, and say, we claim exclusive right to this piece of news, and let the defendant, if he denies our right, say how he got it. Things which are specially important, and which are specially costly to obtain, it would be very easy to identify and to protect. In the matter of Parliamentary debates piracy would not be of so much consequence; no newspaper proprietor would ask for much protection in that matter, but he desires to be protected in the honest enjoyment of the foreign and other news he pays high prices for.

2326. Sir *T. F. Lewis.*] Would you extend your answer to the reports of law proceedings in courts of justice, and also proceedings before the magistrates; would you require protection with reference to those matters?—I do not think it would be very essential. But supposing a very important case to occur, the newspapers employ three or four reporters of skill and character to take a long report, and then if that report was taken wholly and entirely, and if the proprietor of the report chose to complain, it would then, of course, be a question for a jury to say whether or no the man so taking it was justified. It is rather for those points of news in which the English press is unequalled (and there is no press like it), that security is wanted. I have heard a good deal said about the American and the French press, and thinking it possible that a question might be put upon the subject I have brought some specimens with me (*handing in the same*); and if the Committee compare these Paris, New York, Lisbon, Berlin, and Madrid papers with the "Times" or "Daily News," they will see that the newspapers of London, that is to say, the morning papers of London, contain an amount of news which is not contained in any foreign papers. A French paper gives you some very clever, some extremely clever leading articles. In times of excitement, there is a long report of the debates in the Chamber, but there it almost ends: there are no shipping lists, no reports of the markets, no reports of the state of the weather, and no reports of decisions in courts of law. In fact, the Paris journals are different altogether to the English papers

2327. Mr. *Cobden.*] You now speak of French papers, and not of the American?—In the American press you find a great deal of commercial news, and if the Committee compare this American newspaper (*pointing to one*) with the "Times" or "Daily News" of to-day, they will find that the amount

amount of information and news for the people is extremely small. There is an enormous number of advertisements, which are profitable, and there is a quantity of shipping news. Indeed their commercial news is very good in America; but look at the leading article, and you find it is but a small paragraph (*pointing out the same*).

Mr. *F. K. Hunt.*

27 May 1851.

2328. Sir *T. F. Lewis.*] The leading article does not occupy above half a column?—No; and the whole real news in this American paper, which is the best commercial paper of New York, would go into less than one page of a London paper.

2329. Can you give the Committee any information upon this point: of the total number of papers published by the "Daily News" or the "Times," what proportion goes out of London for secondary sale?—I cannot say; I should think it probable that it might be from a quarter to a third.

2330. *Chairman.*] You have stated that at present you are subject to piracy; that you consider the proprietors of newspapers are entitled to have a property in the news which they have laid out money to procure, and you think it probable that there will be more pirates than now if the stamp were removed; but you do not mean the Committee to understand, do you, that as far as the stamp is concerned, you advocate its maintenance on its own merits?—Certainly not; I think that all the papers would improve greatly if the stamp were removed and they had protection from piracy; they are interested in the removal of the stamp, except perhaps the most successful of all, the "Times," which I do not think is so much interested in removing the stamp, because it being now in the first position, any change could not improve but might injure it. I think that the "Daily News," the "Morning Chronicle," and the "Herald" would be improved in their position by the removal of the stamp; I think that the general circulation of papers would be greatly increased, but that some of them would be obliged to infuse new blood and a more popular feeling into their columns generally; for they would doubtless have a number of popular rivals.

2331. Sir *T. F. Lewis.*] How do you contemplate that the London papers would be circulated; by post or otherwise?—At present the bulk of the circulation, all the early circulation of the London morning papers in the provinces, is conducted without the Post Office; they are sent down in large bales by the morning mails; large bales of papers are sent to local agents; and the local agents, I believe, charge some little addition to the price for the papers, to remunerate them for the carriage of them by railway parcel.

 2332. With

Mr. *F. K. Hunt.*

27 May 1851.

2332. With reference to that portion of its circulation, a London paper derives no benefit from the circulation of those papers postage free, does it?—From a portion it does; it is probable that after a paper is taken down into the country by railway, it may be sold and sent by post in the evening. I presume that if Parliament consented to remove the stamp from newspapers, they would probably allow newspapers under an ounce or two ounces to go by post with a penny stamp affixed.

2333. Would that suffice, do you think?—I think it would quite; it seems to me that the great point is that we should not damage the newspapers of England. The London newspapers, on a fair comparison with others, are the most complete, are those upon which the most money is expended, and those upon which most vigilance is exercised, in the world. The proof lies in themselves; they ought not to be damaged by any change in the law in reference to the press. If the Legislature took the penny stamp off, granting to newspaper proprietors a legal property in costly pieces of intelligence, I think that the change would improve the press; it would improve newspapers generally, and it would give every one of them a larger circulation. At present the proprietors in London pay for the costly news I have spoken of, and others steal it. Suppose the India mail, for instance, comes in on a Tuesday morning, is printed in a morning paper, and is taken down a railway line; a copy of the paper is thrown out, say, at Northampton, and if it happens to be the day of publication of the Northampton paper, the agent is there to get this paper, in order that the proprietors may reprint and sell that which cost 100*l.* to proprietors in London, and it is obtained at Northampton for 5*d.* If not protected, the proprietors of newspapers in London would be compelled to give up such things as Indian mails.

2334. Are the leading articles in the principal papers frequently copied?—Yes; but when copied and acknowledged, that is seldom objected to.

2335. Would you extend the copyright to leading articles?—I think the law of copyright in news should be framed in this way; that if a man purchased a thing, whether an Indian mail or a discussion in Parliament, or an article discussing a matter of national importance, if he chose to attach a value to it, he should be enabled to go before a jury and ask them to give him a remedy against a man who had pirated it.

2336. Mr. *G. A. Hamilton.*] The law of copyright now has reference to specific publications or specific designs.

Applying

Mr. *F. K. Hunt.*

27 May 1851.

Applying the principle of copyright in the manner you suggest, would you prevent the publisher of a country newspaper from publishing the report of a battle in India?—After six or eight hours, certainly not. It should be after he had, or might have, received it by way of post; when it had become public property in fact.

2337. Would you prevent his publishing as soon as he could, in order to anticipate the intelligence contained in the London papers, a report of that battle?—The news having been obtained in the way I have mentioned, I think that no London paper would at all object to such a publication as this. If the "Northampton Herald," for instance, should say, "The 'Times' and the 'Daily News' contain an account of a great battle in India, in which 20,000 men have been killed and wounded," no paper would be likely to object to that. But the injustice is this: the expenses of the morning papers are enormous; they have agents where anything is likely to turn out of interest to the public; they bring this information home, and if the paper is printed at five o'clock in the morning, and if the Northampton paper reprints the whole substance of it the same morning at 10 o'clock, the newspaper proprietors in London, who are the real owners of the news, are deprived of the full enjoyment of that to which they are entitled. Any case of police, or any proceeding in a court of law, may be any man's property; for any man can easily go and get it; but news from distant places is another thing. If the stamp were removed, and a copyright in news given for six or eight or ten hours, the best papers would not be injured at all. The London papers would circulate more widely, and people would get newspapers to inform them on political subjects, and get them as cheaply I think as for 2*d.* Not a newspaper like the "Times," nor the "Daily News;" I do not think they would get those at quite so small a price, but they might perhaps have newspapers for 2*d.*

2338. Do you mean a transcript or a copy of those papers? —They might get a summary of them, which should be acknowledged; but I think it should be left in the hands of the owner of the news, whether he would object or not to such a summary; but as the law protects a man who has brought from India a piece of cotton and paid for it, the law ought to protect a man who brings from India a piece of news and paid for it. When news arrives by post by the ordinary mail, it is every man's property; but when it has been brought to this country at great private expense, and at the cost of four sets of proprietors, and it is pirated, that is an injustice; it

 ought

Mr. F. K. Hunt. 27 May 1851.

ought to remain the property of its proprietors till it becomes the property of the public.

2339. The law protects a specific design as regards cotton; the analogy would only go to establish a copyright as far as regards the copying of a particular article, or copying a specific piece of news; but it would not apply to cases where substantially the same intelligence in another form was given?—I should say that if a man owns a piece of cotton or a piece of news, he is entitled to say how much of that may be abstracted by another person with his leave, and how much may not; it is his property till it becomes public property.

2340. *Chairman.*] Do you think it is a foolish apprehension that in other respects the established newspapers would have anything to fear from the rivalry that would rise up in consequence of the removal of the stamp?—I have a very distinct opinion upon that subject. I have been writing in various papers, and have some knowledge of their affairs; for instance, Dickens's "Household Words," which I know enjoys a very wide circulation without any such "protection" as a stamp; and I do not think anybody can bring out a twopenny paper to beat that. Mr. Dickens sells a very large number. And again, you could not bring out any twopenny paper to beat "Punch." Talent protects itself. If the "Times" is the best newspaper in London, it would get the greatest number of purchasers, whether it be stamped or unstamped. The "Daily News" is only a young paper, and has not a tenth part of the age upon it that the "Times" has; yet it occupies, I suppose, the second place on the London press, and (it seems to me) it never need fear the taking off of the stamp.

2341. The advantage in any competition of having an already existing organization and experience in conducting newspapers would of course be all-favourable to the success of the established papers?—Clearly. You could not get up the organization of the "Daily News," for instance, under any circumstances, without the loss of some two or three years; and you could not get up any such papers as we see in London this day without great expenditure of time and money. When any change of the law comes, therefore, a rival could not hope to equal them at once, as you cannot procure all the news and get it prepared for the public in the careful manner in which the present newspaper proprietors prepare it, without a large and expensive staff. If you protect what they produce they will go on in the same way, and the press will not go down from its present level, though the stamp be removed.

2342. Sir *T. F. Lewis.*] What advantage is derived from the

Mr. *F. K. Hunt.*

27 May 1851.

the use of machinery; is it merely rapidity?—Yes, rapidity of production. The "Times" is very greatly interested in having very rapid machinery; but for a paper that circulates only 7,000 a day, an ordinary machine which throws off 4,000 or 5,000 an hour will do. Supposing the House of Parliament sits till two in the morning; the papers have skilful reporters there, who make all haste to the office, and when there would write out the latter part of the debate, say within an hour, which would make it three o'clock; and the paper can be completed and sent to press. Say the early trains go out at a quarter past six, and between three and a quarter past six the printers must produce the number of papers required to supply their country subscribers; and if you want to send away 12,000, a 5,000-per-hour machine will answer that purpose. But if the "Times" wants to send 20,000 by early trains, then they must have a more rapid machine. In that way defective machinery limits the circulation of a paper like the "Times." To supply their large demand, the French papers go to press early in the previous evening. Some London weekly papers have to begin printing long before publication. The "Illustrated News," for instance, is dated on Sunday, but its first edition goes to the press on Thursday night, and they cannot bring up their first news later than Thursday night; they then drop in, every six or 12 hours, a little bit of type with a sort of summary of intelligence; but they begin to print on Thursday night.

2343. Mr. *Rich.*] With regard to the question of protection, you gave as an illustration the Indian news; but the channel for conveying news from India is so narrow that it would be very easy to find out how it was pirated; how would you trace it with regard to continental events?—Sometimes the contest for early intelligence is extremely keen, and it would be worth the while of a paper to keep up a considerable staff, and a considerable amount of efficiency, for the chance every now and then of receiving a very special piece of intelligence. I remember the Revolution of 1848, when the fighting began. The Paris railway stations, and the station of the Northern Railway, among the rest, were all broken up, and there were no trains going, and nothing could be got out of Paris. One of the correspondents of a London paper, the "Morning Post," going down with his despatches, saw a man shot and fall down dead at his feet by the side of the railway. He went back again, and, like others in his position, thought it impossible to get any despatches off. But there was one correspondent in Paris who thought of this expedient:

He

Mr. *F. K. Hunt.*

27 May 1851.

He dressed a man in a blouse, and sent him through the disturbed streets during all the fighting; telling him to get outside the barrier, and then on horseback, and ride down the line till he found a point at which the circulation of the carriages was still in existence. The man did this, the news reached London, and it came to one London paper only. It was the first news of the bloodshed on the barricades. Now, if the paper to which that news was brought could have had the full benefit of it, it would have assisted in making its fortune; but as the law is at present, the temptation was too great for the other daily papers. They took the news from the paper that contained the intelligence alone, and thereby the real owner of it lost almost all the credit of it.

2344. How would you make the law against piracy operate with respect to continental events of importance?—Such events as are so public that any man might get, any man might print an account of, without fear of being challenged; but in the special case—where a set of proprietors send a correspondent, for instance to Hungaria, when that correspondent's despatches first arrived, they should be the copyright property of the paper employing him, leaving the onus with the proprietors to prove their copyright; or rather on any one who pirated out, to show he had a correspondent of his own.

2345. That is where the intelligence is brought by one man; but if events occurred at Paris, at Vienna, or wherever the channel of communication is broad, could you then sustain the exclusive right?—Known events are common property. Events in Paris, for instance, are known in London by post at nine o'clock next morning; but if a set of proprietors of London morning papers have their correspondents in Paris to write out an account of public events there, and they bring despatches to London at half-past four in the morning, surely from half-past four in the morning till the hour when the ordinary post would bring it, that news should belong to those who have paid for it; and they should enjoy it. If we on the "Daily News" get a despatch from Paris, and print it at five o'clock in the morning, to send to Manchester; surely Mr. A. or Mr. B., living in Holywell-street, (publishing a paper at 1½*d.*, into which he has put nothing that he has paid for but the leading article,) should not be entitled at five o'clock to buy a copy of the "Daily News," and to anticipate our sale in London by the reproduction of our despatch. When the ordinary post comes in, it would be his news or anybody's news. I am anxious to put a stress upon this point, because I feel very much

interested

Mr. *F. K. Hunt.*

27 May 1851.

interested in the status of the press in England. As I said before, England has the best papers in the world, and if you meddle with them without giving them some protection with reference to that which they pay for, they will cease to pay for it, and you will cease to have such newspapers as you get now.

2346. Even, then, supposing it possible for those proprietors to fix the piracy upon another, the copyright should hardly extend for 12 hours, because the intelligence would arrive generally within a very few hours after the arrival of your special despatch?—Yes. Supposing I claimed property in a piece of news from Paris, that reached me at my office at five in the morning, I should not bring an action against a man for the piracy of that news, who did not print it till 12 o'clock on the same day; I should know that he would nonsuit me by proving that it might have come by post. I am not sure for how many hours the law ought to give a man the exclusive possession of important intelligence.

2347. You say that you would not complain if the publisher of a country newspaper, immediately he saw the intelligence in the "Daily News," for instance, repeated that news, stating that he had obtained it from the "Daily News"?—I do not think that any set of proprietors would object to that; but I think it should rest with the owner of the intelligence to say whether he was injured or not. The London newspaper proprietors might say, "We will pay our 30,000 *l.* or 40,000 *l.* a year for news," and we will say to A., B., or C., "You may copy our mails always if you will acknowledge them, or you may copy our mails and we will supply you with them for 100 *l.* a year;" but at present things are copied every hour, even in London, things that cost great expense and trouble, without recompense, or even acknowledgment. There is one thing which is now being printed every morning in London, which requires agents all over England and in many parts of Ireland, for its preparation; each agent sends up one line of information about the weather. This has been a most troublesome affair to organize, and it has been necessary to obtain the assistance of the Astronomer Royal, and the heads of all the chief railway lines to complete it. The intelligence is printed in a paper in London, and in the afternoon of each day it is pirated without the slightest acknowledgment. Again, it is necessary in order that a certain London shipping list may be completed every morning, to employ agents at Bristol, at Cork, at Dublin, at Liverpool, and at Gravesend,—all men on salaries,—who send special despatches, for which

railway

Mr. *F. K. Hunt.* 27 May 1851.

railway carriage is paid, and postage is also paid for bringing them to a newspaper office. From the whole of these despatches a man is specially employed to prepare a list of shipping. When complete it is published in a morning paper, and on the same day it has been pirated without the slightest acknowledgment. The law is at present excessively deficient, and judging from the character of certain piratical weekly penny papers, (which do not pay for anything at all, except perhaps a leading article) if you take off the stamp without giving some protection against the evil of piracy, you will bring down the press of London to the level of the character of the American press. The German papers and the French papers are all inferior in amount of information to the English papers; and I think it very desirable, and I suppose all Englishmen must think so, to keep the English papers up to their present standard.

2348. *Chairman.*] Do you think that there would be more pirating if the stamp were removed?—Yes.

2349. Mr. *Rich.*] It would be much more difficult to enforce the law then, would it not?—Yes.

2350. Sir *J. Walmsley.*] If there were more piracy would that prevent you from giving the same amount of information that you do now, and in the same way?—Yes, I think it would. If a morning newspaper procured a costly piece of information, and for the sake of getting it into the country early, began to print it at five o'clock in the morning, and the paper (having a large circulation,) was employed for two hours or three hours (and the "Times" is understood sometimes to be four hours in supplying its country circulation);—if at five o'clock Mr. A. or Mr. B. bought a copy for 5 *d.*, and at once reprinted that news, he would put the "Times" out of the market, by selling it, say for 1 ½ *d.*; and then the proprietors would cease to buy this expensive news, and the papers would cease to be as good as they are now.

2351. *Chairman.*] What is there to prevent a person copying the "Times" as it is (being all ready to purchase the first copy that comes out), and reprinting it two or three hours afterwards, not having paid for any portion of the contents of his paper?—Only his sense of honesty.

2352. And the question is, whether there is not such a sense of honesty in the public, and if they see abuses of this sort, whether they would give encouragement to that sort of piracy?—If a man can buy for 1 *d.* what he must pay elsewhere 4 *d.* or 3½ *d.* for, it is apt to overcome his scruples. There are papers in London now, emanating from Holywell-street,

street, that have a circulation, I am told, of from 60,000 to 100,000. They give large sheets, and the margin of profit is very small, some 8*s.* a thousand only. But the contents are nearly all pirated. They live by stealing their brooms ready made; they take nearly all their articles from other publications. But the public buy them by tens of thousands.

Mr. *F. K. Hunt.*

27 May 1851.

2353. But assuming that the piracy question is disposed of, with regard to the stamp, on its own merits, do you think that the removal of the stamp would have a good educational effect upon the people?—Yes; I think that the law and police reports, for instance, in a newspaper, offer almost the only chance that an uneducated man has of learning what the law is. I think it is most essential that such newspapers as we now have should be sold cheaply, in order that men might learn, and then get a relish for reading the debates and discussions on political subjects. When temperately conducted, political writings are, I think, the very best kind of reading, practically, that Englishmen can obtain. As to the influence of the stamp in improving the character of the writing in newspapers, we may remember that some of the best writing that we have ever had appeared in an unstamped paper,—in Addison's "Spectator."

2354. Mr. *G. A. Hamilton.*] In your opinion is an American paper as good an educational instrument as the "Times"?—The American papers are nearly all advertisements; I have no doubt that they are very valuable in America to the people there, but I do not think they are so good as the English papers. I have brought here some copies to show that our journals have grown up to what they are in spite of the stamp. Here is one (*producing the same*) of Charles the Second, which has no stamp; but shortly after, in Queen Anne's time, they put a stamp on; that has varied in amount at different times; here is a halfpenny stamp in 1734, and in 1796 it is still a halfpenny; later we find it rise to fourpence, but still the papers are seen growing in size and importance; attaining their full vigour, however, with the present reduced penny stamp.

2355. Sir *T. F. Lewis.*] The advertisements in the London papers, judging from their general character, would appear to be more addressed to the London public than to the country public. Have you any opinion as to the value of that portion of the "Times" or the "Daily News" which is devoted to advertisements; or can you state to what extent it is valuable to the country, and whether it assists its circulation or not?—I think a portion of the advertisements, it may be a large

Mr. *F. K. Hunt.*

27 May 1851.

a large portion, are intended for perusal in both town and country.

2356. If it is likely that the removal of the stamp would have a tendency to bring into existence a multitude of local papers in the country market towns, would not that be increased very much by the local advertisements which they would have an opportunity of publishing?—Yes.

2357. Are you at all acquainted with the press of Ireland? —No; at least only by seeing the papers in London.

2358. Are they not written so as to excite and foment antagonistic opinions in Ireland; and do not they tend very much to keep alive local prejudices and local antipathies?—I should be unwilling to give any opinion against the Irish press, as a rule; but I think this, that a paper emanating from the metropolis, having a manifest national character, is much more likely to be useful over the country, as taking a view useful to the entire country, instead of entering into little local bickerings. If the stamp was taken off, postal facilities being retained, the "Times" would be read in the country, and the "Daily News" would be read in all directions, and you would have distributed throughout the breadth of England and Ireland papers with national views.

2359. You think that that would be usefully increased by the removal of the stamp, provided that the circulation of the papers was not encumbered by a heavy postage duty?—Undoubtedly.

2360. You do not apprehend that there would be any tentency of an opposite character, by the multiplication of the number of local newspapers?—No; there would be little papers like the "Cheltenham Looker-On," to give local news, but papers emanating from large towns, such as London, Manchester, and Liverpool, would circulate over the country, and give more than ever a tone to national opinion.

*Veneris,* 30° *die Maii,* 1851

---

MEMBERS PRESENT:

| | |
|---|---|
| Mr. Ewart. | Mr. G. A. Hamilton. |
| Sir J. Walmsley. | Mr. Rich. |
| Mr. Tufnell. | Mr. Cobden. |

THE RIGHT HON. T. MILNER GIBSON IN THE CHAIR.

---

The Reverend *Thomas Spencer*, called in; and Examined.

Rev. *T. Spencer.*

30 May 1851.

2361. *Chairman.*] YOU are a Clergyman of the Established Church, are you not?—Yes, I am.

2362. Have you turned your attention to the effect of the newspaper stamp, with reference to its being an obstacle to the diffusion of knowledge amongst the people?—I have thought of it a great many years; I have long considered it as the greatest obstacle in the way of every movement for the good of the people, and if there were one thing which I should myself wish to do, if I could do no other, it would be to remove that obstacle.

2363. Mr. *Ewart.*] You have had opportunities of coming into contact with a great number of the working classes, have you not?—I have had great opportunities of coming into contact with the working classes; I have been for ten years a guardian of the poor; I have been a leading mover in the temperance question; I have had a great deal to do with peace movements and peace congresses, and this year I have delivered about 60 lectures upon various topics, relating to self-culture, all over England, and I find that the working-classes possess far too little knowledge, because so few take in a paper; so few can afford to take in a paper; so that they can see no answer to the objections which can be raised against any subject, and they are liable to errors on every point.

2364. With reference to the effect of the newspaper stamp in raising the price of newspapers, do you conceive that the poorer classes are not enabled to get newspapers by clubbing together, or going to public-houses where they are taken in?—This very week we are about to petition Parliament from the Temperance Society; the petition was agreed to by the committee

Rev. *T. Spencer.*

30 May 1851.

mittee of that society this very week, on the ground that we consider the stamp duty a premium upon drunkenness. I know, myself, the cases of men who never would have been drunkards but for going to the public-houses to read the newspaper. I was appealed to in the parish of which I was incumbent for 22 years, by the wife and children of a man who was coming home drunk very frequently, and I went to speak to him, and he said, "I tell you, Sir, I never go to the public-house for beer, I go for the news; I have no other way of getting it; I cannot afford to pay five-pence, but unfortunately I go on drinking till I have spent a shilling, and I might as well have bought the paper in the first instance; still that is my reason, my only reason for going to the public-house; I hear people read the paper, and say what is going on in London, and it is the only place where I get the news;" and that is the case with the working classes all over the kingdom. They go to the gin-shop, or the beer-shop, or the public-house; they have no opportunity, generally, of getting at the news, and besides that, there are other inducements to make the news pleasanter there; there is a good deal of society and music, and lighted rooms, and the bribe of the news of the day, which news comes to them in a most garbled form; and when they are in liquor, and have spent their money and made fools of themselves, they are angry with themselves, and angry with society, and are ready to entertain the most desperate feelings against any class, and against any government, and therefore all pot-house politics are the most dangerous of all. There is not the slightest danger to be apprehended from any working-man, a domesticated man and a sober man; there is an innate love of peace and quiet and order in every Englishman if he is not a drunken man.

2365. Mr. *Rich.*] Your experience would induce you to suppose that newspaper reading would be not only the most acceptable but the most instructive description of reading which the people could possess?---If I were a great educator of the people, my first step would be, not in schools, but in the newspaper press; I have not so much opinion of the education of children as some people have; as long as the atmosphere they breathe is so impure, and the fire-side where they must spend part of their time is so prejudicial, they will have their characters formed at home, and not at school; but the newspapers will educate the adult population, the young men and the fathers, and if they are right, their children are sure to be right; this, it appears to me, is the shortest way to get at them; in fact, I could wish to assert, as positively as I may, that it is the way of

Rev. *T. Spencer.*

30 May 1851.

of the Divine Being himself, for in the Bible we have not merely the precepts of religion, but all the news of the day, given up to the day in which the people lived, in the Books of Kings and Chronicles; and in the New Testament, the Acts of the Apostles and everything of importance to the men of that day were recorded for their information, so that they not only knew the history of the world from the beginning and its future destiny, but they knew the passing events of the times in which they moved; and not only so, but our Lord blamed every man, whatever else he knew, if he did not discern the signs of the times, if he did not know what was going on in the day in which he lived, and in which he had duties to perform.

2366. *Chairman.*] If the penny stamp were so reduced, or if the taxes on knowledge were so reduced as to enable the people to obtain newspapers cheaply, there would be a great increase in the demand for newspapers, would there not?—I cannot say how much, I should imagine it would be enormous, indeed I am quite convinced that 100 persons would read newspapers to one who reads them now; go into a small town in England, in such a county as Suffolk or in Devonshire, and you will not find one person in 50 that sees a newspaper; you tell them of anything that is in the "Times," but they do not see the "Times;" if they go to market, or some public-house, they may hear what is going on, but they do not take in newspapers; it is not the habit of the English at all, whereas in the United States almost every person does take in a paper.

2367. And at a very reduced price, do you apprehend that newspapers would become the ordinary reading of the family circle?—Yes, they would become the reading of every family circle; every man would take in his own paper in his own house, as they do in America. I have in my pocket papers from America; they are sold there at from one cent to five cents, perhaps upon the average they are sold at about two or three cents; a cent is a halfpenny. Here is the great "New York Sun," (*producing the same*) which has a circulation of 43,000 at a cent a-piece; this is a halfpenny paper, and I put a few in my pocket in case there should be any doubt as to my statement; I know that some gentlemen think it impossible, but there is the price upon it; this paper has enormous circulation; it takes 40,000 before they get a profit, but the proprietor was making a fortune when I was there; the circulation is stated on the paper to be 43,000; the advertisements are very numerous; everybody can put in an advertisement for 1 *s.* and continue it for 6 *d.*; therefore the advertising is of small cost, having no tax cost, the paper is of small cost, having no

 tax

Rev. *T. Spencer.*

30 May 1851.

tax cost, and there are several times as many advertisements as you would see in a small priced paper in England.

2368. Mr. *Ewart.*] You have a very considerable knowledge of the agricultural districts, have you not?—I have lived a great deal in them.

2369. What, in your opinion, would be the effect of a great reduction in the price of newspapers upon the agricultural labourers?—I believe that nothing would so improve the feelings of agricultural labourers as seeing quietly at their own houses how things were going on. They now hear them from sources which are of a very poisoned nature, and they are very frequently a very disaffected set of men; they have ideas that are very incorrect, and something far more unkind than I think is to be found among the people in towns, for want of this sort of information. They also find that if they are taught to read at schools, they have very little use for it, therefore they have no inducement to send their children to school. Those young men who have been at school have nothing to read, except the Bible, and they get out of the way of reading it; but if they had these newspapers at a halfpenny or a penny, or three halfpence, say a penny on the average, they would get interested in every good thing that was going on, and would take care that every child they had should be taught to read.

2370. You have spoken of agricultural labourers, you have also been mixed up a great deal with the population of towns; do you entertain the same views with regard to the working classes in towns as to the advantage they would derive from cheap newspapers?—Yes; I believe that at present all the advantage of the monopoly of the papers is on the side of bad men and bad principles, and that the difficulty is only on the side of those who wish to do good. If we in the Temperance Society, or in the Peace Society, wish to send right principles all over the community, there is an obstacle which we cannot get over; if it is a little penny tract, you must go to the expense of 5 *l.* to advertise it before it becomes known, the expense of the papers being so great, that people do not take in the very papers in which it is advertised. If these papers were at a small price, people would see them, and the advertisement would therefore be general, at any rate, and whatever you wished to communicate would reach all classes.

2371. Mr. *Rich.*] You state that all the advantages are now on the side of bad men and bad papers?—And bad principles, I said.

2372. How do you show, if the advantages are all on the side

Rev. *T. Spencer.*

30 May 1851.

side of bad men and bad principles, that the newspapers which disseminate those bad principles would become schools of instruction?—I am not speaking of the respectable newspapers of the day, but of those that do not mind breaking the law; there are very many bad publications going on.

2373. You stated that all the advantages were on the side of the bad papers?—I mean the cheap ones, to get at the working classes. If a person wants to corrupt the working classes, all the advantages are on his side; but if he wants to elevate them, all the obstacles are in the way of a person who has that object in view: he will not break the law, he will not publish illegally, he will not go where the gin and beer are in circulation, and therefore he cannot get at the class he wishes to reach.

2374. How do you practically arrive at that conclusion?—Because I perceive that there is a very large circulation of very corrupt publications circulated in a way that no honourable man would stoop to avail himself of.

2375. *Chairman.*] The object of the Newspaper Stamp Act, as avowed, when it was passed, was for the purpose of preventing cheap publications containing news or comments upon news being published; are you of opinion that that was a mistaken policy, and that it has been productive of mischievous results instead of good results?—I am quite of opinion that it was a mistaken policy; I will mention a case in point. When I was in America, there was a great excitement about a war with England; I heard, for 10 days, such warlike speeches in Congress as were never uttered, I think, anywhere else; and on expressing my surprise to Mr. Calhoun, that nobody spoke on the other side, he said, "Our policy is to let the steam off, to let everybody say their say; by-and-by people will be tired of hearing our opponents on the side of war; they will hear us, and we shall by-and-by turn the tide just the other way;" and it turned out so.

2376. Mr. *Rich.*] It would appear from your statement, that those newspapers which disseminate good things let off the steam, and breathe war?—They also let out the antidote, and breathe peace, and there was peace with England just at the time. There were two things that accomplished the peace. Elihu Burritt, one of whose papers I have here, was publishing the "Christian Citizen," and sending what he called "Olive Leaves" to all the papers all over America, recommending peace with England: and at that very time, when the war fever was at its height, Sir Robert Peel's speech on the Corn Laws came, and it was inserted in every paper; wherever I

 travelled

Rev. *T. Spencer.*

30 May 1851.

travelled I found every cent paper filled with that speech: the people said, "England is going to give fair play to America, and we will not have war;" and the man who, from that moment, ventured to talk of war, would have been scouted from society. Those cheap newspapers came to every man until they made him satisfied that it was wiser to be at peace.

2377. Do you think that a country in which a man, who talked of war, would be scouted from society, is a country in which free discussion exists?—In the slave states free discussion does not exist.

2378. Where then is the value of those newspapers which contain so much intelligence?—As to scouting a man from society, I mean that the influence of public opinion would be against him; I mean this, that if you give fair play to truth it really will prevail. Truth has always, in every age, been at first in the minority, and it has always gained the day; and, therefore, if you will only allow free scope to it, everybody could get a paper that would guide them to the truth; now error is advocated; but truth, on every point and on every principle of social order and public morality, will ultimately prevail.

2379. Do you think that truth and falsehood depend upon the question of a penny stamp?—It depends upon the queston of truth being brought into contact with the public mind; in America they have such faith in their public press, that they do not fear any error.

2380. You have stated that you consider the penny stamp is a premium on drunkenness, and that it came within your knowledge that a man attributed, and you agreed with him in attributing his drunkenness to the penny stamp, as he went to the public-house to read the newspaper; this man confessed to you that he spent a shilling a day in drink, stating that the temptation was not the drink, but that it was to hear the newspaper read; now, as the newspaper may be brought to his own door for sixpence, how do you connect drunkenness with the penny stamp?—That is from the infirmity of human nature; a man does not intend to spend a shilling, but being in the habit of drinking, when he begins he is led on, therefore, though he goes to the public-house as a cheap way of getting the newspaper, he spends more than the price of it.

2381. If he goes habitually to the public-house to drink, is not the temptation to get the drink rather than to read, or hear the newspaper read?—No, I believe many people go for the sake of the news to the public-house.

2382. Should you not be inclined to think that a public-house

house where newspapers were read was likely to be more orderly then one where there was no reading at all?—Yes, every place; I would not take the newspapers away from the public-houses, but I would have them at private houses too.

Rev. *T. Spencer.*

30 May 1851.

2383. What induces you to think that an agricultural labourer who comes home from a long day's toil would take in a newspaper, and read it to his family?—People are naturally fond of knowing what is going on; agricultural labourers have no particular wish to be disorderly; they go to the public-house to hear what is going on, and are then led by bad society to become worse than they would be.

2384. Are there not many cheap publications now of a very excellent tendency, that might be read with very great benefit and amusement by a labourer and his family in his own home?—Certainly, but it is the will of the Almighty that a man should know the things that concern himself; the taxes of the day, and the laws concern him; and therefore it is an injustice to keep him from the knowledge of that which affects himself and his children.

2385. Will you state to the Committee whether a man might not with great advantage read, without reference to newspapers, "Chambers's Journal," and publications of that kind, which have a great circulation, and contain much useful information for the lower classes of society?—Certainly; but if he is a good man he would also wish to know, and a man is bound to know what is going on; it is his duty to the Almighty, and he is a bad man if he neglects to know those things in which he is to act a part, and to give an account of himself at a future day.

2386. Do you find that the class referred to do read "Chambers's Journal" and other publications of that kind?—They have not got a habit of reading; and a newspaper would create a love of reading, and form a habit.

2387. Why should not "Chambers's Journal" create a love of reading, and the Bible create a love of reading, and the instruction which they receive at school create a love of reading?—The Bible contained news some thousands of years ago; it contains excellent precepts, but as to the news part of it, the history of the Kings and the Chronicles of old times, that may not affect so much a man at this day, yet it gives him a right to expect to know the events of the present day; and whatever else a man reads, he will desire to know that.

2388. Your opinion is, that unless a man gets a newspaper to read, he will read nothing?—I believe he will not, generally speaking; if he is a very religious man, he will read the Bible.

 2389. But

Rev. *T. Spencer.*

30 May 1851.

2389. But not having a Bible, or not reading it, he will read nothing else but a newspaper?—If he read a newspaper, he would become interested in all the things that were going on, and he would be more likely to read the Bible than if he is sunk in ignorance, and reads nothing.

2390. Without a newspaper, he will read nothing?—Generally speaking, I think so.

2391. *Chairman.*] In fact, the news of the day, when inserted in any publication, renders that publication attractive? —It does; that is one evil which we find in circulating our temperance and peace publications; we have only one topic, and we must not put the news of the day in unstamped ones, and, therefore, they are not sufficiently attractive to be read on their own account; whereas if every little paper were to advocate one great subject, and if you could give the current news, it would take those higher principles to a greater number of readers.

2392. In reference to the mistaken views that have prevailed sometimes in agricultural districts, such as hostility to machinery, and mobs assembling to put an end to improvements of various kinds, under the idea that they interfered with the employment of labour, do not you think that the circulation of a cheap press amongst the people would furnish the means of obtaining access to their minds, and convincing them of the unsoundness of their views?—Certainly, I do; I know some very worthy men in country places that have terrible notions about machinery, and entertain feelings that are quite opposed to their general character. In small towns, and even in large villages, there is always a clergyman, or some other person who would publish a paper for the town or the village if it could be done as cheaply as the repeal of the stamp would allow it to be. Now, everything is difficult; for instance, last week we had a temperance meeting, and we bought 400 copies of a paper to circulate among the subscribers, and we found that we could not send even stamped papers to those in London; we had to send them off to Highgate and into the country, to come back to the people in London, though they were stamped, or there would have been a penny charged on each.

2393. If you had put them in the post in London, to go to the parties to whom they were addressed, there would have been a penny charged?—Yes.

2394. But by sending them first of all to Highgate, they are sent from Highgate into London for nothing?—Yes, and therefore the Post-office has more trouble and expense.

2395. With

Rev. *T. Spencer.*

30 May 1851.

2395. With regard to the effect upon the employment of the people, do you consider that cheap newspapers circulating amongst the labouring classes might facilitate the transfer of labour from one part of the country to another, by making it known where labour was wanted and where labour might be in excess?—Every young man or woman would be on the look-out to see where something was going on. If a paper were accessible, it would give employment in every department of business; and in one department especially it would employ so many more paper-makers, compositors, and literary men, that the employment in that way would be tenfold what it is now in the printing department.

2396. Have you observed, in your intercourse with the labouring classes in the agricultural districts, that there is some little jealousy or suspicion of mere advice; and do you think if facts were communicated and circulated amongst them, they would be more likely to be led by them?—Yes, I believe, as a general rule; or, in many cases, they very much respect the minister of the parish and the country squire; but very frequently there is another feeling; if advice comes from the rich and the great, they look upon it with suspicion; but whatever is in a newspaper they think is law and gospel, and they believe it infallible; they think it is put there by a friend, and with no object to keep them down; and they are more inclined to receive the truth through that channel than in any other way.

2397. With respect to emigration, do you think that it would be assisted, when necessary, by diffusing amongst that class accurate information?—Yes; there is a very great difficulty now in giving and receiving intelligence from abroad; there is a general desire on the part of the working classes to know what the papers contain; and when they are sent, many are lost; they are put in, perhaps, when they are too old, and unless they are put in within eight days, they will not go.

2398. With regard to internal circulation in the United Kingdom, do you think that those cheap newspapers would tend to remove many prejudices that exist in the minds of the people, arising from ignorance, and make them more willing to go where it was obvious their interests would be promoted?—Yes; I think they would remove objections from the minds of ignorant people of every kind respecting emigration, or any other subject.

2399. You spoke of resorting to the post-office at Highgate, in order that a newspaper might be sent from one street to another in London without an extra charge?—Yes.

2400. Does the practice exist in other large towns, that



when

Rev. *T. Spencer.*

30 May 1851.

when they want to diffuse their small publications amongst the people of a particular locality, they are obliged first of all to send them into the country, in order that they may be imported as it were?—I could name several papers, some of which are sent first of all in an immense mass to Kensington every week, and others of which are sent to Acton, where they are put into the post to come into London; and not only so, but in the cases of those that are partly stamped and partly unstamped, it is a direct loss to the Post-office. We, in the Temperance Society, of which I am secretary, are obliged to make that calculation; and for the working of it we have to consider the matter in this way—we pay a boy 6*s.* a week, but if it will cost us less to send a few hundreds by the boy we will send them, and they are unstamped; but if it is too far to send the boy we have stamped ones, and send them by post. The consequence is, that if, instead of the penny stamp there was a halfpenny wrapper to go by post, our boy would not do this, but the Post-office would do the work. I believe every society in London has in the same way calculated, whether it is any cheaper to send the papers round by a boy, and where it is so they use that plan; but where it would cost less to send them by post they always use it; anything that would be sent by a halfpenny wrapper, which I think would pay the post more than the penny stamp does, would supersede this system of sending by a boy instead of the Post-office.

2401. If you had taken a large number of your temperance tracts to the Post-office at St. Martin's-le-grand, they would not have delivered them for you without the charge of a penny upon each?—No.

2402. If you took them to Highgate and put them in, or to Kensington or Acton, would they be subject to the charge of a penny?—No, then they would go free; but a stamped paper if put into any post-office in London will not go to any place within three miles without being charged a penny, and a person therefore, in London, who receives a paper, is unjustly charged a dearer price for it for the sake of those who receive their papers in the country; he has no privilege; he cannot send a paper to a friend in London, nor can it be sent to him.

2403. Is it a common practice to send those papers that are to be distributed in London first of all into the country, in order that they may afterwards come back to London, thereby avoiding the extra charge?—I could mention the names of papers about which I have heard from the proprietors themselves this week; one person sends an immense number to Acton

Acton by the carrier, and they are put into the post-office at Acton; another person sends his newspapers to Kensington, he sends all his numbers that belong to London to Kensington every week, and they come then to the different persons for whom they are intended in London.

Rev. *T. Spencer.*

30 May 1851.

2404. If he had put them into one of the London post-offices the postage would have been charged?—Yes, a penny to each person.

2405. Has not the Post-office far more to do in bringing them from Acton, and delivering them, than if it merely distributed them from the central office?—Yes, a great deal more; if you sent them from London to Acton then you must have somebody to be instructed to send them back again; supposing it was a newspaper published in the Strand, and you wanted to send it to Fleet-street, if you put it into the Post-office a penny is charged, but if you send that paper to a post-office in the country, say to Kensington, Notting-hill, or Acton, or any of those places, then it comes to Fleet-street without any charge whatever.

2406. Mr. *Tufnell.*] Do you think it would give great additional facility if the papers were allowed to circulate in London for a penny stamp?—With a halfpenny wrapper, to be obtained at the Post-office.

2407. But under the present system?—Under the present system it would certainly only fail, because with the penny post, if a man pays a penny on a letter to go to Birmingham it goes, and if he pays a penny to go to the next street, it goes; there is no exception made in favour of the country there, but here the country has all in its own favour; newspapers will go to any distance even in Scotland, but not to any part in London.

2408. Mr. *Ewart.*] Does not that remark apply to all large towns?—Yes, within a town; in fact you must not send the newspapers by post within a town to any party; and the newspaper proprietors send them round to their customers.

2409. Mr. *Rich.*] Are you inclined to recommend a penny wrapper, or a halfpenny wrapper, in substitution for the present stamp?—A halfpenny wrapper, which would more than pay for the penny stamp.

2410. Then your objection to the stamp is not *in toto*, but you wish a substitute for it?—Yes, and in this way, that those who have a paper conveyed to them through the post will have to pay for it, and those who have it at their own homes will have nothing to pay. Now, a newspaper is sent eight or ten times through the post till it is quite old, whereas then it would

Rev. *T. Spencer.*

30 May 1851.

would never go through the post without being properly charged; it would always pay its way.

2411. Your great grievance as to the stamp duty reduces itself to this, that in place of the stamp duty you would put a wrapper round a paper?—Yes, those which go by post.

2412. These small publications, you say, are sent in large numbers, and distributed by private hand, and therefore to stamp them, and to tell the parties that they can use the post, if they please, for nothing, would be giving them no privilege at all?—What we desire is, that our cheap publications should be allowed to go through the post by encircling them with a halfpenny wrapper; that every society engaged in doing good should have that fair opportunity, every literary society and every public body. A gentleman at Tottenham told me that if this was done he would publish a paper at Tottenham, to encourage sanitary principles, and do away with errors among the people; they are now open to infidelity from being so totally ignorant. Half the false charity that exists is because people do not see the cases of imposition which are to be found in the papers, and if they saw these cases of imposition they would then be on their guard; but the great thing necessary now for every movement of our day is a cheap press.

2413. Mr. *Rich.*] And you think that the substitution of a halfpenny wrapper for the penny stamp would create this great moral revolution?—It would be the greatest thing that could be done in this country; I have also to state that there are difficulties, of which some gentlemen are not aware, in the way of getting a small paper before the public.

2414. Sir *J. Walmsley.*] What effect, in your opinion, would the reduction of the penny stamp have upon the demand for literary talent?—It would increase it tenfold, and everything connected with the press, and especially everything connected with the moral and intellectual portion of the press; those which are living by the depraved passions of society get on very well now in their dirty puddles, where nobody sees them; if this could be brought to light, and full scope were allowed for the best men in society, a moral revolution would take place.

2415. Would it increase the remuneration to literary men, do you think?—It would employ a greater number of them.

2416. Would it enhance the value of their labours?—It would enable them to live; I do not know that any one particular individual would receive more; but there would be a great many more of them employed.

2417. Would the quality of the newspaper press be greatly improved?—Certainly.

2418. What

Rev. *T. Spencer.*

30 May 1851.

2418. What effect would a cheap press have on the morals of the people ?—It would give a large scope for every public teacher; every man who wished to combat error would have an opportunity of doing so, and every man who wished to diffuse a good moral principle through the country would have an opportunity to do so, and the papers would become the great teachers of the people. In America, where the press is cheap, there are a great many Sunday religious papers, and they are the most splendid things of the kind that can be conceived. I have a number of them at home, but they are really the writing of the best and cleverest men in the country. Every town has several of these papers, which are taken in by the people. For those who desire to have grave reading, there are most interesting publications, containing right and sound principles.

2419. In your opinion, a reduction of the taxes upon knowledge would tend greatly to improve the tone and morals of the people in general ?—Yes.

2420. *Chairman.*] You have travelled in America, have you not ?—Yes, for half a year.

2421. Mr. *Rich.*] That is the extent of your experience in America ?—Yes; but I have seen a great deal of the Americans.

2422. Mr. *G. A. Hamilton.*] Should you say, on the whole, that the American press was superior, as an educational instrument, to the English press ?—It is superior in coming in contact with the people. I do not say that individual papers are superior to our best papers, but there is a paper for every man; there is a paper to supply that class of society, where there is a vacuum in England. The rich in this country can get those papers and there are very vile papers for the worst of the poor; but there are no papers for the respectable portion of them.

2423. Mr. *Tufnell.*] You stated that the quality of the press would be improved if the stamp were taken away; did you mean the quality of those very low papers, or do you apply that observation to the press generally ?— I believe there are thousands of clergymen and ministers of religion, philanthropic men, who would set up papers; Sir Culling Eardley Eardley conducts a paper, and he can afford it; he conducts the "Christian Times;" and I believe many would take up this plan, because it would be a thing within their reach; whereas at present there are obstacles which are insurmountable. I would mention an obstacle in the way of the "Temperance Chronicle," We are just going to unite the "Temperance

perance

Rev. *T. Spencer.* — 30 May 1851.

perance Chronicle" and the "Temperance Gazette," and it is necessary, in consequence, to come again to Somerset House, because we change our title and printer. We have a paper to fill up; this paper requires that we shall find two persons as sureties for securing the advertisement duty, and at heavy sums of money. It requires that there shall be two persons as securities against the publication of libels, at very large sums of money, and it requires that there shall be two persons to certify to the respectability of the first two, and two more to certify to the respectability of the other two, in reference to libels, and those respectable persons are living in the City. Their time is very valuable, and they exceedingly grudge to come to the Stamp Office, they have to wait there so long; they know that it is a loss of a great deal of time, and there are persons who, on that ground, decline being sureties; and unless that can be done, you cannot even circulate such a little thing as the "Temperance Chronicle." You must get these heavy bonds, and must comply with all these directions; then, I think also, there is an expense incurred to start with, of something like 5 *l.*, at least so our assistant secretary told me; and that that is equivalent to a penny stamp for 1,200 papers. There are obstacles in the way, under the present system, which should not be in the way of a periodical which only seeks the good of the people by bringing the evils of drunkenness and the advantages of sobriety before them.

2424. Mr. *Rich.*] Having stated all these evils and the good likely to arise from the diffusion of useful intelligence among the people, would it not be possible when the obstacles were all removed, that corrupt and flagitious people might be inclined to establish newspapers which would be addressed to the worst passions of mankind, and that those would become very acceptable and very dangerous?—Certainly, that might happen; but there is my perfect faith that, whenever light comes, darkness must flee away. Wherever these bad passions are excited they are just ready to receive the antidote; and, I believe, that, if you only give fair play to truth, a newspaper advocating truth will beat one off the field that advocates error; only let there be no obstacle of great expense, and no legal barrier in the way.

2425. Mr. *Ewart.*] Has your experience in America justified you in that conclusion?—Yes; I never saw so quiet a people.

2426. What species of paper do they prefer?—I have already mentioned that they have all those papers, of which I have

Rev. *T. Spencer.*

30 May 1851.

I have specimens here. These papers show also, from their great number, what the taste of the people is.

2427. You maintain that the good preponderates over the bad where there is free competition?—Yes, I believe that to be so; there is, consequently, a very orderly state of society; there is not only no agitation, but no one that fears agitation; there is no one that fears agitation except in the slave states; and in the slave states I found it very difficult to get at newspapers; in the city of Charlestown I could not buy one; I went to different offices where they were sold, and it was only by having one given to me that I procured one; they said they did not sell them, as they contained advertisements of slaves.

2428. Mr. *Rich.*] Your evidence has only reference to one half of America?—Yes, to the free states; in the slave states newspapers are scarce, and there are obstacles in the way; at New Orleans the cheapest paper is the "Picayune," but there is nothing like a large circulation of papers.

2429. Yet the papers are just as cheap as in the non-slave holding states?—No; in the slave states the slave-holders are afraid of papers being printed, and made accessible to all, and therefore the thing is not at all in the same way as in the free states. If the newspapers were as numerous and as free in their discussion of questions in the slave states as in the free states, slavery would be abolished.

2430. There are no governmental obstacles in America to the circulation of newspapers in the slave states any more than in the free states, are there?—In the slave states there are all sorts of obstacles; a man cannot be a member of the Legislature unless he own slaves. A traveller cannot enter some of the slave states without answering certain questions as to what his object is, whither he goes, and when he comes back. If it was found that he wanted to circulate anything against slavery, or to lecture, or to write, or to publish, he would not be allowed to do so; there are therefore governmental obstacles in the way.

2431. Sir *J. Walmsley.*] Are the slaves allowed to read the newspapers at all?—I think they are not, and that people are forbidden to sell them to the slaves; just as the slaves are kept sober by force of law; any man selling them drink is liable to a penalty.

2432. In the slave states do they teach them to read?—In many states I believe they do not permit them to learn to read.

2433. Mr. *Rich.*] Your experience of the press of America and

Rev. *T. Spencer.*

30 May 1851.

and its beneficial effects is confined to the free states, is it not?—Yes.

2434. You stated that as soon as it was known that Sir Robert Peel had made his speech in favour of free trade, the war-cry which had been strongly raised before in America suddenly ceased, and everybody said, "Now let us have peace with England;" are you not aware that the northern states are the states which are the less inclined to free trade?—There is a great feeling for protection, but it does not mean our protection, but protection to manufactures; they are for free trade in corn, all of them to a man. Their objection to free trade is merely for the purpose of prohibiting English manufactures; even the existence of their cheap press was very much in favour of free trade. In Boston I delivered a lecture on our English corn-laws; and this halfpenny paper (*producing the same*) contained two or three columns of a report of that lecture; and though the editor did not like the argument, the people had an opportunity of reading all that could be said about it, which, if there had been no cheap paper, they could not have done. With respect to the effect of Sir Robert Peel's speech, I happened to know from Mr. Calhoun that there were scores of members in the House of Congress, who had made speeches of the most bloody kind and said the most horrible things, and Mr. Polk, the President, expressed to me his regret on account of their violence. They were printing those speeches to send to their constituents all over the States, in order to get favour with the people; but when Sir Robert Peel's speech came they said, "This will not do, if we send our speeches to Ohio and the other corn-growing states we shall offend them;" and they agreed to burn them, and they did burn them after that speech arrived; they saw that that policy was sound.

2435. Do you consider that the account you have given indicates a strong feeling in favour of the independent expression of public opinion, when they wished to burn the speeches which they themselves had just delivered?—Those persons thought that by getting those warlike speeches into Ohio and other states it would please those who did not like England, because they thought England would not take their corn, but when Sir Robert Peel's speech came, they knew that the people of Ohio would look friendly towards England because of receiving their corn, and, therefore, the speeches for war would not do.

2436. Those speeches must have been delivered either from conviction or not?—They were not delivered from conviction,

but

Rev. T. Spencer.

30 May 1851.

but to please their constituents. I am speaking of the effect upon public opinion, upon the mass of the people. There are members of Congress who speak only with a view to please their constituents.

2437. Mr. *Ewart.*] You mean to state two things: that public opinion finally took the right direction, and that opinion was so powerful, that it turned the Legislature in the direction of public opinion?—Yes.

2438. Mr. *G. A. Hamilton.*] Do you think that public opinion is taking the right direction in America with reference to slavery?—Clearly so; I have received a paper from America with stronger things said about slavery than anything that is said here; and those things are not only written but spoken at the peril of their lives, in a country where slave-owners are. People have said to me, "You must remember that you are in the land of Lynch law." But they are saying now very serious things; they all bent upon putting down slavery.

2439. Mr. *Rich.*] How do you reconcile a land of Lynch law with a land of free discussion?—The former is the state of things in the slave states, where newspapers are very few; in Charlestown, as I mentioned, I could not purchase one paper.

2440. The number of cheap papers is not large in the slave states, is it?—I do not know that they are cheap; in the free states there is a cheap press, but there are some restrictions in the slave states; I do not know, not particularly, but I suppose that one is, that a foreigner may not buy a paper; I could not buy one.

2441. Mr. *Ewart.*] Does Lynch law prevail the most where there is the greatest circulation of newspapers, or where there is the least?—It prevails where there is the least circulation; there is no Lynch law in the free states.

2442. Does not it prevail more in the remoter western districts of America?—I did not go very far west; in places in Connecticut and New Haven a gentleman told me, a clergyman, that they never think of locking their doors, being under no alarm about any property they leave out; they had not a thief or a drunkard in the whole city, and perfect order and quiet prevailed; it is true that they are a very moral people in the free states.

2443. Are they a more temperate people than the English?—Yes; in many towns half the population never drink any alcoholic drink; a great many clergymen are teetotallers, and most of the presidents have been teetotallers; they have a congressional society at Washington, and the last time I spoke in America

Rev. T. Spencer.

30 May 1851.

America was at the State House at Boston, with the Governor of the State in the chair.

2444. Are the seamen generally members of the temperance society?—Many of their vessels are conducted on those principles.

2445. Mr. *Rich.*] Have you seen any returns of the consumption of ardent spirits in the different states?—Not to examine them; I remember going to a strange town, and when I asked persons whether temperance was prosperous there, they have spoken discouragingly of it, and said "No, it was not;" I have said, "What do you mean? I see a great many temperance hotels; are half of your people members of the temperance society?" "I should think so," was the answer. At almost all the hotels at Boston and other cities in the free states you never see anything but water; and if there are several hundred gentlemen and ladies dining you do not see hardly at any hotel in the place any wine or spirits, or anything of the kind.

2446. Mr. *G. A. Hamilton.*] The result of your evidence upon the general question is, that truth, in your opinion, labours under a disadvantage in this country; because those who want to disseminate truth are conscientious, and will not evade the law by sanctioning the issue of cheap unstamped publications?—Yes; I should say, as regards cheap publications, that there are a thousand ways in which there would be instructors of the people, but people cannot now afford to do it.

2447. That is your argument in favour of the reduction of the stamp, is it not?—Yes; and for those papers which are sent through the post I would have a halfpenny wrapper.

2448. Mr. *Ewart.*] Do you feel, in your own case, that you would wish to disseminate sound and wholesome doctrines among the people, and that you cannot do it?—Yes, I would do it; but the cost arising from the penny stamp and other taxes on knowledge prevent it.

2449. You speak from practical and personal experience?—Yes; I should then feel myself at liberty to do ten times the good that I can now do.

2450. Mr. *Tufnell.*] There is no difficulty, is there, in advocating temperance principles, in any paper, without bringing yourself within the operation of the Stamp Act?—No; but I have already stated that we are now under this difficulty. We shall hardly get the next number out, because of the difficulties in the way at Somerset-house; a large portion of our paper is unstamped, and we cannot send it by the post or put in news; but

Rev. *T. Spencer.*

30 May 1851.

but if we could make our paper palatable to everybody that took in the news of the day, a little of the temperance spirit would go along with it, and would be communicated to the masses of the people.

2451. Do you think that the combination of the principles which you advocate, with an article containing news, is a necessary combination for the diffusion of those principles?—Yes, it would be a great aid to us; so much so, that we are now adopting a new plan; instead of relying upon our own paper, we wish to communicate with all the other papers, in order to have our principles added to them.

2452. Mr. *G. A. Hamilton.*] You wish to make truth more attractive, by coupling it with news?—Yes.

Mr. *George Anderson,* called in; and Examined.

Mr. *G. Anderson.*

2453. *Chairman.*] YOU are the manager of a newspaper, are you not?—No, I am not.

2454. Have you had nothing to do with a publication called the "Ratepayer"?—I have written in it; that is all; I am not the publisher or manager of it.

2455. Are you aware of any communications that have passed between the proprietors of the "Ratepayer" and the Board of Inland Revenue?—I have heard that there were some to the effect that they must stamp the paper; it was brought out as a weekly newspaper after it was stamped.

2456. Were you compelled to stamp the whole of the impression of the "Ratepayer"?—It was a monthly publication at first, before it was stamped.

2457. Did they give you the privilege not to stamp it when it was a monthly?—I never heard that they did; it is generally considered a matter of right.

2458. Will you state when you were required to stamp it?—Yes; immediately before it was stamped.

2459. Did the Board of Inland Revenue require you to stamp it when it was a monthly?—Yes, I believe so; the Board of Inland Revenue, when a number was sent up to be assessed for advertisement duty, as I understand, compelled the proprietors to stamp it, or to go through the form usually gone through at the Stamp Office.

2460. Mr. *Cobden.*] It was to be stamped even though it continued to be a monthly publication?—Yes; I supposed it was more for the advertisement duty than anything else.

2461. *Chairman.*] It was required to be stamped whilst it was monthly?—Yes, I believe so.



2462. Did

Mr. *G. Anderson.*

30 May 1851.

2462. Did the Board of Inland Revenue require you to stamp every copy?—I believe every copy was not stamped; some were printed without being stamped, but the Board of Inland Revenue had nothing to do with that question; they could go to law if they chose, and that is all I know about it; it is quite another question as to whether it is a newspaper or not; if it was a weekly affair, it would be a different thing; I have printed newspapers weekly, without touching upon particular subjects, without a stamp; with a stamp and without a stamp, the same as the "Builder."

2463. Mr. *Rich.*] Upon what are called class objects?—Yes; not general newspapers; we always supposed, in publishing class newspapers, that we had liberty to do so at the Stamp Office.

2464. *Chairman.*] The reason why the Board of Inland Revenue required you to stamp the "Ratepayer" was that it was a newspaper?—I do not know as to the reason.

2465. Could there have been any other ground?—I cannot say.

2466. However, your paper was required to be stamped?—Yes.

2467. Do you now stamp the whole of the impression?—The weekly impression, of course; it is a newspaper now.

2468. Did you stamp every copy when it was a monthly?—No, certainly not; I believe they were not all stamped; if it had been mine, I should not have stamped them; I should have stamped a few, merely to go through the form, to prevent any bother.

2469. Mr. *Rich.*] You looked at it as not being within the description of a newspaper?—Certainly.

2470. *Chairman.*] You would have stamped a few?—Yes; it is not worth while to be a victim of the law courts.

2471. You only stamped for appearance sake, and the great bulk circulated unstamped?—Yes; I suppose half-a-dozen were stamped; I do not know; I should not have stamped more.

2472. Mr. *Rich.*] That was when it was a monthly publication, was it not?—Yes, as a weekly publication and a newspaper, containing general news, every number was stamped; of course it was a newspaper.

2473. As a monthly newspaper, you did not think that it fell within the Act?—No.

Mr.

Mr. *Abel Heywood*, called in; and Examined.

Mr. *A. Heywood.*

30 May 1851.

2474. *Chairman.*] YOU reside in Manchester, do you not?—Yes.

2475. What is your occupation?—A bookseller and general publisher, and also a newspaper agent.

2476. You are a member of the town council, are you not?—Yes, and have been for many years.

2477. You have had some experience in your business as to the circulation of small publications in Manchester and its neighbourhood?—Yes.

2478. Do you distribute a good deal of that description of literature through those districts?—Yes, I am the principal publisher for Manchester, for the sale of small publications, and weekly publications which are unstamped. The bulk of those which come direct from London down to Manchester go through my hands, and are sent then to all the surrounding towns round Manchester, extending for 20 miles, in parcels, and re-sold again by other booksellers in those towns.

2479. The whole of this is carried on without any advanvantage from the post?—None of them come through the post; they all come by the London and North-western Railway; they are sent off the evening before, and they arrive in Manchester on the afternoon of the following day.

2480. You then send them into the towns in the neighbourhood to other parties, who distribute them to the particular people in those towns?—Yes, I supply the booksellers with them in the various towns, as I supply the booksellers in Manchester; I do not profess to do much in the retail business; my business is principally wholesale.

2481. Can you give the Committee any idea of the quantity of those small 1 *d.*, 1½ *d.* and 2 *d.* unstamped publications which are circulated in that district?—Yes, I can give you an idea of the number of London publications that come into Manchester every week on the average (I cannot speak exactly), the names of which I can read. This list does not include the whole of them, although it includes the greater portion; those having any sale are included. The principal publications that have the largest sale amongst the penny ones are, the "Family Herald," the "London Journal," and "Reynolds's Miscellany;" these three are the leading publications among the penny press or the cheap publications. The number of the "Family Herald" which circulates

 in

Mr. *A. Heywood.*

30 May 1851.

in Manchester and its neighbourhood I take to be somewhere about 14,000 weekly; my own sale is upwards of 9,000 of it, but I know there are other parties who sell in Manchester besides, and from them I gather the amount which they circulate; in addition to these, some few may come into the town through other channels of which I have no knowledge. At present the "London Journal" circulates to a similar extent, and appears to have run a pretty hard race with the "Herald."

2482. Mr. *Cobden.*] Who publishes "The London Journal"?—The "London Journal" is published by a gentlemen of the name of Stiff, in the Strand; the name which appears upon it is Vickers, in Holywell-street. The "Family Herald" is published by a gentleman of the name of Biggs, in the Strand. The next one in sale to that, of the penny publications, is "Reynolds's Miscellany," and that circulates about one-half, or scarcely one-half, I think, of the number that the "Family Herald" and the "London Journal" circulate; there is also a publisher of the name of Lloyd in London, who publishes a very large number of publications, but his are principally of the novel class; they are rather of the extreme novel class, and deal more in bloody murders and all other crimes which it is possible for the imagination to invent. There is one called "Gentleman Jack," which is I presume a detail of the life of some renowned robber who existed at some period in this country. There is the "Adventures of Captain Hawk" and "Claude Duval the Highwayman." There is the "Hangman's Daughter," "Love and Mystery," "Mable, or the Battle Field," "Mazeppa, or the Wild Horse," the "Adventures of Paul Clifford," the "History of the Life and Adventures of Richard Parker," "Obi, or Three Fingered Jack," the "Adventures of Tom King," the "Black Monk," the "Blighted Heart." This is the class of publications that this gentleman publishes.

2483. Are those separate publications, or are they the various contents of one periodical?—They are separate; they are all now publishing.

2484. They come out periodically?—They come out weekly.

2485. Under those titles?—Yes, and charged a penny.

2486. They are novels, are they not?—Yes, and romances; if one is successful, it will go on to 130 or 140 numbers, if not, he cuts it down to a dozen. Lloyd also publishes a book which is of a little better character, called "Lloyd's Miscellany," which is more approaching to the character of the "London Journal"

Journal" and the "Family Herald," still it falls far beneath them in tone and quality. The average circulation of those I have mentioned, of Lloyd's, will be my own circulation; but from this will be easily obtained the relative difference in the circulation which each periodical has. I sell 100 of the "Black Monk," 100 of the "Blighted Heart," 100 of the "Bridal Ring," and 550 of "Claude Duval;" a great many boys read that, and grown-up people as well as boys buy it; 100 of "Captain Hawk," 400 of "Gentleman Jack," 100 of "Grace Rivers," 50 of the "Hangman's Daughter," 250 of "Kathleen," (which is an Irish story,) 100 of "Love and Mystery," 100 of "Mabel," 250 of "Mazeppa," 350 of "Paul Clifford," 250 of "Richard Parker;" Lloyd has made free with many of the popular names of works that are from time to time being issued by the novelists of the day; 350 of "Three Fingered Jack," and 250 of "Tom King." That includes, I think, the whole of the list Lloyd publishes; he is the principal publisher of cheap romances and novels for the working classes; he frequently sets up a great portion of the matter in his miscellany, and then that matter is laid by in chases, and worked up again, and the penny numbers are lengthened or shortened, according to the demand; I merely give my circulation.

Mr. *A. Heywood*

30 May 1851.

2487. Mr. *Tufnell.*] With regard to the "Family Herald," you gave the whole circulation, did you not?—Yes; then we have Mr. Barker's publication, of which we sell about 1,000. Mr. Barker has gone to America, and his peculiar style of writing is not to be met with.

2488. What publication was that?—It was a comment upon matters connected with "Church and State;" it was rather a political publication, and at one time was selling weekly to the number of about 30,000. Mr. Barker is gone to America, he has sold the paper to some party in London, and the sale is much reduced; I believe the circulation was once 30,000; a very large number was sold in Manchester; about 7,000 weekly. Then we have Beal's broad sheet, of which we sell about 1,500 in Manchester; and latterly there have sprung up two or three Catholic publications, one called the "Catholic Vindicator," and another, called the "Lamp," and those now are selling very well; the entire "Lamp" sale is, in Manchester, about 3,500 weekly.

2489. Mr. *Cobden.*] When was that started?—It has been in existence little more than six months.

2490. Mr. *Rich.*] Do they keep clear of politics?—Yes; they are entirely devoted to religious instruction. The aggregate

Mr. *A. Heywood.*

30 May 1851.

gate sale of the "Lamp" is about 22,000; 3,000 in Manchester weekly; it was 2,000 a few months ago, and I understand that it has been increasing since. We have one called the "Christian Socialist," but that has a very small sale indeed; it advocates socialism upon Christian principles; and I understand that there are some very clever people connected with it; but the sale is very small in Manchester; it would be about 70 copies weekly. Following the order in which I have them down in my list, I come to the "Court of London;" it is a publication of Reynolds's, which professes to detail the scenes which have occurred in connexion with the Court of London; but whether it is true or false, it is not for me to say. This "Court of London" I consider is a test of the taste of the readers generally; I think between this "Court of London" and the others, there is a very wide line of distinction; I have read some portion of it, and it draws scenes of profligacy as strongly as it is possible for any writer to do, and the feelings are excited to a very high pitch by it; indeed some look upon it as an indecent publication; it is not in reality an indecent publication, because I do not believe that any words appear that are vulgar; but certainly the language is of a most exciting kind, and directed to excite the passions of its readers. Now, the circulation of the "Court of London" in Manchester is about 1,500; that is, Manchester and the neighbourhood.

2491. How long has it been published?—It has gone on about four years.

2492. Mr. *Ewart.*] It professes to be an historical account, does it not?—Yes, and George the Fourth, I think, is the principal actor in it; the sale in Manchester is 1,500 on the average; and it shows conclusively to my mind that readers generally are not disposed to buy such publications as this; these 1,500 have to be circulated in Oldham, Bolton and Rochdale, and indeed all the small towns round Manchester—Oldham would take, perhaps, 30; Bolton a few more, and Rochdale a few less; so that the sale in Manchester of this publication, in my opinion, does not reach more than about 700 weekly. Then follows "A History of Wat Tyler," and that has enjoyed a very large sale; the number which we sell of that is 450; it professes to be a history of the life and times of Wat Tyler, and the tendency of it is very good; it is historical. There is no other publication having the same tendency as the "Court of London;" there was, a short time ago, one published called the "Town," which was a vulgar emanation compared with this; but that died from want of support;

Mr. *A. Heywood.*

30 May 1851.

port; there was very little given to it, and it fell through. We have a reprint of "Fox's Book of Martyrs," which is selling very rapidly just at the present juncture; the "Friend of the People" is a weekly publication, edited by Julian Harney; this takes extreme views in politics, its name, before being changed, was the "Red Republican," not the "Friend of the People;" as the "Red Republican" it did not sell, neither with Manchester workmen nor with the workmen anywhere else, and, in order to create a sale, the name was changed to the "Friend of the People;" the circulation in Manchester would be about 250. Now we have one published called "Home," by Mr. Oastler; and the object of the "Home" is to induce the people to change their opinions with regard to free trade, and to have protection again. This I believe is established to circulate the views of the Protectionists, without regard being had to profit; it is sent out to advocate certain opinions upon free trade, and its sale now is about 450 in Manchester. We have another publication called the "Home Circle," which is a very excellent little publication; it is not quite so large as the "Family Herald," devoted to tales and light reading, but quite of an unexceptionable character; my circulation is about 400, and its circulation in Manchester altogether will be about 600 weekly. Next we have the "London Apprentice," which is merely the history of a London apprentice up to the end of his apprenticeship; that is more in the form of a history, and the circulation of it is 400. We have also the "Medical Journal," and a number of others; but of these, whilst there is nothing exceptionable in them, it is hardly worth while to point out the circulation: the principal point would be to show those which differ most from one another. Then we come to Robert Owen's Journal; that advocates socialism. Manchester was considered a stronghold of socialism, and to a certain extent, the views of a great number of the working classes were in favour of socialist principles: the circulation of that does not reach more than 250 a week, and this includes Manchester and the neighbourhood. Then we have the "Reasoner," which is published or edited by a gentleman of the name of Holyoake; this advocates opposite religious principles, or deistical principles, and therefore may be taken as the type of a class. The "Reasoner" will circulate about 400 a week. And then we have "Ruth Maynard," which is a tale; a republication of Shakespeare, and we sell about 150 a week of that; it is published in penny numbers. A working man, who gets anything like decent wages, can afford to buy a copy complete. There are

"Tales

Mr. *A. Heywood.*

30 May 1851.

"Tales of all Nations," the "Bee," and "Tales of Woman's Love." The next we come to is a publication of Mr. Cassell's, the "Working Man's Friend," which is a very excellent publication, and circulates in Manchester about 1,800 weekly. Bulwer's works circulate very little; they are re-issued by Chapman & Hall; they sell better complete than in serial numbers. Then "Chambers's Journal," I could not get exactly the sale of that in Manchester, but I take that upon the same average as I do the rest; my own sale is 1,000 weekly; but this weekly sale does not include the sale in parts. Some booksellers sell them only in monthly parts.

2493. Mr. *Rich.*] About 3,000 altogether?—Yes; the circulation of "Chambers's Papers for the People," the pennyhalfpenny publication, is about 1,200 weekly for Manchester. Of "Eliza Cook's Journal" we sell about 400 weekly, and about one-half more would be something like the number for Manchester. Then we have the "Gardener's Dictionary" and "Hogg's Instructor," which is an excellent work, and sells mostly in Manchester in parts; its weekly sale is not very large. We have a republication of Jerrold's Works; and the "Pathway," published by Cassell, a religious publication, which has a tolerably good sale, considering its religious independence of any particular body; it is published fortnightly, and the sale with myself is 700 each issue. We have also the "Cottage Gardener and Cyclopædia of Botany," and a fortnightly publication, called the "Family Friend," and another, called the "Family Tutor," which sell very well; now, the sale would be about 1,800 of each number. Then we have the "Household Words," by Dickens, and we sell 600 of that in numbers; that is a twopenny one.

2494. *Chairman.*] What is the circulation of the whole?—I cannot tell now; I made out a calculation 18 months ago for the "Morning Chronicle," and I made the average number circulated in Manchester and the neighbourhood at 80,000 a week; but since then I consider that the circulation has increased very rapidly; the "Family Herald" very much, and also the "London Journal," while some of the others have remained stationary.

2495. Mr. *Rich.*] Taking the 80,000, how should you classify them; are the majority of a good tendency?—Yes, most decidedly; I pointed out those upon which there would be differences of opinion; for instance, the "Christian Socialist," the "Court of London," "Owen's Journal," and the "Reasoner;" the "Family Herald" is a miscellaneous journal

Mr. *A. Heywood.*

30 May 1851.

journal of literature, and one that is taken in very generally by the working classes.

2496. Of those 80,000 considerably the larger proportion are of a good tendency?—Yes.

2497. Mr. *G. A. Hamilton.*] Is the style of literature in the "Family Herald" tolerably good?—Yes; the man who edits it is a very clever man indeed.

2498. *Chairman.*] What is its weekly circulation now?—Over 200,000.

2499. Mr. *G. A. Hamilton.*] And what is the circulation of the "London Journal"?—The "London Journal" is not far off the "Family Herald;" they are the two leading publications taken in by the working classes.

2500. Then the other, "Reynolds's Miscellany," what is the circulation of that?—That would be about one-third of the others; its character is similar; the only difference is, that the tales are more strongly imaginative, and deal more in the awful, the wild, and the wonderful; for instance, such tales as the *Wehr Wolf*, and that class.

2501. Mr. *G. A. Hamilton.*] Is information conveyed by them, or are they merely addressed to the imagination?—They are principally tales, but they are made up of translations and selections from books and from various other sources; they have reprinted many of the French novels and some of Lamartine's books have been translated and inserted.

2502. Is there much historical matter in those three publications, the "Family Herald," the "London Journal" and "Reynolds's Miscellany"?—There is less historical matter in the "Family Herald" than in the other two; the "Family Herald" is principally made up of light reading, and there is a peculiar feature about the "Family Herald" which is not possessed by the others, it addresses itself to the fairer sex in a great measure, and to that perhaps may be attributed its very large circulation.

2503. Is there much information contained in these publications which is calculated to be of use to the working classes with regard to machinery, trade and manufactures?—No.

2504. Mr. *Ewart.*] Are the morals and habits of the people likely to be improved by them?—The tone of morality in these publications is quite unexceptionable; I take home the "Family Herald," and read it with a great deal of pleasure, and it is read by every member of my family.

2505. The increase in circulation is the greatest, in your opinion, in the best papers?—Yes, decidedly. The "Family Herald,"

Mr. *A. Heywood.*

30 May 1851.

Herald," during the last twelve months, has increased one-third, with myself.

2506. You are of opinion that the greater demand is towards the good papers, are you not?—Yes.

2507. Mr. *Rich.*] Have all those good papers gone on increasing in their circulation?—Yes, generally.

2508. Mr. *Ewart.*] Has your experience shown that the bad publications put down the good, or that the good publications put down the bad?—I think that the good publications put down the bad. The bad publications are attempted, and they are carried on for a while under various methods; and after getting deeply into debt, they are obliged at last to go out, and perhaps knock up the publisher at the same time.

2509. *Chairman.*] This extensive sale of publications shows that there is a taste and a desire amongst the working classes of those districts to which you have referred for reading, for mental improvement, does it not?—Yes, it does,

2510. And it shows that there is a want of cheap literature amongst those people, does it not?—Yes.

2511. Are you of opinion that a cheap newspaper, for instance, one of those publications containing, in addition to its other matter, the current events of the day, would have an extensive sale?—Yes; I think, for instance, that if the editor of the "Family Herald" were to put in two or three pages of news, along with the matter which he gives weekly to his readers, that the sale would be doubled or trebled very shortly.

2512. You think that a cheap newspaper in a competition with the class of publications which you have mentioned would have an advantage, do you not?—Decidedly.

2513. And, consequently, that the readers would prefer, if they could have it, at the same price, some record of the current events of life?—Yes, I think so; that is the result of my experience. I deal largely in cheap newspapers, as well as in these little publications; and I think I can form an opinion as to the desire of the people to possess newspapers.

2514. Mr. *Ewart.*] With regard to cheap newspapers, does your experience lead you to the same result as in the case of the publications which you mentioned; that the good ones eventually would be preferred to the bad?—With regard to the quality of cheap newspapers, I only know of three that may be considered cheap; namely, "Lloyd's Paper," the "Weekly Times," and the "News of the World." Those three are published at 3 *d.* each; and the sale of the "Weekly Times"

Mr. *A. Heywood.*

30 May 1851.

Times" is much greater with me than the sale of the other two; but whether that arises from any deficiency in the editorial department, I cannot say. The tone in all the papers, I should say, was equally good.

2515. Sir *J. Walmsley.*] What is the quality of the writing in the penny newspapers to which you have referred?—The quality of the writing in the "Family Herald," in the "London Journal," and in "Reynolds's Miscellany" is very good; some of the others I am not sufficiently acquainted with to be able to speak to the quality.

2516. You have stated that some of them are of a pernicious tendency; to what class of readers are those chiefly sold? —I only referred to one; I did not exactly say that it had a pernicious tendency; I said that the "Court of London" might be thought to have, but I have not made use of such an expression.

2517. To what class of readers are those papers to which you have referred as having a very exciting tendency sold?—A great many females buy the "Court of London," and young men; a sort of spreeing young men; young men who go to taverns, and put cigars in their mouths in a flourishing way.

2518. Has the sale of those papers much increased of late? —No; the "Court of London" sold three times the quantity that it sells now, while the better ones have all been increasing.

2519. Mr. *Rich.*] And apparently supplying the want for cheap literature as that want arises?—Yes, I think so.

2520. Sir *J. Walmsley.*] Is the tendency of the more moral newspapers to drive out of the market the immoral newspapers, or the contrary?—Yes, to drive them out.

2521. Would a reduction in the price of newspapers materially tend to diminish the sale of those which you consider pernicious papers?—I think that it would; there is only one that I consider has a pernicious influence; every man who writes a publication has a particular class of people to read it, and from whom he expects support; I believe that it would be almost impossible to put down the "Court of London;" I believe that you could not educate people so that there could not be found 10,000, 15,000, or 20,000 of people in this country disposed to buy it.

2522. If the price of good newspapers were materially reduced, the tendency would be, would it not, to drive such a paper out of the market?—It would have a tendency to reduce such papers; but there is a morbid feeling amongst certain classes, and they will have that description of work if they can

Mr. *A. Heywood.* 30 May 1851.

can get it; the sale being very much more formerly than now; it is evident that the parties themselves who began to take it in have given it up.

2523. Mr. *Rich.*] The result of your experience in Manchester, with regard to the press, shows that in the present state of things the good publications are beating the bad one, does it not?—Yes.

2524. Mr. *G. A. Hamilton.*] Can you state whether the parties who read the "Court of London" for the most part are regular subscribers, or whether they are casual purchasers?—Both; many are regular subscribers, and we have the volumes brought to bind.

2525. *Chairman.*] Have you ever heard that there was any advantage gained by prohibiting the insertion of news in these publications?—No, I have not.

2526. Do you think it would be beneficial that there should be equal facility for diffusing news and facts as for circulating these different publications?—Yes; I think that there ought to be equal facility given to parties, so that they might publish news as easily as they publish the publications that have emanated from the press.

2527. Mr. *Ewart.*] What should you say would be the result of a free publication of news to the population of the country?—All my remarks have reference to the population of Manchester and its neighbourhood; but I believe that it would be very beneficial to the working classes generally.

2528. Would it have a good or a bad effect on their moral character?—It would increase their moral influence and their moral power.

2529. And have a good moral tendency?—Yes, I think so; when the cheap publications commenced, 20 years ago, the sale was very rapid; at that time, there were very few publications of the kind, but every year has increased the number; the good publications have been continually increasing.

2530. Mr. *Rich.*] From what date are you speaking?—I began in 1831; and of a great many then published scarcely one exists now that was published then; they have changed their names, form, and character.

2531. Mr. *Ewart.*] What was the general character of the publications when you began?—The principal one in existence was the "Poor Man's Guardian;" that published reports of meetings in addition to its other matter, and for which I, along with a number of others, were prosecuted.

2532. Mr. *Cobden.*] That was before the stamp duty was reduced to 1 *d.*, was it not?—Yes.

2533. You

Mr. *A. Heywood.* 30 May 1851.

2533. You have given the Committee a list of publications, and also the sale of those publications in the district immediately round Manchester; have you ever formed an opinion what per-centage of the whole circulation of those publications passes through your hands; suppose, for instance, that you have a circulation in Manchester of 1,400 copies of a periodical published in London, have you formed an opinion as to what the whole circulation of that periodical would be altogether, and what per-centage is sold in the immediate neighbourhood of Manchester?—I mentioned the "Lamp' as selling about 3,500 in Manchester; its aggregate sale being 22,000. But it is almost impossible to form an opinion, except I could get the information from the publisher.

2534. According to the figures which you have given, 10 per cent. of those cheap publications must pass through your own hands?—Generally so.

2535. In many cases?—Yes.

2536. Therefore, you have probably the largest experience of any one in the kingdom in the sale of those publications? —I think so; the trade say so.

2537. Have you supplied both stamped and unstamped publications?—Yes.

2538. Is it the result of your 20 years' experience in this business, that you have found that the objectionable publications are short lived, and that those publications which are of the highest intellectual and moral quality have a tendency to increase in circulation?—Yes.

2539. That has been your experience?—Yes; that is my deliberate opinion from the experience which I have had in connexion with the trade.

2540. Do you think that if publications were allowed to insert news as well as literary intelligence, that it would tend to increase the circulation of those papers, and act as a stimulus to the reading habits of the people?—Yes, it would increase the circulation of many of the better class, and decrease the circulation of the worse.

2541. A gentleman who was examined before this Committee, and who represented the "Times," expressed a fear that the removal of the stamp would lead the public to patronise inferior newspapers, and that he should not like the temptation to be put before them lest they should accept things of an inferior kind; but the result of your experience amongst the working people, and their taste for publications is, that they may be safely let to discriminate between the good and bad

Mr. *A. Heywood.*

30 May 1851.

bad newspapers?—I think they may, speaking of the population of Lancashire.

2542. You alluded just now to a publication called the "Red Republican;" that was written very much in the tone and temper of the Red Republicans of Paris, during the Revolution, was it not?—Yes

2543. That had a very small circulation, had it not?—Yes; and they were obliged to change its name.

2544. Therefore, that appeal to the ruffianly passions of our nature was not responded to by the working people?—No.

2545. And that was published at 1 *d.*, was it not—Yes.

2546. Mr. *Tufnell.*] Did that paper change its principles with its name?—No; the principles are exactly the same.

2547. Mr. *Cobden.*] Was it well written in its way?—Yes.

2548. Yet it made no way with the working people?—Very little.

2549. Mr. *Ewart.*] The "Town," which was an indecent publication, disappeared also, did it not?—Yes.

2550. The one was an exceedingly violent political paper, the "Red Republican," and the other an immoral paper, the "Town," and they have both disappeared?—Yes; the "Red Republican" changed its name, and the "Town" was discontinued.

2551. Mr. *G. A. Hamilton.*] Bearing in mind the superior character of the literature of the "Times," do you think if the price of the "Times" was reduced, that its circulation would be increased without its tone being lowered?—Yes; in Manchester I sell the "News of the World," a threepenny paper, to the number of 3,500 every Saturday, and more than 4,000 of the "Weekly Times," and the reason is, that the price is so much lower, it enables a working man better to purchase it; it is also 3 *d.* London papers generally are 6 *d.*, and Manchester papers 4½ *d.*, and they take a threepenny paper, not caring what politics they are; it is not a matter of politics with them, but a question of price; they take it because it is cheap.

2552. If the price of the "Times" were reduced, do you think that the writers of the "Times" would have to write themselves down to the level of the readers?—No; I think that those already in the field would have a great advantage over anybody else coming in.

2553. *Chairman.*] What a working man wants is a record of facts, is it not?—Yes; the current events of the week.

2554. Mr. *Cobden.*] Is the penny stamp an unpopular thing amongst working people?—I do not think it is unpopular; that

that is to say, not to the extent that it was when it was 4*d.* When it was 4*d.* there was a very strong feeling against it; but now whilst they can purchase a cheap paper at 3*d.* of the size which they do now, they have less feeling against it than they had formerly when it was 4*d.*

Mr. *A. Heywood.*

30 May 1851.

2555. Is there any feeling amongst the working people themselves, that the penny stamp is kept on partly with a view of preventing them from getting cheap publications, and having their own organs of the press, and partly for the sake of the tax?—Yes. Particular bodies would issue a publication of their own if it was not for the imposition of the tax. If any particular trade or party chose to publish a record of their proceedings, they come, of course, under the operation of the Stamp Laws, and therefore they are unable to give currency to their peculiar views or opinions, and to that extent the stamp tax prevents them from doing it.

2556. Mr. *Rich.*] You say that the lower classes read the threepenny papers with the news; what are the subjects that are most attractive to them in the newspapers?—I think that foreign news is as attractive as any other matter that appears in them.

2557. If the useful penny papers or publications which you have stated are sold to so large an extent in Manchester, also inserted news, would they be able to furnish that news at the same price at which they now publish their papers?—Yes.

2558. They would have to copy their news from the daily papers, would they not?—Yes; but that is what the cheap papers do now.

2559. Do you not think that a mixture of news in those weekly papers which now contain none, might possibly have a tendency to lower the tone of the other class of writing?—No, I do not think so.

2560. *Chairman.*] The "Poor Man's Guardian" was the paper in reference to which Hetherington was prosecuted, was it not?—Yes, that was the name.

2561. After prosecuting a good many people, it was found out that it was not a newspaper?—Yes; 750, I believe, were prosecuted.

2562. Have you not always felt it rather a difficult matter to tell what is the thing that is liable to the tax?—That was the difficulty with regard to the publication of the "Poor Man's Guardian."

2563. They did not find it out in that case till they had put 750 people to the inconvenience of a prosecution, did they?—

The

Mr. *A. Heywood.* 30 May 1851.

The magistrates convicted at the instance of the prosecution, connected with the Stamp Office; and it was never brought before the Court of King's Bench till Mr. Hetherington brought it forward, and then it was decided that it was not a newspaper.

2564. Were those people put into prison, many of them?—Seven hundred and fifty of them.

2565. And it was decided after all that they had been imprisoned illegally; was any compensation given to them?—I never received any; I was imprisoned four months.

2566. And then it was decided that what you had printed was not news?—Yes.

2567. Do not you think it a very great evil that there should be so much uncertainty in a penal statute?—Yes, I thought so at the time I was prosecuted, in 1832, and I still think so.

2568. Mr. *Rich.*] That was before the alteration in the stamp duty, was it not?—Yes.

2569. At the time that there were a great number of prosecutions?—Yes.

2570. Since then have there been many prosecutions?—None, since the alteration in the stamp duties, to my knowledge.

2571. Practically, as far as your knowledge goes, the present law has worked without much litigation, has it not?—The law is so stringent that no man with any sense would attempt to publish; they not only seize his property but his person; they take the whole plant.

2572. Upon certain points publishers pretty well know when they are within the law and when they are without it, do they not?—Yes, I think so.

2573. *Chairman.*] It was not a question as to the amount of the stamp that constituted the difficulty, but a question as to whether it was news or not?—Yes.

2574. That difficulty has never been removed; they still use the same word "news," do they not, as the thing that is liable to a stamp?—Yes, they do; but the penalties in the present law are more stringent than the former.

2575. You think that the article liable to the tax is as uncertain as ever it was, do you not?—I think not now.

2576. Do you think that they know what is meant by "news" better now than they did formerly?—No; but the difficulty was to understand what constituted a thing a newspaper.

2577. Do they know now?—I believe they do; a man commenting

Mr. *A. Heywood.*

30 May 1851.

commenting upon news of any kind, as far as I understand, is liable to pay the tax.

2578. Are you not aware that the Court of Exchequer is about to decide upon this question?—Yes; but that involves another point.

2579. But you think that they have a clearer idea now of what is "news" than they used to have?—Not with regard to a paper publishing monthly, than they used to have. I still hold the same opinion, that the law allows you to publish within 26 days any news you please without paying the stamp duty.

2580. Mr. *Rich.*] Certain moot points being from time to time brought before the courts of law, and decided, those decisions serve as guides for the future as to the state of the law?—Yes; but I think this point has never been decided upon by a superior court: the Messrs. Chambers, of Edinburgh, published an historical newspaper monthly, some years ago, as Dickens does now, and they were compelled to give it up only from a notice served upon them either from the Court of Exchequer or the Board of Inland Revenue; they did not carry it into court and try the issue, but they gave it up, and since that time several others have been begun in a similar way; but at the slightest notice they have discontinued them.

2581. *Chairman.*] When you said that there had been no prosecutions, the fact is, that the parties discontinued the publications rather than risk them, did they not?—Yes.

2582. Mr. *Rich.*] You would not say that there has been anything like the same number of notices served from the Board of Inland Revenue within the last 10 years as were served at and before the time of the reduction of the stamp duty?—Of course not; the case was rather different then; the Ministry came in under what was understood to be a determination on their part to remove the taxes on knowledge; the publishers plied the Whig Ministry as hard as they could, and published newspapers of all kinds, and at all prices; courting, in fact, prosecutions, for the purpose of breaking through, or compelling the Government to take off the tax.

2583. When the duty was 4 *d.* there naturally would have been a greater temptation to evade the law than when it was a penny, would there not?—I do not know; there was no plunder in it. If a man publishes a penny publication, he must give full value for the penny, or it will not sell; it is a difficult thing to get more than a fair return for his capital.

2584. If I publish a newspaper, say at 3 *d.*, and do not pay the stamp, it is more advantageous to me to keep the news-

 paper

Mr. *A. Heywood.* 30 May 1851.

paper at 3*d.* than to pay the fourpenny stamp, is it not?—Yes, if you give the same size for 3*d.* as the other gives for 7*d.* Before the stamp duty was reduced, Mr. Hetherington started a two-penny paper, and it fell so low in sale, that had not the prosecutors advertised it, he would have been compelled to give it up.

2585. The cheap country newspapers, if the stamp were taken off, would be much smaller, and contain less intelligence than the London ones, would they not?—That would depend upon circumstances: I think that if the trade were thrown open, unless they were restricted, as they are now, in size, we should see larger newspapers than at present, and at a much less price; if it were thrown open, I think we should have halfpenny newspapers and penny newspapers, and every priced newspaper, from a halfpenny upwards to sixpence. I do not see why as good a newspaper as a working man need have cannot be sold for a halfpenny as for 3*d.*, 4*d.* or 6*d.*

2586. Mr. *Ewart.*] You have not mentioned any paper connected with arts or practical manufactures?—Those are principally published monthly, except the "Mechanic's Magazine."

2587. There are such publications?—Yes; there is the "Practical Mechanics' Journal," and one called the "Engineer and Machinist;" one is published in Manchester, and the other in London.

2588. There is a Journal of Design, is there not?—Yes, but I think that its circulation is very much confined.

2589. It is more high priced, is it not?—Yes; it is calculated more for the manufacturers.

2590. Have you any publications connected with moral movements, such as temperance publications, and publications of that kind?—Temperance publications are quite in another clsss; they are published for a body, and are circulated by them; they are sent to the various secretaries of the societies, who circulate them at their meetings; very few of them come through the medium of the booksellers.

2591. Mr. *G. A. Hamilton.*] Religious tracts and publications of that kind are treated in the same way, are they not? —Yes; the great bulk of them are monthly, and thus avoid expense in carriage.

2592. Are they increasing in circulation?—I should say that they are: there is the "Churchman's Penny Magazine," and the "Christian Penny Magazine," with several others; they give a large quantity of matter for the money, and the sale of those two publications is very large; some years ago there were

Mr. *A. Heywood.*

30 May 1851.

were none of that kind, and therefore those may be said to be new.

2593. Mr. *Ewart.*] Would it increase the circulation of such papers as the temperance and religious publications if they were allowed to publish news?—Yes, I think it would.

2594. Mr. *G. A. Hamilton.*] What is the price of the "Family Herald"?—A penny in London, and the same in Manchester.

2595. Is the price of all those publications that have been mentioned the same in Manchester as in London?—Yes; we get the goods down by the London and North Western Railway at 2*s.* a cwt., and the cost, when taken in the gross, is very trifling upon a dozen; the average price the publishers charge them is 8*d.* a dozen, and it will cost half-a-farthing for the carriage; we sell them again at 9*d.* a dozen to the trade; the paper, plain, is almost worth the money.

2596. In point of fact, the buyer pays nothing for the carriage?—No.

2597. Mr. *Rich.*] Do you receive any London daily newspapers?—No, I do not.

2598. Mr. *Ewart.*] Has not the reading portion of the community been greatly benefited by railways?—Yes; we have been benefited in the cost of carriage something like 500 per cent., and benefited in the time also.

2599. *Chairman.*] Is there anything which you have made a note of yourself that you would like to mention?—Only with reference to the operation of the stamp; some think that the penny stamp is proper for the purpose of protecting it in going through the Post-office, and that as the price to be paid for its circulation is only a penny, it is unobjectionable; I have a different opinion; I say that I can get the goods down from London, or any other part of the country, at a very trifling cost, much less than a penny: but if parties choose to send their papers by post, they ought to pay; but it is too bad for the Manchester and other local papers, which have to compete with London, that the London papers should be carried down to Manchester free of any charge, and sold in Manchester, to compete with the Manchester papers; the local papers cannot compete with the London papers on that very ground, but they would the more easily be able to compete if all were free of the present penny stamp; the Manchester papers publish at $4\frac{1}{2}$*d.*, while the London papers can publish theirs at 3*d.*, and by the means of the Post-office offer a larger article for a less sum of money; and I think there would be no injustice to those who choose to have them by post, that they should pay

Mr. *A. Heywood.* 30 May 1851.

pay a penny every time they were posted; not merely the first time, and then to re-post them again and again during 12 months at no cost, but that they should pay a penny for each paper every time they posted it.

2600. Mr. *Ewart.*] Do you think that an increase in the number of local newspapers would be a great benefit to the community?—I think it would; I think there would be a greater and better influence exercised over the public mind in particular localities, if there was less of the general, and more of the local press, and for this reason, that those in the country who take in the London papers know no more about the publishers or editors than the man in the moon; in fact they know nothing about them. But if they bought them from parties whom they knew in their own locality, I say that the influence upon them would be greater than it can possibly be from reading the London papers. In a town like Manchester, though a large one, the readers know the editor and all the parties connected with a paper, and as their characters are free from stain, have considerable influence over their readers.

2601. You would interest a man most effectually through the agency of those subjects which were most familiar to him, would you not?—Yes.

2602. Mr. *Tufnell.*] All those cheap publications come from London, do they not?—Yes, or nearly so.

2603. That is because they could not get them up with the same talent, is it not?—Not exactly; there is not the same facility of production in the country as there is in London.

2604. *Chairman.*] Is it not the fact that those small publications are prevented from giving news, in order that the "Times," and other publications, may be carried free by post?—Yes, I think so.

2605. Therefore, a penalty is imposed upon those smaller publications, in order that others may be carried free by post? Yes, and that is not just.

2606. Mr. *Rich.*] How many of the "Family Herald," and other papers sent down from London, are there in a hundred weight?—About 1,700 copies.

2607. I think you stated that those 1,700 can be sent down for 2*s.*?—Yes.

2608. And you stated also, that those papers are not charged more at Manchester than they are in London?—Yes.

2609. Therefore, I do not quite see how you make out the penalty of a penny, that Manchester pays with reference to London?—

Mr. *A. Heywood.* 30 May 1851.

London?—I was speaking with reference to the newspaper press of Manchester, and other localities.

2610. My question had reference to the transmission of newspapers?—Yes; in Manchester, the sale of course is local, and they sell few of their papers in other parts than the districts around them, and few are sent to London. There is this difference with the London papers, they can come down into the country, at no cost, and compete so successfully with the local press as to prevent its proper expansion. I should mention this: if they had to send them by some other mode of conveyance than by the mail, they would not be able to get them there at the same time, except by a heavy cost upon the paper; for although it only costs 2 *s.* a hundredweight by luggage train, they would, in order to have them out at the same time, have to put on an extra price for cost of carriage: the railway charges are 2 *d.* per pound for all parcels which go by the mail, and therefore any parcel of papers sent from the office of the publisher, and not through the post, would be subject to the payment of 2 *d.* per pound; four or five papers would weigh a pound.

2611. Mr. *Rich.*] Those which are charged 2 *s.* a hundredweight are sent by a slow train?—Yes.

2612. Mr. *G. A. Hamilton.*] They are not so heavy as the "Times"?—No; they are printed on a lighter paper.

2613. Mr. *Rich.*] They would not take them by express?—No, except at the price before stated.

Mr. *Horace Greeley,* called in; and Examined.

Mr. *H. Greeley.*

2614. *Chairman.*] ARE you able to give the Committee any information with respect to the press in the United States, and whether the absence of a stamp in the United States is productive of any bad effects, in your opinion?—I will readily answer your question. We could not comprehend the operation of the stamp; it would be impracticable under our institutions every way. I can state something with regard to what the press is doing in our country, but I cannot imagine the application of the stamp at all; it would require an entire revolution in the habits and feelings of the people generally.

2615. You are the publisher of a newspaper, are you not?—Yes.

2616. What is the name of it?—"The New York Tribune."

2617. At what price is it published?—In the first place, there is a daily journal, that is the size of it—(*producing the same*).—

Mr. *H. Greeley.*

30 May 1851.

*same*).—It is not printed on so good a paper as those in England; it is published daily for one penny.

2618. What is the circulation of that paper?—It is a little under 20,000; I should say 19,000 copies daily.

2619. Is it a paper circulated principally in New York and the neighbourhood, or does it circulate extensively through other parts of the States?—I should say that 10,000 copies are circulated within the city and its vicinity, and then the balance is about equally divided between the mail subscribers and the other towns wherever it is sold, say 5,000 are sold in other towns like Boston, Philadelphia and Albany, and 4,000 sent by mail to subscribers. There is a weekly and semi-weekly in the same form; I must first say, that the daily of that size contains half reading, perhaps, and probably half advertisements, four pages of reading and four of advertisements; that is one penny, or less, by the year; it is five dollars for 313 copies for a year, which is less than a penny when it is subscribed for and is taken from the office by the year.

2620. Can you give the Committee any idea of the number of the New York daily papers that are published?—The number of daily papers that are published in New York are 15 in all, in the city.

2621. Mr. *Cobden.*] How many morning, and how many evening papers are there?—Ten morning and five evening papers; some of the morning papers are also published in the evening; we publish two evening editions, like the "Times" and other papers. There are five distinctive evening papers.

2622. There are fifteen daily papers in New York?—Yes.

2623. What is the population of New York?—Five hundred and seventeen thousand, but with the suburbs 700,000.

2624. Can you inform the Committee what the aggregate circulation of those daily papers is?—There are five of them cheap ones, at 1*d.* or ½*d.*, whose aggregate circulation is a little over 100,000 copies per day; the other ten are sold dearer, that is, at ten dollars per annum, a little more than 1½*d.* each, not 2*d.* a copy. Of those ten, I should say that the average circulation is about 3,000, being 30,000 of the dearer papers, the commercial sheets, and 100,000 of the cheap journals.

2625. The aggregate is 130,000 papers daily?—Yes.

2626. What proportion of those, at a rough guess, should you say are consumed by the 700,000 inhabitants of New York, and what proportion do you suppose are sent to remote distances?—About 60,000 are circulated in the city and its suburbs, and about 45,000 are sent away.

2627. *Chairman.*]

Mr. *H. Greeley.* 30 May 1851.

2627. *Chairman.*] What are the postage regulations in reference to those which are transmitted by post?—The postage has been one cent per copy within the state where it is published, or within 100 miles: if out of the state by the new postage regulations, which will come into effect on the 1st of July, it is reduced about one-half, except for long distances, excluding California, which is also reduced; for 1,000 miles or over the rates will be equal to what they now are; out of the state over 100 miles, it was one cent and a half (three farthings), and a cent within the state, and a cent and a half beyond that; and it is to be reduced one-half, except within certain distances; the average reduction, I think, will be a little more than one-third.

2628. *Chairman.*] It is to be reduced to half a cent within the state, but for all greater distances it is to remain as it was?—No, it is not to remain as it was; but there is a graduated scale increasing, say, over 500 miles, and increasing again over 1,000 miles; it increases because the newspapers constitute the bulk of the mails; and thus for distances over 2,000 miles on this side of the Rocky Mountains, I think the postage will be a little higher than it is now; I think it will be 80 cents per annum for the weekly papers, instead of 78; there is very little increase on distances over 2,000 miles.

2629. The postage is paid every time the paper is sent, is it not?—No, it is generally paid by the quarter; a man pays for his quarter's postage, if a weekly paper, and if in the state, 13 cents, and out of the state 19 cents.

2630. Mr. *Ewart.*] How do the Government check the collection of the postage?—It has not been very closely checked.

2631. Mr. *Tufnell.*] Supposing an individual wants to send a newspaper, how is the postage paid?—He does send it; but I think, since the reduction of the postage five or six years ago, an individual newspaper has to be paid for in advance; if you put in one not coming from a newspaper office, you have to pay in advance.

2632. *Chairman.*] Does the Post-office deliver these papers to the particular parties to whom they are directed?—Yes; but they make some objection to delivering them when we send large packages of papers. By package we send 20 copies a year (weekly) for 20 dollars, a little less than a penny each. They object to the delivering of those without the directions. We send, for instance, a package of 50 to one office, and they have a list of 50 subscribers, and as they come in they deliver the papers to them; but they sometimes say, "No; you must

Mr. *H. Greeley.*

30 May 1851.

must write the names on each of the papers." Of course they must deliver them if the names are on them.

2633. Mr. *Tufnell.*] If they are not delivered, they are called for?—Yes; they are delivered to the gentlemen who have boxes; to the subscribers at their houses; they are not distributed without an extra charge.

2634. Mr. *Rich.*] Where the postage has been either a cent or a cent and a half, that has been irrespective of weight, has it not?—Yes, entirely.

2635. Was there no limit at all?—None.

2636. Hereafter will there be any limit?—I have known journals sent very large as to size; the limit now is 1,900 square inches, and if you exceed that, you pay a double postage.

2637. You stated that the weekly newspapers cost a penny, or two cents?—Yes, when sent to clubs of 20 or more subscribers; we charge more for a single copy of a weekly than of a daily paper, because the advertisements form a great part of the contents of the daily journal. The charge is two dollars a year for a single copy of a weekly paper; that will be twopence each number; but to the clubs it is reduced to one dollar a year, 20 copies for 20 dollars. The object is to get a wider circulation in the different villages by making them cheap. A large number of city papers are taken so as to come to about one penny each to a subscriber, and a halfpenny for his postage.

2638. The publisher does not charge the postage?—No; the postage is paid per quarter in advance, at the Post-office, where the paper is delivered.

2639. *Chairman.*] You do not report, in your papers, the proceedings of the Congress in the way in which they report here the proceedings in Parliament?—No, except in the Washington journals, in which they report them very fully; I think quite as fully as they are reported here. We have a telegraphic report occasionally of a speech by some distinguished statesman, such as Mr. Clay or Mr. Calhoun, or any of the leading men; they are reported fully; but the mass of the speeches are not, except that they are sketched in a telegraphic report, occupying about two columns a day, but stretching sometimes to four or five.

2640. Mr. *Ewart.*] Your newspaper press is of a more local character than the press in this country, is it not?—It is, I presume, more local than the London journals, because its circulation is more circumscribed by the fact that the local journals are so abundant.

2641. *Chairman.*] You go to considerable expense in obtaining

Mr. *H. Greeley.*

30 May 1851.

taining news for your papers from various parts of the world, do not you ?—Yes; but mainly it is by telegraphing from different parts of the country. The leading journals have correspondents; but the great item of expense is telegraphing, and sending off boats sometimes; when steam ships do not touch at Halifax, we sometimes send off boats to intercept them.

2642. You have correspondents in different places, who telegraph up to you any occurrences that may be interesting? —Yes, all over the country; a net-work.

2643. You employ those correspondents to pay constant attention to such things?—Yes; but telegraphing is done mainly by an association, called the Associated Press of New York.

2644. Do you complain of piracy in the United States; for instance, of one publisher who has not himself been at the expense of obtaining news, copying immediately from another? —It is sometimes talked of for effect's sake; yet, on the whole, I would rather that those who do not take it should copy than not. We have six or seven journals in the city, which form a combination, and spend, perhaps, 100,000 dollars a year in telegraphing; and the evening journals all copy from us, and we rather like it.

2645. Have you any protection, in the nature of copyright, to your news?—Not the least; the moment it is out, anybody can take it, and they do take it and issue it.

2646. There is no precaution at all taken against piracy?—No; we only take this precaution; we have, for instance, a very important piece of information, which has cost us 1,000 dollars. We will suppose that two journals take charge of the foreign news, and two journals take charge of another part of the news; and the journals having charge of it, when they send the news round to the others, say, "This is not to be issued till four [or five] o'clock;" and no journal of the combination will let a copy go out of the office till the hour named; it is in the hands of the carriers; but it is not allowed to go out till the hour named, and then nobody can get it.

2647. Supposing it were something of great interest, there would be a continued demand for your paper if you were the only one who could communicate it; and, for a given period, that demand would continue, and you would keep striking off your copies to supply it. Is there nothing to entitle you, having incurred the first expense of obtaining that news, to issue it for any period?—Not for a moment; anybody may print it; but the public are apt to take the paper which has the first news.

2648. They

Mr. *H. Greeley.*

30 May 1851.

2648. They give the preference to the parties who have obtained the news first, and in practice piracy does not inflict injury upon you?—I would choose that they should print it rather than not; they cannot sell as we could. The fact that certain journals have the earliest news soon becomes notorious, and almost every man wants his newspaper with his breakfast, delivered between the hours of five and half-past seven. They take the morning papers to read with their breakfast, and those who take the news after we issue it cannot have it in time to deliver it to a very large number in a suitable morning season, and we regard it as of no consequence.

2649. Mr. *Ewart.*] Does the interest of the intelligence evaporate so soon?—Not that; but a subscriber must have the paper that gives him his news in the morning before he goes to his work.

2650. You retard the publication of news sometimes?—Yes, when we have important intelligence.

2651. Is not that an inconvenience to the public?—We get them out in our regular way, but we do not let a copy go out of the hands of our confidential agents till the hour, say of five o'clock in the morning.

2652. *Chairman.*] At what rate can you print the "New York Tribune"?—Our press will work but 10,000 an hour; there is one faster, an eight-cylinder, which will work 20,000, they say; I call it 18,000.

2653. Mr. *Cobden.*] Do you believe that there is a press at work in New York which will print 18,000 copies an hour?—Yes; I have seen it at work, and it throws off as fast as eight men can feed sheets upon it.

2654. Have you seen the press that is used for the "Times"?—Yes.

2655. Do you consider that the press at New York prints with more rapidity than the one at the "Times" office?—Yes; the press at the "Times" is fed on what I would call a drum or vertical cylinder; we feed on horizontal cylinders, directly on and around our greater or type cylinder. One man stands over the top, and another below, and so on, feeding, and the four cylinders are fed on each side of the large cylinder, on which the form revolves, and they feed the four paper cylinders one above the other on each side of that large cylinder: the sheets are laid over and over on the face as fast as the great cylinder can be turned, and every time it makes one revolution, it has printed eight journals.

2656. Is that machinery used by the proprietor of a penny paper?—Yes; a halfpenny newspaper, "The Sun."

2657. Must

Mr. *H. Greeley.*

30 May 1851.

2657. Must not that require the use of considerable capital? —Yes; "The Sun" concern is worth a quarter of a million dollars; 50,000 *l.* was given for it.

2658. Do you speak of copyright and plant?—There was very little property besides; it was sold for a quarter of a million dollars, and it was very cheap.

2659. Fifty thousand pounds for a halfpenny paper?—Yes.

2660. What is the circulation?—Fifty thousand; but the circulation is a very light matter; there is no profit upon that; but the advertising would be, I suppose, 60*l.* a day, or 300 dollars a day.

2661. Could you furnish the Committee with some statistical information as to the newspaper press of America?—Yes, when our census returns are published. I should say that the whole number of journals printed in the United States is about 3,000 now. If you count, for instance, one daily, with its weekly and semi-weekly all as one paper, the number is 2,500 journals published.

2662. Are there 2,500 with distinct and separate titles?—Yes, distinct establishments; of which about 2,000 are devoted to general intelligence and politics, and the others are devoted to science, religion and education.

2663. And they are published at all intervals, from once a day to once a month?—Yes, some twice or thrice a day.

2664. Mr. *Ewart.*] Your principal profit is derived from advertisements, is it not?—Yes, on daily papers.

Mr. *Henry Watkinson*, called in; and Examined.

Mr. *H. Watkinson.*

2665. *Chairman.*] YOU are the proprietor of the "Spalding Free Press," are you not?—Yes.

2666. Is that a stamped paper?—Yes.

2667. Partly stamped and partly unstamped?—It is wholly stamped.

2668. How long has it been established?—Three years last October.

2669. Was it ever partly stamped and partly unstamped? —I thought of commencing it unstamped; but I found that the editor of the "Wisbeach Advertiser," who had commenced a paper similar to it, had been threatened with a prosecution, so then I felt that it would be a folly on my part, and therefore I felt myself compelled to commence it stamped. It was a monthly publication for three months, in the year 1847, from October to December; I commenced it fortnightly in

Mr. *H. Watkinson.*

30 May 1851.

in 1848, which it continued till 1850; and in the present year I commenced it weekly.

2670. Have you some statement to make to the Committee in reference to the operation of the Newspaper Stamp Act, as giving rise to local persecution?—Yes; but I ought to observe first its effects upon the district. Previously to my paper being published in our purely agricultural district, the great paper published there, the "Stamford Mercury," never entered into any abuses; nothing was described by that paper that could have offended or have any restraint upon the non-stipendiary magistracy; indeed, nothing that would even check the great landlords of that district. All was gently smoothed over in every point of view. But my paper entered fully into the abuses of the magisterial bench, showing particularly that the Spalding bench was composed of six out of eight who were blood relations, whom at any time we might offend against in regard to their tenants, who are located all round, and that we could scarcely go over a stile or a gate without offending some of the family bench whose property lay there. Those matters I so exposed, that it caused a suit of law against me for what was considered a libel upon the gentleman who figured as the chairman, and the case was tried at Lincoln; but yet, it so informed the public mind, that now out of those six, there are only two who really reside in the district, and it was nothing but the exposure of their system, which encouraged the giving of favours and showing kindnesses to their own party, and persecuting the dissenting party, and every one who dared to think contrary to themselves, which my little paper did, as well as giving that kind of expression to public opinion with reference to the great grievance of such a bench, that entirely upset it, and now we have but one or two of all the eight, who dare scarcely sit on the bench, and it requires that a new bench be constituted of the stipendiary class, so that justice should be dispensed.

2671. It was the establishment of this unstamped monthly paper that produced this effect, was it?—Yes.

2672. It improved, in fact, the local news of that district?—Quite so; and so much so that the "Mercury," published at Stamford, has to pay a correspondent 40*l.* or 50*l.* a year now, in order to give a greater supply of news for that district, otherwise it would not have the circulation it used to have. Previously to that it did not pay its correspondent 5*l.*; I mean before mine was established.

2673. What are the complaints which you have to make yourself of the operation of the Newspaper Stamp Act?—In regard

Mr. *H. Watkinson.*

30 May 1851.

regard to the stamp particularly; mainly that were the stamp abolished, where now, from the smallness of wages on the part of the agricultural labourers, we sell only one paper, we should sell at least six papers without the stamp; I am perfectly satisfied of that, because my paper, which is published at 3 *d.*, would be very easily published at 1½ *d.* without a stamp.

2674. The stamp, you say, raises your paper to 3 *d.*?—Yes.

2675. And it could be published at 1½ *d.*?—At 1 *d.* rather than it now is; but at 1½ *d.* certainly; it would even be sold at 1 *d.*, I may say.

2676. How is it that the stamp adds more than its own amount to the price of the paper?—Because there is not one in ten that ever passes through the post of my papers. Six persons unite and pay a halfpenny each in innumerable instances to have my paper, because they cannot individually raise the 3 *d.* when they might 1½ *d.* or 1 *d.*

2677. In point of fact, they have to pay their postage in addition to the stamp on the paper?—They have to pay the stamp without using the post.

2678. Mr. *Rich.*] They pay a halfpenny for having it delivered to them, as well as 1 *d.* for the stamp, do they not?—No, our delivery is free, but they have that stamp to pay; whereas they would not have, and there would be six papers sold at 1½ *d.*, and a poor man could afford that, but not 3 *d.*

2679. You were asked why the penny stamp should make a difference of 1½ *d.*?—That is in regard to the circulation chiefly, and on account of our losses by overprinting or underprinting on account of the stamp.

2680. *Chairman.*] You made some complaints to the Board of Inland Revenue which have not been satisfactorily answered, did you not?—Those have been chiefly in relation to my paper; I have to post to Lincoln two copies every week, and they have compelled me to pay two stamps to post those two copies to the office at Lincoln, which I am compelled by law to send, and they will not allow me for those two stamps; and I complained to the Board of Inland Revenue in that respect.

2681. They compel you to send those two papers?—Yes; on which I have to write my name; and the Board of Inland Revenue compels me to pay those two stamps.

2682. They force you to pay the postage of the two papers that they compel you to send to them?—Yes.

2683. Mr. *Rich.*] Are they stamped newspapers?—Yes; on which we have to sign our name. We have to send up two copies with regard to charging for the advertisement duty, and we are compelled to pay the two stamps.

2684. As

Mr. *H. Watkinson.*

30 May 1851.

2684. As well as the newspaper stamp which is there, do you also affix a postage stamp?—Two stamps, one on each paper.

2685. Two Queen's heads?—Yes; that is the grievance which I complained of to the Board of Inland Revenue.

2686. *Chairman.*] What reason did they give you in explanation?—It is because the Post Office rules are strict in that respect; if you only blot a newspaper with the tip of your finger, you must put a stamp upon it, or it will be charged to the party as postage; but the Board never replied to my letter.

2687. You are compelled by the Board of Inland Revenue to put those signatures to the papers, are you not?—Yes.

2688. And because you do that you become liable to postage?—Yes; but I have only the correspondence between the Post Office and myself on that subject.

2689. Do you consider that the effect of increasing the circulation of local papers would be beneficial to the agricultural labourers and other classes surrounding Spalding?—I believe that from the high price of the present papers through the stamp, very few of them read, and it is entirely through that; but if it were abolished, I have the fullest confidence and belief that all of them nearly would read who could read.

2690. And that you think would tend to keep up a habit of reading, would it not?—Yes.

---

*Martis,* 3° *die Junii,* 1851.

MEMBERS PRESENT.

| | |
|---|---|
| Mr. Tufnell. | Mr. Shafto Adair. |
| Mr. Ewart. | Mr. G. A. Hamilton. |
| Mr. Cobden. | Sir J. Walmsley. |
| Mr. Rich. | |

THE RIGHT HON. T. MILNER GIBSON, IN THE CHAIR.

Mr. *Henry Cole,* was called in; and Examined.

Mr. *H. Cole.*

3 June 1851.

2691. *Chairman.*] YOU have turned your attention to the operation of the newspaper stamp law, and also to the regulations respecting the transmission of printed matters by post, have you not?—For a considerable period, since Mr. Edwin Chadwick

Chadwick first brought forward the subject of taxes on knowledge, which is now some 20 years ago, I have been interested in watching the progress of the subject, and my connexion with the penny postage question led me further to observe the operation of the present law.

2692. You were also somewhat actively engaged in assisting Mr. Rowland Hill previously to the introduction of the penny postage?—Both before the introduction of the penny postage, and subsequently at the Treasury for three years.

2693. You assisted Mr. Hill for three years after the penny postage was introduced?—Yes.

2694. In what capacity was that?—It was to assist generally in carrying out the penny postage.

2695. It was considered, was it not, that the stamp on newspapers was a sort of postage charge for the privilege that was to be extended to newspapers of going by post free?—In all calculations of postage revenue, credit on behalf of the Post Office was taken in respect to the penny charged on newspapers as a postage. If the Committee will refer to the time when Lord Monteagle, then Mr. Spring Rice, brought forward the motion, they will find that he brought it forward particularly as carrying out Sir Edward Lytton Bulwer's proposition that the penny stamp should be considered as a postage. I will presently read a passage from the speech of Lord Monteagle, then Mr. Spring Rice: Sir Edward Lytton Bulwer brought forward a proposition in 1835, that newspapers should be relieved of the fourpenny stamp, and that a penny stamp should be imposed upon those that went through the Post Office as a postage; that proposition was withdrawn or negatived; but in the next year the Chancellor of the Exchequer, then Mr. Spring Rice, brought forward the subject, and he said, "He held that they had a right to the penny stamp, and that it would be essential for the best interests of the press itself, inasmuch as it would afford to newspapers a free circulation by post. He would observe in passing, that no proposition he had ever heard made for establishing a posting duty had appeared to him more desirable in itself, or more favourable to the press than that which he now made; that proposition was to reduce the duty to one penny, allowing that penny for the circulation of the paper by the post. The proposition he (the Chancellor of the Exchequer) had at the time expressed his regret that he could not accede to, by reason of the then state of the finances, but he had also stated that he would take the earliest opportunity himself of bringing forward such a proposition;" that was to treat it as a postage, and

Mr. *H. Cole.*

3 June 1851.

and not as a tax. "He trusted that The House would admit that he had now redeemed his pledge; he had brought forward the distinct and specific proposition which the Honourable Member for Lincoln had expressed his desire to see carried out." That seems to me to make it conclusive that the view at that time was to consider the penny as a postage, rather than as a tax. The whole tone of the speech shows that the tax, as a tax, was held to be an indefensible tax, but that as a postage it was a good thing and a very good bargain.

2696. In the first instance it was a proposition that those that went by post should be charged a stamp, but not the whole impression?—That was the proposition that was first submitted to the House of Commons by Sir Edward Lytton Bulwer.

2697. And not accepted by the Government?—It was not accepted at that time by the Government, but in the next year it was brought forward in an altered shape, and upon grounds which I have quoted from Lord Monteagle's speech.

2698. Mr. *G. A. Hamilton.*] What is the date of that speech?—The 20th of June 1836; it is in Hansard, volume 34, pages 632 and 633.

2699. *Chairman.*] You say that this stamp was considered at that time to be a postage charge, and not a tax upon news; do you consider that it operates as a tax?—Most unquestionably, owing to the altered circumstances of the times: owing to the fact that the great bulk of the London press is now taken out by railways in the morning, and the Post Office not used; and owing to the fact that where the Post Office might be of very great use, the Post Office will not allow newspapers to go through the Post Office without an additional postage; and that seems to lead to the inference that the original idea has been altogether put aside. The Committee are probably aware that you cannot post a newspaper in London to be circulated within the three miles circle without paying an additional penny. I once was witness of something that looked like a pantomime in the matter; 30,000 newspapers were taken down to the Post Office, I saw the proceeding; they were taken down to the superintendent of the district post, and he was asked whether he would like to take them in as then sorted, those for London that were for London, and those for the country that were for the country; he said, "No, it will be a great convenience to take them in; but if you wish to avoid the charge of 1 *d.* upon the London papers, you must take them to Brompton." And accordingly two waggons went to Brompton, to put all the newspapers into the

Brompton

Mr. *H. Cole.*

3 June 1851.

Brompton Post Office without sortation, in order that the newspapers for London should not be assessed with the penny.

2700. In fact, you would lead the Committee to understand that the freedom from postage charge, as an equivalent for the stamp, has not been fairly enjoyed; that as far as London is concerned, for instance, the penny is still charged, although the newspapers are stamped?—Certainly; I know that the postmaster has the power to do so by law; but it seems to me to be an evasion of the Chancellor of the Exchequer's proposal, and an evasion in the precise point where it would tend to cheapen newspapers; because, if the "Times" could circulate all its newspapers direct to its London subscribers, there is no reason why they should not have them for 4*d.*

2701. Mr. *Ewart.*] You mean if the stamp duty were taken off?—I mean, because the newsvenders' discount would thereby be saved; and instead of paying the newsvenders a penny, which the "Times" now allows, the "Times" might send its newspapers direct through the post at once, if the Post Office gave all the necessary facilities. The discount to the newsvenders would be saved.

2702. Mr. *G. A. Hamilton.*] They pay for the distribution twice, do they not; once, according to your view, in paying the stamp, and a second time in paying for the cost of the distribution?—Yes; they are prevented from availing themselves of the Post Office by the additional penny which the Post Office would charge.

2703. *Chairman.*] Your meaning is this, that where freedom from the postage charge is allowed, namely, in the transmission from London to the country, it is not of so much consequence, from the facilities that railways afford, but that where it is charged in the districts, the absence of that charge would be a considerable relief?—Certainly. The practical working in la e times has been that the public can effect the transmission sptedier and better than the Post Office; the railways take the morning papers out of town, the great bulk of them, and the Post Office is not used at all. In the country in local districts, and also in the metropolitan district, you cannot avail yourself of all the privileges of the Post Office, because they have the power of imposing an additional penny for postage.

2704. Mr. *Ewart.*] Therefore those stamped newspapers that go by the railways pay for a postal privilege which they do not use?—Yes.

2705. *Chairman.*] In the case of those 30,000 newspapers that were carted down to Brompton, at whose expense was that; of the parties who wished to transmit them?—Certainly.



2706. The

Mr. *H. Cole.* — 3 June 1851.

2706. The trouble to the Post Office itself was considerably greater, was it not, by their being posted at Brompton, having to bring them from Brompton to London, than if they had been posted, in the first instance, at the General Post Office in London?—A great deal more. There was first the trouble of the carriage from Brompton, and next there was the superseding the sortation that existed when they were proposed to be taken at the head office.

2707. The more the trouble the less they charge; that is to say, when the trouble is great they charge nothing, and when the trouble is small they put on a charge?—That was the practical result.

2708. Did you ever hear, when these matters were discussed, what was the object of so far departing from the understanding when the stamp was imposed, that a penny charge was put on for delivery in London?—I think it was a tenderness for the vested rights of newsvenders, a motive of that kind more than anything else, and a desire, perhaps a natural desire on the part of the Post Office, not to have more work to do than they could help; they saw that the effect of it might be to make them the practical distributors of all the newspapers circulating in London.

2709. And it was for that reason that they were stamped?—You cannot find those motives avowed; but if you look to see what the interests could be that settled a regulation of that sort, they would seem to be those two. In fact, I have heard the expression used in the Post Office, that the desire was not to be troubled with the circulation of the metropolitan newspapers.

2710. Mr. *Rich.*] You say, that if by the payment of a stamp the Post Office were obliged to distribute the London daily newspapers, which are put into the Post Office all over London, the "Times" and other daily newspapers would then be able to distribute them to their customers at 4 *d.*?—I apprehend that they would be able; but whether they would do so, is another consideration.

2711. Why do they not do so now in all great towns in the country, and the country itself?—I apprehend on the whole, that it perhaps would not be profitable to them to have to collect the receipts from their country subscribers, to carry on the daily correspondence connected with it, and to make all the regulations necessary for the transmission and so on; their interest is to get it done by subordinate agencies rather than going to a town directly.

2712. Would not the same objections apply to the London customers?—

customers?—In a less degree; certainly to some extent they would. My answer went to show what could be done if the additional postage were not imposed. Mr. *H. Cole.* 3 June 1851.

2713. You stated at first that it would be burdensome to the Post Office to perform this duty, and now you admit, I think, that it would be hardly profitable, or that it would be cumbrous to the newspaper proprietors themselves, therefore practically it seems better left to the intervention of a third party, namely, the newsvender?—Practically the public have not been able to try the experiment.

2714. You have not been able to try the experiment as far as the country is concerned; but you have in the great towns, as the great towns enjoy the privilege of having the newspapers distributed by the post for a penny?—No. I will point out another obvious disadvantage as respects the country; a reader in Liverpool desires to get a London newspaper at the earliest time; if the Post Office is slow and the railway beats it in speed, it is obvious that the Liverpool reader would not be content to get his newspaper through the Post Office, though he got it a penny less.

2715. You stated that if the penny stamp were abolished, persons in London might get their papers for 4 *d.*, but from the inference you have drawn it would appear that they would not?—I only say that they might, and that the experiment has not yet been tried.

2716. Do you think that the "Times" publishers could afford to distribute them for nothing?—No.

2717. If a newsvender gets a penny profit, would the "Times" do it for nothing?—A penny and something else; some other discount; we have yet to see whether the Post Office would distribute newspapers as quickly as the public wanted them; we have yet to see whether it would not be for the interest of the newspaper proprietors to undertake the circulation themselves; we see a tendency throughout the whole of commerce and commercial relations, at the present time, to get rid of intermediate discounts, and what I desire to show is that the Post Office, by charging this additional 1 *d.*, prevents any experiment of that kind.

2718. *Chairman.*] What you mean to convey to the Committee is, that having obtained the stamp at the Stamp Office, it is rather hard after all that 1 *d.* should be charged for transmission by post?—Yes, having it interpreted according to the Chancellor of the Exchequer's speech, that the stamp is a postage, to be cut off from the use of it as postage at that point

Mr. *H. Cole.*

3 June 1851.

point where it would be most useful, or where it would be likely to be most used.

2719. Mr. *Rich.*] You are aware, are you not, that the Chancellor of the Exchequer contemplated the receipt of a considerable revenue?—Yes, I apprehend so.

2720. Mr. *Ewart.*] Did he take into his contemplation the transmission of large masses of papers as they are sent by the railways?—Hardly at that time I should think.

2721. *Chairman.*] The penny stamp is used as a postage for the transmission of printed matter which does not come under the head of news?—Clearly; you have all kinds of circulars, and things of all sort which avail themselves of the penny stamp as newspapers, wherever it is most economical to do so. I have some cases which when I was bestowing the most attention upon the subject came before my notice. I have here a postage report (*producing the same*) from a committee in the City of London, of which Mr. Bates was chairman: they desired to circulate it cheaply, and they got the publisher of the "Spectator" to make it a supplement to the "Spectator," the object being to transmit this quantity of printed matter all over the country for a penny. Here is an article from a "Quarterly Review" (*producing the same*), which also had a newspaper stamp put on, to be circulated for a penny. Here is a placard (*producing the same*) that was sent all round the country in many thousands; it was sent, availing itself of the passage through the Post Office, as a newspaper.

2722. With respect to the "Spectator," did you transmit the supplement by itself, or conjointly with the newspaper to which it was a supplement?—No, without.

2723. Was not that also contrary to the law, as laid down in the Newspaper Stamp Act, that the supplement should never be sold except with the paper?—The Committee will observe that the stamp of this supplement costs a penny, not a halfpenny; and therefore whether it was or was not a supplement, it was charged with a newspaper stamp.

2724. Was it ever intended that this stamp should have been the means of procuring immunities to printed matter, not news, in the post?—I should think not; but the law being rather loose, people avail themselves of that, which they are able to do, when it is to their interest to do so.

2725. Have you thought generally upon the regulations relating to the transmission of printed matters through the post, as to whether they do not require complete reconsideration?—I think that any modification that takes place in the penny

Mr. *H. Cole.*

3 June 1851.

penny stamp will lead to the reconsideration of the transmission of printed matter generally. There are a number of anomalies. I have heard it said that we are more barbarous than Spain in the transmission of our printed papers; and here is one remarkable anomaly. Here are some printed papers addressed to New York (*producing the same*). Those may be sent for the advantage of the American public for 1 *d.*, whilst the same papers if sent to Canada, or our own colonies, would cost 4*s.* 4*d.*, being considered as letters.

2726. Mr. *Rich.*] They are not stamped?—No.

2727. If they were stamped they could be sent to Canada for 3*d.*, could they not?—If they were converted into newspapers, I think you must pay another penny; but this is common printed matter.

2728. Mr. *S. Adair.*] What would it cost to transmit a paper to Canada?—A stamped paper would cost another penny, I think.

2729. *Chairman.*] Provided it was within eight days of its publication?—Yes. Without a stamp, I apprehend it would be treated as a letter, according to the weight.

2730. Mr. *S. Adair.*] Not as a newspaper?—No, not as a printed matter; it would be treated as a letter.

2731. Mr. *Ewart.*] Does France enjoy the same privilege as the American States in the transmission of printed papers? —No; the Americans had a discussion with us about postage about three years ago, and I think they made it a point of the treaty that they should be able to take our printed matter at the rate of a penny; that is, printed matter under two ounces; so that we give the Americans all the benefit of our intelligence in print, and we cut our colonies off from having it.

2732. *Chairman.*] Your opinion is that this stamp operates as a tax?—Assuredly.

2733. What is your opinion as to the policy of such a tax upon news?—I think it is a tax upon thought and speech, and it is about as defensible in policy as that would be. There is another monstrous inconsistency; every Englishman is supposed to know the law; the State takes no particular pains in making the law known: and to say that nobody shall know the law, except through a paper which is taxed, seems to me to be against the first principles of sound policy altogether. I should express my own opinion better in the words of Lord Brougham, who was then Lord Chancellor, and spoke to that precise point. He says: "I must also add, that I am quite certain if the stamp were taken away, where we circulate useful information to the extent of thousands,

Mr. *H. Cole.*

3 June 1851.

sands, we could circulate useful information to the extent of millions; for we have been trying to get useful publications, not only into parts of the country where men are gregarious, the manufacturing districts, in which they naturally and easily read, but into farm houses and cottages, where the case is different. The great difficulty is, to get the peasants to read; first, because they do not work together; and next, because people working in the open air are sleepy when they come home: but in long winter nights, when they are not so hard worked, and have much more spare time, it is particularly desirable that they should not have recourse to beer shops, or to bad publications. It would be of great advantage if we could furnish them with publications that have a tendency to make men good members of society, rather than those which are now propagated and are read by great numbers, teaching them that the most infamous of characters, a man for instance who is about to be executed for the foulest murder, from the moment he becomes converted to some particular spiritual doctrine is safe from retribution in another world. I cannot conceive a more pernicious doctrine, and all which is said about absolution in the Catholic church is not one whit worse even in its abuse, and I know it is very much abused. Those publications which are in farm houses, to my knowledge for want of better, teach that if a man commits murder, and will only afterwards become a fanatic, he is in acceptance with Heaven, and his murder forgiven him. If a man can have in his cottage, at a cheap rate, accounts of the debates, which they look to with great interest, and which it is their duty as well as their interest to read; the proceedings in courts of justice, which they also are delighted with reading; if in addition to these departments, commonly called the news of the day, we could circulate four pages more, which could all be done for a penny without this pernicious stamp duty, we might give the cottager for one penny a newspaper with wholesome general information, which might be of use to him in various ways, beside giving him all the intelligence of the week. I am quite certain that this would be the effect of repealing the stamp." "If instead of newspapers being sold for 6 *d.* or 1 *s.* they could be sold for a penny, I have no manner of doubt there would immediately follow the greatest possible improvement in the tone and temper of the political information of the people, and therefore of the political character and conduct of the people. It is my decided and deliberate opinion, from very long and anxious consideration, that the danger is not of the people learning too much

Mr. *H. Cole.*

3 June 1851.

much, but knowing too little. It is no longer a question whether they shall read or not; it is no longer a question whether they shall be instructed or not; it is no longer a question whether they shall be politicians, and take part in the discussions of their own interests or not; that is decided long and long ago. The only question to answer, and the only problem to solve is, how they shall read in the best manner, how they shall be instructed politically, and have political habits formed the most safe for the constitution of the country and the best for their own interests." I think these passages say almost all that is to be said upon the political view of the question; I, for one, thoroughly concur in them.

2734. Mr. *Ewart.*] Do you remember Lord Althorpe's opinion upon the same subject?—I believe it was very much to the same effect.

2735. *Chairman.*] Your opinion is, that this tax impedes the diffusion of a knowledge of the law which the State takes no especial mode of dispersing through the country, though it presumes that every man knows the law?—Yes, and I think that is a most crying anomaly. I think even if it could be maintained that people should not discuss politics, at least you should make it as easy as possible to know what the law and its administration are.

2736. Mr. *Tufnell.*] Is it your view that every citizen should know exactly what every law is?—I think it is very desirable that he should know all that affects him.

2737. Do you think that practically you could ever attain that object, so that those who purchased newspapers as well as those who did not should know exactly what every law was?—I think we none of us know what the whole law is; but we all of us have a common sense view of it which we get by reading the newspapers.

2738. Mr. *S. Adair.*] Is not this the fact, that under the original British Constitution, in our early history, care was taken by the then Government to proclaim the law?—I think it was. It was the custom for the laws to be posted on the church doors amongst other things, and probably the clergyman told the people what the law was; but as newspapers are now the great pulpits of the time, I think we should avail ourselves of them for teaching the law, or at all events allow the law to be taught through their means.

2739. Mr. *Ewart.*] Is it not a maxim of the English law that no man is exempt from the operation of the law by pleading ignorance of the law?—Yes.

2740. *Chairman.*] You were concerned very much in the postage

Mr. *H. Cole.*

3 June 1851.

postage matter, and your attention was also called to the reduction of the stamp at the time when it was reduced. Taking the whole into consideration, do you think that since the period when the stamp duty was reduced, the character of the press has improved?—Most decidedly. I would not wish this answer to be taken for more than it is worth. I think that the whole tone of society is improved, and I think that the character of the press is a reflection, more or less, of the spirit of the age. The "Times" has always been a stamped paper; but the "Times" of to-day and the "Times" of 25 years ago are two different things, and the "leaders" are, in my opinion, very much improved.

2741. Were there any predictions that, at the time the stamp was reduced, that the effect would be to deteriorate and injure the tone of the press?—Certainly; very strong predictions.

2742. The same kind of predictions that are now made with regard to the entire removal of the stamp?—Precisely the same, I think.

2743. Mr. *Rich.*] Were there not predictions that the monopoly of the London press would be beaten down, and particularly the monopoly of the leading papers?—I think not, by those who saw farthest into the matter; on the contrary, I think that all those who saw that this avowed penny postage on printed papers was nothing more than a tax, emphatically predicted that it would not break down what is called the monopoly.

2744. You are giving the predictions of those who saw the farthest, as you say. In reply to a question put by the Right honourable Chairman, you gave an answer referring to the predictions of those who saw the least far?—I think the London newspapers themselves were rather apprehensive that their position would be damaged. I think that was the view of the newspapers; but I do not think it was the view of those who were watching the subject.

2745. Were there not a great number of these short-seeing people who said that you would have cheap newspapers of all kinds springing up throughout the country, that would be circulated at 2*d.* and 3*d.*, and disseminate news and be as good as the London newspapers, and considerably enlighten the public?—I think not; I dare say there were some of those people.

2746. Are you aware of a newspaper having been originated which was conducted with great ability, and supported by great capital, and published at 3*d.*?—Yes, I am aware of that. I was, unfortunately, a proprietor of a 3*d.* newspaper, conjointly

Mr. *H. Cole.*

3 June 1851.

conjointly with the late Mr. Charles Buller. He and I, when this tax was altered, attempted to start a threepenny newspaper, and we lost several hundreds of pounds; we found it impossible to maintain the paper at 3*d.*, which was our object. The Committee may know a paper called the "Weekly Chronicle;" it was started at 3 *d.*; I am not sure that it was not started at 2 ½ *d.*, but after a time it was 3 *d.*, and its circulation mounted up to considerably more than 100,000. It was then bought by Mr. H. G. Ward, the present governor of the Ionian Islands, and he found that, in order to keep it at the point of respectability which he desired, the expenses increased, and the result of his experiment was, that he raised the price ultimately to 6 *d.*, going through the different stages of 4 *d.*, 5 *d.*, and 6 *d.*; and his changes in price reduced the circulation, I think, to about 15,000.

2747. The other daily papers, which were published at 3 *d.*, have been also obliged to raise their price, have they not?—There have been only two remarkable cases of daily papers which were published at 3 *d.*; one was not a very creditable one, and the other, which was, was the "Daily News."

2748. The "Daily News" and the "Morning Chronicle" published at 4*d.* at one time, did they not?—"The Morning Chronicle" did not commence by publishing at 4*d.*, but when the present proprietors of the "Morning Chronicle" purchased it, I think they reduced the price to 4 *d.* for a short time.

2749. And then they raised it again?—Yes.

2750. Do you not regard this return to the old price as an indication that those persons had entertained opinions that the taking off of the duty, would enable them to publish at a cheaper rate than they on experience found profitable?—I do not see the connexion between them and the classes first alluded to.

2751. Did it not afford evidence that they had thought their papers could be published profitably at 3 *d.*?—I think they expected it.

2752. Do you not think from their raising the price, that they found their expectations were not realized?—Yes.

2753. Therefore they were mistaken in their expectations?—Yes.

2754. Many persons at that time conversant with newspaper matters, entertained the opinion that the reduction of the duty would enable them to publish newspapers more cheaply than they found on experience to be the case?—I have already said that I have no doubt there was a large percentage

Mr. *H. Cole.* — 3 June 1851.

centage of people who had those expectations; I said also, that those who paid the most attention to the subject did not entertain those expectations. Some sanguine people, like Mr. Charles Buller and myself, tried the experiment.

2755. *Chairman.*] That penny which was left when the stamp was reduced, was called by some noble Lord the worst penny of all; and was not it always foreseen by those who looked deeply into the subject, that the retention of that penny just made the difference between not being able to circulate a cheap paper, and being able to circulate it?—It makes all the difference I think, and for this reason, that in the capital required for the newspaper, the total capital must be paid for. For instance, a newsvender in circulating a paper must be paid for his outlay for these penny stamps; he must have his profit upon the outlay upon the stamps; and therefore it is not the cost of the paper plus the stamp, but it is the total cost of the paper which regulates the price to the public.

2756. Mr. *Tufnell.*] What has the newsvender to do with the stamp?—The newsvender's profit has a great deal to do with it; for instance, I will take the case of a threepenny paper; the custom is to allow to the trade at least 25 per cent. upon the full price, whatever it is: in fact they get nearer 30 per cent. Now a quarter out of 3 *d.* is three farthings, that leaves 2 ¼ *d.* (in some cases the newsvender has been allowed the whole penny), and the penny stamp leaves 1 ¼ *d.*, or only 1 *d.*; if the newspaper is of any size the paper will cost nearly one penny; consequently there is only a farthing left for the payment for composition, and for the proprietor's profit, whatever it may be. But that same newspaper that was published at 3 *d.* could be sold for 1 ½ *d.* without the stamp, because if you take a fourth of 1 ½ *d.*, or a third (I will take a third, giving it more liberally to the newsvender), if you take a third off you leave a penny; then supposing the size of the paper to be reduced a little in proportion, the paper you may assume to cost a halfpenny, and in this case a newspaper proprietor, instead of getting only one farthing out of 3 *d.*, would have a halfpenny to pay himself out of 1 ½ *d.*, with the chances of a greatly increased circulation.

2757. The newsvender gets a discount upon that stamp with which he has nothing to do, does he not?—He has to find the capital for it; the newsvender supplies you with a newspaper, and you probably pay his bill every quarter; he is that outlay out of pocket for the whole price of the paper, whatever it is; therefore the operation of the stamp duty is not merely an additional penny upon every newspaper, but an additional

Mr. *H. Cole.*

3 June 1851.

additional penny, plus the allowances which must be made upon the total outlay.

2758. With regard to this paper which you have mentioned, in which you were concerned in conjunction with Mr. Charles Buller, could you trace its failure to the operation of this penny stamp?—I have traced it to this, that we only got about a farthing out of the 3 *d.*, and that we could have produced that same paper certainly at 2 *d.* with a much better chance of success, and even at 1 ½ *d.*; it was a weekly paper.

2759. Mr. *Rich.*] You are aware that in all these calculations the slightest error, even the smallest fraction of the sum, would lead to very different results?—Certainly; to show how very cheap distribution really is, I may refer to the case of the "Penny Magazine;" that was printed in London, but it was carried all over the whole of England, and delivered at parties' houses; credit was given; the thing cost the public 1 *d.* and the newsvender only got his farthing. In any cheap newspaper I apprehend the newsvender would get his usual distributing price.

2760. *Chairman.*] If there is only this farthing left after paying for the paper, the interest on the capital, and the stamp, how is the editorship and other necessary expenses paid for in this threepenny paper?—It can only be paid for by an enormous circulation; the fraction of a farthing, if you extend the quantity far enough, will make any sum that you like.

2761. Still, whatever the circulation is, it must pay very little for editorship?—The tendency of the penny stamp has been, in all cases of the threepenny papers, to deteriorate the quality extremely, and in fact I might almost say that generally the threepenny papers are mere piracies; the lowest sum is paid for what you might call the fixed expenses of the paper; the printing is bad, the working is bad, the paper is necessarily very thin, and little is spent for editorship; and that must be the case.

2762. Mr. *Tufnell.*] Supposing the penny stamp were abolished, have you ever considered at what price one of the London daily papers, conducted with talent and supported with capital, could be sold for at a profit?—I should say certainly for 3 *d.*; but I should say that after a time you would have a first-rate paper at 2 *d.* in the metropolis.

2763. With expensive arrangements for obtaining foreign news, and reporting the debates daily?—Yes; I think that different arrangements would arise in respect to foreign news; I think that you would get combinations amongst papers much more extensively than you have now. The Committee may be aware

Mr. *H. Cole.* — 3 June 1851

aware that some of the papers join together in league to keep other papers out of their expresses. At the time that the "Daily News" reduced its price to 3*d.*, there was a league among all the morning papers not to allow the "Daily News" to share in those expresses. If the stamp were taken away, I think it would be very desirable to have a short copyright, very short, say six hours. I think it would be quite sufficient; but I think it would deteriorate the character of the press if you allowed everybody to plagiarise instantly those who had obtained information at very great cost.

2764. Would it not give rise to many vexatious prosecutions?—I think not.

2765. Mr. *Rich.*] Without such copyright there would be universal piracy, would there not?—A great deal more than would be wholesome for the public.

2766. Mr. *Ewart.*] Do not you think that the effect of the reduction proposed would be to increase very much the number of local newspapers, as is the case in America?—No doubt; I think that a reduction of the duty would lead to a much freer establishment of newspapers, such as the public wanted; as to the superseding the desire for metropolitan news——

2767. My question referred to an increase in the number of local newspapers?—Certainly there would be an increase.

2768. Mr. *G. A. Hamilton.*] How would you define copyright; would you prohibit the publication of an exact copy of the news, or the substance of the news?—That is a question which requires a great deal of consideration in the answer. I think it would not be difficult to draw a line that should prevent people from being pirates.

2769. Mr. *Ewart.*] Has not such a line been drawn by the introduction of what is called the registration of designs, under a Bill introduced by Sir Emerson Tennent, and by which a short duration of copyright was given to inventions of a fleeting character?—The cases are precisely analogous, and the most remarkable effects upon the honesty of manufacturers has been produced by that Designs Bill, as well as giving great encouragement to designers, and conferring a great benefit on the designs themselves.

2770. Mr. *G. A. Hamilton.*] You say that the cases are analogous; the Copyright of Designs Bill requires, I think, that the design should be registered?—Yes.

2771. And there can be no publication of that design after it has been registered?—No.

2772. Would you require news to be registered; considering how necessary it is that news should be speedily circulated, would

Mr. *H. Cole.*

3 June 1851.

would you prohibit the publication of news for a certain time after the registration of the copyright?—I think measures might be taken to enable proprietors of newspapers to show that they were the first in the field in possession of a particular piece of news; and you might protect them from a flagrant piracy of that news for a few hours; say six hours after the registration.

2773. Mr. *Ewart.*] Would it not be very difficult to define so transient an article as news?—I think it is not at all difficult to prohibit an actual barefaced copy, though the extent to which you would allow other labour to be employed upon the facts taken is a very nice question.

2774. *Chairman.*] It would be for the press, if they had any reason to complain that the law was not adequate to prevent piracy, to come forward and make such proposals as they thought necessary for the purpose?—Yes.

2775. Mr. *Rich.*] Do you think that the press generally would submit to so stringent a law?—I think they would; I think that all the honest press which pays for the news would claim it, and I think that the dishonest would be kept in check by common sense.

2776. *Chairman.*] There are pirates now, and it is only a question of degree whether there would not be rather more pirates then than there are now?—The Committee are aware that now it is piracy in law to take half a dozen lines verbatim from a newspaper; and if it were the interest of people to go to law upon that subject, they would go to law; but the law, in point of fact, recognises such a piracy.

2777. Mr. *Rich.*] At present newspapers do not suffer great practical injury from piracy, do they?—I should say not, broadly speaking; there are some papers which live avowedly by piracy; but it is a satisfactory sign that they are not very much encouraged.

2778. But were the stamp taken off, you think that the number would be so considerably increased as to require rather a stringent law?—A somewhat easier law than exists at present; a law by which a remedy should be more readily obtained than going to Chancery or the Queen's Bench.

2779. Mr. *G. A. Hamilton.*] Does not it appear to you that any restriction of that kind would operate materially as a restriction upon news?—Not in the least; I think it would offer a very great premium for getting the best news. I should think that if news were made more valuable, it would encourage all those who already collect it at great cost, to collect

it

Mr. *H. Cole.*

3 June 1851.

it at still greater cost; and I think that that cost would be divided among a greater number of people.

2780. Take the case of a newspaper having an agent on the Continent; another newspaper having also an agent perhaps in the same place, would not the apprehension of the one agent that the other might transmit intelligence a few hours before himself, operate as a check upon the publication of a second account?—Not at all; you never find that two people do the same thing precisely alike. There would be such a marked difference, and there always is. For instance, if you take the reports of a Member's speech in the House in two newspapers, two pairs of ears listening to precisely the same facts, each represent it so differently that there is inherent evidence that they do not copy one from the other. It is most difficult for any two persons to concur in representing any fact, however precise, in precisely the same form.

2781. You would allow them to publish the same facts, if not in the same form?—Yes; I should give no copyright in "facts," certainly.

2782. Mr. *Rich.*] How would you maintain your law?—The public would settle the matter for themselves. If you gave a short copyright, say for three hours only, the party who really obtained the news would have the ear of the public before the pirate, at least three hours before the pirate; physically, the pirate could not very well get at it, and if you put even a very little impediment in his way, the public would soon determine all the questions unsolved for themselves.

2783. *Chairman.*] When the piracy began have you any doubt, if it were necessary, that it could be dealt with?—Not the slightest.

2784. Mr. *S. Adair.*] In respect of the metropolitan press, your copyright would be a defence against third editions. For instance, a newspaper states that its publication commences at such an hour; a third edition of another paper is published, say five or six hours afterwards; and unless the time has expired which you assign as the limit of the copyright, it would have no right to publish any portion of that which was contained in the impression of which I spoke at first?—Not without its leave.

2785. Mr. *G. A. Hamilton.*] Did you not state that, in your opinion, the character of the press would be deteriorated by taking off the stamp, unless copyright were provided?—That would require rather a long answer. I said at first that I thought the character of the press is very much influenced by the tone of society; I think that the tone of society, now especially,

Mr. *H. Cole.*

3 June 1851.

especially, is against piracy; it is considered improper, and therefore, though I should expect if you took off the tax without giving a copyright, that you would for some time have a horde of pirates striving to struggle into existence, I think that society in the long run would more or less put them down. I think that there would be an advantage in having the copyright simultaneously with the reduction.

2786. Mr. *Rich.*] Then you abandon your opinion as to the necessity of a law against piracy, do you not?—No, I do not abandon my opinion; I think it a desirable thing. If you ask me whether I would like to have the stamp off newspapers with or without a copyright, I should say "with a copyright." But if you say, "You shall have it without a copyright," I should say, "I am thankful, but I should be better satisfied with a copyright." If the press and the interests connected with the press were tightly pinched by the consequences, they would find a remedy.

2787. Would not the existence of this copyright tend to lodge a great power in the hands of newspapers?—I think not.

2788. Would not the gaining of this early and exclusive intelligence tend to increase their circulation?—Certainly; but it is open to anybody to procure it.

2789. It would be open to anybody after six hours delay? —I mean the first getting at the intelligence, not after the copyright. It is as free to you or to me, if disposed to do so, to go to Calcutta for information, just as much as to the "Times."

2790. But certain papers having obtained a position in the country, and having large capital and considerable experience at their command, would be more likely to maintain their ascendency, would they not, than any individual struggling against them without being protected by this law of copyright? —Being already in the field, they would have that advantage no doubt.

2791. Would not that advantage be increased by a law of copyright?—No.

2792. Would such straggling papers be enabled to maintain their existence without it; you say that a paper would be able to publish intelligence by going to the expense of sending to Calcutta for it?—So far as the present press are already existing, and experienced and practised in the way of getting information from Calcutta, they would have that advantage. But it is open to anybody else to do it, and to bring better if they can; therefore there is nothing in that. Then, as respects the law of copyright, I would say, that if the "Times" got its

Mr. *H. Cole.* — 3 June 1851.

its information from Calcutta, and had been at all the trouble and cost of it, I would not allow anybody to pilfer that information within some short period of time.

2793. *Chairman.*] After the paper is purchased from the paper manufacturer it has to be sent to the Stamp Office to be stamped before news can be printed upon it, has it not?—Yes.

2794. Consequently you could not combine the paper making and printing, so as to carry them on in one establishment, whilst the stamp exists; but could it be done if the stamp were removed?—I believe the time will come when, if paper makers are not compelled to cut their paper into sheets for the convenience of stamping, you will have paper making and printing going on under the same roof.

2795. Would you say that the maintenance of the stamp prevents mechanical improvements?—Certainly.

2796. Mr. *S. Adair.*] Did not your previous answer refer rather to the excise upon paper?—It applies to the excise to some extent, and it applies also to the stamp, it being necessary to have the paper cut into certain sheets that the stamps may be put upon them; but there is every reason to think that in the progress of printing, the type will be printed from cylinders continuously on sheets of paper; and one impediment to doing that at present is the necessity of having the sheets cut up and sent down to the Stamp Office.

2797. They would be able to print many more in an hour if it could be done continuously, than by the other operation, would they not?—Vastly more. Mr. Rowland Hill invented a machine somewhat in principle like the present "Times" machinery. The type was placed round the cylinder, and the cylinder had a continuous motion. It is intended always to roll, and to give an impression like the calico printing. That was done, I think, in anticipation of the tax being altogether taken away. It was just at that period; but the maintenance of this 1 *d.* tax, and compelling the sheets to be cut up, prevent that improvement going on.

2798. *Chairman.*] It wars against a paper that is a very cheap paper, depending upon an extensive circulation?—Certainly.

2799. Because it is necessary, in order to give news, that it should be struck off rapidly?—Certainly.

2800. The circulation could not be obtained which is necessary for a cheap paper, could it?—I would not quite say that it tends in that direction strongly at present. The "Times" machine enables you to get very numerous impressions in an hour;

Mr. *H. Cole.*

3 June 1851.

hour; but a printing press that had not breaks in its cylinder like the "Times" cylinder, but where the type was always continuous would go on with much greater rapidity, and to that extent the stamp operates as a drag upon all improvements in rapid printing.

2801. You state that you have been more or less familiar with this subject for the last 25 years, and that you have given your attention to it ever since Mr. Chadwick commenced the agitation. Did you ever hear anybody give any clear definition of what the thing is that is liable to the tax, the news?—If you take the statute itself, and lawyers differ very much upon it, you find that during the 25 years there has been every conceivable twisting and turning to evade the tax. I have attempted to show that the first intention, or at all events the declared intention was, that it should not be considered a tax, but that it should be a postage.

2802. But still it only applies to a certain thing; it is a postage regulation if you please, but it is a postage regulation affecting only things that contain news; therefore it is still necessary to define this news which brings a publication under the operation of the Act?—So difficult is it to define "news," that I think if you attempted to carry out the principle fairly you would have to put the penny tax upon every sheet of paper that is printed, certainly upon every periodical publication: there is not a single periodical publication which does not find it necessary in some way or other to comment upon passing events or to state passing events; therefore the only way of honestly carrying out the tax would be to tax every sheet of paper, every printed sheet of periodical literature.

2803. You would say, would you not, that a thing so difficult of definition as news, is not a fit subject for a tax?—I should not put it upon the mere ground of the technical difficulty of applying it, but upon the much higher ground of the great impolicy of it.

2804. Even if it were not impolitic to do it, would it not be technically extremely difficult?—I think it would be next to impossible to do it fairly without a positive tax upon every sheet of periodical literature, in fact upon almost every book. If the phase of the law is adopted, that you must not speak of passing events, every book, if it looks to have any publicity at all, must speak of passing events.

2805. You must not speak of passing events unless your price is above 6 *d.*, or the paper is above two sheets; it is the smaller publications that are not allowed to comment on passing events?—That is one difficulty of the law; but according

Mr. *H. Cole.*

3 June 1851.

ing to some interpretations of the law the "Quarterly Review" would be a newspaper. If the Committee read the opinions expressed by the judges the other day, it will be seen that they questioned whether any periodical publication could speak of an event of yesterday without being subject to the tax; at all events it was thrown out as a doubt whether they ought not to be taxed.

2806. Do you think that the maintenance of the stamp upon newspapers tends to prevent the publication of libellous matter?—Not in the least. I might call the attention of the Committee to the fact that our press was much more libellous when the stamp was highest than it is now when it is lowest; that is a fact which cannot be disputed; the "John Bull" and similar papers were much more fruitful and lively in personal libels 20 years ago, when we had a fourpenny stamp, than now.

2807. Mr. *Rich.*] You assigned general reasons in your evidence why the tone of the press had become ameliorated independently of that?—Yes.

2808. *Chairman.*] The preambles of one or two of these various Acts which are consolidated into the present Newspaper Stamp Act, set forth, as the ground for imposing the stamp, that it was to prevent not only private libels, but public libels and seditious writings of a character likely to create contempt for the institutions of the country. Do you believe that the maintenance of this last penny in the least degree operated to carry out the intentions of those ancient legislators?—Not at all. The Committee are perhaps aware when the stamp tax was first introduced, that the greatest advocate for the stamp was Dean Swift, who was the greatest libeller this country has ever seen. I will read this passage from Lord Brougham, which expresses my own views on the tax preventing libels: "I have always considered that the laws made to restrain the press, though intended to check libel, have a very obvious tendency to lessen the security against libel. Whatever makes the trade of a newspaper precarious, whatever exposes those who conduct it to greater hardships, to more oppressions than the rest of their countrymen endure, whatever singles them out from the rest of the community as a suspected and slighted or a maltreated class, a class for whom there is one law, one rule of conduct, there being another for the rest of the community, tends, *pro tanto,* to lessen the respectability of those who resort to that profession. Whatever makes them dependent more upon the caprice of prosecutors, whether public or private, whatever exposes

Mr. *H. Cole.*

3 June 1851.

exposes them more than the rest of their fellow-subjects to penal visitations of courts and magistrates in general, has a direct tendency to lessen the respectability of the profession, and of those who engage in it. In my time there have been two remarkable instances of injurious proceedings in this respect, the one by the law, the other by the practice of judges. I allude, first, to the making a conviction for a second offence (which was one of the Six Acts of 1819) punishable by banishment, though that has never been put in force; and I allude, next, to the tendency which has been observed on the part of several judges, (I am sorry to say it, but I am bound to give my opinion,) a tendency to consider that the editors of newspapers are not entitled to protection, when they complain of injuries to their character, in the same measure in which the rest of the community are entitled. I cannot conceive any course more effectual to destroy the respectability of a class of men than that a judge, when summing up to a jury on the trial of a cause in which the individuals of that profession complain of injury to their character by libel or slander, should treat them as though they were persons who had no right to complain of slander, who had no character to lose, and should direct the jury not to regard the character of those individuals as the subjects of judicial redress. When I was at the bar, I remember a case of the editor of a newspaper prosecuting another editor for one of the foulest libels I ever read; and the learned judge who tried the cause, and who is now no more, said it was only the editor of a newspaper who had been libelled, and therefore he did not think it a case for conviction, though it would have been quite an undefended cause, and the conviction a matter of course, if any other person had been prosecutor. There was an acquittal accordingly; just as if a newspaper editor may be with impunity slandered by any one who chooses. I cannot imagine any principle more directly tending to lower the character of those in whose hands the press is (meaning by the press the newspaper press), and to throw that press into the hands of persons disreputable and capable of abusing its power by dealing in libel, either for lucre of gain, or to gratify private malice."

2809. It would appear that Lord Brougham, when Lord Chancellor, was against taking the especial securities against libels on the part of newspaper proprietors, and objected to singling them out particularly from the rest of society as persons who should be subject to such restrictions?—Certainly.



Mr.

Mr. *William Henry Smith*, called in; and Examined.

Mr. *W. H. Smith.*

3 June 1851.

2810. Mr. *Rich.*] YOU are a Distributor of Newspapers for the London Press, are you not?—Yes, a Newspaper Agent.

2811. Have you been long so?—For upwards of 60 years my house has been carrying on the business.

2812. Do you carry on a considerable business?—A very large one.

2813. What proportion of the London daily papers do you consider that you transmit to the provinces?—About one-seventh of all that are published in London.

2814. Of all the daily papers?—Yes.

2815. Can you give a rough estimate of the number?—I should think that the circulation of the daily papers scarcely exceeds 60,000.

2816. Of those you transmit about one-seventh, do you not?—Yes.

2817. In London and in the provinces?—Chiefly in the provinces; to a very small extent in London; my circulation is chiefly confined to those persons who may be coming to town for a season.

2818. Do you transmit much of the weekly press also?—A smaller proportion than of the daily papers by far.

2819. What proportion do you imagine of the newspapers which are sent to the provinces is sent through the Post Office?—It would be difficult to say what proportion of the newspapers generally is sent through the post; but in the first instance a very small proportion of the morning papers is sent through the Post Office; the majority are sent by railway trains to large towns in the country.

2820. Will you explain how they are sent, and the cost of sending them?—We obtain the papers at an early hour, about five o'clock in the morning, from the offices by carts; they are then made up in parcels for the principal towns, and we dispatch them by the first trains, at six or half-past six; then a second dispatch is made by the Post Office to the country villages, chiefly in the neighbourhood of large towns, and to distant parts of Scotland which are not reached by the parcels, and the dispatch of the morning papers then ceases. In the evening the papers are made up chiefly in single copies for the distant parts of the country; but the second editions are forwarded also by parcels to the large towns, in order to save the expense of a halfpenny postage which is charged by the Post Office, and to ensure an earlier delivery.

2821. Mr.

Mr. *W. H. Smith.*

3 June 1851.

2821. Mr. *Ewart.*] Paying the postage is the exception, not the rule?—Yes, in the first instance.

2822. Mr. *Rich.*] With regard to the daily papers sent to the great towns with which the railways communicate, they receive them very rapidly, and at no additional cost whatever to the receivers?—Scarcely any; the cost is paid by the agent in the country, who is glad to make an arrangment for receiving them by train, in order to attract to himself the whole of the business of the district; the cost averages a farthing a paper.

2823. It has been stated to this Committee, that at Manchester and some of the larger towns, a charge is made of a penny for the early delivery of the "Times" or other morning papers, as soon as the train arrives; do you imagine that practice prevails to any extent?—Certainly not in the large towns.

2824. Generally persons receive their early "Times" newspaper for 5*d.* do they not?—If they are disposed to pay promptly for the paper. But where a person takes long credit, in fact here in London, a higher price would be charged; but the agents in Manchester would all of them be very glad to supply the "Times" at a fraction over 5*d.* per copy, or 1 *l.* 13*s.* 6*d.* a quarter, if paid in advance.

2825. To their regular subscribers?—Yes.

2826. Mr. *Cobden.*] Do they deliver them for that?—They do.

2827. Mr. *Rich.*] Are you aware whether the railway companies are in the habit of transmitting newspapers to individuals living on the line, or near the line, where large masses of papers cannot be sent?—The North-western Railway Company, the Great Western, the South-eastern, and two or three other companies, charge a guinea per annum for a single newspaper, and half a guinea additional for every extra paper put in the same packet and conveyed to certain stations, and delivered by the clerks to persons residing within a reasonable distance of the line.

2828. Then two papers sent to an individual living near a railway station, would be received from London at a cost of not more than a halfpenny?—Not more than that. The cost in bulk, in sending large quantities to Manchester and Liverpool, is scarcely a farthing a copy.

2829. With regard to that portion of the press which is partly stamped and partly unstamped, such as the "Athenæum" and the "Builder," are any unstamped copies of those papers sent to the great towns in parcels?—The "Athenæum" and the

Mr. *W. H. Smith.*

3 June 1851.

the "Builder," and some other publications, are sent extensively to Manchester and Liverpool, and always blank copies are sent, because the conveyance is much cheaper than the posting charge of a penny would be.

2830. Does a regular subscriber to the "Athenæum" at Manchester receive his "Athenæum" unstamped at Manchester at the same price as he would receive it at his house in town?—Yes; but he has this disadvantage, that he cannot send it off again; a stamp would enable him to send it to any friend in the country; it is mostly filed; but with regard to newspapers, after they are read in the first instance, they are forwarded almost invariably to other persons to read.

2831. Mr. *Ewart.*] Would the Post Office have time to examine whether the stamp was attached to the paper if it was sent to a friend?—Probably not; but the clumsy way in which a person not accustomed to it would fold it up, would attract attention probably.

2832. Mr. *Rich.*] From your experience in the transmission of newspapers, have you found it to be a very great convenience to the middle classes to have the power of re-transmitting the newspapers?—It is carried on to a most enormous extent, and it reduces the cost of the paper to those least able to pay for it, to a perfectly wonderful extent; I have no doubt that every daily paper published in London is read by three or four distinct persons.

2833. By means of this re-transmission practically, the cost of the "Times" to each individual is reduced to a penny or 2 *d.*?—I know a case quite well; I was in the country, and a clergyman told me that the "Times" only cost him a penny. It was forwarded first and read at a news-room in Norwich; it was sent off from that room in the afternoon to some person residing in that city, and next morning forwarded by the Post Office to a village about eight or nine miles off, and then it travelled round the country in two or three quarters.

2834. Should you say that this class of persons was very numerous?—I should think so; exceedingly numerous.

2835. And by them the charge of a penny for each re-transmission would be felt as a considerable tax?—It would; it would operate in fact to prevent them probably from taking a paper at all, unless it was a weekly paper.

2836. By that means, although if the penny stamp were taken off, and although the number of newspapers published might be increased, yet it would not necessarily follow that the number of persons reading the newspapers would be so largely increased?—Certainly not.

2837. Mr.

Mr. *W. H. Smith.*

3 June 1851.

2837. Mr. *Ewart.*] Would not the taking off of the stamp duty lead to the establishment of a great number of local newspapers in different parts of the country?—It might do so, and probably would do so, in some of the smaller towns.

2838. Therefore, in that direction, there would be greater facilities given?—They would still require postal communication to bring the papers into those remote districts.

2839. Mr. *Cobden.*] You have mentioned the case of a gentleman who receives the "Times" paper for one penny, how old must the "Times" be before it is reduced to the value of a penny?—I can hardly speak of the value of the "Times" when it reached him; it cost him only a penny.

2840. How many days old must a paper be before it sinks to the value of a penny?—He received it the second morning after publication.

2841. After it had gone through several hands?—Three persons; an incalculable number in the first instance, because it went to the news-room, and then to a private individual.

2842. Probably it was not the cleaner for the number of hands it had gone through?—This was a news-room in which no kind of refreshment was allowed. It was a perfectly clean paper.

2843. I presume that the reason why this individual was content with the "Times" paper two days old was, that it was not convenient for him to pay the price for a new paper, or on the day of publication?—Yes, I have no doubt that was so.

2844. Otherwise, I presume this gentleman shared the common feelings of our nature, namely, that he would have liked to have his news at an earlier date?—No doubt, if he could have had as good an article for what he paid for it.

2845. You stated, did you not, that newspapers were transmitted very frequently through the post?—I think ultimately there is scarcely a newspaper published in London which is not transmitted through the post.

2846. Did you not state that the London daily papers were transmitted more than once through the post, generally?—On the average, I should think that the London daily papers are transmitted at least three times through the post; between twice and three times; I can hardly say exactly.

2847. Supposing that the compulsory stamp were removed from newspapers, you would contemplate, I presume, that there would be cheaper newspapers published than at 5*d.*?—Probably there would be.

2848. You are aware, are you not, of the existence of many unstamped

Mr. *W. H. Smith.*

3 June 1851.

unstamped publications enjoying a very good character in families, such as the "Family Herald," with an enormous circulation?—Yes.

2849. The Committee have been informed that 200,000 copies of the "Family Herald" are circulated for a penny each, weekly?—Yes.

2850. Do you think that there would not be equally cheap newspapers published if there were no stamp?—I do not think it would be possible to provide newspapers to meet the taste of the public, unless they fell very greatly, for a penny.

2851. Would you consider it probable that a newspaper might be published for 2 *d.* without a stamp?—If it borrowed extensively from other newspapers; but it would not be possible to publish a newspaper to the full as good a paper as the "Times" for less than the difference which the stamp would make.

2852. Mr. *Rich.*] That is, a penny difference?—Yes; for 4 *d.*

2853. Mr. *Cobden.*] Do not you think that the daily newspapers would be published at all prices, from a penny upwards, to suit the different classes of people, if there were no stamp?—I think that attempts would be made, but unless the tone of the press were lowered very extensively, those attempts would fail.

2854. Do you think it impossible to have a cheaper article maintaining a respectable tone; for instance, what is your opinion of the tone of that penny publication called the "Family Herald?"—The "Family Herald" is altogether distinct from a newspaper, it contains a number of scraps very well got up; it is respectably done, and there are short articles, novels in point of fact, interesting and exciting matter, both very cheap and got up without any regard to the times, or those accidents which are inseparable from newspapers.

2855. But it avoids improper matter, does it not?—Yes.

2856. Will it not be to the interest of the publishers of a newspaper to maintain a high moral tone, if they wished for a large circulation in families?—I do not know that a newspaper avoiding improper matter, and preserving a high moral tone, would get a large circulation.

2856*. Do you think that the general taste is for low and immoral?—No, I do not; but I do not think it would be possible for a newspaper publisher, at a penny or 2 *d.*, to publish at a profit without pandering to a very immoral taste.

2857. You consider that newspapers would be published at all

all prices, from a penny upwards, but that the cheap ones would not be so respectable in their tone?—I think that attempts would be made to establish them; as shortly after the reduction of the stamp on newspapers an attempt was made to establish them at a very low price, but the attempt failed.

Mr. *W. H. Smith.*

3 June 1851.

2858. Supposing that the stamp were removed from newspapers, and that they were allowed to be transmitted through the post once on the payment of a penny, would not the revenue derived by the Post Office be comparatively very much greater than it is now in consequence of the papers going three or more times through the post for a penny?—I think not, because the newsvenders, into whose hands the first publication of a newspaper is confided almost entirely, would immediately contrive means by which the papers should be delivered at a very small cost, and we could derive a very profitable trade by conveying newspapers to any part of the United Kingdom for a halfpenny a copy.

2859. Are those papers which are sent off to individuals two or three days after they are published, sent to the towns, or sent to isolated houses or remote districts?—I think that the towns generally are supplied with information in the first instance, and the individuals in the towns, or the news-rooms in the towns, send those newspapers afterwards to the more remote districts, to villages and to persons living away from the large towns.

2860. You could not compete with the Post Office for the supply of isolated houses and remote villages, could you?—We should do it to a very great extent round Manchester; we could do it for, certainly, 15 miles.

2861. You did not speak of the immediate neighbourhood of Manchester when you said people were content with newspapers two days old, did you?—I have no doubt that there is a very great number of people residing in the immediate neighbourhood of Manchester who are content with papers in that way.

2862. Do you think that you could so compete with the Post Office as to prevent them purchasing their papers, and having them sent through the post?—We should not do it to prevent them purchasing their papers, but to get a profit out of the difference.

2863. And you would establish a successful competition with the Post Office?—Yes.

2864. Why do you not do that now?—Because the stamp of one penny conveys newspapers without any charge or expense to us at all, to all those districts; and unless we can

save

Mr. *W. H. Smith.*

3 June 1851.

save time, and therefore accomplish a business connexion, it is not to our advantage to pay the expense of transmitting those papers by railway.

2865. Would not the revenue of the Post Office be compensated if, instead of carrying a newspaper three times for one penny, they carried a newspaper only once?—I do not think that they would carry it once; I think that they would only take newspapers to those remote districts at a very great expense to themselves.

2866. You think that they would have none to transmit, in consequence of your successful rivalry?—I think that the general rivalry of persons engaged in the newspaper business would be such as to prevent the Post Office from carrying any newspapers for the postage charge of a penny to any town in England.

2867. Do you think that the Post Office revenue is derived chiefly from the fact of their carrying the same paper three times for a penny?—If you consider the stamp as a postage revenue it would be so.

2868. In fact, the Post Office is not getting a penny per newspaper for carrying, but only one-third of a penny?—Probably not.

2869. You think, do you, that they do not get more than one-third of a penny for carrying newspapers?—I think not.

2870. You are aware, are you not, that the stamp was not contemplated as a postage?—Probably it was not contemplated, but it is a very great indirect advantage to the public, because those persons who obtain a newspaper at a reduced price are not those who could afford to pay a higher price for it; they are content to take a little news for a small cost.

2871. Still looking at it as a Post Office revenue, so far as the Post Office derives any revenue from the carrying of newspapers, the Post Office would be indemnified if they carried only one-third that they do now, if they got one penny for each?—Probably they would; but I do not think that they would carry the number.

2872. Mr. *Rich.*] You have stated that ultimately the Post Office in reality carries all the newspapers; that you send them by railway or otherwise, first, but ultimately the Post Office take them up and deliver them to some person?—Yes.

2873. And thereby the Post Office fulfils the expectation held forth by Mr. Spring Rice in 1836, that it should transmit the newspapers for a penny?—Just so.

2874. *Chairman.*] It charges a penny in particular places, not universally. If a person wishes to transmit a paper from one

Mr. *W. H. Smith.*

3 June 1851.

one street in the west of London, to another street in London on the east, a penny is still charged for the postage, is it not? —Yes; that is an additional charge of a penny.

2875. Therefore it is only to keep the newsvenders out of towns that the Post Office gives this advantage?—To keep them out of London.

2876. Mr. *Rich.*] You stated that you sent them to the great towns, and that in the great towns many reading societies sent them on to other individuals?—Yes.

2877. You stated that you sent your newspapers to the great towns now by railway?—Yes.

2878. And those newspapers are sent from the individuals who read them there, to their subscribers in towns and other districts?—Yes.

2879. Those newspapers are put into the post in the great towns to which you have sent them?—They are put into the Post Office. Supposing that we send papers to Manchester; a large quantity of papers are read in Manchester, and by the afternoon a paper is posted by the individual who reads the paper to his friend 20 or 30 miles off, and they probably would be posted a second time by that person on the second day; that is the course pursued.

2880. Which duty is done by the Post Office, is it not?—Yes.

2881. You have stated that the "Times" newspaper, or a morning paper, was read on the second morning; do you mean 24 or 48 hours afterwards?—Forty-eight hours afterwards.

2882. You know, do you not, that a great number of persons take in papers which are published on alternate days?—Yes, a great number.

2883. Would not many persons prefer a daily paper a day old, receiving that paper every day, rather than a paper that they receive thrice a week only?—There is a large class who take in the three day papers which are published, such as reprints of the "Times," and others; in the first instance they always endeavour to get a second-hand paper in preference to a reprint; and if some difficulty arises so that they cannot find some person to join with them, they then take the three-day papers, reprints.

2884–8. Are you aware of the number of daily papers that were distributed by yourselves prior to the taking off of the duty in 1836?—I have a Table with me which will show.

[*The following Table was handed in:*]

RETURN

RETURN of DAILY PAPERS sent to *Liverpool* and *Manchester*.

| — | 31 Aug. 1836. Stamp 4 *d.* Price of Paper 7 *d.* | | 30 July 1837. Stamp 1 *d.* Price Reduced to 5 *d.* | | 1 July 1846. | | | 26 Jan. 1847. | 31 Jan. 1849. | 3 June 1851. | |
|---|---|---|---|---|---|---|---|---|---|---|---|
| | Times. | Other Papers. | Times. | Other Papers. | Times at 5 *d.* | Other Daily Papers at 5 *d.* | Daily News at 2½ *d.* | Daily News at 2½ *d.* | Daily News at 3 *d.* | Times at 5 *d.* | Other Papers at 5 *d.* |
| Liverpool - - - | 127 | 481 | 148 | 577 | 437 | 413 | 277 | 163 | 134 | 506 | 411 |
| Manchester - - | 88 | 543 | 117 | 606 | 734 | 504 | 290 | 235 | 180 | 848 | 434 |

The number in Manchester of the "Times" and other papers is 1,282 to-day, and a small number sent independently of our agency, probably 400 or 500 altogether between the towns. I should observe that the "Daily News" was published in 1846 at 2½ *d.*, and the number taken of the "Daily News" in Manchester, at that time, was 290. The number of papers taken at 5 *d.*, double the price, was 1,238.

2889. In what interval of time?—At the same time, in July 1846; and on the 26th of January 1847 it raised its price to 3 *d.* It had in the meantime lost the circulation of 65 copies in Manchester. It was raised again on the 1st of February 1849 to 5 *d.*, and between the date at which the first increase in the price was made from 2½ *d.* to 3 *d.* it lost a circulation of 55 copies; and on the 31st of January 1849, when it was still at 3 *d.*, the circulation in Manchester was 180 copies, distributed by ourselves.

2890. *Chairman.*] With respect to class publications, you stated that when they were stamped they had the same advantages as newspapers?—They have.

2891. But they are not obliged to stamp their whole impression?—No, they are not.

2892. But a newspaper is obliged to stamp its whole impression, is it not?—Yes.

2893. Do you think it right to give the same postal advantages to a class publication as to a newspaper; that the one should be obliged to stamp all its impressions, and the other only such a portion as it thinks fit?—I hardly wish to express an opinion upon that point, but the one always was published as a periodical not coming under the operation of the stamp laws; and they applied to the Government for permission to stamp, in order that it might pass through the Post Office at a very

Mr. *W. H. Smith.*

3 June 1851.

very small charge. The other is a newspaper coming under the stamp duty.

2894. As a matter of fact, in order that a newspaper may obtain its postal privilege, it is obliged to submit to a greater burthen than a class publication has to submit to in order to enjoy the same privileges, is it not?—I do not think it a burthen for a newspaper.

2895. Is it not a greater amount of tax, if it is obliged to stamp every copy in order that some may go by post, while the "Athenæum" for instance, is only obliged to stamp those that go by post, or those that it thinks fit to stamp: does not the "Times" thereby, for the postal privilege, submit to a greater charge than the "Athenæum"?—My own opinion is that the "Times" is in a more favourable position than the "Athenæum," in this respect, that a very large proportion of the "Times" circulation is sent by post.

2896. But they stamp that proportion that is not sent, do they not?—Yes; but I think that the proportion that is not sent by post is very inconsiderable.

2897. In the case of the "Athenæum" they can leave unstamped as many as they please; whereas in the other case they must stamp every copy, must they not?—Yes.

2898. Then as far as it goes the one is in a more disadvantageous position than the other?—If you could trace a copy of the "Times" to one individual, never passing through the post, then to that extent, and those numbers of the "Times" which might be used by a subscriber and never be used again, and never having occasion to pass though the post, the "Times" would be at a disadvantage, as compared with the "Athenæum."

2899. If it were an advantage, in point of fact, to stamp the whole impresssion rather than a part, would not the "Athenæum" do it, and would not "Punch" stamp every impression if it were an advantage to do so?—Probably it would; but the cases are not at all similar; the "Athenæum" and "Punch" are publications which are kept for reference and amusement, and the charge is so small weekly, but the "Times" is not.

2900. Mr. *Cobden.*] Do you think that "Punch" is kept for reference?—Yes; or to be torn up.

2901. *Chairman.*] In the first instance, you say that these newspapers are sent by railway?—Yes, they are.

2902. Then in the first instance the recipients would get them for a penny less if there were no stamp?—Probably they would.

2903. Would they not?—Yes, those that are sent by railway;

Mr. *W. H. Smith.*

3 June 1851.

way; that is, provided no other means existed of sending them than by post and paying a penny; but it would clearly be to the interest of a newsvender in any town, supposing he had a connexion in that town within his grasp, to get as high a price as he could, and he would probably charge something additional, but he does not do so now. If the "Times" was 4*d.*, and the postage charge was 1 *d.* in a small town, an additional 1 *d.* would be charged by the newsman in delivering it to his subscriber, because he would say, "You must pay that 1 *d.* if you have it through the post, and you shall pay it to me, because I convey it, and save you the trouble of delivery by post."

2904. Speaking of those large towns, Manchester and Liverpool, the first recipients of the "Times," if the stamp were removed, would get it from you for 1 *d.* less than they now get it?—Perhaps they would. I am not clear that they would, but probably they would, because there would be competition.

2905. You would be able to supply the first class of recipients for 1 *d.* less, would you not?—Yes; in Manchester and Liverpool.

2906. Is not that the most considerable class?—So far as we are concerned it is, decidedly.

2907. Which is the most numerous class?—Those who read the paper at second-hand.

2908. The man who receives it first, obtains it for 1 *d.* less? —Yes.

2909. Therefore, even supposing a postage to be paid, it is not at all clear that that postage charge is to be 1 *d.*, and the second man could get it for at least as small a price as he got it before, when the stamp was on?—I do not think that that is correct. These papers are taken by two or three parties together, and they pay the cost together; so that, if the paper being sent by post, costs 7 *d.* or 8 *d.*, instead of 5 *d.*, as it now does, it stands to reason, and it is perfectly clear, that the division of that 7 *d.* or 8 *d.* must be larger than that of 5 *d.* between the three or four persons.

2910. You began by saying, that first of all they were sent by railway to the large towns, and then that the parties who received them in the large towns transmitted them to other individuals by post?—Yes.

2911. With regard to that first case of transmission, the second recipients would stand in the same position as they did before, after the postage charge was put on, even though that postage charge was 1 *d.*; because the first person having got it for 1 *d.* less, the cost of the paper would be to the second person

Mr. *W. H. Smith.*

3 June 1851.

person just what it was before?—Yes; but he would be in this position, he would be required to put a stamp at the extra cost of 1 *d.* to himself, in sending it forward to the person who took it the second time.

2912. The charge would be the same, would it not?—The charge of the paper would be the same, but he would have to pay the postage stamp out of pocket.

2913. If *A.* had to send a paper to *B.*, and to stamp it, of course the charge to *B.* would be plus the stamp; I am supposing this to be a business transaction, and not a mere matter of fancy, but that parties arrange to take a paper in succession, would not the second receiver get it for the same charge as he does now?—The second receiver would.

2914. Can you inform the Committee what proportion of the whole recipients of the "Times" those third parties would be?—I cannot tell; I should think that the third recipients form a very large proportion.

2915. If the postage charge were a halfpenny instead of a penny, then the third recipient would still be in the same position as he is now, would he not?—Yes, he would be.

2916. And until you got to the fourth man there would be no increased charge?—Supposing the postage to be a halfpenny, but you would be carrying on a very large business.

2917. Mr. *Ewart.*] Do not you think that the effect of the removal of the stamp duty would be that those second and third parties, those ultimate parties whom the paper reaches at present, would be supplied with local papers?—I do not think there would be many local papers in the country; not daily papers.

2918. I mean local newspapers?—Almost every one who now takes a London paper, also sees a country paper.

2919. Did you not say that you thought the result would be that the local press would considerably increase?—So they would.

2920. Do not you think it is desirable that a person should be made acquainted with the news of his own neighbourhood, as touching him the most nearly?—It may be so; but I have always observed that the tendency of things is decidedly in favour of the London press; every change has been in favour of the London press.

2921. Sir *J. Walmsley.*] You have stated that certain papers are kept for reference; "Punch" and the "Athenæum"?—Yes.

2922. Have you ever formed any estimate as to the extent to which the "Times" is kept for reference?—I should think that

Mr. *W. H. Smith.*

3 June 1851.

that the "Times" is only kept for reference in public establishments, and by persons having frequent occasion to refer to what has been said and done in past years.

2923. And for general reference?—Yes.

2924. To what extent?—A very small extent, compared with the whole circulation.

2925. Have you any idea, comparing it with any other publication; you referred to "Punch" being kept for the purpose of reference; you would say, would you not, that the "Times" would be kept much more for the purpose of reference than "Punch"?—Yes; it is very unpleasant to say that the "Times" is not kept, being so much the better article; I think it is not.

2926. You are aware that all the City companies, a great number of solicitors, and a great many associations, keep the "Times," knowing its superior character, and containing information upon which they can rely as a book of reference? —I am afraid that if the individual cases in which the "Times" is kept for reference were calculated, they would be found to be exceedingly small as compared with its circulation.

2927. But to the extent that it is kept for reference, the "Times" is damnified by the penny stamp?—To that extent, whatever the extent may be; but it amounts to a very small per-centage upon the circulation of the paper.

2928. Mr. *Rich.*] The papers which you mentioned as being kept for reference publish indexes, do they not?—Yes, they do, but the "Times" does not.

2929. Do the "Athenæum" and "Spectator" publish indexes?—Yes, they do.

2930. *Chairman.*] You are a news agent, are you not?—Yes.

2931. Were the London news agents favourable to the reduction of the stamp on newspapers?—I think not, on the whole, on this ground, that in the last reduction a reduction of their profits was made; which was a very reasonable objection, and that reduction was not rapidly made up by the increase of business.

2932. They were unfavourable to the reduction of the stamp duty in 1836; do you suppose that a similar feeling would induce the London news agents, as a rule, to be unfavourable to the abolition of the stamp now?—I think that, as a body, the London newspaper agents would be unfavourable to it now. As an individual, and considering only my own interests, I should strongly desire it; because, having a very large business already in those manufacturing towns, it would concentrate

concentrate that business still more in my own hands, and I could afford to convey newspapers for very much less than the Post Office, let them do what they choose.

2933. The feeling among the newsvenders is, that the first effect is to create a loss of profit, and that it takes time, by an increase of business, to replace that loss?—Yes, that would be the feeling of the trade; the feeling generally would be, with any small newspaper agent, that the means in the hands of a person doing a large business would be such as to enable him to take away the business of the smaller agents.

2934. Mr. *Rich.*] It appears by a Return to the House of Commons, that the London press increased, from 1841 to 1848, from 100 to 150 newspapers, and the number of advertisements from 658,114 to 863,888; while the provincial newspapers increased only from 223 newspapers to 238, with 723,744 advertisements in 1841, and 804,268 in 1848. If the increase of the London press, under the reduction of the duty which took place in 1836, has been so great in proportion to that of the provincial press within those seven years, do not you think that the London newsvenders would generally feel that any further reduction would tend to increase the London press, and thereby increase their business and improve their interests?—I think newspaper agents generally would not; because, as I mentioned before, it would confine the business in the hands of those persons who have influence enough to supply the large towns, and all the towns in the kingdom, at a less cost than the Post Office would charge; therefore the tendency of any change of that kind would be to concentrate the business into fewer hands.

2935. Mr. *Cobden.*] You stated, did you not, that the whole circulation of the daily press in London was 60,000?—I have estimated it at that.

2936. Is that of morning and evening papers?—Yes; I have taken the two together.

2937. What proportion of them should you take to be of the evening press, and what of the morning press?—I think the circulation of the evening press can scarcely exceed 9,000.

2938. Then you would consider the circulation of the morning newspaper press to be a little over 50,000?—Quite that.

2939. It was stated in evidence by the gentlemen who conducts the "Times," that their circulation is 39,000?—It is so, no doubt.

2940. Do you consider that the whole of the other morning papers,

Mr. *W. H. Smith.*

3 June 1851.

papers do not publish more than 12,000?—I am afraid they do not, or not much more; I should be sorry to say anything that would be considered erroneous.

2941. Have you any means of knowing what the circulation has been within the last 10 years; has the circulation of the daily press increased much since the stamp was reduced to a penny?—The circulation of the "Times" has increased enormously, but the circulation of the other papers has gradually decreased in every case. With regard to the circulation of the other morning papers in Manchester and Liverpool, there are fewer now by a great deal than there were in 1836.

2942. That is to say, there are fewer "Heralds," and "Posts," and "Chronicles," and "Advertisers," sent to Manchester now than there were in 1836?—Yes, the only exception is in favour of the "Advertiser," and that is because it has employed a sporting editor.

2943. All the competitors of the "Times," with the exception of the "Advertiser," have fallen off in circulation since 1836?—Very much indeed.

2944. Mr. *Ewart.*] Will you give the Committee the ratio of the increase on the one hand, and the decrease on the other?—I find that in 1836 there were 481 other papers circulated in Liverpool, copies of all the other papers besdes the "Times;" and in Manchester 543. Now in the two towns of Manchester and Liverpool the total number circulated of the other papers is 806, and of the "Times" 1,282. The circulation of other papers in Liverpool and Manchester together was 1,024, and it has fallen to 806; while the "Times" has risen from 215 to 1,282.

2945. Mr. *Cobden.*] Taking the total circulation of the London daily press, has there been an aggregate increase during the last 15 years?—There has been, decidedly.

2946. To what extent do you suppose the circulation of the London daily press has increased since the stamp was reduced? —I think they may have increased by at least one-third since the stamp duty was reduced.

2947. And that one-third has been wholly absorbed by the "Times"?—Entirely, and more.

2948. Has the circulation of evening papers diminished since the establishment of railroads generally?—It has. I should say that the number I have given the Committee includes the evening papers also; so that the number I have now mentioned, namely 806, is the total number of all the other papers, morning and evening, circulated in Mauchester and Liverpool.

2949. Then

*Mr. W. H. Smith.*

3 June 1851.

2949. Then the "Times" paper circulates more than all the other papers, morning and evening?—Yes.

2950. Has there been a falling off in the circulation of the evening press since railroads were generally established?—Yes.

2951. People take in the morning papers instead of the evening?—Yes, they do; they get them in Birmingham at eleven, in Manchester at two, and in Liverpool at two o'clock.

2952. The gentleman who conducts the "Times" stated to the Committee that the publication of the supplement had been attended the day before with no profit to them, for the cost of the paper, the printing, and the stamp, just amounted to the sum that was paid for advertisements; and he stated that they found it necessary to discourage the sale of the "Times" newspaper, for if the sale continued to an indefinite extent, the proprietors would be involved in serious loss; do you encounter any difficulty in obtaining the "Times," owing to their discouraging the sale?—We know nothing of the reasons which prevent us from obtaining the papers.

2953. Do you experience, at times, a difficulty in getting as many as you wish?—Very frequently.

2954. The difficulty that is avowed is, that they have not time to print them?—Yes, that is it; and in most cases I believe it is so.

2955. They have not time to print as many as they have a demand for?—Yes; we require about 5,000 copies of the "Times" before six o'clock, when a very much smaller number would suffice us for any other paper; and it is sometimes difficult to get 5,000 copies printed before six o'clock.

2956. You do, practically, encounter a difficulty in getting as many as you wish?—Quite so.

2957. *Chairman.*] They can always print at the same rate, can they not?—Not always; they have a new vertical machine which will print at the rate of 10,000 an hour, but if any accident happens to that machine, they have the old machines to go upon.

2958. But barring accidents they can always print at the same rate?—Yes.

2959. Sometimes upon particular occasions, as for instance, when the exhibition was opened, you were able to obtain a very greatly increased number of the "Times," were you not?—It was remarkable that on that morning the "Times" was later in going to press than usual, and we were unable to get what we required in the first instance; after the trains had gone, the increased numbers were useless to us.

 2960. Why

Mr. *W. H. Smith.*

3 June 1851.

2960. Why should they at one time be unable to give you this increased supply that you wish for, if they have been able to furnish it at another; you are aware that upon particular occasions, when there is some event of great public interest, the whole number of impressions is very much greater?—Yes.

2961. Then inasmuch as the "Times," barring accidents, can always print, if it pleases, at the same rate, why at one time should you be able to obtain an increased quantity when you cannot do so at another?—The "Times" will always supply to the ordinary number, as soon as they possibly can, for the subscribers, but any extra demand is placed behind other orders, and will only be supplied, probably, in the order in which the demand is created; consequently if the paper itself is late in going to press, the extra demand would not be supplied in time to render it of any service to you.

2962. However, practically it is a fact that you sometimes cannot get as many of the "Times" as the public would buy of you?—Quite so.

2963. Mr. *Rich.*] If, as it has been stated, the "Times" loses upon its supplement when it exceeds the number of 39,000, it would naturally be to their interest to print with so little expedition that their general delivery should not exceed very much that amount?—Yes, but I think it is very rarely done; there may occasionally be obstacles in the way.

2964. If it is so, it is a proof that there is an outstanding demand for the "Times" greater than the "Times" is able to gratify?—Yes, on occasions of extraordinary interest it is so.

2965. But if the duty were taken off the stamped newspapers generally, it would enable the "Times" to publish more than those 39,000 copies, which is the limit at which it, supplement can now be published profitably, would it not?—It would do so, but the charge would be 4 *d.*, and in such a case they would get the profit of the halfpenny, which they now pay as a stamp on the supplements. The difference of the halfpenny would make the thing profitable.

2966. If there is this outstanding demand already for the "Times," would not the taking off of the duty on newspapers be more beneficial to the "Times" than any other newspaper, inasmuch as it would find a body of persons ready to take it who at this moment can hardly get it?—It would apply chiefly to occasions of great interest and importance. I take it that those who would be ordinary subscribers, are already supplied regularly; but on occasions of great importance an extra demand springs up for the "Times," and unfortunately there is scarcely any other paper that can be supplied.

2967. It

Mr. *W. H. Smith.*

3 June 1851.

2967. It has been stated that the demand for the "Times" occasionally is felt by those conducting it to exceed the supply that they are willing to give?—On particular occasions it is so.

2968. Therefore they would profit more, would they not, by taking off the duty than any other newspaper?—Yes, they would.

2969. Sir *J. Walmsley.*] You stated, did you not, that the circulation of the morning and evening papers amounted to 60,000?—It is an estimate that I have formed since I came into this room; I should think that it very little exceeds that number.

2970. You gave 39,000 for the "Times," 9,000 for the evening circulation, and 12,000 for the daily circulation?—Yes.

2971. Could you give the Committee the data upon which you arrived at that estimate?—There might be a difference of 2,000 or 3,000 in the number divided between the morning papers; I should be sorry to give my own opinion, unless the Committee requested it, as to the comparative circulation.

2972. Would a reduction in the price of a newspaper by the abolition of the penny stamp tend to increase the quantity circulated generally?—I think not, unless the price were reduced very much below 4 *d.*, which I think would be the first price.

2973. You do not think that the abolition of the penny stamp would have a material influence upon the increase and sale of papers?—The increase would not be great upon the present morning papers.

2974. Would the reduction be confined to the penny stamp, or would there be a greater reduction?—No newspapers can be published at present, such as the present morning papers, at less than the net amount which they now receive.

2975. If there were any great increase in the circulation in consequence of the reduction of the 1 *d.* stamp, seeing that the "Times," according to the evidence given before this Committee, has reached its maximum circulation, that increase must be shared among the other morning papers, must it not?—If the stamp were taken off altogether it would be taken off the supplements as well as off the "Times." The consequence of that would be that the "Times" would save the halfpenny which they now pay on the supplement, and be able to print the paper at a profit.

2976. Then the only limit to the circulation of the "Times" would be the quantity which they could throw off in a given time?—When an extra demand arose.

2977. That would be the only limit?—Yes.



Mr.

Mr. *Horace Greeley*, called in; and further Examined.

Mr. *H. Greeley*.

3 June 1851.

2978. *Chairman*.] WITH reference to the "Sun" paper, you stated in your last examination that the circulation was large, but that the profit derived therefrom was from the advertising?—The profit is nothing on the circulation. I will state how in our country, there being no duty on the advertisements, the prices are very much less for advertising. The prices range from 25 cents up to any amount, that is to say, 25 cents is the lowest; for instance, the advertisement of a religious meeting, or any public gathering, will be some 25 cents, or 1 *s.* of the money of this country; the consequence is that the amount of their advertisements is enormous. Every religious meeting, or meeting to take place of any religious society, benevolent or philanthropic, is advertised in all the journals, and forms a very large proportion of our receipts, though the receipts in each case are very small. We regard those as a portion of the news of the day; and advertising, which possesses a public interest, is done at a less price than advertisements intended for the pecuniary profit of the advertiser. Now an advertisement duty would destroy new papers. Its operation is this; your duty is the same on an advertisement in a journal where it is worth ten times as much, for instance, in a journal with 50,000 circulation, as in a journal with 2,000, although the value of the article is 20 times as much in the one case as in the other: the duty operates precisely as though you were to lay a tax of 1 *s.* a day on every day's labour that a man were to do; on a man's labour which is worth, say 2 *s.*, it would be destructive; while by that man who earns 20 *s.*, it would be very lightly felt. It would entirely destroy new papers. An advertisement is worth but a certain amount, and the public soon get an idea of what it is worth; you put a duty on advertising, and you prevent any advertisements coming to a new establishment. To those people who advertise in the "Sun" and our well-established journals, they could afford in charge a price to include the duty, and do very well; but in a new concern the advertisements would not be worth the amount of the duty, and the consequence would be that they would be utterly withheld. Now the advertisements are one main source of the value of daily papers, and thousands of business men take them in mainly for those advertisements. For instance, at one time, in New York, our auctioneers were appointed by law, and were of course party politicians, and one journal, which was high in the confidence of the party in power, obtained not a law but

Mr. *H. Greeley.*

3 June 1851.

but an understanding that all the auctioneers appointed should advertise in that journal. Now though that journal has ceased to be of that party, and the auctioneers are no longer appointed by the State, yet that journal has almost a monopoly of the auctioneers' business, because at a certain time all the auctioneers were obliged to advertise in that paper; consequently, all the men who buy and sell at auction were obliged to take the paper; and now, although the necessity has gone away, yet still every advertiser by auction must advertise in that journal, because he knows that purchasers are looking there, and every purchaser by auction must take that journal in, because he knows that the advertisements by auction will be there, without regard to the goodness of the paper, but simply because of its containing those advertisements, all the great dry goods interest, with the corresponding interests, must take that paper, and they continue to take it; and precisely in that way the advertising duty is an enormous help to any paper which has the most circulation; it tends to throw the advertising always on the greatest concern, and the persons who take, as I know men in this town do take, one journal mainly for its advertisements, must take the "Times," because everything is advertised there; consequently they do take it, and advertisers must advertise in it for the same reason. If we had a duty on advertisements now, I will say not only that it would be impossible to build a new concern up in New York against the competition of the older ones, but it would be impossible to preserve the weaker papers from being swallowed up by the stronger ones.

2979. Mr. *Cobden.*] Do you consider that the fact which you have heard stated, that the "Times" newspaper for the last 15 years has been increasing so largely in its circulation is to be accounted for mainly by the existence of the advertisement duty?—Yes; much more than by the stamp. The limited circulation of papers generally is caused by the stamp. But the advantage of any one journal must be caused by the advertising duty, which in effect is charging ten times as much for an advertisement in one paper as in another. An advertisement in the "Times" may be worth 5 *l.*, while in another paper it is worth only 1 *l.*, but the duty is the same.

2980. *Chairman.*] Then the advertisement duty must really destroy all the advertisements that are not worth the duty?—Yes, that and something more; you cannot publish them for nothing; the advertising duty not being graduated, it is the same as so much on each without regard to size.

2981. Mr. *Rich.*] The greater the number of comparatively

Mr. *H. Greeley.*

3 June 1851.

tively small advertisements in papers, the greater the advantage to their proprietors?—Yes; I should say, suppose the cost of a small advertisement to be 5*s.*, (the usual charge in the "Times,") if you have to pay 1*s.* or 1*s.* 6*d.* duty, it is not worth the duty in a journal with a fourth part of the circulation of the "Times."

2982. *Chairman.*] Your meaning is, with regard to the stamp, that the stamp wars against the advertisement duty, and that the advertisement duty wars against the stamp?—I say that the stamp duty wars against a greater circulation of newspapers, and the advertisement duty wars against all others in favour of one.

2983. Does not it appear to you inconsistent that if a Government is disposed to tax the press, it should impose two sorts of tax; the one tending to lessen the amount received from the other?—I should think that it tends that way.

2984. Both combine in keeping down the press, though one lessens the amount of revenue receivable from the other?—Yes.

2985. Mr. *Rich.*] If the one tends to prevent the existence of a leviathan paper, to that extent it would not tend to keep down the press, would it?—The one tends to throw all the business on one concern.

2986. But the other stamp duty has not that effect, has it?—I do not think it has particularly that effect.

2987. Then by that means it would not have so injurious an effect as the advertisement duty?—It would not have as unequal and as monopolising an effect as the advertisement duty.

2988. *Chairman.*] Supposing it is admitted that the Government has a right to tax the press, and there are three kinds of taxes on the press, first on the paper, then on the stamp, and then on the advertisements that are inserted in the paper, does not it appear to you that the operation of these taxes must be hostile to one another: in the first place, by lessening the circulation of the papers by means of the stamp duty, you diminish the consumption of paper, and therefore lessen the amount of paper duty; and secondly, by diminishing the number of papers sold through the stamp, you lessen the number of advertisements in the papers, and therefore the receipts from the advertisement duty?—I should say, that if the Government were simply as a matter of revenue to fix a duty, say of a halfpenny per pound, or something like that, on paper, it would be easily collected, and produce more money: and then a law

Mr. *H. Greeley.*

3 June 1851.

a law which is equal in its operation does not require any considerable number of officers to collect the duty, and it would require no particular vigilance, and the duty on paper alone would be most equal and most efficient as a revenue duty.

2989. It is clear then that the effect of the stamp and advertisement duty is to lessen the amount of the receipt from the duty on paper?—Enormously. I see that the circulation in London is but 60,000 against 130,000 in New York city, while the tendency is more to concentrate on London than on New York. Not a tenth part of the daily papers in the United States are printed in New York city.

2990. Mr. *Cobden.*] Do you consider that there are upwards of a million daily papers issuing from the daily press in the United States?—I should say about a million; I cannot say upwards. I think there are about 250 daily journals published in the United States.

2991. You would consider that there are a million of daily papers issuing from the press in the United States?—I think very nearly that.

2992. You stated that there are 15 daily papers in New York; how many are there in Boston?—Twelve, I think.

2993. What is the population of Boston?—Boston contains but about 140,000 inhabitants, but Massachussetts is much more compactly peopled and better supplied with railways. All the towns in Massachussets and in New England take more or less of the Boston daily papers.

2994. What number of daily papers are published in Philadelphia?—Philadelphia has 10, I think; they are not so many in number, but one or two have a much larger circulation.

2995. How many in Baltimore?—Six.

2996. How many in New Orleans, should you think?—Ten or 12, I think.

2997. At what amount of population of a town in America do they generally begin to have a daily paper; they first of all begin with a weekly paper, do they not?—Yes. With regard to newspapers, the general rule is this, that each county will have one; in all the Free States, if a county has a population of 20,000 it has two, one of each party; the general average is about one local journal in the agricultural counties for 10,000 inhabitants; a county containing 50,000 has five journals which are generally weekly papers; and when a town grows to have as many as 15,000 inhabitants, or thereabout, then it has a daily paper; sometimes that is the case when it has as few as 10,000; it depends more on the business of the place, but 15,000 may be stated as the average at which a daily

Mr. *H. Greeley.* 3 June 1851.

daily paper commences; at 20,000 they have two, and so on; in central towns like Buffalo, Rochester, Troy, and such towns, they have from three to five daily journals, each of which prints a semi-weekly or a weekly journal.

2998. Mr. *Rich.*] Have those papers much circulation outside the towns in which they are published?—The county is the general limit, though some pervade a judicial district including five or six counties.

2999. They do not penetrate into counties and towns in which other papers are published?—Not as a rule, but the Buffalo papers will have a circulation round Lake Erie, which is a country easily reached by them.

3000. Would the New York papers, for instance, have much circulation at Charleston?—The "New York Herald," I think, which is considered the journal the most friendly to southern interests, has a considerable circulation there.

3001. Independently of peculiar reasons, they would not circulate in the more distant States?—To a certain extent, the leading political journal of one party would be taken by the leading politicians in other States; and if it is a business journal, there is one I know particularly that has a very large circulation among the pork-buyers and the grain-buyers throughout the Free Western States, having relations with New York. They want fuller reports of the markets than those the telegraph brings them.

3002. Substantially, the newspaper of any of those States finds the bulk of its readers within its own State?—Yes; the Washington papers are an exception.

3003. The New Orleans papers would have but little circulation in New York, for instance?—No.

3004. Mr. *Ewart.*] The circulation is more local than in this country, is it not?—Yes.

3005. *Chairman.*] When a person proposes to publish a paper at New York, is he required to go to any office to register himself?—No, not at all.

3006. Is he required by law to give any security that he will not insert libels or seditious matter?—No.

3007. He merely publishes a paper at his own will and pleasure, without consulting any public authority?—Yes.

3008. If he should libel anybody in his paper, he would be liable to an action at law, would he not?—To two actions, civil and criminal.

3009. Then a newspaper publisher is not subject to any liability more than other persons?—No more than one starting a blacksmith's shop.

3010. They

Mr. *H. Greeley.*

3 June 1851.

3010. They do not presume, in the United States, that because a man is going to print news in a paper he is going to libel?—No, nor do they presume that his libelling would amount to much unless he is a responsible character.

3011. Mr. *Cobden.*] Are there not many actions brought in America for libel?—Very few indeed, unless founded on police reports, such as the report of a man being arrested on the charge of swindling, or the like of that.

3012. Are you not permitted by the law of America to publish the police reports?—No, it is not regarded as lawful even to say that John Jones was arrested for swindling; it is not a privileged publication; he might show a damage in that case and convict you, even though it was the fact that he was so arrested for swindling, unless you could prove that he was actually a swindler; that rule is derived from your courts.

3013. Mr. *Rich.*] Does that practically occur?—Yes, though it is very rare.

3014. Mr. *Cobden.*] From what you have stated with regard to the circulation of the daily press in New York, it appears that a very large proportion of the adult population must be customers for them there?—Yes, I think three-fourths of all the families take in a daily paper of some kind.

3015. The purchasers of the daily papers must consist of a different class from those in England; mechanics must purchase them?—Every mechanic takes a paper, or nearly every one.

3016. At what time does he buy his paper?—He subscribes to an office. The carrier of a paper is the owner of a certain ward of the city; it is a property of his own; on the "Sun" I have known one sold for 700 dollars; that is, the privilege of buying the papers at the office at 70 cents a hundred, and serving them to subscribers, and getting one dollar a hundred for them. In every particular ward of the city the carrier has a property in the right to receive the journals for the ward, and to distribute them in that ward.

3017. Then the working class receive their papers regularly through the carrier in the morning?—Yes.

3018. What time are they delivered in the morning?—Between six and seven as a rule.

3019. Do those people generally get them before they leave home for their work?—Yes, and you are complained of if you do not furnish a man with his newspaper at his breakfast; he wants to read it between six and seven usually.

3020. Then a shipbuilder, or a cooper, or a joiner takes in his daily paper in the morning, and reads it at his breakfast time?—

Mr. *H. Greeley.*

3 June 1851.

time?—Yes, and he may take it with him to read at his dinner, between 12 and one; but the rule is that he wants his paper at his breakfast.

3021. After he has finished his breakfast or dinner he may be found reading the daily newspaper, just as the people of the upper classes do in England?—Yes, if they do.

3022. And that is quite common, is it not?—Almost universal, I think. There is a very poor class, a good many foreigners, who do not know how to read, but no native, I think.

3023. Mr. *Ewart.*] To a working man, what is the cost of a newspaper?—He may obtain one for 3 *d.* a week, or a halfpenny a day.

3024. Mr. *Rich.*] Do the agricultural labourers read much? —Yes, they take our weekly papers, which they receive through the post generally.

3025. *Chairman.*] Is there any sending of papers from one person to another person; a person having bought a paper and read it, does he send it to a friend by post?—There has been a little of that; it is often done when there is a marriage or a death, or some piece of information that you want your friend to know in another country.

3026. It is not done for the purpose of economy, and to share the expenses of the paper between different persons?—No, they are so cheap that it is not worth while.

3027. Mr. *Rich.*] The transmission by post would be nearly as expensive as the cost of the paper, would it not?—Quite so, as they send them in separately, and the post offices do not like to receive them in that way.

3028. Mr. *Ewart.*] When you can get them so easily, you need not transmit them?—No.

3029. Mr. *Cobden.*] The working people in New York are not in the habit of resorting to public-houses to read the newspapers, are they?—Yes, they are, but not to read the papers.

3030. They resort to public-houses to drink spirits, or anything else?—A good many of them do; it is not the general practice, but still there are quite a class who do so.

3031. The newspaper is not the attraction to the public-house?—No; I think a very small proportion of our reading class go there at all; those that I have seen there are mainly the foreign population, those who do not read.

3032. *Chairman.*] Are there any papers published in New York, or in other parts, which may be said to be of an obscene or immoral character?—We call the "New York Herald" a very bad paper, those who do not like it; but that is not the cheapest.

3033. Have

Mr. *H. Greeley.*

3 June 1851.

3033. Have you heard of a paper called the "Town," published in this country, with pictures of a certain character in it, an unstamped publication; have you any publications in the United States of that character?—Not daily papers. There are weekly papers got up from time to time, called the "Scorpion," the "Flash," the "Whip," and so on, whose purpose is to extort money from parties who can be threatened with exposure of immoral practices, or for visiting infamous houses.

3034. Mr. *Ewart.*] Will you look at that paper (*The "Town" being handed to the Witness*)?—There was a class of weekly papers got up there that were printed for two or three months; I do not know of any one being continued any considerable time; if one dies, another is got up, and that goes down.

3035. They do not last, do they?—No, and I suppose they do not here; but the cheap daily papers, the very cheapest, are as a whole, I think, quite as discreet in their conduct and conversation as other journals; they do not embody the same amount of talent, they devote themselves mainly to news; they are not party journals, they are nominally independent, that is, of no party; they are not given to harsh language with regard to public men, they are very moderate.

3036. Is scurrility or personality common to the publications in the United States?—It is not common; it is much less frequent than it was, but it is not absolutely unknown.

3037. *Chairman.*] In the transmission of papers by post is a distinction made between newspapers and other printed matter?—There is a distinction; other printed matter goes by weight, two cents and a half being charged for the first ounce, and one cent for every succeeding ounce. I believe that is the rate of postage there; but it is reduced by the new law.

3038. There is a less rate of postage applied to newspapers than to other printed matter?—Yes.

3039. What do you call a newspaper; where do you draw the line between what comes under the postage rate and what is liable to a higher rate?—The rule has been that everything printed as often as once a week was a newspaper; the others are generally regarded as magazines and periodicals.

3040. If it is only printed once; for instance, supposing that you printed any particular fact in a paper published to distribute all through the country, would that come under the printed-matter rate, or under the newspaper rate?—If it had the appearance of a newspaper and was said to be published weekly,

Mr. *H. Greeley.*

3 June 1851.

weekly, of course it would come under the newspaper rate; but if not, or was not to be published as a periodical, it would be regarded as other printed matter. There is no carefulness about these matters. One postmaster would call a thing a newspaper, and another would not, and they often refer to the postmaster-general, and he decides.

3041. Has there ever been any proposition made in the United States with a view to control the press; for instance, that it should be liable to a stamp duty, and give security in the same manner as is required in France?—I have heard a suggestion that it might be well to charge one cent on a copy, and let it go free through the post; but not by any number of persons. Some have said that it would improve the character of the press; but it was never seriously taken up. I have seen it in newspapers as a suggestion.

3042. Mr. *Cobden.*] What is the circulation of the "New York Herald?"—I think 25,000.

3043. Has its circulation been increased during the last few years, or otherwise?—I think it has rather increased; not diminished.

3044. Is that an influential paper in America?—I think not.

3045. It has a higher reputation probably in Europe than at home?—A certain class of journals in this country find it their interest or pleasure to quote it a good deal.

3046. *Chairman.*] As the demand is extensive, is the remuneration for the services of literary men who are employed on the press good?—The prices of literary labour are more moderate than in this country. The highest salary, I think, that would be commanded by any one connected with the press would be 1,000*l.*, the highest that could be thought of; I have not heard of higher than 600*l.*

3047. Mr. *Rich.*] What would be about the ordinary remuneration?—In our own concern it is, besides the principal editor, 300*l.* down to 100*l.*; I think that is the usual range.

3048. *Chairman.*] Are your leading men in America, in point of literary ability, employed from time to time upon the press as an occupation?—It is beginning to be so, but it has not been the custom. There have been leading men connected with the press, but the press has not been usually conducted by the most powerful men. With a few exceptions, the leading political journals are conducted ably, and this is becoming more general; and with a wider diffusion of the circulation, the press is more able to pay for it.

3049. Mr. *Rich.*] Is it a profession apart?—No; usually the

Mr. *H. Greeley.*

3 June 1851.

the men have been brought up to the bar, to the pulpit, as printers, and so on; they are not originally literary men.

3050. *Chairman.*] Your extensive circulation of those cheap papers is based to some extent upon the fact that your whole population can read?—Yes.

3051. I presume that the non-reading class in the United States is a limited one?—Yes; except in the Slave States.

3052. Do not you consider that newspaper reading is calculated to keep up a habit of reading?—I think it is worth all the schools in the country. I think it creates a taste for reading in every child's mind, and it increases his interest in his lessons; he is attracted to study from the habit of always seeing a newspaper and hearing it read, I think.

3053. Supposing that you had your schools as now, but that your newspaper press were reduced within the limits of the press in England, do not you think that the habit of reading acquired at school would be frequently laid aside?—I think that the habit would not be acquired, and that often reading would fall into disuse.

3054. Mr. *Rich.*] Does not the habit of reading create a demand for newspapers, rather than the supply of newspapers create a habit of reading?—I should rather say that the capacity that is obtained in the schools creates a demand for newspapers.

3055. The greater number of persons who read in the United States accounts for the greater number of newspapers that are published, does it not?—There is no class in the Free States who do not know how to read, except the immigrant class.

3056. But in proportion to the number of persons who can read will be the number of papers supplied?—Yes.

3057. *Chairman.*] But the means of obtaining cheap newspapers enables people to keep up their reading, does it not?—Yes.

3058. Mr. *Ewart.*] Must not the contents of a newspaper have a great effect upon the character of the population, and give a more practical turn to their minds?—I should think the difference in intelligence would be very great between a population first educated in schools, and then acquiring the habit of reading journals, and an uneducated non-reading.

3059. If a man is taught to read first, and afterwards applies his mind to the reading of newspapers, would not his knowledge assume a much more practical form than if that man read anything else?—Every man must be practical. I think that the capacity to invent or to improve a machine, for instance,

Mr. *H. Greeley.*

3 June 1851.

instance, is very greatly aided by newspaper reading; by the education afforded by newspapers.

3060. Having observed both countries, can you state whether the press has greater influence on public opinion in the United States than in England, or the reverse?—I think it has more influence with us; I do not know that any class is despotically governed by it, but the influence is more universal; every one reads it and talks about it with us, and more weight is laid upon intelligence than on editorials; the paper which brings the quickest news is the one looked to.

3061. The leading article has not so much influence as it has in England?—No; the telegraphic despatch is the great point.

3062. Mr. *Cobden.*] You stated, did you not, that your New York paper contains two or three columns of telegraphic news?—Three to five columns in times of Congresses and Legislative sessions; always from one to five columns.

3063. Do you, in New York, publish any telegraphic report of the proceedings in your Legislature at Albany?—Every day.

3064. To what extent would the proceedings be telegraphed from Albany?—From half a column to two columns; sometimes three columns when the matter is of great interest.

3065. Observing our newspapers, and comparing them with the American papers, do you find that we make much less use of the electric telegraph for transmitting news to newspapers than in America?—Not a hundredth part as much as we do.

3066. That is a considerable item of expense there, is it not?—Enormous; but it is cheaper with us than with you.

3067. An impression prevails in this country that our newspaper press incurs a great deal more expense to expedite news than you do in New York; are you of that opinion?—I do not know what your expense is; I should say that 100,000 dollars a year are paid by our association of the six leading daily papers, beside what each gets separately for itself.

3068. £. 20,000 a year are paid by your association, consisting of six papers, for what you get in common?—Yes; we telegraph a great deal in the United States. For instance: the Scientific Association held its annual meeting in Cincinnati this year, and we had telegraphic reports from that place, though we, and I presume other journals, had special reporters to report the proceedings at length; so we have reports every day 1,000 miles,—from New Orleans daily, and St. Louis, and other places.

*Veneris*, 20° *die Junii*, 1851.

MEMBERS PRESENT.

Mr. Shafto Adair.
Sir Joshua Walmsley.
Mr. Cobden.
Mr. Ewart.
Mr. G. A. Hamilton.
Mr. Rich.
Mr. Sotheron.

THE RIGHT HON. T. MILNER GIBSON IN THE CHAIR.

*Thomas Keogh*, Esq., called in; and further Examined.

*T. Keogh*, Esq.

20 June 1851.

3069. Mr. *Rich.*] YOU have seen the statement made by Mr. Bucknall with regard to the proceedings of the Board of Inland Revenue; have you any explanation to make thereon?—Yes; the circumstances that occurred I wish to state to the Committee exactly as they took place. It appears that on the 15th of April 1851 this gentleman wrote to the Board this very brief letter: "Gentlemen,—Will you have the goodness to inform me if I am liable to any penalty for issuing the enclosed without the stamp, and whether the Board of Inland Revenue will enforce the same." The paper which accompanied this letter is a newspaper without any doubt or question; it contains the Parliamentary debates, and many other articles of public intelligence; and as we had had a correspondence with Mr. Bucknall on previous occasions——

3070. Mr. *S. Adair.*] What was the date of the letter?—The 15th of April 1851; we were able to see that Mr. Bucknall was just as conversant with the law relating to newspapers as we were ourselves, and therefore the order made upon the letter, the paper being marked vol. 1, No. 10, and 10 numbers of it must have appeared, and being unstamped, was, "Inform the party that the Board are surprised at this inquiry, and that they do not believe that he can be ignorant that the printing and publishing of a newspaper without stamps subjects him to penalties. Let the sub-distributor at Stroud be directed to obtain unstamped copies of this paper, and forward them to this office, and let the solicitor proceed upon the annexed copy; inform the party that the Board have ordered a prosecution." Our notion of the thing was this, that he had issued 10 publications of this

 paper

*T. Keogh,* Esq.

20 June 1851.

paper without stamps, and that he asked what we considered to be a perfectly unnecessary question on his part, whether he could publish those without stamps, and whether we would enforce the penalties that he might incur by so doing. We thought it a very bold and curious proceeding, but it turned out afterwards that this gentleman had really printed one copy of this particular day's publication for the purpose of addressing this letter to the Board, and that the remainder of the copies of the paper were all stamped, as well as all the preceding numbers down to No. 10; that he had in fact stamped them as newspapers from the commencement as well as every other copy of the publication of this day, Friday, the 28th of March; and when he explained and made a declaration, as the Board required him to do, that no other copy than this particular one was published without a stamp, they at once directed the prosecution to be withdrawn.

3071. Sir *J. Walmsley.*] Was he put to any expenses?—No; the prosecution was entirely withdrawn, without any costs being charged.

3072. *Chairman.*] The penalty would have been 20*l.* for each copy, would it not?—Yes.

3073. As there was only one copy, why was the writ for 100*l.*?—That is merely the form of the writ; it directs that if he does not appear he shall be subject to a penalty; that is the ordinary form of subpœna.

3074. He was under the impression from his correspondence that you had sued him, or were about to sue him, for 100*l.*?—If you issue a writ of subpœna from the Court of Exchequer, it runs in that form, "that you be and appear in Court, and herein fail not, under a penalty of 100*l.*" The penalty sued for, whether 20*l.* or any other amount, is not mentioned in the writ.

3075. Mr. *Rich.*] A question was asked you with respect to the number of prosecutions that had taken place; are you prepared with a statement in answer to that question?—I do not recollect any such question being put to me; but I have obtained at the request of the Honourable Chairman a list of all the cases in which cautions have been given to publishers of newspapers within the last three years (*the same being handed in by the Witness*). The truth is, that these cautions have only begun to be issued within the last two or three years. These attempts to steer just beyond the line of the law have only arisen within that period. In prior years we had not to deal with any such persons.

3076. Have you any statement to make with regard to the prosecutions

*T. Keogh*, Esq.

20 June 1851.

prosecutions and the correspondence that you have had with the press regarding the transgression of the law with respect to stamps?—I have. I wish to state that with the general body of the newspaper press, we have no controversies or disputes whatever; the questions that have arisen are merely with regard to those publications that have started up within the last three years, which are just on the line between what is not liable and what is. The parties who publish those papers seem to understand the law very well; but in the cases where we have interfered they have overstepped the proper limits while professing to observe them, and it is with those parties that we have discussions, and not with the general body of the regular newspaper press, with whom we never have any disputes whatever.

3077. *Chairman.*] Should you say that a reprint of an article on the Exhibition from the "Times" (*handing the same to the Witness*), was an illegal thing or not, being without a stamp?—This copy of a publication as to the Exhibition was shown to me on my attendance here on Tuesday last, when the Committee did not sit, and I confess that it very much surprised me. I knew the great accuracy and regularity of the "Times" in all its proceedings; and I was surprised to see this, because I do think it a transgression of the law. However, I have inquired upon the subject at Somerset House, and the Registrar of Newspapers informs me that this was sent from the "Times" office with the name of the publisher upon it, and with the publication of that day, and that he certainly did not observe it. That is all the excuse that he offered, for not bringing it under the notice of the Board.

3078. It would have been his duty to have intimated to the "Times" that it was an illegal proceeding?—It would.

3079. But it escaped his attention?—Yes, it did.

3080. Mr. *Rich.*] In fact, what you would prosecute would be any attempt to evade the law continuously, not an occasional oversight on the part of the paper, that by its general practice showed a willingness to act within the law?—Yes. In a case of this kind, where a lapse from the general regularity of the paper has occurred, under, as I conceive, some erroneous impression, for it cannot be from any other cause, we should only call, as we shall call upon the "Times," for payment of the duties on the number of copies issued; but as to any penal prosecution, we should not think of it in a case where we knew that the parties had no intention of evading the duty.



3081. Mr.

T. Keogh, Esq.

20 June 1851

3081. Mr. *Sotheron.*] Suppose that you thought proper to enforce the law to the utmost, what is the amount of penalties which would have been incurred for that illegal publication? —The penalty of 20 *l.* for every copy that was published.

3082. Do you happen to know how many copies were published?—I do not know.

3083. Mr. *Rich.*] But such a penalty never would have been enforced?—It may be said in the same way that the penalty for committing the most trifling offence against the customs is confiscation of the cargo of a vessel; but the Commissioners never would think of confiscating a cargo.

3084. *Chairman.*] How are the "Times" to know, when they send a paper of this sort to the Board of Inland Revenue, and no notice is taken of it, that it is an illegal thing; and what is to prevent their doing so again unless they receive an intimation to that effect?—I dare say that they did think it legal, or perhaps had not given much consideration to the subject. It is quite certain that they did not want to conceal the transaction, because they sent in a copy, and it will remain with the Board of Inland Revenue to take such notice of it as they think fit.

3085. Will it be brought before the Board?—Yes, immediately.

3086. There is a paper called the "Mirror of the Time," (*the same being handed to the Witness*), which is published weekly, which contains a great deal of direct news, and a great deal of comments upon news. It is a paper that attacks political parties strongly, and perhaps coarsely, and it is published without a stamp. Has your attention been called to that paper?—I may mention that that paper has just been registered as a newspaper.

3087. But it was not till recently?—No.

3088. Had the Board called the attention of the parties to it?—No; it was a voluntary proceeding of the parties.

3089. How long has it been in existence without a stamp? —I do not know. What I recollect about that paper is, that it came to the registrar of newspapers as a monthly publication; as a magazine, in fact, being bound up in a yellow cover, and it is presented merely for the assessment of the advertisement duty.

3090. Mr. *Rich.*] That is just one of those cases of evasion which you have described, is it not?—This paper, from the cursory glance I have taken at it, seems hardly to contain observations upon public occurrences. I observe one paragraph upon the meeting of the Athenæum Society at Manchester.

T. Keogh, Esq.

20 June 1851.

Manchester. Now it is a very questionable thing whether the meeting of the Athenæum Society, a soirée, or something of that sort, can be considered public intelligence, and of course any observations upon it would not be objectionable. Therefore I am not sure that this publication, though published within 26 days, is liable to the duty upon newspapers. However, the parties have not hitherto considered that they were liable, and they have merely presented this at the Stamp Office in a monthly form, four weekly numbers stitched together as a magazine, for the purpose of assessing the advertisement duty. It cannot be liable as a newspaper, except in commenting upon public news within 26 days; if it were monthly, it would not be liable at all.

3091. *Chairman.*] Is it for the purpose of postage that it is registered as a newspaper, or do they stamp every impression? —That I cannot tell; it is likely that they desire to insert matters of intelligence so as to give their paper more interest.

3092. Do not you think that it would be rather a hard case for the Board of Inland Revenue to prevent persons from replying to those attacks in an unstamped periodical as the attacks are allowed to be made without a stamp; and if they continue to make these attacks without a stamp, would it not be fair to allow the replies to be made on unstamped paper? As those are remarks upon the recent transactions of the day, of course the replies must be remarks upon the recent transactions of the day, and would it be competent to reply to the remarks to be found in that paper without a stamp?— To judge of this, I must look at the tenor of the articles, which I have not seen (*the Witness referred to the paper*). This appears to be a vulgar tirade against the honourable Member for the West Riding, and I should not consider that the reply to it would be liable to be treated as public news, or comments upon public news.

3093. This is a slip reprinted from the "English Churchman;" has your attention been called to it (*a paper being shown to the Witness*)? Would that come under the same head as the "Wakefield Examiner"?—On the spur of the moment I should say that it would. But on looking at the paper again, there is nothing to show when it was printed. The matter published is Lord John Russell's letter to the Bishop of Durham about the Papal aggression. Then there is a variety of observations upon Lord John Russell's conduct; but there is nothing to indicate whether this was published recently or six months ago.

 3094. Mr.

*T. Keogh,* Esq.

20 June 1851.

3094. Mr. *Rich.*] In order to give the answers to the questions put to you, would it not require time to consider and to make references?—Perhaps it would.

3095. And to compare the different papers?—Yes; but no consideration will enable me to find out when this was published. This is a comment upon the letter of Lord John Russell, dated November the 4th, meaning of course November the 4th, 1850, and this may have been published within this week, for aught I know.

3096. *Chairman.*] In the case of the "Wakefield Examiner," the publisher was prosecuted and fined for reprinting a slip from his own newspaper. Now that is a slip of the same sort reprinted from the "English Churchman" newspaper, and it seems to run on all fours with the "Wakefield Examiner" case. You say that perhaps it was reprinted some time after the date of the newspaper in which it was first contained. How long after the date of a newspaper does the law permit a person to reprint its contents without a stamp?—The law says nothing specifically upon the subject; but if what is printed be "public news, intelligence, or occurrences," it is liable to a stamp. The circumstances that occurred in the case of the Wakefield paper, if I recollect them rightly, were these: that a report was given of a trial at the assizes, and this trial was very interesting in that part of the country. It was an action for slander, and I think that the persons connected with one of the parties were very desirous that this trial should be circulated as widely as possible in that locality, and accordingly they did not depend upon the newspaper, but went to the proprietor and got him to reprint the trial on sheets of paper, and the reprint of this trial interfered with the forthcoming publication of another newspaper proprietor, who complained to the Board of being thus forestalled, and the Board would perhaps not have been particularly anxious to press the case unless they had been urged to do so by this rival proprietor; but there was no doubt of the liability of the party.

3097. Will you look at the second slip, which is a reprint of a meeting; in what way does that differ?—I do not know whether there is anything in this. It does not follow that because this has been published in a newspaper that it is news. There is a great deal of the contents of a newspaper that is not public news. This seems to be some gossip about the election of a proctor, or convocation clerk, for the diocese of Peterborough.

3098. Is not the election of a proctor or convocation clerk of of a diocese public intelligence?—I cannot say without knowing more of the circumstances. *T. Keogh,* Esq.

20 June 1851.

3099. Mr. *Rich.*] Would not that depend upon how the matter is treated, and would it not require you to read it through to be able to give an answer?—To be sure. I dare say that if these two papers do contain matter which would subject them in an equal degree to the newspaper duty, as in the case of the Wakefield newspaper, that the Board, if they were brought before them, would take the same course; I believe they would, but I cannot say with certainty, these matters involving always questions of discretion.

3100. *Chairman.*] Will you look at those papers now that your attention is called to them?—It is impossible for me to consider them with that degree of accuracy to give an answer. The reprinting of slips may occur; but to suppose that we have a knowledge of every such circumstance is quite a mistake. I do not know from what source these have been collected; and it is probable that we have never seen them or known anything about them. I never saw them, or heard of them before.

3101. Mr. *Cobden.*] Here is a reprint of a New Zealand paper; will you look at that (*a paper being handed to the Witness*)?—It was brought to my notice for the first time two days ago. I think it is a fraud, and I have taken the proper steps to have it investigated. I never heard of it before.

3102. Sir *J. Walmsley.*] There is in the Act of Parliament, is there not, a penalty of 20*l.* imposed upon every copy of each newspaper printed without a stamp?—Yes.

3103. Is that penalty not intended, or was it not rather intended to intimidate persons from acting contrary to the law, than with any view on the part of the Board to enforcing such a penalty?—All penalties are enacted with that intention; penalties regarding the revenue are always in the hands of the Commissioners of that revenue; and it is the intention, in giving to the Commissioners the power of remitting the whole, or retaining any part of a penalty, that they shall measure the punishment which the party deserves, and inflict only a proportionate penalty.

3104. Then to your knowledge no such penalty has ever been enforced, nor ever will be?—No, not as a whole penalty.

3105. Then does not it follow that such a penalty is an improper one to insert in the Act of Parliament?—I do not see that; a case might arise in which it might be desirable



to

*T. Keogh,* Esq.

20 June 1851.

to inflict the full penalty; but I am not aware that any such has occurred. But then the question is as to the multiplication of penalties; for instance, if there were 5,000 copies of this slip of the "Times" printed without stamps, the party would incur penalties to the amount of 5,000 multiplied by 20, which would be 100,000*l.*, and the Board would not think of inflicting that penalty; that is an absurdity.

3106. Then a great offender, who printed 20,000 copies, would get off for the same amount, 20 *l.*, that a person who printed one copy of another publication would?—No, we should not think of imposing a penalty upon anybody printing one copy, if that really was the amount of the offence; but such a thing has never occurred as prosecuting for one penalty. The common offence is, that a man publishes some of his newspapers stamped, and some unstamped, or altogether unstamped.

3107. It would be equally an infraction of the law with one as with 20,000, would it not?—To be sure.

3108. Mr. *Sotheron.*] You find practically some difficulty in drawing a distinction between what comes under the head of a newspaper, and what does not?—We find none at all; the difficulties have been raised and suggested by the parties interested, but we have never experienced the least difficulty.

3109. If you were speaking the sense of the Board, do you think that any fresh legislation is required to enable you to distinguish between what fairly should be stamped and what need not be stamped?—We do not think any further legislation necessary; we have never ourselves experienced any difficulty in determining what is a newspaper.

3110. Mr. *Cobden.*] Is the Board quite clear what the decision of the Judges will be in the case of Mr. Dickens's paper?—Their opinion is quite confident upon the subject, and they expect that the opinion of the Court will be in accordance with it.

3111. Mr. *Sotheron.*] Have you had occasion in the course of the last three years to give several intimations to parties that unless they ceased to publish certain matters, or registered, and paid the stamp duty, they would be proceeded against?—The intimation is this, it being observed that their paper contains either news or comments upon public news, that it will be necessary, if they continue to insert such matter, that they should register the paper as a newspaper, and pay the duty upon it, or discontinue the insertion of such matter.

3112. What has been the result for the most part; have they

they discontinued it, and complied with the law?—In a great many instances the parties adopt the suggestion of the Board, and either exclude the matter or register.

*T. Keogh,* Esq.

20 June 1851.

3113. Do you think that the present law, as understood by the Board in reference to newspaper stamps, is in a satisfactory state?—I do not think that there is the least difficulty in interpreting it.

3114. Do not you think that some hardship is inflicted upon parties who afford a great deal of information to the public, and yet just happen to trench within the line which is drawn by the Board, which makes them liable to a stamp? —I think there can be no hardship in persons being kept within the limits which the law imposes.

3115. Mr. *Ewart.*] Are not those limits very much undefined?—We think not; we think there is no difficulty.

3116. Mr. *Rich.*] Your experience leads you to think that those persons who do transgress the law do so knowingly?—My experience leads me to think that they transgress the law with a profession of their belief that they are keeping within it. But I believe that this is in most instances only a profession, and that the parties have no real difficulty if they desire to confine themselves within the proper limit.

3117. They go, as one of the witnesses expressed it, as near the wind as they can?—Yes.

3118. Mr. *Sotheron.*] Is it the fact that several publications within the last three years have been set up, as it were, upon the chance of being pulled down, and have gone on for a certain time before information has been given to the Board of Inland Revenue?—That I have no doubt has occurred, particularly in London, where the opportunities of observation are not the same as exist in the country.

3119. Have the number of intimations given by the Board increased in a progressive ratio during the last three years?—They have increased in these proportions: in 1848, there were two; in 1849, there were seven; in 1850, there were 12; and in 1851, at the middle of which we have only arrived, there are seven.

3120. Mr. *Ewart.*] That is only up to the present date? —Yes.

3121. Mr. *Sotheron.*] Does not that increasing number give you reason to anticipate that the number will be continually on the increase?—I do not know that. If it be found that those attempts, just keeping on the line of the law, are generally unsuccessful, and that the parties must either exclude such matter from their papers or register them

*T. Keogh*, Esq.

20 June 1851.

them as newspapers, I do not see why there should be an increase.

3122. You are unable to state in the cases where intimations have been given to papers or publications, for how long a time they have been going on before those intimations were given?—That may be or may not be; in certain papers they state the numbers; in the "Mirror of the Time," which has been shown to me, the number is 22; and if that particular were given, we should know how long it had been in existence.

3123. *Chairman.*] Is there anything further that you wish to add to your evidence?—No.

Mr. *Henry Rust*, called in; and Examined.

Mr. *H. Rust*.

3124. *Chairman.*] YOU appear before this Committee to represent Messrs. Savory & Company, do you not?—A. B. Savory and Sons.

3125. They register a publication called "Savory's Newspaper," do they not?—"Price Current" is the name of it; I have a copy of it here (*producing the same*). The title of it is "Savory and Sons' Price Current Newspaper;" the word "newspaper" merely applies to the stamp.

3126. You enter into all the securities and obligations that the publisher of an ordinary newspaper does?—Exactly the same in every respect.

3127. You give security that you will not libel any one, or publish any blasphemous or seditious libel?—Every form is gone through, the same as if it were a public newspaper.

3128. And you declare it to be a newspaper?—I do not know; I think it is declared to be a "Price Current."

3129. As you are not required by law to stamp the paper upon which you print your "Price Current," why do you do it?—We do it to enable us to send it through the Post Office into the country.

3130. You do it for the purpose of obtaining the privilege of going free by post?—Yes.

3131. What would you have to pay in postage if you did not do this, and if you put it into the post in the ordinary way?—We should not do that; at least I do not think we should.

3132. How much does your "Price Current" weigh?—The stamped one is under two ounces, I think; I am not certain; but it is the limit that is allowed for stamped publications to pass through the post; just under two ounces.

3133. What

Mr. *H. Rust.*

20 June 1851.

3133. What would be the postage on that?—Fourpence.

3134. If you sent it regularly by post, you would pay 4*d.*, would you not?—Yes; but the Committee will understand that we should not do so.

3135. But if you did you would have to pay 4*d.*?—Yes. When we do send any by post, otherwise than the stamped ones, it is this copy, which is exactly the same (*handing the same to the Committee*), only it is on better paper, and then we pay 6*d.* We send several of those when we are out of print of the stamped ones.

3136. Practically, you get them carried for you for 1*d.*? —Yes.

3137. Supposing that you were permitted, in virtue of a penny stamp, to send this by post, instead of getting stamped paper as you now do for each copy, you would stand in the same position, would you not?—The same position exactly we should be in if they stamped it.

3138. You would stamp it and send it by post?—Yes.

3139. In point of fact, would not that plan save the trouble also of having to enter into all those securities that you will not libel, and so forth?—That trouble would then be saved, but we have gone through that process.

3140. Supposing you had not gone through all that process, and had been permitted merely to stamp it with a penny stamp, that would have been a more convenient arrangement for you than the present one, would it not?—I presume so. I am not aware that publishing a price current like that is contrary to law, and therefore I presume that, being stamped, and having a postage stamp affixed to it, it would go through the post if the law were so.

3141. You were at the trouble, in order to get the privilege of obtaining stamped paper, of going to the Board of Inland Revenue and giving those securities?—Yes.

3142. And of obtaining bondsmen, were you not?—Yes.

3143. If it had been in your power to put on a penny stamp, which would carry the paper through the post, you would have saved all that trouble?—Yes.

3144. As far as the pecuniary arrangement goes, you would have stood in the same position?—In saying yes, I suppose you allude to a stamp being placed upon it in the same way as it is placed on a letter.

3145. A stamp which would frank it, supposing it went in virtue of a penny stamp?—If it would frank it in virtue of the penny stamp we should use the stamp, but whether we should have to give security or not I do not know.

3146. You

Mr. *H. Rust.*

20 June 1851.

3146. You do not, I think, understand my question. You were asked whether if you had been able to stamp your "Price Current" with a penny stamp, you would not, in a pecuniary point of view, have stood in exactly the same position as you now do, being able to send it in virtue of its being printed on stamped paper?—Just the same.

3147. Then in the case of your paper going in virtue of the stamp, you would have saved the trouble of going to the Stamp Office to give those securities, would you not?—I answer to the best of my knowledge, that in practice it would certainly be so; but I do not know whether, irrespective of the stamp, such a thing would be allowed to be circulated through the country previously to our getting permission from the authorities at Somerset House.

3148. Supposing it were allowed in virtue of a penny stamp, what would you do?—Then we should avail ourselves of the stamp, and not take any trouble in the matter.

3149. In fact, you get no greater pecuniary advantage by the present arrangement than the stamp gives you, and you have the additional trouble to find securities that you will not libel anybody?—Yes.

3150. Therefore, supposing that the penny stamp would carry four ounces of such printed matter as yours through the post, namely, two of your numbers, you would be in a better position than you are now?—It would be an advantage undoubtedly if the weight were slightly increased. I do not know that we should avail ourselves of the full four ounces, as it would not answer in business to have a pamphlet of a size to weigh four ounces.

3151. Could you not send two numbers to some person in the country to distribute them for you?—No, we never do that; we never find any of our customers so liberal as to do that.

3152. You do not send more than one to the same individual?—We do not at the same time send more than one to the same individual; never by any chance. They are circulated from a directory when we circulate them without orders. In the usual way they are sent in reply to applications by letter.

3153. You would have no reason to complain then if a penny stamp would frank them once through the Post Office, if an arrangement were made by which you were relieved from obtaining stamped paper at the Stamp Office?—Not at all; we should like it better; indeed if the weight were slightly increased it would be a great advantage to us. By

comparing

comparing the two, the Committee will see the superiority of the unstamped one. *Mr. H. Rust.*

*20 June 1851.*

3154. Mr. *Rich.*] Upon what grounds should you request the privilege of sending these prices current by a penny wrapper or a penny stamp, as described by the honourable Chairman?—I believe the fact of sending the "Price Current" in that form through the Post Office originated from reading a paragraph in the "Times" newspaper, which stated that Government allowed publications under such a weight to pass through the post free.

3155. Provided that you make a declaration that it is for the purpose of a newspaper?—Yes; on reading that it immediately occurred to Mr. Savory that it would be an advantage to us to circulate our book in that form; before that we had an uncut sheet; in 1845 it was a sheet.

3156. Do you imagine that the Board of Inland Revenue would grant you a penny stamp to send your book through the Post Office, unless you made some declaration similar to that which you have made in order to obtain your stamp?—No, they would not do so; I believe not.

3157. Therefore without that you would have no privilege of sending this book more than anybody else?—No.

3158. What proportion out of the whole number which you dispatch do those which you send by post bear to those which you send by railway or other means of transmission?—I have not the particulars of the exact number of those which we have printed that are unstamped, but I think it is something like 5,000 a year, the unstamped ones; and we circulate by post say from 1,000 to 1,500 a year; there are about 5,000 unstamped ones, and 1,200 others. In 1851, in consequence of the Exhibition, we have sent a great many through the country by means of the Post Office; but in all probability we should not do that again for a series of years.

3159. On the whole it might be inferred, from your sending so many as 1,200 a year, that you find it an advantage to be allowed so to transmit your paper?—Yes, a great advantage undoubtedly; we have applications for it every morning; as certain as the post comes in we have applications for that pamphlet, and our business is transacted to a great extent by it. It is a complete list of our stock, without any exaggeration or puff, or anything of that kind; simply a list of the stock, and parties write their orders from that book.

3160. If this privilege were withdrawn, you would then have recourse to sending them as you now do, and you would not

Mr. *H. Rust.*

20 June 1851.

not take advantage of the Post Office at all?—We should still send just exactly those that were asked for, and no more; now we frequently send others. For instance, in reading a newspaper, if we see what we consider an opportunity, and some probability of its being useful, we send a price current.

3161. What diminution would it make in the number transmitted were you to send them only when called for, paying the regular price according to the weight?—I should think that we should send not more than 700 a year by post.

3162. Rather more than one-half?—Yes. We give away over the counter more than 100 a week of unstamped ones. Very many parties who call for it, when we say that we have one for the post, take it, to go through the post instead. If it were not conveyed by post we should circulate a great many free.

3163. Your stamped circulation now amounts to about 1,200 a year, does it not?—Yes.

3164. And you expect that if the privilege of sending by post for a penny were withdrawn your circulation then by stamps, according to weight, would fall down to 700?—Yes, quite tha.t

3165. *Chairman.*] Is there any second sending of your circulars; if you send one to a person in the country, does he send it on to another?—We have no means of knowing whether they ever do so. It has occurred that one price current has been twice sent in this way: a price current is sent by post, and when it arrives the person to whom it is sent is dead, and it is then returned to us.

3166. That would be an exceptional case?—Yes; the number is very trifling indeed; I apprehend, out of the number that we send, it is not three per cent.

3167. If it were the law that all printed matter, up to the weight of two ounces, should be carried by post, with a penny stamp affixed thereto, would you be satisfied with that arrangement?—Quite so.

3168. It would save all persons who wanted to circulate these things the trouble of going to the Board of Inland Revenue, and finding securities against libel and sedition? —Yes.

3169. Mr. *Rich.*] You are aware that that would include a total alteration of the present rates of conveying stamped papers that are not newspapers; you say that the book I had in my hand would cost rather more than 2 *d.*?—No, the one in your hand would cost 6 *d.*

3170. Therefore

Mr. *H. Rust.*

20 June 1851.

3170. Therefore the alternative put to you by the honourable Chairman involves an alteration of the charges now made by the Post Office, namely, a reduction from 6*d.* to 1 *d.*?—No. This we do not circulate through the post but very seldom, and having had the privilege of stamping all along, it would really make no difference to us.

3171. Do not you see that to enable you to send the book which I hold in my hand, if unstamped, through the Post Office, there must be a reduction in the present rate of charges from 6 *d.* to 1 *d.*?—Yes.

3172. Mr. *S. Adair.*] I observe that the stamp is on the title page in the stamped copy; is it invariably on the title page?—As it is there, it always is.

3173. Is that stamp impressed before or after the printing?—I do not know.

*William Edward Hickson*, Esq., called in; and Examined.

*W. E. Hickson*, Esq.

3174. *Chairman.*] YOU were associated with Mr. Senior and Lord Overstone in the Hand-loom Inquiry Commission, were you not?—I was.

3175. Did that inquiry give you an opportunity of making yourself acquainted with the state of mind of the working classes?—Very generally as to the state of the working classes of this country, and also as to the state of mind of the working classes of other countries. I took a very active part in the proceedings of the Commission, and personally visited the hand-loom weavers in almost every part of this country, including the sister kingdom of Ireland. I have also,—as a member of a Board of Guardians, and as an old educationist,—all my life more or less employed in connexion with school associations, in founding them, or taking an active part in promoting the interests of the working classes, as connected with popular instruction,—had perhaps more opportunity than falls to the lot of most persons of ascertaining with tolerable accuracy what the state of mind of the working classes is in this country.

3176. What is your opinion of a newspaper as an educational instrument amongst the working classes?—I have entertained a strong opinion upon this subject for some years. Prior even to the formation of the Hand-loom Inquiry Commission, I took, in 1836, a very active part with Lord Brougham and other educationists in favour of the total abolition of the newspaper stamp. It was at that time proposed to reduce the fourpenny stamp to a penny, and

*W. E. Hickson*, Esq.

20 June 1851.

and I at that time saw, and many other persons saw with me, that a great part of the object that we had in view, namely, making use of newspapers as educational implements, would be frustrated entirely if the abolition was not adopted, instead of a mere reduction to 1*d.* Lord Brougham strongly denounced the last penny as the worst penny of the four; and I entertained with him, and many other persons, a very decided opinion to the same effect. I remember stating at the time when we went up as a deputation to Mr. Spring Rice, and when, subsequently, we went to Lord Melbourne (I attended two deputations in 1836 to these different Ministers on this particular question, the question of reduction or abolition), that our object would be so completely frustrated, that the mere reduction from 7*d.* to 5*d.* as the price of a daily newspaper would not have the effect of allowing a single new daily newspaper to be started in the United Kingdom. I stated that very confidently at that time, and it was one of my predictions which appears to have been verified to the letter. In the United States, I believe that daily newspapers are published to the extent of 250: in this country, including the evening press, there are only 10 published.

3177. Mr. *Cobden.*] Are there not more daily papers now than at that time?—I believe I am strictly accurate in saying that there is not one more.

3178. Mr. *Rich.*] Are you aware that a formal return, which is before me, states that the London papers have increased from 100 to 150?—I am speaking of the daily and the evening papers; of the diurnal journals published in Great Britain. There is no increase whatever; I say no increase, but it is possible that there may be a difference now of one.

3179. Mr. *Ewart.*] You speak of papers coming out every day?—Yes.

3180. *Chairman.*] The original intention, or rather the original demand, was to abolish the stamp altogether; why was the penny retained?—Of course I can only give an opinion; we considered at that time that the Government were afraid of the possibility of a more strongly developed democratic tendency in an absolutely free press.

3181. Was there any opposition to the entire removal of the stamp from any established newspaper?—We considered so; and of the evidence that there was an opposition, one fact made a strong impression upon my mind, as showing the *animus* of the stamped press. That fact was this: that one

*W. E. Hickson*, Esq.

20 June 1851.

one of the largest public meetings I ever attended in my life was held in reference to the question of the reduction or abolition of the newspaper stamp duty; it was held at Guildhall, and it was crowded to overflowing; the members of the committee, of which I was one, had the greatest difficulty in getting on to the platform. The proceedings were of a very animating and exciting description, and speeches were delivered at very considerable length, but not a single report of any one of the speeches, and no notice whatever of that public meeting, was published in any of the journals the next day.

3182. You infer from that circumstance that their feeling was, that the abolition of the stamp was against their interest, and that they did not wish to give any publicity to this meeting?—Undoubtedly. We always considered that the reduction was a measure framed in support of the interests of the stamped press, rather than the interests of the public. As far as the existing stamp was concerned at that time, we were not asking Government for any change, because that was a point virtually carried; we regarded that as a *fait accomplis.* Unstamped papers were then circulating, according to the statement of Mr. Spring Rice himself in the House of Commons, to the extent of 200,000 weekly; and the Government admitted that it was impossible to carry on the stamp at its then existing rate. That question was decided; and it only remained to be determined whether the whole fourpenny stamp was to be taken off, or a penny should be retained. Upon that subject there was a very active agitation in 1836, in promoting which the gentlemen of the stamped press took no part; but they took every means to suppress all notice of our proceedings.

3183. Was it their idea that the retention of this remaining penny, this worst penny of the whole, as Lord Brougham called it, would protect, to a certain degree, the stamped press from the competition of the unstamped press?—Yes, that was my strong impression, and I stated it very frequently to different public men with whom I was in communication at that time, and it was with extreme disappointment that we found our views were over-ruled. I recollect the arguments I used then, and I would use them now; the price of a daily newspaper published at 5*d.* is a subscription of 6*l.* 10*s.* per annum; and that is a subscription that not one person in perhaps 1,000 in this country is able to afford; it is a subscription to a club at the West End. We know from existing returns that the number of subscribers to daily newspapers is extremely limited; that the market is a fixed



quantity.

*W. E. Hickson*, Esq.

20 June 1851.

quantity. The existing circulation is only to the extent of 60,000, I believe, of direct subscribers to the existing daily journals. If I started a daily journal to-day, I could not calculate upon any increased number of subscribers; I must obtain my sale by robbing some of the existing journals of a portion of their circulation, as the "Times" is doing at this present moment.

3184. You cannot get beyond the limit?—No.

3185. Mr. *Cobden*.] Who had the charge of the question of Newspaper Stamps in 1836 in the House of Commons?—Sir Edward Bulwer Lytton was the most active person.

3186. He had the charge of the question?—Yes.

3187. And he compromised it for a permanent fixed duty with the Government?—Yes; if we could have over-ruled the opinions of Sir Edward Bulwer Lytton we might possibly have succeeded at that time, but we were not so far fortunate. The reduction it should be borne in mind was not a total reduction of 3*d.* to 1*d.*; the stamp of 4*d.* was subject to a discount of 20 per cent., which reduced the actual charge upon the public to 3*d.* and the fifth of one penny; I do not know whether it has been brought out in evidence, but it should be observed that that fifth of a penny the proprietors of the existing stamped journals put into their pockets, and gave the public the benefit only of the reduction of 2*d.* The price of the "Times" was reduced from 7*d.* to 5*d.*, and the odd 1*d.* the "Times" retained for their own benefit; I calculated the same year, that upon their then circulation, the Government had given them actually a bonus of 2,500*l.* a year. Their circulation was then about 10,000, and 10,000 fifths of 1*d.* daily, amount to 2,500 *l.* a year, so that our feeling was very indignant, that after all our exertions we should only have succeeded in obtaining a measure so completely in the interest of the stamped journals, that if the proprietor of the "Times" had been the Chancellor of the Exchequer, he could not have more effectually attained his own object; first of obtaining a bonus, and next of securing himself against any competition.

3188. Mr. *S. Adair*.] Have you given your attention to the history of the newspaper press of this country?—I have generally read the history of the newspaper press.

3189. With regard to the state of the newspaper press, during the great civil war, are you aware that during that struggle 110 papers were published in Great Britain?—I am aware that a great number were published at that time, but I cannot speak accurately to the fact.

3190. At

*W. E. Hickson*, Esq.

20 June 1851.

3190. At that time there was no restriction on the press?—I am aware that in the first instance there was no restriction.

3191. *Chairman.*] Did not the "Spectator" give the public the full benefit of the reduction?—Some of the weekly papers did, but I cannot speak with accuracy on that subject.

3192. None of the London morning papers gave the public the benefit of the full reduction?—None of the London morning papers at that time did.

3193. May not the penny stamp be defended on fiscal grounds; supposing we give up the old notion that it is necessary to restrain the press by a stamp on political grounds, may it not be proper, in a fiscal point of view, to levy a tax upon every newspaper?—I think not; it appears to me, that neither upon the fiscal part of the question, nor the moral part, nor the political part of the question, nor, indeed, in any way is the present stamp defensible; it certainly is not defensible on fiscal grounds as it now exists. It is very easy to show that by a different mode of stamping newspapers, by an *ad valorem* duty instead of a fixed duty, the evils which now result from the stamp would not be produced to precisely the same mischievous extent. A penny stamp is now a duty of 20 per cent. upon a newspaper published at 5 *d.*; but it is 100 *l.* per cent. upon a newspaper published at 1 *d*; it is not, therefore, merely a fiscal duty, but it is a prohibitory duty; it is a duty belonging to the old *regime* of protection; I believe the only prohibitory duty now remaining on the statute book. It is a duty absolutely prohibitory to the circulation of cheap political journals, or journals of any kind containing intelligence. If I were in the position of the Chancellor of the Exchequer, and really *bonâ fide* circumstances went to show that the penny stamp was important as a matter of revenue, the way I should obtain the revenue would be by charging a five per cent. *ad valorem* duty, allowing the public to publish newspapers at any price they pleased. If a duty of five per cent. were levied upon a daily journal published at a penny, it would first of all allow it to exist, which the present stamp does not, and the newspaper circulation, increased but fivefold, would produce a larger revenue than the existing stamp produces.

3194. Mr. *Rich.*] You state that the present duty is a prohibitory duty, and that with regard to the object of the reduction of the duty in 1836, from 4 *d.* to 1 *d.*, there has been a complete failure; how do you reconcile that statement with the fact, that the number of newspaper stamps issued in the year

*W. E. Hickson*, Esq.

20 June 1851.

year 1835 was, in round numbers, 28,000,000, and that it has gone on steadily increasing from that time to the present year, when it amounts to 65,000,000?—I did not state that the effect of the reduction was a complete failure in every sense of the word. I am aware that there has been an increase in the number of journals. I stated that it was a failure as regards the publication of any new daily journals. Certainly it has not been altogether a failure as regards the publication of weekly journals, but it has been a failure in reference to the daily journals, and the object which we as educationists had primarily in view, that of enabling us to reach the mind of the lowest stratum of the community, which we do not by any means do now.

3195. Do you not conceive that the newspapers, the stamps for which have increased more than 100-fold, in a period so short as has elapsed between 1836 and 1851, must not, when the stamps amount to the enormous number of 65,000,000 issued, reach down to the very lowest persons who are able to read?—Undoubtedly they do not.

3196. Does not your experience among the lower orders lead you to know that the "Times" or other daily papers are in almost every house of resort where persons who can read are to be found?—My experience teaches me directly the contrary, and that reminds me of another point with regard especially to the "Times," and with regard to the question about the inferior class of publications which would be called into existence if the penny stamp were removed, and I attended to day as much to speak to that point as any other, because it is really an important one. I do not dispute the fact, and I am prepared to admit that if the penny stamp were removed there would be a host of journals inferior to the "Times" called into existence. I think it most desirable that they should be called into existence, and for this simple reason, that my experience as an educationist has shown me that journals so well written as the "Times," and so classically written as the "Times," really overshoot the comprehension of the working classes of the community. I was not aware of the fact till I tried the experiment practically. I formed in the village where I am now living, when I first went there, an evening class of adult labourers, and as I was then very much interested in some very able articles that were being published in the "Times," I thought I would read them to them in the evening; but I found that we did not get on at all; and upon cross-examination of some of my auditors afterwards, I discovered, to my surprize, that I could not

*W. E. Hickson*, Esq

20 June 1851.

not read 20 lines of the leading article of the "Times" without finding that there were 20 words in it which none of my auditors understood. I remember one passage which not one of the agricultural labourers to whom I was reading understood at all. The editor was speaking of some operations of our fleet in the channel; the word "operations" puzzled them, the word "fleet" puzzled them; they did not know what a fleet was, and they had not the slightest idea of what the "channel" meant.

3197. What kind of paper would you propose to address to people who do not know the meaning of the word "operations," and who do not know the meaning of the "channel" or the "fleet"?—My view with regard to newspapers is the same as regards school-books; we want books addressed to classical students in schools of the higher class, and we want primers containing words of one or two syllables, for those who are learning to read; and the newspapers that would reach the minds of agricultural labourers would be newspapers, like school primers, not such as I myself should read, but such as would be read by a person just two or three degrees above their own class. The case is the same as it is with regard to Baptist preachers and Wesleyan preachers, and the classical men who come from our own universities to preach in our neighbourhood. In my neighbourhood we have Baptist chapels and Wesleyan chapels, and the working classes are there to be found. We have classically educated rectors and curates, but when the working classes attend their churches, if you ask them what they have understood of the sermon, you find that it amounts to nothing, and that the familiar discourses of preachers not so well educated are better adapted for their case.

3198. My question was, what kind of newspaper would you address to those people who do not understand the meaning of the word "operations," or the word "channel"?—I should not myself perhaps try the experiment of publishing a newspaper addressed to the agricultural labourers; I should perhaps distrust my own ability; but I am certain that the kind of newspaper which they would encourage would be one that related to local events which they really understood. They would not encourage a paper that discussed the operations of a fleet in the channel, but I think they would encourage a paper that gave a good account of some trial at Maidstone assizes; they would encourage a paper that gave a good account of some farmer's stackyard having been burnt down, and what steps were taken in consequence; and they would encourage

*W. E. Hickson*, Esq.

20 June 1851.

encourage a paper that gave an account of what became of a ship that sailed with some families from their neighbourhood with which they might be connected.

3199. Are not all these subjects to be found in the "Times"?—Not to the extent that is desired for local information.

3200. It has been stated in evidence, that the parts of a paper which the lower classes like to read, are the debates in Parliament, and proceedings before courts of justice, and the police courts; are not these subjects to be found well reported in the "Times"?—It would be possible to make a smaller journal in large type out of the "Times," which would perhaps be suitable in some cases.

3201. Mr. *Ewart.*] The most probable way of getting at the minds of the labouring population of this country, both manufacturing and agricultural would be, would it not, by appealing through the known to the unknown; for instance, by taking those things most familiar to them in the local districts, and making them the means of exciting their interest? —Yes, that is decidedly my opinion; it has been a great mistake, though I shared in it myself, to suppose that the daily papers are the papers most interesting to those who are permanently resident in distant local districts; I find even with myself coming to London occasionally only as I do now, that I really take more interest in the "Maidstone Gazette" than I do in the "Times" paper, though I read both; if it was merely from the difference of the advertisements, that would be one consideration; I am sometimes a buyer of stock, and I want to know what the price of heifers and horses is, and what the price of corn is especially, not at Mark-lane as the "Times" gives it, but at Maidstone Market.

3202. Do you happen to know that where the newspaper press is left free, without a stamp, local news circulates most rapidly; what, for instance, is the result in America; is it not that the newspapers are principally local?—I think so.

3203. *Chairman.*] Would not emigration be one subject upon which the local papers would give information to the agricultural labourers, and would not they obtain through them accurate knowledge of what had become of the ships that had carried out families from their neighbourhood?—Yes; a few weeks ago a poor woman applied to me in very great distress about a report which had reached her, that the ship in which her son had sailed a few weeks previously for New York, had been lost with all hands on board, and she could obtain no information anywhere in the district. There were no means,

though

though she could read and write, within five miles of getting to see a daily paper to give any information about the shipping. At small beershops and public-houses it is very rare that you find even a weekly paper; and I obtained the information for this poor woman by inquiries in London. With regard to the subject of emigration generally, I have been often struck with the great difficulty (till the current fairly sets in, one carrying another along with him) that there is in getting the working classes to understand that when you are recommending them to go abroad you are promoting a measure that is in their interest; a difficulty arising from their knowing nothing whatever of the configuration of the globe, or the countries that exist upon it, and getting none of that scattered information which we are so familiar with from the paragraphs in newspapers.

3204. Sir *J. Walmsley.*] You were asked by the Honourable Member for Richmond, whether you were not aware that the "Times" newspaper was read in all the places of public resort in the kingdom; do you know the amount of the circulation of the "Times" newspaper daily?—I am aware that it fluctuates, but I cannot speak to the present amount.

3205. Do you know that its circulation is about 39,000? —I have heard that it is about 30,000.

3206. Do you know the number of places of public resort in the kingdom?—I cannot speak to the number; there are a great many.

3207. Do you know that they exceed many hundreds of thousands?—I am aware it is more or less the public establishments and institutions that take in the "Times."

3208. Mr. *Rich.*] My question had reference to the number of places of public resort, where papers were taken in?—Yes.

3209. *Chairman.*] You are not yourself favourable, if I understand you correctly, to raising money by taxing newspapers?—Certainly not.

3210. But if that were necessary to be done, what plan would you impose?—Then I should propose a five per cent. *ad valorem* duty.

3211. Rather than the penny stamp, which you complain of as a prohibitory duty upon cheap newspapers?—Yes, that was precisely my point. I think that a five per cent. *ad valorem* duty would now be received as a most ungenerous and ungracious act; but if the revenue were in such straits as to render the imposition of a tax necessary, that would be a more legitimate mode of raising the duty, the present mode being prohibitory to cheap publications.

 3212. Comparing

*W. E. Hickson,* Esq.

20 June 1851.

3212. Comparing the receipt of some 300,000*l.* to the public revenue with the effect that is produced by the prevention of cheap newspapers, do not you think that the State, in reference to its general policy, gets that small return upon very dear terms?—I think so. Indeed upon moral grounds, if the Government really are at all in earnest in their efforts for raising the intellectual status of the working classes of this country, I cannot imagine a more disastrous mode of defeating their object than by retaining the penny stamp. With regard to education, though I have been all my life actively engaged in promoting schools for teaching reading and writing, yet of course every one who has considered the subject of education, must know that education does not consist in merely elementary matters of that kind, and that true education consists in the teaching of events. The wisest man is he who observes most of what is passing in the world, and makes the best observations upon them, and if you repress the newspaper, which is a record of events, and, in fact, the only record of events that is accessible to persons who are stationary, and do not travel, as the mass of the working classes are, you repress the most important implement of education. I am speaking merely in reference to newspapers as records of events. I am not so very earnest about the circulation of newspaper editorial leading articles. What I rely upon most as a means of quickening the intelligence of the working classes, is placing before them a daily record of what is going on in the world, and if you wish to prohibit editorial articles, I should be willing to compromise with you.

3213. Mr. *Ewart.*] Are you aware that in local newspapers in America editorial leading articles form a very small portion of the contents, and that current news forms the largest portion?—Yes, I have frequently looked over them.

3214. Sir *J. Walmsley.*] Did you not state that an *ad valorem* duty of five per cent. should be placed on newspapers?—No; I should deprecate that; but I merely brought it forward in illustration of the fact, that we are now, in continuing the penny stamp, adhering, in defiance of the principles professed by our Government, to the old protection *regime,* and maintaining a prohibitory duty on cheap publications.

3215. What do you mean by a five per cent. *ad valorem* duty?—A five per cent. *ad valorem* duty would allow a newspaper to be published at a penny, and there would be five per cent. charged upon that penny.

3216. Mr.

*W. E. Hickson*, Esq.

20 June 1851.

3216. Mr. *Rich.*] You state that a five per cent. *ad valorem* duty should be charged upon a penny newspaper; how would you send that newspaper?—I am not prepared with the details of any scheme to be carried out.

3217. With a five per cent. *ad valorem* duty upon a penny newspaper, at what charge would you transmit that paper, or without the duty how would you transmit it?—That is a question upon which I am not prepared to speak. I should calculate upon the newspapers an increase over the existing circulation of at least fivefold. Then it would be a question for the consideration of the Post-office whether that fivefold increase could be carried by the present postage franchise or not.

3218. If I understand you rightly, your notion of taking off the penny stamp would involve the substitution of a penny postage stamp, or a stamp of rather less value for transmission by post?—Yes; in the present case, I am in favour of a postage stamp duty. If the present stamp were taken off entirely, it would be but just to do so.

3219. If you state that the imposition of a penny stamp upon a newspaper published at a penny is a prohibitory duty, would not the imposition of a penny postage stamp upon a penny newspaper be an equally prohibitory and injurious duty?—Undoubtedly not.

3220. Would not that be a duty of 100 per cent., whereas in reference to the "Times," which is published at 5*d.*, the transmission of its papers for a penny would be a duty of one-fifth of that amount?—I cannot understand how the abolition of the penny stamp would operate as a prohibitory duty, when any number of daily journals might at once spring into existence at the price of the present penny stamp.

3221. You have spoken of the inequality of the pressure of the penny stamp now upon papers published at 5 *d.*, and upon papers published at a penny; will you state whether the same inequality would not exist in charging a penny for the transmission by post of a paper which was published at 5*d.*, and the same for another paper which was published at a penny?—As far as the postage stamp is concerned, of course there would be the same inequality, but then I have never defended the existing postage system. It appears to me that that is a part of our objection, and a part of our case against the existing system. We now give to the proprietors of the "Times" a positive bonus as against the proprietors of local newspapers, who get no advantage whatever by the postage stamp. We give it to the daily journals. Why should they not

*W. E. Hickson*, Esq.

20 June 1851.

not have the monopoly solely of the circulation which legitimately belongs to them, namely, their local circulation?

3222. If the stamp duty were taken off to-morrow, would you send a paper, published at a penny in London, through the post, at the same, or at a lower price than a paper published in London and charged 5 *d.*?—I should leave Mr. Rowland Hill or the authorities at the Post Office to settle that question. I should view the postage question principally in reference to the weight and distribution, which are the two elements: the distribution would remain the same in the one case as the other, and as far as I am concerned I should make no difference; the weight would make some difference, and on that account a large heavy paper ought to be charged a trifle more than a lighter one.

3223. You would charge, would you not, according to the weight of the paper?—Yes.

3224. And not according to the value of the paper?—No.

3225. Then you abandon all notion of an *ad valorem* duty for the transmission of newspapers by post?—Yes; that has nothing to do with the question.

3226. You do not advocate sending the newspapers through the post gratis, do you?—Certainly not.

3227. And the charge would be borne equally by all papers, without any reference whatever to their cost?—Without any reference to their cost when they used the post.

3228. Do you not therefore perceive that precisely the same prohibitory duty under a new name, which you now so strongly denounce with regard to the penny stamp, would be in operation with regard to newspapers sent through the post? —As far as distant places are concerned, there is no doubt that it might operate in that way; but it would not as an absolutely prohibitory duty, because for local purposes newspapers do not require to be sent by post, and they could be published at any price it pleased the proprietors to publish them at.

3229. Mr. *Ewart.*] As the probable result of a change in the law would be a vast increase in the number of local newspapers, the question of the payment of postage upon those papers would not arise, as they would be circulated through the several districts probably by messengers?—Yes.

3230. Might not this arise, that papers from London might be sent down into the country by weight in large numbers together, as they are now, in masses?—Undoubtedly.

3231. Are you aware whether that is done now?—Yes, it is, I believe, done to a very great extent.

3232. *Chairman.*]

3232. *Chairman.*] You wish to make no suggestion as to what amount should be charged for the transmission of printed matter by post; you would leave that to be settled by the proper authorities; all you wish to speak to is the effect of the penny stamp upon newspapers?—Yes.

*W. E. Hickson,* Esq.

20 June 1851.

3233. Mr. *Ewart.*] You speak of an existing evil, but you do not suggest any remedy?—No.

3234. *Chairman.*] In reference to a previous part of your evidence, is there not a great deal of matter in the London papers relating to the different routs and parties given in town, with the names of the persons who attend them, which cannot have much interest for mechanics and working people, either in this town or any other town in the kingdom?—I should think it had not.

3235. It is of no use putting into the hands of an artisan at Birmingham a record of an evening rout which might be found in the "Morning Post," or the details of the ladies' dresses, and the number of the carriages that attended?—No.

3236. Is it not a hard case that a labouring man, in order to get at the news which he wants, should be obliged to purchase intelligence such as I have described, namely, as to who attended the routs in London, and as to the dresses of the ladies who went to Court?—Yes; and it is an additional objection that when he gets it at all under the existing system, it is only by frequenting the public-house.

3237. Mr. *S. Adair.*] You spoke of the slowness of the intelligence of your rustic auditors in respect to matters not immediately within their usual scope of observation?—Yes.

3238. I apprehend that you would attribute that to a lack of that current knowledge which is conveyed in newspapers? —Yes; they want local information.

3239. In addition to local information, you would desire, would you not, that general broad questions of policy might be well considered in those local newspapers?—I have not the slightest doubt that the first operation of the reduction of the stamp would be that we should see an inferior class of journals. I have not the slightest doubt also that in a few years we should see a prodigious improvement in the quality of those journals; the penny stamp has nothing to do with the quality of newspaper matter, though that has been sometimes urged in argument; and I might mention that in regard to the stamped press itself, there has been a most decided improvement since the reduction of the duty, as compared with the stamped press before the newspaper fourpenny stamp was reduced. I remember the kind of controversy that

*W. E. Hickson*, Esq.

20 June 1851.

that existed between "Cobbett's Register" and the "Times" newspaper; and the sort of language which the "Times" editor used occasionally to apply, speaking of Cobbett, and Cobbett's rejoinder of "the bloody old 'Times;'"—both being high-priced stamped journals. Since the newspaper stamp has been reduced we have seen a greatly improved tone.

3240. With respect to that particular class of intelligence, and the education of the people we have been speaking of, in your village for instance, they would after a short time probably be able to enter into great questions of policy, as set forth in the local journals?—I think so. What would be of interest to them would be first the events connected with their immediate parish, seeing something in print relating to a person whose name they knew. What would interest them by-and-by would be the affairs relating to their own county. By-and-by, again, what would interest them would be the affairs relating to their own country; and so on, until they took an interest in the affairs of mankind at large. I have been struck, as an educational question, with the effect of newspapers in reference to the mere elementary art of reading. I have often observed that boys at the National British schools, and others, are taught apparently to read, and after a few years appear to have forgotten almost the whole of what they were taught, so as not to be able to read. I have endeavoured to ascertain the cause of it, and have found that the reason was this, that all the knowledge acquired at school was just to spell painfully through a chapter in the New Testament, and that nothing was afterwards put into their hands that had sufficient novelty to induce them to keep up the habit of reading till they had overcome the mechanical difficulty, and found a pleasure in the art. After trying various experiments, and putting into their hands books of all kinds, such as "Chambers's Journal" and the penny magazines, I have found that the only effectual thing to induce them to keep up or to create the habit of reading was some local newspaper. If you began in that way, by asking them to read an account of somebody's rick that was burnt down, you would find that you would succeed.

3241. Your residence is in Kent, is it not?—Yes.

3242. It was in Kent that the unhappy insurrection called Thom's insurrection took place?—Yes, in the neighbourhood of Canterbury.

3243. The partial success that Thom met with was attributable, was it not, to the gross ignorance of the poor in the neighbourhood in which he appeared?—Yes.

3244. Are

*W. E. Hickson*, Esq.

20 June 1851.

3244. Are you acquainted with that neighbourhood?—Yes, not minutely; but I can speak generally with regard to the state of mind of the lower classes in Kent. Close to my residence there is a large group of the followers of Joanna Southcote. One would scarcely believe that at this time of day, and after she has been dead so long, that there should be bearded followers of hers about our country;—the disciples of such an impostor. These people live within a mile of my residence. One is a blacksmith, who may be seen at work at his forge every day, with a long beard reaching down to his middle. I have conversed with the working people there lately, with reference to the subject of the Great Exhibition, and I have been very much struck with the fact, that notwithstanding all the interest that has been excited throughout the country, there, within 20 miles of London, the interest has not reached to the labouring classes; they know nothing about it, or what they know is not sufficient to excite an interest; and if you offered to pay their expenses, they would view the matter with indifference.

3245. Mr. *Cobden*.] The agitation of the question has never reached them, because they are not in the habit of seeing the periodical press?—Yes; I attribute it solely to that. I would mention this fact, that 10 days ago I made a job for a country journeyman carpenter in London, and I sent him to London, and gave him a week's work in London, with the view that he might go to see the Exhibition, furnishing him with the opportunity, but he never availed himself of it.

3246. Mr. *Rich*.] You have stated, with regard to young persons, that after they have been taught to read their interest flags; and if they attempt a chapter in the Bible, they hammer through it; and that "Chambers's Journal," and the "Penny Magazine," have failed to induce them to take any pleasure in reading; but that an effective stimulus was supplied by asking them to read an account in a provincial newspaper of the burning of a haystack in their neighbourhood?—Yes; or some corresponding event, having a strong exciting interest.

3247. Do you conceive that accounts of murders and burnings of ricks are exactly the subjects which are best calculated to humanise the mind and affections, and most conducive to the formation of moral habits?—I will answer that question by reference to my own experience. My experience is this: that what interested me most of all in newspaper reading, and what first formed the habit of reading with me, was reading the accidents and offences in the "Examiner" newspaper.

*W. E. Hickson*, Esq.

20 June 1851.

paper. There were two volumes which my father had had bound up for the years 1808 and 1809; and when I was just beginning to read I got hold of them, and I read through the accidents and offences in those two volumes. Now, I should never look at those accidents and offences, but I read the leading articles. So that it really produced this effect: it was the means of developing my intellectual powers, and I believe that a similar kind of reading would produce the same effect generally throughout the country.

3248. You are aware of the immense circulation of the "Penny Magazine" formerly, and of "Chambers's Journal," and many of those publications which seem in Kent to be not very popular, but which are largely circulated in the manufacturing districts?—Yes; but that has been almost exclusively confined to the middle classes. I never did know of a poor man taking in the "Penny Magazine."

3249. How do you define "the middle classes"?—Generally by "the middle classes" I mean persons not dependent upon weekly wages; I never myself knew a working man who was dependent upon weekly wages take in the "Penny Magazine" for any series of numbers. "Chambers's Journal" I read myself.

3250. Do not you think that among the working classes, the artisans in the great manufacturing towns are in the habit of reading such works in their homes?—Undoubtedly. I should make an exception; I do remember having seen, in one instance, a number of "Chambers's Journal" in a cottage in the neighbourhood of Newcastle.

3251. How do you account for the enormous circulation of such publications?—I think that the circulation of "Chambers's Journal" is chiefly among small shopkeepers, not among those dependent upon weekly wages; not certainly among any portion of the working classes earning less than 16*s.* a week. In the manufacturing districts, amongst the factory operatives, there is a very large section of the community called the working classes, whose wages are from 40*s.* to 50*s.* a week.

3252. Is it not much more desirable that the minds of the people should be formed, and good examples inculcated by reading publications of that kind than by reading such accounts as you have described, namely, descriptions of murders, burnings, and outrages?—In the first instance, I want to create a habit of reading, and I think that events of the most exciting kind have that tendency; I do not prefer their reading accounts of the burning of hayricks, or murders, but

an

an account of such an event as a shipwreck, for instance, of a ship which they knew had gone out with emigrants on board, with some of whom they might have had a personal acquaintance, such an event would interest them by exciting their minds.

3253. The burning of ricks has been very prevalent in the county in which you reside; and I ask you whether you consider it conducive to the moral interests of the lower orders, that accounts of rick burnings should be the subjects in which they should take the most delight?—I really do think it desirable that the agricultural labourers of this country should read a little more than they do now about rick burnings, and if they did read more about them, I think there would be fewer ricks burnt.

3254. You are aware of the effects of sympathy or association of ideas upon the human mind?—That belongs to the present system more than it would to the new one. They meet at a beershop, for instance, to discuss the subject of their grievances; some one perhaps expresses a strong opinion about some farmer having refused to give a certain rate of wages. One says, "I wish somebody would burn down his ricks for him next week;" and some one of the party there does it. Now if they could read a paper containing an account about rick-burnings, the paper would perhaps inform them that they would do the farmer, after all, no mischief, because his stacks were insured; readers are not rioters; readers are not rick-burners.

3255. Mr. *Ewart*.] You think that reading upon the subject would lead to reasoning on the subject?—Yes, reading leads to reasoning.

3256. Mr. *Cobden*.] You have been a long time paying attention to educational questions, have you not?—Yes, the whole of my life.

3257. You have been engaged in some inquiries upon the subject of education, have you not?—In a sort of semi-official capacity I have, as also in my private capacity continually.

3258. May not the Committee gather from your remarks that you are of opinion that the publications which have been brought out at a cheap rate, originally under the plea of benefiting the working classes, have missed their aim, and have been generally circulated among the middle classes?—I think so; they have generally overshot the comprehension of their readers, or they have not sufficiently entered into subjects adapted to their sympathies.

3259. You would include "Chambers's Journal" and the

*W. E. Hickson*, Esq.

20 June 1851.

the "Penny Magazine" among the number?—Yes; as relating too much to events past, and too little to events present.

3260. Is there not some misapprehension with regard to the effect of mechanics' institutes, as to their influence upon the working classes; are the members of these institutions really of the mechanic class generally?—I have generally observed that they have been almost always composed of the middle classes; in some instances, in the manufacturing districts, there have been mechanics' institutes that embraced a large portion of the working classes; but generally mechanics' institutes have been almost exclusively composed of the middle classes of the community; and I should notice with regard to newspapers, that many of those institutions have failed, from the fact of their not having a newsroom.

3261. And you are aware probably, that now in the mechanics' institutes in the north of England the newsroom is found to be the greatest attraction?—Yes.

3262. And they are constantly increasing and extending the newsrooms?—Yes, I am aware of that.

3263. You are of opinion, are you not, that cheap newspapers circulated amongst the working classes would stimulate the habit of reading, and prepare the people for reading something better than cheap newspapers?—That is precisely my view.

3264. But that their appetite would be created and excited by having access to cheap newspapers?—Yes.

3265. Mr. *Ewart*.] Is not the same process of mind observable even in the better classes of society, who, if left to read what they like best, will choose interesting and exciting events to read?—Yes.

3266. Is it not the fact, that in education you begin by presenting to children something that excites them in order to lead them onwards?—Yes; the most attractive of all school books that was ever written, is the history of Jack the Giant Killer; I do not know what the circulation is, but I am sure it is immense. When I am teaching little children myself, if I find a boy more particularly slow of comprehension, I generally put Jack the Giant Killer, as a stimulant, into his hand.

# LIST OF APPENDIX.

## Appendix, No. 1.

Papers furnished by T. Keogh, Esq.:



## Appendix, No. 2.





Appendix,

## Appendix, No. 3.



## Appendix, No. 4.

# APPENDIX.

## Appendix, No. 1.

### PAPERS furnished by *T. Keogh*, Esq.

App. No. 1.

PAGE.



— No. 1. —

STATEMENT of the Net Produce of the STAMP DUTY on NEWSPAPERS in the United Kingdom, for the Years 1848, 1849, and 1850.

| YEAR. | AMOUNT. |
|---|---|
| | £. |
| 1848 - - | 353,011 |
| 1849 - - | 348,206 |
| 1850 - - | 350,418 |

App. No. 1.

— No. 2. —

STATEMENT of the Expenses connected with the STAMPING of NEWSPAPERS in *London, Edinburgh,* and *Manchester*; as returned to The House of Commons on the 28th of January 1850.

AN estimate "of the annual expense of collecting the Stamp Duty on Newspapers; stating the number and wages of persons employed at Somerset House, and in Edinburgh and Manchester, in stamping the paper; the annual cost of machinery, and the expense of clerks, including those who receive the money for stamps."

| — | Number of Persons Employed. | Wages of Persons Employed. | Other Expenses. | | | TOT L | | |
|---|---|---|---|---|---|---|---|---|
| | | £. | £. | s. | d. | £. | s. | d. |
| Somerset House - | 41 | 3,991 | 489 | – | – | 4,480 | – | – |
| Edinburgh - - | 6 | 399 | 32 | 15 | – | 431 | 15 | – |
| Manchester - | 6 | 620 | 637 | 7 | 3 | 1,257 | 7 | 3 |
| | 53 | 5,010 | 1,159 | 2 | 3 | 6,169 | 2 | 3 |

*Note.*—Machinery is not employed in the stamping of newspapers, nor are any clerks exclusively employed to receive the money for the stamps.

(signed) *L. S. Lyne,* A. &. C. G.

Accountant and Compt.-General's Office,
Inland Revenue, Somerset House,
28 January 1850.

— No. 3. —

INSTANCES of NEWSPAPERS Published on Unstamped Paper in *London, Edinburgh* and *Manchester*.

THE following London Newspapers have issued unstamped copies, and have been excused from the penalties on payment of the duties:

"Sun."
"Indian News."
"Era."
"Home News."

The

The following Edinburgh papers have printed on unstamped paper, and have been excused from penalties on payment of the duties:

| | |
|---|---|
| " Edinburgh Weekly Courant." | " Edinburgh Saturday Evening Post." |
| " Edinburgh Weekly Chronicle." | " Edinburgh Monthly Advertiser." |
| " Edinburgh Observer." | |

The following Manchester papers have printed on unstamped paper, and have been excused from penalties on payment of the duties:

| | |
|---|---|
| " Manchester Times." | " Manchester Argus." |

---

— No. 4. —

COPY of MEMORIAL from the Newspaper Proprietors of *Glasgow* to the Lords of the Treasury.

UNTO the Right Honourable the Lords Commissioners of Her Majesty's Treasury; the MEMORIAL of the undersigned Newspaper Proprietors of *Glasgow* and its Vicinity,

Humbly sheweth,

THAT your Memorialists have long and patiently suffered a heavy loss and inconvenience from the mode in which they derive their stamps, which your Lordships may be aware are in Scotland only to be obtained in Edinburgh.

That the monopoly in favour of Edinburgh has frequently compelled your Memorialists to procure their supplies from Manchester, where your Lordships may probably know that newspaper stamps are also issued.

That your Memorialists are ignorant of any reason why Edinburgh or Manchester should have this privilege confined to them, while the injustice of not including Glasgow and its vicinity must be obvious to your Lordships, when it is stated that a vast amount of stamps are required for Glasgow, above either Edinburgh or Manchester; and it is hoped your Memorialists may be pardoned for stating that they consider the Press of Glasgow in every respect as much entitled to your Lordships' consideration as either of those cities. That your Lordships cannot fail to observe that much expense, delay, and inconvenience is, by the present system, entailed upon your Memorialists, independent of the risk of damage in the transit, which often occurs to a serious extent, and which would be completely obviated by simply stamping their papers in Glasgow. That your Memorialists are all equally desirous that no additional expenditure should be caused to Her Majesty's Government by the concession urged in the Memorial, and would respectfully suggest to your Lordships that the Excise Office would be a fit and proper place to have their papers stamped, and where your Memorialists understand there is at all times a staff sufficient for such a duty, without any increased demand upon the revenue.



That

App. No. 1.

That it is from a thorough conviction of your Memorialists that their views can be carried out without any additional charge upon the Government, that they now tender this Memorial, and they trust that your Lordships will forthwith cause an order to be issued, for ever putting an end to this long-endured grievance.

(signed)

*George Onham & Co.*, Proprietors of "Glasgow Herald."
*Peter Mackenzie & Co.*, Proprietors of "Scotch Reformers' Gazette."
*James Hedderwich & Son*, Proprietors of "Glasgow Citizen."
*James Hill Keppin & Co.*, Proprietors of "Glasgow Chronicle."
*George M. Dalry*, for Proprietors of "Saturday Post."
*James Macnab*, for Proprietors of "Glasgow Constitutional."
*A. Smith*, for Proprietors of "Glasgow Examiner."
*John Alexander*, for Proprietors of "Glasgow Courier."
*Hy. Nisbet*, Publisher of "Christian News."
*Robert Munsie*, for Proprietors of "Scottish Guardian."
*John Blackie*, Jun., for W. Blackie, Proprietor of "National Advertiser."
*Scott & Mackenzie*, Proprietors of "Greenock Advertiser."
*William Wilson*, Proprietor of "Renfrewshire Advertiser."
*Robert Somers*, Proprietor of "Scottish Times."

---

TREASURY MINUTE, 9 January 1849.

ACQUAINT parties that my Lords have had the subject of their Memorial under consideration, but are not at present prepared to sanction the establishment of another stamping establishment in North Britain.

---

— No. 5. —

Complaint as to "PUNCH" Publishing on Unstamped Paper.

To the Commissioners of Inland Revenue.

Gentlemen,

BY the Act 6 & 7 Wm. 4, c. 76, it is enacted, that no one under severe penalties, shall publish a newspaper on paper not duly stamped; and in the schedule at the end of the Act, a newspaper is defined to be "any paper containing public news, intelligence or occurrences, printed in any part of the United Kingdom, to be dispersed and made public;" and again, "any paper containing any public news, intelligence or occurrences, or any remarks or observations thereon," at intervals not exceeding 26 days.

I beg to call your attention to the fact, that a newspaper registered at Somerset House, and entitled "Punch," and printed by William Bradbury, of No. 13, Upper Woburn-place, in the parish of St. Pancras, and Frederick Mullett Evans, of No. 7, Church-row, Stoke Newington,

Newington, both in the County of Middlesex, printers, at their office in Lombard-street, in the precinct of Whitefriars, in the City of London; and published by them at No. 85, Fleet-street, in the parish of St. Bride, in the City of London, is in the habit of circulating unstamped, the country edition alone being stamped. App. No. 1.

That "Punch" is as much a newspaper as the "Times," or the Morning Chronicle," will appear in examining three or four numbers. Almost every number contains public news, intelligence or occurrences, to say nothing of remarks and observations thereon; it even ventures to report public meetings, and debates in Parliament. In laying this information before your Board, I think it sufficient to specify the following articles in the enclosed number of "Punch," which was published as aforesaid, on Saturday the 16th February 1850:

"Mr. Punch on Church and State Education."
"Louis Napoleon, Spare that Tree."
"Punch, Parliamentary Hodge Podge."
"The Credit of an Emperor."
"Affair of Hungary."
"Our Colonial Experience."
"Mr. Horsman's Anatomy."
"Our Foreign Feud."
"Wit and Wisdom in the House of Lords."
"The Worst of Taxes."
"A Minister is Infallible."
"Nothing Like Grog."

Should the Board imagine that this number of "Punch," is an exception to the general rule, I am prepared to show that the reverse is the fact, the violation of the law on the part of this paper is wilful and systematic, and that justice to the rest of the press requires that it should be put an end to.

I remain, &c.
(signed) *William Gellen,*
34, Museum-street, Bloomsbury.

2 April 1850.

---

(Copy Solicitor's Report.)

I do not think that this publication can be considered a newspaper; it contains nothing that can be properly termed public news, intelligence or occurrences, and it would be straining the words of the Act to call the reference made in it to public matters, remarks or observations upon news.

(signed) *Hugh Tilsley.*

9 April 1850.

(Copy Board's Minute.)

Read 11 April 1850.

*J. T.*
C. P. R.

---

App. No. 1.

To the Commissioners of Inland Revenue.

Gentlemen, 34, Museum-street, Bloomsbury.

It recently appeared in print, that you intended to proceed against a penny publication, published in the city of Norwich, on the grounds that it came within the law's grasp as a newspaper.

Now I am a poor man, and feel a strong repugnance to tyranny of any description, and in this instance the case is so clear, of "one law for the rich, and another for the poor," that I should not fulfil my mission as a man, if I did not protest against such a system of favouritism; and now for proofs: "Punch" frequently quotes largely, and a work just come out, "Dickens's Household Narrative" cannot be considered by any one as otherwise than a newspaper. Now it is so manifest an injustice to debar the poor man from his modicum of political or other intelligence, that any well-constituted mind must shudder at the continuance of a law that should never have passed, and at the present time, totally unfitted the increasing knowledge of the people. It may live in your remembrance, that I enclosed a copy of "Punch" some time since, in reference to the same matter, but I received no communication, which I trust will either cause you to alter the law, or else give a shadow of a reason for its continuance.

I am, &c.
(signed) *William Gellen.*

---

Inland Revenue, Somerset House.
Sir, 11 May 1850.

Having laid before the Board your letter of the instant, I am directed to state, that they do not think it necessary or desirable to enter into any discussion with you on the subject therein referred to, in which you appear to have no personal concern.

I am, &c.
(signed) *Thomas Keogh.*

Mr. William Gellen, 34, Museum-street,
Bloomsbury.

---

— No. 6. —

Instances of Applications from Parties to pay Duties on Unstamped Copies, and the Correspondence thereon.

---

16, Great Windmill-street, Haymarket,
Sir, 10 April 1848.

As printer of the "Northern Star" newspaper, I have to inform you, that 1,000 copies of that paper were yesterday printed on unstamped paper.

The demand for the "Northern Star" was so much beyond our calculation, that, although we had provided ourselves with an extra supply of stamps, we found ourselves obliged to print the above-named quantity on blank paper.

Yours, &c.
(signed) *D. McGowan.*

J. Timm, Esq., Somerset House.

Stamps and Taxes,
17 April 1848.

Sir,

THE Board having had before them your letter of the 10th instant, as to your having published certain copies of the "Northern Star" newspaper without stamps, I am directed to acquaint you, that on your making a declaration before a magistrate, as to the number so printed, the Board will, on this occasion, allow the duty in respect thereof to be received without penalty; but I am to observe that a similar indulgence will not be extended to you in future, as the Board consider it incumbent on all newspaper proprietors, especially since the reduction of the duty, to keep a sufficient supply of stamps on hand to guard against all emergencies.

I am to add, that the duty for the unstamped copies must be paid immediately, to Wm. Everett, esq., Receiver-general, at this office.

I am, &c.
(signed) *Thos. Keogh.*

To Mr. McGowan, Printer,
16, Great Windmill-street,
Haymarket.

---

Sir,

Stamps and Taxes, 15 Feb. 1849.

I AM directed to call your attention to the Board's letter of the 17th April last, and to require you immediately to pay the duty on the unstamped copies of the "Northern Star" newspaper therein alluded to.

I am, &c.
(signed) *Thos. Keogh.*

Mr. D. McGowan, Printer,
16, Great Windmill-street,
Haymarket.

---

MR. MCGOWAN thought that this was paid at the time; he is very much surprised to find it was not; he must trouble the office to send him copy of his letter, as neither the publisher nor he can recollect how many unstamped sheets were used on the occasion alluded to.

Windmill-street, 22 February 1849.

---

Inland Revenue Somerset House,
28 February 1849.

Sir,

WITH reference to your letter of the 22d instant, I am directed by the Board to enclose herewith a copy of your application of the 10th of April last.

I am, &c.
(signed) *Thomas Keogh.*

Mr. D. McGowan, Printer,
16, Great Windmill-street,
Haymarket.

---

App. No. 1.

Sir, Inland Revenue, 13 April 1849.

I AM directed to call your immediate attention to the Board's letters of the 17th April 1848, and the 15th and 28th February 1849, and I am to acquaint you, that if the duty on the unstamped copies of the "Northern Star" newspaper therein referred to, be not paid forthwith, a prosecution will be instituted for the penalties.

I am, &c.

Mr. D. McGowan, Printer, (signed) *Thos. Keogh.*
16, Great Windmill-street.

---

16, Great Windmill-street,
Sir, 17 April 1849.

MR. MCGOWAN is away from the office; he will return on Saturday or Monday morning, and shall immediately attend to your letter of the 13th, respecting the unpaid stamps for the "Northern Star" newspaper.

I am, &c.
(signed) *James McGowan.*

To Thos. Keogh, Esq.,
Inland Revenue, Somerset House.

---

"Dundee Advertiser" Office,
Sir, 2 February 1849.

WE are very sorry in having again to trouble you about a mistake we have made in selling nine blanks instead of stamped newspapers. These blanks were intended for binding and private purposes connected with ourselves, and were carried during the bustle of a second edition from the machine-room to the publishing office, and sold by mistake for stamped copies; the error originated in these blank copies not having been put properly aside, and thereafter carried to the publishing office and sold, under the impression that they were stamps instead of blanks.

We are very sorry for what has occurred, and shall be glad to make affidavit to the above statements and repay the stamp duty as formerly authorized. Trusting this shall satisfy, we remain,

Yours, &c.

Angus Fletcher, &c. (signed) *Thos. Young.*
Edinburgh.

---

Inland Revenue, Somerset House, London,
Sir, 8 February 1849.

I HAVE laid before the Board your report of the 3d instant, with a letter from the publisher of the "Dundee Advertiser" relative to the sale of certain unstamped copies of that paper; and in reply I am directed to acquaint you, that the Board consent to the duty being received on a declaration as to the number printed, but the party should be cautious against the occurrence of a similar irregularity.

I am, &c.

A. Fletcher, Esq. (signed) *Thomas Keogh.*
Inland Revenue, Edinburgh.

---

App. No. 1.

To the Board of Commissioners of Inland Revenue, Somerset House, London.

"Liverpool Times" Office,
9 April 1849.

Gentlemen,

HAVING been disappointed in my usual number of stamps for the publication of the "Liverpool Times" of the 5th instant, and the demand being so great on that day in consequence of the recent awful murders of Mrs. Henrickson, her children, and servant, I was obliged to use 500 sheets of unstamped paper, which I shall have pleasure in paying the amount for stamps into the office of the distributor of stamps in Liverpool, or wherever you may request the amount to be paid. Below I append the affidavit of the person who printed the papers on that day. (See page 492, for affidavit.)

I am, &c.
*pro Thomas Baines,*
(signed) *John Benson.*

---

Inland Revenue, Somerset House,
19 April 1849.

Sir,

THE Board having had before them your letter of the 9th instant, as to your having published certain copies of the "Liverpool Times" newspaper without stamps, I am directed to acquaint you that the Board will, on this occasion, allow the duty in respect thereof to be received without penalty; but I am to observe, that a similar indulgence will not be extended to you, as the Board consider it incumbent on all newspaper proprietors, especially since the reduction of the stamp, to keep a sufficient supply on hand to guard against all contingencies.

I am to add, that the duty for the unstamped copies must be paid immediately to the Receiver-general, at this office, instead of to the distributor.

I am, &c.
(signed) *Thomas Keogh.*

To Mr. Thomas Baines,
"Liverpool Times" Office,
10, Castle-street, Liverpool.

---

"Liverpool Times" Office,
20 April 1849.

Gentlemen,

ACCOMPANYING I forward you a post-office order for the amount of duty on 500 impressions of "Liverpool Times," printed upon unstamped paper.

I am, &c.
*pro Thomas Baines,*
(signed) *John Benson.*

To the Board of Inland Revenue,
&c. &c. &c.

App. No. 1.

(Affidavit.)

Borough of Liverpool in the County Palatine of Lancaster, } to wit.

I, *George Arrowsmith*, printer, of Liverpool, in the county of Lancaster, in the United Kingdom of Great Britain and Ireland, do solemnly and sincerely declare, that I printed for Thomas Baines, of 10, Castle-street, Liverpool, 500 sheets of unstamped paper for the "Liverpool Times" on the 5th day of April 1849.

---

AT *Elgin*, the 20th Day of April 1849.

In presence of *Patrick Cameron*, Esq., one of Her Majesty's Justices of Peace for *Elginshire*.

Compeared *Alexander Russell*, Printer and Publisher of the "Elgin Courant" Newspaper, who being solemnly sworn, depones, that on the 5th April current, he sent an order to Messrs. Cowan & Co., papermakers in Edinburgh, along with a remittance for 2,000 stamps for said newspaper; that notwithstanding the deponent's instructions to transmit the same by the "Duke of Richmond" steamer on the 10th current, the said Messrs. Cowan & Co. were prevented from doing so in consequence of a holiday at the Stamp Office; that the deponent having full confidence that the stamps would be sent him by the same conveyance on the 17th, waited for their arrival, but found to his great disappointment that they had not been sent by her: that the deponent's supply of stamps being deficient for his publication of this day, he was most reluctantly compelled to print and publish said deficiency on plain paper, amounting to 125 sheets, the stamp-duty of which he has this day paid to the stamp distributor of Elgin. All which is truth, as the deponent shall answer to God.

(signed) *Alex. Russell.*
*Pat. Cameron*, J. P.

---

Inland Revenue, Edinburgh,
30 April 1849.

Sir,

I beg respectfully to enclose an affidavit, by the publisher of the "Elgin Courant," showing the circumstances under which 125 copies of the impression of the "Courant" of the 20th instant were printed on unstamped paper. On inquiry, I find that the facts therein stated are correct, and as no similar irregularity has occurred with this paper for many years back, I submit that the duty thereon be received without penalties.

I have, &c.
(signed) *A. Fletcher.*

Thomas Keogh, Esq.

---

App. No. 1.

Inland Revenue, Somerset House,
London, 4 May 1849.

Sir,

HAVING laid before the Board your report of the 30th ultimo, with an affidavit from the publisher of the "Elgin Courant," relative to 125 copies of the paper having been published on unstamped paper, I am directed to acquaint you that the Board have been pleased to consent to the duties being received.

You will at the same time caution the party against a repetition of the offence.

I have, &c.
(signed) *Thomas Keogh.*

To A. Fletcher, Esq.,
Inland Revenue, Edinburgh.

---

Inland Revenue, Edinburgh,
25 September 1849.

Sir,

I BEG to enclose letter and relative affidavit from the publisher of the "Aberdeen Herald," respecting the publication of 750 supplement sheets on unstamped paper on the 24th instant, and respectfully request to be favoured with the instructions of the Board thereon.

I may mention that this is the first offence on the part of the publisher of this paper for many years.

I have, &c.
(signed) *A. Fletcher.*

Thomas Keogh, Esq.

---

Inland Revenue, Somerset House,
London, 29 September 1849.

Sir,

I HAVE laid before the Board your letter of the 25th instant, forwarding an application from the publisher of the "Aberdeen Herald" newspaper, for permission to pay duty on 750 supplements printed on unstamped paper.

In reply, I am directed to authorize you to receive the duty in question, cautioning the party against a repetition of the offence.

The papers enclosed by you are returned herewith.

I have, &c.
(signed) *Thomas Keogh.*

A. Fletcher, Esq.

---

Inland Revenue, Edinburgh,
21 November 1849.

Sir,

I BEG to enclose a letter from the publisher of the "Nairnshire Mirror" newspaper, and relative affidavit respecting the publication of 180 copies on unstamped paper on the 20th ultimo, and respectfully request to be favoured with the instructions of the Board thereon.

I may mention that this is not the first offence on the part of the publisher of the "Mirror," as he printed 85 copies on unstamped paper on 16th October 1847.

I have, &c.
(signed) *A. Fletcher.*

Thomas Keogh, Esq.

---

App. No. 1.

"Mirror" Office, Nairn,
19 November 1849.

Sir,

I BEG leave to transmit the accompanying declaration with regard to the number of unstamped sheets issued by me in a recent publication of the "Nairnshire Mirror" newspaper, but I am at a loss to know to whom to remit the duty. Perhaps you will have the kindness to inform me on this subject.

I have, &c.
(signed) *C. Macwatt.*

A. F. Fletcher, Esq.
Solicitor of Stamps, Edinburgh.

---

At Nairn, the 19th day of November, Eighteen hundred and forty-nine years.

I, *Charles Macwatt,* Printer, in Nairn, do hereby solemnly and sincerely declare, that on the 20th day of October last, I published 180 copies of the "Nairnshire Mirror" newspaper on unstamped paper, and intimated in the same publication that I had so published part of that impression of the paper; that my reason for so publishing on unstamped paper arose from the following cause:—That on the twelfth day of October aforesaid, I transmitted the duty for a greater number of stamps than was necessary for the said publication; but as alleged by the stationer to whom the order was sent, and indorsed on the invoice transmitted to the stamp-office at Elgin, the stamps could not be obtained from the stamp-office in Edinburgh in time for transmission by the steamer of the week of publication, and only arrived by mail on the nineteenth day of October, being the afternoon of the day immediately preceding the day of publication, and after the paper had gone to press; that under these circumstances I was compelled to publish part of my impression on unstamped paper; and I make this solemn declaration believing the same to be true, and by virtue of the provisions of an Act made and passed in the sixth year of his late Majesty William the Fourth, chapter 62, intituled, An Act to repeal an Act, &c.

(signed) *C. Macwatt.*

Declared before me, Isaac Kitchen, Esquire, one of Her Majesty's Justices of Peace for the county of Nairn, on the nineteenth day of November, eighteen hundred and forty-nine years.

(signed) *Isaac Kitchen.*

---

Sir, Inland Revenue, 27 November 1849.

I HAVE laid before the Board your letter of the 21st instant, with an application from the publisher of the "Nairnshire Mirror," to pay the duty on certain unstamped copies of that paper.

In reply, I am directed to acquaint you that the Board have consented to the duties being received; you will however caution the party, that in case of any similar infringement of the law in future, the penalties will be certainly enforced.

I am, &c.
(signed) *Thomas Keogh.*

A. Fletcher, Esq., &c. &c.

App. No. 1.

"Era" Newspaper, Catherine-street,
Strand, 3 June 1850.

Gentlemen,

I HUMBLY beg to solicit your pardon and indulgence. Yesterday morning we had an extra demand for the above journal, and through neglect of not providing to meet the same, we were out of stamps, necessitating us to machine one ream (500 copies) with blank sheets. Trusting you will allow me to pay immediately the price of 500 stamps, and promising to be more careful for the future to prevent a repetition, I anxiously wish to know how to act, and

Remain, &c.
(signed) *Frederic Ledger,*
Printer and Publisher of
"Era" Newspaper.

To Her Majesty's Commissioners
of Inland Revenue, Somerset House.

---

Sir, Inland Revenue, 8 June 1850.

HAVING laid before the Board your letter of the 3d instant, I am directed in reply to state, that on the present occasion they have consented to receive the duty in respect of the unstamped copies of the "Era," on your making a statutory declaration before a magistrate as to the number so published.

I am however to observe, that the Board will not pass over a similar irregularity on any future occasion, as they consider it incumbent on all proprietors of newspapers (especially since the reduction in the duty) to keep a supply of stamps on hand adequate to all emergencies.

I am, &c.
(signed) *Thomas Keogh.*

Mr. Frederic Ledger,
"Era" Newspaper Office, Catherine-street,
Strand.

---

To the Honourable the Commissioners of Stamps and Taxes.

ON Friday last, the 25th day of February, the pressman of the Evening "Sun" Newspaper, 112, Strand, having, from the unexpected increase of sale of the "Sun," used and printed 1,312 sheets of blank paper without being stamped, begs leave to pray your Honourable Board to allow payment to be received on account of the number printed, and further to pray your Honourable Board to dispense with any penalty that may have been incurred, and your Memorialist will ever pray.

(signed) *George Murden,*
Pressman to the
"Sun" Newspaper, 112, Strand.

28 February 1848.

---

App. No. 1.

Sir, Stamps and Taxes, 14 March 1848.

THE Board having had before them your letter of the 28th ultimo, as to your having published certain copies of the "Sun" newspaper without stamps, I am directed to acquaint you, that on your making a declaration before a magistrate as to the number so printed, the Board will, on this occasion, allow the duty in respect thereof to be received without penalty; but I am to observe, that a similar indulgence will not be extended to you on any future occasion, as the Board consider it incumbent on all newspaper proprietors (especially since the reduction of the stamp) to keep a sufficient supply on hand to guard against all emergencies.

I am to add, that the duty for the unstamped copies must be paid immediately to William Everett, esq., the Receiver-general, at this office.

I am, &c.
(signed) *Thomas Keogh.*

Mr. George Murden,
"Sun" Newspaper-office, 112, Strand.

---

Honourable Sirs, Old Bailey, 22 March 1850.

I RESPECTFULLY beg to be allowed to pay the duty on 1,000 copies of the "Indian News," No. 182, printed on unstamped paper, which I was obliged to avail myself of this morning, having inadvertently mitted to fetch away the stamped paper from Somerset-house. I shall do my utmost to avoid the occurrence of a similar circumstance.

I am, &c.
(signed) *A. E. Murray.*

The Honourable
the Commissioners of Stamps.

---

Sir, Stamps and Taxes, 28 March 1850.

I HAVE laid before the Board your letter of the 22d instant, requesting, under the circumstances therein stated, to be allowed to pay the duty of 1,000 copies of the "Indian News," printed by you on unstamped paper.

In reply, I am directed to inform you that the Board consent to accept the duty as requested, on your making a statutory declaration of the number of copies, but I am to warn you against a repetition of the offence.

I am, &c.
(signed) *Thomas Keogh.*

Mr. A. Murray,
"Indian News" Office, Old Bailey.

Honorable Sirs, 15, Old Bailey, 2 August 1850.

I RESPECTFULLY beg to be allowed to pay the duty on 700 copies of the last No. of the "Home News," which I was obliged to print on unstamped paper. The circumstance arose from the inability of the stationer to send the paper to the Stamp-office in time to be stamped; owing to delay in its non-arrival, caused by an accident occurring to the machinery of the steamer. I may as well mention, that on the day of publication I received from the stationer 3,500 stamps, but unfortunately not in time to save me the necessity of printing the 700 copies on unstamped paper; the duty on which, I now respectfully beg to be allowed to pay. The edition consisted of 3,200 copies; 2,500 of which were on stamped, and 700 on unstamped paper.

I am, &c.
(signed) *A. E. Murray.*

To the Honorable the Commissioners of Stamps, &c. &c.

---

Inland Revenue, Somerset House,
9 August 1850.

Sir,

I HAVE laid before the Board your letter of the 2d instant, requesting that the duty may be received on certain copies of a publication entitled "Home News," printed on unstamped paper. In reply, I am directed to call upon you for a statutory declaration of the number so printed.

I am, &c.
(signed) *Thomas Keogh.*

Mr. A. E. Murray,
15, Old Bailey.

---

(DECLARATION.)

I, *Alexander Elder Murray*, printer, 15, Old Bailey, do solemnly and sincerely declare, that I have printed 700 copies of No. 86, of the "Home News" on unstamped paper, and no more.

---

Inland Revenue, Somerset House,
16 August 1850.

Sir,

THE Board have had before them your declaration of the 14th instant, of the number of copies of No 86, of the publication entitled "Home News," printed on unstamped paper; and I am to inform you that the Board have, on this occasion, been pleased to direct that the duties be received, and that they should be immediately paid to the Receiver-general at this office.

I am, however, at the same time to observe, that a similar indulgence will not be extended to any similar infringement of the law, it being incumbent on the proprietors of newspapers to keep a sufficient supply of stamps on hand to guard against emergencies.

I am, &c.
(signed) *Thomas Keogh.*

Mr. A. E. Murray,
15, Old Bailey.

---

App. No. 1.

"Mercury" Office, Liverpool,
10 January 1851.

Gentlemen,

WE respectfully beg to state for your information, that this day, having an extra demand for our paper, we were compelled to print supplements on unstamped paper to the amount of two thousand (2,000) copies; the usual form has been applied for to the office in Manchester.

We are, &c.
*Egerton Smith & Co.*
(signed) *Robert Long.*

The Honourable
Commissioners of Stamps.

---

Inland Revenue, Somerset House, London,
18 January 1851.

Gentleman,

MR. BISCHOFF, the distributor at Liverpool, having forwarded to the Board your communication of the 10th instant in regard to your having issued on that day certain supplements of the "Liverpool Mercury" on unstamped paper, I am directed to acquaint you that the Board have been pleased on the present occasion to allow the duties to be received without penalty, on your making a declaration before a magistrate as to the number of unstamped copies so published.

I am, however, to observe that the Board will not on any future occasion pass over such an irregularity, as they consider it incumbent on all proprietors of newspapers, especially since the reduction of the stamp, to keep a sufficient supply on hand to guard against all emergencies.

I am to add that the duties should be paid immediately to the Receiver-general at this office, and not to the distributor.

I am, &c.
(signed) *Thomas Keogh.*

Messrs. Egerton Smith & Co.
Liverpool.

---

## Appendix, No. 2.

A RETURN of PROSECUTIONS in respect of Violations of the NEWSPAPER STAMP ACTS, for the Three Years ended September 1836, when the present Act came into operation. App. No. 2.

| DEFENDANT. | RESULT OF PROCEEDINGS. |
|---|---|
| Year ending September 1834: | |
| In the EXCHEQUER: | |
| Charles Penny - - - - | Verdict given for 120 *l.* penalties. |
| George Patchett - - - - | - - Stayed on payment of duties evaded, and 2 *l.* costs. |
| W. M. Knight and others - - | - - Stayed on payment of duties evaded, 2 *l.* 6 *s.*; costs, 2 *l.* |
| Henry Hetherington - - - | Verdict given for 120 *l.*, and costs. |
| John Cleave - - - - | Verdict given for 100 *l.* and costs. |
| Eneas MacKenzie - - - | - - Stayed on payment of mitigated penalty, 5 *l.*, and duty evaded, 4 *l.* 0 *s.* 8 *d.* |
| Before MAGISTRATES: | |
| ——— Walker, Norwich - - | Fined 10 *s.* |
| John Smith, Strand - - - | - - Fined 20 *l.*; committed for non-payment. |
| George Baker, Worcester - - | - - Fined 10 *l.*; committed for non-payment. |
| ——— Wastneys, Newcastle - | Fined 20 *l.* - - ditto. |
| Charles Puttock, Grafton-street, Soho. | „ 5 *l.* |
| John Clements, Little Pulteney-street | „ 5 *l.* |
| John Cleave, Shoe-lane - - | „ 5 *l.* |
| Richard Egan Lee, Holborn - - | „ 40 *l.*; warrant issued for committal. |
| John Cleave, Shoe-lane - - | „ 5 *l.* |
| Edmund Wastneys, Newcastle - | „ 20 *l.*; committed. |
| Edward Somerside, Winlaton, Durham. | „ 20 *l.* ditto. |
| Edmund Stallwood, Holborn - | Fined 40 *l.*; committed. |
| Isabella Rose, Southampton - - | „ 5 *l.* ditto. |
| William Nicholls, John-street, Tottenham-court-road. | Withdrawn; error in name. |



(*continued*)

App. No. 2.

| DEFENDANT. | RESULT OF PROCEEDINGS. |
|---|---|
| James Watson, City-road - - | Fined 20 *l.*; committed. |
| W. N. Fagnoit, Great Wild-street | Withdrawn; error as to parish. |
| Richard Pears, Holywell-lane, Curtain-road. | |
| Thomas Heins, Middle-row, Holborn. | Not proceeded with. |
| Worthy Worthington George Nicholls, John-street, Tottenham-court-road. | Fined 20 *l.*; committed. |
| Alice Mann, Leeds - - - | „ 5 *l.* |
| Henry Hetherington, 126, Strand - | „ 40 *l.* |
| John Sharp, Kent-street, Southwark | „ 5 *l.* |
| John Dredge, 67, High street, Whitechapel. | „ 5 *l.* |
| Benjamin Sampson, Boyce-street, Brighton. | „ 20 *l.* |
| Patrick Thomas Bready, Sheffield - | „ 20 *l.*; committed. |
| Edward Gleave - - - - | „ 20 *l.* ditto. |
| Susannah Wotton, Grape street, Stockport - - - - | „ 5 *l.*; given up. |
| James Acland, Hull - - - | „ 100 *l.* |
| John Chappell, Hotwell-road, Clifton | „ 10 *l.*; committed. |
| Jeremiah Cruse, 67, Whitechapel-road. | Not proceeded with. |
| James Guest, 91, Steelhouse-lane, Birmingham. | Fined 25 *l.*; committed. |
| Richard Jenkinson, 6, Church street, Birmingham. | „ 5 *l.* ditto. |
| Julius Faulkner, 5, Stafford-street, Birmingham. | „ 20 *l.* ditto. |
| William Plastans, 55, Dale-end, Birmingham. | „ 10 *l.* ditto. |
| William Guest, Birmingham - | „ 15 *l.* ditto. |
| Thomas Watts, Birmingham - | „ 10 *l.* ditto. |
| William Augustus Kentish, Birmingham. | Withdrawn. |
| William Hickling, Coventry - | Fined 5 *l.* |
| Alexander Yates, Coventry - - | „ 10 *l.*; committed. |
| Year ending September 1835: | |
| In the EXCHEQUER: | |
| William Rickerby - - - | - - Stayed on payment of duty evaded, 6 *l.* 19 *s.*; costs, 1 *l.* |
| John P. Eve - - - - | Proceedings stayed. |
| W. Allbut and another - - | Stayed on payment of 2 *l.* for costs. |
| J. Vincent and another - - | The like. |

App. No. 2.

| DEFENDANT. | RESULT OF PROCEEDINGS. |
|---|---|
| P. Perring - - - - - | - - Stayed on payment of duty evaded, 7 *l.* 1 *s.* 8 *d.*, and costs, 1 *l.* |
| J. Lloyd - - - - - - | Stayed. |
| Prentice and Cathrall - - - | Stayed on payment of 2 *l.* for costs. |
| J. Hardinge Veitch - - - | Stayed. |
| G. Fall - - - - - - | Stayed on payment of 20 *s.* for costs. |
| T. L. Holt - - - - - | Stayed. |
| J. Keys - - - - - - | Stayed. |
| Before MAGISTRATES: | |
| John Smith - - - - - | Fined 40 *l.*; committed. |
| George Jeffery - - - - | " 20 *l.* ditto. |
| Charles Miller Hucklebridge - | " 20 *l.* ditto. |
| Thomas Heins - - - - - | " 20 *l.* ditto. |
| Joseph Harris - - - - - | " 20 *l.* ditto. |
| Joshua Hobson - - - - - | " 20 *l.* ditto. |
| William Jones - - - - - | " 20 *l.* ditto. |
| Thomas Collumbell - - - | " 5 *l.* |
| Alexander Yates - - - - - | " 10 *l.*; committed. |
| Samuel Goodwin - - - - | " 20 *l.*; not enforced. |
| Samuel Hulley - - - - - | Not proceeded with. |
| Charles Woodall - - - - | Fined 20 *l.*; committed. |
| A person, name unknown, serving at the shop of Thomas Harris. | " 20 *l.* ditto. |
| Elizabeth Smith - - - - - | " 10 *l.* ditto. |
| John Pugh - - - - - - | " 10 *l.*; not enforced. |
| William Burnett - - - - - | " 10 *l.*; committed. |
| Benjamin Cousins - - - - | " 20 *l.* |
| William Nicholas Fagnoit - - | " 20 *l.* |
| William French - - - - - | " 10 *l.*; not enforced. |
| John Sharp - - - - - | " 10 *l.* ditto. |
| Francis Needham - - - - | " 20 *l.*; committed. |
| John Meredith - - - - - | " 5 *l.* ditto. |
| Thomas Millard - - - - - | Not proceeded with. |
| William Pearce - - - - - | Ditto. |
| John Speacklam - - - - - | Fined 5 *l.*; committed. |
| William Slater - - - - - | " 5 *l.* ditto. |
| George Broughton - - - - | " 5 *l.*; not enforced. |
| George Tomkins - - - - - | Not to be found. |
| George Johnson - - - - - | Absconded. |
| George Turner - - - - - | Ditto. |
| Jane Barlow - - - - - | Withdrawn. |
| Year ending September 1836: | |
| In the EXCHEQUER: | |
| William Houston - - - - | Stayed. |
| J. Cleave - - - - - - | Verdict given for 620 *l.* and costs. |
| G. B. Batchelor - - - - - | - - Stayed on payment of mitigated penalty, 2 *l.* |

(*continued*)

App. No. 2.

| DEFENDANT. | RESULT OF PROCEEDINGS. |
|---|---|
| Before MAGISTRATES: | |
| Joseph Ashton - - - - | Absconded. |
| William Sletor - - - - | Fined 10 *l.*; committed. |
| ——— Crocker - - - - | „ 80 *l.* |
| Richard Egan Lee - - - | Not proceeded with. |
| Robert Stevens - - - - | Ditto. |
| Alexander Yates - - - - | Not to be found. |
| William Paul Staines - - - | Fined 20 *l.*; committed. |
| John Riches - - - - | „ 10 *l.* ditto. |
| ——— Jenkins - - - - | Dismissed. |
| Mary Ann Beales - - - | Fined 10 *l.*; committed. |
| Joshua Hobson - - - - | „ 80 *l.* ditto. |
| Alice Mann - - - - | „ 100 *l.* ditto. |
| William Stockbridge - - - | „ 15 *l.* |
| Charles Dade Blanchard - - | „ 20 *l.*; committed. |
| John Smith - - - - | „ 20 *l.* ditto. |
| Patrick Thomas Bready - - | „ 10 *l.* ditto. |
| ——— Croker - - - - | „ 10 *l.* ditto. |
| William Nicholas Fagnoit - - | „ 20 *l.*; absconded. |
| James Reeve - - - - | „ 20 *l.*; committed. |
| John Mark - - - - | „ 20 *l.* ditto. |
| Abel Heywood - - - - | „ 15 *l.* ditto. |
| Thomas Martin - - - - | „ 5 *l.* |
| Thomas Hutton - - - - | „ 5 *l.* |
| John Day - - - - | „ 15 *l.*; committed. |
| Joseph Bell - - - - | „ 5 *l.* |
| John Pickering - - - - | „ 5 *l.* |
| Edward Gleave - - - - | „ 5 *l.*; committed. |
| James Ibbotson - - - - | „ 20 *l.* ditto. |
| ——— Bready - - - - | „ 10 *l.* ditto. |
| John Pugh - - - - | Absconded. |
| Wife of John Smith - - - | Dismissed. |
| Christopher Tinker - - - | Fined 80 *l.*; committed. |
| James Osborne - - - - | „ 60 *l.* ditto. |
| William Jones - - - - | „ 5 *l.* |
| Ann Jackson - - - - | „ 20 *l.*; committed. |
| Joseph Lawson - - - - | „ 5 *l.* |
| Mary Hobson - - - - | „ 5 *l.* |
| John Sharp - - - - | „ 40 *l.*; committed. |
| William Ants - - - - | Dismissed: misnomer. |
| William Paul Staines - - - | Absconded. |
| John Parker - - - - | Fined 10 *l.*; committed. |
| William Barker - - - - | „ 5 *l.* |
| Joshua Hobson - - - - | Dismissed. |

App. No. 2.

A RETURN of PROSECUTIONS in respect of Violations of the NEWSPAPER STAMP ACTS, for the Three Years ended 1st June 1851.

| DEFENDANT. | RESULT OF PROCEEDINGS. |
|---|---|
| **Year ended 1st June 1849:** | |
| In the EXCHEQUER: | |
| Thomas Piers Healey - - - | Discontinued. |
| John and Henry Cox - - - | - - Proceedings stayed on the paper being registered. |
| William Strange - - - - | - Ditto - - - ditto. |
| Oscar Hart - - - - - | Proceedings stayed. |
| J. B. F. Leach - - - - | - - Stayed on payment of duty evaded, 17 *s.* |
| **Year ending 1st June 1850:** | |
| In the EXCHEQUER: | |
| Thomas Smith - - - - | - - Stayed on payment of mitigated penalty of 2 *l.* |
| Thomas Micklekwaite - - - | - - Stayed on payment of duty evaded, 8 *s.* 4 *d.* and costs. |
| Charles Yeates - - - - | - - Stayed on payment of mitigated penalty of 2 *l.* |
| Rowland Hill - - - - | - - Stayed on payment of mitigated penalty of 1 *l.* |
| **In the EXCHEQUER,** | |
| **Year ending 1st June 1851:** | |
| Messrs. Bradbury & Evans - - | Case still pending. |
| Samuel Greenwood - - - - | - - Stayed on payment of 10 *l.*, to cover the duties evaded, and costs. |
| Henry Barrass, jun. - - - | - - Stayed on payment of 2 *l.* mitigated penalties, 1 *l.* 1 *s.* 11 *d.* duties evaded, and 2 *l.* 5 *s.* 6 *d.* costs. |
| William Elliott - - - - | - - Stayed on payment of duties evaded. |
| Samuel George Bucknall - - | Proceedings stayed. |

App. No. 2.

CASES in which the Solicitor of INLAND REVENUE has, during the last Three Years, written to Caution the PUBLISHERS of UNSTAMPED NEWSPAPERS against incurring further Liabilities, or has in any way interfered with such Publications where no Prosecution has been instituted. The particulars complained of can only be designated as News in a general way. In some instances the character of the News may, perhaps, be inferred from the Title of the Publication.

| Date of Letter. | Party Written to. | Title and other Description of Publication. |
|---|---|---|
| 1848: | | |
| 1 July - | Mr. Shaw, Manchester - | - - Manchester News, Manchester Standard, Oldham News. |
| 29 „ - | - - Mr. B. S. Treanor, Stalybridge. | The Truth Teller. |
| 1849: | | |
| 23 February - | - - Mr. Joseph Lawson, Bradshaw-gate, Bolton. | - The Bolton Reform Advocate. |
| 8 March - | - Mr. J. Noble, Market-place, Boston. | - - Noble's Great Northern, East Lincolnshire, &c. Monthly Time Tables, and General Advertiser. |
| 10 „ - | Mr. H. T. Jennings, Bath - | - - The Bath and Clifton Looker-on. |
| 12 „ - | - - Mr. J. Bannister, Knaresborough. | - - Bannister's Northern Luminary. |
| 24 April - | - Messrs. Matthews, 44, Broad-street, Bristol. | - - Handbill; Execution of Sarah H. Thomas. |
| 4 May - | - - Mr. J. Beck, 8, Upper-parade, Leamington. | - - Beck's Weekly List of Visitors. |
| 5 November | - - Mr. J. Goodfellow, Fisherton, Salisbury. | - - The Wiltshire Game Law Reporter. |
| 1850: | | |
| 11 February - | - - Mr. Isaac Latimer, Journal Office, Plymouth. | - - A paper containing an account of the opening of Parliament, and the Queen's Speech. |
| 6 March - | - Mr. T. Smith, 42, Mincing-lane. | Commercial Daily List. |
| 7 „ - | - - Messrs. Jarrold, 47, St. Paul's Church-yard. | The Reformer. |

App. No. 2.

| Date of Letter. | Party Written to. | Title and other Description of Publication. |
| --- | --- | --- |
| 1850: | | |
| 15 March - | - - Mr. A. Reid, 117, Pilgrim-street, Newcastle-on-Tyne. | Reid's Newcastle Diary. |
| 20 " - | - - Mr. W. H. Oliver, High-street, Lowestoft. | East Anglian Record. |
| 6 May - | - - Mr. C. B. Merry, Well-street, Bedford. | The Bedford Charity Record. |
| 19 June - | - - Mr. H. Ward, 8, Upper Dorset-place, Kennington. | The Ratepayer. |
| 23 July - | - - Mr. G. Batters, 17, Chapel-bar, Nottingham. | - - The Nottinghamshire Advertiser. |
| 9 August - | - - Mr. S. Greenwood, 17, North-gate, Wakefield. | - - Paper containing an account of the Trial, Fermandez *v.* Horner. |
| 12 " - | - - Mr. J. Chandler, 12, Clemen's-street, Leamington Spa. | - - A paper containing the report of the Temperance Festival. |
| 30 " - | - - Mr. J. T. Morris, Aldersgate-street. | Railway Times. |
| 10 December | Mr. J. Macaulay, Reading - | Berkshire Independent. |
| 1851: | | |
| 15 January - | - Mr. C. Kertsey, 118, Whitechapel. | The Parochial Informer. |
| 29 " - | - Mr. T. J. Potter, 60, Tabernacle-walk, Finsbury. | - - The Ratepayer and Tower Hamlets Reporter. |
| 1 March - | Mr. Lambert, Wakefield - | - A paper (or "slip") called "The Resignation of the Ministry." |
| 12 " - | Mr. J. Jares, Barnstaple - | - The Barnstaple and North Devon Miscellany. |
| 25 " - | Mr. S. Webb, Bilston - - | - - South Staffordshire Iron District Advertiser. |
| 26 " - | - - Mr. T. Hardcastle, Figtree-place, Sheffield. | Sheffield Pictorial. |
| 3 April - | - - Mr. Effingham Wilson, 11, Royal Exchange. | The Natal Journal. |

19 June 1851.

App. No. 2.

A RETURN of the CORRESPONDENCE which has taken place during the last Three Years between the Solicitor of the BOARD of INLAND REVENUE and the Publishers of UNSTAMPED NEWSPAPERS, in the Cases in which the Publishers have been cautioned that their Papers have contained News or comments upon News.

---

Stamps and Taxes, Somerset House,
London, 1 July 1848.

Sir,

I HAVE now before me copies of three newspapers, respectively entitled "Manchester Standard," "Manchester News," and "Oldham News," printed and published by you, but which are not registered at this office. I need scarcely point out to you the irregularity of printing or publishing a newspaper without first making a proper declaration and giving the necessary securities, nor the liabilities incurred by it. I trust that I shall shortly receive the instructions for preparing such documents, so that the law may be complied with in reference to future numbers, if the papers are to be continued; and in the meanwhile I shall be happy to submit to the Board any statement you may think proper to make in respect of the penalties to which you have already subjected yourself.

I am, &c.
(signed) *J. Timm*,
Solicitor for Stamps and Taxes.

Mr. Shaw, Printer,
186, Oxford Road, Manchester.

*Note.*—The papers were immediately discontinued, and no proceedings were taken.

---

Stamps and Taxes, Somerset House,
London, 29 July 1848.

Sir,

AN unstamped paper, being the first number of a publication called "The Truth Teller," printed and published by you, having been brought under the notice of the Commissioners of this Board, I am directed by them to communicate with you on the subject of it. The Commissioners do not suppose that you entertain any intention of violating the law, either by evading the newspaper stamp duty or omitting the other statutory requisites, and they are desirous of cautioning you against involving yourself in the liabilities which attend any such illegal course. A paper containing public news, intelligence, or occurrences, or, if published at intervals not exceeding 26 days, remarks or observations thereon, is a newspaper, and cannot therefore be lawfully printed or published without stamps, nor until the necessary declaration be made, and securities given. No. 1 of the

the "Truth Teller" contains matter of this description, and the printing and publishing of that paper has rendered you liable to severe penalties. I trust, however, that you will in future numbers, if the publication be continued, cautiously avoid a recurrence of this irregularity, either by refraining from inserting therein all articles of the nature alluded to, or by duly registering it as a newspaper, for which latter purpose I refer you to the stamp office at Manchester, where proper instructions will be given you.

I am, &c.
(signed) *J. Timm,*
Solicitor for Stamps and Taxes.

Mr. B. S. Treanor,
Melbourne Street, Staleybridge.

---

Melbourne Street, Staleybridge,
8 August 1848.

Sir,

YOUR communication respecting my small publication, the "Truth Teller," came duly to hand, and for the very kind manner in which you have warned me of the danger I was incurring, I beg to express my warmest acknowledgments.

I trust you will assure the Commissioners that it is not my intention to violate the law in any particular; and the violation which it seems did take place, was entirely owing to my ignorance of the law.

I send you herewith No. 2 of the "Truth Teller," and you will find that the comments upon occurrences, &c., are carefully left out.

I am, &c.
(signed) *B. S. Treanor.*

The Solicitor to the Commissioners of
Stamps and Taxes, London.

---

Stamps and Taxes, Somerset House,
London, 23 February 1849.

Sir,

I HAVE before me your letter of the 16th instant, addressed to this Board, together with copies of the first four numbers of the "Bolton Reform Advocate," and I beg to state that these publications are a newspaper, and that by printing and publishing it without stamps, and without complying with the other requisites of the law, all parties connected with it have incurred serious penalties, and that the matter will be brought under the consideration of the Board in the course of a day or two, with the view to such measures being adopted against yourself as may be thought necessary.

I am, &c.
(signed) *J. Timm,*
Solicitor of Stamps and Taxes.

Mr. Jos. Lawson,
News Agent, Bradshawgate, Bolton.

*Note.—*

App. No. 2.

*Note.*—In consequence of the foregoing letter, Sir Joshua Walmsley sought an interview with the Solicitor of Stamps and Taxes, who addressed to Sir Joshua a letter of which the following is a copy:—

" Sir, " 27 February 1849.

"I HAVE received your note of yesterday, and beg to reply to it. I shall be happy to see you any day that it may be convenient to yourself, either at this office before 11 o'clock, or at the Excise Office, in Broad-street, after that hour. I may, however, perhaps, save you trouble by informing you what has been done in the case of the " Bolton Reform Advocate." The matter has been before the Commissioners of this Board, both on the report of the registrar of newspapers, and on a voluntary communication made to them by Mr. Lawson, the publisher, from whom I have this morning also received a letter stating that the paper has been discontinued; they have directed me to take no measures against Mr. Lawson, relying upon his statement that no further numbers will be published.

" I have, &c.
(signed) *J. Timm*,
Solicitor of Inland Revenue."

" Sir J. Walmsley, M.P.,
101, Westbourne-terrace, Hyde Park."

---

Inland Revenue, Somerset House,
London, 10 March 1849.

Sir,

THE "Bath and Clifton Looker-on" having been brought under my notice, I beg to inform you that by publishing it on unstamped paper, and without having previously registered it as a newspaper, very serious penalties have been incurred. As I observe by No. 2 of the publication that it is your intention to stamp it, I beg to suggest the propriety of your doing so without delay, and not to incur any further liability by publishing it again in its present form; for this purpose the necessary instructions should be immediately given at the stamp office, Bath, in order that the documents, &c., may be prepared.

I am, &c.
(signed) *J. Timm*,
Solicitor of Inland Revenue.

Mr. H. T. Jennings,
" Bath and Clifton Looker-on" Office,
4, Princes Buildings, Bath.

---

Sir, 4, Princes Buildings, Bath.

I RECEIVED this morning your communication respecting the " Bath and Clifton Looker-on." I beg to state that when I undertook to publish the same, I had no intention of committing an illegal act. As I do not possess a share in the publication I would not have undertaken to be the agent of the proprietor without, in the first place, being persuaded of its legality.

The

The "Builder," "Athenæum," "Literary Gazette" and "Chat," together with many other publications of the same class, being issued without stamps caused me to embark in this undertaking with confidence. As however it appears that I am mistaken, the publication of the "Looker-on" is postponed for a week, until the necessary forms are gone through.

I beg to apologise for thus troubling you, and likewise to thank you for your kindness in warning me for the future.

I am, &c.
(signed) *Henry T. Jennings.*

J. Timm, Esq.
Solicitor of Inland Revenue.

---

Inland Revenue, Somerset House,
London, 8 March 1849.

Sir,

The first No. of an advertising sheet published by you entitled "Noble's Great Northern, East Lincolnshire, &c. Monthly Time Tables and General Advertiser," has been brought to the notice of the Commissioners of this Board, and I have to intimate to you that by inserting in it articles of news, whereby it has become a newspaper, you have incurred serious liabilities; and I write to caution you against a repetition of that course if you desire to avoid the consequences of an infringement of the law. Should you intend to publish a newspaper you should make application to the distributor of stamps for the district and give the necessary instructions, with the view to the proper documents being prepared and stamps issued.

You will deliver copies of the different Nos. to the distributor, in order that the advertisement duties may be assessed, whatever may be the character of the paper in future.

I am, &c.
(signed) *J. Timm.*
Solicitor of Inland Revenue.

Mr. T. Noble, Printer,
Market-place, Boston.

---

Inland Revenue, Somerset House,
London, 12 March 1849.

Sir, "Burniston's Northern Luminary."

This publication having been brought under my notice, I have to inform you that it is a newspaper, and that by publishing it as such you are incurring heavy penalties. I beg therefore to suggest the propriety of your immediately registering it as a newspaper or discontinuing to publish it. If you adopt the former course you must give the necessary instructions for the documents at the Stamp Office at York, without delay.

I am, &c.
(signed) *J. Timm,*
Solicitor of Inland Revenue.

Mr. J. Burniston, Printer, &c.
Knaresborough.

*Note.*—This paper was discontinued.

Inland

App. No. 2.

Inland Revenue, Somerset House, London,
24 April 1849.

Gentlemen,

A PRINTED paper entitled "Execution of Sarah Ann Thomas," printed and published by you, has been brought to the notice of this Board. I have therefore to intimate to you that by publishing such paper, which is a newspaper, on unstamped paper, and without in other respects complying with the requisites of the law, you have incurred serious penalties. The Commissioners are ready however to attend to any explanation you may think proper to give as to the irregularity, and any statement you may send to me upon the subject shall be submitted to them.

I am, &c.
(signed) *J. Timm,*
Solicitor of Inland Revenue.

Messrs. Mathews, Printers,
44, Broad Street, Bristol.

---

44, Broad Quay, Bristol,
25 April 1849.

Sir,

In reply to yours of yesterday, we beg to say that we must plead entire ignorance of the existence of any law which we have infringed in issuing the tract referred to. We have nothing in Hansard's instructions to printers which at all deals with the question. We have also inquired at the stamp office to-day, and can get no infor mation on the subject. We most certainly would not knowingly lay ourselves open to the penalties of infringement. You would therefore greatly oblige by stating where the information can be obtained. We have for many years (in common, with our brethren in the profession) printed reports and tracts on passing subjects, and cannot therefore perceive wherein we have offended.

We are, &c.
(signed) *Mathews, Brothers.*

J. Timm, Esq.

---

Inland Revenue, Somerset House,
London, 26 April 1849.

Gentlemen,

I HAVE received your letter of the 23d instant, in explanation of the publishing by you of the tract, as you term it, entitled "Execution of S. H. Thomas," and in reply beg to furnish you with the necessary information for your future guidance. A newspaper is defined to be "any paper containing public news, intelligence, or occurrences printed in any part of the United Kingdom, to be dispersed and made public." The paper in question, with the exception perhaps of that which relates to the history of the criminal, is from beginning to end within this description of matter. This Board is not disposed, I apprehend, to treat the present case as a wilful infringement of the law, and the notice thus taken will probably be deemed sufficient.

I am, &c.
(signed) *J. Timm,*
Solicitor of Inland Revenue.

Messrs. Mathews, Printers,
44, Broad Quay, Bristol.

---

Inland

App. No. 2.

Inland Revenue, Somerset House,
London, 4 May 1849.

Sir,

I HAVE to acquaint you that your paper called "Beck's Weekly List of Visitors," &c. has come under the notice of this office; and referring to the article in No. 11, entitled "The Forthcoming Season," I write to suggest that you be careful to avoid infringing the law relating to newspapers, by withholding all kinds of public news, intelligence, or occurrences, whether political or otherwise, and whether of a local or general character, as the insertion of any such matter will render your publication a newspaper, and involve you in serious penalties unless the paper be stamped.

I am, &c.
(signed) *J. Timm*,
Solicitor of Inland Revenue.

Mr. J. Beck, 8, Upper Parade,
Leamington.

---

Inland Revenue, Somerset House,
London, 5 November 1849.

Sir,

A PAPER called the "Wiltshire Game Laws Reporter," published by you, having been brought to the notice of this Board, I beg to inform you that penalties have been incurred for printing and publishing the same on unstamped paper, and without having first made the usual declaration and given the necessary securities.

Perhaps this intimation will be sufficient to induce you to forego any further responsibility. Should you however intend to continue the publication, you had better, without delay, send me, through the distributor, instructions for preparing the necessary documents.

I am, &c.
(signed) *J. Timm*,
Solicitor of Inland Revenue.

Mr. J. Goodfellow, Fisherton,
Salisbury.

---

Office of the "Wiltshire Game Law Reporter,"
Fisherton, Salisbury, 6 November 1849.

Sir,

As soon as the first number of my weekly periodical appeared I sent two copies to Mr. Tugwell, the distributor of stamps at Devizes, for advice how to pay the advertisement duty, and for instruction that I may not sin in ignorance. I believed as there was no other character of news but prosecutions under the existing Game Laws inserted in my periodical that I should be held just as harmless from penalties as the occasional publishers of criminal trials, and that the law held no penalty for so doing. You will perceive, Sir, my desire to comply with the law by forthwith asking for instruction of the distributor of stamps for this district. As it is my intention to continue this publication, when I have complied with the law, may I beg you to furnish me with instruction how I am to proceed, the bond or security required, whether there

App. No. 2.

there are any expenses attending it, and the amount, and the safe, proper, and expeditious course to pursue, to attain that object? As it appears I have done wrong I hope it will be considered that it was not my intention, wish or desire to break the law, but above all, not in any way to defraud Her Majesty's revenue; most humbly begging your consideration of this reply to your favour of this morning received,

I am, &c.

J. Timm, Esq. (signed) *James Goodfellow.*

*P.S.*—I beg to add that Mr. Tugwell has given me no intimation to desist in the publication, or I should at once have done so.

---

Inland Revenue, Somerset House,
London, 7 November 1849.

Sir,

I AM this morning in receipt of your letter; and with reference thereto I beg to enclose a printed form, which you will be so good as to fill accurately under each head, and return to Mr. Tugwell, who will forward it to me, when I will prepare and send down the necessary documents. You should instruct some friend in London to bespeak the die of Mr. Halfhide the engraver in Coventry-street, Haymarket.

I am, &c.

Mr. James Goodfellow. (signed) *J. Timm,*
Solicitor of Inland Revenue.

---

Inland Revenue, Somerset House,
London, 11 February 1850.

Sir,

I BEG to inform you that the Board has received information of your having printed and circulated an unstamped newspaper containing an account of the opening of Parliament, and the Queen's Speech. I give you this intimation to afford you an opportunity of showing any reason why a prosecution should not be commenced against you for the same.

I am, &c.
(signed) *J. Timm,*
Solicitor of Inland Revenue.

Mr. Isaac Latimer,
Plymouth Journal Office,
Plymouth.

---

Inland Revenue, Somerset House,
6 March 1850.

Sir,

THE notice of this Board has been directed to an article of public news contained in your Commercial Daily List of 9th and 16th of November last, under the head "City of London Union," of a character

App. No. 2.

racter which cannot lawfully be published in any but a stamped newspaper, and I have therefore been desired by the Commissioners to draw your attention to the circumstance with the view to prevent any further similar irregularity.

I am, &c.
(signed) *J. Timm.*
Solicitor of Inland Revenue.

Mr. T. Smith,
42, Mincing-lane, City.

---

"Price Current Office," 43, Mincing-lane,
8 March 1850.

Sir,

I AM in receipt of your letter of the 6th instant, calling my attention to a notice of the Honourable Board of Inland Revenue, relative to an article of public news contained in my Daily List of the 9th and 16th November last, under the head "City of London Union," such article being of a character which cannot be lawfully published in any but a stamped newspaper. In reply, I beg to say that no such irregularity shall again occur, which, as I have before stated to the Honourable Board of Commissioners, was solely intended for the "Mercantile Journal," and which, through inadvertence of my compositor, was inserted in the list, during my absence, in consequence of severe indisposition. Sincerely thanking the Honourable Board for their kind consideration,

I am, &c.
(signed) *Thos. Smith.*

J. Timm, Esq.

---

Inland Revenue, Somerset House,
7 March 1850.

Gentlemen,

THE attention of this Board having been directed to some articles of public news contained in Nos. 1 and 2 of your publication the "Reformer," under the head the "Record of Progress," of a character that cannot legally be published in any but a stamped newspaper, I have been desired to acquaint you with the circumstance, and to caution you against any further insertion of like matter.

I am, &c.
(signed) *J. Timm,*
Solicitor of Inland Revenue.

Messrs. Jarrold & Sons,
47, St. Paul's Churchyard.

---

Norwich, 12 March 1850.
(Jarrold & Sons.)

Sir,

I HAVE received your intimation that the intelligence given in the "Reformer," under the heading "Record of Progress" cannot be lawfully inserted in any but a stamped newspaper.

I should feel greatly obliged if you would inform me on what grounds the "Gentleman's Magazine," "United Service Magazine," "Tait's Edinburgh Magazine," "Christian Observer," "Eclectic Review,"

App. No. 2.

Review," "People's Journal," with others that I might name (including unstamped copies of the "Freeholder," "Athenæum," &c.) are permitted to furnish similar information?

Also, why the origans of societies of a literary, philanthropic and religious character should be allowed to contain details of their respective operations, whilst that privilege is denied to a journal of a political association?

Thanking you for your caution, and soliciting information upon these points,

I am, &c.

J. Timm, Esq, *The Editor of the "Reformer."*

---

Inland Revenue, Somerset House,
London, 13 March 1850.

Gentlemen,

I AM this morning in receipt of a letter written without signature, but purporting to come from the editor of the "Reformer," and as it is written in reference to mine of the 7th instant, addressed to you, I reply to it as proceeding from you. The publications to which allusion is made are not before me either officially or otherwise. I know therefore nothing of their contents, but assuming them to be unstamped papers, and to contain matter which they ought not to publish, it is not for me to offer any explanation upon the subject, nor can the circumstance justify irregularities in others. I may, however remark, as I am aware that the subject has been under notice, in reference more particularly to learned societies, that articles, although relating to the transactions of such societies, and therefore savouring of public news and intelligence, yet, as partaking of the character of a review, are not looked upon as matters to be objected to in unstamped publications. So also with regard to dramatic performances, and such like.

I am, &c.
(signed) *J. Timm.*

Messrs. Jarrold & Sons.

---

Inland Revenue, Somerset House,
London, 15 March 1850.

Sir,

THE attention of this office having been called to some articles of public news and intelligence contained in your publication, "Reid's Newcastle Diary," of the 13th instant, under the head, "House of Commons," which cannot lawfully be published in any unstamped paper,

I write to caution you against any further irregularity of the kind, and your involving yourself in further liability.

I am, &c.
(signed) *J. Timm,*
Solicitor of Inland Revenue.

Mr. A. Reid, 117, Pilgrim-street,
Newcastle-on-Tyne.

---

Publishing

App. No. 2.

Publishing Offices, 117, Pilgrim-street,
Sir, Newcastle-on-Tyne, 16 March 1850.

I HAVE received your letter cautioning against inserting information in "Reid's Weekly Diary" not allowed in unstamped papers, and am anxious to obey the law, but which is most difficult to know what is permitted and what is not.

If you could enclose me a copy of the law on this subject it would prevent this, as I cannot learn from the authorities here where to draw the line.

I am, &c.
J. Timm, Esq. (signed) *Andrew Reid.*

---

Inland Revenue, Somerset House,
Sir, London, 18 March 1850.

IN answer to your letter of the 16th instant, I beg to say that the news and intelligence that may be published in an unstamped publication must consist of "matters wholly of a commercial nature." I do not see how any doubt could have arisen as to the articles of news contained in your paper under the head "House of Commons," which are entirely political.

I am, &c.
(signed) *J. Timm.*
Mr. A. Reid, 117, Pilgrim-street, Solicitor of Inland Revenue.
Newcastle-on-Tyne.

---

Inland Revenue, Somerset House,
Sir, London, 20 March 1850.

THE attention of this office having been drawn to some articles of public news and intelligence contained in your paper called the "East Anglian Record," of the 1st instant, which cannot lawfully be published in an unstamped publication, I write to caution you against a repetition of any such irregularity, and your involving yourself in further liability.

I am, &c.
(signed) *J. Timm,*
Mr. W. H. Oliver, Solicitor of Inland Revenue.
Printer, High-street, Lowestoft.

*Note.*—This paper was duly registered as a newspaper.

---

Inland Revenue, Somerset House,
Sir, London, 6 May 1850.

THE first number of a paper called the "Bedford Charity Record" is now before me, and as it appears to be a newspaper, and is not


stamped

App. No. 2.

stamped or registered as such, I write to bring to your notice the liabilities you have incurred by printing and publishing it, with a view to preventing a recurrence of the irregularity.

I am, &c.
(signed) *J. Timm.*
Solicitor of Inland Revenue.

Mr. C. B. Merry,
Printer, Well-street, Bedford.

---

Sir, Bedford, 5 June 1850.

I RECEIVED a courteous letter from you respecting the publication of the "Bedford Charity Record," which being confined entirely to matters relating to the Bedford Charity, and not a single article relating to anything else, was not thought by me to require a stamp, not containing anything like general news. But the words of the Act, if literally construed, would apply to a common hand-bill or report of the proceedings of any society. I expect, however, it would be of little use to argue that point or any other against your opinion. The article respecting the protection society did not relate to an agricultural society, but a Bedford Charity Protection Society, established to watch the proceedings of the trustees, I have therefore discontinued it, but should I hereafter make up my mind to publish with a stamp, what securities would you require for the advertisement duty, which I should calculate not to exceed 1 *l.* a month, and that would be immediately demanded by the Stamp Office, so that any security would be merely nominal. Have the goodness therefore to inform me what security would be required; and also state what other forms would be necessary. My printing press was registered in 1815.

I remain, &c.
(signed) *C. B. Merry.*

J. Timm, Esq.

*P.S.*—Whether stamped or unstamped the publication would be beneficial to the revenue.

---

Inland Revenue, Somerset House,
London, 6 June 1850.

Sir,

WITH reference to your letter received this morning, I beg to hand to you a printed form of instructions for the necessary documents required to be prepared and completed previously to the printing of any newspaper. This form, when filled up, should be returned to me through the stamp office in your town.

I am, &c.
(signed) *J. Timm,*
Solicitor of Inland Revenue.

Mr. C. B. Merry, Bedford.

---

Inland

Inland Revenue, Somerset House,
19 June 1850.

Sir,

An unstamped newspaper, entitled the "Ratepayer," having come under the notice of this Board, I am directed to call your attention to the serious liabilities you have incurred by printing and publishing it without complying with the requisites of the law, and to caution you against a repetition of the irregularity.

I am, &c.
(signed) *J. Timm*,
Solicitor of Inland Revenue.

Mr. Henry Ward, Printer,
8, Upper Dorset Place, Kennington.

*Note.*—This paper was afterwards duly registered as a newspaper.

---

Inland Revenue, Somerset House,
London, 23 July 1850.

Sir,

The attention of this Board having been drawn to a publication called the "Nottinghamshire Advertiser," containing articles of public news and intelligence, and printed and published by you upon unstamped paper, I am instructed to caution you against any future irregularity of the kind, and your involving yourself in further liability.

I am, &c.
(signed) *J. Timm*,
Solicitor of Inland Revenue.

Mr. G. Batters,
Advertiser Office, 17, Chapel Bar, Nottingham.

---

Inland Revenue, Somerset House,
London, 12 August 1850.

Sir,

The attention of this Board having been drawn to a publication printed and published by you called the "Report of Temperance Festival," &c., (being one of a series of tracts called Miscellaneous Tracts) which is of a nature that cannot lawfully be printed on unstamped paper, I write to caution you against any further irregularity of the kind, and your involving yourself in further liability.

I am, &c.
(signed) *J. Timm*,
Solicitor of Inland Revenue.

Mr. J. Chandler, Printer,
12, Clemens-street, Leamington Spa.

---

 Inland

App. No. 2.

Inland Revenue, Somerset House,
London, 11 December 1850.

Sir,

A NEWSPAPER called the "Berkshire Independent," which appears to have been printed and published by you, having been brought to the notice of the Commissioners of this Revenue, I have to acquaint you that by printing and publishing the same without stamps, and without having made the declaration and given the securities required by law, you have incurred serious penalties; I therefore give you this intimation in order that you may avoid incurring further liabilities.

I am, &c.
(signed) *J. Timm,*
Solicitor of Inland Revenue.

Mr. J. Macaulay,
113, Broad-street, Reading.

*Note.*—The paper was immediately registered as a newspaper.

---

Inland Revenue, Somerset House,
15 January 1851.

Sir,

THE attention of this Board having been drawn to a periodical paper printed and published by you, called the "Parochial Reformer," containing public news and intelligence, and subject to the duty and regulations relating to newspapers, I am directed to communicate with you respecting it. I beg, therefore, to intimate to you that by printing and publishing the paper in question without stamps, and without previously complying with the requisites of the law, you have incurred serious penalties, and to caution you against involving yourself in further liability.

I shall be happy to submit to the Board any statement you may think proper to send to me, showing why proceeding should not be instituted against you for the penalties already incurred.

I am, &c.
(signed) *J. Timm,*
Solicitor of Inland Revenue.

Mr. C. Kertsey,
118, Whitechapel.

---

Inland Revenue, Somerset House,
29 January 1851.

Sir,

A NEWSPAPER, called the "Ratepayer and Tower Hamlets Reporter," which appears to have been printed and published by you, having been brought to the notice of the Commissioners of this Revenue, I have to acquaint you that by printing and publishing the same without stamps, and without having made the declaration and given

given the securities required by law, you have incurred serious penalties. I, therefore, give you this intimation in order that you may avoid incurring further liabilities.

I am, &c.
(signed) *J. Timm*,
Solicitor of Inland Revenue.

Mr. T. J. Potter,
60, Tabernacle Walk, Finsbury.

*Note.*—This paper was afterwards duly registered as a newspaper.

---

Inland Revenue, Somerset House, London.
12 March 1851.

Sir,

YOUR publication, called the "Barnstaple and North Devon Miscellany," has been under the notice of this Board in reference to the Newspaper Act. I have to inform you that a weekly publication containing any remarks or observations upon news, intelligence, or occurrences, is a newspaper, and cannot be lawfully published without being duly registered at this office, and stamped. I write, therefore, to caution you against the insertion of articles of this kind in any future numbers, that you may avoid the liability to the serious penalties imposed for an infringement of the Act alluded to.

I am, &c.
(signed) *J. Timm*,
Solicitor of Inland Revenue.

Mr. J. Jones, Printer,
Quay, Barnstaple.

*Note.*—This paper was afterwards duly registered as a newspaper.

---

Inland Revenue, Somerset House, London,
25 March 1851.

Sir,

SOME numbers of a publication, called the "South Staffordshire Iron District Advertiser," printed and published by you, and containing as well public news, intelligence, and occurrences, as remarks and observations on such matters, having been brought to the notice of this office, I beg to intimate to you that by printing and publishing the paper in question without stamps, and without having previously complied with the requisites of the law with respect to newspapers, you have rendered yourself liable to heavy penalties, and to caution you against further involving yourself in liability.

I am, &c.
(signed) *J. Timm*,
Solicitor of Inland Revenue.

Mr. S. Webb,
Oxford-street, Bilston, Staffordshire.

---

App. No. 2.

Inland Revenue, Somerset House,
London, 26 March 1851.

Sir,

An unstamped paper, called the "Sheffield Pictorial," printed and published by you, and containing public news, intelligence, and occurrences, having been brought to the notice of this office, I have to inform you that in the event of any further numbers being issued without stamps, and without a compliance in other respects with the law relating to newspapers, the Commissioners of this Board will deem it incumbent upon them to institute proceedings against you for the penalties incurred by your so doing.

I am, &c.
(signed) *J. Timm*,
Solicitor of Inland Revenue.

Mr. T. Hardcastle,
Fig-tree Place, Sheffield.

---

Inland Revenue, Somerset House,
3 April 1851.

Sir,

Some numbers of a paper, called the "Natal Journal," printed and published by you, and containing public news, intelligence, and occurrences, having been brought to the notice of this office, I have to inform you that in the event of any further numbers being issued without stamps, and without a compliance in other respects with the law relating to newspapers, the Commissioners of this Board will deem it incumbent upon them to institute proceedings against you for the penalties incurred by your so doing.

I am, &c.
(signed) *J. Timm*,
Solicitor of Inland Revenue.

Mr. Effm Wilson,
11, Royal Exchange.

*Note.*—This paper was afterwards duly registered as a newspaper.

---

Inland Revenue, Somerset House,
London, 3 April 1851.

Sir,

A publication, called the "Tenterden Free Press," printed and published by you, and containing public news, intelligence, and occurrences, having been brought to the notice of this office, I beg to intimate to you that by printing and publishing the paper in question without stamps, and without having previously complied with the requisites of the law with respect to newspapers, you have rendered yourself liable to heavy penalties, and to caution you against further involving yourself in liability.

I am, &c.
(signed) *J. Timm*,
Solicitor of Inland Revenue.

Mr. S. Ballard,
London House, Tenterden.

---

London

App. No. 2.

London House, Tenterden, Kent,
Sir, 7 April 1851.

I WAS induced to publish the "Tenterden Free Press" on the recommendation of Chambers' Journal, that every town should possess a small monthly 1*d.* sheet to enable the townsmen to advertise, &c., and seeing that Mr. Dickens had commenced one on the same plan, I had no idea I should infringe the law if I avoided political news, which I have done. If it would not trespass too much on your time, will you inform me if there are any requisitions of the law on complying with which I shall be enabled still to issue the paper on an unstamped sheet as heretofore, as I find many magazines give a summary of political as well as general news monthly?

I am, &c.

J. Timm, Esquire. (signed) *Saml Ballard.*

---

Inland Revenue, Somerset House,
Sir, London, 8 April 1851.

IN reply to your letter of the 7th instant, I beg to say than an unstamped sheet of paper containing news, intelligence, or occurrences, cannot lawfully be published.

I may state with reference to Mr. Dickens's publication, that if you refer to his "Household Narrative," a prosecution against the printer for penalties respecting it is now pending.

I am, &c.

(signed) *J. Timm,*
Solicitor of Inland Revenue.

Mr. S. Ballard,
London House, Tenterden.

# Appendix, No. 3.

LIST of MECHANICS' and other LITERARY and SCIENTIFIC INSTITUTIONS in *Lancashire* and *Cheshire*, specifying those which have NEWSROOMS; referred to in the Evidence of Mr. *Thomas Hogg*.

| | LANCASHIRE. | TITLE OF INSTITUTION. | News Room. |
|---|---|---|---|
| | Ashton - - - - | Mechanics' Institution - - - | 1 |
| | Bacup - - - - | Ditto - - ditto - - - - | 1 |
| | Blackburn - - - | Ditto - - ditto - - - - | 1 |
| | Blackley - - - | Ditto - - ditto - - - - | 1 |
| 5 | Bolton - - - - | Ditto - - ditto - - - - | 1 |
| | Besses - - - - | Co-operative Society - - - | 1 |
| | Bridgehall - - - | Lyceum - - - - - - | 1 |
| | Burnley - - - - | Mechanics' Institution - - - | 1 |
| | Bury - - - - | Ditto - - ditto - - - - | 1 |
| 10 | Chadderton - - - | Literary Institution - - - - | ? |
| | Clitheroe - - - | Mechanics' Institution - - - | 1 |
| | Colne - - - - | Ditto - - ditto - - - - | 1 |
| | Crawshaw Booth - - | Ditto - - ditto - - - - | 1 |
| | Darwen - - - - | Ditto - - ditto - - - - | 1 |
| 15 | Denton - - - - | Ditto - - ditto - - - - | ? |
| | Droylsden - - - | Ditto - - ditto - - - - | 1 |
| | Facit - - - - | People's Institute - - - - | 1 |
| | Failsworth - - - | Mechanics' Institution - - - | 1 |
| | Farnworth and Kensley - | Mutual Improvement Society - - | 1 |
| 20 | Fleetwood - - - | Mechanics' Institution - - - | 1 |
| | Haslingden - - - | Ditto - - ditto - - - - | 1 |
| | Heywood - - - | Ditto - - ditto - - - - | 1 |
| | Ditto - - - | Church Institute - - - - | 1 |
| | Hoddlesden - - - | Mechanics' Institution - - - | 1 |
| 25 | Lancaster - - - | Ditto - - ditto - - - - | 1 |
| | Ditto - - - | Athenæum - - - - - | ? |
| | Lees - - - - | Mechanics' Institution - - - | 1 |
| | Leigh - - - - | Ditto - - ditto - - - - | 1 |
| | Levenshulme - - - | Ditto - - ditto - - - - | ? |
| 30 | Liverpool - - - | Ditto - - ditto - - - - | 0 |
| | Ditto - - - - | Collegiate Institution - - - - | 0 |
| | Liverpool - - - | Northern Mechanics' - - - - | 1 |
| | Ditto - - - - | Booth Educational - - - - | 0 |
| | Ditto - - - - | Brougham Institute - - - - | 1 |
| 35 | Ditto - - - - | Tuckerman Institute - - - - | 1 |
| | Manchester - - - | Mechanics' Institute - - - - | 1 |
| | Ditto - - - - | Athenæum - - - - - | 1 |
| | Ditto - - - - | Ancoats Lyceum - - - - | 1 |
| | Ditto - - - - | Miles' Platting Institute - - - | 1 |

| | LANCASHIRE. | TITLE OF INSTITUTION. | News Room. |
|---|---|---|---|
| 40 | Manchester | Salford Mechanics' Institute | 1 |
| | Ditto | Harpurhey Mechanics' Institute | 1 |
| | Ditto | Rusholme | 1 |
| | Middleton | Mechanics' Institute | 1 |
| | Mossley | Ditto - - ditto | 1 |
| 45 | Oldham | Lyceum | 1 |
| | Ditto | Low Moor Institute | 1 |
| | Ditto | Hurlworks Institute | ? |
| | Ormskirk | Literary and Scientific Institute | 1 |
| | Padiham | Mechanics' Institute | 1 |
| 50 | Patricroft | Ditto - - ditto | 1 |
| | Park Lane | Ditto - - ditto | 1 |
| | Pendleton | Ditto - - ditto | ? |
| | Prescot | Educational Institute | 0 |
| | Preston | Institute for Diffusion of Knowledge | 1 |
| 55 | Ditto | Literary and Philosophical | 1 |
| | Radcliffe | Mutual Improvement Society | 1 |
| | Ramsbottom | Ditto - - ditto | 0 |
| | Rawtenstall | Mechanics' Institute | 1 |
| | Rhodes' Works | Ditto - - ditto | 0 |
| 60 | Rochdale | Athenæum | 1 |
| | Ditto | People's Institute | 1 |
| | Royton | Mechanics' Institution | 1 |
| | Ditto | Mutual Improvement Society | 1 |
| | Tyldesley | Mechanics' Institution | 1 |
| 65 | Ulverstone | Athenæum | 1 |
| | Ditto | Mutual Improvement Society | 1 |
| | Warrington | Mechanics' Institution | 1 |
| | Wavertree | Ditto - - ditto | ? |
| | Wigan | Ditto - - ditto | 0 |
| 70 | Wootton | Ditto - - ditto | 1 |
| | Worsley | Library and Institute | 1 |
| | Altrincham | Literary Institution | 1 |
| | Chester | Mechanics' Institution | 1 |
| | Congleton | Ditto - - ditto | 1 |
| 75 | Crewe | Ditto - - ditto | 1 |
| | Dinting Vale | Library | 1 |
| | Dukinfield | Village Library | 1 |
| | Hollingworth | Young Men's Association | 0 |
| | Macclesfield | Useful Knowledge Society | 1 |
| 80 | Middlewich | Literary and Scientific Institution | 1 |
| | Nantwich | Mechanics' Institute | 1 |
| | Northwich | Public Institute | 0 |
| | Runcorn | Church | ? |
| | Sandbach | Literary and Scientific Institution | 1 |
| 85 | Stockport | Mechanics' Institution | 1 |
| | Tarporley | Ditto - - ditto | 1 |
| 87 | Tintwistle | Mutual Improvement Society | ? |

Of 87 Institutions, 69, or a little more than 9-10ths, have news rooms.

# Appendix, No. 4.

A RETURN of the Number of NEWSPAPER STAMPS at One Penny issued to the
1837 to 1850 inclusive, specifying each Newspaper by Name, and

## LONDON PAPERS.

| | 1837. | 1838. | 1839. | 1840. | 1841. |
|---|---|---|---|---|---|
| Atlas | 105,000 | 140,000 | 136,500 | 125,000 | 90,541 |
| Athenæum | 30,250 | 55,650 | 63,500 | 70,000 | 68,900 |
| Anti-Slavery Reporter | - | - | - | 38,374 | 47,150 |
| Allen's Indian Mail | - | - | - | - | - |
| Ayton's Corn Report | - | - | - | - | - |
| A. Cook's Price Current | - | - | - | - | - |
| Anning & Cobb's Circular | - | - | - | - | - |
| A. Dennistown's Circular | - | - | - | - | - |
| Australian Gazette | - | - | - | - | - |
| Architect and Building Gazette | - | - | - | - | - |
| A. & B. Kenny's Price Current | - | - | - | - | - |
| Age | 127,030 | 120,500 | 105,500 | 96,000 | 74,000 |
| Argus | - | - | 134,500 | 142,000 | 50,500 |
| African Colonizer | - | - | - | 10,250 | 6,874 |
| Art Union | - | - | 29,400 | 22,500 | 26,750 |
| Academic Circular | - | - | - | - | 5,000 |
| Australian Record | - | - | - | - | 11,700 |
| Anti-Monopolist | - | - | - | - | - |
| Amateur and Working Gardener's Gazette | - | - | - | - | - |
| Army and Navy Register | - | - | - | - | 9,243 |
| Agriculturist Monthly Journal | - | - | - | - | - |
| Art Manufactory Circular | - | - | - | - | - |
| Assurance Gazette | - | - | - | - | - |
| A. & R. Nisbett's Price Current | - | - | - | - | - |
| Agricultural Advertiser | - | - | - | - | - |
| Art Circular | - | - | - | - | - |
| Age and Argus | - | - | - | - | - |
| Builder | - | - | - | - | - |
| Bradshaw's Railway Guide | - | - | - | - | - |
| Bible Society Reporter | - | - | 2,000 | 2,250 | 2,200 |
| Bent's Literary Advertiser | 13,000 | 13,950 | 16,250 | 18,250 | 18,500 |
| Bell's New Weekly Messenger | 215,000 | 162,050 | 138,000 | 70,250 | 123,500 |
| Bell's Life in London | 851,000 | 1,040,000 | 1,180,500 | 1,173,500 | 1,029,000 |
| Bell's Weekly Messenger | 789,000 | 898,250 | 926,000 | 906,000 | 883,000 |
| Britannia | - | - | 66,600 | 161,000 | 199,500 |
| British Indian Advocate | - | - | - | - | 18,500 |
| British Millenial Harbinger | - | - | - | - | - |
| British Banner | - | - | - | - | - |
| British Statesman | - | - | - | - | - |
| Brown's Western Visitor | - | - | - | - | - |
| British Queen | - | - | - | 2,000 | 93,000 |
| British Lion | - | - | - | - | - |
| Brokers' Circular | - | - | - | - | - |
| British Annals of Medicine | 8,550 | — | | | |
| British Standard | 17,500 | — | | | |
| British Beacon | 8,500 | — | | | |
| British Monitor | 1,500 | — | | | |

## - - - - - Appendix, No. 4.

undermentioned Newspapers in *England, Ireland, Scotland* and *Wales,* from the Year
the Number of Stamps issued each Year to each Newspaper.

### - - - - - - LONDON PAPERS.

| 1842. | 1843. | 1844. | 1845. | 1846. | 1847. | 1848. | 1849. | 1850. |
|---|---|---|---|---|---|---|---|---|
| 125,000 | 107,000 | 87,000 | 84,000 | 72,000 | 83,250 | 85,500 | 90,668 | 98,000 |
| 75,000 | 78,000 | 93,250 | 103,500 | 117,000 | 117,500 | 125,500 | 127,500 | 144,158 |
| 37,200 | 40,500 | 34,400 | 28,500 | 12,150 | 18,000 | 12,125 | 12,000 | 12,000 |
| - - | - - | - - | 29,550 | 28,750 | 26,750 | 24,000 | 28,725 | 23,600 |
| - - | - - | - - | - - | - - | - - | - - | - - | 1,000 |
| - - | - - | - - | - - | - - | - - | - - | - - | 1,250 |
| - - | - - | - - | - - | - - | - - | - - | 4,220 | 5,350 |
| - - | - - | - - | - - | - - | 1,640 | 1,000 | 1,000 | 3,500 |
| - - | - - | - - | - - | - - | - - | - - | - - | 3,500 |
| - - | - - | - - | - - | - - | - - | - - | 17,700 | 16,200 |
| - - | - - | - - | - - | - - | - - | - - | - - | 1,500 |
| 62,400 | 36,000 | — | | | | | | |
| 86,800 | 38,850 | — | | | | | | |
| — | | | | | | | | |
| 27,000 | 25,500 | 1,000 | 6,500 | 870 | 21,000 | 5,000 | — | |
| 9,000 | 6,500 | 5,750 | — | | | | | |
| 14,350 | 7,300 | 2,800 | — | | | | | |
| - - | 5,000 | 11,500 | 6,000 | — | | | | |
| - - | - - | 8,450 | 40,680 | 18,063 | — | | | |
| 7,050 | — | | | | | | | |
| - - | - - | - - | - - | - - | - - | 11,298 | 150 | — |
| - - | - - | - - | - - | - - | - - | 1,500 | — | |
| - - | - - | - - | - - | - - | - - | 2,500 | — | |
| - - | - - | - - | - - | - - | - - | 775 | 984 | 1,300 |
| - - | - - | - - | - - | 20,050 | — | | | |
| - - | - - | - - | - - | - - | - - | - - | - - | 750 |
| - - | 23,500 | 77,500 | 16,500 | — | | | | |
| - - | 17,490 | 20,344 | 19,750 | 23,450 | 36,925 | 38,105 | 46,425 | 54,456 |
| - - | - - | - - | 124,450 | 101,700 | — | | | |
| 2,000 | 8,000 | 8,250 | 9,600 | 10,350 | 11,500 | 11,000 | 12,250 | 11,850 |
| 18,000 | 18,000 | 16,500 | 14,750 | 12,250 | 13,000 | 13,500 | 11,087 | 13,500 |
| 117,750 | 97,250 | 77,250 | 66,255 | 54,000 | 44,450 | 31,500 | 27,500 | 20,250 |
| 1,014,000 | 992,500 | 948,000 | 1,520,500 | 1,250,000 | 1,311,000 | 1,236,500 | 1,176,500 | 1,285,500 |
| 847,000 | 785,250 | 780,000 | 735,000 | 733,000 | 760,000 | 743,000 | 709,000 | 703,500 |
| 289,000 | 261,500 | 258,000 | 257,000 | 252,331 | 216,000 | 203,300 | 182,350 | 163,875 |
| - - | - - | - - | 2,830 | 1,250 | 4,222 | 800 | — | |
| - - | - - | - - | - - | - - | - - | - - | - - | 3,000 |
| - - | - - | - - | - - | - - | - - | 568,000 | 305,750 | 229,900 |
| 48,245 | 3,300 | — | | | | | | |
| - - | - - | - - | - - | - - | 5,030 | — | | |
| 99,000 | 28,000 | — | | | | | | |
| - - | 19,500 | — | | | | | | |
| - - | - - | 11,020 | 1,800 | — | | | | |

| | 1837. | 1838. | 1839. | 1840. | 1841. |
|---|---|---|---|---|---|
| LONDON PAPERS—*continued.* | | | | | |
| Baptist Guardian | - | - | - | - | - |
| Bankrupt and Insolvent Register | - | - | - | - | - |
| Brown & Co.'s Price Current | - | - | - | - | - |
| Byrne's Emigrant Journal | - | - | - | - | - |
| Bentell's Price List | - | - | - | - | - |
| Book Reporter | - | - | - | - | - |
| Busche & Co.'s Trade Report | - | - | - | - | - |
| British Emancipator | - | 83,500 | 35,000 | 850 | — |
| Bombay Times | - | - | - | 1,000 | — |
| Bedwell & Co.'s Circular | - | - | 2,500 | — | |
| Barber & Nephew's Price Current | - | - | - | - | 900 |
| British Army Dispatch | - | - | - | - | - |
| Botanical Gazette | - | - | - | - | - |
| Beacon | - | - | - | - | - |
| Course of the Exchange | 340 | 360 | 360 | 12,500 | 11,750 |
| Courier | 424,500 | 398,000 | 355,000 | 243,000 | 209,000 |
| County Herald | 47,500 | 46,500 | 43,000 | 37,000 | 44,000 |
| County Chronicle | 73,500 | 81,500 | 80,500 | 80,500 | 79,000 |
| Champion and Weekly Herald | 145,280 | 29,925 | 94,939 | 48,300 | — |
| Court Journal | 53,785 | 86,500 | 99,000 | 74,000 | 76,000 |
| Circular to Bankers | 22,000 | 23,000 | 8,000 | 21,000 | 28,500 |
| Commercial Daily List | - | 32,050 | 29,550 | 14,300 | 15,000 |
| Commercial Gazette | - | 20,000 | 37,200 | 11,900 | — |
| Court Gazette | - | 82,000 | 76,800 | 1,000 | 37,915 |
| Cinque Port Chronicle | - | - | - | 26,888 | 26,500 |
| Colonial Gazette | - | - | - | 55,000 | 52,000 |
| Christian Examiner | - | - | - | 20,000 | 13,000 |
| Charter | - | - | 182,625 | 20,650 | — |
| Conservative Journal | - | - | 69,000 | 89,000 | 69,300 |
| Constitutionalist | 116,120 | - | 36,750 | 74,500 | — |
| Cousins & Kemp's Tea Circular | - | - | 5,700 | — | |
| Clark & Row's Circular | - | - | 2,750 | — | |
| Commercial Traveller | - | - | - | - | - |
| Critic | - | - | - | - | - |
| Church and State Gazette | - | - | - | - | - |
| Christian Spectator | - | 15,000 | 64,000 | 70,000 | 61,000 |
| Commercial Review | - | - | - | - | - |
| Cole's Price Current | - | - | - | - | - |
| Colonial Church Chronicle | - | - | - | - | - |
| Champion | — | | | | |
| Christian Advocate | 47,807 | 44,621 | 33,500 | — | |
| Church of England Family | 2,000 | — | | | |
| Carlton Chronicle | 20,500 | — | | | |
| Chartist | - | - | 83,750 | — | |
| Crown | - | 32,650 | 16,525 | — | |
| C. Pidding's China Olio | - | - | - | - | - |
| Church Chronicle | - | - | - | - | - |
| Churton's Register | - | - | - | - | - |
| Corrie & Co.'s Circular | - | - | - | - | - |
| Course of the Exchange | - | - | - | - | - |
| Court Gazette | — | | | | |
| City Chronicle | - | - | - | 40,340 | 77,100 |
| Carlisle, Capel & Co. | - | - | - | - | - |
| Continental Echo | - | - | - | - | - |
| Citizen | - | - | - | - | - |
| Church Intelligencer | - | - | - | - | - |
| Chemical Gazette | - | - | - | - | - |
| Courier de Londres et de Paris | — | | | | |
| Chambers' Journal | - | - | - | - | - |
| Cox Savory's Price Current | - | - | - | - | - |
| Cicerone | — | | | | |
| Chapman's Weekly Magazine | — | | | | |
| Cerberus | - | - | - | - | - |

| 1842. | 1843. | 1844. | 1845. | 1846. | 1847. | 1848. | 1849. | 1850. |
|---|---|---|---|---|---|---|---|---|
| - - | - - | - - | 11,000 | — | | | | |
| - - | - - | - - | - - | - - | 9,100 | — | | |
| - - | - - | - - | - - | - - | - - | - - | 1,000 | 1,500 |
| - - | - - | - - | - - | - - | - - | - - | - - | 4,000 |
| - - | - - | - - | - - | - - | - - | - - | - - | 3,000 |
| - - | - - | - - | - - | - - | - - | - - | - - | 1,000 |
| - - | - - | - - | - - | - - | - - | - - | - - | 2,000 |
| 2,100 | 3,150 | 15,000 | 3,900 | 4,640 | 2,980 | 1,250 | 876 | 1,350 |
| - - | - - | - - | - - | - - | - - | 26,100 | 34,900 | 36,900 |
| - - | - - | - - | - - | - - | - - | - - | - - | 696 |
| - - | - - | - - | - - | 7,600 | — | | | |
| 10,800 | 9,900 | 10,400 | 12,000 | 13,200 | 9,600 | 9,600 | 7,800 | 7,800 |
| 93,500 | — | | | | | | | |
| 40,000 | 38,000 | 38,324 | 41,500 | 37,000 | 36,000 | 27,500 | 30,500 | 26,500 |
| 79,500 | 74,500 | 72,000 | 67,100 | 68,940 | 79,000 | 74,500 | 77,000 | 72,000 |
| 58,500 | 40,400 | 42,100 | 40,700 | 41,500 | 37,697 | 26,007 | 18,559 | 17,543 |
| 17,000 | 25,750 | 25,500 | 27,000 | 25,500 | 27,200 | 26,000 | 23,300 | 25,448 |
| 17,000 | 17,500 | 19,000 | 25,400 | 26,700 | 29,000 | 22,000 | 25,200 | 27,000 |
| 41,400 | 36,250 | 34,850 | 33,739 | 9,190 | — | | | |
| — | | | | | | | | |
| 38,000 | 37,000 | 61,250 | 33,000 | 32,000 | 1,000 | — | | |
| 12,000 | 14,000 | 14,000 | 13,500 | 12,025 | 10,500 | 8,650 | — | |
| 46,000 | 12,250 | — | | | | | | |
| 43,000 | 32,900 | 27,500 | 24,850 | 27,100 | 30,000 | 9,850 | - - | 4,000 |
| - - | 1,500 | 23,650 | 61,125 | 55,975 | 52,600 | 16,000 | 13,030 | 20,500 |
| 200,700 | 66,000 | 37,000 | 47,000 | 53,250 | 48,000 | 43,000 | 41,000 | 44,000 |
| 61,500 | 62,000 | 61,250 | 35,000 | 31,000 | 21,000 | 20,000 | 25,050 | 25,300 |
| 1,400 | 1,000 | 2,000 | 1,000 | 1,700 | 1,055 | 2,200 | 2,200 | 2,500 |
| - - | - - | - - | - - | - - | 501 | 480 | 240 | 480 |
| - - | - - | - - | - - | - - | 2,500 | 4,200 | 3,900 | 4,160 |
| - - | - - | 33,000 | 1,500 | — | | | | |
| - - | - - | - - | 2,500 | — | | | | |
| - - | - - | - - | 2,500 | — | | | | |
| - - | - - | 2,000 | 3,000 | - - | - - | 3,000 | — | |
| - - | - - | - - | 12,000 | — | | | | |
| 71,350 | 67,350 | 61,100 | 51,750 | — | | | | |
| - - | - - | 1,500 | 3,000 | 3,500 | 2,500 | 2,250 | 2,250 | — |
| - - | - - | - - | 3,200 | 6,500 | — | | | |
| - - | - - | - - | 4,460 | - - | - - | - - | 11,500 | — |
| 52,000 | 52,700 | 32,000 | - - | - - | - - | - - | 14,700 | — |
| 5,000 | 1,500 | 2,000 | 1,500 | — | | | | |
| - - | - - | 7,000 | — | | | | | |
| - - | - - | - - | - - | 4,000 | — | | | |
| - - | 21,150 | — | | | | | | |

| — | 1837. | 1838. | 1839. | 1840. | 1841. |
|---|---|---|---|---|---|
| LONDON PAPERS—*continued.* | | | | | |
| Catholic | - | - | - | - | - |
| Commonweal | - | - | - | - | - |
| Censor | - | - | - | - | - |
| Croskill's Implement | - | - | - | - | - |
| Christian Times | - | - | - | - | - |
| Critical Register | — | | | | |
| Colonial Dispatch | — | | | | |
| City of London | - | - | - | - | - |
| Church Times | - | - | - | - | - |
| Cottage Gardener | - | - | - | - | - |
| Church Missionary Intelligencer | - | - | - | - | - |
| Catling & Co.'s Circular | - | - | - | - | - |
| C. Priex Current | — | | | | |
| C. Imer, Pollet & Co.'s Trade Report | - | - | - | - | - |
| Church Chronicle | - | - | - | - | - |
| Colman's & Stolterfoht's Report | - | - | - | - | - |
| Commonwealth | - | - | - | - | - |
| Catholic Standard | - | - | - | - | - |
| Cream & Co.'s Monthly | - | - | - | - | - |
| Cocks' Musical Miscellany | - | - | - | - | - |
| Chemical Gazette | - | - | - | - | - |
| C. C. Brockner's Bereting | - | - | - | - | - |
| C. Rekul's Prix Current | - | - | - | - | - |
| Davison's & Gordon's Circular | - | - | - | - | - |
| Darton & Clark's Catalogue | - | - | - | - | - |
| Daily News | - | - | 3,500 | - | - |
| Deutche Londoner Zeitung | - | - | - | - | - |
| Devaux Circular | - | - | - | - | - |
| Domestic Economy | - | - | - | - | - |
| Dorson, Son & Hill's Circular | - | - | 600 | — | |
| Daily Dispatch | - | - | - | - | 1,260 |
| Douglas Jerrold's Weekly | - | - | - | - | - |
| Daily Advertiser | - | - | - | - | - |
| D. Birket & Co.'s Price Current | - | - | - | - | - |
| Evangelical Christendom | - | - | - | - | - |
| Ecclesiastical Review | - | - | - | - | - |
| Evening Chronicle | 220,000 | 236,000 | 226,500 | 219,500 | 204,000 |
| Evening Mail | 318,000 | 275,000 | 360,000 | 380,000 | 445,000 |
| Examiner | 204,275 | 267,965 | 290,345 | 311,825 | 319,700 |
| Ecclesiastical Gazette | - | 79,750 | 126,600 | 139,300 | 143,975 |
| Era | - | 127,000 | 187,500 | 176,500 | 245,000 |
| English Churchman | - | - | - | - | - |
| Economist | - | - | - | - | - |
| Edwards & Matthias' Price Current | - | - | - | - | - |
| Express | - | - | - | - | - |
| Ellis' London Price Current | — | | | | |
| English Journal of Education | - | - | - | - | - |
| E. Bush & Co.'s Trade Report | - | - | - | - | - |
| Educational Times | - | - | - | - | - |
| English Gentleman | - | - | - | - | - |
| Evening Star | - | - | - | - | - |
| Emigration Gazette | - | - | - | 5,000 | 2,000 |
| Eddows' Journal | — | | | | |
| Educational Record | - | - | - | - | - |
| Evans & Trokes' Circular | - | - | - | - | - |
| Eagle & Courier | - | - | - | - | - |
| Ellis & Hales' Price Current | - | - | - | - | - |
| English Mail | - | - | - | - | - |
| Emigrant | - | - | - | - | - |
| Eliza Cook's Journal | - | - | - | - | - |
| English Newspaper | 3,000 | — | | | |
| Expositor | - | - | - | - | - |
| East India Circular | — | | | | |

| 1842. | 1843. | 1844. | 1845. | 1846. | 1847. | 1848. | 1849. | 1850. |
|---|---|---|---|---|---|---|---|---|
| 40,500 | — | | | | | | | |
| - - | - - | - - | - - | 1,340 | 100 | — | | |
| - - | - - | - - | - - | 1,750 | — | | | |
| - - | - - | - - | - - | - - | - - | 8,000 | 2,950 | 4,000 |
| - - | - - | - - | - - | - - | - - | 25,500 | 131,121 | 94,000 |
| - - | - - | - - | - - | - - | - - | 45,110 | 12,750 | — |
| - - | - - | - - | - - | - - | - - | - - | 11,500 | — |
| - - | - - | - - | - - | - - | - - | 9,000 | 27,009 | 24,000 |
| - - | - - | - - | - - | - - | - - | - - | 14,700 | 10,550 |
| - - | - - | - - | - - | - - | - - | - - | - - | 11,500 |
| - - | - - | - - | - - | - - | - - | - - | - - | 1,700 |
| - - | - - | - - | - - | 7,050 | — | | | |
| - - | - - | - - | - - | - - | - - | 5,440 | 7,000 | 8,500 |
| - - | - - | - - | - - | - - | - - | - - | 5,000 | |
| - - | - - | - - | - - | - - | - - | - - | 20,950 | 80,950 |
| - - | - - | - - | - - | - - | - - | - - | - - | 960 |
| - - | - - | - - | - - | - - | - - | - - | - - | 5,300 |
| - - | - - | - - | - - | - - | - - | - - | - - | 1,500 |
| - - | - - | - - | - - | - - | - - | - - | - - | 3,500 |
| - - | - - | - - | - - | - - | - - | - - | - - | 3,094 |
| - - | - - | - - | - - | - - | - - | - - | - - | 1,000 |
| - - | - - | - - | - - | 3,099 | 2,000 | 2,000 | 2,600 | 4,000 |
| - - | - - | - - | - - | 3,520,500 | 3,477,009 | 3,530,638 | 1,375,000 | 1,152,000 |
| - - | - - | - - | - - | 19,028 | 11,790 | 13,440 | 12,480 | 11,122 |
| - - | - - | - - | - - | - - | - - | - - | 3,000 | 5,509 |
| - - | - - | - - | - - | - - | - - | - - | - - | 2,000 |
| — | | | | | | | | |
| - - | - - | - - | - - | 229,000 | 417,200 | 252,502 | — | |
| - - | - - | - - | - - | - - | 18,947 | 12,600 | — | |
| - - | - - | - - | - - | - - | - - | - - | - - | 3,500 |
| - - | - - | - - | - - | - - | 20,250 | 12,600 | 11,050 | 9,100 |
| - - | - - | - - | - - | - - | 1,500 | — | | |
| 194,000 | 150,000 | 144,000 | 134,000 | 93,000 | 39,600 | — | | |
| 475,009 | 500,000 | 550,000 | 525,009 | 530,000 | 550,000 | 600,000 | 675,000 | 650,000 |
| 318,550 | 292,750 | 268,609 | 265,775 | 250,500 | 222,009 | 276,000 | 218,825 | 228,228 |
| 159,050 | 134,750 | 147,000 | 159,264 | 134,200 | 159,000 | 132,350 | 144,600 | 144,300 |
| 240,500 | 210,500 | 221,000 | 201,000 | 169,551 | 228,000 | 230,500 | 191,500 | 221,600 |
| - - | 56,150 | 81,500 | 86,590 | 111,500 | 95,957 | 104,250 | 80,709 | 79,000 |
| - - | 31,500 | 92,950 | 150,500 | 175,475 | 233,109 | 225,000 | 200,500 | 199,000 |
| - - | - - | - - | - - | - - | 1,010 | 344 | 1,090 | 1,160 |
| - - | - - | - - | - - | 169,009 | 778,714 | 888,080 | 964,000 | 766,950 |
| - - | - - | - - | - - | - - | 4,500 | 2,500 | 2,000 | 2,500 |
| - - | - - | - - | - - | - - | 9,000 | 6,909 | 23,009 | 14,000 |
| - - | - - | - - | - - | - - | 6,400 | 13,500 | 14,200 | 12,500 |
| - - | - - | - - | 42,500 | 29,148 | — | | | |
| 91,350 | 19,790 | — | | | | | | |
| 29,500 | 13,009 | — | | | | | | |
| - - | - - | - - | - - | - - | - - | 8,500 | 15,850 | — |
| - - | - - | - - | - - | - - | - - | 650 | 500 | — |
| - - | - - | - - | - - | - - | - - | 10,000 | — | |
| - - | - - | - - | - - | - - | - - | - - | 600 | 1,500 |
| - - | - - | - - | - - | - - | - - | 6,280 | — | |
| - - | - - | - - | - - | - - | - - | 14,452 | 16,725 | — |
| - - | - - | - - | - - | - - | - - | 3,000 | 15,000 | 600 |
| - - | - - | - - | - - | - - | - - | - - | - - | 9,000 |

| ——— | 1837. | 1838. | 1839. | 1840. | 1841. |
|---|---|---|---|---|---|
| LONDON PAPERS—*continued.* | | | | | |
| Emigration Messenger | - | - | - | - | - |
| Eyre, Evans & Co.'s Circular | - | - | - | - | - |
| Ewart & Co.'s Tea Circular | - | - | - | - | - |
| Edwards & Short's Circular | - | - | 2,188 | — | - |
| East India Telegraph | - | - | - | 10,329 | 18,000 |
| Englische Correspondinz | - | - | - | - | - |
| East Anglian Circular | - | - | - | - | 4,000 |
| English Chronicle | - | - | - | 120,500 | 116,875 |
| English Churchman | - | - | - | - | - |
| Euterpean | - | - | - | - | - |
| English Review | - | - | - | - | - |
| Financial and Commercial Record | 3,840 | 7,680 | 5,760 | 9,600 | 7,680 |
| Farmers' Journal | - | - | 6,000 | 51,850 | 9,544 |
| Fiscon & Co.'s Circular | - | - | 2,000 | — | - |
| Forbes & Co.'s Circular | - | - | 1,000 | 1,500 | 2,000 |
| Finley, Hodson & Co.'s Circular | - | - | - | - | 1,000 |
| F. Huth & Co.'s Circular | - | - | - | - | - |
| F. Gade's Market Report | - | - | - | - | - |
| Forrester's Monthly Miscellany | - | - | - | - | - |
| Fry, Griffith & Co.'s Price Current | - | - | - | - | - |
| Family Times | - | - | - | - | - |
| Friend of the Africans | - | - | - | - | 4,750 |
| Fine Arts Journal | - | - | - | - | - |
| Forrester | - | - | - | - | - |
| Financial and Commercial Record | - | - | - | - | - |
| Farmers' Chronicle | - | - | - | - | - |
| Fine Arts Union | — | | | | |
| Forrester | - | - | - | - | - |
| Freemasons' Journal | - | - | - | - | - |
| Fonetic Nuz | - | - | - | - | - |
| Frolic & Co.'s Statement | - | - | - | - | - |
| Great Northern Railway Reporter | - | - | - | - | - |
| Gardeners' and Farmers' Journal | - | - | - | - | - |
| Gas Gazette | - | - | - | - | - |
| Gospel Standard | - | - | - | - | - |
| Gardeners' Gazette | - | - | - | - | 3,850 |
| Globe | 864,000 | 920,000 | 900,000 | 997,800 | 1,069,000 |
| Gardeners' Chronicle | - | - | - | 20,000 | 208,000 |
| General Advertiser | - | - | - | - | - |
| Guardian | - | - | - | - | - |
| Grocers' Circular | - | - | - | - | - |
| Gardeners' Florist and Agriculturist | - | - | - | - | - |
| Gazette of Fashion | - | - | - | - | - |
| Great Gun | - | - | - | - | - |
| Gardener | - | - | - | - | - |
| Gospel Banner | - | - | - | - | - |
| Gray & Co.'s Overland Price Current | - | - | - | - | - |
| Gibbs & Co.'s Market Report | - | - | - | - | - |
| Green & Co.'s Monthly Guide | 65,000 | 16,000 | — | | |
| Gore's General Advertiser | 325 | - | - | - | - |
| Green, Wilsons & Co.'s Circular | - | - | 1,830 | — | |
| Giles' Price Current | — | | | | |
| Giles' Mark Lane Express | - | - | - | - | - |
| General Commercial Intelligencer | - | - | - | - | - |
| Gospel Magazine | - | - | - | - | - |
| Hodgkinson & Co.'s Circular | - | - | 1,000 | — | |
| Holt's Weekly Chronicle | - | 24,625 | — | | |
| Howard & Son's Price Current | - | - | - | - | - |
| Historic Times | - | - | - | - | - |
| Herald of Fashion | - | - | - | - | - |
| Harvey & Co.'s Price Current | — | | | | |
| Homœopathic Times | - | - | - | - | - |

| 1842. | 1843. | 1844. | 1845. | 1846. | 1847. | 1848. | 1849. | 1850. |
|---|---|---|---|---|---|---|---|---|
| - - | - - | - - | - - | - - | - - | - - | - - | 1,700 |
| - - | - - | - - | - - | - - | - - | - - | - - | 500 |
| - - | - - | - - | - - | - - | - - | - - | - - | 1,940 |
| — | | | | | | | | |
| - - | - - | - - | - - | - - | - - | - - | - - | 1,560 |
| - - | - - | 750 | — | | | | | |
| 122,548 | 115,500 | — | | | | | | |
| - - | - - | - - | 86,500 | — | | | | |
| - - | - - | - - | - - | - - | - - | - - | 1,150 | — |
| - - | - - | - - | - - | - - | - - | - - | - - | 19,450 |
| 6,720 | 8,000 | — | | | | | | |
| — | | | | | | | | |
| 2,000 | 2,000 | 2,000 | 2,000 | 2,000 | 2,000 | 2,000 | 2,000 | 2,000 |
| - - | - - | 1,500 | 880 | 650 | 750 | 870 | 1,246 | 2,082 |
| - - | 1,500 | 1,500 | 1,500 | 1,500 | 2,350 | 10,300 | 6,960 | 13,500 |
| - - | - - | - - | - - | - - | - - | - - | 500 | 1,500 |
| - - | - - | - - | - - | - - | - - | 920 | — | |
| 1,950 | 4,570 | 3,600 | 6,700 | 4,870 | 2,760 | — | | |
| - - | - - | - - | - - | 64,200 | 93,800 | — | | |
| 9,190 | 4,850 | 4,575 | 4,500 | 1,875 | — | | | |
| - - | - - | - - | - - | - - | 2,890 | — | | |
| - - | - - | - - | - - | 23,270 | 29,650 | — | | |
| - - | - - | 8,000 | 6,000 | — | | | | |
| - - | - - | - - | 1,200 | 800 | — | | | |
| - - | - - | - - | 34,150 | 24,350 | — | | | |
| - - | - - | - - | - - | 3,500 | — | | | |
| - - | - - | - - | - - | - - | - - | 10,000 | — | |
| - - | - - | - - | - - | - - | - - | - - | - - | 5,000 |
| - - | - - | - - | - - | - - | 1,900 | 13,000 | 19,500 | 11,000 |
| - - | - - | - - | - - | - - | 69,770 | 118,250 | 91,500 | 60,500 |
| - - | - - | - - | - - | - - | 5,250 | — | | |
| - - | - - | - - | - - | - - | 1,000 | 1,918 | 750 | 640 |
| 44,800 | 14,800 | 42,675 | 56,750 | 75,600 | 84,500 | 141,000 | 121,250 | 121,600 |
| 1,101,050 | 948,125 | 875,000 | 852,000 | 764,000 | 690,000 | 720,000 | 640,000 | 585,000 |
| 188,502 | 267,000 | 428,022 | 391,021 | 410,000 | 406,000 | 382,000 | 385,019 | 338,000 |
| - - | - - | 610 | 1,240 | 4,860 | 2,690 | — | | |
| - - | - - | - - | - - | 60,000 | 82,350 | 116,250 | 131,000 | 187,825 |
| - - | - - | - - | - - | 2,050 | 2,640 | — | | |
| - - | - - | - - | - - | - - | 15,055 | 12,210 | 936 | — |
| - - | - - | - - | - - | - - | 3,600 | 6,100 | 6,750 | 7,645 |
| - - | - - | 5,500 | 14,750 | — | | | | |
| - - | - - | 1,024 | 108 | — | | | | |
| - - | - - | - - | - - | - - | 750 | 750 | 1,200 | 1,030 |
| - - | - - | - - | - - | - - | - - | - - | 800 | 700 |
| - - | - - | - - | - - | - - | - - | - - | 3,590 | 4,000 |
| - - | 600 | — | | | | | | |
| - - | - - | - - | - - | - - | - - | - - | - - | 14,500 |
| - - | 22,300 | — | | | | | | |
| - - | - - | - - | - - | - - | - - | - - | - - | 1,500 |
| - - | - - | - - | - - | - - | 1,000 | 10,000 | 4,260 | 3,050 |
| - - | - - | - - | - - | - - | - - | - - | 245,590 | 85,503 |
| - - | - - | - - | - - | - - | - - | 1,524 | 520 | — |
| - - | - - | - - | - - | - - | - - | - - | 7,500 | 12,800 |

| —— | 1837. | 1838. | 1839. | 1840. | 1841. |
|---|---|---|---|---|---|
| LONDON PAPERS—*continued.* | | | | | |
| Herapath's Journal | - - | - - | - - | - - | - - |
| Herald of Peace | - - | - - | - - | - - | - - |
| Home News | - - | - - | - - | - - | - - |
| Hoffman's Price Current | - - | - - | - - | - - | - - |
| Hulbert, Layton & Co.'s Circular | - - | - - | - - | - - | - - |
| Hermen, Sillen & Sons' Bericht | - - | - - | - - | - - | - - |
| Hugh, Low & Co.'s Plant List | - - | - - | - - | - - | - - |
| Howitt's Journal | - - | - - | - - | - - | - - |
| H. S. Floud & Co.'s Price Current | - - | - - | - - | - - | - - |
| Historical Register | - - | - - | - - | - - | - - |
| Hong Kong Circular | - - | - - | - - | - - | - - |
| Household Words | - - | - - | - - | - - | - - |
| Harrison & Brothers' Price Current | - - | - - | - - | - - | - - |
| Household Narrative | - - | - - | - - | - - | - - |
| H. Roberts & Co.'s Price Current | - - | - - | - - | - - | - - |
| Howard's Circular | - - | - - | - - | - - | - - |
| Journal of Gaslighting | - - | - - | - - | - - | - - |
| Journal of Public Health | - - | - - | - - | - - | - - |
| Illustrated London News | - - | - - | - - | - - | - - |
| John Bull | 201,000 | 226,000 | 227,000 | 219,000 | 201,000 |
| Jurist | 100,600 | 108,000 | 78,000 | 87,500 | 85,913 |
| Justice of the Peace | 13,000 | 78,700 | 93,550 | 108,400 | 122,850 |
| Indian News | - - | - - | - - | 11,550 | 23,500 |
| Johnson & Kenney's Price Current | - - | - - | - - | - - | - - |
| Inquirer | - - | - - | - - | - - | - - |
| Jewish Chronicle | - - | - - | 9,950 | 37,500 | - - |
| Journal of Commerce | - - | - - | - - | - - | - - |
| Journal | - - | - - | - - | - - | - - |
| Journal of Education | — | - - | - - | - - | - - |
| Indian Mail | - - | - - | - - | - - | - - |
| Iron Times | - - | - - | - - | - - | - - |
| John Straite's Price Current | - - | - - | - - | - - | - - |
| Joe Miller the Younger | - - | - - | - - | - - | - - |
| Illustrated Polytechnic Review | - - | - - | - - | - - | - - |
| Illustrated Weekly Times | — | | | | |
| Illustrated London Life | - - | - - | - - | - - | - - |
| Illustrated Weekly | - - | - - | - - | - - | - - |
| J. P. Mason & Co.'s Overland Circular | - - | - - | - - | - - | - - |
| Journal of Public Health | - - | - - | - - | - - | - - |
| Joint Stock Company Law Journal | - - | - - | - - | - - | - - |
| Justice | - - | - - | - - | - - | - - |
| Jerrold's Weekly News | - - | - - | - - | - - | - - |
| J. Still & Co.'s Price Current | - - | - - | - - | - - | - - |
| J. Teesdale's Sale List | - - | - - | 3,000 | — | |
| J. Peram's Circular | | - - | 4,638 | — | |
| J. Wylie's Tea Circular | | - - | 1,347 | — | |
| Inventors' Advocate | - - | - - | - - | 44,850 | 32,480 |
| J. Edwards' Tea Circular | - - | - - | 800 | — | |
| Kunhards, Arndes & Co.'s Bericht | - - | - - | - - | - - | - - |
| Kirkman, Brown & Co.'s Price Current | - - | - - | - - | - - | - - |
| Kumpt & Fekenstern's Statement | - - | - - | - - | - - | - - |
| London Mercury | 177,000 | - - | - - | - - | - - |
| L'Echo de Savenarola | - - | - - | - - | - - | - - |
| Lancet | - - | - - | - - | - - | - - |
| L'Observateur Français | - - | - - | - - | - - | - - |
| London Mercantile Journal | 19,500 | 20,600 | 17,900 | 17,500 | - - |
| Legal Observer | 4,500 | - - | - - | - - | - - |
| Literary Gazette | 21,550 | 24,512 | 27,030 | 27,530 | 37,600 |
| Literary Circular | - - | - - | - - | - - | 6,450 |
| Le Courrier de l'Europe | - - | - - | - - | 53,250 | 89,500 |
| Law Gazette | 282 | 351 | 414 | 400 | 375 |
| Law Chronicle | 4,184 | 4,501 | 4,419 | 4,000 | 3,500 |
| London Gazette | 160,000 | 160,000 | 150,000 | 155,000 | 200,000 |

| 1842. | 1843. | 1844. | 1845. | 1846. | 1847. | 1848. | 1849. | 1850. |
|---|---|---|---|---|---|---|---|---|
| - | 75,775 | 95,500 | 334,500 | 123,500 | 96,000 | 94,500 | 95,000 | 96,300 |
| - | - | 1,000 | 5,000 | 6,750 | 6,400 | 8,000 | 9,450 | 12,350 |
| - | - | - | - | - | 75,500 | 72,500 | 70,000 | 78,700 |
| - | - | - | - | - | - | 3,800 | 8,950 | 8,200 |
| - | - | 1,000 | 700 | 800 | 500 | 1,000 | 2,200 | 3,000 |
| - | - | - | - | - | 2,000 | 2,000 | 2,000 | 2,000 |
| - | - | - | - | - | - | 2,000 | 3,000 | 2,000 |
| - | - | - | - | 2,000 | 8,600 | 2,000 | — | |
| 2,660 | 1,368 | 1,850 | 3,750 | — | | | | |
| - | - | 50,000 | — | | | | | |
| - | - | - | 25,000 | — | | | | |
| - | - | - | - | - | - | - | - | 23,000 |
| - | - | - | - | - | - | - | - | 2,500 |
| - | - | - | - | - | - | - | - | 2,640 |
| - | - | - | - | - | - | - | - | 6,100 |
| - | - | - | - | 2,000 | — | | | |
| - | - | - | - | - | - | - | 8,100 | 8,252 |
| - | - | - | - | - | 4,000 | 10,200 | 6,700 | — |
| 932,950 | 2,110,353 | 2,532,000 | 2,618,800 | 2,367,067 | 2,267,601 | 2,964,658 | 3,600,169 | 3,467,007 |
| 185,000 | 168,000 | 147,000 | 132,000 | 132,000 | 118,000 | 118,500 | 120,000 | 110,000 |
| 85,794 | 93,936 | 95,960 | 94,500 | 83,400 | 83,200 | 84,887 | 84,800 | 83,325 |
| 115,850 | 105,552 | 123,550 | 96,558 | 99,600 | 95,050 | 99,775 | 89,010 | 85,075 |
| 27,775 | 21,800 | 21,150 | 30,175 | 36,995 | 31,650 | 29,750 | 34,000 | 36,400 |
| - | - | - | 860 | 1,746 | 1,940 | 2,055 | 1,236 | — |
| 19,800 | 47,000 | 55,000 | 54,000 | 51,000 | 48,000 | 43,150 | 49,440 | 49,075 |
| - | - | 26,600 | 53,200 | 45,860 | 37,000 | 35,000 | 28,000 | 24,000 |
| - | - | - | 2,375 | 3,390 | 5,574 | 8,204 | 8,120 | 8,622 |
| - | - | - | - | 15,450 | 6,550 | — | | |
| - | 16,350 | 13,050 | 1,400 | - | - | - | - | 500 |
| - | - | - | 233,300 | 41,000 | — | | | |
| - | - | 480 | 990 | 360 | - | - | 220 | 450 |
| - | - | - | 7,000 | — | | | | |
| - | 17,830 | 2,100 | — | | | | | |
| - | 77,000 | — | | | | | | |
| - | - | - | - | - | - | 10,500 | — | |
| - | - | - | - | - | - | 1,250 | 1,500 | 2,000 |
| - | - | - | - | - | 4,000 | 10,250 | 6,700 | — |
| - | - | - | - | - | - | 6,000 | 1,000 | — |
| - | - | - | - | - | - | 5,500 | — | |
| - | - | - | - | - | - | 97,000 | — | |
| - | - | - | - | - | - | - | 1,500 | — |
| — | | | | | | | | |
| - | - | - | - | - | - | - | 2,000 | — |
| - | - | - | - | - | - | 1,000 | 1,750 | 2,000 |
| - | - | - | - | - | - | - | 2,000 | — |
| - | - | - | - | - | 26,500 | 12,550 | — | |
| - | - | - | - | - | 2,600 | 3,000 | 3,000 | 3,000 |
| - | - | 60,350 | 51,290 | 48,000 | 46,635 | 52,300 | 53,775 | 63,812 |
| - | - | - | 85,500 | 70,300 | 86,707 | 31,850 | — | |
| 42,583 | 23,436 | 21,807 | 20,000 | 19,000 | 16,000 | 15,000 | 17,500 | 14,500 |
| - | - | 7,000 | 10,500 | 8,500 | 8,000 | 8,000 | 5,500 | 6,500 |
| 28,760 | 20,518 | 19,530 | 18,000 | 29,500 | 25,358 | 25,700 | 26,850 | 26,300 |
| 12,000 | 10,700 | 11,500 | 8,500 | 9,950 | 11,100 | 7,550 | 14,100 | 14,350 |
| 92,750 | 80,500 | 90,400 | 114,200 | 87,000 | 48,000 | 77,100 | 70,500 | 67,000 |
| 400 | 400 | 325 | 275 | 175 | 175 | — | | |
| 3,000 | 3,500 | 4,000 | 3,500 | 3,000 | 3,000 | — | | |
| 235,000 | 240,000 | 314,096 | 822,000 | 440,000 | 170,000 | 245,000 | 210,000 | 180,000 |

| | 1837. | 1838. | 1839. | 1840. | 1841. |
|---|---|---|---|---|---|
| LONDON PAPERS—*continued.* | | | | | |
| Littledale & Co.'s Circular | - | - | - | - | - |
| Lloyd, Matheson & Co.'s Price Current | - | - | - | - | - |
| London Price Current | 1,500 | - | 3,000 | - | - |
| Life Assurance Record | - | - | - | - | - |
| Lumley's Advertiser | - | - | 18,600 | 39,000 | 22,225 |
| Law Times | - | - | - | - | - |
| Lean's Engine Reporter | - | - | 1,500 | 2,000 | - |
| Lord and Co.'s Price Current | - | - | - | - | - |
| London Commercial Record | - | - | - | - | - |
| Lloyd's Weekly London | - | - | - | - | - |
| London Medical Gazette | - | - | - | - | - |
| London and Liverpool Advertizer | - | - | - | - | - |
| Law Student's Magazine | - | - | - | - | - |
| Lewis & Peat's Price Current | - | - | - | - | - |
| Laing & Broxner's Price Current | - | - | - | - | - |
| Ladies' Journal | - | - | - | - | - |
| Lloyd's Liverpool Railway Times | - | - | - | - | - |
| London Mail | - | - | - | 22,950 | 40,000 |
| London Railway | - | - | - | - | - |
| Legal Record | - | - | - | - | - |
| Law Intelligencer | - | - | - | - | - |
| La Essoca | - | - | - | - | - |
| London Monthly Overland Mail | - | - | - | 3,851 | 13,035 |
| London Southern Advertiser | — | | | | |
| Lyre | — | | | | |
| London Mercury | — | | | | |
| Leech and Co.'s Market Report | - | - | - | - | - |
| Le Spectateur de Londres | - | - | - | - | - |
| Lilley's Furniture Sale Circular | - | - | - | - | - |
| London Telegraph | - | - | - | - | - |
| Ladies' Companion | - | - | - | - | - |
| London City Mission Magazine | — | | | | |
| London New Price Current | - | - | - | 6,500 | — |
| London Journal | 46,000 | — | | | |
| London Journal and Pioneer | - | - | - | - | - |
| London Dispatch | 370,750 | 259,000 | 121,250 | — | |
| London Journal (Kidd's) | — | | | | |
| London Pilot | - | - | - | - | 250 |
| Leader | - | - | - | - | - |
| Lucy, Son, & Co.'s Price Current | — | | | | |
| Life | - | - | - | - | - |
| Lord's Price Current | — | | | | |
| London Review | - | - | - | - | - |
| Leisure Moments | — | | | | |
| London Medical Examiner | - | - | - | - | - |
| London Mercantile Journal | - | - | - | - | - |
| Leisure Moments | - | - | - | - | - |
| London Musical Gazette | - | - | - | - | - |
| London City Mission Magazine | - | - | - | - | - |
| London Journal of Commerce | - | - | - | 37,500 | 103,000 |
| Legal Guide | - | - | - | - | - |
| London and Southern Advertiser | - | - | - | - | - |
| Lyre | - | - | - | - | - |
| London Price Current | - | - | - | - | - |
| Lloyd's Illustrated London | - | - | - | - | - |
| Medical Protection Circular | - | - | - | - | - |
| Melley, Romily, & Co.'s Circular | - | - | - | - | - |
| Monthly Digest | - | - | - | - | - |
| M. & K. Keightly & Co.'s Price Current | — | | | | |
| Mackey's Price Current | - | - | - | - | - |
| Mark Lane Express | 161,000 | 180,750 | 237,250 | 238,000 | 231,000 |
| Mining Journal | 66,000 | 71,000 | 68,500 | 72,600 | 74,407 |

| 1842. | 1843. | 1844. | 1845. | 1846. | 1847. | 1848. | 1849. | 1850. |
|---|---|---|---|---|---|---|---|---|
| - - | - - | 3,888 | 5,184 | 4,758 | 5,434 | 7,412 | 3,956 | 7,212 |
| - - | - - | - - | - - | 1,250 | 1,750 | 2,050 | 2,000 | 1,000 |
| 6,500 | 7,000 | 6,000 | 5,500 | 4,950 | 4,700 | 4,325 | 3,420 | 3,147 |
| - - | - - | - - | - - | - - | 27,900 | 4,340 | — | |
| 18,000 | 20,000 | 25,000 | 29,000 | 23,064 | 29,713 | 29,228 | 31,700 | 33,020 |
| - - | 104,250 | 151,048 | 156,750 | 156,000 | 164,500 | 138,100 | 125,750 | 139,100 |
| 2,000 | 5,000 | 1,000 | 1,500 | 1,000 | 1,000 | 1,500 | 1,000 | 1,000 |
| 1,072 | 1,000 | 1,000 | 1,000 | 1,000 | 1,000 | 1,000 | 1,259 | 1,000 |
| - - | - - | 16,860 | 23,820 | 25,030 | 34,200 | 36,420 | 32,210 | 35,750 |
| 1,719,000 | 1,110,353 | 2,372,027 | 2,777,432 | 2,663,500 | 1,69[illegible],500 | 1,776,577 | 2,431,450 | 2,559,000 |
| - - | - - | - - | 7,252 | 9,000 | 9,000 | 10,500 | 13,300 | 12,000 |
| - - | - - | - - | - - | - - | 35,975 | — | | |
| - - | - - | - - | 2,960 | 14,750 | 12,650 | 8,250 | 5,800 | 3,800 |
| - - | - - | - - | - - | - - | 6[illegible]4 | 1,200 | 1,440 | 2,160 |
| - - | - - | - - | - - | - - | 4,100 | 2,500 | 1,000 | 2,000 |
| - - | - - | - - | - - | - - | 1,050 | — | | |
| - - | - - | - - | 6,500 | — | | | | |
| 39,000 | 39,424 | 37,000 | 83,291 | 52,500 | — | | | |
| - - | - - | - - | 2,000 | — | | | | |
| - - | - - | 3,750 | 1,000 | — | | | | |
| - - | 3,100 | — | | | | | | |
| 14,016 | — | | | | | | | |
| 5,209 | — | | | | | | | |
| - - | - - | - - | - - | - - | - - | 3,200 | 2,000 | 3,100 |
| - - | - - | - - | - - | - - | - - | 13,5[illegible]0 | — | |
| - - | - - | - - | - - | - - | - - | 6,840 | 216 | 432 |
| - - | - - | - - | - - | - - | - - | 403,500 | — | |
| - - | - - | - - | - - | - - | - - | - - | 2,000 | 14,500 |
| - - | - - | - - | 59,856 | 23,425 | — | | | |
| — | | | | | | | | |
| - - | - - | - - | - - | - - | - - | - - | - - | 116,275 |
| - - | - - | - - | - - | - - | - - | - - | - - | 7,500 |
| - - | - - | - - | - - | - - | - - | - - | 500 | 500 |
| - - | - - | - - | - - | - - | - - | - - | - - | 800 |
| 25,483 | 25,000 | 21,807 | 20,000 | 19,000 | 16,000 | 15,000 | 17,000 | 14,500 |
| - - | - - | - - | - - | - - | - - | - - | - - | 2,000 |
| - - | - - | - - | - - | - - | - - | - - | 18,000 | — |
| - - | - - | - - | - - | - - | - - | - - | 3,200 | 5,375 |
| 92,600 | 68,020 | 22,500 | — | | | | | |
| 3,459 | 5,000 | — | | | | | | |
| 10,850 | 10,452 | — | | | | | | |
| 2,160 | — | | | | | | | |
| - - | 6,000 | — | | | | | | |
| 80,000 | — | | | | | | | |
| - - | - - | - - | - - | - - | - - | - - | - - | 11,350 |
| - - | - - | - - | - - | - - | - - | - - | - - | 5,300 |
| - - | - - | - - | - - | - - | - - | - - | - - | 6,800 |
| - - | - - | - - | - - | - - | - - | - - | - - | 1,000 |
| 218,500 | 220,500 | 232,000 | 229,500 | 245,000 | 317,000 | 280,750 | 237,250 | 248,000 |
| 73,500 | 77,000 | 78,750 | 97,500 | 91,500 | 100,500 | 96,500 | 106,500 | 107,000 |

| —— | 1837. | 1838. | 1839. | 1840. | 1841. |
|---|---|---|---|---|---|
| LONDON PAPERS—*continued.* | | | | | |
| Morning Advertiser - - - - - - | 1,380,000 | 1,565,225 | 1,535,000 | 1,550,000 | 1,470,000 |
| Morning Chronicle - - - - - - | 1,940,000 | 2,750,000 | 2,028,000 | 2,075,500 | 2,079,000 |
| Morning Herald - - - - - - | 1,928,000 | 1,925,000 | 1,820,000 | 1,956,000 | 1,630,000 |
| Morning Post - - - - - - | 735,000 | 875,000 | 1,006,000 | 1,125,000 | 1,165,210 |
| Magnet - - - - - - | 194,500 | 224,500 | 209,000 | 207,650 | 213,750 |
| Metropolitan Conservative Journal - - - | 73,850 | 113,500 | 36,500 | — | |
| Mining Gazette - - - - - - | 9,300 | — | | | |
| Moor's Stock List - - - - - - | 494 | 498 | 500 | 950 | — |
| Marylebone Journal - - - - - | 2,000 | — | | | |
| Medical Times - - - - - - | - - | - - | - - | 14,598 | 18,524 |
| Madras Spectator - - - - - | - - | - - | 600 | — | |
| Musical World - - - - - - | - - | - - | 4,500 | 3,250 | 4,800 |
| Moffatt & Co.'s Tea List - - - - | - - | - - | - - | - - | 14,000 |
| Monthly Times - - - - - - | - - | - - | - - | - - | - - |
| Municipal and Poor-law Gazette - - - | - - | - - | - - | - - | - - |
| Missionary Herald - - - - - | - - | - - | - - | - - | - - |
| Musical Examiner - - - - - - | - - | - - | - - | - - | - - |
| Medical Argus - - - - - - | - - | - - | - - | - - | - - |
| Musical Times - - - - - - | - - | - - | - - | - - | - - |
| Money Market Examiner - - - - | - - | - - | - - | - - | - - |
| Midland Florist - - - - - - | - - | - - | - - | - - | - - |
| Missionary Magazine and Chronicle - - | - - | - - | - - | - - | - - |
| Merridew & Delmar's Price Current - - | - - | - - | - - | - - | - - |
| Macnaughton and Parry's Price Current - | - - | - - | - - | - - | - - |
| M'Kenzie's Railway Time Table - - - | - - | - - | - - | - - | - - |
| Monthly Colonial Market Report - - - | - - | - - | - - | - - | - - |
| Mechanics' Magazine - - - - - | - - | - - | - - | - - | - - |
| Magistrate - - - - - - - | - - | - - | - - | - - | - - |
| Milner, Broathwick & Co.'s Price Current | - - | - - | - - | - - | - - |
| M. R. Knightly - - - - - - | - - | - - | - - | - - | - - |
| Monthly Digest - - - - - - | - - | - - | - - | - - | - - |
| Missionary Magazine and Chronicle - - | - - | - - | - - | - - | - - |
| National Society, Monthly - - - - | - - | - - | - - | - - | - - |
| Nautical Standard - - - - - - | - - | - - | - - | - - | - - |
| Norton, Kilburn & Co.'s Circular - - | - - | - - | - - | - - | - - |
| New Zealand Journal - - - - - | - - | - - | - - | 18,000 | 20,450 |
| Nonconformist - - - - - - | - - | - - | - - | - - | 43,000 |
| Naval and Military Gazette - - - - | 63,336 | 76,650 | 88,725 | 94,665 | 94,500 |
| Nicholson's Price Current - - - - | - - | - - | - - | 14,500 | 14,000 |
| National Temperance Chronicle - - - | - - | - - | - - | - - | - - |
| Northern Star - - - - - - | - - | - - | - - | - - | - - |
| News of the World - - - - - | - - | - - | - - | - - | - - |
| Notes and Queries - - - - - - | - - | - - | - - | - - | - - |
| Nestle, Andrew & Co.'s Price Current - | - - | - - | - - | - - | - - |
| National - - - - - - - | - - | - - | - - | - - | - - |
| Nonconformist Elector - - - - - | - - | - - | - - | - - | - - |
| National Protector - - - - - | - - | - - | - - | - - | - - |
| New Farmers' Journal - - - - - | 20,000 | 10,000 | - - | - - | 42,325 |
| National Record - - - - - - | - - | - - | - - | - - | - - |
| New Age - - - - - - - | - - | - - | - - | - - | - - |
| Nicholson's Weekly Register - - - - | - - | - - | - - | - - | - - |
| National Advertiser - - - - - | - - | - - | - - | 2,000 | 28,000 |
| News and Sunday Globe and Herald - - | 62,720 | 101,000 | 48,000 | — | |
| Newsman's Weekly Chronicle - - - | 29,000 | — | | | |
| News - - - - - - - - | 66,936 | — | | | |
| Nisbett's Price Current - - - - - | - - | - - | - - | - - | - - |
| Observer - - - - - - - | 299,000 | 275,000 | 118,500 | 216,000 | 182,500 |
| Old England - - - - - - | - - | - - | 33,500 | 191,000 | 111,100 |
| Ostel & Le Page's Circular - - - - | - - | - - | - - | - - | 500 |
| Overland Despatch - - - - - | - - | - - | - - | - - | - - |
| Oxberry's Weekly Budget - - - - | - - | - - | - - | - - | - - |
| Overland News - - - - - - | - - | - - | - - | - - | - - |

| 1842. | 1843. | 1844. | 1845. | 1846. | 1847. | 1848. | 1849. | 1850. |
|---|---|---|---|---|---|---|---|---|
| 1,445,000 | 1,534,000 | 1,415,000 | 1,440,000 | 1,480,000 | 1,500,000 | 1,538,000 | 1,528,220 | 1,549,843 |
| 1,918,500 | 1,784,000 | 1,628,000 | 1,554,000 | 1,356,000 | 1,233,000 | 1,150,304 | 937,500 | 912,547 |
| 1,559,500 | 1,516,000 | 1,608,070 | 2,018,025 | 1,752,500 | 1,510,000 | 1,335,000 | 1,147,000 | 1,139,000 |
| 1,195,025 | 1,900,000 | 1,002,000 | 1,200,500 | 1,450,500 | 990,100 | 964,500 | 905,000 | 828,000 |
| 210,500 | 212,550 | 199,750 | 202,950 | 215,175 | 210,290 | 260,958 | 257,000 | 246,050 |
| 22,555 | 34,710 | 77,500 | 95,220 | 82,150 | 76,520 | 81,615 | 82,150 | 70,833 |
| 3,410 | 7,890 | 8,200 | 11,641 | 14,680 | 16,446 | 15,652 | 15,432 | 14,712 |
| 10,000 | 10,000 | 11,000 | 4,000 | — | | | | |
| 21,250 | 31,025 | 21,500 | 42,256 | 32,900 | 26,697 | 8,350 | — | |
| - - | - - | 25,400 | — | | | | | |
| - - | - - | 5,550 | 6,700 | 4,000 | 4,000 | 2,000 | 3,720 | 4,000 |
| - - | - - | 5,684 | — | | | | | |
| - - | - - | 4,600 | — | | | | | |
| 6,450 | 4,150 | 3,000 | 3,500 | 1,500 | 9,500 | 10,700 | 9,000 | 10,000 |
| - - | - - | - - | - - | - - | - - | 6,000 | 35,725 | 17,200 |
| - - | - - | - - | - - | - - | - - | 1,000 | — | |
| - - | - - | - - | - - | - - | - - | 2,500 | — | |
| - - | - - | - - | - - | - - | - - | 956 | - | 900 |
| - - | - - | - - | 12,000 | - - | 680 | 12,000 | 1,240 | 960 |
| - - | - - | - - | - - | - - | 1,650 | 700 | — | |
| - - | - - | - - | - - | - - | - - | - - | 880 | 800 |
| - - | - - | - - | - - | - - | 1,000 | 5,100 | 8,000 | 9,100 |
| - - | - - | - - | - - | - - | - - | - - | 800 | 14,025 |
| - - | - - | - - | - - | - - | - - | - - | 2,000 | 3,000 |
| - - | - - | - - | - - | - - | - - | - - | - - | 4,000 |
| - - | - - | - - | - - | - - | - - | - - | - - | 6,800 |
| - - | - - | - - | - - | - - | - - | - - | - - | 3,722 |
| - - | - - | - - | - - | - - | - - | 7,498 | 67,500 | 43,200 |
| - - | - - | - - | - - | 36,500 | 55,000 | 52,948 | 44,000 | 40,000 |
| - - | 2,000 | 3,000 | 2,500 | 3,000 | 3,500 | 3,000 | 3,500 | 4,000 |
| 22,100 | 21,750 | 19,514 | 14,750 | 10,000 | 7,800 | 9,925 | 10,000 | 7,850 |
| 110,850 | 115,900 | 117,064 | 108,500 | 113,500 | 118,550 | 145,850 | 146,500 | 154,175 |
| 96,920 | 91,447 | 89,720 | 89,187 | 95,000 | 88,000 | 80,724 | 73,800 | 60,320 |
| 12,500 | 11,500 | 14,238 | 8,000 | 10,600 | 12,000 | 7,000 | 7,750 | 6,500 |
| - - | 4,500 | 9,000 | 15,850 | 14,200 | 10,500 | 18,000 | 13,000 | 4,090 |
| - - | - - | - - | 337,500 | 322,000 | 455,000 | 626,500 | 361,500 | 246,000 |
| - - | 101,205 | 674,018 | 1,251,150 | 1,878,500 | 1,981,853 | 2,478,955 | 2,806,767 | 2,926,269 |
| - - | - - | - - | - - | - - | - - | - | 4,000 | 12,500 |
| - - | - - | - - | - - | - - | 1,920 | 480 | 1,450 | 2,839 |
| - - | - - | - - | - - | 11,150 | 2,461 | 1,262 | 698 | — |
| - - | - - | - - | - - | 11,000 | — | | | |
| - - | - - | - - | - - | - - | 8,000 | — | | |
| 79,532 | 73,700 | 71,250 | 60,234 | 55,755 | — | | | |
| - - | - - | - - | 7,000 | — | | | | |
| - - | - - | - - | 6,056 | — | | | | |
| 101,000 | - - | 12,675 | — | | | | | |
| 169,000 | 35,500 | — | | | | | | |
| - - | - - | 910 | 450 | - - | 450 | 11,000 | 1,700 | — |
| 210,000 | 141,500 | 154,500 | 149,000 | 177,500 | 212,000 | 281,000 | 360,500 | 324,000 |
| 11,700 | — | | | | | | | |
| 2,060 | 1,700 | 810 | — | | | | | |
| 500 | 1,500 | 2,000 | 4,000 | 4,000 | 3,000 | — | | |
| 250 | 250 | 324 | — | | | | | |
| - - | - - | - - | 29,000 | — | | | | |

| —— | 1837. | 1838. | 1839. | 1840. | 1841. |
|---|---|---|---|---|---|
| LONDON PAPERS—*continued.* | | | | | |
| Pawnbrokers' Circular | - | - | - | - | - |
| Principality | - | - | - | - | - |
| Post-office Official Monthly Director | - | - | - | - | - |
| Patent Journal | - | - | - | - | - |
| Perry's Bankrupt Gazette | 17,927 | 21,049 | 21,830 | 24,938 | 27,560 |
| Pharmaceutical Times | - | - | - | - | - |
| Patriot | 229,500 | 228,500 | 266,500 | 302,300 | 261,000 |
| Price Current (Prince's) | - | - | - | 15,000 | 7,500 |
| Public Ledger | 65,350 | 104,500 | 140,600 | 140,000 | 140,000 |
| Publishers' Circular | 20,000 | 85,750 | 105,674 | 66,300 | 60,900 |
| Pawnbrokers' Gazette | - | 2,850 | 24,950 | 27,830 | 29,700 |
| Parish Choir | - | - | - | - | - |
| Punch | - | - | - | - | - |
| Presbyterian | — | | | | |
| Patry Pasteur's Price Current | - | - | - | - | - |
| Price Current of Leather | - | - | - | - | - |
| Peace Advocate | - | - | - | - | - |
| Protestant Magazine | - | - | - | - | - |
| Phonetic News | - | - | - | - | - |
| Protestant World | - | - | - | - | - |
| Pictorial Times | - | - | - | - | - |
| Public Societies Reporter | - | - | - | - | - |
| Puppet Show | - | - | - | - | - |
| Publisher | - | - | - | - | - |
| Protestant Elector | - | - | - | - | - |
| Presbyterian Messenger | - | - | - | - | - |
| Peuples | - | - | - | - | - |
| Prophetic Herald | - | - | - | - | - |
| Protection Alliance | - | - | - | - | - |
| Pandora | - | - | - | - | - |
| Provincial Medical Journal | - | - | - | 12,000 | 36,250 |
| Pioneer | - | - | - | - | - |
| Pilot | - | - | - | - | - |
| Planet | - | 246,000 | 141,500 | 110,100 | 102,250 |
| Philanthropist | - | - | - | - | - |
| Poor-law Guide | - | - | - | - | - |
| Phœnix | — | | | | |
| Parish Law Recorder | 1,200 | — | | | |
| Parish Law Recorder | — | | | | |
| Parthenon | - | - | 11,700 | 700 | — |
| Protection | - | - | 15,300 | 3,000 | 3,000 |
| Parson, Day & Co.'s Market Report | - | - | - | - | - |
| Primitive Church Magazine | - | - | - | - | - |
| Provident Philantrophist | - | - | - | - | - |
| Protectionist | - | - | - | - | - |
| Payne's Time Table | - | - | - | - | - |
| Racing Calendar | 38,400 | 37,100 | 25,775 | 36,225 | 39,225 |
| Record | 278,000 | 302,500 | 313,000 | 323,500 | 333,000 |
| Railway Times | 8,000 | 92,900 | 114,000 | 134,975 | 135,075 |
| Rippon and Burton's Price Current | - | - | - | 500 | 1,900 |
| Railway Magazine | - | - | 25,500 | 72,500 | 70,000 |
| Ripley and Brown's Circular | - | - | - | - | - |
| Railway Chronicle | - | - | - | - | - |
| Railway Record | - | - | - | - | - |
| Railway Bill and Advertiser | - | - | - | - | - |
| Railway Herald | - | - | - | - | - |
| Railway Telegraph | - | - | - | - | - |
| Railway World | - | - | - | - | - |
| Railway Courier | - | - | - | - | - |
| Railway Express | - | - | - | - | - |
| Railway Director | - | - | - | - | - |
| Railway Standard | - | - | - | - | - |

| 1842. | 1843. | 1844. | 1845. | 1846. | 1847. | 1848. | 1849. | 1850. |
|---|---|---|---|---|---|---|---|---|
| - - | - - | - - | - - | - - | - - | - - | 6,000 | — |
| - - | - - | - - | - - | - - | 20,500 | 64,680 | 58,610 | 28,000 |
| - | - - | - - | - - | - - | - - | - - | 1,929 | 2,880 |
| - - | - - | - - | - - | - - | 2,500 | 7,200 | 8,900 | 8,600 |
| 30,879 | 3,938 | 32,359 | 27,410 | 29,630 | 28,971 | 48,833 | 65,413 | 88,226 |
| - - | - - | - - | - - | 18,250 | 47,220 | 33,175 | 12,875 | — |
| 42,500 | 264,000 | 245,000 | 231,500 | 225,000 | 210,000 | 174,076 | 155,000 | 139,000 |
| 1,000 | 11,500 | 10,500 | 10,500 | 9,500 | 8,600 | 7,600 | 7,500 | 8,500 |
| 139,000 | 130,000 | 140,000 | 130,000 | 140,000 | 131,000 | 140,000 | 130,000 | 150,000 |
| 57,570 | 20,250 | 25,500 | 19,000 | 54,500 | 65,550 | 61,532 | 58,900 | 60,900 |
| 31,800 | 27,190 | 41,900 | 41,100 | 40,950 | 41,300 | 40,000 | 39,050 | 39,900 |
| - - | - - | - - | - - | 2,000 | 2,000 | 1,675 | 1,950 | 1,800 |
| - - | 63,000 | 237,083 | 149,491 | 509,492 | 409,110 | 390,385 | 345,864 | 345,050 |
| - - | - - | - - | 3,700 | 2,500 | 3,800 | 3,000 | 3,400 | 4,000 |
| - - | - - | - - | - - | - - | - - | 2,000 | 7,000 | 7,500 |
| - - | - - | - - | - - | 3,920 | 12,000 | 2,600 | 1,900 | 2,250 |
| - - | - - | - - | - - | - - | - - | - - | 5,225 | 4,250 |
| - - | - - | - - | - - | - - | - - | - - | 34,405 | — |
| - - | - - | - - | - - | - - | - - | - - | 5,000 | 1,000 |
| - - | 547,000 | 607,190 | 539,185 | 901,000 | 385,800 | 14,500 | — | |
| - - | - - | - - | - - | - - | - - | 1,000 | — | |
| - - | - - | - - | - - | - - | - - | 2,686 | — | |
| - - | - - | - - | - - | - - | 3,000 | — | | |
| - - | - - | - - | - - | - - | 37,329 | — | 4,270 | 4,725 |
| - - | - - | - - | ,000 | 9,500 | 9,325 | 7,125 | | |
| - - | - - | - - | - - | - - | 61,500 | — | | |
| - - | - - | - - | - - | 9,136 | — | | | |
| - - | - - | - - | - - | 1,000 | — | | | |
| - - | - - | 1,500 | 1,150 | — | | | | |
| 69,068 | 79,875 | 102,320 | 100,500 | — | | | | |
| - - | - - | - - | 22,500 | — | | | | |
| - - | - - | 18,500 | 2,000 | — | | | | |
| 89,500 | 69,600 | 4,750 | — | | | | | |
| - - | 5,250 | 3,500 | — | | | | | |
| - - | 26,900 | — | | | | | | |
| — | | | | | | | | |
| - - | - - | - - | - - | - - | - - | - - | - - | 11,000 |
| - - | - - | - - | 9,600 | 3,425 | 400 | - | - - | 1,600 |
| - - | - - | - - | - - | - - | 1,500 | 200 | — | |
| - - | - - | - - | - - | - - | - - | - - | - - | 3,500 |
| - - | - - | - - | - - | - - | - - | - - | - - | 2,000 |
| 38,075 | 37,850 | 39,200 | 39,675 | 45,625 | 45,900 | 43,450 | 51,050 | 45,900 |
| 342,000 | 351,500 | 353,500 | 356,100 | 358,500 | 361,500 | 361,500 | 366,000 | 390,500 |
| 139,000 | 155,000 | 184,452 | 355,350 | 242,500 | 195,500 | 137,250 | 113,200 | 85,700 |
| 650 | 850 | 1,790 | 1,250 | 1,350 | 850 | 1,000 | 750 | 600 |
| 75,750 | — | | | | | | | |
| 2,000 | 2,000 | 3,000 | 3,000 | 4,000 | 3,000 | 4,000 | 4,000 | 4,000 |
| - - | - - | 76,500 | 144,000 | 106,500 | 66,200 | 50,300 | 39,000 | — |
| - - | - - | 75,000 | 186,500 | 115,000 | 93,000 | 67,475 | 54,500 | 31,750 |
| - - | - - | 168,500 | 26,000 | 82,200 | — | | | |
| - - | - - | - - | 59,240 | 21,000 | 5,500 | — | | |
| - - | - - | - - | 22,275 | 5,075 | — | | | |
| - - | - - | - - | 10,500 | 7,500 | 1,300 | — | | |
| - - | - - | - - | 5,500 | 2,000 | — | | | |
| - - | - - | - - | 24,000 | 3,850 | — | | | |
| - - | - - | - - | 68,000 | 17,000 | — | | | |
| - - | - - | - - | 14,500 | 34,000 | — | | | |

| — | 1837. | 1838. | 1839. | 1840. | 1841. |
|---|---|---|---|---|---|
| LONDON PAPERS—*continued.* | | | | | |
| Railway Gazette | - | - | - | - | - |
| Railway Mail | - | - | - | - | - |
| Railway Monthly Magazine | - | - | - | - | - |
| Railway Chart | - | - | - | - | - |
| Rambler | - | - | - | - | - |
| Reformer | - | - | - | - | - |
| Reid's Time Table | - | - | - | - | - |
| Randel's Price Current | - | - | - | - | - |
| Rennie & Co.'s Price Current | - | - | - | - | - |
| Robards & Co.'s Price Current | - | - | - | - | - |
| Ragged School Union Magazine | - | - | - | - | - |
| Railway Examiner | - | - | - | - | - |
| Railway Critic | - | - | - | - | - |
| Railway King | - | - | - | - | - |
| Railway Engine | - | - | - | - | - |
| Railway Advertiser | - | - | - | - | - |
| Railway Argus | - | - | - | - | - |
| Richardson, Brothers & Co.'s Circular | - | - | - | - | - |
| Rucker & Bencroft's Price Current | - | - | - | - | - |
| Reporter | - | - | - | - | - |
| R. Gibbs & Co.'s Circular | - | - | - | - | - |
| Reynolds's Weekly | - | - | - | - | - |
| Schroder & Co.'s Market Report | - | - | - | - | - |
| Stilt, Conborough & Stilt's Price Current | - | - | - | - | - |
| Sailors' Magazine | - | - | - | - | - |
| Suse & Sibeth's Bericht | - | - | - | - | - |
| Scordet, Meyer & Co's. Price Current | - | - | - | - | - |
| Stitts, Day & Co.'s Price Current | - | - | - | - | - |
| Standard of Freedom | - | - | - | - | - |
| Solicitors' Register | - | - | - | - | - |
| Sunday Times | 407,000 | 695,000 | 690,000 | 1,050,000 | 1,100,000 |
| Shipping Gazette | 237,630 | 316,976 | 349,000 | 386,000 | 408,000 |
| Standard | 1,330,000 | 1,075,000 | 1,030,000 | 1,040,000 | 1,025,000 |
| St. James's Chronicle | 657,000 | 707,500 | 674,500 | 692,000 | 676,000 |
| Sun | 794,000 | 1,344,000 | 1,231,000 | 1,281,000 | 1,225,000 |
| Spectator | 135,000 | 158,000 | 176,000 | 182,000 | 185,000 |
| Satirist | 164,200 | 154,500 | 149,500 | 194,027 | 162,000 |
| Slack's Price Current | - | - | - | - | - |
| Sidney's Emigrants' Journal | - | - | - | - | - |
| South Australian News | - | - | - | - | - |
| Shuttleworth & Co.'s Tea List | - | - | 2,000 | - | - |
| Spirit of the Age | - | - | - | - | - |
| Sporting Life | - | - | - | - | - |
| Sunday School Magazine | - | - | - | - | - |
| Sportsman's Magazine | - | - | - | - | - |
| Sargant, Gorden & Co.'s Circular | - | - | - | - | - |
| Savings Bank Circular | - | - | - | - | - |
| Sail & Son's Price Current | - | - | - | - | - |
| Spirit of the Times | - | 2,018 | 904 | - | - |
| Sentinel | - | - | - | - | - |
| Stock Exchange Express | - | - | - | - | - |
| South London News | - | - | - | - | - |
| Steam Times | - | - | - | - | - |
| Shareholder | - | - | - | - | - |
| South Western Standard | - | - | - | - | - |
| Savory & Son's Price Current | - | - | - | 15,220 | - |
| Shetland Journal | - | - | - | - | - |
| Sunday Evening Globe | - | - | - | - | - |
| Surrey Standard | 19,000 | 36,500 | — | | |
| Sunbeam | - | 7,275 | 3,040 | — | |
| Social Reformer | - | - | 6,500 | — | |
| Southern Star | - | - | - | 44,750 | — |

| 1842. | 1843. | 1844. | 1845. | 1846. | 1847. | 1848. | 1849. | 1850. |
|---|---|---|---|---|---|---|---|---|
| - - | - - | - - | - - | 5,000 | 74,420 | 33,874 | 19,000 | 13,000 |
| - - | - - | - - | 10,160 | 500 | — | | | |
| - - | - - | - - | - - | - - | 1,271 | — | | |
| - - | - - | - - | 6,000 | — | | | | |
| - - | - - | - - | - - | - - | 3,000 | 40,500 | — | |
| - - | - - | - - | - - | - - | - - | 17,300 | — | |
| - - | - - | - - | - - | - - | - - | - - | 1,400 | 1,500 |
| - - | - - | - - | - - | - - | - - | - - | - - | 4,000 |
| - - | - - | - - | - - | - - | - - | - - | - - | 4,250 |
| - - | - - | - - | - - | - - | - - | - - | - - | 2,350 |
| - - | - - | - - | - - | - - | - - | 548 | 5,000 | 6,524 |
| - - | - - | - - | 11,000 | — | | | | |
| - - | - - | - - | 11,500 | — | | | | |
| - - | - - | - - | 6,500 | — | | | | |
| - - | - - | - - | 43,000 | — | | | | |
| - - | - - | - - | 4,360 | — | | | | |
| - - | - - | - - | 1,500 | — | | | | |
| - - | - - | - - | - - | - - | - - | - - | 2,000 | 2,000 |
| - - | - - | - - | - - | - - | - - | 850 | - - | 600 |
| - - | - - | - - | - - | - - | - - | 1,450 | 10,200 | 9,725 |
| - - | - - | - - | - - | - - | - - | - - | - - | 1,000 |
| - - | - - | - - | - - | - - | - - | - - | - - | 275,250 |
| - - | - - | - - | - - | - - | - - | - - | - - | 2,800 |
| - - | - - | - - | - - | - - | - - | - - | 1,380 | 2,000 |
| - - | - - | - - | - - | - - | 1,400 | 4,300 | 2,822 | 2,050 |
| - - | - - | - - | - - | - - | 11,918 | 8,472 | 20,198 | 21,764 |
| - - | - - | - - | - - | - - | - - | 4,130 | 5,040 | 7,718 |
| - - | - - | - - | - - | - - | 7,000 | 6,500 | 3,000 | — |
| - - | - - | - - | - - | - - | - - | 185,000 | 288,500 | 168,500 |
| - - | - - | - - | - - | 24,120 | 22,675 | 18,150 | 27,900 | 250 |
| 1,080,000 | 915,000 | 880,500 | 945,500 | 932,500 | 785,000 | 757,000 | 735,000 | 675,000 |
| 383,588 | 400,000 | 385,500 | 385,500 | 407,112 | 429,500 | 414,000 | 475,000 | 459,500 |
| 1,000,000 | 920,000 | 867,000 | 846,000 | 780,000 | 659,500 | 652,500 | 539,000 | 492,000 |
| 627,000 | 593,000 | 651,000 | 611,000 | 593,500 | 530,000 | 496,000 | 467,000 | 451,000 |
| 1,173,000 | 1,098,000 | 868,000 | 1,098,500 | 1,104,000 | 909,000 | 893,312 | 873,000 | 834,500 |
| 188,000 | 188,500 | 166,000 | 135,000 | 194,000 | 174,100 | 174,000 | 161,000 | 152,500 |
| 151,500 | 128,500 | 78,100 | 72,000 | 66,100 | 61,800 | 62,200 | 33,500 | — |
| - - | - - | 500 | 300 | 250 | 600 | 300 | 550 | 500 |
| - - | - - | - - | - - | - - | - - | 3,000 | 18,000 | — |
| - - | - - | - - | - - | 2,960 | 5,300 | 5,550 | 5,280 | 4,800 |
| - - | - - | - - | - - | - - | 19,000 | 26,000 | 18,000 | 20,000 |
| - - | - - | - - | - - | - - | - - | 33,050 | 10,900 | — |
| - - | - - | - - | - - | - - | 1,260 | 7,750 | — | |
| - - | - - | - - | - - | - - | - - | 2,000 | 500 | — |
| - - | - - | - - | 13,300 | 5,290 | 1,910 | — | | |
| 1,500 | 2,000 | 3,000 | 2,000 | 3,000 | 3,000 | — | | |
| - - | - - | 1,550 | 4,225 | 3,850 | 1,750 | — | | |
| - - | - - | - - | 3,000 | 2,000 | - - | - - | - - | 1,000 |
| - - | - - | - - | - - | - - | 18,000 | — | | |
| - - | 67,050 | 68,000 | 49,500 | 13,000 | — | | | |
| - - | - - | - - | 23,000 | 3,500 | — | | | |
| - - | - - | - - | - - | 11,500 | — | | | |
| - - | - - | - - | 6,500 | — | | | | |
| - - | - - | - - | 17,550 | — | | | | |
| - - | - - | 8,000 | — | | | | | |
| - - | 5,160 | - - | 3,000 | 1,200 | 1,000 | 1,500 | 1,000 | 555 |
| - - | - - | - - | - - | - - | 11,500 | 13,900 | — | |
| - - | - - | - - | - - | - - | 31,189 | — | | |

| —— | 1837. | 1838. | 1839. | 1840. | 1841. |
|---|---|---|---|---|---|
| LONDON PAPERS—*continued.* | | | | | |
| Sharpe's London Magazine | - | - | - | - | - |
| South Australian Record | - | - | - | - | 26,200 |
| Southern Gas Circular | - | - | - | - | - |
| Times | 3,065,000 | 3,065,000 | 4,300,000 | 5,060,000 | 5,650,000 |
| Trade List | 1,500 | 3,000 | 2,000 | 12,000 | 10,000 |
| True Sun, Daily | 398,000 | — | | | |
| Temperance Journal | - | - | 14,188 | 14,053 | 12,912 |
| Temperance Recorder | - | - | - | - | 1,500 |
| Tablet | - | - | - | 57,000 | - |
| Temperance Record | — | | | | |
| True Tablet | - | - | - | - | 99,700 |
| The Friend | - | - | - | - | - |
| The League | - | - | - | - | - |
| The Institute | - | - | - | - | - |
| The Labourer's Friend | - | - | - | - | - |
| The Churchman | - | - | - | - | - |
| The Wesleyan | - | - | - | - | - |
| The Balance | - | - | - | - | - |
| The Universe | - | - | - | - | - |
| The Merchant | - | - | - | - | - |
| The Lady's | - | - | - | - | - |
| Teetotal Times | - | 4,000 | 4,000 | - | - |
| Temperance News | - | - | - | - | - |
| The Freeholder | - | - | - | - | - |
| Trade Protection Record | - | - | - | - | - |
| Truman and Rouse's Monthly Circular | - | - | - | - | - |
| The Country Gentleman | - | - | - | - | - |
| T. Cox Savory's Price Current | - | - | - | - | - |
| Thomson & Son's Monthly Circular | - | - | - | - | - |
| The Forceps | - | - | - | - | - |
| T. Moffit & Co.'s Price Current | - | - | - | - | - |
| Theological Register | - | - | - | - | - |
| The Freeholder | - | - | - | - | - |
| T. J. & T. Powell's Price Current | - | - | - | - | - |
| The Working Man's Friend | - | - | - | - | - |
| The Scholar | - | - | - | - | - |
| The Surplice | - | - | - | - | - |
| United Service Gazette | 62,000 | 77,750 | 78,500 | 86,500 | 85,200 |
| United Gardener's Journal | - | - | - | - | - |
| Universal Corn Reporter | 4,950 | 4,950 | 15,870 | 10,024 | 8,836 |
| Voluntary | - | - | - | - | - |
| Voice of Israel | - | - | - | - | - |
| Voice of Jacob | - | - | - | - | - |
| Voice of the People | - | - | - | - | - |
| Vegetarian Advocate | - | - | - | - | - |
| Weekly News | - | - | - | - | - |
| Weekly Monthly Orthodox | — | | | | |
| Working Man's Charter | - | - | - | - | - |
| Weekly Dispatch | 2,606,000 | 2,691,000 | 2,750,000 | 2,275,000 | 2,975,000 |
| Weekly Chronicle | 2,712,500 | 1,681,000 | 1,342,720 | 1,128,152 | 1,700,500 |
| Watchman | 145,700 | 137,150 | 215,200 | 210,000 | 207,000 |
| W. Thacker & Co.'s Overland Circular | - | - | - | - | - |
| Weekly Tribune | - | - | - | - | - |
| Wood & Samuel's Price Current | - | - | - | - | - |
| Willis's Price Current | - | - | - | - | - |
| Wesleyan Notices | - | - | - | - | - |
| Weekly Register | - | - | - | - | - |
| Weekly Times | - | - | - | - | - |
| W. Jameson & Son's Bericht | - | - | - | - | - |
| Weekly Evangelist | - | - | - | - | - |
| Wesleyan Times | - | - | - | - | - |
| Ward's Commercial Assistant | - | - | - | - | - |
| Weekly Railway | - | - | - | - | - |

| 1842. | 1843. | 1844. | 1845. | 1846. | 1847. | 1848. | 1849. | 1850. |
|---|---|---|---|---|---|---|---|---|
| - - | - - | - - | - - | 5,000 | 3,500 | — | | |
| — | | | | | | | | |
| - - | - - | - - | - - | - - | - - | - - | - - | 600 |
| 6,305,000 | 6,250,000 | 6,900,000 | 8,100,000 | 8,950,000 | 9,205,230 | 11,025,500 | 11,300,000 | 11,900,000 |
| 10,000 | 12,000 | 12,000 | 11,000 | 13,476 | 15,500 | 12,000 | — | |
| - - | - - | - - | - - | - - | 1,239 | — | | |
| 7,600 | 9,050 | 8,500 | 8,000 | — | | | | |
| 41,400 | 177,500 | 178,100 | 179,000 | 190,000 | 199,716 | 212,550 | 190,600 | — |
| 106,000 | — | | | | | | | |
| - - | 12,650 | 11,960 | 14,742 | 21,950 | 22,250 | 22,500 | 19,000 | 18,000 |
| - - | 167,000 | 1,041,000 | 738,000 | 503,000 | — | | | |
| - - | - - | 400 | 475 | - - | - - | - - | - - | 24,000 |
| - - | - - | 6,100 | 8,400 | 8,300 | 7,800 | 8,105 | 8,700 | 8,400 |
| - - | - - | 45,200 | 24,000 | — | | | | |
| - - | - - | 27,092 | 110,275 | 176,859 | 123,850 | 93,500 | — | |
| - - | - - | - - | 5,000 | 22,400 | — | | | |
| - - | - - | - - | 20,000 | 52,000 | 61,000 | 35,000 | — | |
| - - | - - | - - | - - | 65,650 | 37,000 | 39,000 | 29,500 | 21,000 |
| - - | - - | - - | - - | 20,000 | 300,166 | 382,385 | 337,025 | 258,000 |
| - - | - - | - - | - - | 8,900 | 4,000 | 3,000 | 6,500 | 3,250 |
| - - | - - | - - | - - | 1,200 | — | | | |
| - - | - - | - - | - - | - - | - - | - - | - - | 14,800 |
| - - | - - | - - | - - | - - | - - | - - | 14,500 | 300 |
| - - | - - | - - | - - | - - | - - | 499 | 2,250 | 3,000 |
| - - | - - | - - | - - | - - | - - | - - | - - | 2,000 |
| - - | - - | - - | 6,000 | 4,180 | 4,200 | 5,500 | 4,000 | 800 |
| - - | - - | - - | - - | - - | - - | - - | - - | 7,550 |
| - - | - - | - - | 1,500 | 4,000 | — | | | |
| - - | - - | - - | - - | 1,000 | 1,500 | - - | - - | 1,500 |
| - - | - - | - - | - - | 9,250 | 6,500 | — | | |
| - - | - - | - - | - - | - - | - - | - - | 200 | — |
| - - | - - | - - | - - | - - | - - | - - | - - | 800 |
| - - | - - | - - | - - | - - | - - | - - | - - | 6,250 |
| - - | - - | - - | - - | - - | - - | - - | - - | 2,100 |
| - - | - - | - - | 18,000 | 66,000 | — | | | |
| 88,700 | 89,800 | 82,000 | 76,000 | 72,000 | 68,000 | 63,072 | 66,550 | 72,700 |
| - - | - - | - - | 90,210 | 84,500 | 46,140 | — | | |
| 5,000 | 4,750 | 4,250 | 3,730 | 2,950 | 3,200 | 2,880 | 2,240 | 1,970 |
| 6,000 | 3,000 | 3,000 | — | | | | | |
| - - | - - | - - | 4,000 | 4,000 | 4,000 | — | | |
| - - | - - | 7,500 | 9,500 | 10,250 | 7,526 | 2,779 | — | |
| - - | - - | - - | - - | - - | - - | 20,000 | — | |
| - - | - - | - - | - - | - - | - - | 2,075 | - - | 2,970 |
| - - | - - | - - | - - | - - | - - | - - | 53,250 | 74,600 |
| - - | - - | - - | - - | - - | - - | 10,000 | — | |
| 3,275,000 | 2,865,000 | 2,600,000 | 2,457,000 | 2,421,500 | 2,203,500 | 2,112,790 | 2,250,000 | 1,950,000 |
| 925,000 | 692,000 | 373,000 | 315,000 | 260,000 | 171,000 | 152,000 | 116,800 | 85,000 |
| 209,000 | 170,000 | 156,500 | 169,500 | 175,500 | 175,000 | 158,000 | 182,000 | 209,000 |
| - - | - - | 3,250 | 2,000 | 4,500 | 4,000 | 4,500 | 3,525 | 3,000 |
| - - | - - | - - | - - | - - | - - | - - | 20,050 | 29,400 |
| - - | - - | - - | - - | - - | 2,830 | 3,040 | 4,200 | 4,010 |
| - - | - - | - - | - - | - - | 13,600 | 15,600 | 17,150 | 17,580 |
| - - | - - | - - | 5,000 | 24,000 | 21,775 | 14,075 | 8,500 | 14,600 |
| - - | - - | - - | - - | - - | - - | - - | 2,268 | — |
| - - | - - | - - | - - | - - | 805,580 | 1,077,033 | 1,808,190 | 2,037,703 |
| - - | - - | - - | - - | - - | 4,000 | 6,000 | 6,000 | 8,000 |
| - - | - - | - - | 40,600 | — | | | | |
| - - | - - | - - | - - | - - | - - | - - | 308,000 | 466,900 |
| - - | - - | - - | - - | - - | - - | - - | - - | 500 |
| - - | - - | - - | - - | - - | - - | 33,000 | 25,850 | — |

| —— | 1837. | 1838. | 1839. | 1840. | 1841. |
|---|---|---|---|---|---|
| LONDON PAPERS—*continued.* | | | | | |
| Wild's Law Catalogue | - | - | - | - | - |
| Water Cure Journal | - | - | - | - | - |
| Weekly Telegraph | - | - | - | - | - |
| Watson's Catalogue | - | - | - | - | - |
| Wilkinson's Price Current | - | - | - | - | - |
| Woolwich Gazette | - | - | - | - | - |
| West Indian Mail | - | - | - | - | - |
| Wesleyan Chronicle | - | - | - | - | - |
| Weekly Post | 21,250 | — | | | |
| Weekly True Sun | 449,551 | 329,500 | 201,400 | 163,140 | 33,000 |
| Weekly Express | - | - | - | - | - |
| Weekly and Monthly Orthodox | - | - | - | - | - |
| Working Man's Charter | - | - | - | - | - |
| W. Bargett's Corn Circular | - | - | - | - | - |
| Woodhouse's Price Current | - | - | - | - | - |
| W. S. Buxton's Price Current | - | - | - | - | - |
| Wright, Young & Co.'s Price Current | - | - | - | - | - |
| Weekly Corn Report | - | - | - | - | - |
| Young England | - | - | - | - | - |

## ENGLISH PROVINCIAL PAPERS.

| | 1837. | 1838. | 1839. | 1840. | 1841. |
|---|---|---|---|---|---|
| Aylesbury News | 38,500 | 42,500 | 52,500 | 49,000 | 43,500 |
| Albion, Liverpool | 111,500 | 156,000 | - | 162,500 | 168,500 |
| American News Letter | - | - | - | - | - |
| Anti-Corn Law Circular | - | - | 99,935 | 172,600 | 118,700 |
| British Record | - | - | - | - | - |
| Bath Herald | 46,000 | 57,000 | 48,000 | 50,000 | 11,000 |
| Bath Chronicle | 67,000 | 70,000 | 70,500 | 71,950 | 76,000 |
| Bath Journal | 43,000 | 47,000 | 54,000 | 72,000 | 67,000 |
| Bath and Clifton Looker-on | - | - | - | - | - |
| Bath and Cheltenham Gazette | 47,500 | 52,000 | 55,250 | 55,500 | 57,000 |
| Berwick Advertiser | 29,000 | 32,500 | 33,000 | 38,000 | 36,000 |
| Berwick Warder | 27,500 | 35,000 | 30,000 | 39,000 | 36,000 |
| Bradshaw's Railway Guide | - | - | - | - | - |
| Brighton Gazette | 57,000 | 64,000 | 63,600 | 57,000 | 60,500 |
| Brighton Guardian | 65,000 | 70,000 | 73,000 | 60,000 | 66,000 |
| Brighton Herald | 49,000 | 55,000 | 56,000 | 56,000 | 53,000 |
| Barbour's Circular | - | - | - | - | - |
| Bedford Times | - | - | - | - | - |
| Bedford Mercury | 18,600 | 32,000 | 24,125 | 25,000 | 26,245 |
| Bristol Journal | 78,000 | 97,000 | 96,000 | - | - |
| Bristol Temperance Herald | - | - | - | - | - |
| Bath and Devizes Guardian | 37,000 | 33,150 | 19,000 | — | |
| Beacon | 19,965 | 15,350 | — | | |
| Berkshire Chronicle | 35,000 | 28,000 | 43,000 | 41,000 | 42,000 |
| Birmingham Advertiser | 54,000 | 65,000 | 72,500 | 80,000 | 55,000 |
| Birmingham Gazette (Aris's) | 154,000 | 167,000 | 165,000 | 151,500 | 148,500 |
| Bucks Advertiser and Aylesbury News | - | - | - | - | - |
| Birmingham Journal | 131,100 | 138,000 | 130,500 | 106,500 | 105,000 |
| Birmingham Herald | 233,500 | 183,000 | — | | |
| Birmingham Philanthropist | 21,000 | 5,500 | — | | |
| Blackburn Gazette | 14,250 | 11,070 | 11,100 | 10,500 | 10,055 |
| Brighton Patriot | 42,000 | 34,000 | 17,950 | — | |
| Bristol Mercury | 124,000 | 132,000 | 142,000 | 168,000 | 197,000 |
| Bristol Mirror | 118,000 | 131,000 | 137,000 | 111,000 | 106,000 |
| Bristol Advocate | 22,000 | — | | | |

| 1842. | 1843. | 1844. | 1845. | 1846. | 1847. | 1848. | 1849. | 1850. |
|---|---|---|---|---|---|---|---|---|
| - - | - - | - - | - - | - - | 7,000 | 7,500 | — | |
| - - | - - | - - | - - | - - | 1,500 | 2,420 | 505 | 500 |
| - - | - - | - - | - - | - - | - - | - - | 16,000 | — |
| - - | 1,000 | - - | 1,000 | 1,000 | 4,000 | 2,500 | - - | 1,350 |
| - - | - - | - - | - - | - - | - - | 1,000 | 850 | 1,000 |
| 2,200 | 10,150 | 10,755 | 7,425 | 3,500 | — | | | |
| - - | - - | - - | - - | 4,500 | 750 | — | | |
| - - | 4,000 | 24,000 | — | | | | | |
| — | | | | | | | | |
| - - | 10,250 | — | | | | | | |
| - - | - - | - - | - - | - - | - - | - - | 2,220 | — |
| - - | - - | - - | - - | - - | - - | - - | 7,000 | — |
| - - | - - | - - | - - | - - | - - | - - | - - | 11,000 |
| - - | - - | - - | - - | - - | - - | - - | - - | 500 |
| - - | - - | - - | - - | - - | - - | - - | - - | 1,200 |
| - - | - - | - - | - - | - - | - - | - - | - - | 1,000 |
| - - | - - | - - | - - | - - | - - | - - | - - | 3,840 |
| - - | - - | 10,000 | 10,000 | — | | | | |

- - - - ENGLISH PROVINCIAL PAPERS.

| 1842. | 1843. | 1844. | 1845. | 1846. | 1847. | 1848. | 1849. | 1850. |
|---|---|---|---|---|---|---|---|---|
| 27,500 | 40,000 | 40,000 | 51,500 | 46,000 | — | | | |
| 163,300 | 169,500 | 164,000 | 161,000 | 159,500 | 141,000 | 153,900 | 160,250 | 176,000 |
| 4,000 | 15,100 | 12,500 | 7,200 | — | | | | |
| 82,552 | 115,670 | — | | | | | | |
| - - | - - | - - | - - | - - | - - | - | 28,000 | — |
| 48,000 | 44,000 | 42,000 | 39,000 | 42,000 | 41,000 | 36,00 | 34,000 | 37,000 |
| 79,000 | 76,000 | 74,500 | 82,000 | 75,500 | 74,500 | 74,000 | 74,500 | 81,000 |
| 61,000 | 54,000 | 48,000 | 50,000 | 51,000 | 58,500 | 52,015 | 56,000 | 50,000 |
| - - | - - | - - | - - | - - | - - | - - | 4,000 | — |
| 51,000 | 53,000 | 43,000 | 46,000 | 49,000 | 40,500 | 49,000 | 45,000 | 44,000 |
| 40,000 | 38,000 | 42,000 | 36,000 | 40,000 | 41,000 | 43,500 | 45,000 | 42,000 |
| 30,500 | 33,250 | 28,625 | 24,000 | 27,000 | 24,000 | 26,000 | 23,025 | 25,000 |
| - - | - - | - - | - - | 7,586 | 6,950 | 27,000 | 34,750 | 27,100 |
| 61,000 | 65,500 | 70,000 | 59,500 | 63,000 | 55,000 | 63,500 | 55,000 | 62,000 |
| 64,000 | 66,000 | 48,000 | 50,000 | 50,000 | 50,000 | 50,000 | 45,000 | 48,000 |
| 54,000 | 59,000 | 44,000 | 41,000 | 44,000 | 52,000 | 65,000 | 53,000 | 65,000 |
| - - | - - | - - | 410 | 3,157 | 2,740 | 3,130 | 3,560 | 3,400 |
| - - | - - | - - | 9,000 | 21,000 | 23,000 | 26,300 | 26,000 | 26,000 |
| 27,000 | 28,000 | 21,000 | 22,000 | 16,100 | 14,000 | 12,000 | 12,037 | 16,000 |
| - - | - - | 48,000 | 63,200 | 69,000 | 56,000 | 69,500 | 77,000 | 59,500 |
| 8,000 | 9,500 | 11,000 | 17,000 | 12,000 | 18,000 | 15,000 | 20,000 | 12,000 |
| 42,000 | 42,000 | 40,000 | 25,000 | 39,500 | 33,000 | 37,350 | 37,000 | 40,500 |
| 65,000 | 61,500 | 55,000 | 49,000 | 30,100 | 57,250 | 7,350 | — | |
| 144,000 | 132,000 | 142,000 | 108,000 | 120,000 | 114,000 | 132,000 | 106,000 | 120,000 |
| - - | - - | - - | - - | - - | 37,000 | 36,000 | 48,000 | 36,000 |
| 98,000 | 90,000 | 109,200 | 218,500 | 260,000 | 338,500 | 421,500 | 409,250 | 390,000 |
| 16,500 | 4,000 | — | | | | | | |
| 209,000 | 221,000 | 233,000 | 252,000 | 272,000 | 250,300 | 275,000 | 277,500 | 267,000 |
| 132,500 | 135,000 | 129,000 | 132,050 | 127,000 | 136,000 | 143,000 | 143,000 | 137,000 |

| | 1837. | 1838. | 1839. | 1840. | 1841. |
|---|---|---|---|---|---|
| ENGLISH PROVINCIAL PAPERS—*continued.* | | | | | |
| Bucks Gazette | 13,000 | 11,250 | 17,500 | 9,500 | 9,000 |
| Bucks Herald | 19,000 | 24,000 | 26,500 | 30,000 | 40,238 |
| Bury and Suffolk Herald | 22,500 | 24,000 | 26,000 | 28,112 | 28,000 |
| Bury and Norwich Post | 84,000 | 87,500 | 90,500 | 89,000 | 84,100 |
| Bristol Gazette | 28,000 | 34,500 | 45,000 | 33,000 | 30,000 |
| Boston Herald | 10,118 | 11,500 | 9,000 | 12,000 | 9,0[illegible]0 |
| Bradford Observer | 23,000 | 32,500 | 34,0[illegible]0 | 27,879 | 31,000 |
| Bath Post | 6,500 | - - | 29,500 | 13,200 | — |
| Bath Figaro | - - | 5,000 | — | | |
| Bolton Free Press | 6,000 | 34,000 | 40,000 | 36,000 | 43,000 |
| Bristol Examiner | - - | - - | - - | - - | - - |
| Bucks Chronicle | - - | - - | 1,250 | 2,150 | - - |
| Buxton Herald | - - | - - | - - | - - | - - |
| Blackburn Standard | 15,000 | 22,000 | 24,000 | 27,000 | 30,750 |
| Bolton Chronicle | 53,018 | 43,012 | 50,000 | 42,500 | 39,000 |
| Banbury Chronicle | - - | - - | - - | - - | - - |
| Banbury Guardian | - - | - - | - - | - - | - - |
| Bridgewater Times | - - | - - | - - | - - | - - |
| Barnes' Colonial Circular | - - | - - | - - | - - | - - |
| Bedford Standard | - - | - - | - - | - - | - - |
| Birmingham Mercury | - - | - - | - - | - - | - - |
| Bolton Times | - - | - - | - - | - - | - - |
| British Record of Medicine | - - | - - | - - | - - | - - |
| Blackburn Mercury | - - | - - | - - | - - | - - |
| Bury and Suffolk Farmers' Journal | - - | - - | - - | - - | - - |
| Bradford Herald | - - | - - | - - | - - | 1,000 |
| Cambridge Chronicle | 64,608 | 71,550 | 79,250 | 86,100 | 86,000 |
| Canterbury Weekly Journal | 30,000 | 30,000 | 30,000 | 25,500 | 18,000 |
| Carlisle Journal | 97,700 | 100,000 | 102,000 | 106,565 | 115,000 |
| Carlisle Patriot | 28,404 | 42,000 | 56,000 | 43,000 | 50,000 |
| Cheltenham Chronicle | 42,000 | 56,000 | 43,000 | 50,000 | 44,000 |
| Cheltenham Journal | 19,300 | 25,000 | 35,000 | 30,000 | 30,000 |
| Cheltenham Free Press | 38,975 | 51,000 | 43,000 | 30,000 | 30,000 |
| Cheltenham Looker On | 15,264 | 29,250 | 18,000 | 24,000 | 24,000 |
| Chester Chronicle | 85,000 | 88,000 | 96,000 | 95,500 | 100,000 |
| Chester Courant | 44,296 | 48,000 | 52,000 | 52,000 | 60,000 |
| Chester Gazette | 50,085 | 52,000 | 33,000 | 31,000 | — |
| Chester Reformer | 39,000 | - - | 32,000 | — | |
| Colchester and Chelmsford Gazette | 22,650 | — | | | |
| Chelmsford Chronicle | 89,500 | 101,500 | 95,500 | 107,000 | 102,300 |
| Cornwall Royal Gazette | 28,733 | 45,000 | 48,000 | 53,500 | 58,200 |
| Coventry Herald | 33,000 | 39,300 | 42,000 | 50,000 | 39,000 |
| Coventry Standard | 36,000 | 34,000 | 40,000 | 35,000 | 37,000 |
| Cumberland Pacquet | 36,500 | 37,300 | 56,280 | 50,000 | - - |
| Chard Union Gazette | 1,500 | 4,000 | 4,000 | 1,240 | — |
| Cambridge Advertiser | 8,150 | 1,000 | 45,500 | 34,500 | 37,000 |
| Cambridge Independent Press | - - | - - | 54,500 | 121,188 | 115,000 |
| Cockermouth Miscellany | - - | - - | - - | - - | - - |
| Catholic Instructor | — | | | | |
| Cornish Mining Company | - - | - - | - - | - - | - - |
| Cornwall Weekly Times | - - | - - | - - | - - | - - |
| Cator's Circular | - - | - - | - - | - - | - - |
| Cheltenham Parish Register | - - | - - | - - | - - | - - |
| Dorset County Chronicle | 68,700 | 85,000 | 78,000 | 74,000 | 96,000 |
| Durham Chronicle | 48,000 | 47,922 | 50,500 | 46,000 | 68,737 |
| Durham Advertiser | 30,500 | 35,900 | 40,500 | 40,000 | 40,000 |
| Devonport Telegraph | 40,500 | 41,000 | 40,000 | 26,000 | 46,200 |
| Devonport Independent | 34,200 | 33,500 | 34,100 | 41,650 | 41,440 |
| Derbyshire Advertiser | - - | - - | - - | - - | - - |
| Devonshire Chronicle | 12,270 | 11,850 | 11,500 | 21,400 | 25,500 |
| Derby Mercury | 61,000 | 55,500 | 67,[illegible]00 | 71,000 | 80,000 |
| Derby Reporter | 68,500 | 58,500 | 56,000 | 60,000 | 60,000 |

| 1842. | 1843. | 1844. | 1845. | 1846. | 1847. | 1848. | 1849. | 1850. |
|---|---|---|---|---|---|---|---|---|
| 5,200 | 12,600 | 6,500 | 8,000 | 5,575 | 6,000 | 5,250 | 3,625 | — |
| 35,500 | 36,810 | 33,235 | 34,500 | 29,000 | 37,000 | 30,000 | 31,000 | 38,500 |
| 26,500 | 41,000 | 48,450 | 57,000 | 58,500 | 58,500 | 36,000 | 42,000 | — |
| 94,750 | 91,000 | 91,000 | 92,500 | 91,000 | 99,500 | 82,000 | 86,000 | 103,000 |
| 38,000 | 32,000 | 18,000 | 30,000 | 30,000 | 32,000 | 40,000 | 30,000 | 40,000 |
| 12,050 | 12,500 | 27,725 | 27,[illegible]00 | 25,000 | 27,000 | 25,000 | 25,000 | 34,500 |
| 36,000 | 55,500 | 48,000 | 54,000 | 54,000 | 54,000 | 55,598 | 39,435 | 55,000 |
| 25,100 | 27,000 | 29,000 | 27,000 | 27,000 | 9,500 | — | | |
| - - | - - | - - | - - | - - | - - | - - | 3,000 | 54,750 |
| - - | - - | - - | - - | - - | - - | - - | 37,500 | 30,000 |
| 5,000 | 7,500 | 5,000 | 6,500 | 7,000 | 6,000 | 6,500 | 8,000 | 4,000 |
| 28,100 | 27,000 | 27,000 | 28,000 | 33, 00 | 44,300 | 28,330 | 31,000 | 28,000 |
| 37,500 | 33,500 | 34,000 | 40,500 | 67,709 | 60,000 | 66,000 | 71,250 | 72,000 |
| - - | - - | - - | - - | - - | - - | 36 | — | |
| - - | 23,000 | 28,000 | 32,000 | 32,000 | 36,000 | 34,000 | 41,000 | 36,000 |
| - - | - - | - - | 7,000 | 26,133 | 32,000 | 30,000 | 18,000 | 16,900 |
| - - | - - | - - | - - | - - | - - | - - | 1,200 | 3,200 |
| 4,000 | - - | - - | - - | - - | - - | 13,000 | — | |
| - - | - - | - - | - - | - - | - - | 23,500 | 193,000 | 150,000 |
| - - | - - | - - | - - | - - | 1,000 | 7,650 | — | |
| - - | - - | - - | - - | - - | 1,000 | 7,100 | 2,800 | — |
| - - | 9,700 | 14,000 | 13,000 | 5,600 | — | | | |
| - - | - - | 9,000 | — | | | | | |
| 27,550 | — | | | | | | | |
| 89,750 | 89,175 | 86,500 | 85,950 | 85,250 | 87,000 | 80,700 | 96,550 | 105,100 |
| 24,000 | 12,000 | 18,000 | 18,000 | 9,000 | 18,000 | 9,000 | 13,000 | 13,000 |
| 112,000 | 114,000 | 118,000 | 147,000 | 156,000 | 11[illegible],000 | 166,000 | 168,000 | 168,000 |
| 41,000 | 45,100 | 51,421 | 38,000 | 45,000 | 38,685 | 60,900 | 58,000 | 64,000 |
| 45,100 | 51,421 | 38,000 | 45,000 | 38,685 | 60,900 | 58,000 | 61,000 | 56,000 |
| 30,025 | 30,000 | 30,000 | 30,000 | 25,000 | 30,000 | 23,500 | 35,000 | 30,000 |
| 30,000 | 30,000 | 35,000 | 36,000 | 36,000 | 36,000 | 43,000 | 29,000 | 31,400 |
| 26,000 | 28,000 | 26,500 | 24,500 | 25,000 | 30,238 | 22,000 | 31,000 | 27,200 |
| 96,000 | 88,000 | 76,000 | 86,000 | 80,000 | 72,000 | 66,000 | 55,500 | 66,000 |
| 53,000 | 47,000 | 56,050 | 61,000 | 58,000 | 60,000 | 54,000 | 55,500 | 58,000 |
| 106,000 | 113,000 | 114,000 | 118,500 | 108,750 | 117,000 | 137,750 | 114,000 | 110,300 |
| 54,000 | 47,000 | 51,500 | 50,000 | 53,500 | 54,000 | 50,000 | 52,500 | 65,000 |
| 39,000 | 43,000 | 42,500 | 42,000 | 42,000 | 42,000 | 42,500 | 46,000 | 42,000 |
| 39,150 | 39,150 | 39,000 | 42,325 | 44,000 | 42,000 | 37,500 | 42,500 | 42,000 |
| 37,000 | 44,350 | 40,000 | 50,000 | 41,300 | 40,000 | 40,000 | 40,000 | 40,000 |
| 37,000 | 36,000 | 36,000 | 34,125 | 36,900 | 36,550 | 35,000 | 25,000 | 8,150 |
| 116,000 | 110,000 | 123,000 | 128,500 | 121,000 | 127,500 | 126,000 | 138,000 | 121,000 |
| - - | - - | 6,000 | — | | | | | |
| - - | - - | - - | - - | 6,500 | — | | | |
| - - | - - | - - | - - | - - | - - | 4,500 | — | |
| - - | - - | - - | - - | - - | 1,135 | 4,000 | — | |
| - - | - - | - - | - - | - - | - - | - - | 1,000 | — |
| 72,000 | 70,000 | 73,000 | 79,500 | 76,000 | 73,800 | 69,000 | 65,500 | 62,900 |
| 59,175 | 58,475 | 53,000 | 69,100 | 50,000 | 59,500 | 66,000 | 59,000 | 56,500 |
| 40,000 | 40,000 | 24,500 | 25,000 | 25,000 | 30,000 | 29,000 | 40,050 | 29,900 |
| 30,000 | 26,600 | 34,000 | 28,000 | 31,500 | 31,900 | 26,600 | 36,125 | 26,500 |
| 42,000 | 32,700 | 33,000 | 40,000 | 40,600 | 44,000 | 34,700 | 37,000 | 30,750 |
| - - | - - | - - | - - | 35,000 | 23,420 | 24,000 | 23,000 | 20,500 |
| 25,300 | 21,000 | 18,750 | 23,500 | 16,500 | 21,000 | 20,000 | 18,000 | 12,000 |
| 80,975 | 80,000 | 80,000 | 80,000 | 79,000 | 75,000 | 75,000 | 85,750 | 70,000 |
| 60,000 | 117,000 | 90,000 | 105,000 | 110,000 | 115,000 | 105,000 | 105,500 | 110,000 |

| — | 1837. | 1838. | 1839. | 1840. | 1841. |
|---|---|---|---|---|---|
| ENGLISH PROVINCIAL PAPERS—*continued.* | | | | | |
| Derbyshire Courier | 33,400 | 37,500 | 39,500 | 43,000 | 35,000 |
| Dover Telegraph | 20,000 | 26,000 | 28,500 | 28,000 | 29,300 |
| Dover Chronicle | 15,000 | 16,500 | 27,000 | 24,000 | 23,000 |
| Doncaster Gazette | 84,000 | 96,000 | 120,000 | 119,000 | 117,050 |
| Doncaster Chronicle | 31,168 | 40,000 | 42,000 | 39,000 | 54,000 |
| Devizes and Wiltshire Gazette | 37,900 | 51,000 | 49,000 | 48,000 | 50,000 |
| Du Fays & Co.'s Trade Report | - | - | - | - | - |
| Darlington and Stockton Times | - | - | - | - | - |
| Exeter Flying Post | 54,500 | 60,000 | 104,000 | 72,000 | 91,000 |
| Exeter and Plymouth Gazette | 103,000 | 119,500 | 124,000 | 111,500 | 121,500 |
| Essex Standard | 53,600 | 63,000 | 64,800 | 65,100 | 79,500 |
| Essex, Herts, and Kent Mercury | 42,678 | 64,400 | 68,000 | 66,000 | 43,150 |
| Essex and Suffolk Times | 4,000 | 31,500 | 17,000 | 16,500 | 2,855 |
| Eastern Counties Herald | - | 73,300 | 159,000 | 165,500 | 156,000 |
| Essex Herald | 44,250 | 51,500 | 55,250 | 59,000 | 58,000 |
| Essex, Herts, and Suffolk Mercury | - | - | - | - | - |
| Eddowes' Journal | - | - | - | - | - |
| European Times | - | - | - | - | - |
| European Mail | - | - | - | - | - |
| Falmouth Express and Colonial Journal | - | 28,662 | 24,500 | 12,500 | — |
| Fleetwood Chronicle | - | - | - | - | - |
| Farmers' Herald | - | - | - | - | - |
| Fraser's Circular | - | - | - | - | - |
| Fraser & Co.'s Price Current | - | - | - | - | - |
| Falmouth Packet | 36,000 | 37,500 | 31,002 | 35,050 | 35,075 |
| Felix Farley's Bristol Journal | - | - | - | 64,000 | 72,000 |
| Gloucester Journal | 98,175 | 98,800 | 102,800 | 108,000 | 112,000 |
| Gloucestershire Chronicle | 56,500 | 69,000 | 66,000 | 69,000 | 67,000 |
| Gravesend Journal | 11,000 | — | | | |
| Greenwich Gazette | 8,000 | 37,000 | 51,550 | — | |
| Greenwich Patriot | 3,000 | 18,378 | — | | |
| Gateshead Observer | 7,500 | 99,232 | 108,000 | 108,000 | 108,000 |
| Great Northern Advertiser | - | - | - | - | 233,000 |
| General Commercial Intelligencer | — | | | | |
| Great Western Advertiser | - | - | - | - | - |
| Hadwen's Circular | - | - | - | - | - |
| Higgins' Gazette | 1,084 | - | - | - | - |
| Hereford Journal | 85,550 | 84,200 | 85,100 | 86,550 | 89,175 |
| Hereford Times | 76,064 | 52,750 | 90,000 | 101,000 | 111,789 |
| Hampshire Guardian | - | - | - | - | - |
| Hampshire Chronicle | 58,750 | 68,500 | 77,000 | 56,000 | 69,500 |
| Hampshire Advertiser | 100,000 | 144,000 | 77,000 | 104,125 | 100,500 |
| Hampshire Independent | 90,000 | 67,550 | 69,000 | 70,000 | 75,500 |
| Hertford County Press | 35,000 | 37,100 | 34,000 | 31,920 | 42,025 |
| Halifax Guardian | 20,000 | 16,650 | 38,000 | 33,090 | 41,000 |
| Herts Reformer | 40,000 | - | 51,000 | 46,500 | 41,000 |
| Hull Advertiser | 99,940 | 74,000 | 81,000 | 177,000 | 95,000 |
| Hull Packet | 65,196 | 52,000 | 51,354 | 84,500 | 47,000 |
| Hampshire Telegraph | 134,500 | 145,000 | 129,000 | 168,500 | 203,000 |
| Harrogate Advertiser | 4,000 | 7,630 | 7,500 | 18,000 | 12,000 |
| Harrogate Herald | - | - | - | - | - |
| Hastings and St. Leonard's News | - | - | - | - | - |
| Harrogate Herald | - | - | - | - | - |
| Hampshire and West Sussex Standard | - | - | - | - | 13,500 |
| Hull Rockingham | 35,000 | 35,000 | 35,000 | 35,000 | 38,000 |
| Hull Times | - | - | 40,000 | 40,000 | 36,200 |
| Hull Saturday Journal | 21,500 | 11,000 | 20,000 | — | |
| Huntingdon Gazette | 99,000 | 115,000 | 54,000 | — | |
| Harrogate Weekly Gazette | 500 | 900 | 2,900 | 3,000 | 800 |
| Ipswich Journal | 76,900 | 94,000 | 101,100 | 115,000 | 104,000 |
| Ipswich Express | - | - | 13,000 | 28,000 | 47,000 |

| 1842. | 1843. | 1844. | 1845. | 1846. | 1847. | 1848. | 1849. | 1850. |
|---|---|---|---|---|---|---|---|---|
| 40,000 | 28,000 | 35,000 | 42,000 | 36,150 | 44,000 | 39,500 | 44,500 | 25,100 |
| 28,500 | 27,500 | 29,000 | 29,300 | 29,250 | 27,925 | 26,455 | 26,475 | 21,100 |
| 27,500 | 26,000 | 20,500 | 21,000 | 20,000 | 21,000 | 22,000 | 17,000 | 21,500 |
| 115,000 | 112,000 | 103,000 | 106,000 | 111,000 | 109,000 | 109,000 | 107,700 | 109,000 |
| 53,000 | 50,000 | 55,000 | 55,000 | 64,000 | 55,000 | 55,000 | 60,000 | 55,000 |
| 50,000 | 51,000 | 51,000 | 55,000 | 52,500 | 53,000 | 53,250 | 57,000 | 54,000 |
| - - | 4,000 | 9,000 | 5,160 | 11,000 | 11,000 | 7,000 | 4,000 | 6,000 |
| - - | - - | - - | - - | - - | 16,500 | 44,100 | 46,100 | 34,000 |
| 89,000 | 99,000 | 79,000 | 92,730 | 80,000 | 88,000 | 81,000 | 100,000 | 99,500 |
| 122,500 | 120,000 | 130,000 | 90,500 | 98,000 | 99,150 | 118,500 | 117,000 | 120,000 |
| 72,800 | 73,400 | 71,400 | 72,200 | 71,400 | 74,200 | 71,400 | 71,400 | 70,000 |
| 39,900 | 26,100 | — | | | | | | |
| — | | | | | | | | |
| 153,000 | 120,350 | 129,000 | 106,000 | 98,000 | 87,000 | 87,000 | 77,000 | 96,730 |
| 64,000 | 64,500 | 66,000 | 65,500 | 74,000 | 79,000 | 83,000 | 80,500 | 85,500 |
| - - | 7,600 | — | | | | | | |
| - - | - - | 84,600 | 82,500 | 88,500 | 96,000 | 88,000 | 102,000 | 109,000 |
| - - | 50,650 | 50,520 | 78,000 | 76,000 | 101,450 | — | | |
| - - | - - | - - | - - | - - | 15,000 | 43,700 | 14,000 | — |
| - - | - - | 1,920 | 9,030 | 10,560 | 13,504 | 8,440 | 10,500 | 8,960 |
| 1,500 | 7,075 | 6,900 | 8,525 | 9,500 | 9,960 | 9,288 | 8,275 | 10,000 |
| - - | - - | - - | - - | - - | - - | 1,500 | 4,500 | — |
| - - | 1,000 | 4,000 | 6,350 | 5,380 | 6,000 | 3,800 | - - | 4,500 |
| 30,200 | 22,900 | 23,800 | 24,500 | 22,500 | 17,000 | 500 | — | |
| 73,500 | 69,000 | 56,000 | 970 | — | | | | |
| 112,000 | 107,500 | 116,000 | 98,703 | 117,000 | 115,000 | 120,000 | 123,922 | 108,000 |
| 67,000 | 63,000 | 39,000 | 66,450 | 65,500 | 55,000 | 55,000 | 56,000 | 65,500 |
| 101,000 | 110,000 | 120,000 | 110,000 | 120,000 | 110,000 | 102,000 | 65,000 | 101,000 |
| 99,175 | 52,200 | — | | | | | | |
| - - | 5,000 | 252,050 | 239,500 | 138,000 | 37,500 | — | | |
| - - | - - | - - | - - | - - | - - | - - | 480 | 1,920 |
| - - | - - | - - | - - | - - | - - | - - | 1,386 | 1,084 |
| 81,046 | 78,756 | 72,825 | 72,800 | 70,600 | 69,000 | 65,000 | 56,000 | 60,000 |
| 120,650 | 123,200 | 136,500 | 152,750 | 148,800 | 172,000 | 176,000 | 190,550 | 203,500 |
| - - | - - | - - | 6,000 | 16,500 | 27,200 | 29,500 | 28,000 | 1,100 |
| 76,885 | 66,000 | 70,000 | 63,000 | 65,000 | 70,000 | 74,000 | 40,711 | 56,750 |
| 104,000 | 110,325 | 118,000 | 126,500 | 133,000 | 136,500 | 133,500 | 133,500 | 140,500 |
| 54,250 | 66,000 | 67,350 | 66,000 | 70,250 | 72,000 | 78,000 | 78,000 | 69,000 |
| 30,100 | 39,400 | 41,000 | 25,925 | 32,500 | 39,000 | 38,000 | 39,000 | 36,000 |
| 56,000 | 59,000 | 74,000 | 69,000 | 82,000 | 117,450 | 109,000 | 102,000 | 124,000 |
| 35,500 | 35,998 | 40,000 | 36,000 | 31,000 | 31,000 | 32,000 | 33,732 | 35,500 |
| 93,000 | 95,000 | 99,000 | 114,000 | 106,000 | 108,000 | 104,000 | 130,000 | 99,625 |
| 51,950 | 68,500 | 60,000 | 79,500 | 85,500 | 96,000 | 123,000 | 89,425 | 99,500 |
| 156,000 | 177,000 | 192,000 | 164,000 | 166,200 | 164,500 | 164,500 | 175,000 | 135,500 |
| 11,000 | 13,000 | 15,000 | 14,000 | 14,250 | 16,250 | 18,500 | 18,750 | 18,500 |
| - - | - - | - - | - - | - - | 16,000 | 6,720 | - - | 7,000 |
| - - | - - | - - | - - | - - | - - | 14,400 | 28,000 | 29,250 |
| - - | - - | - - | - - | - - | - - | - - | 6,760 | — |
| 52,000 | - - | 11,000 | — | | | | | |
| 25,000 | 27,500 | 6,500 | — | | | | | |
| 5,000 | — | | | | | | | |
| — | | | | | | | | |
| 112,500 | 105,000 | 105,000 | 112,000 | 112,000 | 101,000 | 108,000 | 111,000 | 109,350 |
| 54,000 | 34,000 | 47,300 | 45,000 | 39,100 | 48,000 | 52,000 | 49,800 | 14,000 |

| | 1837. | 1838. | 1839. | 1840. | 1841. |
|---|---|---|---|---|---|
| ENGLISH PROVINCIAL PAPERS—*continued.* | | | | | |
| Jones, Gibson & Orde's Circular | - - | - - | - - | - - | - - |
| Jones, Gibson & Orde's Woolwich Mercury | - - | - - | - - | - - | - - |
| Kent Herald | 59,000 | 66,000 | 52,500 | 65,000 | 52,500 |
| Kentish Independent | - - | - - | - - | - - | - - |
| Kendal Mercury | 40,300 | 40,000 | 30,000 | 35,250 | 41,500 |
| Kentish Champion | - - | - - | - - | - - | - - |
| Kentish Standard | - - | - - | - - | - - | - - |
| Kentish Gazette | 43,500 | 42,677 | 51,500 | 54,000 | 56,000 |
| Kentish Observer | 30,000 | 36,000 | 30,000 | 30,000 | 30,000 |
| Kentish Chronicle | 20,400 | 8,300 | — | | |
| Kidderminster Messenger | 51,875 | 58,350 | 5,000 | — | |
| Kent and Surrey Patriot | - - | 9,055 | 4,925 | — | |
| Lancaster Gazette | 24,000 | 29,000 | 27,000 | 31,000 | 30,500 |
| Lancaster Guardian | 34,000 | 33,742 | 30,000 | 32,000 | 33,000 |
| Leamington Spa Courier | 40,500 | 44,550 | 52,000 | 52,000 | 52,000 |
| Leamington Chronicle | 20,308 | 20,850 | 31,000 | 22,000 | 18,000 |
| Leeds Intelligencer | 143,000 | 173,000 | 173,000 | 213,500 | 187,000 |
| Leeds Mercury | 397,000 | 459,[illegible]28 | 527,000 | 493,500 | 517,000 |
| Leeds Times | 159,000 | 132,000 | 118,000 | 169,500 | 182,000 |
| Leicester Chronicle | 39,500 | 52,000 | 37,000 | 33,500 | 37,500 |
| Leicester Herald | 14,000 | 18,000 | 15,000 | 13,500 | 13,000 |
| Leicester Journal | 53,000 | 71,175 | 61,500 | 79,500 | 76,251 |
| Leicestershire Mercury | 44,900 | 60,000 | 6[illegible],500 | 43,000 | 47,600 |
| Lincoln Standard | 5,650 | 12,625 | 20,500 | 2,000 | 10,250 |
| Lincolnshire Chronicle | 65,400 | 76,000 | 77,525 | 81,000 | 84,000 |
| Liverpool Advertiser | 56,000 | - - | 73,600 | 75,000 | 74,000 |
| Lincolnshire Times | - - | - - | - - | - - | - - |
| Leamington Magnet | - - | - - | - - | - - | - - |
| Liverpool European Times and Chronicle | - - | - - | - - | - - | - - |
| Liverpool Chronicle | 85,000 | 96,000 | 97,000 | 104,000 | 117,500 |
| Liverpool Courier | 70,500 | 88,300 | 121,197 | 100,000 | 117,500 |
| Liverpool Journal | 42,025 | 71,880 | 63,139 | 82,100 | 85,828 |
| Liverpool Mail | 166,600 | 123,500 | 201,000 | 177,000 | 189,000 |
| Liverpool Mercury | 277,000 | 333,000 | 386,000 | 400,000 | 363,000 |
| Liverpool Standard | 87,000 | 91,000 | 90,000 | 104,500 | 115,000 |
| Liverpool Telegraph | 9,340 | 4,000 | - - | - - | - - |
| Liverpool Times | 25,000 | 50,000 | 48,000 | 68,000 | 83,000 |
| Liverpool Free Press | 6,000 | — | | | |
| Liverpool Express | - - | - - | - | - - | - - |
| Loughborough Telegraph | 8,840 | - - | 2,000 | — | |
| Lancaster Herald | - - | 35,000 | — | | |
| Leeds Conservative Journal | - - | - - | - - | - - | - - |
| Liverpool Mercantile Gazette | - - | - - | 51,900 | 56,000 | 55,500 |
| Leamington Looker-on | - - | - - | - - | - - | - - |
| Lynn Advertiser | - - | - - | - - | - - | 3,000 |
| Liverpool Advertiser (Gore's) | - - | 69,500 | - - | 75,000 | - - |
| Liverpool Price Current | - - | - - | - - | - - | - - |
| Liverpool Weekly News | - - | - - | - - | - - | - - |
| Liverpool Review | - - | - - | - - | - - | - - |
| Lincolnshire Advertiser | - - | - - | - - | - - | - - |
| Macclesfield Courier and Herald | 62,500 | 62,500 | 70,374 | 65,000 | 68,000 |
| Maidstone Gazette | 64,500 | 72,500 | 74,374 | 78,000 | 76,500 |
| Maidstone Journal | 48,000 | 58,000 | 54,000 | 52,100 | 59,000 |
| Manchester and Salford Advertiser | 184,500 | 196,000 | 181,000 | 140,000 | 93,000 |
| Manchester Chronicle | 58,500 | 73,200 | 159,000 | 143,500 | 137.750 |
| Manchester Courier | 142,500 | 142,000 | 233,240 | 239,500 | 276,000 |
| Manchester Guardian | 486,740 | 545,000 | 602,000 | 609,000 | 637,451 |
| Manchester Times | 161,225 | 148,300 | 144,000 | 126,250 | 120,700 |
| Myre's Mercantile Advertiser | 50,000 | 52,000 | 4,500 | — | |
| Manchester Trade Report | - - | - - | - - | - - | - - |
| Manchester Spectator | - - | - - | - - | - - | - - |
| Manchester Gazette | - - | - - | - - | - - | - - |

| 1842. | 1843. | 1844. | 1845. | 1846. | 1847. | 1848. | 1849. | 1850. |
|---|---|---|---|---|---|---|---|---|
| - - | 1,480 | 1,750 | 1,200 | 1,200 | 1,100 | 2,250 | 2,500 | 2.512 |
| - - | - - | 2,000 | 7,250 | 11,500 | 1,400 | 17,500 | 17,000 | 15,000 |
| 56,389 | 65,500 | 50,000 | 60,000 | 55,000 | 55,000 | 55,000 | 50,000 | 50,000 |
| - - | 28,050 | 34,485 | 31,000 | 24,000 | 21,500 | 22,500 | 23,500 | 22,000 |
| 42,700 | 46,000 | 46,000 | 54,500 | 56,500 | 50,500 | 51,000 | 48,000 | 44,000 |
| - - | - - | 8,500 | — | | | | | |
| 4,900 | — | | | | | | | |
| 58,000 | 60,000 | 53,000 | 46,000 | 54,000 | 49,500 | 51,500 | 52,850 | 50,000 |
| 28,000 | 24,000 | 24,000 | 30,000 | 24,000 | 24,000 | 15,000 | 20,000 | 21,000 |
| 33,000 | 33,000 | 24,000 | 36,000 | 26,094 | 22,991 | 26,250 | 38,250 | 37,000 |
| 26,150 | 27,375 | 31,500 | 29,000 | 31,000 | 35,000 | 47,500 | 41,000 | 29,500 |
| 48,000 | 48,000 | 44,000 | 52,000 | 51,500 | 52,000 | 51,500 | 54,000 | 50,000 |
| 14,975 | — | | | | | | | |
| 188,500 | 190,000 | 200,000 | 210,000 | 208,500 | 201,480 | 220,174 | 200,000 | 180,000 |
| 513,000 | 459,006 | 464,190 | 489,250 | 500,000 | 500,000 | 521,000 | 459,000 | 459,000 |
| 163,000 | 176,000 | 204,000 | 241,000 | 234,650 | 254,000 | 281,500 | 250,000 | 251,000 |
| 36,000 | 39,000 | 41,000 | 38,000 | 41,000 | 37,000 | 33,150 | 33,000 | 33,000 |
| 9,640 | — | | | | | | | |
| 84,000 | 71,500 | 61,000 | 72,000 | 63,500 | 60,500 | 55,000 | 63,000 | 51,500 |
| 38,000 | 32,000 | 34,000 | 46,050 | 39,950 | 41,875 | 40,500 | 47,000 | 59,175 |
| 10,000 | 9,000 | 7,180 | 6,432 | 6,850 | 7,300 | — | | |
| 84,250 | 87,000 | 61,000 | 61,500 | 70,000 | 56,000 | 70,000 | 56,000 | 77,875 |
| — | | | | | | | | |
| - - | - - | - - | 30,000 | - - | 20,500 | - - | - - | 39,500 |
| - - | - - | - - | - - | - - | - - | - - | 6,000 | — |
| - - | - - | - - | - - | - - | 10,000 | 144,650 | - - | 203,550 |
| 104,000 | 80,000 | 78,000 | 73,000 | 93,500 | 239,960 | 137,500 | 108,500 | — |
| 117,000 | 105,000 | 108,000 | 89,000 | 120,000 | 133,000 | 169,200 | 154.000 | 143,000 |
| 73,000 | 57,000 | 82,500 | 124,000 | 140,500 | 389,000 | 420,000 | 434,000 | 352,000 |
| 151,500 | 130,000 | 150,500 | 146,500 | 165,000 | 189,000 | 171,000 | 168,000 | 155,000 |
| 367,000 | 361,500 | 372,000 | 379,000 | 457,000 | 161,500 | 728,000 | 643,648 | 544,750 |
| 126,000 | 97,000 | 82,000 | 100,000 | 113,000 | 145,000 | 123,400 | 100,000 | 60,000 |
| - - | - - | - - | - - | 3,840 | 6,950 | 8,000 | 8,000 | 6,000 |
| 72,000 | 33,500 | 51,000 | 55,000 | 53,000 | 151,000 | 90,000 | 68,460 | 78,600 |
| - - | - - | - - | - - | 10,000 | 30,000 | — | | |
| 33,000 | — | | | | | | | |
| 51,500 | 56,000 | 34,000 | 45,000 | 48,600 | 47,000 | 48,000 | 36,000 | 44,000 |
| 4,500 | 4,500 | — | | | | | | |
| 18,000 | 19,350 | 30,000 | 24,000 | 35,000 | 30,000 | 30,000 | 39,000 | 32,750 |
| 74,000 | 74,000 | 74,000 | 61,500 | 70,000 | 66,000 | 41,000 | 60,500 | 25,000 |
| - - | - - | - - | 9,700 | 19,167 | 29,077 | 4,592 | - - | 1,240 |
| - - | - - | - - | - - | 28,000 | 90,883 | — | | |
| - - | - - | - - | - - | 900 | 2,400 | 1,200 | 5,300 | 500 |
| - - | 1,500 | 4,500 | - - | 1,490 | 12,150 | 14,738 | 7,146 | 1,800 |
| 60,000 | 63,000 | 60,000 | 39,000 | 60,000 | 44,000 | 55,000 | 72,500 | 66,000 |
| 76,000 | 76,500 | 86,000 | 96,250 | 102,000 | 111,000 | 109.000 | 113,500 | 106.950 |
| 58,000 | 64,250 | 58,400 | 56.000 | 57,000 | 62,500 | 55,000 | 54.750 | 53,000 |
| 97,000 | 115,500 | 129,000 | 134,000 | 83,000 | 76,000 | 41,000 | — | |
| 63,000 | — | | | | | | | |
| 330,000 | 296,000 | 271,500 | 2[illegible]0,000 | 278,000 | 256,758 | 235,000 | 215,000 | 236,250 |
| 710,000 | 761,800 | 859,000 | 967,000 | 1,002,000 | 1,00[illegible],000 | 968,000 | 940,000 | 940,000 |
| 139,650 | 173,000 | 134,000 | 149,800 | 111,000 | 135,000 | 234,350 | 68,460 | 78,600 |
| - - | 300 | 732 | 2,060 | 2,302 | 3,292 | 3,640 | 5,450 | 4,000 |
| - - | - - | - - | - - | - - | - - | - - | 130,450 | 108,500 |
| - - | - - | - - | - - | - - | - - | - - | 1.090 | 3,440 |

| —— | 1837. | 1838. | 1839. | 1840. | 1841. |
|---|---|---|---|---|---|
| ENGLISH PROVINCIAL PAPERS—*continued.* | | | | | |
| Midland Counties Herald | - - | 100,000 | 297,500 | 292,000 | 287,000 |
| Manchester Journal | - - | 31,000 | 81,750 | — | |
| Macclesfield Chronicle | - - | - - | - - | - - | - - |
| Midland Monitor | - - | - - | - - | - - | 75,600 |
| Manchester Herald | - - | - - | - - | - - | - - |
| Mendet's Trade Report | - - | - - | - - | - - | - - |
| Midland Observer | - - | - - | - - | - - | - - |
| Melton Recorder | - - | - - | - - | - - | - - |
| Manchester Examiner | - - | - - | - - | - - | - - |
| Manchester Argus | - - | - - | - - | - - | - - |
| Midland Gazette | - - | - - | - - | - - | - - |
| Manchester Express | - - | - - | - - | - - | - - |
| Manchester Price Current | - - | - - | - - | - - | - - |
| Manchester Spectator | - - | - - | - - | - - | - - |
| Manchester Zwitchanbart Circular | - - | - - | - - | - - | - - |
| Newark Times | - - | - - | - - | - - | 20,000 |
| New Cambridge Advertiser | - - | - - | - - | - - | - - |
| North Devon Advertiser | - - | - - | - - | 18,000 | 1,800 |
| Newcastle Advertiser | - - | - - | - - | - - | - - |
| North Oxfordshire Monthly Times | - - | - - | - - | - - | - - |
| Northampton Herald | 6,325 | 93,300 | 82,000 | 105,500 | 110,500 |
| Northampton Mercury | 87,500 | 104,000 | 103,000 | 101,800 | 101,800 |
| Nottingham Guardian | - - | - - | - - | - - | - - |
| Nottingham Journal | 85,000 | 100,000 | 100,000 | 99,000 | 106,000 |
| Nottingham and Newark Mercury | 60,500 | 60,300 | 59,000 | 60,000 | 56,750 |
| Nottingham Review | 80,000 | 98,000 | 98,000 | 101,000 | 111,000 |
| Norwich Mercury | 105,303 | 116,000 | 140,500 | 132,000 | 137,000 |
| Norfolk Chronicle | 116,500 | 130,000 | 134,000 | 139,000 | 148,000 |
| North Devon Journal | 45,000 | 23,825 | 21,500 | 20,500 | 25,500 |
| Newcastle Guardian | - - | - - | - - | - - | - - |
| Newcastle Journal | 116,500 | 155,000 | 180,500 | 49,000 | 152,100 |
| Newcastle Courant | 150,725 | 162,546 | 203,500 | 198,000 | 198,700 |
| Newcastle Chronicle | 158,850 | 168,500 | 166,500 | 156,500 | 154,000 |
| Norfolk News | - - | - - | - - | - - | - - |
| North and South Shields' Gazette | - - | - - | - - | - - | - - |
| National Temperance Advocate | - - | - - | - - | - - | - - |
| New Orleans Price Current | - - | - - | - - | - - | - - |
| National Advertiser | - - | - - | - - | - - | - - |
| National Temperance Magazine | - - | - - | - - | - - | - - |
| Norfolk and Norwich Monitor | - - | - - | - - | - - | 1,500 |
| Northern Star | 52,000 | 572,640 | 1,851,000 | 976,500 | 706,000 |
| Northern Times | - - | - - | 20,000 | 58,000 | 40,675 |
| New Moral World | - - | - - | - - | 6,500 | 15,500 |
| Norwich Protestant Herald | - - | - - | - - | - - | 2,960 |
| North Derbyshire Chronicle | 32,000 | — | | | |
| Northern Liberator | 20,000 | 68,100 | 125,500 | 90,323 | — |
| Newcastle Police Gazette | — | | | | |
| Oxford Journal | 101,000 | 105,000 | 117,500 | 109,700 | 120,000 |
| Oxford City and County Chronicle | 59,300 | 65,900 | 69,000 | 75,000 | 71,000 |
| Oxford Herald | - - | 57,500 | 65,000 | 59,000 | 60,500 |
| Pickford's Circular | - - | - - | - - | - - | - - |
| Port of Tyne Pilot | - - | - - | - - | - - | - - |
| Poole and South Western Herald | - - | - - | - - | 34,490 | 40,200 |
| Port of Portsmouth Guardian | - - | - - | - - | - - | - - |
| Portsmouth Times and Naval Gazette | - - | - - | - - | - - | - - |
| Payne's Leicester Advertiser | - - | - - | - - | - - | - - |
| Preston Chronicle | - - | - - | - - | - - | 8.000 |
| Preston Pilot | 65,050 | 70,500 | 75,500 | 100,000 | 93,000 |
| Preston Guardian | 24,600 | 28,700 | 30,600 | 33,000 | 30,000 |
| Plymouth Herald | - - | - - | - - | - - | - - |
| Plymouth and Devonport Journal | 44,250 | 40,000 | 46,000 | 49,000 | 54,000 |
| Plymouth Times | 33,000 | 29,500 | 33,755 | 32,500 | 29,000 |
| | - - | - - | - - | - - | - - |

| 1842. | 1843. | 1844. | 1845. | 1846. | 1847. | 1848. | 1849. | 1850. |
|---|---|---|---|---|---|---|---|---|
| 286,000 | 284,000 | 280,000 | 315,000 | 296,000 | 305,143 | 306,000 | 312,000 | 312,000 |
| 24,000 | 38,100 | 29,500 | 30,000 | 27,000 | 24,000 | 24,000 | 2,000 | — |
| 48,000 | 9,800 | — | | | | | | |
| - - | 59,310 | — | | | | | | |
| - - | - - | 310 | 682 | — | | | | |
| - - | - - | 20,700 | — | | | | | |
| - - | - - | - - | - - | 2,530 | — | | | |
| - - | - - | - - | 5,000 | 288,970 | 353,000 | 483,700 | 609,850 | 553,560 |
| - - | - - | - - | 25,325 | — | | | | |
| - - | - - | - - | 960 | 6,500 | 1,500 | 1,000 | — | |
| - - | - - | - - | - - | 10,000 | 61,100 | — | | |
| - - | - - | - - | - - | - - | 1,150 | - - | - - | 877 |
| - - | - - | - - | - - | - - | - - | - - | - - | 108,500 |
| - - | - - | - - | - - | - - | - - | - - | 14,000 | 14,500 |
| 7,500 | — | | | | | | | |
| - - | - - | - - | - - | - - | - - | - - | - - | 8,430 |
| 18,500 | 15,000 | 17,000 | 15,000 | 14,000 | 1,500 | 14,500 | - - | 52,100 |
| - - | - - | 48,000 | 31,717 | — | | | | |
| - - | - - | - - | - - | - - | - - | - - | 1,260 | 560 |
| 110,000 | 104,500 | 106,000 | 108,000 | 107,000 | 100,000 | 93,000 | - - | 90,000 |
| 96,000 | 88,000 | 88,000 | 80,000 | 85,500 | 88,000 | 80,000 | 88,000 | 89,000 |
| - - | - - | - - | - - | 37,750 | 55,000 | 41,788 | 46,000 | 17,000 |
| 101,000 | 79,800 | 114,000 | 116,000 | 118,000 | 70,000 | 72,400 | 95,000 | 71,000 |
| 54,000 | 56,000 | 54,000 | 60,000 | 66,000 | 34,000 | 45,000 | 48,000 | 32,500 |
| 111,000 | 109,000 | 121,000 | 103,000 | 104,000 | 100,000 | 90,000 | 81,000 | 85,000 |
| 135,000 | 145,000 | 130,000 | 117,000 | 130,000 | 112,000 | 92,000 | 167,762 | 105,600 |
| 153,000 | 164,000 | 152,700 | 152,000 | 151,000 | 146,000 | 148,500 | 138,000 | 144,000 |
| 28,750 | 26,000 | 28,825 | 36,500 | 36,500 | 42,500 | 38,200 | 52,650 | 51,200 |
| - - | - - | - - | - - | 59,000 | 67,800 | 106,444 | 136,500 | 135,500 |
| 124,500 | 121,500 | 101,000 | 121,500 | 138,500 | 122,500 | 117,500 | 110,500 | 119,815 |
| 204,000 | 214,000 | 215,000 | 222,000 | 151,000 | 262,000 | 272,500 | 260,000 | 250,000 |
| 150,000 | 132,000 | 100,500 | 100,000 | 145,500 | 149,000 | 164,000 | 151,000 | 148,000 |
| - - | - - | 10,000 | 73,000 | 100,000 | 164,000 | 151,750 | 222,060 | 150,000 |
| - - | - - | - - | - - | - - | - - | - - | 57,475 | 11,000 |
| - - | - - | - - | - - | 1,850 | - - | - - | 8,400 | — |
| - - | - - | - - | - - | - - | - - | 200 | 1,440 | 1,920 |
| - - | - - | - - | - - | - - | - - | 29,000 | 1,200 | — |
| - - | - - | - - | - - | - - | 250 | — | | |
| 1,500 | 1,500 | 2,150 | 11,900 | — | | | | |
| 651,000 | 454,500 | 384,000 | — | | | | | |
| 42,527 | 24,000 | — | | | | | | |
| 12,500 | — | | | | | | | |
| 2,400 | — | | | | | | | |
| 112,000 | 112,500 | 112,500 | 107,500 | 110,000 | 105,000 | 105,000 | 102,500 | 102,500 |
| 86,500 | 70,000 | 64,000 | 66,500 | 69,000 | 65,000 | 60,000 | 60,000 | 64,400 |
| 70,000 | 62,500 | 38,375 | 41,000 | 40,000 | 30,000 | 38,000 | 15,000 | 31,000 |
| - - | - - | - - | - - | - - | 400 | 690 | 900 | 1,610 |
| 26,500 | — | | | | | | | |
| - - | - - | 28,000 | 31,500 | 26,000 | 27,000 | 30,000 | - - | 20,000 |
| - - | - - | - - | - - | - - | - - | - - | - - | 31,500 |
| - - | - - | - - | - - | - - | - - | - - | - - | 35,000 |
| 100,000 | 102,000 | 108,000 | 101,000 | 95,000 | 101,000 | 96,000 | 88,000 | 71,975 |
| 90,000 | 96,000 | 50,500 | 58,900 | 63,500 | 74,500 | 63,500 | 66,000 | 63,000 |
| 36,000 | 33,000 | 28,000 | 30,000 | 36,300 | 47,000 | 48,750 | 45,000 | 47,875 |
| - - | - - | 96,000 | 137,000 | 169,380 | 199,750 | 194,500 | 241,000 | 261,000 |
| 49,000 | 56,000 | 43,000 | 58,000 | 60,000 | 64,000 | 56,000 | 61,050 | 64,000 |
| 25,000 | 28,700 | 25,500 | 33,000 | 40,000 | 35,000 | 46,200 | 64,801 | 68,705 |
| 31,000 | 34,000 | 17,000 | 27,000 | 24,000 | 24,000 | 27,000 | 14,000 | 19,000 |

| — | 1837. | 1838. | 1839. | 1840. | 1841. |
|---|---|---|---|---|---|
| ENGLISH PROVINCIAL PAPERS—*continued.* | | | | | |
| Penzance Gazette | - | - | 6,124 | 16,070 | 19,000 |
| Penzance Journal | - | - | - | - | - |
| Poole and Dorsetshire Herald | - | - | - | - | - |
| Provincial Medical Journal | - | - | - | - | - |
| Preller's & Fromnell's Liverpool Courier | — | | | | |
| Portsea and Isle of Wight Journal | - | - | - | - | - |
| Pilot, Birmingham | - | - | - | - | - |
| Prophetic Herald | - | - | - | - | - |
| Pilot | - | - | 18,500 | - | - |
| Plymouth and Devonport Weekly Journal | - | - | - | - | - |
| Paisley Advertiser | — | | | | |
| Reading Mercury | 127,500 | 137,500 | 143,700 | 150,700 | 154,500 |
| Rochester Gazette | 3,000 | 4,000 | 3,000 | 3,000 | 3,000 |
| Sherborne Journal | 71,000 | 78,200 | 72,030 | 69,000 | 64,000 |
| Stamford Mercury | 378,400 | 391,000 | 438,000 | 430,000 | 483,000 |
| Star in the East | 26,600 | 40,000 | 39,540 | 6,250 | — |
| Somerset County Gazette | 31,500 | 31,880 | 32,300 | 57,350 | 47,000 |
| Sussex Advertiser | 53,736 | 55,500 | 47,575 | 51,950 | 17,000 |
| Sheffield Independent | 66,500 | 66,000 | 108,500 | 118,000 | 121,000 |
| Sheffield Iris | 44,000 | 40,500 | 44,000 | 36,500 | 16,500 |
| Staffordshire Advertiser | 193,500 | 194,500 | 221,500 | 216,000 | 234,000 |
| Staffordshire Examiner | 40,000 | 51,250 | 53,000 | 45,000 | 41,500 |
| Shrewsbury Chronicle | 129,000 | 115,000 | 136,000 | 120,000 | 120,000 |
| Suffolk Chronicle | 124,000 | 130,000 | 135,000 | 120,000 | 121,000 |
| Sherborne Mercury | - | - | 34,400 | 30,000 | 34,100 |
| Salisbury and Wiltshire Herald | 37,000 | 37,000 | 46,000 | 34,000 | 45,000 |
| Surrey Standard | - | - | 26,000 | 33,000 | 4.700 |
| Sunderland Herald | 41,000 | 58,419 | 66,500 | 49,000 | 54,000 |
| Sussex Agricultural Express | 79,500 | 85,250 | 111,000 | 120,730 | 151,500 |
| Salisbury Journal | — | | | | |
| Sheffield Chronicle | 35,000 | 23,870 | — | | |
| Staffordshire Mercury | - | - | 46,000 | 52,000 | 50,000 |
| Salopian Journal | 56,000 | 65,700 | 75,000 | 85,000 | 71,000 |
| Scarborough Herald | 8,400 | 8,300 | 9,500 | 7,350 | 10,250 |
| Stockport Advertiser | 32,500 | 32,500 | 32,500 | 30,000 | 31,150 |
| Suffolk Literary Chronicle | 500 | 500 | — | | |
| Sunderland Beacon | 10,000 | 41,000 | 25,750 | — | |
| Sheffield Mercury | 95,975 | 92,500 | 90,750 | 90,000 | 60,700 |
| Shetland Journal | - | - | 10,550 | — | |
| Somerset County Herald | - | - | - | - | - |
| Sheffield Free Press | - | - | - | - | - |
| Sheffield Times | - | - | - | - | - |
| Shields Gazette | - | - | - | - | - |
| Stroud Free Press | - | - | - | - | - |
| Shrewsbury News | - | - | - | 55,000 | 72,070 |
| Stockport Chronicle | - | - | - | 32,000 | 32,000 |
| Shrewsbury Reporter | - | 52,500 | 6,000 | — | |
| Sheffield Patriot | - | 6,000 | 29,000 | 24,000 | 12,581 |
| Staffordshire Gazette | - | 5,000 | 62,735 | 62,100 | 56,500 |
| Shropshire Conservative | - | - | - | 18,000 | 31,100 |
| Swansea Journal | — | | | | |
| Scarborough Herald | - | - | - | - | - |
| Sunderland Times | - | - | - | - | - |
| Salisbury and Winchester Journal | 150,000 | 147,000 | 151,000 | 147,000 | 145,500 |
| Southport Visitor | - | - | - | - | - |
| Sussex Advertiser and Surrey Gazette | - | - | - | - | - |
| Scarborough Gazette | - | - | - | - | - |
| Scarborough Record | - | - | - | - | - |
| Surrey Mercury | - | - | - | - | - |
| Sussex Express and Surrey Standard | - | - | - | - | - |
| Stockport Mercury | - | - | - | - | - |
| Sunday School Magazine | - | - | - | - | - |

| 1842. | 1843. | 1844. | 1845. | 1846. | 1847. | 1848. | 1849. | 1850. |
|---|---|---|---|---|---|---|---|---|
| 20,050 | 22,000 | 23,500 | 29,000 | 29,000 | 16,375 | 10,000 | 8,191 | 9,267 |
| - - | - - | - - | - - | - - | 15,500 | 20,775 | 21,175 | 14,975 |
| - - | - - | - - | - - | 25,000 | 30,000 | 30,000 | 30,000 | 8,450 |
| - - | - - | - - | - - | 75,000 | 43,100 | 54,300 | 28,500 | 41,500 |
| - - | - - | - - | - - | - - | 4,000 | 8,000 | — | |
| - - | - - | - - | 67,000 | 15,500 | — | | | |
| - - | - - | - - | 6,000 | — | | | | |
| - - | - - | 5,000 | — | | | | | |
| - - | - - | 24,500 | — | | | | | |
| 164,075 | 165,950 | 169,950 | 174,430 | 181,750 | 187,500 | 190,740 | 188,000 | 206,700 |
| 2,000 | 3,000 | 4,500 | 5,000 | 6,000 | 5,000 | 5,000 | 5,000 | 5,500 |
| 70,000 | 75,000 | 69,000 | 81 000 | 81,050 | 79,500 | 78,500 | 76,000 | 84,000 |
| 494,000 | 520,000 | 520,000 | 588,025 | 588,000 | 571,000 | 572,700 | 598,000 | 581,500 |
| 42,700 | 40,000 | 33,000 | 41,500 | 34,000 | 45,000 | 33,000 | 23,000 | 38,500 |
| 29,035 | 43,400 | 46,500 | — | | | | | |
| 123,500 | 134,600 | 131,999 | 156,000 | 174,000 | 168,500 | 170,000 | 190,000 | 207,000 |
| 17,000 | 27,125 | 28,000 | 35,500 | 34,500 | 26,500 | 21,000 | — | |
| 248,500 | 255,500 | 259,500 | 287,800 | 271,750 | 299,000 | 325,000 | 327,500 | 333,500 |
| 28,100 | — | | | | | | | |
| 132,080 | 123,000 | 126,000 | 135,000 | 125,000 | 132,000 | 123,000 | 124,425 | 107,000 |
| 125,000 | 120,000 | 120,000 | 110,000 | 120,000 | 110,000 | 110,000 | 111,000 | 110,000 |
| 27,500 | 32,500 | 28,500 | 37,500 | 36,000 | 30,000 | 30,000 | 28,000 | 32 000 |
| 50,000 | 15,000 | 34,500 | 33,000 | 27,000 | 27,000 | 25,500 | 18,500 | 20,000 |
| — | | | | | | | | |
| 50,000 | 59,000 | 60,000 | 70,000 | 82,000 | 77,000 | 100,500 | 100.000 | 104,000 |
| 150,000 | 144,000 | 154,500 | 172,500 | 22,500 | — | | | |
| 60,304 | 41,500 | 36,000 | 53,150 | 65,250 | 52,500 | 17,500 | — | |
| 84,500 | 12,000 | — | | | | | | |
| 10,200 | 10,450 | 12,550 | 14,700 | 3,550 | — | | | |
| 29,150 | 27,500 | 28,000 | 27,100 | 28,100 | 27,500 | 29,000 | 27,500 | 28,500 |
| 71,500 | 72,650 | 64,000 | 70,000 | 67,000 | 54,000 | 37,000 | — | |
| - - | 14,000 | 14,000 | 31,500 | 26,000 | 27,000 | 30,000 | 32,000 | 28,000 |
| - - | - - | - - | - - | - - | - - | - - | - - | 5,000 |
| - - | - - | - - | - - | 47,000 | 87,000 | 121,500 | 155,000 | 132,000 |
| - - | - - | - - | - - | - - | - - | - - | - - | 40,700 |
| - - | - - | - - | - - | - - | - - | - - | - - | 2,500 |
| 63,000 | 39,000 | 10,000 | — | | | | | |
| — | | | | | | | | |
| — | | | | | | | | |
| 7,000 | — | | | | | | | |
| 36,200 | 18,000 | 29,000 | 25,500 | 24,000 | 20,000 | 21,000 | 20,000 | 20,000 |
| 10,200 | 10,400 | 12,550 | 14,700 | 3,560 | — | | | |
| - - | 3,000 | 20,000 | 28,000 | 14,000 | 15,000 | 17,000 | 14,200 | 12,000 |
| 150,000 | 150,000 | 140,000 | 111,000 | 139,000 | 134,500 | 136,000 | 120,000 | 120,000 |
| - - | - - | 11,464 | 12,800 | 12,500 | 12,000 | 13,500 | 14,850 | 17,000 |
| - - | - - | - - | 50,500 | 43,250 | 49,440 | 50,500 | 56,500 | 57,000 |
| - - | - - | - - | 17,000 | 21,393 | 35,500 | 17,500 | 28,850 | 33,750 |
| - - | - - | - - | 9,000 | 12,250 | 7,500 | — | | |
| - - | - - | - - | 5,225 | 3,099 | 7,774 | 540 | — | |
| - - | - - | - - | - - | 148,000 | 168,000 | 192,000 | 184,000 | 192,000 |
| - - | - - | - - | - - | - - | 18,750 | 13,000 | 12,500 | 14,980 |
| - - | - - | - - | - - | 480 | 5,880 | — | | |

| —— | 1837. | 1838. | 1839. | 1840. | 1841. |
|---|---|---|---|---|---|
| ENGLISH PROVINCIAL PAPERS—*continued.* | | | | | |
| Southampton Chronicle | - - | - - | - - | - - | - - |
| Spalding Free Press | - - | - - | - - | - - | - - |
| Shaw's Circular | - - | - - | - - | - - | - - |
| Stroud Observer | — | | | | |
| Torquay and Tor Directory | - - | - - | - - | - - | - - |
| Truth Seeker | - - | - - | - - | - - | - - |
| Taunton Courier | 26,450 | 28,000 | 30,000 | 31,000 | 32,500 |
| Ten Towns Messenger | - - | 12,000 | 71,825 | 69,000 | 66,000 |
| Teignmouth Gazette | - - | - - | - - | - - | - - |
| Tavistock Monthly Advertiser | - - | - - | - - | - - | - - |
| Temperance Gazette | - - | - - | - - | - - | - - |
| Tyne Mercury | 32,500 | 28,500 | 46,000 | 24,550 | 24,000 |
| Truro Gazette | 6,500 | — | | | |
| Torquay Chronicle | - - | - - | - - | - - | - - |
| Tyne Courier | - - | - - | - - | - - | - - |
| Ulverstone Advertiser | - - | - - | - - | - - | - - |
| Wigan Times | - - | - - | - - | - - | - - |
| Wakefield Examiner | - - | - - | - - | - - | - - |
| Wolverston Advertiser | — | | | | |
| Warwick Advertiser | 60,987 | 64,538 | 66,000 | 75,000 | 77,025 |
| West Kent Guardian | 8,500 | 7,000 | 16,500 | 28,850 | 26,525 |
| West Briton and Cornwall Advertiser | 115,500 | 93,500 | 98,000 | 88,500 | 101,000 |
| West Briton Advocate | - - | 3,000 | — | | |
| West of England Conservative | 26,672 | 34,750 | 46,000 | 31,500 | 42,000 |
| West Riding Herald | 39,000 | 31,000 | 35,000 | 33,000 | 23,000 |
| Western Herald | 16,685 | — | | | |
| Western Luminary | 31,500 | 27,900 | 31,900 | 35,000 | 36,000 |
| Western Times | 86,000 | 98,500 | 112,500 | 95,500 | 114,000 |
| Westmorland Gazette | 20,000 | 30,000 | 30,000 | 37,500 | 33,000 |
| Whitehaven Herald | 37,100 | 34,500 | 38,500 | 44,700 | 38,000 |
| Wigan Gazette | 28,500 | 28,550 | 31,800 | 25,500 | 22,000 |
| Windsor and Eton Express | 39,750 | 41,000 | 36,000 | 40,000 | 42,000 |
| Wiltshire Independent | 59,750 | 54,975 | 26,500 | 38,000 | 37,500 |
| Wilts and Gloucestershire Standard | 24,368 | 26,538 | 22,500 | 23,550 | 26,900 |
| Wolverhampton Chronicle | 63,700 | 58,015 | 60,300 | 63,800 | 67,900 |
| Worcestershire Guardian | 49,325 | 50,000 | 85,000 | 37,000 | 40,000 |
| Worcester Herald | 94,000 | 108,400 | 108,750 | 103,500 | 96,750 |
| Worcester Journal (Berrow's) | 64,000 | 94,500 | 79,500 | 89,175 | 111,000 |
| Wisbeach Gazette | 6,000 | 6,000 | — | | |
| Warwickshire Times | - - | 15,000 | — | | |
| Wakefield Journal | - - | - - | - - | - - | 1,000 |
| Winsleydale Advertiser | - - | - - | - - | - - | - - |
| Westonian and Somerset Mercury | - - | - - | - - | - - | - - |
| Weston-super-Mare Gazette | - - | - - | - - | - - | - - |
| West of England Advertiser | — | | | | |
| Worcester Chronicle | 8,000 | 75,500 | 75,000 | 73,450 | 93,150 |
| Weekly Register | - - | - - | - - | - - | - - |
| Woolwich Gazette | - - | - - | - - | - - | - - |
| Wisbeach Advertiser | - - | - - | - - | - - | - - |
| Yorkshire Gazette | 97,050 | 101,500 | 111,500 | 144,400 | 112,950 |
| Yorkshire Racing Calendar | 2,920 | 3,300 | 2,700 | 4,800 | 4,200 |
| York Herald | 206,500 | 158,100 | 173,000 | 171,500 | 162,800 |
| Yorkshireman | 59,137 | 85,250 | 114,905 | 122,000 | 120,000 |
| Yeovil Times | - - | - - | - - | - - | - - |
| York Monthly Advertiser | - - | - - | - - | - - | - - |
| York Courant | 124,900 | 103,900 | 173,000 | 154,000 | 116,000 |
| York Chronicle | 28,000 | 15,000 | 20,000 | 3,200 | — |

| 1842. | 1843. | 1844. | 1845. | 1846. | 1847. | 1848. | 1849. | 1850. |
|---|---|---|---|---|---|---|---|---|
| - - | - - | - - | - - | - - | 1,000 | - - | 988 | — |
| - - | - - | - - | - - | - - | 2,000 | 4,000 | 5,000 | 6,000 |
| - - | - - | - - | - - | - - | - - | - - | 14,100 | — |
| - - | - - | - - | 2,060 | 14,000 | 28,000 | 25,000 | 28,000 | 28,100 |
| - - | - - | - - | 1,999 | 2,892 | 1,507 | 3,308 | 2,444 | 1,664 |
| 28,000 | 30,000 | 25,000 | 25,000 | 24,500 | 22,000 | 18,000 | 15,754 | 14,000 |
| 52,000 | 60,140 | 48,000 | 32,500 | 39,500 | 26,500 | 28,000 | 10,300 | 10,300 |
| - - | - - | - - | - - | - - | - - | - - | 2,880 | 5,000 |
| - - | - - | - - | - - | - - | 2,192 | — | | |
| - - | - - | - - | - - | 9,750 | 6,000 | — | | |
| 21,000 | 29,000 | 36,500 | 36,000 | 2,000 | — | | | |
| - - | - - | - - | - - | - - | - - | - - | - - | 2,920 |
| - - | - - | - - | - - | - - | - - | - - | - - | 4,000 |
| - - | - - | - - | - - | - - | - - | - - | - - | 48,000 |
| - - | - - | - - | - - | - - | - - | - - | - - | 22,375 |
| - - | - - | - - | - - | - - | - - | - - | - - | 40,800 |
| 77,000 | 66,000 | 71,500 | 71,500 | 60,000 | 60,500 | 55,000 | 55,000 | 57,000 |
| 26,000 | 22,800 | 22,800 | 20,500 | 13,500 | 13,100 | 13,000 | 9,700 | 550 |
| 105,000 | 97,000 | 102,000 | 108,000 | 135,500 | 132,500 | 124,000 | 110,000 | 132,500 |
| 31,000 | 31,000 | 28,500 | 33,000 | 29,500 | 33,067 | 27,500 | 33,800 | 40,000 |
| — | | | | | | | | |
| 34,070 | 34,000 | 29,000 | 36,000 | 30,000 | 33,000 | 27,000 | 33,000 | 27,000 |
| 114,000 | 116,000 | 124,500 | 142,500 | 148,500 | 171,000 | 183,000 | 185,500 | 191,000 |
| 33,000 | 21,000 | 32,180 | 31,000 | 43,800 | 36,000 | 36,000 | 37,000 | 39,350 |
| 32,135 | 40,000 | 25,000 | 35,000 | 30,000 | 31,000 | 25,500 | 25,000 | 27,000 |
| 2,500 | — | | | | | | | |
| 42,000 | 38,000 | 38,000 | 42,000 | 40,000 | 38,000 | 37,750 | 36,000 | 38,000 |
| 37,500 | 42,000 | 36,000 | 37,000 | 41,000 | 33,000 | 33,000 | 30,000 | 33,000 |
| 28,800 | 25,000 | 31,200 | 31,350 | 29,100 | 28,000 | 26,500 | 26,465 | 25,500 |
| 71,000 | 67,000 | 74,000 | 79,700 | 75,000 | 83,825 | 88,986 | 89,494 | 89,500 |
| 40,000 | 46,700 | 54,500 | 29,000 | — | | | | |
| 116,000 | 123,000 | 113,000 | 102,000 | 111,500 | 132,500 | 123,375 | 141,975 | 144,000 |
| 105,000 | 104,000 | 100,000 | 59,000 | 104,700 | 72,500 | 101,000 | 104,600 | 85,000 |
| 37,000 | 23,000 | 25,000 | 27,100 | 39,000 | 41,000 | 29,900 | 27,500 | 24,000 |
| - - | 1,000 | 6,650 | 7,000 | 7,000 | 7,000 | 6,000 | 1,000 | |
| - - | - - | - - | 2,440 | 5,000 | 4,942 | 500 | — | |
| - - | - - | - - | 6,000 | 6,900 | 6,000 | 7,000 | 8,000 | 6,000 |
| 100,000 | 98,000 | 86,000 | 37,000 | 77,875 | 82,000 | 88,000 | 83,000 | 87,480 |
| - - | - - | - - | - - | - - | 137,000 | 160,000 | 105,000 | 82,000 |
| 2,200 | 10,150 | 10,755 | 7,425 | 3,500 | 500 | 18,000 | 3,962 | 5,325 |
| - - | - - | - - | 5,000 | 11,000 | 13,000 | 12,000 | 10,000 | 10,000 |
| 147,950 | 156,000 | 117,000 | 131,337 | 143,000 | 156,000 | 156,000 | 143,000 | 143,000 |
| 3,600 | 3,050 | 2,700 | 2,475 | 2,900 | 4,500 | 2,900 | 2,900 | 2,950 |
| 106,000 | 124,000 | 136,500 | 140,000 | 161,000 | 165,000 | 177,500 | 221,000 | 196,000 |
| 123,000 | 132,000 | 110,000 | 114,000 | 110,000 | 129,000 | 145,000 | 184,000 | 161,000 |
| - - | - - | - - | - - | - - | 15,800 | 33,000 | 26,400 | 27,250 |
| - - | - - | - - | - - | - - | - - | - | 7,400 | — |
| 90,000 | 80,000 | 66,000 | 73,000 | 71,000 | 47,000 | 17,500 | — | |

# IRISH NEWSPAPERS. - - - - - -

| —— | 1837. | 1838. | 1839. | 1840. | 1841. |
|---|---|---|---|---|---|
| Dublin: | | | | | |
| „ Saunders' News Letter | 316,175 | 570,000 | 596,000 | 566,400 | 636,000 |
| „ Morning Register | 191,100 | 193,500 | 140,500 | 119,000 | 118,000 |
| „ Freeman's Journal | 112,392 | 158,500 | 171,000 | 201,575 | 204,075 |
| „ Morning Herald | - - | - - | 40,000 | — | |
| „ Evening Mail | 270,000 | 456,000 | 456,000 | 439,000 | 348,000 |
| „ Evening Post | 129,025 | 274,875 | 237,400 | 296,000 | 235,000 |
| „ Evening Freeman | 41,100 | 50,884 | 48,000 | 46,500 | 38,550 |
| „ Evening Packet | 147,700 | 282,000 | 233,000 | 245,000 | 244,000 |
| „ Pilot | 88,250 | 127,500 | 98,500 | 120,275 | 114,475 |
| „ Record | 37,451 | 117,525 | — | | |
| „ Statesman and Record | - - | - - | 116,900 | 90,000 | 78,150 |
| „ Gazette | 85,000 | 9,142 | 2,500 | 13,500 | 20,000 |
| „ Standard | 22,275 | 11,662 | — | | |
| „ Paddy Kelly's Life in Dublin | 7,500 | 2,250 | — | | |
| „ Weekly Register | 16,500 | 110,375 | 111,500 | 132,500 | 113,500 |
| „ Weekly Freeman | 52,500 | 117,500 | 130,400 | 182,500 | 145,000 |
| „ Warder | 76,462 | 99,925 | 101,425 | 93,700 | 99,425 |
| „ General Advertiser | - - | 306,000 | 313,000 | 248,000 | 398,000 |
| „ Temperance Gazette | 12,000 | 60,450 | 33,280 | — | |
| „ Mercantile Advertiser | 11,500 | 23,000 | 20,500 | 20,000 | 17,500 |
| „ Norney's Corn Circular | 2,000 | 9,800 | 2,400 | — | |
| „ Christian Journal | 6,864 | 21,700 | 14,800 | 17,400 | 17,300 |
| „ Racing Calendar | 1,150 | 900 | 1,500 | 1,370 | 1,270 |
| „ United Service Journal | 550 | — | | | |
| „ Satirist | 3,600 | — | | | |
| „ Observer | 1,000 | — | | | |
| „ Protestant Guardian | - - | - - | 31,500 | — | |
| „ Bankrupt Calendar | - - | - - | 3,850 | 2,570 | 2,370 |
| „ Philanthropist | - - | - - | 9,700 | - - | - - |
| „ Monitor | - - | - - | 1,300 | 109,650 | 110,650 |
| „ Weekly Herald | - - | - - | 4,800 | 27,810 | 36,920 |
| „ Medical Press | - - | - - | 2,400 | 40,200 | 40,100 |
| „ Christian Examiner | - - | - - | - - | 14,400 | 16,900 |
| „ Ecclesiastical Journal | - - | - - | - - | - - | 13,550 |
| „ Irishman | - - | - - | - - | 14,750 | 72,360 |
| „ The World | - - | - - | - - | - - | 66,250 |
| „ Allen's Irish Land Schedule | - - | - - | - - | - - | - - |
| „ Nation | - - | - - | - - | - - | - - |
| „ Irish Friend | - - | - - | - - | - - | 20,910 |
| „ Advocate Industrial Journal | - - | - - | - - | - - | - - |
| „ Nation Advertiser | - - | - - | - - | - - | - - |
| „ Old Ireland | - - | - - | - - | - - | - - |
| „ Messenger | - - | - - | - - | - - | - - |
| „ Irish Railway Gazette | - - | - - | - - | - - | - - |
| „ United Irishman | - - | - - | - - | - - | - - |
| „ Tablet | - - | - - | - - | - - | - - |
| „ Commercial Journal | - - | - - | - - | - - | - - |
| „ Commercial Record | - - | - - | - - | - - | - - |
| „ Constitutional and Church Sentinel | - - | - - | - - | - - | - - |
| „ Irish Jurist | - - | - - | - - | - - | - - |
| „ Liberator | - - | - - | - - | - - | - - |
| „ Inspector | - - | - - | - - | - - | - - |
| „ Steeple Chase Calendar | - - | - - | - - | - - | - - |
| „ Missionary Herald | - - | - - | - - | - - | - - |
| „ Farmers' Gazette | - - | - - | - - | - - | - - |
| Dublin and Cork Price Current | - - | - - | - - | - - | - - |
| „ Catholic Magazine | - - | - - | - - | - - | - - |
| „ Evening Herald | - - | - - | - - | - - | - - |

- - - - - IRISH NEWSPAPERS.

| 1842. | 1843. | 1844. | 1845. | 1846. | 1847. | 1848. | 1849. | 1850. |
|---|---|---|---|---|---|---|---|---|
| 696,000 | 720,000 | 732,000 | 726,000 | 790,000 | 768,000 | 796,000 | 705,000 | 756,000 |
| — | | | | | | | | |
| 222,500 | 211,000 | 466,000 | 429,000 | 446,500 | 426,000 | 424,000 | 475,000 | 442,000 |
| 450,000 | 450,000 | 444,000 | 372,000 | 396,000 | 408,000 | 441,000 | 346,000 | 315,000 |
| 256,000 | 216,000 | 296,000 | 255,000 | 260,000 | 234,500 | 210,000 | 184,500 | 162,000 |
| 41,000 | 87,500 | 66,000 | 75,000 | 81,000 | 66,000 | 71,000 | 72,000 | 54,000 |
| 275,000 | 196,000 | 282,000 | 238,000 | 233,000 | 214,500 | 209.000 | 181,500 | 173,000 |
| 127,500 | 98,169 | 170,876 | 129,750 | 120,850 | 81,162 | 43,150 | 6,100 | 1,000 |
| 27,550 | 62,000 | 45,295 | 52,500 | 44,500 | — | | | |
| 11,000 | 5,000 | 27,295 | 37,400 | 6,000 | 18,500 | 14,000 | 16,000 | 30,000 |
| 120,500 | 84,500 | 101,000 | 139,000 | 100,500 | 77,000 | 62,500 | 40,000 | 11,625 |
| 142,500 | 167,000 | 283,000 | 207,000 | 210,000 | 237,000 | 235,500 | 168,000 | 120,000 |
| 142,000 | 89,000 | 148,000 | 145,500 | 116,500 | 108,000 | 108,500 | 118,000 | 118,000 |
| 347,450 | 346,750 | 345,725 | 490,450 | 481,750 | 495,500 | 474,500 | 520,500 | 530,000 |
| 15,000 | 17,500 | 12,500 | 14,500 | 7,500 | 10,000 | 10,000 | 10,000 | 7,500 |
| 7,400 | 7,500 | 5,000 | 2,500 | 2,644 | — | | | |
| 700 | 1,000 | 760 | 970 | 1,220 | 1,200 | 800 | 980 | 885 |
| 2,800 | 3,350 | 2,400 | 2,400 | 8,000 | 13,400 | 10,000 | 5,000 | 7,000 |
| - - | - - | - - | - - | - - | 5,000 | 2,500 | — | |
| 92,500 | 77,100 | 82,760 | 30,699 | — | | | | |
| 8,218 | - - | - - | - - | 15,000 | 39,500 | 16,500 | 47,500 | — |
| 38,500 | 31,650 | 32,000 | 14,000 | 26,500 | 22,000 | 26,792 | 24,750 | 24,562 |
| 12,600 | 14 500 | 16,750 | 10,400 | 20,000 | 10,400 | 12,000 | 12,500 | 12,500 |
| 24,000 | 20,500 | 18,000 | 16,500 | 16,000 | 11,500 | 11,500 | 12,400 | 12,500 |
| 8,750 | — | | | | | | | |
| 49,600 | 46,500 | 44,500 | 44,350 | 30,913 | 39,893 | 60,790 | 37,550 | 31,400 |
| - - | - - | - - | - - | - - | - - | - - | - - | 39,700 |
| - - | - - | 94,000 | 318,000 | 299,500 | 267,000 | 153,000 | 155,500 | 108,500 |
| — | | | | | | | | |
| - - | - - | - - | - - | - - | - - | - - | 45,400 | 42,000 |
| - - | - - | - - | - - | - - | - - | - - | - - | 61,000 |
| - - | - - | - - | - - | 2,500 | — | | | |
| - - | - - | - - | - - | - - | - - | - - | - - | 9,525 |
| - - | - - | 7,500 | 32,000 | 25,500 | 22,475 | 27,500 | 20,000 | 5,000 |
| - - | - - | - - | - - | - - | - - | 13,000 | — | |
| - - | - - | - - | - - | - - | - - | - - | - - | 162,300 |
| - - | - - | - - | - - | - - | - - | - - | 46,950 | 60,500 |
| 123,500 | — | | | | | | | |
| - - | - - | - - | - - | - - | - - | - - | - - | 7,695 |
| - - | - - | - - | - - | - - | - - | - - | - - | 1,300 |
| - - | - - | - - | - - | - - | - - | - - | - - | 750 |
| - - | - - | - - | - - | - - | - - | - - | - - | 6,700 |
| - - | - - | - - | - - | - - | - - | - - | 2,970 | 1,463 |
| - - | - - | - - | - - | - - | - - | - - | - - | 6,000 |
| - - | - - | - - | 138,000 | 127,500 | 123,000 | 94,775 | 80,425 | 96,625 |
| - - | - - | - - | - - | - - | - - | - - | - - | 7,324 |
| - - | - - | - - | - - | - - | - - | 1,275 | 300 | — |
| - - | - - | - - | - - | - - | - - | 16,500 | — | |

| — | 1837. | 1838. | 1839. | 1840. | 1841. |
|---|---|---|---|---|---|
| IRISH NEWSPAPERS—*continued.* | | | | | |
| Dublin: | | | | | |
| ,, Farmers' Journal | - | - | - | - | - |
| ,, Sporting Chronicle | - | - | - | 7,500 | 12,500 |
| ,, Mercantile Register | - | - | - | - | 17,500 |
| ,, Protestant Journal | - | - | - | - | - |
| ,, Press | - | - | - | - | - |
| ,, Examiner (Christian) | - | - | - | - | - |
| ,, Amateur | - | - | - | - | - |
| ,, Protestant Dependent | - | - | - | 14,000 | — |
| Belfast Commercial Chronicle | 71,500 | 113,211 | 112,000 | 115,000 | 115,000 |
| ,, News Letter | 70,000 | 118,000 | 119,000 | 108,000 | 100,000 |
| ,, Standard | - | 16,000 | - | 4,500 | 2,500 |
| ,, Reformer | - | 20,000 | 12,000 | 8,000 | 4,825 |
| ,, Northern Whig | 58,000 | 145,000 | 149,000 | 119,000 | 174,500 |
| ,, Ulster Times | 49,168 | 133,000 | 138,000 | 131,500 | 120,000 |
| ,, Christian Patriot | - | | 32,500 | 15,000 | — |
| ,, Guardian | 16,175 | — | | | |
| ,, Vindicator | - | - | - | 90,000 | 86,500 |
| ,, Patriot | — | | | | |
| ,, Banner of Ulster | - | - | - | - | - |
| ,, Mercantile Register | - | - | - | - | - |
| ,, Mercantile Journal | - | - | - | 14,750 | 72,325 |
| ,, Northern Herald | 875 | — | | | |
| ,, Ulster Missionary | - | - | - | - | 3,360 |
| ,, Ulster Churchman | - | - | - | - | 15,500 |
| Athlone Sentinel | 5,150 | 6,000 | 5,500 | 4,000 | 5,000 |
| ,, Independent | 6,025 | 1,500 | — | | |
| ,, Conservative | - | 4,000 | — | | |
| [An]glo Celt | - | - | - | - | - |
| [A]rmagh Guardian | - | - | - | - | - |
| Achill Missionary Herald | - | 15,000 | 29,020 | 59,500 | 27,000 |
| Ballina Advertiser | - | - | - | - | 8,500 |
| ,, Chronicle | - | - | - | - | - |
| Ballyshannon Herald | 11,001 | 7,000 | 10,500 | 13,000 | 5,300 |
| Cork Constitution | 164,000 | 163,000 | 173,500 | 187,500 | 204,000 |
| ,, Standard | 18,584 | 64,000 | 63,000 | 57,500 | 35,000 |
| ,, Southern Reporter | 185,575 | 197,500 | 193,000 | 190,000 | 200,000 |
| ,, Evening Herald | 38,175 | — | | | |
| ,, Advertiser | 36,000 | - | - | 60,500 | 71,000 |
| ,, People's Press | 1,500 | — | | | |
| ,, Examiner | - | - | - | - | - |
| Connaught Journal | - | - | 4,500 | — | |
| Coleraine Chronicle | - | - | - | - | - |
| Carlow Sentinel | 14,550 | 12,500 | 15,000 | 12,500 | 15,000 |
| Clare Journal | 8,500 | 5,000 | 16,000 | 9,500 | 20,000 |
| Clonmel Herald | 10,575 | 7,500 | 5,000 | 7,400 | — |
| ,, Advertiser | 18,500 | 14,000 | 3,000 | — | |
| ,, Chronicle | - | - | - | - | - |
| Downpatrick Recorder | 5,000 | 37,000 | 30,000 | 29,000 | 30,000 |
| ,, Chronicle | - | - | - | - | 20,400 |
| ,, Irishman | - | - | - | - | - |
| Drogheda Journal | 27,600 | 28,182 | 24,718 | 17,362 | 4,900 |
| ,, Conservative | - | 10,000 | 17,534 | 20,000 | 20,500 |
| ,, Argus | 18,900 | 15,500 | 20,000 | 25,000 | 32,500 |
| Dundalk Democrat | - | - | - | - | - |
| Enniskillen Chronicle | 14,700 | 11,500 | 12,000 | 13,000 | 16,000 |
| Enniskillener | 5,795 | — | | | |
| Fermanagh Impartial Reporter | 14,750 | 13,500 | 13,000 | 12,500 | 12,500 |

| 1842. | 1843. | 1844. | 1845. | 1846. | 1847. | 1848. | 1849. | 1850. |
|---|---|---|---|---|---|---|---|---|
| 32,125 | - - | - - | 10,620 | 90,750 | 34,500 | — | | |
| — | | | | | | | | |
| — | | | | | | | | |
| - - | - - | - - | 36,000 | 51,000 | 43,500 | 90,300 | — | |
| - - | - - | - - | - - | - - | - - | - - | 89,000 | 12,500 |
| - - | - - | - - | - - | - - | - - | - - | 8,000 | 12,500 |
| - - | - - | - - | - - | - - | - - | - - | 5,000 | — |
| 122,500 | 120,000 | 110,000 | 110,000 | 110,000 | 89,500 | 90,000 | 90,000 | 90,000 |
| 91,000 | 77,000 | 84,000 | 72,000 | 70,000 | 66,000 | 70,000 | 75,500 | 72,500 |
| — | | | | | | | | |
| — | | | | | | | | |
| 203,950 | 209,000 | 220,000 | 225,000 | 234,000 | 242,000 | 272,500 | 282,500 | 285,500 |
| 101,000 | 52,500 | — | | | | | | |
| 95,000 | 80,000 | 87,500 | 87,000 | 88,000 | 51,500 | 40,000 | 18,000 | 54,750 |
| 72,000 | 121,000 | 79,000 | 73,000 | 100,000 | 86,500 | 92,000 | 90,000 | 123,400 |
| - - | - - | - - | - - | - - | - - | - - | - - | 12,500 |
| 43,000 | - - | 15,000 | — | | | | | |
| — | | | | | | | | |
| — | | | | | | | | |
| 5,500 | 7,500 | 9,000 | 5,500 | 2,500 | 5,000 | 5,000 | 5,000 | 2,500 |
| - - | - - | - - | - - | 22,500 | 18,000 | 17,500 | 17,500 | 20,000 |
| - - | - - | 5,500 | 30,000 | 25,227 | 29,500 | 32,500 | 32,500 | 34,750 |
| 32,000 | 28,000 | 31,500 | 28,500 | 31,500 | 22,500 | 47,000 | 36,500 | 32,000 |
| — | | | | | | | | |
| - - | - - | - - | - - | - - | - - | - - | 5,100 | 52,500 |
| 10,500 | 7,000 | 10,000 | 5,000 | 7,500 | 7,750 | 6,700 | 5,500 | 2,500 |
| 216,000 | 216,000 | 224,000 | 207,000 | 208,000 | 228,000 | 216,025 | 204,000 | 180,000 |
| — | | | | | | | | |
| 185,000 | 205,000 | 140,500 | 152,500 | 172,000 | 145,000 | 167,000 | 141,500 | 168,000 |
| — | | | | | | | | |
| 106,000 | 128,000 | 113,000 | 184,000 | 167,000 | 199,500 | 210,025 | 103,000 | 161,500 |
| - - | - - | 19,000 | 30,500 | 39,000 | 33,000 | 32,500 | 30,000 | 42,000 |
| 21,000 | 15,000 | 15,000 | 15,500 | 17,000 | 17,500 | 15,000 | 17,500 | 15,000 |
| 18,500 | 8,000 | 15,000 | 23,000 | 13,500 | 16,500 | 17,500 | 18,000 | 19,000 |
| - - | - - | - - | - - | - - | - - | - - | - - | 10,000 |
| 30,000 | 25,000 | 25,000 | 25,500 | 34,500 | 25,000 | 30,000 | 25,000 | 20,000 |
| — | | | | | | | | |
| - - | - - | - - | - - | - - | - - | - - | 36,500 | — |
| — | | | | | | | | |
| 23,500 | 18,000 | 22,000 | 20,000 | 12,500 | 17,500 | 12,500 | 5,000 | 7,500 |
| 38,000 | 32,500 | 32,500 | 32,500 | 41,500 | 31,500 | 30,000 | 29,000 | 25,000 |
| - - | - - | - - | - - | - - | - - | - - | 5,500 | 22,500 |
| 16,000 | 12,000 | 16,000 | 8,000 | 22,000 | 15,000 | 15,000 | 10,000 | — |
| 15,000 | 25,000 | 20,000 | 25,000 | 32,500 | 29,500 | 27,500 | 25,000 | 22,500 |

| —— | 1837. | 1338. | 1839. | 1840. | 1841. |
|---|---|---|---|---|---|
| IRISH NEWSPAPERS—*continued.* | | | | | |
| Galway Journal | - - | - - | - - | - - | 10,500 |
| „ Weekly Register | 14,055 | 3,625 | 9,500 | — | |
| „ Patriot | 23,850 | 16,250 | 10,000 | 5,000 | — |
| „ Advertiser | - - | - - | - - | 14,009 | 9,500 |
| „ Vindicator | - - | - - | - - | - - | - - |
| „ Mercury | - - | - - | - - | - - | - - |
| Kerry Evening Post | 14,575 | 15,500 | 13,750 | 15,250 | 25,000 |
| „ Examiner | - - | - - | - - | 19,000 | 21,000 |
| King's County Chronicle | - - | - - | - - | - - | - - |
| Kilkenny Journal | 21,975 | 28,500 | 24,000 | 25,000 | 25,000 |
| „ Moderator | 24,300 | 25,000 | 27,000 | 25,000 | 25,000 |
| Lurgan Chronicle | - - | - - | - - | - - | - - |
| „ Independent | - - | - - | - - | - - | - - |
| Leinster Express | 26,901 | 30,000 | 25,687 | 37,900 | 38,615 |
| „ Independent | 9,061 | 14,750 | 13,125 | 8,350 | 4,000 |
| „ Reformer | - - | - - | - - | 12,500 | 35,175 |
| Limerick Chronicle | 176,062 | 170,500 | 198,000 | 158,500 | 200,000 |
| „ Star and Evening Post | 28,500 | 46,500 | 11,000 | — | |
| „ Times | 12,200 | 2,000 | — | | |
| „ Standard | - - | 48,000 | 56,000 | 62,000 | 57,500 |
| „ Reporter | - - | - - | 33,025 | 33,025 | 65,000 |
| „ Examiner | - - | - - | - - | - - | - - |
| Londonderry Journal | 25,288 | 40,120 | 46,737 | 37,500 | 41,500 |
| „ Sentinel | 61,900 | 61,660 | 52,123 | 63,000 | 59,500 |
| „ Standard | 20,000 | 56,480 | 46,827 | 54,500 | 61,500 |
| Longford Journal | - - | - - | 3,000 | 8,000 | 8,500 |
| „ Messenger | 300 | 2,000 | — | | |
| Leitrim Journal | - - | - - | - - | - - | - - |
| Meath Herald | - - | - - | - - | - - | - - |
| Mayo Constitution | 21,962 | 15,250 | 21,175 | 18,500 | 17,500 |
| „ Telegraph | 23,650 | 21,000 | 17,000 | 22,500 | 22,500 |
| „ Mercury | - - | - - | - - | 6,300 | 10,500 |
| Nenagh Guardian | - - | - - | 20,000 | 32,500 | 24,000 |
| „ Chronicle | - - | - - | - - | - - | - - |
| Newry Telegraph | 86,500 | 93,000 | 107,850 | 105,500 | 115,000 |
| „ Examiner | 82,016 | 86,250 | 77,000 | 72,500 | 60,000 |
| „ Standard | - - | - - | - - | 17,500 | 15,500 |
| Northern Standard | - - | - - | 2,500 | 17,500 | 15,000 |
| Roscommon Gazette | 4,225 | 7,662 | 7,500 | 7,500 | 7,500 |
| „ Journal | 7,888 | 9,303 | 6,000 | 7,167 | 10,549 |
| „ Messenger | - - | - - | - - | - - | - - |
| Robins of Munster | - - | - - | - - | - - | - - |
| Sligo Guardian | - - | - - | - - | - - | - - |
| „ Chronicle | - - | - - | - - | - - | - - |
| „ Journal | 13,074 | 10,175 | 7,750 | 10,075 | 12,500 |
| „ Champion | 8,150 | 12,650 | 15,800 | 16,500 | 12,900 |
| Strabane Morning Post | 3,218 | 450 | — | | |
| Tipperary Free Press | 34,850 | 33,000 | 38,500 | 38,500 | 37,000 |
| „ Constitution | 29,925 | 36,000 | 36,000 | 37,500 | 30,000 |
| „ Vindicator | - - | - - | - - | - - | - - |

| 1842. | 1843. | 1844. | 1845. | 1846. | 1847. | 1848. | 1849. | 1850. |
|---|---|---|---|---|---|---|---|---|
| — | | | | | | | | |
| — | | | | | | | | |
| — | | | | | | | | |
| 37,000 | 31,500 | 32,000 | 26,500 | 35,000 | 32,500 | 27,700 | 32,500 | 34,000 |
| - - | - - | - - | 16,500 | 18,250 | 16,125 | 12,725 | 14,425 | 12,500 |
| 22,500 | 15,000 | 17,400 | 20,000 | 22,000 | 18,500 | 17,500 | 17,500 | 17,500 |
| 28,500 | 20,625 | 20,477 | 18,000 | 14,500 | 13,500 | 13,500 | 5,000 | 4,500 |
| - - | - - | - - | 2,500 | 20,000 | 15,325 | 20,000 | 17,500 | 17,500 |
| 30,000 | 27,000 | 20,250 | 25,000 | 25,000 | 24,500 | 23,500 | 17,500 | 20,000 |
| 25,000 | 27,000 | 25,000 | 25,000 | 27,500 | 22,500 | 27,500 | 25,000 | 25,000 |
| - - | - - | - - | - - | - - | - - | - - | - - | 11,875 |
| - - | - - | - - | - - | 2,500 | 10,000 | 12,500 | 10,000 | 3,250 |
| 35,000 | 25,000 | 35,850 | 35,500 | 30,000 | 32,000 | 34,176 | 37,500 | 31,000 |
| — | | | | | | | | |
| — | | | | | | | | |
| 205,000 | 181,500 | 180,000 | 190,500 | 190,000 | 205,000 | 250,000 | 193,500 | 165,000 |
| 2,400 | — | | | | | | | |
| 63,000 | 57,000 | 55,000 | 47,500 | 50,000 | 40,000 | 39,500 | 29,000 | 37,000 |
| - - | - - | - - | - - | 116,000 | 55,500 | 65,000 | 60,500 | 60,000 |
| 38,500 | 43,000 | 35,000 | 34,500 | 38,000 | 36,500 | 32,500 | 30,000 | 26,000 |
| 63,500 | 61,000 | 60,500 | 50,500 | 63,000 | 56,000 | 49,125 | 59,675 | 60,000 |
| 65,000 | 67,500 | 71,500 | 68,000 | 51,500 | 90,000 | 103,500 | 102,000 | 97,000 |
| 12,000 | 6,000 | 9,000 | 9,000 | 9,000 | 9,000 | 12,000 | 9,000 | 9,000 |
| - - | - - | - - | - - | - - | - - | - - | - - | 2,500 |
| - - | - - | - - | 9,000 | 12,500 | 5,000 | 2,760 | 5,400 | 12,500 |
| 24,000 | 25,000 | 19,375 | 12,000 | 15,000 | 14,500 | 11,000 | 10,500 | 10,500 |
| 18,000 | 18,025 | 21,000 | 15,000 | 28,500 | 15,000 | 15,000 | 15,000 | 15,000 |
| — | | | | | | | | |
| 20,000 | 20,000 | 22,500 | 25,500 | 24,750 | 22,500 | 20,000 | 20,000 | 20,000 |
| - - | - - | - - | - - | - - | - - | - - | - - | 18,000 |
| 120,700 | 109,000 | 123,000 | 119,150 | 130,500 | 107,500 | 120,000 | 107,500 | 110,000 |
| 50,000 | 41,000 | 37,500 | 40,500 | 30,000 | 34,500 | 32,000 | 30,250 | 27,500 |
| — | | | | | | | | |
| 17,500 | 17,500 | 17,500 | 20,000 | 17,500 | 17,500 | 17,500 | 17,500 | 15,000 |
| 7,500 | 9,000 | 9,500 | 7,500 | 18,500 | 10,625 | 8,250 | 6,000 | 3,525 |
| 6,161 | 6,403 | 5,000 | 5,000 | 2,500 | 4,959 | 16,000 | 1,825 | 2,750 |
| - - | - - | - - | - - | - - | - - | - - | 10,000 | 9,525 |
| - - | - - | - - | - - | - - | - - | - - | - - | 45,000 |
| - - | - - | - - | - - | - - | - - | - - | 20,000 | 7,550 |
| - - | - - | - - | - - | - - | - - | - - | - - | 16,000 |
| 8,000 | 10,000 | 10,000 | 7,500 | 7,750 | 7,500 | 7,500 | 7,500 | 5,000 |
| 12,750 | 10,000 | 10,000 | 12,500 | 10,000 | 12,500 | 7,500 | 7,500 | 7,500 |
| 32,500 | 26,000 | 32,000 | 32,000 | 32,000 | 32,000 | 32,000 | 28,000 | 24,000 |
| 30,000 | 27,500 | 25,175 | 32,500 | 22,450 | 16,550 | 7,500 | — | |
| - - | - - | - - | 50,000 | 66,000 | 59,000 | 62,000 | 50,000 | 17,000 |

| —— | 1837. | 1838. | 1839. | 1840. | 1841. |
|---|---|---|---|---|---|
| IRISH NEWSPAPERS—*continued.* | | | | | |
| Tuam Herald - - - - - - - | - - | 8,500 | 12,750 | 12,500 | 13,000 |
| Tyrawley Herald - - - - - - | - - | - - | - - | - - | - - |
| Tyrone Constitutional - - - - - | - - | - - | - - | - - | - - |
| Tralee Mercury - - - - - - | 11,300 | 15,000 | 15,000 | 7,500 | — |
| ,, Chronicle - - - - - - | - - | - - | - - | - - | - - |
| Ulster Gazette - - - - - - | - - | - - | - - | - - | - - |
| ,, Conservative - - - - - | - - | - - | - - | - - | - - |
| Westmeath Guardian - - - - - | 2,900 | 7,242 | 9,897 | 10,914 | 11,090 |
| Western Star - - - - - - - | - - | - - | - - | - - | - - |
| Waterford Chronicle and Weekly ditto - - | 46,785 | 42,500 | 36,000 | 44,150 | 44,750 |
| ,, Freeman - - - - - - | - - | - - | - - | - - | - - |
| ,, Mirror - - - - - - | 27,180 | 17,900 | 23,000 | 25,000 | 22,500 |
| ,, Mail - - - - - - | 21,875 | 30,708 | 30,000 | 27,500 | 27,500 |
| ,, News Letter - - - - - | - - | - - | 10,800 | 7,200 | 9,700 |
| ,, Evening News - - - - - | - - | - - | - - | - - | - - |
| Wexford Independent - - - - - | 36,637 | 35,500 | 37,000 | 40,500 | 35,000 |
| ,, Conservative - - - - - | 21,400 | 25,000 | 22,500 | 25,000 | 25,000 |
| ,, Freeman - - - - - - | 18,100 | 3,500 | — | | |
| ,, Guardian - - - - - - | - - | - - | - - | - - | - - |

## SCOTCH PAPERS. - - - - - - -

| | 1837. | 1838. | 1839. | 1840. | 1841. |
|---|---|---|---|---|---|
| Aberdeen Herald - - - - - - | 110,000 | 84,000 | 100,000 | 125,000 | 112,000 |
| ,, Journal - - - - - - | 124,125 | 137,000 | 119,500 | 130,000 | 133,800 |
| ,, Constitutional - - - - - | 21,500 | 44,000 | 42,500 | 44,500 | 38,500 |
| ,, Banner - - - - - - | - - | - - | - - | 41,900 | 71,700 |
| ,, North of Scotland Gazette - - | - - | - - | - - | - - | - - |
| ,, Scottish Farmer - - - - | - - | - - | - - | - - | - - |
| ,, Family Journal - - - - | - - | - - | - - | - - | - - |
| ,, Review - - - - - - | - - | - - | - - | - - | - - |
| Ayr Advertiser - - - - - - | 57,000 | 57,000 | 66,500 | 72,000 | 70,200 |
| ,, Observer - - - - - - | 39,500 | 37,600 | 42,250 | 41,000 | 46,500 |
| ,, Examiner - - - - - - | - - | 21,000 | 26,600 | — | |
| ,, Watchman - - - - - - | - - | - - | - - | - - | - - |
| ,, and Renfrew Agriculturist - - | - - | - - | - - | - - | - - |
| ,, News Letter - - - - - | - - | - - | - - | - - | - - |
| ,, North British Agriculturist - - | - - | - - | - - | - - | - - |
| Arbroath Journal - - - - - - | 3,000 | 19,900 | 21,025 | 15,000 | 14,790 |
| ,, Herald - - - - - - | - - | 3,50 0 | 14,000 | — | |
| ,, Guide - - - - - - | - - | - - | - - | - - | - - |
| Alloa Advertiser - - - - - - | - - | - - | - - | - - | - - |
| Banffshire Journal - - - - - | - - | - - | - - | - - | - - |
| Banff Advertiser - - - - - - | - - | - - | - - | - - | - - |
| ,, Reporter - - - - - - | - - | - - | - - | - - | - - |
| Brechin Advertiser - - - - - | - - | - - | - - | - - | - - |
| Clackmannan Advertiser - - - - | - - | - - | - - | - - | - - |
| Dunfermline Advertiser - - - - - | - - | - - | - - | - - | - - |
| Dingwall Ross Advertiser - - - - | - - | - - | - - | - - | - - |
| Dumfries Courier - - - - - - | 100,000 | 100,500 | 96,000 | 96,000 | 103,000 |
| ,, Herald - - - - - - | 31,500 | 40,560 | 40,000 | 42,000 | 42,000 |

| 1842. | 1843. | 1844. | 1845. | 1846. | 1847. | 1848. | 1849. | 1850. |
|---|---|---|---|---|---|---|---|---|
| 15,000 | 14,500 | 12,500 | 15,500 | 12,750 | 12,000 | 15,000 | 12,500 | 12,500 |
| - - | - - | 10,000 | 14,000 | 11,250 | 10,750 | 12,750 | 10,000 | 10,000 |
| - - | - - | - - | 17,000 | 12,000 | 8,000 | 10,000 | 20,000 | 18,000 |
| - - | 6,000 | 20,000 | 17,500 | 12,230 | 18,500 | 14,000 | 13,000 | 16,250 |
| - - | - - | - - | 39,000 | 31,500 | 22,500 | 18,000 | 15,000 | 11,500 |
| - - | - - | - - | 40,000 | 22,850 | — | | | |
| 12,000 | 7,762 | 12,400 | 19,000 | 14,500 | 15,536 | 15,000 | 12,800 | 18,000 |
| - - | - - | - - | - - | 13,000 | 13,000 | 13,500 | 10,500 | 12,500 |
| 45,000 | 43,300 | 2,250 | - - | 18,000 | 30,500 | 27,000 | 5,000 | 10,000 |
| - - | - - | - - | 17,500 | 30,000 | 7,500 | — | | |
| — | | | | | | | | |
| 30,500 | 23,500 | 25,000 | 25,000 | 25,000 | 25,000 | 27,000 | 30,800 | 30,250 |
| 7,200 | 9,600 | 8,600 | 12,600 | 9,106 | 9,600 | 14,372 | 2,400 | 10,000 |
| - - | - - | - - | - - | - - | - - | - - | 9,360 | 10,000 |
| 32,500 | 39,000 | 44,000 | 41,500 | 46,000 | 57,500 | 69,000 | 47,000 | 46,500 |
| 25,000 | 22,500 | 22,500 | 22,500 | 16,500 | — | | | |
| - - | - - | - - | - - | - - | 5,000 | 12,500 | 17,500 | 18,625 |

## SCOTCH PAPERS.

| 1842. | 1843. | 1844. | 1845. | 1846. | 1847. | 1848. | 1849. | 1850. |
|---|---|---|---|---|---|---|---|---|
| 102,000 | 88,000 | 71,000 | 100,000 | 103,000 | 98,500 | 99,500 | 123,000 | 78,000 |
| 130,000 | 116,025 | 138,200 | 110,000 | 120,250 | 138,000 | 148,000 | 175,240 | 161,000 |
| 24,000 | 24,500 | 12,000 | — | | | | | |
| 42,000 | 46,000 | 34,000 | 31,200 | 28,500 | 27,870 | 22,000 | 27,000 | 15,500 |
| - - | - - | - - | 87,500 | 97,000 | 76,500 | 62,500 | 42,000 | 29,750 |
| - - | - - | 2,500 | 7,500 | 13,000 | 9,500 | 10,500 | 10,000 | 7,510 |
| - - | - - | - - | - - | 4,500 | 5,252 | — | | |
| - - | 24,000 | 16,000 | 1,000 | — | | | | |
| 69,500 | 65,375 | 67,325 | 72,000 | 80,000 | 80,000 | 80,000 | 88,000 | 88,000 |
| 38,960 | 40,900 | 42,800 | 41,000 | 41,000 | 40,000 | 44,000 | 44,000 | 20,400 |
| - - | 5,500 | 7,275 | 17,625 | 24,400 | 35,775 | 24,600 | — | |
| 15,500 | 28,000 | 18,700 | — | | | | | |
| - - | - - | 6,120 | 8,000 | 7,200 | 5,040 | 3,620 | 2,880 | 2,760 |
| - - | - - | - - | - - | - - | - - | - - | 38,500 | — |
| 14,000 | — | | | | | | | |
| 16,980 | 20,191 | 21,000 | 22,500 | 20,000 | 21,770 | 20,750 | 22,000 | 18,000 |
| - - | - - | 480 | 3,840 | 3,840 | 4,800 | 4,800 | 4,968 | 15,772 |
| - - | - - | - - | 7,000 | 17,050 | 21,000 | 22,000 | 26,000 | 26,350 |
| - - | - - | - - | - - | - - | 3,000 | — | | |
| - - | - - | - - | - - | - - | - - | - - | - - | 4,000 |
| - - | - - | - - | - - | 17,000 | 15,500 | 15,500 | 16,000 | 16,000 |
| - - | - - | 2,314 | 2,952 | 4,168 | 3,180 | 3,625 | 3,920 | 3,500 |
| - - | - - | - - | - - | - - | - - | 1,000 | 2,000 | 2,000 |
| 26,600 | 30,700 | 28,600 | 22,700 | 26,000 | 25,000 | 25,000 | 13,400 | — |
| 103,800 | 103,000 | 97,000 | 96,500 | 106,000 | 108,000 | 108,500 | 110,000 | 104,000 |
| 42,500 | 38,500 | 48,500 | 48,000 | 40,000 | 34,300 | 34,500 | 32,000 | 32,000 |

| — | 1837. | 1838. | 1839. | 1840. | 1841. |
|---|---|---|---|---|---|
| SCOTCH PAPERS—*continued.* | | | | | |
| Dumfries Times | 55,000 | 64,000 | 67,000 | 61,000 | 52,000 |
| ,, Galloway Register | 660 | 24,150 | 27,000 | 32,000 | 22,500 |
| ,, Standard | - - | - - | - - | - - | - - |
| ,, Eskdale Advertiser | - - | - - | - - | - - | - - |
| Dundee Courier | - - | - - | - - | 18,775 | 26,500 |
| ,, Herald | - - | - - | - - | - - | - - |
| ,, Chronicle | 27,000 | 28,000 | 32,760 | 34,195 | 45,000 |
| ,, Northern Warder | - - | - - | - - | - - | 51,500 |
| ,, Commercial Journal | - - | - - | - - | - - | - - |
| ,, Advertiser | - - | - - | - - | 67,925 | 78,541 |
| Edinburgh Courant | 252,550 | 263,050 | 275,050 | 274,150 | 280,100 |
| ,, Mercury | 111,013 | 108,312 | 123,000 | 126,000 | 126,000 |
| ,, Advertiser | 140,000 | 138,000 | 148,000 | 142,000 | 143,000 |
| ,, Gazette | 6,844 | 8,000 | 11,000 | 11,000 | 12,000 |
| ,, Journal | 81,283 | 93,000 | 78,000 | 70,000 | 67,500 |
| ,, Chronicle | 60,000 | 48,900 | 42,450 | 55,000 | 32,000 |
| ,, Scotsman | 264,362 | 271,000 | 253,000 | 250,592 | 268,000 |
| ,, North British Advertiser | 376,712 | 397,250 | 148,000 | 142,000 | 143,000 |
| ,, Ladies' Own Journal | - - | - - | - - | - - | - - |
| ,, Saturday Post | 53,739 | 54,400 | 51,000 | 44,000 | 80,000 |
| ,, Scottish Jurist | 2,880 | 3,132 | 4,800 | 3,360 | 4,320 |
| ,, Missionary Record, Church of Scotland | - - | - - | - - | - - | - - |
| ,, Missionary Record, Children's | - - | - - | - - | - - | - - |
| ,, Witness | - - | - - | - - | 155,500 | 195,000 |
| ,, Weekly Register | - - | - - | - - | - - | - - |
| ,, North British Express | - - | - - | - - | - - | - - |
| ,, Missionary Record | - - | - - | 10,950 | 22,390 | 40,780 |
| ,, Free Church Children's Record | - - | - - | - - | - - | - - |
| ,, The News | - - | - - | - - | - - | - - |
| ,, Monthly Telegraph | - - | - - | - - | - - | - - |
| ,, Free Church Magazine | - - | - - | - - | - - | - - |
| ,, Railway Gazette | - - | - - | - - | - - | - - |
| ,, Christian Treasury | - - | - - | - - | - - | - - |
| ,, Scottish Express | - - | - - | - - | - - | - - |
| ,, United Presbyterian Magazine | - - | - - | - - | - - | - - |
| ,, United Presbyterian Record | - - | - - | - - | - - | - - |
| ,, Juvenile Magazine | - - | - - | - - | - - | - - |
| ,, Chambers' Journal | - - | - - | - - | - - | - - |
| ,, Scottish Register | — | - - | - - | - - | - - |
| ,, British League | — | - - | - - | - - | - - |
| ,, Temperance Review | - - | - - | - - | - - | - - |
| ,, Leith Herald | - - | - - | - - | - - | - - |
| ,, Scottish Agriculturist Insurance | - - | - - | - - | - - | - - |
| ,, Hogg's Instructor | - - | - - | - - | - - | - - |
| ,, Ladies' Review | - - | - - | - - | - - | - - |
| ,, Free Church Educational Journal | - - | - - | - - | - - | - - |
| ,, Chronicle Magazine | - - | - - | - - | - - | - - |
| ,, Eastern Female Friend | - - | - - | - - | - - | - - |
| ,, Christian Magazine | - - | - - | - - | - - | - - |
| ,, Scottish Christian Journal | - - | - - | - - | - - | - - |
| ,, Brydon's Musical Journal | - - | - - | - - | - - | - - |
| ,, Nelson's Trade List | - - | - - | - - | - - | - - |
| ,, Lawson & Son's List | - - | - - | - - | - - | - - |
| ,, Scottish Magazine | - - | - - | - - | - - | - - |
| ,, Leith Commercial List | - - | - - | - - | - - | 8,000 |
| ,, Midlothian Advertiser | - - | - - | - - | - - | - - |
| ,, North British Agriculturist | - - | - - | - - | - - | - - |
| ,, Range & Co.'s Report | - - | - - | - - | - - | - - |
| ,, Examiner | - - | - - | - - | - - | - - |
| ,, Mitchell & Co.'s Market Report | - - | - - | - - | - - | - - |
| ,, Monthly Advertiser | - - | - - | - - | - - | - - |
| ,, Market Report | - - | - - | - - | - - | - - |

| 1842. | 1843. | 1844. | 1845. | 1846. | 1847. | 1848. | 1849. | 1850. |
|---|---|---|---|---|---|---|---|---|
| 47,300 | — | | | | | | | |
| 24,952 | 18,986 | — | | | | | | |
| - - | 25,000 | 35,500 | 30,000 | 35,000 | 30,000 | 29,500 | 33,250 | 34,000 |
| - - | - - | - - | - - | - - | - - | - - | 12,000 | 2,880 |
| 24,000 | 22,000 | 22,500 | 19,000 | 18,000 | 20,150 | 24,000 | 29,250 | 30,000 |
| 11,475 | 15,000 | — | | | | | | |
| 23,020 | — | | | | | | | |
| 40,000 | 40,000 | 37,000 | 84,725 | 87,775 | 74,500 | 70,000 | 67,500 | 78,000 |
| - - | - - | - - | - - | - - | - - | - - | - - | 4,000 |
| 72,500 | 67,500 | 78,000 | 114,500 | 145,000 | 143,000 | 150,000 | 136,000 | 123,000 |
| 280,000 | 274,000 | 258,000 | 253,000 | 242,000 | 240,000 | 243,000 | 241,000 | 255,000 |
| 135,000 | 117,000 | 100,200 | 101,000 | 105,000 | 106,000 | 107,500 | 110,500 | 106,512 |
| 147,000 | 144,000 | 141,200 | 143,000 | 149,000 | 145,000 | 149,000 | 150,000 | 151,000 |
| 16,000 | 13,000 | 12,000 | 15,000 | 14,000 | 15,000 | 16,500 | 22,370 | 20,000 |
| 65,000 | 47,250 | 40,750 | 41,000 | 34,000 | 38,000 | 9,100 | — | |
| 46,650 | 53,925 | 155,450 | 138,000 | 155,456 | 160,000 | 30,250 | — | |
| 294,900 | 267,000 | 250,037 | 248,050 | 272,000 | 284,500 | 302,000 | 299,000 | 301,000 |
| 512,000 | 514,000 | 590,000 | 608,500 | 611,150 | 612,850 | 638,500 | 649,000 | 659,000 |
| - - | - - | 4,000 | 18,000 | 22,000 | 27,000 | 31,500 | 34,000 | 42,000 |
| 86,500 | 72,000 | 107,650 | 133,500 | 124,500 | 108,000 | 102,000 | 95,600 | 86,700 |
| 3,840 | 5,760 | 4,800 | 5,760 | 6,240 | 7,200 | 6,460 | 7,480 | 8,500 |
| - - | - - | - - | 28,725 | 34,994 | 37,113 | 34,550 | 27,980 | 32,610 |
| - - | - - | - - | - - | - - | - - | - - | 1,400 | 2,820 |
| 251,437 | 350,000 | 296,000 | 270,000 | 268,000 | 267,000 | 251,000 | 265,000 | 266,000 |
| - - | 327,925 | 295,000 | 267,100 | 250,000 | 89,000 | — | | |
| - - | - - | - - | - - | 38,000 | 33,300 | 77,550 | 11,750 | — |
| 37,960 | 24,060 | 31,062 | 25,950 | 29,700 | 33,300 | 27,604 | 34,400 | 34,780 |
| - - | - - | - - | - - | 2,320 | 3,300 | 3,126 | 3,086 | 2,820 |
| - - | - - | - - | - - | - - | 27,980 | 112,750 | 128,300 | — |
| - - | - - | 1,050 | 2,450 | 2,700 | 2,200 | 1,440 | 1,400 | 1,020 |
| - - | - - | 9,752 | 8,500 | 7,680 | 7,950 | 10,300 | 8,100 | 9,680 |
| - - | - - | - - | 40,500 | 49,500 | 40,000 | 29,250 | 20,500 | 16,000 |
| - - | - - | - - | 2,800 | 2,448 | 1,680 | 3,300 | 7,450 | 11,000 |
| - - | - - | - - | - - | - - | - - | 132,000 | 111,425 | 110,000 |
| - - | - - | - - | - - | - - | 800 | 2,100 | 2,150 | 2,785 |
| - - | - - | - - | - - | - - | 10,000 | 23,360 | 21,760 | 19,300 |
| - - | - - | - - | - - | - - | 700 | 4,050 | 4,600 | 5,000 |
| - - | - - | 10,153 | 15,000 | 15,000 | 12,000 | 9,600 | 9,600 | 9,600 |
| - - | - - | - - | 7,368 | 13,137 | 7,468 | 2,880 | — | |
| - - | - - | - - | - - | - - | 240 | 3,072 | 312 | 120 |
| - - | - - | - - | - - | - - | - - | - - | - - | 31,890 |
| - - | - - | - - | - - | - - | - - | 240 | 3,360 | 2,200 |
| - - | - - | - - | - - | - - | - - | - - | 1,700 | — |
| - - | - - | - - | - - | - - | - - | 6,600 | 1,500 | — |
| - - | - - | - - | - - | - - | - - | - - | 950 | 3,950 |
| - - | - - | - - | - - | 2,920 | 696 | 650 | 1,368 | 900 |
| - - | - - | - - | - - | - - | - - | - - | 2,550 | — |
| - - | - - | - - | - - | - - | - - | - - | 2,020 | — |
| - - | - - | - - | - - | - - | - - | - - | 400 | — |
| - - | - - | - - | - - | - - | 500 | 480 | 480 | 480 |
| - - | - - | - - | - - | - - | - - | - - | 3,000 | 7,500 |
| - - | - - | - - | - - | - - | - - | - - | - - | 480 |
| 14,037 | — | | | | | | | |
| - - | - - | - - | - - | - - | - - | - - | - - | 149,000 |
| - - | - - | - - | - - | - - | - - | - - | - - | 70,300 |
| - - | - - | - - | - - | - - | - - | - - | - - | 1,000 |
| - - | - - | - - | - - | - - | - - | - - | - - | 7,000 |
| - - | - - | - - | - - | - - | - - | - - | - - | 120 |
| - - | - - | - - | - - | - - | - - | - - | - - | 800 |
| - - | - - | - - | - - | - - | - - | - - | - - | 3,000 |

| ——— | 1837. | 1838. | 1839. | 1840. | 1841. |
|---|---|---|---|---|---|
| SCOTCH PAPERS—*continued.* | | | | | |
| Edinburgh Musical Journal | - - | - - | - - | - - | - - |
| ,, Neal, Hemp & Co's Price Current | - - | - - | - - | - - | - - |
| ,, Young & Co's. Catalogue | - - | - - | - - | - - | - - |
| ,, C. D. Young's ditto | - - | - - | - - | - - | - - |
| ,, Berry & Co's. Report | - - | - - | - - | - - | - - |
| ,, Maxwell & Co's. Market Beriting | - - | - - | - - | - - | - - |
| ,, M'Lean & Co's. Price Current | - - | - - | - - | - - | - - |
| ,, Grand Lodge of Scotland Report | - - | - - | - - | - - | - - |
| ,, Northern Ensign | - - | - - | - - | - - | - - |
| ,, Evening Post and Scottish Journal | - - | - - | - - | - - | - - |
| ,, Observer | - - | - - | - - | 65,000 | 30,000 |
| ,, True Scotsman | - - | - - | - - | 43,590 | 67,700 |
| ,, Literary Circular | - - | - - | - - | 10,000 | - - |
| ,, Scottish Pilot | - - | - - | - - | 35,250 | 27,450 |
| ,, Intelligencer | - - | - - | - - | 11,000 | 7,150 |
| ,, National | - - | - - | - - | - - | - - |
| ,, Local Advertiser | - - | - - | - - | 4,000 | 5,000 |
| ,, Phœnix | - - | - - | - - | - - | 23,500 |
| Elgin Courant | 18,000 | 20,848 | 28,000 | 25,000 | 31,000 |
| ,, Courier | - - | - - | - - | - - | - - |
| Fife Herald | 42,000 | 41,869 | 41,000 | 38,000 | 41,500 |
| ,, Journal | 22,200 | 28,050 | 30,000 | 28,000 | 30,500 |
| ,, Advertiser | - - | - - | - - | 500 | - - |
| Forres Gazette | 3,920 | 4,222 | 6,500 | 8,000 | 5,500 |
| Falkirk Herald | - - | - - | - - | - - | - - |
| Glasgow Courier | 120,000 | 142,000 | 143,000 | 160,000 | 150,000 |
| ,, North British Mail | - - | - - | - - | - - | - - |
| ,, Chronicle | 62,020 | 68,000 | 66,500 | 68,750 | 59,500 |
| ,, Herald | 265,000 | 280,000 | 304,900 | 333,000 | 319,641 |
| ,, Saturday Evening Post | 22,700 | 46,200 | 61,000 | 74,000 | 105,500 |
| ,, Scottish Guardian | 118,000 | 120,200 | 132,475 | 124,000 | 120,000 |
| ,, Constitutional | 46,500 | 40,000 | 64,110 | 99,090 | 127,739 |
| ,, Scottish Reformers' Gazette | 99,850 | 112,500 | 120,000 | 123,960 | 144,840 |
| ,, Scottish Temperance Review | - - | - - | - - | - - | - - |
| ,, Citizen Scots' Times | 33,750 | 37,000 | 32,700 | — | |
| ,, Christian News | - - | - - | - - | - - | - - |
| ,, Day Star | - - | - - | - - | - - | - - |
| ,, British Friend | - - | - - | - - | - - | - - |
| ,, Examiner | - - | - - | - - | - - | - - |
| ,, Liberator | 87,000 | 13,000 | — | | |
| ,, Railway and Shipping Journal | - - | - - | - - | - - | - - |
| ,, Shipping List | - - | - - | - - | - - | 12,000 |
| ,, Magazine on Punishment | - - | - - | - - | - - | - - |
| ,, The Mail | - - | - - | 21,000 | 26,000 | 24,000 |
| ,, Daily Mail | - - | - - | - - | - - | - - |
| ,, North British Telegraph | - - | - - | - - | - - | - - |
| ,, Grain Market | - - | - - | - - | - - | - - |
| ,, Practical Mechanics' Journal | - - | - - | - - | - - | - - |
| ,, Murray's Time Table | - - | - - | - - | - - | - - |
| ,, Milne & Co's. Corn Circular | - - | - - | - - | - - | - - |
| ,, Sentinel | - - | - - | - - | - - | - - |
| ,, Argus | 114,500 | 116,000 | 107,300 | 97,000 | 104,000 |
| ,, Citizen | - - | - - | - - | - - | - - |
| ,, Journal | - - | - - | - - | 14,500 | 16,050 |
| ,, Patriot | - - | - - | - - | 68,500 | 59,185 |
| ,, Scottish Times | - - | - - | - - | 12,000 | 2,000 |
| ,, Scottish Temperance Journal | - - | - - | - - | 1,920 | 2,922 |

| 1842. | 1843. | 1844. | 1845. | 1846. | 1847. | 1848. | 1849. | 1850. |
|---|---|---|---|---|---|---|---|---|
| - - | - - | - - | - - | - - | - - | - - | - - | 100 |
| - - | - - | - - | - - | - - | - - | - - | - - | 4,980 |
| - - | - - | - - | - - | - - | - - | - - | - - | 27,500 |
| - - | - - | - - | - - | - - | - - | - - | - - | 9,300 |
| - - | - - | - - | - - | - - | - - | - - | - - | 6,000 |
| - - | - - | - - | - - | - - | - - | - - | - - | 7,000 |
| - - | - - | - - | - - | - - | - - | - - | - - | 4,000 |
| - - | - - | - - | - - | - - | - - | - - | - - | 450 |
| - - | - - | - - | - - | - - | - - | - - | - - | 1,128 |
| - - | - - | - - | - - | 43,500 | — | | | |
| 60,000 | 50,000 | 42,500 | — | | | | | |
| 17,050 | 6,000 | — | | | | | | |
| 2,000 | 10,000 | — | | | | | | |
| 13,860 | — | | | | | | | |
| 10,140 | — | | | | | | | |
| 14,500 | — | | | | | | | |
| 14,500 | — | | | | | | | |
| — | | | | | | | | |
| 29,000 | 25,800 | 27,500 | 26,950 | 28,000 | 25,000 | 30,000 | 26,000 | 30,000 |
| - - | - - | - - | 16,000 | 17,000 | 23,000 | 16,150 | 18,500 | 19,350 |
| 39,300 | 39,500 | 36,000 | 47,850 | 48,820 | 38,500 | 34,000 | 36,500 | 37,500 |
| 28,000 | 26,000 | 28,000 | 32,000 | 31,300 | 38,200 | 30,000 | 27,000 | 28,500 |
| 18,825 | 14,675 | - - | - - | 2,000 | 4,840 | 12,710 | 9,325 | 11,000 |
| 4,900 | 7,000 | 5,500 | 6,120 | 5,500 | 5,800 | 5,500 | 4,998 | 5,750 |
| - - | - - | - - | - - | 6,000 | 7,700 | 8,000 | 8,700 | 13,600 |
| 150,000 | 150,500 | 139,500 | 140,000 | 140,000 | 135,000 | 110,900 | 100,000 | 100,000 |
| - - | - - | - - | - - | - - | 435,980 | 558,000 | 243,350 | 229,000 |
| 78,500 | 28,000 | 63,100 | 56,000 | 79,950 | 76,309 | 68,000 | 78,000 | 78,000 |
| 348,620 | 358,000 | 366,250 | 380,000 | 397,931 | 390,000 | 390,000 | 390,000 | 391,000 |
| 176,000 | 188,300 | 180,050 | 207,250 | 248,000 | 271,600 | 374,000 | 459,000 | 458,000 |
| 90,000 | 121,000 | 87,000 | 100,000 | 110,000 | 113,000 | 107,000 | 110,000 | 110,100 |
| 110,000 | 81,000 | 75,000 | 98,000 | 80,000 | 90,000 | 79,850 | 62,500 | 73,000 |
| 203,850 | 172,000 | 135,000 | 140,000 | 131,000 | 160,000 | 129,000 | 121,000 | 122,000 |
| 960 | 1,200 | 3,370 | 3,500 | 2,000 | 2,000 | 10,890 | 12,950 | 5,760 |
| - - | - - | - - | - - | 22,640 | 79,829 | 75,680 | 79,624 | 81,000 |
| - - | - - | - - | - - | 2,640 | 6,379 | 5,330 | 4,920 | 2,880 |
| - - | 18,000 | 21,500 | 18,500 | 22,000 | 23,200 | 16,000 | 18,000 | 19,500 |
| - - | - - | 95,000 | 114,000 | 129,500 | 112,800 | 139,000 | 138,000 | 150,000 |
| - - | - - | - - | 13,000 | 39,000 | 36,000 | 26,000 | 19,500 | 17,500 |
| 48,500 | 36,000 | 33,000 | 21,000 | — | | | | |
| - - | - - | - - | - - | 2,600 | — | | | |
| 18,000 | 15,000 | 9,000 | - - | - - | - - | - - | 74,750 | 73,464 |
| - - | - - | - - | - - | - - | - - | - - | 234,690 | 229,000 |
| - - | - - | - - | - - | - - | - - | 2,590 | 7,460 | 17,720 |
| - - | - - | - - | - - | - - | - - | - - | - - | 1,200 |
| - - | - - | - - | - - | - - | - - | - - | 290 | 911 |
| - - | - - | - - | - - | - - | - - | - - | - - | 960 |
| - - | - - | - - | - - | - - | - - | - - | - - | 3,000 |
| - - | - - | - - | - - | - - | - - | - - | - - | 78,000 |
| 104,020 | 54,000 | 16,000 | 66,000 | 82,000 | 57,800 | 57,501 | — | |
| 14,500 | 108,000 | 101,500 | 81,000 | 116,000 | 126,000 | 121,000 | 113,500 | 110,000 |
| 14,000 | 12,000 | 6,000 | 6,000 | 9,000 | — | | | |
| — | | | | | | | | |
| — | | | | | | | | |
| — | | | | | | | | |

| | 1837. | 1838. | 1839. | 1840. | 1841. |
|---|---|---|---|---|---|
| SCOTCH PAPERS—*continued.* | | | | | |
| Greenock Advertiser | 57,022 | 55,000 | 62,000 | 66,325 | 73,500 |
| „ Record | - - | - - | - - | - - | - - |
| Galashiels Border Advertiser | - - | - - | - - | - - | - - |
| Inverness Courier | 57,600 | 58,200 | 64,000 | 61,500 | 68,487 |
| „ Advertiser | - - | - - | - - | 31,000 | 26,000 |
| „ Journal | - - | - - | - - | - - | - - |
| „ Herald | - - | - - | - - | - - | - - |
| Kelso Mail | 50,000 | 49,000 | 43,000 | 52,000 | 50,000 |
| „ Chronicle | 34,000 | 34,000 | 34,000 | 28,000 | 30,000 |
| „ Fear Tathicknain Beann | - - | - - | - - | - - | - - |
| Kinross Advertiser | - - | - - | - - | - - | - - |
| Kirkaldy Recorder | - - | - - | - - | - - | - - |
| Kilmarnock Journal | 25,812 | 24,250 | 24,400 | 23,000 | 25,000 |
| „ Herald | - - | - - | - - | - - | - - |
| Lanark Advertiser | - - | - - | - - | - - | - - |
| Montrose Review | 47,975 | 63,000 | 63,000 | 62,000 | 65,109 |
| „ Standard | 15,000 | 16,000 | 16,000 | 16,000 | 18,000 |
| Nairn Mirror | - - | - - | - - | - - | 8,000 |
| Peebles Advertiser | - - | - - | - - | - - | - - |
| Paisley Advertiser | 32,000 | 29,200 | 33,500 | 30,000 | 30,000 |
| Perth Courier | 19,000 | 18,000 | 24,000 | 18,000 | 21,072 |
| „ Advertiser | 39,500 | 41,500 | 45,980 | 61,200 | 60,000 |
| „ Constitutional | 37,000 | 37,500 | 29,000 | 29,100 | 32,000 |
| „ Chronicle | 28,225 | 20,960 | 19,800 | 22,000 | 18,000 |
| „ Independent | - - | - - | - - | 14,280 | 14,200 |
| Renfrew Advertiser | - - | - - | - - | - - | - - |
| Stirling Journal | 36,000 | 39,500 | 45,000 | 42,000 | 38,000 |
| „ Observer | 42,750 | 42,000 | 39,000 | 48,150 | 44,000 |
| Stonehaven Journal | - - | - - | - - | - - | - - |
| Stranraer Galway Register | - - | - - | - - | - - | - - |
| Thurso Caithness Chronicle | - - | - - | - - | - - | - - |
| Wigtonshire Free Press | - - | - - | - - | - - | - - |
| Wick John O'Groat's Journal | 39,750 | 33,500 | 37,300 | 37,500 | 37,000 |
| „ Northern Star | 18,720 | 12,000 | 3,500 | — | |

| 1842. | 1843. | 1844. | 1845. | 1846. | 1847. | 1848. | 1849. | 1850. |
|---|---|---|---|---|---|---|---|---|
| 65,000 | 64,125 | 57,000 | 52,000 | 58,000 | 68,000 | 60,000 | 62,500 | 65,480 |
| - - | - - | - - | - - | - - | - - | - - | - - | 8,640 |
| - - | - - | 27,000 | 25,000 | 26,000 | 24,200 | 23,175 | 19,170 | 22,000 |
| 58,750 | 60,750 | 62,200 | 74,000 | 88,000 | 93,525 | 94,000 | 96,000 | 90,000 |
| 26,000 | 24,000 | 18,000 | 16,000 | 18,500 | 17,000 | 11,000 | 48,000 | 80,000 |
| - - | 33,500 | — | | | | | | |
| - - | - - | 2,400 | — | | | | | |
| 30,000 | 43,000 | 43,000 | 43,000 | 44,000 | 43,000 | 40,000 | 44,000 | 41,000 |
| 22,000 | 27,000 | 25,000 | 24,000 | 27,250 | 22,900 | 26,000 | 27,900 | 28,000 |
| - - | - - | - - | - - | - - | - - | 11,000 | 5,500 | 165 |
| - - | - - | - - | - - | - - | - - | 1,750 | 1,460 | 3,650 |
| - - | - - | - - | - - | - - | - - | 3,525 | 3,528 | — |
| 14,036 | 21,000 | 21,500 | 20,000 | 20,700 | 11,000 | 17,000 | 19,000 | 19,000 |
| - - | - - | - - | 28,620 | 30,825 | 32,100 | 12,334 | — | — |
| - - | - - | - - | - - | - - | - - | - - | 150 | 1,343 |
| 58,500 | 60,000 | 55,048 | 61,150 | 67,000 | 72,000 | 67,200 | 71,000 | 65,500 |
| 37,000 | 16,000 | 18,000 | 18,000 | 16,000 | 19,000 | 36,000 | 44,500 | 59,000 |
| 6,500 | 6,500 | 4,000 | 8,500 | 8,000 | 9,000 | 9,500 | 8,500 | 8,000 |
| - - | - - | - - | 2,285 | 2,900 | 3,622 | 3,908 | 2,138 | 4,272 |
| 27,000 | 21,000 | 10,325 | — | | | | | |
| 18,000 | 18,000 | 18,000 | 22,000 | 21,000 | 15,000 | 18,875 | 15,000 | 65,000 |
| 55,000 | 51,500 | 51,000 | 48,000 | 52,000 | 56,000 | 60,000 | 68,000 | 65,000 |
| 24,000 | 24,000 | 24,000 | 16,000 | 24,000 | 23,000 | 17,000 | 17,000 | 16,000 |
| 3,500 | — | | | | | | | |
| 14,880 | 5,280 | — | | | | | | |
| - - | - - | 18,000 | 31,000 | 28,000 | 28,500 | 36,500 | - - | 7,000 |
| 34,000 | 37,000 | 32,000 | 28,000 | 36,000 | 30,000 | 30,000 | 31,050 | 28,000 |
| 34,299 | 34,650 | 33,750 | 32,650 | 30,000 | 30,000 | 30,000 | 32,500 | 32,500 |
| - - | - - | - - | - - | 10,000 | 11,500 | 8,450 | 8,800 | 7,750 |
| - - | - - | 3,870 | 5,700 | 18,000 | 3,000 | — | | |
| - - | - - | - - | - - | - - | 8,110 | — | | |
| - - | 49,500 | 32,000 | 28,580 | 28,000 | 38,000 | 30,000 | 35,000 | 35,000 |
| 35,000 | 31,500 | 31,600 | 32,000 | 37,000 | 41,000 | 43,500 | 41,000 | 36,150 |

## WELSH PAPERS. - - - - -

| —— | 1837. | 1838. | 1839. | 1840. | 1841. |
|---|---|---|---|---|---|
| Cambrian | 89,000 | 92,500 | 90,500 | 91,000 | 90,000 |
| Carmarthen Journal | 47,118 | 39,000 | 40,000 | 48,100 | 48,000 |
| Carnarvon and Denbigh Herald | 39,700 | 42,345 | 36,400 | 37,650 | 39,450 |
| Cornubian | — | | | | |
| Cronid Yr Oes | 5,400 | 20,750 | 17,850 | 9,000 | — |
| Cylchgrawn Rhydidd | - - | - - | - - | - - | 4,350 |
| Chronicle Cymru | - - | - - | - - | - - | - - |
| Llanelly Advertiser | - - | - - | - - | - - | - - |
| Merthyr Guardian | 61,475 | 46,000 | 46,000 | 44,500 | 50,880 |
| ,, Chronicle | 18,300 | — | | | |
| Monmouthshire Merlin | - - | - - | 100,000 | 74,000 | 74,000 |
| ,, Beacon | 9,000 | 37,000 | 38,500 | 23,000 | 29,000 |
| ,, Gazette | - - | - - | - - | - - | - - |
| ,, Advertiser | - - | - - | - - | 4,000 | 6,380 |
| North Wales Chronicle | 22,836 | 20,500 | 24,000 | 22,000 | 24,000 |
| ,, Gazette | - - | - - | - - | - - | - - |
| Pembrokeshire Herald | - - | - - | - - | - - | - - |
| Silurian | 41,950 | 36,500 | 35,0 00 | 30,000 | 27,000 |
| South Wales Reporter | 5,500 | — | | | |
| Swansea Journal | - - | - - | - - | - - | - - |
| ,, and Glamorgan Herald | - - | - - | - - | - - | - - |
| ,, and Neath Advertiser | - - | - - | - - | - - | - - |
| Tenby and Pembrokeshire Chronicle | - - | - - | - - | - - | - |
| Udgorn Cymru | - - | - - | - - | - - | - - |
| Welshman | 51,276 | 44,500 | 37,000 | 35,200 | 42,950 |
| Y Bryton | 8,000 | 6,281 | 6,000 | 3,000 | — |
| Y Papyz Newydd Cymreag | 2,700 | — | | | |
| Y Protestant | - - | - - | - - | 32,000 | 18,600 |
| Yr Amseram | - - | - - | - - | - - | - - |
| Yr Yypinr | - - | - - | - - | - - | - - |
| Y Cymro | - - | - - | - - | - - | - - |
| Y Geimogneth | - - | - - | - - | - - | - - |

Registrar of Warrants Office, Inland Revenue,
Somerset House, 23 July 1851.

## - - - - - WELSH PAPERS.

| 1842. | 1843. | 1844. | 1845. | 1846. | 1847. | 1848. | 1849. | 1850. |
|---|---|---|---|---|---|---|---|---|
| 84,000 | 84,000 | 70,000 | 67,967 | 40,475 | 68,000 | 68,000 | 72,000 | 61,000 |
| 44,000 | 41,050 | 51,900 | 40,800 | 77,000 | 40,180 | 40,700 | 39,000 | 36,435 |
| 41,100 | 40,500 | 42,000 | 41,000 | 48,000 | 51,450 | 57,900 | 66,000 | 77,500 |
| 2,600 | — | | | | | | | |
| 10,600 | — | | | | | | | |
| - - | - - | - - | - - | - - | - - | 2,110 | — | |
| 58,000 | 45,000 | 39,500 | 46,000 | 51,600 | 62,000 | 70,000 | 63,000 | 62,998 |
| 60,500 | 64,000 | 64,600 | 63,000 | 66,000 | 72,000 | 75,000 | 75,000 | 82,500 |
| 27,000 | 29,000 | 26,500 | 27,500 | 27,000 | 27,000 | 26,000 | 26,500 | 27,500 |
| - - | - - | - - | - - | - - | - - | - - | - - | 3,440 |
| — | | | | | | | | |
| 27,000 | 22,150 | 22,000 | 22,000 | 22,250 | 22,500 | 18,000 | 15,400 | 38,600 |
| - - | - - | - - | - - | - - | - - | - - | - - | 2,100 |
| - - | 6,000 | 32,000 | 30,600 | 42,000 | 36,700 | 36,000 | 42,700 | 36,000 |
| 29,000 | 23,425 | 23,000 | 25,500 | 22,072 | 23,000 | 20,036 | 22,000 | 19,000 |
| 1,000 | 35,800 | 32,100 | 13,500 | — | | | | |
| - - | - - | - - | - - | - - | 20,000 | 48,500 | 44,000 | 48,000 |
| - - | - - | - - | - - | - - | - - | - - | 1,000 | 1,000 |
| - - | - - | - - | - - | 19,200 | 14,815 | — | | |
| - - | - - | - - | - - | - - | - - | - - | 960 | — |
| 46,000 | 45,000 | 47,650 | 44,000 | 48,000 | 49,000 | 44,000 | 39,000 | 36,000 |
| 10,500 | 12,000 | 10,500 | 11,000 | 7,500 | 8,000 | 3,000 | — | |
| - - | 9,000 | 17,950 | 43,775 | 64,000 | 50,240 | 40,600 | 101,280 | 86,975 |
| - - | - - | - - | 3,600 | — | | | | |
| - - | - - | - - | - - | - - | 2,000 | 28,884 | 19,137 | 22,000 |
| - - | - - | - - | - - | - - | - - | - - | - - | 204 |

*W. Watson*, Registrar.

# ANALYSIS OF INDEX.

ALPHABETICAL and CLASSIFIED LIST of the PRINCIPAL HEADINGS in the following INDEX, with the Paging at which they will be respectively found.

# INDEX.

[*N.B.*—In this Index, the *Figures* following *Rep.* refer to the Page of the Report; those following the Names of the Witnesses to the Questions of the *Evidence*, and those following *App.* to the Page of the Appendix.]

## A.

*Acts of Parliament.* The duty on newspapers is imposed by the Act 6 & 7 Will. 4, c. 76; amount of the duty, *Rep.* 4——Reference to the Acts of Parliament which regulate the proceedings; nature and object of the various sections of the Act 6 & 7 Will. 4, c. 76, *Timm* 4——The principal Act is the 6 & 7 Will. 4, c. 76, which imposes the present stamp duty of one penny upon newspapers, and a halfpenny upon supplements, *ib.*——Section 4 of the Act 6 & 7 Will 4, c. 76, declares that the newspapers mentioned in the schedule shall be subject to the regulations of this Act, *ib.*——And that it shall be sufficient to describe any such paper as is contained in this schedule by the word "newspaper," *ib.*——The whole of the Acts of Parliament bearing upon the question of the newspaper press were consolidated by the Act 6 & 7 Will. 4, c. 76, except the 60 Geo. 3, and 1 Will. 4, *ib.* 14–16.

*See* also *Transmission of Newspapers*, 2.

*Ad Valorem Duty.* Witness does not see his way clear as to the adoption of an *ad valorem* duty upon newspapers, or an *ad valorem* duty upon letters, *Russell* 1530, 1531——If it is necessary to obtain a revenue from newspapers, witness would propose obtaining it by charging an *ad valorem* duty, allowing the public to publish newspapers at any price they please, *Hickson* 3193. 3209–3212. 3214–3233.

*ADVERTISEMENT DUTY:*

1. *Generally.*
2. *Injurious effects of the Advertisement Duty.*

1. *Generally:*

The 11th section of the Act 6 & 7 Will. 4, c. 76, directs that the printers and publishers of a newspaper shall give security for the payment of the advertisement duty by bond, with sufficient securities, to the satisfaction of the Commissioners, *Timm* 5——The 13th section of the Act 6 & 7 Will. 4, c. 76, directs that copies of newspapers shall be delivered to the Commissioners of Stamps and Taxes by the printer, for the purpose of assessing the advertisement duty, and also for the purpose of being filed as evidence, *ib.*——A printed copy of every pamphlet or paper containing advertisements is to be delivered to the Commissioners, that they may assess the duty upon the advertisements contained in it, *ib.*——Observations relative to the advertisement duty, *Cassell* 1337, 1338.

2. *Injurious effects of the Advertisement Duty:*

The effect of the advertisement duty in a commercial town like Liverpool is most injurious, *Whitty* 644–648——Evidence showing that the advertisement duty is evaded by advertisements being inserted in books; this is a great injury to newspapers and periodicals, *Collett* 965–971——All the newspaper proprietors regard the advertisement duty as the greatest oppression which they have to suffer, *ib.* 997. 1017, 1018——Difficulties which publishers have to contend with by the regulations as to advertisement duty; evil effects thereof, *Cassell* 1431–1438.

Remarks generally as to the evil effects of the duty on advertisements, as pressing unjustly on certain newspapers, *Greeley* 2978–2989——The advertisement

Report, 1851—*continued.*

*ADVERTISEMENT DUTY*—continued.

2. *Injurious effects of the Advertisement Duty*—continued.

tisement duty tends to limit the circulation of newspapers, while the revenue arising from the penny stamp depends upon the number circulated, *Greeley* 2978-2988——From this it appears inconsistent that if Government is disposed to tax the press, it should impose two sorts of tax, the one tending to lessen the amount received from the other, *ib.* 2982-2988.

*See* also *Paper Duty.* *Penny Newspapers.*

*Advertisements.* With respect to papers printed at less intervals than twenty-six days, containing any, or principally, advertisements, being legally liable to duty, the Committee are of opinion that the circulation of these papers must be restricted by the stamp, and the facilities to the public of advertising being thereby considerably lessened, *Rep.* 6——One definition of a newspaper in the Act is, "Any paper printed in any part of the United Kingdom, weekly, or oftener, or at intervals not exceeding twenty-six days, containing only, or principally, advertisements," *Keogh* 499——This law is not violated; there are a great number of these advertising publications which are registered, and pay the duty with perfect regularity; witness never heard of their being published without a stamp, *ib.* 499, 500.

The advertisements are the chief element of profit to which the proprietors of newspapers look, *Collett* 997——Remarks relative to the advertisements contained in the London papers, *Hunt* 2355——It is likely that the removal of the stamp would have a tendency to bring into existence a number of local papers in the country market towns; the local advertisements would afford an opportunity for their establishment, *ib.* 2356-2360——The principal profit derived by the American newspapers is from the advertisements, *Greeley* 2664——Amount charged for advertisements in the American papers; large amount of income received from advertisements, *ib.* 2978.

*See* also *Circulation.* *Expense of Newspapers.* "*Stroud Observer.*" "*Times,*" The.

*Agents.* Objection of the news agents to the reduction of the newspaper stamp in 1836, in consequence of the reduction of their profits; they are also unfavourable to the removal of the penny stamp from the same cause, *Smith* 2930-2934——The tendency of the abolition of the stamp would be to concentrate the news agents' business into fewer hands; witness would be able to convey newspapers at a much less cost than the Post-office, *ib.* 2932-2934.

*See* also *Newsvenders.* *Railways.* "*Times,*" The.

*Agricultural Labourers.* Frequency of agricultural labourers forming themselves into clubs for the purpose of subscribing to a newspaper; the removal of the stamp would be an advantage to this class of the community, *Cassell* 1429——Opinion that nothing would have so great an effect in improving the feelings of agricultural labourers as a reduction in the price of newspapers, *Spenser* 2367-2369. 2383-2391——Opinion that the abolition of the stamp would lead to increased reading habits among the agricultural classes, by enabling them more frequently to obtain newspapers, *Watkinson* 2689, 2690.

*See* also *Working Classes.*

Report, 1851—*continued.*

*AMERICAN PRESS:*

1. *Generally.*
2. *Local Character of the American Press.*
3. *Comparison between the Character of the English and of the American Press.*
4. *Comparison between the Price.*

1. *Generally:*

Witness cannot comprehend the operation of the stamp on newspapers; it would be impracticable under the institutions of America, *Greeley* 2614——Statistical information as to the newspaper press of America, *ib.* 2661–2663——Observations on the suggestion in the United States to control the press, by making newspapers liable to stamp duty, and requiring the publishers to give security, as in France, *ib.* 3041.

2. *Local Character of the American Press:*

Remarks relative to the character of the Americans, and the American papers; they are superior to the English press in coming in contact with the people, *Spenser* 2420–2422. 2425–2445——The newspaper press of America is more local in its character than the British press; manner in which news is obtained, *Greeley* 2639–2 44——Evidence as to the number of newspapers in America, and their circulation; their circulation is more local than that of the British press, *ib.* 2990–3004 ——The newspaper press has much greater influence upon the public opinion in the United States than in this country, *ib.* 3060, 3061.

3. *Comparison between the Character of the English and of the American Press:*

Character of the papers published in America; nature of the talent employed on them, *Whitty* 613–617——Witness considers that the freedom of the press in America acts as a kind of safety-valve for public opinion, *ib.* 640–642——In regard to moral character, the American press is quite equal to our own, *ib.* 660–666. 673. 691–704——Witness is aware that in this country an opinion prevails extensively, adverse to the respectability of the American press, but it is an entirely wrong one, *ib.* 665——Scurrility or personality is not common to the publications of America, *Greeley* 3035, 3036.

Inferiority of the American newspapers to the English papers; the worst of ours are better than the best of theirs, *Morris* 2114–2120. 2147——Inferiority of both the American and French newspapers to the English papers, in point of news, *Hunt* 2326–2328. 2347.

4. *Comparison between the Price:*

As regards price, taking quantity for quantity, the price in Ameriea is less than one-third of our own, *Whitty* 667–668——This is a great anvantage to any community having a free constitutional government, *ib.* 669——If we were free in England from the taxes on knowledge, as they are popularly called, we should have as cheap and as good a press as they have in America, and a much better one than we have now, *ib.* 670–673. 691–704——Remarks relative to the cheap publication of newspapers in America; the removal of the stamp would not enable British publishers to publish newspapers on equal

Report, 1851—*continued.*

*AMERICAN PRESS*—continued.

4. *Comparison between the Price*—continued.

equal terms with the Americans, in consequence of advertisement duty, *Cassell* 1430, 1431. 1438——Impossibility of newpapers being published in England as cheaply as in America, even if the stamp be abolished, *Russell* 1576–1578.

*See* also *Advertisements. Copyright of News. Editors. Electric Telegraph. Libel. Low Publications. New York.* "*New York Herald.*" "*New York Tribune.*" *Penny Newspapers. Postage. Price of Newspapers. Printing Machinery. Transmission of Newspapers,* 3. *Working Classes.*

*Anderson, George.* (Analysis of his Evidence.)—Has written for the publication called the "Ratepayer," but is not connected with the paper in any other way, 2453, 2454——Remarks relative to the publication of the "Ratepayer" as a monthly unstamped periodical; communication received from Board of Inland Revenue requiring that paper to be stamped, 2455–2473——Since the communication from the Board of Inland Revenue, the paper has been stamped, and is now a weekly newspaper, 2462–2472.

"*Annual Register.*" Grounds on which witness forms the opinion that the "Annual Register" does not come within the scope of the law, *Timm* 128–145.

*Applegarth's Printing Press.* See *Printing Machinery.*

"*Athenæum,*" The. Frequency of news being published in the "Athenæum," which is to a great extent unstamped, *Bucknall* 1113. 1140.

*See* also *Class Publications. Partly Stamped Publications.*

B.

*Bad Publications.* Opinion that improper papers are read very extensively by the working and poorer classes for the want of better; illustration of this opinion, *Whitty* 587–590——If good newspapers were sold at a low price there would be few or no bad publications issued; grounds for this assertion, *ib.* 598–601. 674–690. 706–721——Demoralising effect of the low-priced unstamped periodicals and novels; the removal of the stamp duty would enable useful information to be circulated, which would drive out bad publications, *Bucknall* 1215–1225.

*See* also *Immoral Publications. Low Publications. Obscene Publications. Pernicious Publications.*

*Blasphemous Publications.* See *Libel.*

*Bokenham, William.* (Analysis of his Evidence.)—Superintending President of the Inland Office of the Post Office, 1973——The transmision of newspapers comes under witnesses's immediate supervision, 1974——Witness concurs in the estimate prepared by Mr. Hill, as to the average number of newspapers transmitted

Report, 1851—*continued.*

*Bokenham, William.* (Analysis of his Evidence)—*continued.* transmitted through the London Post Office, 1975, 1976——Examination to which newspapers are subject to detect fraud and evasion of postage, 1977–1989. 2004, 2005——A strict and effectual examination of all newspapers would be the cause of considerable expense and delay in the transmission of the mails, 1985——There are no systematic frauds carried on to any extent; they are usually individual attempts at evasion, 1986–1989.

Opinion that the present arrangement of newspaper stamps is a defective arrangement as regards the postal revenue, 1990-1992——Some few unstamped editions of periodicals are occasionally mistaken for newspapers and sent duty free; it would cost more to detect these abuses than the revenue is now defrauded of, 1993–1996. 2009–2011——All unstamped publications that are detected are charged as unpaid letters; they are universally refused, and there exists no means of tracing the party who post them, 1997–2003——Great increase of labour would result from the stamps on newspapers having to be obliterated, 2006–2115.

*Bradbury & Evans,* Messrs. Messrs. Bradbury & Evans are very extensive publishers of publications, which, however excellent, are very questionable as to their legality, *Collett* 908——Instances of this in "Punch," the "Lady's Magazine," the "Household Narrative," and "Household Words," *ib.*

*Brougham,* Lord. See *Abolition of the Duty,* 1. *Libel.*

*Bucknall Samuel George.* (Analysis of his Evidence.)—Printer and publisher at Stroud, in Gloucestershire, 1096, 1097——Has been engaged in publishing the "Stroud Observer" and the "Stroud Free Press," 1098, 1099——Evidence generally as to the nature of the "Stroud Observer," and the suppression of that paper by the Board of Inland Revenue, 1099 *et seq.*——Pecuniary loss to witness from the suppression of the "Stroud Observer;" extensive circulation of that paper; only three numbers were published, 1099–1105. 1118, 1119. 1142. 1176——Communication which passed between witness and the Board of Inland Revenue, which led to the suppression of the "Stroud Observer," 1106, 1107. 1113, 1114. 1135——Statement as to what passed at an interview witness had with Mr. Keogh, the secretary to the Board of Inland Revenue, with respect to the pending prosecution for the publication of the "Stroud Observer," on unstamped paper, 1108–1113——Remarks relative to the publication of Hansard's Parliamentary Debates, on two penny sheets of unstamped paper, 1113. 1140. 1157. 1160——Frequency of news being publishsd in the "Athenæum," which is to a great extent unstamped, 1113. 1140.

Witness considers that it is a great hardship on him to be prevented from publishing the "Stroud Observer," while so many unstamped papers of the same class are allowed to be published by other parties, 1113. 1135. 1142, 1143. 1177. 1198——Witness would not have dropped the "Stroud Observer" had he been in a pecuniary position to have defended himself in a court of law, as he considers he had not acted illegally; it would have been a very expensive undertaking, 1114-1117. 1163, 1164. 1171–1175——Extensive circulation of the "Stroud Observer" among the poorer class of operatives; the

Report, 1851—*continued.*

*Bucknall, Samuel George.* (Analysis of his Evidence)—*continued.*

the suppression of this paper was a great hardship on this class of the community, 1119, 1120. 1152–1156——It would not have paid to have stamped the "Stroud Observer;" it would not have sold at the increased price, 1121 ——Loss to the revenue by the suppression of the "Stroud Observer," of the amount arising from advertisement duty; this was a large amount considering the nature of the publication, 1122. 1144–1146.

Witness is now engaged in the publication of a stamped paper, the "Stroud Free Press;" price and circulation of this paper, 1123–1134——Publication of the "Law Journal," containing legal reports, on unstamped paper, 1136, 1137——Remarks as to the publication of an unstamped paper, the "Rugby Morning Advertiser;" this contains the same description of information as the "Stroud Observer," yet it has not been suppressed, 1138, 1139—— Opinion as to what does, and what does not constitute news, within the meaning of the Act, 1141. 1183–1184——Remarks as to the circulation of newspapers in Stroud; great wish among the people for a cheap local organ like the "Stroud Observer," 1146-1154——Average circulation of unstamped publications in Stroud; the number is very small, 1161, 1162.

Evidence relative to the publication of the "Dunfermline Journal," an unstamped paper, 1165, 1166. 1198–1200——Communication sent by the Inland Revenue Board to the publishers of the "Freeholder," an unstamped monthly paper; this has been entirely disregarded, and the publication continued, 1167–1169. 1178–1181——Though witness's publication was suppresed, richer publishers have been allowed to go on publishing precisely the same kind of works, they having the means of withstanding the threats of the Board of Inland Revenue, 1173–1177. 1184–1186——Proceedings at present being taken against the publishers of "Dickens's Household Narrative," to decide the legality of publishing an unstamped monthly periodical containing news, 1182, 1183.

Evidence generally relative to witness having sent an unstamped copy of the "Stroud Free Press" to the Board of Inland Revenue, and the proceedings of the Board against witness, although no copy of that publication was sold, or ever left witness's printing office, 1187–1197——Reason for witness sending on unstamped copy of that paper to the Inland Revenue Board, 1195. 1200–1203——The "Stroud Free Press" is at present carried on at a loss; could it be published without a stamp it would yield a good profit, 1203—— Expenses attending the obtaining of stamped paper from Somerset House for country newspapers; establishing district offices in various parts of the country would lessen this expense, 1204–1211——General effect of the stamp duty in preventing the diffusion of knowledge amongst the people, 1212–1215—— Demoralizing effect of the low-priced unstamped periodicals and novels; the removal of the stamp duty would enable useful information to be circulated, which would drive out the bad publications, 1215–1225.

Opinion that the tone of the press has greatly improved within the last few years; instance of this in the character of the "Weekly Dispatch," 1225–1229. 1254, 1255——Beneficial effect of free competition in newspapers, as leading to the improved character of the press; the operation of the Stamp Act limits the market and prevents newspapers being published, 1229–1235.

 1255,

Report, 1851—*continued.*

*Bucknall, Samuel George.* (Analysis of his Evidence)—*continued.*
1255, 1256——Observations as to the expense of conducting and publishing newspapers, and the profits arising from the advertisements, 1235–1246——Enormous circulation of pernicious publications at the present time; this is increased from the difficulties in the way of buying a higher priced paper, 1247–1249. 1262–1270——The reduction of the taxes upon knowledge would greatly improve the general tone of the press, and also the general condition of society, 1250——This would lead to an increased demand for literary men, and give the publishers the means to remunerate them better, 1251–1253——Remarks contained in a pamphlet, intituled the "Power of the Press," disclosing the extent and influence of the cheap, scurrilous and baneful publications, 1247. 1261, 1262——Opinion that a cheap newspaper would rival the present pernicious publications in point of interest with the lower orders, and lead to a great moral improvement, 1256–1259.

*Bunting, Christopher James.* (Analysis of his Evidence.)—Was connected with the "Norwich Reformer," 2239——Evidence relative to the "Norwich Reformer," an unstamped paper; nature of its contents; suppression of the paper by the Board of Inland Revenue from its not being stamped, 2240–2272——The newspaper stamp is extremely unpopular with the whole of the working classes, 2273–2280——The professed efforts of the Government to forward education among the labouring classes, are laughed at whilst the newspaper stamp and other taxes upon knowledge are retained, 2279, 2280——The facilities of transmission by post are valueless to most of the provincial papers, 2281–2291.

Great desire on the part of the working classes to obtain newspapers; they take more interest in reading the passing events than in such works as "Chambers' Journal," 2292–2309——The majority of the local newspapers are of a character more likely to do good than harm to the labouring classes, 2308, 2309——There is no disposition amongst the people to disagree, on religious grounds, as to the propriety of removing the existing taxes on knowledge, 2310–2314.

C.

*Capital.* See *Character of the Press,* 1. *Cheap Newspapers.*

*Cassell, John.* (Analysis of his Evidence.)—Is engaged in literary matters and in publishing works of different kinds, 1271, 1272——Witness is publisher of a monthly periodical, intituled the "Freeholder," 1273, 1274——Circumstances which led to the establishment of the "Freeholer" as an unstamped publication; character of this periodical, 1275–1280——Notice received by witness from the Board of Inland Revenue, that the "Freeholder," was liable to stamp duty; no proceedings have been taken under that notice, and witness continues the publication of the paper, 1275–1289——Large number of monthly unstamped publication in existence; almost every religious and philanthropic movement has its monthly organ, 1277——Enumeration of several of the monthly and weekly unstamped publications, which are registered as newspapers, 1277

Observations

Report, 1851—*continued.*

*Cassell, John.* (Analysis of his Evidence)—*continued.*

Observations as to the prosecution at present pending against the publisher of Dickens's "Household Narrative;" the whole question as to the liability of publications hinges upon this trial, 1283–1290——In the event of its being decided that the "Household Narrative" ought to be stamped, all monthlies will have to be stamped; but there will be great difficulty in drawing a distinction between what is an ordinary periodical and what constitutes a newspaper, 1291–1296. 1299——On those occasions a discretion must be exercised by the proper authorities as to the carrying out of the law, 1297——Inconvenience to the trade from the existing uncertainty as to the liability of publications to the stamp duty; the settlement of the question would be very satisfactory to the trade, 1298, 1299——Carrying out the present Stamp Act literally, and with the extreme rigour of the law, would be very oppressive, not only to capitalists, but it would arrest the moral and social progress of the people, 1300–1306.

Difficulties in defining what constitutes a newspaper; witness would consider it a very dangerous power for any man to be entrusted with the definition of what constitutes a newspaper, 1307–1311——There are a number of magazines giving comments upon the events of the month; were they debarred from so doing they would be dropped, and the beneficial effect to the working classes impeded, 1312–1314——Publication of unstamped Temperance Journals, in Jersey and the Isle of Man, these have been discontinued in consequence of their not being allowed to pass through the Post-office without having a postage lable affixed, 1315–1319——It would materially assist the objects of the moral and religious movements were their monthly organs permitted to contain news, and narratives of passing events, 1320, 1321——Remarks relative to the publication entitled, the "Working Man's Friend;" superior character of this work, 1322, 1323——The taste of the working classes is an elevated taste, and requires a high order of talent to suit it; improvement taking place in cheap literature generally, 1324.

If the greatest liberty were allowed to the publication of cheap literature, by the abolition of the stamp and paper duty, the superior class of periodicals would effectually counteract the influence of the more immoral publications, 1326——Vast improvement which has taken place both in the stamped and unstamped periodical publications of late years, 1327——If the decision with respect to the "Household Narrative" be favourable to Mr. Dickens, it will have a beneficial effect, as far as montly publications are concerned, 1328, 1329——In the event of the decision going against the "Household Narrative," the "Working Man's Friend" would be liable to the stamp duty; witness would be obliged, in that case, to increase the price of that publication, 1331–1344——Observations relative to the advertisement duty, 1337, 1338——Obliging witness to stamp the "Working Man's Friend" would entirely destroy it, 1345–1348.

[Second Examination.]—Were witness precluded from commenting upon the interesting public events of the day, in the "Working Man's Friend," it could not be carried on successfully, 1349–1354——Taking the whole number of newspapers published, a very small proportion pass through the Post-office, therefore the stamp levied for the facilities afforded by the Post-office is no advantage

Report, 1851—*continued.*

*Cassell, John.* (Analysis of his Evidence)—*continued.*
advantage, but the contrary, 1355-1360——Facilities afforded by the railways for the conveyance of the daily newspapers into the country; consequently, to a great extent, the public do not avail themselves of the Post-office, and the stamp is useless, 1355——The removal of the stamp duty, and charging a penny for newspapers transmitted through the post, might affect the revenue at first, but it would ultimately prove a benefit, 1361.

Grounds on which witness founds his opinion that the revenue would derive a benefit by the abolition of the stamp duty on newspapers, 1361-1414——It would be a great advantage to the whole community to abolish the stamp duty on newspapers, charging a penny for their transmission through the Post-office, 1361-1373——The competition among newspapers would be greatly increased by the removal of the stamp duty, 1415, 1416——Great number of people employed in the production of a newspaper; limiting the number of newspapers limits the employment of labour in producing them, 1417-1420——Opinion that a higher description of talent would be employed upon the unstamped press, which would lead to a greater demand for the services of literary men, 1421-1423.

The present stamp on newspapers acts as a protection to the proprietors from increased competition, 1424, 1425——The abolition of the stamp would lead to a complete revolution in the newspaper press, 1425——Repealing the penny stamp would decidedly increase the circulation of local newspapers; this would be an advantage to the different districts in the country in which they were published, 1426-1429——Frequency of agricultural labourers forming themselves into clubs for the purpose of subscribing to a newspaper; the removal of the stamp would be an advantage to this class of the community, 1429——Remarks relative to the cheap publication of newspapers in America; the removal of the stamp would not enable British publishers to publish newspapers on equal terms with the Americans, in consequence of the advertisement duty, 1430, 1431. 1438——Difficulties which publishers have to contend with by the regulations as to advertisement duty; evil effects thereof, 1431-1438.

Opinion that in the event of the removal of the stamp duty, penny newspapers might be established, and circulated with profit, 1439, 1440——Existing practice among the evening and weekly papers to copy from the daily morning papers; this is not an unfair proceeding, or any infringement of copyright, 1441-1450——Evidence as to how far any advantage would result from allowing country newspapers to be published without the stamp, the London papers still retaining the stamp for transmission through the post, 1451-1463——Manner in which the country newspapers would obtain their news in the event of the stamp being abolished, and the number of papers was increased; how far it would be fair for them to copy from the London papers, who have been at the expense of obtaining the news, 1451, 1452——Many of the newspaper proprietors might imagine that the removal of the penny stamp would affect their interests, 1463.

*Catalogues.* See *Prices Current.* *Tradesmen's Catalogues.*

*Censorship.* The result of witness's inquiries has been, that we are living under a disguised censorship of the press, *Collett* 737. 749——Generally where there

*Censorship*—continued.

there is an avowed censorship of the press there are no taxes on knowledge, no stamp duty, and generally no paper duty, *Collett* 737——Existence of a censorship of the press at the present time; explanation as to the form in which it exists, *Morris* 2208–2210. 2219.——*See* also *American Press.*

" *Chambers's Journal.*" See *Cheap Publications. Scotland.*

*CHARACTER OF THE PRESS:*

1. *Opinions that the Stamp keeps up the Tone of the Press.*
2. *Opinions that it has not this effect, and that its Abolition would improve the Character of Newspapers.*

1. *Opinions that the Stamp keeps up the Tone of the Press:*

Witness is decidedly of opinion that the stamping of newspapers is some security for their respectability, *Keogh* 421——Witness regards the registration and the duty, combined together, as securing a press of a high description, such as exists in this country, and perhaps exists in no other, *ib.* 482. 485. 490, 491——Abolishing the newspaper stamp would very likely have the effect of destroying those papers possessing the least public confidence; the papers of established reputation would not be affected, *Morris* 2024–2027. 2063–2069——Opinion that the stamp improves the character of newspapers; provided it was increased it would improve them still more, *ib.* 2155–2164.

The tone of the press has greatly improved since the reduction of the stamp from fourpence to a penny, still witness considers that great deterioration would be caused by the removal of the penny stamp, *Morris* 2179–2193. 2201–2218——Manner in which witness considers that the penny stamp tends to improve the tone of the press, *ib.* 2196–2200. 2221, 2222——Importance of the proprietors of newspapers being large capitalists, as having the effect of keeping up the respectable character of the press, *ib.*——The improved tone of the press of late years arises entirely from the great improvement in the manners, tastes, and feelings of the nation, *ib.* 2216–2218. 2220.

2. *Opinions that it has not this effect, and that its Abolition would improve the Character of Newspapers:*

Conclusion arrived at by the Committee, that the opinion which prevails to some small extent, that the maintenance of the stamp has the effect of rendering newspapers more respectable, does not rest on any good foundation, *Rep.* 10——Witness considers that cheapness would have a good effect on the quality of the newspapers, *Whitty* 602–609. 611——Opinion that the tone of the press has greatly improved within the last few years; instance of this in the character of the "Weekly Dispatch," *Bucknall* 1225–1229. 1254, 1255——Beneficial effect of free competition in newspapers, as leading to the improved character of the press; the operation of the Stamp Act limits the market, and prevents newspapers being published, *ib.* 1229–1235. 1255, 1256——Vast improvement which has taken place both in the stamped and unstamped periodicals of late years, *Cassell* 1327.

The removal of the stamp would increase the circulation of the higher description of newspapers, provided they are not encumbered by a heavy postage

Report, 1851—*continued.*

*CHARACTER OF THE PRESS*—continued.

2. *Opinions that it has not this effect, &c.*—continued.

postage duty, *Hunt* 2359——At the present all the advantage of the monopoly of the newspapers is on the side of bad men and bad principles, and the difficulty is only on the side of those who wish to do good; how witness arrives at this conclusion, *Spenser* 2370-2379——Evidence showing the manner in which the newspaper press of the country would be improved by the abolition of the stamp, *ib.* 2423, 2424——Improved character of the press since the reduction of the stamp duty; the whole tone of society has improved, and the character of the press is a reflexion of the tone of the age, *Cole* 2740——At the time of the reduction of the stamp duty, there were many predictions that the effect would be to deteriorate and injure the tone of the press, *ib.* 2741-2744.

*See* also *American Press,* 3. *Local Newspapers,* 3. *Penny Newspapers. Scotland. Taxes on Knowledge.*

*Cheap Newspapers.* Observation of the Committee that the evidence taken before them shows that great moral advantages may be expected to follow the establishment of cheap local newspapers, *Rep.* 10, 11——Witness has published a high-priced paper and also a low-priced paper, *Whitty* 569, 570——The high-priced paper answered witness's purpose best, but it did not answer the public purpose so well, *ib.* 571, 572——Opinion that cheap newspapers would pay a great deal better to the proprietors than the present high-priced papers, *ib.* 573. 612——If good newspapers were cheap, the buyers and readers would increase twenty or thirty fold, *ib.* 573-586. 601-609. 628-635——Still witness does not consider that the country would be inundated with cheap papers; a large capital being required to start them, *ib.* 609. 630-635.

Witness is aware that the London daily papers incur an immense expense for news; if sold cheap they could afford this expense and much more, *Whitty* 618——No penny or twopenny paper would ever produce the income of the "Times" if the stamp duty were taken off, nor would the "Times" do it if this were done, *ib.* 619——Grounds on which witness forms the opinion that the working classes would prefer to purchase a cheap newspaper to any other kind of cheap periodical publication, *Collett* 922-928——A cheap press would have the best possible effect, *Whitty* 636-639; *Spenser* 2392-2398. 2417-2419——Experiments which have been tried for maintaining a cheap newspaper in London, all of which have failed through the operation of the penny stamp, *Cole* 2745-2761——Manner in which witness connects these failures with the operation of the penny stamp, *ib.* 2755-2761.

In the event of the stamp being abolished it is most probable that there would be cheaper newspapers established, *Smith* 2847——Witness is prepared to admit that if the penny stamp were removed there would be a host of inferior journals to the "Times" called into existence, *Hickson* 3196——Reason why it is desirable they should be called into existence, *ib.*——Cheap newspapers circulated amongst the working classes would stimulate the habit of reading, and prepare the people for reading something better; nature of the

Report, 1851—*continued.*

*Cheap Newspapers*—continued.

the information and intelligence which such papers should contain, *Hickson* 3197–3208. 3212, 3213. 3234–3255. 3263–3266.

*See* also *Bad Publications.* *Character of the Press*, 2. *Emigration. Mechanics' Institutions.* *Penny Newspapers.* *Pernicious Publications.* "*Stroud Observer.*" *Working Classes.*

*Cheap Publications.* Of the number of cheap publications in circulation, considerably the larger proportion are of a good tendency, *Haywood* 2496–2504. Rapid increase of good cheap publications within the last twenty years, *ib.* 2529–2532——The publications which have been brought out at a cheap rate originally, under the plea of benefiting the working classes, such as the "Penny Magazine," "Chambers's Journal," &c., have missed their aim, and have been generally circulated among the middle classes, *Hickson* 3256–3259.

*See* also *Comments on News.* *Immoral Publications.* *Unstamped Publications.* *Weekly Publications.* *Working Classes.*

"*Christian Socialist,*" The. See *Partly Stamped Publications.*

*Circulars.* See *Prices Current.* *Tradesmen's Catalogues.*

*Circulation.* With regard to the operation of the stamp on the established newspapers it is obvious that, by increasing their cost, it limits the field of their circulation, *Rep.* 7——One element in the profit of newspapers is the circulation; a reduction in the price would of course add greatly to their circulation, *Collett* 998, 999——And an increase of circulation would also greatly increase the advertisements, if there were no advertisement duty, *ib.* 1000. 1017, 1018——Removing the stamp from newspapers and preventing their passing through the post free, would tend to limit their circulation within the locality of their publication, *Morris* 2089–2091——But allowing newspapers to pass through the post on the payment of a penny, instead of the present stamp, would not limit the circulation, *ib.* 2092, 2093——The abolition of the stamp would cause an enormous increase in the sale of newspapers, by the reduction of the price, *Spenser* 2366, 2367——If small weekly publications were allowed to insert news as well as literary intelligence, it would tend to increase the circulation of those papers, and act as a stimulus to the reading habits of the people, *Haywood* 2540——The stamp duty on newspapers tends greatly to limit their circulation by increasing the price, *Watkinson* 2673–2679. 2689, 2690.

*See* also *Abolition of the Duty*, 2. *Advertisement Duty*, 2. *Advertisements.* *American Press*, 2. *Daily Papers.* *Evening Papers.* *Libellous Publications.* *Monopoly.* "*New York Herald.*" *Provincial Newspapers.* "*Stroud Free Press.*" "*Stroud Observer.*" *Supplements to Newspapers.* "*Times,*" The. *Weekly Publications.*

*Class Publications.* The Board of Inland Revenue have not usually interfered with class publications confined to particular subjects, in consequence of the insertion therein of some trifling paragraphs of public news, *Rep.* 5——Exception to this rule in the case of the "Norwich Reformer," *ib.* 5, 6——Witness would say that such papers as the "Athæneum," &c., the "Builder," &c.

*Class Publications*—continued.

&c., do not serve the purpose of newspapers generally, *Timm* 52–54——Although certain class publications, such as the "Legal Observer, the "Lancet," the "Builder," &c., may sometimes contain what is, strictly speaking, news, still witness does not consider he could get a jury to say that they were newspapers, published unstamped, *ib.* 88–96. 113, 114——At the present time, any paper that confines its news to class news is not held to be a newspaper, unless that class news have some special relation to politics; instances of the "Musical Word," the "Legal Observer," and the "Builder," *Collett* 741——Remarks relative to the publications connected with moral and religious movements, as also with arts and manufactures; the circulation would be increased by their being allowed to publish news, *Haywood* 2586–2593——With respect to class publications, they have the same advantages as newspapers, when stamped, although they are not obliged to stamp the whole of their impressions; witness does not consider this any hardship on the newspapers, *Smith* 2890–2900.

*See* also "*Law Journal.*" "*Legal Observer.*" *Temperance Society.*

*Cole, Henry.* (Analysis of his Evidence.)—Has paid great attention to the operation of the newspaper stamp law, 2691——Was actively engaged in assisting Mr. Rowland Hill previously to the introduction of the penny postage, 2692–2694——At the time of the reduction of the stamp duty on newspapers, and the penny stamp fixed, it was considered as a postage duty, affording newspapers a free circulation by post; it was not considered a tax, 2695–2698. 2801——From the altered circumstances of the times the stamp is no longer a postage charge, it operates as a tax upon news, 2699——The great bulk of the London press is now taken out by railways in the morning, and the Post-office very little used, 2699. 2703——Great injustice and inconvenience of a postage of a penny being charged on all newspapers transmitted post within the three-mile circle, 2699–2707——Instance of a large number of newspapers being taken from London and posted at Brompton, in order to avoid the additional postage payable within the London district, 2699. 2705, 2706.

By the present arrangement, the stamped newspapers that go by the railway pay for a postal privilege which they do not use, 2704——Reason which led to the additional postage charge being placed on newspapers circulating within the London district, 2708, 2709——Opinion that were the newspapers allowed to pass within the London district without the impost of additional postage, the proprietors would be enabled to reduce the price of their papers, 2710–2718——At the time the penny stamp on newspapers was fixed it was contemplated that the revenue arising therefrom would be considerable, 2719——Great extent to which the penny stamp is used, as a postage, for the transmission of printed matter which does not come under the head of news; objectionable nature of this practice, 2721–2731.

Strong objections to the stamp on newspapers, it acts as a tax on knowledge; the policy of such a tax is not defensible, 2732–2739——Improved character of the press since the reduction of the stamp duty; the whole tone of society has improved, and the character of the press is a reflection of the tone of the age, 2740——At the time of the reduction of the stamp duty there

Report, 1851—*continued.*

*Cole, Henry.* (Analysis of his Evidence)—*continued.* there were many predictions that the effect would be to deteriorate and injure the tone of the press, 2741–2744——Experiments which have been tried for maintaining a cheap newspaper in London, all of which have failed, through the operation of the penny stamp, 2745-2761——Manner in which witness connects these failures with the operation of the penny stamp, 2755–2761——Opinion that in the event of the abolition of the penny stamp, the London daily papers, conducted with talent and supported with capital, could be sold at a profit for two pence or three pence, 2762, 2763.

In the event of the removal of the stamp, it would be very desirable to give the newspapers a short copyright, of say six hours; without such a copyright there would be universal piracy, 2763–2765. 2785, 2786——The abolition of the penny stamp would have the effect of increasing the number of local newspapers, 2766, 2767——Evidence generally as to the manner in which a law of copyright of news might be established, 2768–2792——The maintenance of the stamp on newspapers prevents mechanical improvements in the printing, by obliging the paper to be cut into certain sheets that the stamps may be put upon them, 2793–2800——Great difficulties in defining what is news and liable to the stamp duty; anything so difficult of definition as news is not a fit subject for a tax, 2801–2805——It would be next to impossible to levy the stamp with perfect justice, unless it was placed upon every printed sheet of periodical literature, in fact upon almost every book, 2802–2805.

Reference to the opinions expressed by the Judges, whether any periodical publication could speak of an event of yesterday without being subject to the tax, 2805——Opinion that the maintenance of the stamp on newspapers does not in the least tend to prevent the publication of libellous matter, 2806–2809——Reference to the opinion expressed by Lord Brougham, that though the laws made to restrain the press were intended to check libel, they have a very obvious tendency to lessen the security against libel, 2808, 2809.

*Collett, Collett Dobson.* (Analysis of his Evidence.)—Has been secretary for the last two years to a society, the special object of which has been to get rid of all the taxes on knowledge, and particularly the newspaper stamps, 734–735——Since witness has been secretary to this society, he has turned his attention to everything connected with newspapers, and has endeavoured to obtain all the information he could from every part of the country, 736——Conclusions witness has come to with regard to the mode in which the law is administered as to the stamping of news, 737 *et seq.*——The result of his inquiries has been, that we are living under a disguised censorship of the press, 737. 749——Generally where there is an avowed censorship of the press there are no taxes on knowledge, no stamp duty, and generally no paper duty, 737——From time when the stamp duty was first imposed, in the reign of Queen Anne, the number of newspapers has been very much diminished, 737.

Evidence showing that the meaning of the word "newspaper," the taxable articles called news, has changed from time to time 737–739——From that time to this the amount of revenue derived from newspaper stamps has never been

Report, 1851—*continued.*

*Collett, Collett Dobson.* (Analysis of his Evidence)—*continued.*

been so large as to be a serious matter of consideration, 737——Amount derived from before the reduction, from fourpence to a penny, and amount derived since 737——Reference to the number of unstamped newspapers issued about the time of the Reform Bill, 737——Opinion that the penny stamp has something of the same effect in driving the poorer classes to the unstamped press that the higher rate of of stamp used to have, but not to the same extent, 738——Evidence showing that the penny stamp does prevent the penny newspapers altogether, 738——A bad penny paper has but little circulation, and it requires a large capital to bring out a good penny paper, 738——Opinion that at the present time there is no definite meaning whatever attached to the term "newspaper," by the Stamp-office, 739 *et seq.*

About the time of the unstamped newspapers, from 1832 to 1836, there was a very definite meaning attached to it, 739——Any paper at that time that was issued oftener than once a month was put down if it contained a very small quantity of news, 739, 740——Instance of a paper called the "Harlequin," which related merely to theatricals, ; but as it gave reports and criticisms on the plays, it was deemed to contain news, and was put down, 739–741. 747——At the present time any paper that confines its news to class news, is not held to be a newspaper, unless that class news have some special relation to politics ; instances of the "Musical World," the "Legal Observer," and the "Builder," 741——Instance of the "Norwich Reformer," the organ of the Parliamentary Reform Association in Norwich, which, from its containing a column, called "Record of Progress," was demed to be a newspaper; proceedings taken by the Stamp-office with respect to this paper, and correspondence on the subject, 742–749. 758.

Opinion that the Stamp-office has a dangerous discretion as to whom they shall pick out for prosecution and whom not, 747–758——Cases of what witness considered to be a violation of the law, and which he got laid before the Board of Inland Revenue at the time of the threatened prosecution of the "Norwich Reformer;" these cases were similar to that of this paper; result of this proceeding, 758 *et seq.*——One of these cases was that of "Punch ;" grounds on which witness asserts that this publication comes under the definition of a newspaper; it comments on the public events of the day, 758. 760–775——"Punch" is as much a newspaper, according to the law, as the "Times" and "Morning Chronicle," 758——Another case brought under the notice of the Board through witness as a violation of the law was the "Reasoner ;" particulars relative to this case, 758——Another intimation was sent to the Board by a friend of witness's as respects the "Democratic Review," a Chartist paper, 758, 759.

Witness classes the faults of the Board of Inland Revenue under six heads, 776——Witness would say, in the first place, they defraud (speaking technically) the Post-office revenue, by giving to publications a false certificate of their being newspapers; way in which witness arrives at this conclusion, 776–808——This may be the fault of the law, but if so it should be altered, 789. 795–798. 805——The Board of Inland Revenue ought not to allow of any newspaper circulating under the two heads of stamped and unstamped, 789–803——The second fault witness finds with them, and which is a part of the first,

Report, 1851—*continued.*

*Collett, Collett Dobson.* (Analysis of his Evidence)—continued.

first, is, that they favour a number of registered newspapers at the expense of the rest, by allowing them to circulate a part of their impression without a stamp, thus encouraging unfair competition, 808 *et seq.*——And a great number of these actually contain that news which the law declares ought not to be contained at all, 808——Evidence showing how this regulation acts as regards unfair competition; complaints which have been made on the subject by the proprietors of the "Coventry Herald," the "Leader," and the "Caledonian Mercury," 809-812——Witness's next complaint is, that the Board neglect to enforce the law in London; instance of this in the case of the "Household Narrative," 812 *et seq.*

[Second Examination.]—Witness does not think there is any intention at all on the part of the Board of Inland Revenue to trouble themselves as to what the politics or utility of a paper may be; they simply consider that a good newspaper is a taxable article, but if it is bad they consider it is not a taxable article, and leave it alone; they do not take a political view of the case, they merely take a fiscal view of it, 843-855.

Grounds on which witness makes the assertion that the "Legal Observer" is a newspaper, 855-863——Slips or parts of a newspaper printed on a separate paper are prohibited in the country but allowed in London, 864——Instances illustrating this statement, 865-869. 873-893——If newspaper stamps were altogether abolished, it would not be possible to permit the circulation of the London papers by post free of cost, 870-872——Witness delivers in a half year's numbers of Dickens's "Household Words," showing that they contain comments and observations on news, 893-908——Witness considers that the reprinting of a speech delivered in Parliament, and published by Ridgway, is news, and liable to a stamp, 893-900.

Witness is aware that the Board of Inland Revenue is carrying on a prosecution against Dickens, for the publication of his "Household Narrative," 901——But he does not consider that this prosecution can altogether be considered *bonâ fide*; grounds on which witness forms this opinion, 901-908——If the Board had wished to try the case thoroughly they should also have proceeded against the other publications of the same publishers, 908——Bradbury & Evans are very extensive publishers of publications, which, however excellent, are very questionable as to their legality, 908——Instances of this in "Punch," the "Lady's Magazine," the "Household Narrative," and "Household Words," 908——Evidence showing that the "Household Words" contains very frequently comments on news, 908——The "Mirror of the Time" is also a publication contrary to the law; it is constantly publishing political articles, 908, 909.

Witness delivers in copies of three illegal papers, one of them called the "Expositor;" it is a paper partly stamped and partly unstamped; it has no business to contain news, 910-912——Witness could produce nearly fifty papers unstamped that illegally publish news, intelligence, or occurrences, or remarks or observations thereon, 910, 911——Instance of this in the case of "Punch," 913——Instance also of a paper called the "Red Republican," which contains political articles every week, 914, 915——Mischievous and bad publications usually fall off after a short time for want of support and notice,

*Collett, Collett Dobson.* (Analysis of his Evidence)—*continued.*

notice, 915. 918, 919——A prosecution by the Board of Inland Revenue would no doubt tend very much to increase the circulation of papers of this description by giving them publicity, 916–921——Still, if the law cannot be put in force, or the Government officers will not put it in force, or a jury will not give a verdict, then witness would say the law is bad, and should be altered, 917–920.

Grounds on which witness forms the opinion that the working classes would prefer to purchase a cheap newspaper to any other kind of cheap periodical publication, 922–927——Many of the working classes now club together to take newspapers, even when they do not altogether approve of them, for they feel it necessary to have something of the kind, 927——This has been very much the case with respect to the "Northern Star," 927——Witness is quite convinced that a good paper, a moderate paper, would have a much better chance of circulation than any of the merely violent publications, 927–929——Suggestions as to the transmission of newspapers through the Post-office, supposing the stamp to be abolished, 930 *et seq.*——In the first place, witness would propose that the management of the newspaper postage should be left entirely to the Post-office, 930——In the second place, witness would suggest that newspapers should be sent in a stamped envelope, 930. 985–989——Under the present system of stamping newspapers, by letting the stamp remain inside it is quite possible to defraud the Post-office; evidence showing that the Post-office is so defrauded, 930–950.

There is no doubt that it is the desire of the artisans and mechanics, and the various branches of the industrial classes, to get rid of the stamp on newspapers, 951-953——Opinion that if the stamp were taken off they would get their newspapers at all prices, from a halfpenny up to four-pence or five-pence, 954–964. 972–978——Evidence showing that the advertisement duty is evaded by advertisements being inserted in books; this is a great injury to newspapers and periodicals, 965-971——The working classes decidedly consider that the Government cannot be supposed really to care about education so long as they leave a tax which prohibits self-education, 979——There is no doubt that the dissemination of such knowledge as a newspaper circulates would have a tendency to promote the spread of education, and would have a beneficial effect, 979-984. 991–996. 1005-1016.

Taking off the stamp, and only making those papers pay a tax which went through the Post-office, would no doubt increase the number of local papers with extracts from the London papers, 985-996. 1005–1016——But witness does not believe that the London papers would be injured thereby, as he does not consider that their circulation would be diminished, 985-996. 1004——The advertisements are the chief element of profit to which the proprietors of newspapers look, 997——All the newspaper proprietors regard the advertisement duty as the greatest oppression which they have to suffer, 997. 1017, 1018——The next element is the profit on the circulation; a reduction in the price would of course add greatly to their circulation, 998, 999——And an increase of circulation would also greatly increase the advertisements if there were no advertisement duty, 1000. 1017, 1018.

A reduction in the price would enable the proprietors to pay more for the literary

Report, 1851—*continued.*

*Collett, Collett Dobson*—(Analysis of his Evidence)—*continued.* literary talent employed, and they would consequently obtain higher literary talent, 1001–1003——There are many party papers, the organs of a particular set of opinions, which are published even at a loss to the proprietors; among these may be named the "Christian Socialist," the "Red Republican," the "Reasoner," the "People," &c., 1019–1021——Witness delivers in a statement showing the effect of political agitation upon the number of newspapers, 1021.

*Comments on News.* Mr. Keogh and Mr. Timm are of opinion that any paper containing remarks on public news, printed at less intervals than twenty-six days, where the price is less than sixpence, or the size less than two sheets, is legally liable to stamp duty, *Rep.* 4——Observation of the Committee, that the evidence taken before them shows the great difficulty of defining remarks on news, *ib.* 6——It appears that with respect to comments on news in cheap publications, the law has been allowed to some extent to sleep, *ib.* 6, 7——If the law imposing a stamp on observations or public intelligence were carried out, nearly all the printed periodical matter, and a large portion of occasional printed matter, would be subjected to the stamp duty, *ib.* 7——On the other hand, if it be understood that the law is not to be fully observed, much unequal competition must continue to arise between the different publishers, *ib.*——And the Board of Inland Revenue will continue to be placed in the undesirable position of having to decide upon what periodicals the law is to be enforced, and in what cases its provisions may be dispensed with, *ib.*

Comments or observations may be published without a stamp, provided they are published at intervals exceeding twenty-six days, *Timm* 23——They may be published without a stamp at a less interval than twenty-six days, provided they contain a quantity of paper at least equal to two sheets, each sheet containing a quantity not less than twenty-one inches in length and seventeen in breadth, and that the publication shall be published for sale at a sum not less than 6 *d.*, *ib.* 24–32——A person may comment and observe upon news, at intervals exceeding twenty-six days, without a stamp, *Keogh* 504——But if he comments upon news at intervals of less than twenty-six days the price must be 6 *d.* or above, and the size of the publication must be two sheets of certain dimensions; probable object of this regulation, *ib.* 504–513. 518.

*See* also *Magazines.* *News*, 2. *"Punch."* *Weekly Publications.* *"Working Man's Friend."*

*Commercial Towns.* See *Advertisement Duty*, 2.

*Competition.* The competition among newspapers would be greatly increased by the removal of the stamp duty, *Cassell* 1415, 1416——The present stamp on newspapers acts as a protection to the proprietors from increased competition, *ib.* 1424, 1425——The abolition of the stamp would lead to a complete revolution in the newspaper press, *ib.* 1425——Many of the newspaper proprietors might imagine that the removal of the penny stamp would affect their interests, *ib.* 1463——Doubts as to whether the abolition of the penny stamp would lead to any increase in the number of newspapers published, *Russell* 1602–1612——The established newspapers have nothing to fear from the competition that would result from the removal of the stamp on newspapers

*Competition*—continued.

papers; the best newspapers would always get the greatest number of purchasers, whether stamped or not, *Hunt* 2340, 2341.

*See* also *Character of the Press*, 2.

*Copyright of News.* Reference by the Committee to the proposition which has been made, that some short privilege of copyright should be conferred on the established newspapers, particularly the London daily press, *Rep.* 11——Necessity for some law being established, giving the morning papers, paying for Indian and other news, a copyright in that news for a certain number of hours, *Hunt* 2319–2325. 2333–2339——Piracy of news is carried on to a great extent, to the serious loss of the leading daily papers; this would be greatly increased in the event of the removal of the stamp, unless some law of copyright was established, *ib.* 2319–2326. 2334–2339. 2348–2352——Manner in which the law might be framed to prevent the piracy of articles of news, by papers not contributing to the despatches, *ib.* 2343–2347.

The newspaper press of America does not possess any protection in the nature of copyright of news, *Greeley* 2644–2648——In the event of the removal of the stamp, it would be very desirable to give the newspapers a short copyright of, say, six hours; without such copyright there would be an universal piracy, *Cole* 2763–2765. 2785, 2786——Evidence generally as to the manner in which a law of copyright of news might be established, *ib.* 2768–2792.

*See* also *Evening Papers.*

*Country Newspapers.* See *Local Newspapers.*

*Country Readers.* The recipients of the London newspapers in the country would not obtain their papers any cheaper from the removal of the stamp, whereas those parties to whom they are now retransmitted free would have to pay a postage charge, *Smith* 2901–2916.

## D.

*Daily Papers.* Proportion of the morning daily papers that go out of London for secondary sale, *Hunt* 2329——Statement of the number of daily papers distributed by witness's house prior to the reduction of the stamp in 1836, and since that period, showing the great increase, *Smith* 2884–2889——Evidence generally relative to the circulation of the daily morning and evening press in London, showing the increase and decrease of the several papers, *ib.* 2935–2949. 2969–2971——None of the London morning papers gave the public the full benefit of the reduction of the duty from fourpence to a penny in 1836; some of the weekly papers did so, *Hickson* 3187. 3191, 3192.

*See* also *Abolition of the Duty*, 1. *Advertisements.* *Copyright of News.* *Evening papers.* *Price of Newspapers.* "*Times,*" The.

*Declarations.* See *Registration of Newspapers.*

***Democracy.*** See ***Abolition of the Duty*, 1.**

***Dickens,***

Report, 1851—*continued.*

*Dickens,* Mr. *Charles.* See "*Household Words.*" "*Narrative of Current Events.*"

*Dies for Stamping.* The third section of the Act 6 & 7 Will. 4, c. 76, provides for the preparing, under the directions of the Commissioners of Inland Revenue, of proper dies for the stamping of each newspaper, *Timm* 4.

*Draft Reports.* Draft report proposed by Mr. Milner Gibson, chairman of the Committee, *Rep.* 18–23——Draft report proposed by Mr. Rich, *ib.* 24–32.

*Drunkenness.* See *Working Classes.*

"*Dunfermline Journal.*" Evidence relative to the publication of the "Dunfermline Journal" on unstamped paper, *Bucknall* 1165, 1166. 1198–1200.

*Duty.* Publications on which the duty is declared to be payable according to the Act 6 & 7 Will. 4, c. 36, *Rep.* 4——Net produce of these duties in the year 1850, and on the average of the three years 1848, 1849, and 1850, *ib.*——Three classes of publications legally liable to the newspaper stamp, according to the evidence of Mr. Keogh and Mr. Timm, *ib.*——A proprietor pays the duty before he receives the stamps, *Keogh* 286——No stamps are issued but those that are paid for; no credit is given, *ib.* 395–397.

*See* also *Abolition of the Duty.* *Advertisement Duty.* *Paper Duty.* *Reduction of the Duty.* *Stamp Duties.*

## E.

*Edinburgh.* How far Edinburgh possesses any advantage over Glasgow and other places in Scotland, from there being a stamping department established there, *Russell* 1474–1477.

*See* also *Scotland.* *Stamping Establishments.*

*Editors.* How far able literary men are employed on the newspaper press of America; average amount of remuneration given for the services of literary men; the prices of literary labour are more moderate than in this country, *Greeley* 3046–3049.——*See* also *Literary Talent.*

EDUCATION:

1. *Importance of Newspapers as a means of Education for the People.*
2. *Objection to Newspapers as a source of Education.*

1. *Importance of Newspapers as a means of Education for the People:*

The dissemination of such knowledge as a newspaper circulates would have a tendency to promote the spread of education, and would have a beneficial effect, *Collett* 979–984. 991–996. 1005–1016; *Hunt* 2353——The working classes decidedly consider that the Government cannot be supposed really to care about education, so long as they leave a tax which prohibits self-education, *Collett* 979.——For certain subjects, witness considers newspapers a good source

Report, 1851—*continued.*

*EDUCATION*—continued.

1. *Importance of Newspapers,* &c.—continued.

source of information for the members of mechanics' institutions, *Hogg* 1054–1058. 1069–1073——Opinion as to the general effect of the stamp duty in preventing the diffusion of knowledge amongst the people, *Bucknall* 1212–1215——The professed efforts of the Government to forward education among the labouring classes are laughed at, whilst the newspaper stamp and other taxes upon knowledge are retained, *Bunting* 2279, 2280——The removal of the stamp would have a good educational effect, *Hunt* 2353.

The newspaper stamp is a great obstacle in the way of every movement for the diffusion of knowledge and the good of the people, *Spenser* 2362——Evidence generally in support of this opinion, *ib.* 2363 *et seq.*——Strong objections to the stamp on newspapers; it acts as a tax on knowledge; the policy of such a tax is not defensible, *Cole* 2732–2739——Opinion that newspaper reading is calculated to keep up the habit of reading; the newspaper is worth all the schools in the country, *Greely* 3050–3059——As an educationist witness has taken an active part in promoting the interests of the working classes, as connected with popular instruction, *Hickson* 3175.

2. *Objection to Newspapers as a source of Education:*

Witness does not look upon newspapers as a means of educating the people, *Russell* 1613–1615.

*See* also *Tax on Knowledge.* *Working Classes.*

*Electric Telegraph.* Great extent to which the electric telegraph is used by the newspapers in America; it is not used to near so great an extent by the newspapers in this country, *Greely* 3062–3068——The expense of electric telegraph despatches is enormous, but it is cheaper in America than in this country, *ib.* 3066–3068.

*Emigration.* Emigration would be very much assisted by the circulation of a cheap newspaper press, *Spenser* 2397, 2398.

*Employment of Labour.* Great number of people employed in the production of a newspaper; limiting the number of newspapers limits the employment of labour in producing them, *Cassell* 1417–1420.

*Envelopes.* Witness would suggest that newspapers should be sent into the country in a stamped envelope, *Collett* 930. 985–989——Convenience of adopting stamped wrappers for newspapers, *Hill* 1903, 1904.

*See* also *Postage Labels.*

*Established Newspapers.* See *Abolition of the Duty,* 1. *Character of the Press,* 1. *Circulation.* *Competition.* *Reduction of the Duty.*

*EVASIONS OF POSTAGE:*

1. *Extent to which, and manner in which Evasions of Postage take place.*
2. *Difficulties in the way of detecting and preventing such Evasions.*

1. *Extent*

Report, 1851—*continued.*

*EVASIONS OF POSTAGE*—continued.

1. *Extent to which, and manner in which Evasions of Postage take place:*

All newspapers with writing on them are liable to be surcharged; there is no time to examine all newspapers to see whether they have writing on them, *Parkhurst* 1681–1686——Various kinds of evasion arising out of the present newspaper arrangements; frequency of parties writing in newspapers, or enclosing articles which are liable to postage, *Hill* 1693——The principal evil resulting from the system of evasion is that it begets a habit of fraud and trickery on the part of the public, *ib.* 1723——Any privilege possessed by newspapers involves evasion, but the precautions recommended would greatly lessen the amount of the risk, *ib.* 1905–1908——There are no systematic frauds carried on to any extent; they are usually individual attempts at evasion, *Bokenham* 1986–1989——Some few unstamped editions of periodicals are occasionally mistaken for newspapers and sent duty free; it would cost more to detect these abuses than the revenue is now defrauded of, *ib.* 1993–1996. 2009–2011——Great extent to which the penny stamp is used as a postage, for the transmission of printed matter which does not come under the head of news; objectionable nature of this practice, *Cole* 2721–2731.

2. *Difficulties in the way of detecting and preventing such Evasions:*

Great difficulties in the way of preventing the evasions of the postage charge which take place under cover or pretence of stamped newspapers, *Rep.* 9——Impossibility of examining every parcel of newspapers to ascertain whether they bear the stamp; such an examination would require the force to be increased to an enormous extent, and would necessarily delay the delivery, *Parkhurst* 1657–1664——In the event of the fraud being detected, and the postage as for a letter charged, the party to whom it is addressed may refuse to receive it, and there is no means of reaching the party who posted it, *ib.* 1665–1672——The detection of fraud in such cases does not lead at all to the prevention of it, *ib.* 1673——No effective examination is at present made to ascertain whether any evasion takes place with regard to newspapers; it is impossible under existing circumstances, *Hill* 1704——It would be possible to do so, but it would be attended with a great deal of labour and expense, which it would be unwise to incur, *ib.* 1705–1711. 1732–1736.

Unstamped newspapers, when detected, are liable to postage as letters; this cannot be enforced unless the parties forwarding the paper are discovered, *Hill* 1712–1731——Great difficulty in detecting enclosures in newspapers; under any arrangement a considerable loss of revenue must arise from this system of fraud, *ib.* 1894–1902——Examination to which newspapers are subject to detect fraud and evasion of postage, *Bokenham* 1977–1989. 2004, 2005——A strict and effectual examination of all newspapers would be the cause of considerable expense and delay in the transmisssion of the mails, *ib.* 1985.

*See* also *Folding Newspapers. Partly Stamped Publications. Postage. Postage Labels. Prosecutions. Unstamped Publications.*

Report, 1851—*continued.*

"*Evening Mail.*" The "Times" is published three times a week, under the head of the "Evening Mail," without the advertisements, for circulation in the country, *Morris* 2146.

*Evening Papers.* Existing practice among the evening and weekly papers to copy from the daily morning papers; this is not an unfair proceeding, or any infringement of copyright, *Cassell* 1441–1450——The circulation of evening newspapers has greatly diminished since the establishment of railways; people in the country now get the early morning papers instead of the evening, *Smith* 2948–2951.

*Expense of Newspapers.* Observations as to the expense of conducting and publishing newspapers, and the profits arising from the advertisements, *Bucknall* 1235–1246.

"*Expositor,*" The. Witness delivers in copies of three illegal papers, one of them called the "Expositor;" it is a paper partly stamped and partly unstamped; it has no business to contain news, *Collett* 909. 912.

*Extracts from Newspapers.* If a person extract parts of a newspaper, and publish them on unstamped paper, it renders him liable to a penalty of twenty pounds for every copy, if what he extracts is news, *Timm* 98–101——Case in which the publisher of the "West Riding Examiner" republished from his own paper 2,000 copies of a report of a particular trial; notice of an action was given him for the full amount of penalties, but he was let off on the payment of the small penalty of ten pounds, *ib.* 102–112. 115–121——If witness were aware that it was a common practice in London to publish separate parts of a newspaper upon unstamped paper, he would consider it his duty to interfere in such cases, provided the matter so printed were news, *ib.* 156–173——It would not be fair upon the regular newspapers to allow extracts from these papers, such as the Queen's speech or the financial statement of the Chancellor of the Exchequer, to be printed and circulated on unstamped paper; if this were to come under observation it would not be allowed, *Keogh* 537–547.

Slips, or parts of a newspaper printed on a separate paper, are prohibited in the country, but allowed in London, *Collett* 864——Instances illustrating this statement, *ib.* 865–869. 873–893——Witness considers that the reprinting of a speech delivered in Parliament, and published by Ridgway, is news, and liable to a stamp, *ib.* 893–900——Reasons why no notice has been taken by the Board of a reprint of an article on the Exhibition, from the "Times," issued without a stamp, *Keogh* 3077–3085——The law says nothing specifically as to how long after the date of a newspaper a person is permitted to reprint its contents without a stamp, *ib.* 3093–3101——But if what is printed be public news, intelligence, or occurrences, it is liable to a stamp, *ib.* 3096.

*See* also *Local Newspapers,* 2. "*Times,*" The.

## F.

*Filing Newspapers.* Remarks relative to newspapers being kept for reference; to whatever extent papers are kept for reference they are damnified by the penny stamp, *Smith* 2921–2929.

*Folding*

Report, 1851—*continued.*

*Folding Newspapers.* Under the present system of stamping newspapers, by letting the stamp remain inside it is quite possible to defraud the Post-office; evidence showing that the Post-office is so defrauded, *Collett* 930–950——Insisting upon the stamp being folded so as to appear on the outside of the papers would tend to check evasion, but would be attended with great difficulties, *Hill* 1696–1701. 1739–1745. 1817, 1818——In folding the newspapers witness would recommend their being folded so as to expose the title of the paper, *ib.* 1892, 1893. 1899, 1900.

*Frauds.* See *Evasion of Postage,* 1. 2.

*Free Press.* See *Abolition of the Duty,* 1. *American Press,* 3.

"*Freeholder,*" The. Communication sent by the Inland Revenue Board to the publishers of the "Freeholder," an unstamped monthly paper, as to its liability to the stamp duty; this has been entirely disregarded and the publication continued, *Bucknall* 1167–1169. 1178–1181——Circumstances which led to the establishment of the "Freeholder" as an unstamped publication; character of this periodical, *Cassell* 1275–1280——Notice received by witness from the Board of Inland Revenue, that the "Freeholder" was liable to stamp duty; no proceedings have been taken under that notice, and witness continues the publication of the paper, *ib.* 1275–1289.

*French Press.* Witness has a very high opinion of the French press; they have greatly improved since the stamp duty have been imposed upon them, *Morris* 2148–2159. 2167–2178.——*See* also *American Press,* 3.

## G.

*Glasgow.* See *Edinburgh.*

*Greeley, Horace.* (Analysis of his Evidence.)—Witness cannot comprehend the operation of the stamp on newspapers; it would be impracticable under the institutions of America, 2614——Remarks relative to the publication, price, and circulation of the "New York Tribune," 2616–2619——Number of daily papers published in New York; average circulation of those papers, 2620–2626——Postal regulations of America for the transmission of newspapers, 2627–2638——The newspaper press of America is more local in its character than the British press; manner in which news is obtained, 2639–2644——The newspaper press of America does not possess any protection in the nature of copyright of news, 2644–2648——The publishers in America frequently retard the publication of important intelligence in their newspapers; cause of this, 2648–2651.

Powerful machinery employed in printing newspapers in America; the press of New York prints with greater rapidity than the "Times," 2652–2655——Description of the machinery used in printing the American paper the "Sun;" capital employed on that paper, extent of its circulation, 2655–2660——

Report, 1851—*continued.*

*Greeley, Horace.* (Analysis of his Evidence)—*continued.*

2660——Statistical information as to the newspaper press of America, 2661-2663——The principal profit derived by the American newspapers is from the advertisements, 2664.

[Second Examination.]—Evil effects of the duty on advertisements, as pressing unjustly on certain newspapers, 2978-2989——Amount charged for advertisements in the American papers; large amount of income received from advertisements, 2978——The advertisement duty tends to limit the circulation of newpapers; while the revenue arising from the penny stamp depends upon the number circulated, 2978-2988——From this it appears inconsistent that if Government is disposed to tax the press, it should impose two sorts of tax, the one tending to lessen the amount received from the other, 2982-2988——The effect of the stamp and advertisement duty must be to lessen the amount of the receipt from the duty on paper, 2988, 2989——Instead of the three taxes, the stamp, advertisement, and paper duties, a paper duty alone would be the most equal and most efficient as a revenue duty, 2988, 2989.

Evidence as to the number of newspapers in America, and their circulation; their circulation is more local than that of the British press, 2990-3004——Persons about to establish a newspaper in America do not have to register nor give security not to publish libels or seditious matter; they are not subject to any liability more than any other trade, 3005-3010——Very few actions for libel are brought against the newspaper press of America, 3011-3013——Great extent to which the working classes of America are subscribers to newspapers; cost of the papers, 3014-3024——The newspapers are but seldom transmitted through the post from one person to another; they are so cheap it is not worth while, 3025-3028.

Existence of a low class of publications in America whose purpose is to extort money from parties who can be threatened with exposure, 3032-3035——Scurrility or personality is not common to the publications of America, 3035, 3036——Distinction made by the Post-office in America in the charge for the transmission of newspapers and other printed matter; manner in which it is decided what constitutes a newspaper, 3037-3040——Remarks relative to the suggestion in the United States to control the press, by making newpapers liable to stamp duty, and requiring the publishers to give security, as in France, 3041——Extent of the circulation of the "New York Herald;" character of this paper, 3042-3045——How far able literary men are employed on the newspaper press of America; average amount of remuneration given for the services of literary men; the prices of literary labour are more moderate than in this country, 3046-3049.

Opinion that newspaper reading is calculated to keep up the habit of reading; the newspaper is worth all the schools in the country, 3050-3059——The newspaper press has much greater influence on public opinion in the United States than in this country, 3060, 3061——Great extent to which the electric telegraph is used by the newspapers in America; it is not used to near so great an extent by the newspapers in this country, 3062-3068——The expense of electric telegraph despatches is enormous, but it is cheaper in America than in this country, 3066-3068.

Report, 1851—*continued.*

## H.

*Halfpenny Postage.* See *Postage.*

" *Hansard's Debates.*" Witness does not look upon " Hansard's Debates" as a newspaper; it is rather a work conducive to history than the diffusion of news, *Keogh* 554-558——Remarks relative to the publication of Hansard's Parliamentary Debates on twopenny sheets of unstamped paper, *Bucknall* 1113. 1140. 1157-1160.

" *Harlequin,*" The. Instance of a paper called the " Harlequin," which related merely to theatricals; but as it gave reports and critiques on the plays, it was deemed to contain news, and was put down, *Collett* 739-741. 747.

*Haywood, Abel.* (Analysis of his Evidence.)—Bookseller and publisher at Manchester; has been a member of the town council for many years, 2474-2476——Has great experience in the circulation of small publications which are unstamped, 2477, 2478——None of the unstamped penny publications are sent through the post; they are distributed to the booksellers in the various towns by the railways, 2479, 2480. 2594-2598. 2606-2613——Detail as to the name, quality, and circulation of the various cheap unstamped publications at one penny and three halfpence, 2481-2502. 2533-2537——Of the number of cheap publications in circulation, considerably the larger proportion are of a good tendency, 2496-2504——Increased circulation of the best description of publications; the good publications always have a tendency to put down the bad, 2505-2508. 2515-2519. 2523——The extensive sale of publications shows a taste among the working classes for reading and mental improvement, and a general desire for cheap literature, 2509, 2510.

General desire among the working classes for newspapers; extensive sale of the cheap weekly newspapers, 2511-2514——Were the publishers of weekly periodicals allowed to put a few pages of news in their works, the circulation would be enormously increased, 2511——Reducing the price of newspapers would have a tendency to diminish the sale of pernicious penny publications, 2520-2523——No advantage is gained by prohibiting the insertion of news in the penny weekly publications, 2525——Beneficial effects would result from the free publication of news to the population of the country, 2526-2529——Rapid increase of good cheap publications within the last twenty years, 2529-2532——The result of witness's experience has proved that the objectionable publications are short-lived, and that those of the highest intellectual and moral quality have a tendency to increase in circulation, 2538, 2539——If the small weekly publications were allowed to insert news as well as literary intelligence, it would tend to increase the circulation of those papers, and act as a stimulus to the reading habits of the people, 2540.

Opinion that the working classes might be safely left to discriminate between the good and bad newspapers; the removal of the stamp would not lead them to patronise inferior papers, 2541-2550——If the price of the " Times" was reduced, its circulation would be increased without its tone being lowered, 2551,

Report, 1851—*continued.*

*Haywood, Abel.* (Analysis of his Evidence)—*continued.*
2551, 2552——The working classes do not care so much about politics, all they want are the current events of the week, 2551-2553——The stamp is not so very unpopular with the working classes; they consider it is kept on partly with a view of preventing them from getting cheap publications and having their own organs, and partly for the sake of the tax, 2554, 2555——Witness does not consider that allowing a mixture of news in the penny weekly publications would have a tendency to lower the tone of the other class of writing, 2556-2559.

Remarks relative to the prosecution of 750 parties in connexion with the "Poor Man's Guardian," which prosecution was afterwards decided to be illegal, 2560-2568——There have been no prosecutions under the stamp duty of late years, as all parties have ceased to publish on receiving notice from the Board of Inland Revenue, 2569-2584——Difficulties in ascertaining what constitutes a newspaper, and renders it liable to the stamp duty, 2571-2584——In the event of the abolition of the stamp, and no limit being placed on the size of newspapers, papers will be published all sizes and all prices, 2585——Remarks relative to the publications connected with moral and religious movements, as also with arts and manufactures; the circulation would be increased by their being allowed to publish news, 2586-2593.

The present effect of the stamp on newspapers is to tax all readers of papers, that a few persons choosing to send their papers through the post may do so free of charge, 2599——Witness considers this unjust; a penny postage should be charged on newspapers each time they are sent through the post, 2599-2610——Opinion that an increase in the number of local newspapers would be a great benefit to the community, 2600, 2601.

*Hickson, William Edward.* (Analysis of his Evidence.)—Was associated with Mr. Senior and Lord Overstone in the Hand-loom Inquiry Commission, 3174——This inquiry gave witness an opportunity of making himself acquainted very generally with the state of mind of the working classes of this and of other countries, 3175——As an educationist witness has taken an active part in promoting the interests of the working classes, as connected with popular instruction, 3175.

Strong exertions made by witness in connexion with other parties to obtain a total abolition of the stamp, at the time it was reduced from 4*d.* to 1*d.*; 3176 *et seq.*——At that period Lord Brougham strongly denounced the last penny as the worst penny of the four, and witness entertained with him and many other persons a very decided opinion on the same subject, and in the same direction, 3176. 3183——There are no more daily papers now than there were at that time, 3177-3179——It was supposed by witness's party at that time that the penny was retained by the Government, as they were afraid of the possibility of a more strongly developed democratic tendency in an absolutely free press, 3180——The total abolition was opposed by the entire of the established newspaper press, 3181——They fancied it would protect them in a certain degree from the competition of an unstamped press, 3181-3187——None of the London morning papers gave the public the full benefit of the reduction; some of the weekly papers did so, 3187. 3191-3192.

Reasons

Report, 1851—*continued.*

*Hickson, William Edward.* (Analysis of his Evidence)—*continued.*

Reasons why witness does not consider that the penny stamp can be defended on fiscal grounds, 3193——If it is necessary to obtain a revenue from newspapers, witness would propose obtaining it by charging an *ad valorem* duty, allowing the public to publish newspapers at any price they please, 3193. 3209–3212. 3214–3233——Even though the number of stamps issued for newspapers has increased from 28,000,000 in 1836 to the enormous number of 65,000,000 at the present time, witness is of opinion that newspapers have not reached down to the comprehension of the very lowest persons who are able to read, 3194–3195——Witness is prepared to admit that if the penny stamp were removed there would be a host of inferior journals to the "Times" called into existence, 3196——Reason why it is desirable they should be called into existence, 3196.

The writing of the "Times" really overshoots the comprehension of the labouring classes, 3196——Cheap newspapers circulated amongst the working classes would stimulate the habit of reading, and prepare the people for reading something better; nature of the information and intelligence which such papers should contain, 3197–3208. 3212–3213. 3234–3255. 3263–3266——Witness is not prepared to make any suggestion as to the charge for the transmission of newspapers by post, if the stamp should be abolished, 3217–3233——The publications which have been brought out at a cheap rate originally, under the plea of benefiting the working classes, such as the "Penny Magazine," "Chambers's Journal," &c., have missed their aim, and have been generally circulated among the middle classes, 3256–3259.

As regards the mechanics' institutes witness has generally observed that they have been almost always composed of the middle classes, 3260——Still in some of the manufacturing districts they embrace a large portion of the working classes, 3260——Many of these institutions have failed from their not having a news-room; the news-room is found the greatest attraction, 3260–3262.

*Hill, Rowland.* (Analysis of his Evidence.)—Secretary to the Postmaster-general, 1687——Existing arrangements at the Post-office in reference to the transmission of newspapers by post, 1688 *et seq.*——Weekly return made by the Stamp-office to the Postmaster-general of all newly-registered papers; the Postmaster-general decides whether they are newspapers or not, 1689. 1691——By a Treasury Minute dated 1838, any publication which bears a newspaper stamp is allowed to go free through the Post-office, provided it does not exceed two ounces in weight, 1689, 1690——The regulations respecting newspapers are very much evaded, and probably the admission of portions of an impression may tend to promote that evasion, 1692–1749——Various kinds of evasion arising out of the present newspaper arrangements, 1693.

Allowing publishers to stamp a portion of their impressions leads to unstamped copies being passed through the Post-office without detection; instance of this with regard to "Punch," the "Athenæum," &c., 1693, 1694——Detection does not invariably follow cases of fraud in sending unstamped publications through the Post-office, 1695——Insisting upon the stamp being folded so as to appear on the outside of the papers would tend to check evasion, but

Report, 1851—*continued.*

*Hill, Rowland.* (Analysis of his Evidence)—*continued.*

but would be attended with great difficulties, 1696–1701. 1739–1745——Rendering it necessary that all newspapers should have a stamp affixed to them would not prevent articles liable to postage being enclosed, although it would prevent any evasion as to sending unstamped publications, 1702, 1703——No effective examination is at present made to ascertain whether any evasion takes place with regard to newspapers; it is impossible under existing circumstances, 1704.

It would be possible to examine all newspapers, but it would be attended with a great deal of labour and expense, 1705–1711——Unstamped newspapers when detected are liable to postage as letters; this cannot be enforced unless the parties forwarding the paper are discovered, 1712–1731——Great number of newspapers sent through the Post-office by the newsvenders, 1729–1731. 1737, 1738——The cost of an efficient scrutiny as to newspapers would be so large that it would be unwise to incur it, 1732–1736——The cases of fraud in sending unstamped publications by the post are not very numerous, 1746–1748——There is no limit as to the number of newspapers sent through the post in bundles; frequency of large bundles weighing 10 or 20 pounds passing through the post, 1750, 1751.

Defective nature of the arrangements as to the transmission of certain impressions of various publications through the post, by reason of the stamp; frequency of evasion from the whole of the impressions not being stamped, 1752–1769——Limitation as to the size of the sheets of paper stamped for newspapers, 1767–1769——There is no restriction as to the age of newspapers sent through the Post-office, except as to the colonial or foreign posts; frequency of papers passing and repassing through the post, 1770–1777——Frequency of bundles of old newspapers for waste paper being sent through the post free of charge, 1772–1774——Newspapers are the only packets transmitted through the Post-office which are allowed the privilege of being twice sent without any additional charge, 1778, 1779——Sending a newspaper twice through the post is an abuse of the privilege of the stamp, yet it is within the letter of the law, and an alteration of the law would be required to prevent it, 1780–1784.

The only means of preventing newspapers being sent more than once through the post is to obliterate the stamp, 1785–1792——This plan has been rejected on the ground that the trouble and expense of applying it would be greater than the advantage gained would justify, 1785–1789——Witness has no doubt but that the Treasury have the power of making any alteration in the present regulations for the transmission of newspapers through the post, 1793——Opinion that in the event of the stamp being abolished from newspapers, they should be allowed to pass through the post by affixing a penny postage stamp, or using stamped covers, 1794–1804. 1876–1881——Objections to allowing newspapers to be sent through the post without pre-payment, 1800. 1882, 1883——Witness would not extend that privilege to all printed matter until it had been tried in a limited form on the regular newspaper press, when, if it should be considered safe to extend it, all printed matter might be included in the arrangement, 1805, 1806. 1810, 1811.

Placing the whole of the postal arrangements under the management of the Postmaster-general

Report, 1851—*continued.*

*Hill, Rowland.* (Analysis of his Evidence)—*continued.*

Postmaster-general would not be any more convenient than the existing system; the course is now open to the Postmaster-general to advise the Treasury upon any subject of inconvenience, 1807–1809——In the event of the stamp duty on newspapers being abolished, and a postage being fixed for their transmission through the post, a large proportion of the newspapers will be forwarded by railway, 1812–1815. 1830-1832——Loss of revenue which will result from the proposed substitution of a postage rate on newspapers when transmitted through the post, and the abolitionof the stamp duty, 1813–1816——There would be great difficulty in obliging people so to fold their newspapers that the present stamp would appear on the outside, 1817, 1818——Frequency of old newspapers being sent through the post as a token of news, in substitution for a letter, whereby the postage is evaded; this practice has materially decreased since the introduction of the penny postage, 1819–1822.

Memorandum as to the number of newspapers passing through the post-office, and estimate of the amount likely to arise from a penny postage on newspapers, 1823. 1870——Evidence upon the subject of witness's estimate of the number of papers likely to be sent through the post at a penny postage, 1824–1841. 1957–1960——Great number of newspapers sent by the railways at the present time, for the purpose of early delivery; extra charge made by the newsvenders for these early copies in the country, 1826-1832. 1842–1851——In the event of the stamp on newspapers being abolished, whether the papers would be dispatched through the post-office or by other means, would depend upon the comparative excellence of the means employed by the post-office and the news agent, 1851——Under the existing arrangements at the post-office, newspapers could be carried profitably at a postage rate of a penny each, 1852–1854. 1860–1863. 1873-1875——If the newspapers were removed altogether from the post-office, it would be impossible to make anything like a corresponding reduction in the expenses of the establishment, 1855. 1872.

Extra charge made by newsvenders for the early newspapers in the country, which are sent down by railway; how far witness considers the post-office would be able to compete with these newsvenders in the delivery of newspapers at a penny each, 1856-1869. 1932–1954. 1961-1969——Manner in which witness considers that carrying newspapers at a penny each would be profitable to the post-office, 1871–1875——In the event of a postage rate being fixed upon newspapers, the weight should be limited; average weight of the "Times," the "Weekly Despatch," &c., 1884-1891——In folding the newspapers witness would recommend their being folded so as to expose the title of the paper, 1892, 1893. 1899, 1900——Great difficulty in detecting enclosures in newspapers; under any arrangement a considerable loss of revenue must arise from this system of fraud, 1894–1902——Convenience of adopting stamped wrappers for newspapers, 1903, 1904——Any privilege possessed by newspapers involves evasion, but the precautions recommended would greatly lessen the amount of the risk, 1905–1908.

Detail of a plan proposed by witness by which the post-office could deliver newspapers at a uniform postage of a halfpenny; great difficulties attending the carrying out of this plan, 1909–1913. 1920–1954. 1961–1968——Heavy bags which

Report, 1851—*continued.*

*Hill, Rowland.* (Analysis of his Evidence)—*continued.*
which many of the postmen have to carry; assistance is afforded them when the bags are unusually heavy, 1914–1919——At present the post-office does not take credit for the portion of the postage which comes under the head of newspaper stamps; the money received for newspaper stamps all goes into the account of the Inland Revenue, 1955, 1956——There are very few of the letter carriers that could not bear a very large increase of burden, 1970——Obliterating the stamps on the covers of newspapers would be a great addition to the present labour in the post-office 1971, 1972.

*Hogg, Thomas.* (Analysis of his Evidence.)—Has been connected with mechanics' institutions since January 1842; chiefly as secretary, 1022, 1023——Number of these institutions in Lancashire, Cheshire, and Yorkshire, 1024——Is secretary to the thirty or forty institutes which have formed themselves into a union in Lancashire and Cheshire, 1025–1028——Nearly the whole of these institutions have news rooms, 1029. 1049——The great exception is that at Liverpool, 1029. 1050——Many of these news rooms are the most attractive departments of these mechanics' institutions, 1030——In all large towns they are generally very well supplied with papers; but in the small towns there is generally the greatest difficulty in getting a good supply, 1031. 1033. 1063–1065——The first great difficulty which these institutes have to contend with is the want of funds, 1032. 1047——There is a great want of interest on the part of the working classes to attend them, though the institutions bear their name and were established by them, 1032.

Opinion that if the price of newspapers were low, and the supply large, the working classes would attend these institutions in greater numbers; many of them now prefer the public-house, where they can find a newspaper, 1033–1037. 1042–1048. 1062. 1068——Witness considers that there are many collateral advantages that would follow from inducing the working classes to attend the news rooms of these institutions, 1037——Many of the wealthier and influential founders and supporters of these institutions withdrew their support when the news rooms were added to them, 1040——They feared that the introduction of newspapers would introduce party politics, 1040–1046——By good management, however, this fear has proved to be groundless, 1040–1046. 1051–1053——For certain subjects witness considers newspapers a good source of information for the members of mechanics' institutions, 1054–1058. 1069–1073——Economical plans which these institutions are obliged to adopt in consequence of the expense of the papers, 1059.

A petition to the House of Commons was presented by the union of mechanics' institutions in Lancashire and Cheshire, praying for the repeal of the stamp-duty, the advertisement duty, and the paper duty, 1060–1061. 1095——Way in which they interfere with the prosperity of these institutions, 1061, 1062. 1082–1085——Opinion that introducing news rooms into each of the mechanics institutes in the country would not have a tendency to take the mechanics from more solid pursuits than newspaper reading, 1067–1075——It would take them rather from worse pursuits, and lift them up rather than bring them down, *ib.*

The newspapers are usually supplied to these institutions by agents in the towns,

*Hogg, Thomas.* (Analysis of his Evidence)—*continued.*
towns, which entails the charge of an extra penny on the paper, 1076–1081. 1092–1094——The proportion of artisans who attend these institutions is, generally speaking, rather upon the decrease; causes to which this may be attributed, 1086–1089——Reasons for the decrease in the encouragement given to these institutions by the higher classes of manufacturers and persons in that position, 1090, 1091.

"*Household Narrative.*" See "*Narrative of Current Events.*"

"*Household Words.*" Witness delivers in a half-year's number of Dickens's "Household Words," showing that they contain comments and observations on news, *Collett* 893. 908.

*Hunt, Frederick Knight.* (Analysis of his Evidence.)—Sub-editor of the "Daily News," 2315–2318——Opinion that the removal of the stamp would be beneficial, 2319. 2330, 2333——Necessity for some law being established giving the morning papers paying for Indian and other news a copyright in that news for a certain number of hours, 2319–2325. 2333–2339——Piracy of news is carried on to a great extent, to the serious loss of the leading daily papers; this would be greatly increased in the event of the removal of the stamp, unless some law of copyright was established, 2319–2326. 2334–2339. 2348–2352——Inferiority of both the American and French newspapers to the English papers in point of news, 2326–2328. 2347——Proportion of the morning daily papers that goes out of London for secondary sale, 2329——In the event of the stamp on newspapers being removed, they should be allowed to pass through the post on payment of a penny; this would be satisfactory, 2331–2333.

The established newspapers have nothing to fear from the competition that would result from the removal of the stamp on newspapers; the best newspapers would always get the greatest number of purchasers, whether stamped or not, 2340, 2341——Importance of superior machinery for the purpose of printing sufficient copies of the morning papers for early circulation, 2342——Manner in which the law might be framed to prevent the piracy of articles of news, by papers not contributing to the dispatches, 2343–2347——Importance of newspapers as a means of education for the people; the removal of the stamp would have a good educational effect, 2353——Remarks relative to the various stamp duties that have been imposed on newspapers since the time of Queen Anne; the papers have grown up to their present perfection in spite of the stamp, 2354.

Remarks relative to the advertisements contained in the London papers, 2355——It is likely that the removal of the stamp would have a tendency to bring into existence a number of local papers in the country market towns; the local advertisements would afford an opportunity for their establishment, 2356. 2360——Opinion that a paper emanating from the metropolis, having a manifest national character, is much more likely to be useful to the country than small local papers confined to little local bickerings, 2358–2360——The removal of the stamp would increase the circulation of the higher description of newspapers, provided they are not encumbered by a heavy postage duty, 2359.

Report, 1851—*continued.*

## I.

*Immoral Publications.* If the greatest liberty were allowed to the publication of cheap literature by the abolition of the stamp and paper duty, the superior class of periodicals would effectually counteract the influence of the more immoral publications, *Cassell* 1326——Witness is not aware of a single unstamped periodical of an evil tendency, published in Scotland; cause to which this is attributable, *Russell* 1482, 1483.

*See* also *Bad Publications. Low Publications. Obscene Publications. Pernicious Publications.*

*Infractions of the Law.* The Board of Inland Revenue are guided in their proceedings against parties for any infractions of the law rather by what a jury would say than by their own discretion and judgment in the case, *Timm* 174–178.

*Inland Revenue Board.* Heads under which witness classes the faults of the Board of Inland Revenue, *Collett* 776——Witness would say, in the first place, they defraud (speaking technically) the Post-office revenue, by giving to publications a false certificate of their being newspapers; way in which witness arrives at this conclusion, *ib.* 776–808——This may be the fault of the law, but if so, it should be altered, *ib.* 789. 795-798. 805-808——The second fault witness finds with them, and which is a part of the first, is that they favour a number of registered newspapers at the expense of the rest, by allowing them to circulate a part of their impression without a stamp, thus encouraging unfair competition, *ib.* 808 *et seq.*——And a great number of these actually contain that news which the law declares ought not to be contained at all, *ib.* 808——Evidence showing how this regulation acts as regards unfair competition; complaints which have been made on the subject by the proprietors of the "Coventry Herald," the "Leader," and the "Caledonian Mercury," *ib.* 809–812——Witness's next complaint is, that the Board neglect to enforce the law in London; instance of this in the case of the "Household Narrative," *ib.* 812 *et seq.*

Witness does not think there is any intention at all on the part of the Board of Inland Revenue to trouble themselves as to what the politics or utility of a paper may be; they simply consider that a good newspaper is a taxable article, but if it is bad they consider it is not a taxable article, and leave it alone; they do not take a political view of the case, they merely take a fiscal view of it, *Collett* 843–855——With the general body of the public newspaper press the Board have had no controversies or disputes whatever, *Keogh* 3076.

*See* also *News*, 2. 3. *Post Office. Prosecutions. Secretary to the Board. Solicitor to the Board. "Stroud Free Press." "Stroud Observer."*

## J.

*Jersey.* Publication of unstamped temperance journals in Jersey and the Isle of Man; these have been discontinued in consequence of their not being allowed to pass through the Post-office without having a postage label affixed, *Cassell* 1315–1319.

Report, 1851—*continued.*

## K.

*Keogh, Thomas.* (Analysis of his Evidence.)—Assistant Secretary to the Board of Inland Revenue, 269——All the secretarial business relating to newspapers or stamps is brought under witness's notice, 270, 271——Every letter from the Board on the subject of the newspaper press is signed by witness; he writes on the part of the Board, 272, 273——Witness is aware of the views taken by the Board as to the law relating to newspaper stamps, and of the practice that prevails under that law, 274, 275——Evidence relative to the limited number of stamping places in the United Kingdom, and the inconvenience arising therefrom; nature of the complaints which have been made to the Board of Inland Revenue on this subject, 284. 288–290.

Some years ago there was but one place for stamping, 284——London was the only place; and then the papers in the north of England and some of the papers in Scotland pressed very hard to have an establishment at Edinburgh, 284——This was conceded, and very shortly afterwards Manchester was established, 284——There is no doubt the necessity of sending so far for stamped paper does require newspaper proprietors to keep a large supply of stamped paper than they would otherwise keep, 285——But it was conceived when the duty was reduced from 4*d.* to 1*d.* that this would not be a very great evil or hardship upon the newspaper proprietors, 285–287.

A proprietor pays the duty before he receives the stamps, 286. 395–397——The south of England is of course supplied from London, 291——Evidence showing that allowing the paper for newspapers to be stamped wherever there is a stamp office or a collection of excise, would be likely to lead to fraud, and would also cause a large increase of expense, 292, 293. 296–314. 337–339. 348–351——Witness does not believe that the proprietors of newspapers deal directly with the paper manufacturers for their supply of paper, but deal with the agents in London, who, if the proprietors are proprietors of country papers, forward the paper ready stamped to them, 315–336. 364–369——So that a proprietor of a paper, say in Cornwall, would not be under the necessity of sending his paper up to London in the first instance to have it stamped, 315–336——Even newspapers in the neighbourhood of Manchester, where there is a stamping establishment, are supplied with their paper from London, 320–336. 340, 341.

There may have been occasions in which delay and loss have accrued to the proprietors of newspapers from their having to get their paper stamped at a distance; but this has been from the neglect of the parties themselves, 342——Applications have been made by parties to be allowed, in a case of sudden emergency, to print upon unstamped paper, they agreeing to pay the stamp duty afterwards, 343——Where the transaction is one that occurs for the first time it is always passed over on the payment of the duties, but it would not be granted beforehand, 343–347. 352–363. 370. 385–389——How far there is any distinction in the course pursued with respect to the stamping of newspapers and the stamping of deeds and bills, and documents of that kind, 371–383.

The stamp office only supply stamps on paper of their own to their distributors in the country; this is the only way in which the Stamp-office can be said

*Keogh, Thomas.* (Analysis of his Evidence)—*continued.*

said to keep any stock of stamps, 372, 373. 375, 376——Newspaper proprietors send their own paper to the office to be stamped, 374——The public in London send in all their own paper and parchment and every other thing requiring a stamp, to be stamped, just as the newspaper proprietors do, 375——Impracticability of printing stamps for newspapers as stamps for deeds are prepared, and supplying the stamp distributors in the country with them and allowing them to send them to the newspapers, 384——Impossibility of providing paper of all the sizes that would be required, 384——It might be possible to devise means by which stamps could be attached to newspapers by labels, but witness never heard of such a proposition, 385, 386——Stamping the paper for newspapers by hand is found preferable to doing it by machinery, 390-393——Short period of time taken when a person applies for stamps before he is supplied with them, 394-395.

Newspaper proprietors do not give sureties for newspaper stamps; the sureties are for the duties upon advertisements, 398——If the stamps are spoiled, or if a newspaper becomes defunct having on hand a certain supply of stamps, or if it changes in size, a return is made by the Stamp-office if the stamps are brought back, 399——If the paper is printed on, no return is made, 400——The Board of Inland Revenue holds that any paper containing public news, intelligence, or occurrences is a newspaper and subject to the stamp duty, 401——Any party printing and dispersing public news on unstamped paper is liable to a penalty of 20 *l.*; 402——If the printing of news were to occur on a piece of cotton, witness does not think the law would comprehend that, 403——The law requires that any person wishing to be entitled to print public news, &c. upon stamped paper, must enter into securities that he will not libel anybody, 404-410——This does not apply to the printing of publications descanting on the concerns of private families or private individuals, as was the case in a publication called "Sam Sly," 405-409——Witness is not aware that this difference between public and private news has ever been brought to an issue, 411. 413, 414.

One advantage of registering every newspaper is, that it affords an easy means of proving the fact of publication, 411, 412. 421-422——There would have been difficulty in this in the case of the publication above-named, as if the party defamed were desirous of obtaining compensation by law, he would have to prove the publication by the common-law course, 411, 412——Definition of what witness considers news under the terms of the Act, 415-420. 427-432. 444-447——The 38 and 60 Geo. 3 merely require sureties against the publication of blasphemous or seditious libels in newspapers, 421-423——Witness is decidedly of opinion that the stamping of newspapers is some security for their respectability, 421——Lord Abinger's Act first extended this security to libels and defamations against individuals, 423-426. 433-443.

In witness's opinion a publication such as "Sam Sly," containing nothing else than paragraphs relating to the private characters of individuals would in no sense be a newspaper, nor would this matter be public news, intelligence, or occurrences, 429. 433. 444-447——Witness considers such a paper would not have much circulation, 437-439——If one of these papers, all of which are watched, began to insert public news, the party would be warned that he was rendering

Report, 1851—*continued.*

*Keogh, Thomas.* (Analysis of his Evidence)—*continued.*

rendering himself subject to the laws relating to newspapers, and if he persisted he would be prosecuted or compelled to register and take out stamps, 437–441 ——Having registered he becomes more accessible to prosecution by the parties whom he has libelled, 442, 443.

Evidence on the subject of the return delivered in by Mr. Timm of the 53 registered newspapers published without stamps; they do not contain that matter upon which the newspaper duty is imposed, viz. public news, intelligence, or occurrences, 448–452——Amongst these papers is the "Legal Observer," 453——The reason why this paper is not stamped is that it has been held that a paper addressed to one particular subject, and which only inserts in its paper something bearing upon that subject, is not to be considered a newspaper within the contemplation of that expression, 453–463—— If upon consideration of the contents of this paper, or any other, the Board were of opinion that it contained anything which fell within the liability imposed upon newspapers they would prosecute for the penalty, 464–470—— Grounds on which witness forms the opinion that if newspapers could be put in competition as regards price with such publications as "The Town," an infamous and obscene paper, published at a penny, they would not be likely entirely to divert the minds of the reading public from such works, 471–498. 501–503.

Witness regards the registration and the duty combined together as securing a press of a high description, such as exists in this country, and perhaps exists in no other, 482. 485. 490, 491——Such papers as "The Town" are not required to be registered; the Newspaper Stamp Act has no relation to them, 483–484. 486–489——One definition of a newspaper in the Act is, "Any paper printed in any part of the United Kingdom weekly, or oftener, or at intervals not exceeding 26 days, containing only or principally advertisements," 499——This law is not violated; there are a great number of these advertising publications which are registered, and pay the duty with perfect regularity; witness never heard of their being published without a stamp, 499, 500——A person may comment and observe upon news at intervals exceeding 26 days without a stamp, 504——But if he comments upon news at intervals of less than 26 days the price must be 6*d.* or above, and the size of the publication must be two sheets of certain dimensions; probable object of this regulation, 504–513. 518——Many of the 53 registered publications are of less price than 6*d.*, and smaller in size than the size set forth, and published at less intervals than 26 days; but the question is, do they comment on public news; if so, they would be subject to the newspaper duty, 505, 506. 509—— With regard to the Board of Inland Revenue enforcing these conditions of high price and large size, they look to the law as it stands, 514——If they consider it is infringed they endeavour to enforce it; giving notice to the parties of the position in which they stand, and if they resist of course they are prosecuted, 514——The discretion of the Board in instituting a prosecution is governed by their estimate of the opinion the jury is likely to form of the publication, 514. 517——"Punch," for instance, which is of small size, and under 6*d.*, is a peculiar publication; their comments are merely a joke on the public events of the day, and it would be ridiculous to notice them with a view to prosecution, 515, 516. 518.



Way

Report, 1851—*continued.*

*Keogh, Thomas.* (Analysis of his Evidence)—*continued.*

Way in which the return of the 53 registered publications was made up, 521, 522——Opinion that allowing merchants to transmit their prices current, and tradesmen their catalogues, through the post if stamped in the same way as newspapers, produces a large sum to the revenue, 523–532——These papers would not be published or transmitted to near the extent they now are if they had not this privilege; but this is a matter for the Post-office itself, 523–532——The Board is now conducting a case against a "Narrative of Current Events," 533——Several monthly publications have received intimations from the Stamp-office that they contained matters that render them liable to the newspaper stamp, 534. 550–558——The decision on the "Narrative of Current Events" case will decide this class of cases, 534, 535——The larger magazines do not fall within this category, 536.

It would not be fair upon the regular newspaper to allow extracts from these papers, such as the Queen's speech or the financial statement of the Chancellor of the Exchequer, to be printed and circulated on unstamped paper; if this were to come under observation it would not be allowed, 537–547——The Board have received a request from newspaper proprietors, whose papers are undoubtedly newspapers, to be put on the footing of papers that are not newspapers at all, 548, 549. 551, 552——Witness does not look upon "Hansard's Debates" as a newspaper; it is rather a work conducive to history than diffusion of news, 554–558.

[Second Examination.]—Evidence in explanation of the threatened prosecution of Mr. Bucknall for publishing several copies of a newspaper without being stamped, as referred to in Mr. Bucknall's evidence, 3069–3074——Witness delivers in a statement of all the cases in which cautions have been given to publishers of newspapers within the last three years, 3075——These cautions have only begun to be issued within the last two or three years, 3075. 3111, 3112——These attempts to steer just beyond the line of the law have only arisen within the last three years, 3075. 3111, 3112——In former years the Board had not to deal with any such persons, 3075, 3076——With the general body of the public newspaper press the Board have had no controversies or disputes whatever, 3076.

Reasons why no notice has been taken by the Board of a reprint of an article on the Exhibition from the "Times" issued without a stamp, 3077–3085——A paper called the "Mirror of the Time" has not been brought specifically under the notice of the Board as to whether it was a newspaper or not; it has just been registered as a newspaper, 3086–3092——The law says nothing specifically as to how long after the date of a newspaper a person is permitted to reprint its contents without a stamp, 3093–3101——But if what is printed be "public news, intelligence, or occurrences," it is liable to a stamp, 3096——Although a penalty of 20*l.* is imposed by the Act of Parliament on every copy of a newspaper printed without a stamp, still no such penalty would ever be enforced as a whole, 3102.

Witness does not consider that any further legislation is necessary to enable the Board of Inland Revenue to distinguish between what fairly should be stamped and what need not be stamped, 3108, 3109——The present law, as understood by the Board in reference to newspaper stamps, is in a satisfactory state;

Report, 1851—*continued.*

*Keogh, Thomas.* (Analysis of his Evidence)—*continued.*
state; there is not the least difficulty in interpreting it, 3113–3115——Several publications have been set up as it were upon the chance of being pulled down, and have gone on for a certain time before information has been given to the Board of Inland Revenue, 3116–3122——If it be found that these attempts, just keeping on the line of the law, are generally unsuccessful, and that the parties must either exclude such matter from their papers or register them as newspapers, there is no reason why they should increase, 3116–3122.

*Keogh,* Mr. See "*Stroud Observer.*"

## L.

*Labels.* See *Postage Labels.*

*Labouring Classes.* See *Agricultural Labourers.* *Education,* 1. *Working Classes.*

"*Lancet,*" The. See *Class Publications.*

"*Law Journal.*" Publication of the "Law Journal," containing legal reports on unstamped paper, *Bucknall* 1136, 1137.

"*Legal Observer.*" The reason why the "Legal Observer" is not stamped is that it has been held that a paper addressed to one particular subject, and which only inserts in its paper something bearing upon that subject, is not to be considered a newspaper within the contemplation of that expression, *Keogh* 453–463——If upon consideration of the contents of this paper or any other, the Board were of opinion that it contained anything which fell within the liability imposed upon newspapers, they would prosecute for the penalty, *ib.* 464–470——Grounds on which witness makes the assertion that the "Legal Observer" is a newspaper, *Collett* 855–863.

*See* also *Class Pablications.*

*Legislative Interference.* Witness does not consider that any further legislation is necessary to enable the Board of Inland Revenue to distinguish between what fairly should be stamped and what need not be stamped, *Keogh* 3108, 3109——The present law as understood by the Board in reference to newspaper stamps is in a satisfactory state; there is not the least difficulty in interpreting it, *ib.* 3113–3115.

*Letter Carriers.* Heavy bags which many of the postmen have to carry; assistance is afforded them when the bags are unusually heavy, *Hill* 1914–1919 ——There are very few of the letter carriers that could not bear a very large increase of burden, *ib.* 1970.

*Libel.* The Act of the 60 Geo. 3, c. 9, provides for sureties for the payment of fines on conviction of any printer or publisher for the publication of a blasphemous or seditious libel, *Timm* 10——Extension of the provisions of this Act by the 1 Will. 4, c. 73, *ib.* 10–13——The law requires that any person wishing to be entitled to print public news, &c. upon stamped paper, must enter

Report, 1851—*continued.*

*Libel*—continued.

enter into securities that he will not libel anybody, *Keogh* 404–410——This does not apply to the printing of publications descanting on the concerns of private families or private individuals, as was the case in a publication called "Sam Sly," *ib.* 405–409——Witness is not aware that this difference between public and private news has ever been brought to an issue, *ib.* 411. 413, 414.

The 38th and 60th Geo. 3 merely require sureties against the publication of blasphemous or seditious libels in newspapers, *Keogh* 421–423——Lord Abinger's Act first extended this security to libels and defamations against individuals, *ib.* 423–426. 433–443——Opinion that the maintenance of the stamp on newspapers does not in the least tend to prevent the publication of libellous matter, *Cole* 2806–2809——Reference to the opinion expressed by Lord Brougham, that though the laws made to restrain the press were intended to check libel, they have a very obvious tendency to lessen the security against libel, *ib.* 2808, 2809——Persons about to establish a newspaper in America do not have to register or give security not to publish libels or seditious matter; they are not subject to any liability more than any other trade, *Greeley* 3005–3010——Very few actions for libel are brought against the newspaper press of America, *ib.* 3011–3013.

*Libellous Publications.* In witness's opinion, a publication such as "Sam Sly," containing nothing else than paragraphs relating to the private characters of individuals, would in no case be a newspaper, nor would this matter be public news, intelligence, or occurrences, *Keogh* 429–433. 444–447——Witness considers such a paper would not have much circulation, *ib.* 437–439——If one of these papers, all of which are watched, began to insert public news, the party would be warned that he was rendering himself subject to the laws relating to newspapers, and if he persisted, he would be prosecuted or compelled to register and take out stamps, *ib.* 437–441——Having registered he becomes more accessible to prosecution by the parties whom he has libelled, *ib.* 442, 443.

*Literary Talent.* A reduction in the price would enable the proprietors to pay more for the literary talent employed, and they would consequently obtain higher literary talent, *Collett* 1001–1003——The reduction of the taxes on knowledge would lead to an increased demand for literary men, and give the publishers the means to remunerate them better, *Bucknall* 1251–1253——Opinion that a higher description of talent would be employed upon the unstamped press, which would lead to a greater demand for the services of literary men, *Cassell* 1421–1423——The abolition of the penny stamp would increase the demand for literary talent, and increase the remuneration of literary men, *Spenser* 2414–2417.

*See* also *American Press*, 3. *Editors.*

*Literary and Scientific Institutions.* See *Mechanics' Institutions.*

*LOCAL*

Report, 1851—*continued.*

*LOCAL NEWSPAPERS:*

1. *Increase in the Number of Local Newspapers which may be expected from the Abolition of the Stamp.*
2. *How far such Increase would be injurious to the London Papers.*
3. *Advantages which would result to the Country Districts from their Increase.*

1. *Increase in the Number of Local Newspapers which may be expected from the Abolition of the Stamp:*

The removal of the stamp and the substitution of a postal rate might have the effect of encouraging small local newspapers, *Russell* 1479–1487——Opinion that a paper emanating from the metropolis, having a manifest national character, is much more likely to be useful to the country than small local papers, confined to little local bickerings, *Hunt* 2358–2360——The abolition of the penny stamp would have the effect of increasing the number of local newspapers, *Cole* 2766, 2767——Taking off the penny stamp would lead to the establishment of a great number of local newspapers, but they would still require postal communication to bring the papers into the remote districts, *Smith* 2837, 2838. 2917–2920.

2. *How far such Increase would be injurious to the London Papers:*

Taking off the stamp, and only making those papers pay a tax which went through the Post-office, would no doubt increase the number of local papers with extracts from the London papers, *Collett* 985–996. 1005–1016——But witness does not believe that the London papers would be injured thereby, as he does not consider that their circulation would be diminished, *ib.* 985–996. 1004——Evidence as to how far any advantage would result from allowing country newspapers to be published without the stamp, the London papers still retaining the stamp for transmission through the post, *Cassell* 1451–1463——Manner in which the country newspapers would obtain their news in the event of the stamp being abolished and the number of papers increased; how far it would be fair for them to copy from the London papers which have been at the expense of obtaining the news, *ib.* 1451–1462.

Objections to the removal of the penny stamp, as it would have the effect of giving rise to the growth of local newspapers of an inferior quality, and the most struggling papers in the large towns would be killed off by them, *Russell* 1547–1575. 1579–1595. 1606——Witness considers the metropolitan papers a greater advantage than local papers for the circulation of sound intelligence, *ib.* 1599——The provincial newspapers are enabled to publish more cheaply than the daily papers, as they are published but once or twice a week, and they copy all their articles from the daily papers, *Morris* 2112, 2113.

3. *Advantages which would result to the Country Districts from their Increase:*

Repealing the penny stamp would decidedly increase the circulation of local newspapers; this would be an advantage to the different districts in the country in which they were published, *Cassell* 1426–1429——The majority of the local newspapers are of a character more likely to do good than harm to the labouring classes, *Bunting* 2308, 2309——Opinion that an increase in the number

Report, 1851—*continued.*

*Local Newspapers*—continued.

3. *Advantages which would result to the Country Districts,* &c.—continued.

number of local newspapers would be a great benefit to the community, *Haywood* 2600, 2601——Advantages of local newspapers in correcting local abuses, *Watkinson* 2670–2672.

*See* also *Advertisements. American Press,* 2. *Extracts from Newspapers. Provincial Newspapers. Stamping Establishments. Transmission of Newspapers,* 1.

*London District.* Recommendation of the Committee that the charge of a penny for the transmission of stamped newspapers from one part of the London district to another be abolished, *Rep.* 8, 9——Inconvenience of a charge being made for the transmission of newspapers from one part of London to another; this is avoided by posting them out of the London district; this applies also to all the large towns, *Spenser* 2392–2394. 2399–2408——It would give great additional facility if the newspapers were allowed to circulate in London for a halfpenny wrapper, *ib.* 2406–2413. 2447——Great injustice and inconvenience of a postage of a penny being charged on all newspapers transmitted by post within the three-mile circle, *Cole* 2699–2707——Instance of a large number of newspapers being taken from London and posted at Brompton, in order to avoid this additional charge, *ib.* 2699. 2705, 2706——Object with which the additional postage charge on newspapers circulating within the London district was made, *ib.* 2708, 2709; *Smith* 2874, 2875——Opinion that were the newspapers allowed to pass within the London district without the impost of additional postage, the proprietors would be enabled to reduce the price of their papers, *Cole* 2710–2718.

*London Papers.* See *Daily Papers.*

*Low Publications.* Existence of a low class of publications in America, whose purpose is to extort money from parties who can be threatened with exposure, *Greeley* 3032–3035.

*See* also *Bad Publications. Immoral Publications. Libellous Publications. Obscene Publications. Pernicious Publications.*

## M.

*Magazines.* Magazines have, from the time that the newspaper stamp duty has been imposed, obtained a character different in some respects from that of a newspaper, *Timm* 146——Although they may contain news in one article, yet generally they are filled with other matter than is common to newspapers, *ib.* 146–148——If the decision of the court should be that Dickens's "Household Narrative" is a newspaper, such decision would not carry with it and include the large monthly publications, such as the "New Monthly Magazine," *ib.* 149–155——Their contents are totally different from Dickens's paper, *ib.* 149——There are a number of magazines giving comments upon the events of the month; were they debarred from so doing they would be dropped, and the beneficial effect to the working classes impeded, *Cassell* 1312–1314.——*See* also *Monthly Publications.*

*Manchester.* See *Stamping Establishments.*

*Mechanics'*

Report, 1851—*continued.*

*MECHANICS' INSTITUTIONS:*

1. *Generally.*
2. *Benefits which have resulted from the addition of News-rooms to these Institutions.*
3. *Further Benefits which would probably result if Newspapers could be obtained more cheaply.*

1. *Generally:*

Number of Mechanics' Institutes in Lancashire, Cheshire, and Yorkshire, *Hogg* 1024——Witness is secretary to the 30 or 40 institutes which have formed themselves into a union in Lancashire and Cheshire, *ib.* 1025–1028——Nearly the whole of these institutions have news-rooms, *ib.* 1029–1049——The great exception is that at Liverpool, *ib.* 1029–1050.

Many of the wealthier and influential founders and supporters of these institutions withdrew their support when the news-rooms were added to them, *Hogg* 1040——They feared that the introduction of newspapers would introduce party politics, *ib.* 1040–1046——By good management, however, this fear has proved to be groundless, *ib.* 1040–1046. 1051–1053——The proportion of artisans who attend these institutions is, generally speaking, rather on the decrease; causes to which this may be attributed, *ib.* 1086–1089——Reasons for the decrease in the encouragement given to these institutions by the higher classes of manufacturers and persons in that position, *ib.* 1090–1091——List of mechanics' and other literary and scientific institutions in Lancashire and Cheshire, specifying those which have news-rooms, *App.* 522.

2. *Benefits which have resulted from the addition of News-rooms to these Institutions:*

The news-rooms are the most attractive departments in many of the Mechanics' Institutions, *Hogg* 1030——Witness considers that there are many collateral advantages which would follow from inducing the working classes to attend the news-rooms of these institutions, *ib.* 1037——Opinion that introducing news-rooms into each of the mechanics institutes in the country would not have a tendency to take the mechanics from more solid pursuits than newspaper reading, *ib.* 1067–1075——It would take them rather from worse pursuits, and lift them up rather than bring them down, *ib.* 1067–1075.

As regards the mechanics' institutes, witness has generally observed that they have been almost always composed of the middle classes, *Hickson* 3260——Still in some of the manufacturing districts they embrace a large portion of the working classes, *ib.*——Many of these institutions have failed from their not having a news-room; the news-room is found the greatest attraction, *ib.* 3260–3262.

3. *Further Benefits which would probably result if Newspapers could be obtained more cheaply:*

In all the large towns the news-rooms of these institutes are generally very well supplied with papers; but in the small towns there is generally the greatest difficulty in getting a good supply, *Hogg* 1031–1033. 1063–1065——The first great difficulty which these institutes have to contend with is the want of funds, *ib.* 1032–1047——There is a great want of interest on the

part

*MECHANICS' INSTITUTIONS*—continued.

3. *Further Benefits which would probably result,* &c.—continued.

part of the working classes to attend them, though the institutions bear their name, and were established by them, *Hogg* 1032——Opinion that if the price of newspapers were low, and the supply large, the working classes would attend these institutions in greater numbers; many of them now prefer the public-house where they can find a newspaper, *ib.* 1033–1037. 1042–1048. 1062–1068.

Economical plans which these institutions are obliged to adopt in consequence of the expense of the papers, *Hogg* 1059——A petition to the House of Commons was presented by the union of mechanics' institutions in Lancashire and Cheshire, praying for the repeal of the stamp duty, the advertisement duty, and the paper duty, *ib.* 1060, 1061. 1095——Way in which they interfere with the prosperity of these institutions, *ib.* 1061, 1062. 1082–1085——The newspapers are usually supplied to these institutions by agents in the towns, which entails the charge of an extra penny on the paper, *ib.* 1076–1081. 1092–1094.——*See* also *Education,* 1.

*Middle Classes.* See *Cheap Publications. Mechanics' Institutions. Old Newspapers.*

"*Mirror of the Time.*" The "Mirror of the Time" is a publication contrary to the law; it is constantly publishing political articles, *Collett* 908, 909——A paper called the "Mirror of the Time" has not been brought specifically under the notice of the Board, as to whether it was a newspaper or not; it has just been registesed as a newspaper, *Keogh* 3086-3092.

*Monopoly.* The penny stamp decidedly operates to create a monopoly, *Whitty* 620——The effect of abolishing the stamp and advertisement duties would be to equalize a great deal the circulation of newspapers, and to give a decided preference to the best ones, *ib.* 621–627.

*Monthly Publications.* Several monthly publications have received intimations from the Stamp-office that they contained matters that render them liable to the newspaper stamp, *Keogh* 534. 550–558——The decision in the "Narrative of Current Events" case will decide this class of cases, *ib.* 534, 535——The larger magazines do not fall within this category, *ib.* 536——Large number of monthly unstamped publications in existence; almost every religious and philanthropic movement has its monthly organ, *Cassell* 1277——Opinion that it would materially assist the objects of the moral and religious movements, were their monthly organs permitted to contain news and narratives of passing events, *ib.* 1320, 1321.

*See* also *Magazines.* "*Narrative of Current Events.*" *Registration of Newspapers.*

"*Morning Chronicle.*" See "*Punch.*"

*Morning Papers.* See *Daily Papers. Printing Machinery.*

*Morris,*

Report, 1851—*continued.*

*Morris, Mowbray.* (Analysis of his Evidence.)—Manager of the "Times" newspaper, 2016——Nature of the duties performed by witness as manager, 2017, 2018——Total amount paid by the "Times" for penny stamps, including also halfpenny stamps for supplements, 2019–2021——The stamp is paid for by the public in the shape of an additional charge upon the papers, 2022, 2023——Abolishing the newspaper stamp would very likely have the effect of destroying those papers possessing the least public confidence, the papers of established reputation would not be affected, 2024–2027. 2063–2069——Remarks as to the stamp duty payable on supplements of the "Times;" this tends to limit the circulation, as the losses upon the supplement destroy the profit of the paper, 2028–2050——The stamp on the supplement is extremely unjust, as it consists entirely of advertisements, on each of which a duty is paid, 2051–2054.

The stamp duty acts as a protection to the inferior class of newspapers, and tends to limit the circulation of the leading newspapers by reason of the duty on the supplements, 2055–2070——It is quite possible to have a uniform stamp of a fixed denomination without reference to size; the supplement is just as much part of the paper as page No. 6, and there is no reason why a particular page should be stamped, 2070——Object of limiting the superficial extent of newspapers when Lord Monteagle's Stamp Act passed, 2071——As far as those newspapers are concerned that are sent by post a service is rendered for the penny stamp, 2072–2075——Very few of the morning papers are transmitted into the country by post; they are usually sent by the railway, and an additional charge made by the newsvenders for the express, 2076–2078.

Calculations bearing upon the statement with regard to the effect of the stamp duty on the supplement, 2079–2084——In the event of the stamp being abolished, witness conceives it would be the duty of every paper to reduce the price exactly the amount of the stamp, 2085, 2086. 2146——It might be possible to publish and maintain at a profit a newspaper at a penny, but not such a paper as the people are accustomed to, 2087, 2088——Removing the stamp from newspapers, and preventing their passing through the post free, would tend to limit their circulation within the locality of their publication, 2089–2091——Allowing newspapers to pass through the post on the payment of 1 *d.* instead of the present stamp, would not limit the circulation, 2090, 2093——The expenses of producing a good newspaper render it impossible to work it for 1 *d.* a copy, 2094–2096.

Remarks relative to the penny newspapers published in America, 2095–2097. 2147——Superiority of the machinery used for newspaper printing in England to that used in America; Applegath's machinery is superior to anything in use in any part of the world, 2098–2107——A good newspaper could not even be maintained at 2 *d.*, 2108–2111——The provincial newspapers are enabled to publish more cheaply than the daily papers, as they are published but once or twice a week, and they copy all their articles from the daily papers, 2112, 2113——Inferiority of the American newspapers to the English papers, 2114. 2120. 2147——Publication of an account of the opening of the Exhibition on unstamped paper, as it was published in the "Times;" opinion that it did not require a stamp, 2121–2133——The

Queen's

Report, 1851—*continued.*

*Morris, Mowbray.* (Analysis of his Evidence)—*continued.*

Queen's speech is printed and published almost immediately it is delivered in the House of Parliament, without a stamp, 2133.

Manner in which the paper for the "Times" is obtained and stamped; expense to the proprietors of the newspaper in fetching the paper from the Stamp-office to their printing office, 2134–2140——Advantages which the established newspapers experienced from the reduction of the stamp duty, in former times, 2141–2145.——The "Times" is published three times a week under the head of the "Evening Mail," without the advertisements, for circulation in the country, 2146——Witness has a very high opinion of the French press, they have greatly improved since the stamp duty has been imposed upon them, 2148–2159. 2167–2178——The stamp improves the character of newspapers; provided it was increased, it would improve them still more, 2155–2164——It is not advisable to remove the stamp from off newspapers, 2164. 2199——The stamp on the supplements has the effect of restricting the circulation of newspapers; it is a heavy burthen, and ought not to be imposed on any ground whatever, 2165, 2166.

The tone of the press has greatly improved since the reduction of the stamp from from 4 *d.* to 1 *d.*; still witness considers that great deterioration would be caused by the removal of the penny stamp, 2179–2193. 2201–2218——The chief ground upon which witness advocates the retention of the stamp duty on newspapers is, that an excellent revenue is raised without imposing any sensible burden, 2193–2195——Manner in which the penny stamp tends to improve the tone of the press, 2196–2200. 2221, 2222——Importance of the proprietors of newspapers being large capitalists, as having the effect of keeping up the respectable character of the press, 2196–2200. 2221, 2222——The removal of the penny stamp would lead to the establishment of cheap newspapers, containing violent doctrines dangerous to the public peace and morals, 2201–2215.

Existence of a censorship of the press at the present time; explanation as to the form in which it exists, 2208–2210. 2219.——The improved tone of the press of late years arises entirely from the great improvement in the manners, tastes, and feelings of the nation, 2216–2218. 2220——Witness cannot see the justice of allowing publishers to stamp portions of their impressions for obtaining the facilities of transmission by post, the regular newspapers being obliged to stamp all their impressions, 2223–2225——It is witness's conviction, that if the stamp duty were removed from newspapers, the commercial advantages of the "Times" would be enormous, from the increased circulation, but witness would be sorry to see the stamp abolished, as it might lead the public to patronize inferior papers, 2225–2238——Whatever is done with the stamp on the newspaper itself, the stamp on the supplement ought decidedly to come off, 2226–2231. 2236.

## N.

"*Narrative of Current Events.*" Grounds of the proceedings which have been commenced against the publishers of a "Narrative of Current Events," edited by Dickens, and nature of these proceedings, *Timm* 59–66——Lengthened

examination

Report, 1851—*continued.*

" *Narrative of Current Events*"—continued.

examination on the subject of the prosecution pending against Dickens's "Narrative of Current Events," with the grounds for witness's coming to the conclusion that it is undoubtedly in its present form, and at the present interval of publication, a newspaper, *Timm* 202-268——The Board of Inland Revenue is carrying on a prosecution against Dickens for the publication of his "Household Narrative," *Keogh* 533; *Collett* 901——Witness does not consider that this prosecution can altogether be considered *bonâ fide*; grounds on which witness forms this opinion, *Collett* 901-908——If the Board had wished to try the case thoroughly, they should also have proceeded against the other publications of the same publishers, *ib.* 908.

Proceedings are at present being taken against the publishers of Dickens's "Household Narrative," to decide the legality of publishing an unstamped monthly periodical containing news, *Bucknall* 1182, 1183——Observations as to the prosecution at present pending against the publisher of Dickens's "Household Narrative;" the whole question as to the liability of such publications hinges upon this trial, *Cassell* 1283-1290——But there will be great difficulty in drawing a distinction between what is an ordinary periodical and what constitutes a newspaper, *ib.* 1291-1296. 1299——On these occasions a discretion must be exercised by the proper authorities as to the carrying out of the law, *ib.* 1297——If the decision with respect to the "Household Narrative" be favourable to Mr. Dickens, it will have a beneficial effect as far as monthly publications are concerned, *ib.* 1328, 1329.

*See* also *Magazines. Monthly Publications. " Working Man's Friend."*

" *New Monthly Magazine.*" See *Magazines.*

*New Publications.* Several publications have been set up, as it were, upon the chance of being pulled down, and have gone on for a certain time before information has been given to the Board of Inland Revenue, *Keogh* 3116-3122——If it be found that these attempts, just keeping on the line of the law, are generally unsuccessful, and that the parties must either exclude such matter from their papers, or register them as newspapers, there is no reason why they should increase, *ib.* 3116-3122.

*See* also *Starting Newspapers.*

*New York.* Number of daily papers published in New York; average circulation of those papers, *Greeley* 2620-2626.

" *New York Herald.*" Extent of the circulation of the "New York Herald;" character of this paper, *Greeley* 3042-3045.

" *New York Tribune.*" Remarks relative to the publication, price, and circulation of the "New York Tribune," *Greeley* 2516-2519.

*NEWS:*

Report, 1851—*continued.*

*NEWS:*

1. *Generally.*
2. *Difficulties in defining what constitutes News.*
3. *Test at the Board of Inland Revenue as to whether a Publication is a Newspaper or not.*

1. *Generally:*

Statement of the Committee that, apart from fiscal considerations, they do not consider that news is of itself a desirable subject of taxation, *Rep.* 12.

2. *Difficulties in defining what constitutes News:*

Observations of the Committee on the difficulty that the officers of the Board of Inland Revenue find in defining what is news, *Rep.* 5——Statement of the Committee that the Board of Inland Revenue, according to the evidence of their secretary, recognise a difference, hard to be understood, between public and private news, and draw a distinction unknown to the law between public and class news, *ib.*——Evidence showing that the meaning of the word "newspaper," the taxable articles called "news," has changed from time to time, *Collett* 737–739——At the present time there is no definite meaning whatever attached to the term "newspaper" by the Stamp-office, *ib.* 739 *et seq.*——About the time of the unstamped papers, from 1832 to 1836, there was a very definite meaning attached to it, *ib.* 739——Any paper at that time that was issued oftener than once a month was put down, if it contained a very small quantity of news, *ib.* 739, 740.

Inconvenience to the trade from the existing uncertainty as to the liability of publications to the stamp duty; the settlement of the question would be very satisfactory to the trade, *Cassell* 1298, 1299——Difficulties in defining what constitutes a newspaper; witness would consider it a very dangerous power for any man to be entrusted with the definition of what constitutes a newspaper, *ib.* 1307–1311——Difficulties in ascertaining what constitutes a newspaper, and renders it liable to the stamp duty, *Haywood* 2571–2584; *Cole* 2801–2805——It would be next to impossible to levy the stamp with perfect justice, unless it was placed upon every printed sheet of periodical literature; in fact, upon almost every book, *Cole* 2802–2805——Reference to the opinion expressed by the judges, whether any periodical publication could speak of an event of yesterday without being subject to the tax, *ib.* 2805.

3. *Test at the Board of Inland Revenue as to whether a Publication is a Newspaper or not:*

In the Schedule (A.) of the Act 6 & 7 Will. 4, c. 76, there are the definitions of what, in law, are to be deemed newspapers; nature of these definitions, *Timm* 4. 17–22——The first section of this Act (6 & 7 Will. 4, c. 76) imposes duties on newspapers contained in the above-named schedule, *ib.* 4——Under the Acts in no case must facts, intelligence, occurrences, or anything that can come within the description of public news, be printed on any material without a stamp, *ib.* 15. 17–22——The test at the Board of Inland Revenue whether a given publication is a newspaper or not, is, whether it contains public news, intelligence, or occurrences, or comments or observations thereon, published at less intervals than twenty-six days, *ib.* 55–57——The Board has never found itself in any great practical difficulty in deciding what is news and what is not, *ib.* 58.

The

*NEWS*—continued.

3. *Test at the Board of Inland Revenue, &c.*—continued.

The Board of Inland Revenue holds, that any paper containing public news, intelligence, or occurrences, is a newspaper, and subject to the stamp duty, *Keogh* 401——If the printing of news were to occur on a piece of cotton, witness does not think the law would comprehend that, *ib.* 403——Definition of what witness considers news, under the terms of the Act, *ib.* 415–420. 427–432. 444–447——Opinion as to what does and what does not constitute news, within the meaning of the Act, *Bucknall* 1143. 1183, 1184.

*See* also *Acts of Parliament.* "*Athenæum,*" The. *Class Publications. Comments on News. Extracts from Newspapers.* "*Legal Observer.*" *Magazines.* "*Narrative of Current Events.*" *Notices to Publishers. Pamphlets. Penalties. Prosecutions.* "*Punch.*" *Registration of Newspapers. Weekly Publications.*

*News Rooms.* See *Mechanics' Institutions.*

*Newspapers.* From the time when the stamp duty was first imposed, in the reign of Queen Anne, the number of newspapers has been very much diminished, *Collett* 737.

*Newsvenders.* Extra charge made by newsvenders for the early newspapers in the country, which are sent down by railway; how far witness considers the Post-office would be able to compete with these newsvenders in the delivery of newspapers at a penny each, *Hill* 1856–1869. 1932–1954. 1961–1969——Very little revenue would arise from a penny postage for the conveyance of newspapers, as the newsvenders would immediately contrive means by which the papers should be delivered at a very small cost, *Smith* 2858–2873——The newsvenders would be able to establish a successful competition with the Post-office in the distribution of newspapers, *ib.* 2863–2871.

*See* also *Agents. Railways. Transmission of Newspapers.*

"*Northern Star.*" See *Working Classes.*

"*Norwich Reformer.*" Instance of the "Norwich Reformer," the organ of the Parliamentary Reform Association in Norwich, which, from its containing a column called "Record of Progress," was deemed to be a newspaper; proceedings taken by the Stamp-office with respect to this paper, and correspondence on the subject, *Collett* 742–749. 758——Cases of what witness considered to be a violation of the law, and which he got laid before the Board of Inland Revenue at the time of the threatened prosecution of the "Norwich Reformer;" these cases were similar to that of this paper; result of this proceeding, *ib.* 758 *et seq.*——Evidence relative to the "Norwich Reformer," an unstamped paper; nature of its contents; suppression of the paper by the Board of Inland Revenue, from its not being stamped, *Bunting* 2240–2272.

*See* also *Class Publications.*

*Notices to Publishers.* Statement of all the cases in which cautions have been given to publishers of newspapers within the last three years, *Keogh* 3075——These cautions have only begun to be issued within the last two or three years, *ib.* 3075. 3111, 3112——These attempts to steer just beyond the line of the law have only arisen within the last three years, *ib.*——In former years the Board had not to deal with any such persons, *ib.* 3075, 3076.

Report, 1851—*continued.*

*Notices to Publishers*—continued.

Cases in which the solicitor of Inland Revenue has, during the last three years, written to caution the publishers of unstamped newspapers against incurring further liabilities, or has in any way interfered with such publications where no prosecution has been instituted, *App.* 504——Return of the correspondence which has taken place during the last three years between the solicitor of the Board of Inland Revenue and the publishers of unstamped newspapers, in the cases in which the publishers have been cautioned that their papers have contained news or comments upon news, *ib.* 506.

*See* also *"Freeholder,"* The. *Monthly Publications.* *Prosecutions.*

## O.

*Obliteration of Stamps.* Frequency of newspapers passing several times through the Post-office; impossibility of preventing this as the stamp is not obliterated, *Parkhurst* 1653–1656——The only means of preventing newspapers being sent more than once through the post would be to obliterate the stamp, *Hill* 1785–1792——This plan has been rejected on the ground that the trouble and expense of applying it would be greater than the advantage gained by it would justify, *ib.* 1785–1789. 1971, 1972——Great increase of labour would result from the stamps on newspapers having to be obliterated, *Bokenham* 2006–2015.

*Obscene Publications.* If newspapers could be put in competition, as regards price, with such publications as the "Town," an infamous and obscene paper, published at a penny, they would not be likely entirely to divest the minds of the reading public from such works, *Keogh* 471–498. 501–503——Such papers are not required to be registered; the Newspaper Stamp Act has no relation to them, *ib.* 483, 484. 486–489——The publication of unstamped newspapers very much reduced the sale of the penny papers of an obscene and improper character; still these unstamped papers were not very good themselves, *Whitty* 590–597.——*See* also *Immoral Publications.*

*Old Newspapers.* There is no limit of time that prevents a newspaper being carried within the United Kingdom in virtue of the penny stamp, *Parkhurst* 1674–1680——Frequency of bundles of old newspapers sold for waste paper being sent through the post free of charge, *Parkhurst* 1677; *Hill* 1750, 1751. 1772–1774——There is no restriction as to the age of newspapers sent through the Post-office, except as to the colonial or foreign posts; frequency of papers passing and repassing through the Post-office, *Hill,* 1770–1777——Newspapers are the only packets transmitted through the Post-office which are allowed the privilege of being twice sent without any additional charge, *ib.* 1778, 1779——Sending a newspaper twice through the post is an abuse of the privilege of the stamp, yet it is within the letter of the law, and an alteration of the law would be required to prevent it, *ib.* 1780–1784——Frequency of newspapers being sent through the post several times; this power of re-transmission by means of the stamp is a great convenience to the middle classes, *Smith* 2829–2834. 2839–2846. 2876–2883.

## P.

*Pamphlets.* Great advantage would result from pamphlets advocating temperance and other principles being allowed to contain news, *Spencer* 2450–2452.

*See* also *Advertisement Duty,* 1.

*Paper*

Report, 1851—*continued.*

*Paper Duty.* The effect of the stamp and advertisement duty must be to lessen the amount of the receipts from the duty on paper, *Greeley* 2988, 2989—— Instead of the three taxes, the stamp, advertisement, and paper duties, a paper duty alone would be the most equal and most efficient as a revenue duty, *ib.*

*Parkhurst, Rodae.* (Analysis of his Evidence.)--Senior clerk in the secretary's office of the Post-office, 1618——Regulations as to the transmission of newspapers by post, 1619–1623——The permission of the Postmaster-general is necessary for the transmission of any publications not strictly newpapers through the post by the penny stamp; manner in which this permission is obtained, 1624–1628. 1635–1638——Power of the Treasury to lay down any regulations as to the transmission of newspapers through the Post-office; they could at their discretion put a charge upon all newspapers, 1629–1633.

In the event of unstamped publications being sent through the Post-office they are charged as letters when detected; impossibility of examining every parcel, 1639–1650——Every precaution is taken against this system of fraud that the machinery of the Post-office will allow; cases of fraud are very rare now, 1643-1651——Provided a stamp was placed on the outside of every newspaper detection of frauds would be far more easy than at present, 1652——Frequency of newspapers passing several times through the Post-office; difficulty in the way of preventing this as the stamp is not obliterated, 1653–1656.

Impossibility of examining every parcel of newspapers to ascertain whether they bear the stamp; such an examination would require the force to be increased to an enormous extent, and would necessarily delay the delivery, 1657–1664——In the event of such fraud being detected, and the postage as for a letter charged, the party to whom it is addressed may refuse to receive it, and there is no means of reaching the party who posted it, 1665–1673——There is no limit of time that prevents a newspaper being constantly carried within the United Kingdom, in virtue of the penny stamp, 1674-1680——Frequency of large bundles of newspapers being sent through the post after being sold as waste paper, 1677——All newspapers with writing on them are liable to be surcharged; there is no time to examine all newspapers to see whether they have writing on them, 1681–1686——Newspapers containing writing can be sent through the Post-office, provided they are prepaid with a postage stamp, 1681. 1685.

*Partly Stamped Publications.* Applications have been made from the proprietors of newspapers, who are now under the necessity of stamping every copy that they publish, to be allowed the privilege that the fifty-three registered newspapers enjoy, of only stamping that portion which goes by post, *Timm* 179; *Keogh* 548, 549. 551, 552——The law prevents the Board from granting these applications, *Timm* 180——Evidence showing that there is a wide distinction between the case of the proprietors who stamp all their impressions and the publications of the applicants for this privilege, as it is termed, *ib.* 181–194——The Board of Inland Revenue ought not to allow of any newspaper circulating under the two heads of stamped and unstamped, *Collett* 789–803.

Witness does not approve of the system of allowing publishers of periodicals to stamp a portion of their impressions for the purpose of sending them

 through

*Partly Stamped Publications*—continued.

through the post; such a system is not defensible, *Russell* 1532–1542——The regulations respecting newspapers are very much evaded, and probably the admission of portions of an impression may tend to promote this evasion, *Hill* 1692. 1749——Allowing publishers to stamp a portion of their impressions leads to unstamped copies being passed through the post-office without detection; instance of this with regard to "Punch," the "Athenæum," &c., *ib.* 1693, 1694——Defective nature of the arrangements with respect to the transmission of certain impressions of various publications through the post by reason of the stamp; frequency of evasion from the whole of the impressions not being stamped, *ib.* 1752–1769——Witness cannot see the justice of allowing publishers to stamp portions of their impressions for obtaining the facilities of transmission by post, such as the "Athenæum" and "Punch," the regular newspapers being obliged to stamp all their impressions, *Morris* 2223–2225.

*See* also "*Athenæum,*" The. *Class Publications.* "*Expositor,*" The. *Prices Current.* "*Punch.*" *Transmission of Newspapers,* 1.

*Party Papers.* There are many party papers, the organs of a particular set of opinions, which are published even at a loss to the proprietors; among these may be named the "Christian Socialist," the "Red Republican," the "Reasoner," the "People," &c., *Collett* 1019–1021.

*Peace Society.* See *Temperance Society.*

*Penalties.* Every person who prints a newspaper without a stamp is liable to a penalty of 20*l.* for every copy of the same, *Timm* 7–9. 37, 38; *Keogh* 402——But no penalty can be recovered beyond the copies which the Board may have in their possession and be able to give in as evidence, *Timm* 8——Although a penalty of 20*l.* is imposed by the Act of Parliament on every copy of a newspaper printed without a stamp, still no such penalty would ever be enforced as a whole, *Keogh* 3102.

*See* also *Extracts from Newspapers.* *Libel.* *Registration of Newspapers.*

"*Penny Magazine.*" See *Cheap Publications.*

*Penny Newspapers.* If the stamp were taken off newspapers, and the duty off advertisements, the papers might be sold at a penny, the same as they are in America, and be as well conducted as the "Times," *Whitty* 610. 622——Evidence showing that the penny stamp does prevent the penny newspapers altogether, *Collett* 738——A bad penny paper has but little circulation, and it requires a large capital to bring out a good penny paper, *ib.*——In the event of the removal of the stamp duty, penny newspapers might be established and circulated with profit, *Cassell* 1439, 1440.

It might be possible to publish and maintain at a profit a newspaper at a penny, but not such a paper as the people are accustomed to, *Morris* 2087, 2088——The expenses of producing a good newspaper render it impossible to work it for a penny a copy, *ib.* 2094–2096——Evidence relative to the penny newspapers published in America, *ib.* 2095. 2997. 2147——

A good

Report, 1851—*continued.*

*Penny Newspapers*—continued.

A good newspaper could not even be maintained at two pence, *ib.* 2108–2111——It would be impossible to provide newspapers for a penny, even were the stamp taken off; it would not make more difference in the price of the papers than the amount of the stamp, unless the quality was very much deteriorated, *Smith* 2848–2857.

*Penny Postage.* Frequency of old newspapers being sent through the post as a token of news, in substitution for a letter, whereby the postage is evaded; this practice has materially decreased since the introduction of the penny postage, *Hill* 1819–1822.

*Penny Publications.* See *Cheap Publications.* *Weekly Publications.*

"*People,*" The. See *Party Papers.*

*Pernicious Publications.* Mischievous and bad publications usually fall off after a short time for want of support and notice, *Collett* 915. 918, 919——A prosecution by the Board of Inland Revenue would no doubt tend very much to increase the circulation of papers of this description, by giving them publicity, *ib.* 916–921——Still if the law cannot be put in force, or the Government officers will not put it in force, or a jury will not give a verdict, then witness would say the law is bad and should be altered, *ib.* 917–920——Enormous circulation of pernicious publications at the present time; this is increased from the difficulties in the way of buying a higher-priced paper, *Bucknall* 1247–1249. 1262–1270.

Remarks contained in a pamphlet entitled "The Power of the Press," disclosing the extent and influence of the cheap scurrilous and baneful publications, *Bucknall* 1247. 1261, 1262——A cheap newspaper would rival the present pernicious publications in point of interest with the lower orders, and lead to a great moral improvement, *Bucknall* 1256–1259; *Haywood* 2538, 2539——The removal of the penny stamp would lead to the establishment of cheap newspapers, containing violent doctrines, dangerous to the public peace and morals, *Morris* 2201–2215——Reducing the price of newspapers would have a tendency to diminish the sale of pernicious penny publications, *Haywood* 2505–2508. 2515–2523.

*See* also *Bad Publications.* *Immoral Publications.* *Obscene Publications.*

*Personality.* See *American Press,* 3.

*Piracy.* See *Copyright of News.* *Local Newspapers,* 2.

*Political Agitation.* Witness delivers in a statement showing the effect of political agitation upon the number of newspapers, *Collett* 1021.

"*Poor Man's Guardian.*" Evidence as to the prosecution of 750 parties in connexion with the "Poor Man's Guardian," which prosecution was afterwards decided to be illegal, *Haywood* 2560–2568.

*Poorer Classes.* The penny stamp has something of the same effect in driving the poorer classes to the unstamped press that the higher rate of stamp used to have, but not to the same extent, *Collett* 738.

*See* also *Working Classes.*

Report, 1851—*continued.*

***POSTAGE:***

1. *Recommendations that the Stamp Duty should be Abolished, substituting a charge of a Penny for Transmission by Post.*
2. *Objections to such an Alteration.*
3. *Impracticability of transmitting Newspapers Free by Post.*
4. *Charge for Postage in America.*

1. *Recommendations that the Stamp Duty should be Abolished, substituting a charge of a Penny for Transmission by Post:*

It would be a great advantage to the whole community to abolish the stamp duty on newspapers, charging a penny for their transmission through the Post-office, *Cassell* 1361-1373—— Newspapers containing writing can be sent through the Post-office, provided they are prepaid with a penny stamp, *Parkhurst* 1681-1685——Memorandum as to the number of newspapers passing through the Post-office, and estimate of the amount likely to arise from a penny postage on newspapers, *Hill* 1823-1841. 1870. 1957-1960——Under the existing arrangements at the Post-office, newspapers could be carried profitably at a postage rate of a penny each, *Hill* 1852-1854. 1860-1863. 1873-1875——Manner in which witness considers that carrying newspapers at a penny each would be profitable to the Post-office, *ib.* 1871-1875.

In the event of a postage rate being fixed upon newspapers, the weight should be limited; average weight of the "Times," the "Weekly Dispatch," &c., *Hill* 1884-1891——Detail of a plan proposed by witness, by which the Post-office could deliver newspapers at a uniform postage of a halfpenny; great difficulties attending the carrying out of this plan, *ib.* 1909-1913. 1920-1954. 1961-1968——In the event of the stamp on newspapers being removed, they should be allowed to pass through the post on payment of a penny; this would be satisfactory, *Hunt* 2331-2333——Witness concurs in the estimate prepared by Mr. Hill as to the average number of newspapers transmitted through the London Post-office, *Bokenham* 1975, 1976——Witness is not prepared to make any suggestion as to the charge for the transmission of newspapers by post if the stamp should be abolished, *Hickson* 3217-3233.

2. *Objections to such an Alteration:*

Objections to the removal of the newspaper stamp, and the substitution of a postage upon the papers, *Russell* 1494-1508——From the altered circumstances of the times the stamp is no longer a postage charge; it operates as a tax upon news, *Cole* 2699——The abolition of the stamp, and the charge of a penny for each re-transmission, would be felt as a considerable tax, *Smith* 2835, 2836.

3. *Impracticability of transmitting Newspapers Free by Post:*

If newspaper stamps were altogether abolished, it would not be possible to permit the circulation of the London papers by post free of cost, *Collett* 870-872——Witness does not consider the stamp a tax, but a payment made to the Post-office for services, which could not be so efficiently performed in any other way for much more cost, *Russell* 1471. 1478. 1600, 1601. 1615——Objections to allowing newspapers to be sent through the post without prepayment, *Hill* 1800. 1882, 1883.

4. *Charge*

*POSTAGE*—continued.

4. *Charge for Postage in America:*

Amount of the postage charged on newspapers in America, *Russell* 1576. 1596–1598.

*See* also *Country Readers. Envelopes. Evasions of Postage. London District. Newsvenders. Obliteration of Stamps. Old Newspapers. Partly Stamped Publications. Postmaster-General. Prices Current. Railways. Revenue. Transmission of Newspapers. Treasury,* The.

*Postage Labels.* It might be possible to devise means by which stamps could be attached to newspapers by labels, but witness never heard of such a proposition, *Keogh* 385, 386——Provided a stamp were placed on the outside of every newspaper, detection of frauds would be far more easy than at present, *Parkhurst* 1652——Rendering it necessary that all newspapers should have a stamp affixed to them, would not prevent articles liable to postage being inclosed, although it would prevent any evasion as to sending unstamped publications, *Hill* 1702, 1703——In the event of the stamp being abolished from newspapers, they should be allowed to pass through the post by affixing a penny postage stamp, or using stamped covers, *ib.* 1794–1804. 1876–1881——Witness would not extend that privilege to all printed matter until it had been tried in a limited form on the regular newspaper press, when, if it should be considered safe to extend it, all printed matter might be included in the arrangement, *ib.* 1805, 1806. 1810, 1811.

*Postmaster-General.* The permission of the Postmaster-general is necessary for the transmission of any publications not strictly newspapers through the post by the penny stamp; manner in which this permission is obtained, *Parkhurst* 1624–1628. 1635–1638——Weekly return made by the Stamp-office to the Postmaster-general of all newly registered papers; the Postmaster-general decides whether they are newspapers or not, *Hill* 1689. 1691.

*Post Office.* If a revenue is to be derived from the postage of newspapers it is worthy of consideration whether it would not be simpler and more economical that the collection of such revenue should be managed, as in the case of letters, directly by the Post-office, rather than indirectly by another department, *Rep.* 9——The management of the newspaper postage should be left entirely to the Post-office, *Collett* 930——The present practice is for the Post-office to carry everything by post that bears the penny stamp; by this means the regulation of the postage is taken out of the hands of the Postmaster-general and placed in those of the Board of Inland Revenue, *Russell* 1543–1546——Objectionable nature of this plan; the postage regulations should be left entirely in the hands of the Post-office, *ib.* 1546.

Existing arrangements at the Post-office in reference to the transmission of newspapers by post, *Hill* 1688 *et seq.*——Placing the whole of the postal arrangements under the management of the Postmaster-general would not be any more convenient than the existing system; the course is now open to the Postmaster-general to advise the Treasury upon any subject of inconvenience, *ib.* 1807–1809——If the newspapers were removed altogether from the Post-office, it would be impossible to make anything like a corresponding reduction in

Report, 1851—*continued.*

*Post Office*—continued.

in the expenses of the establishment, *Hill* 1855. 1872——At present the Post-office does not take credit for the portion of the postage which comes under the head of newspaper stamps; the money received for newspaper stamps all goes into the account of the Inland Revenue, *ib.* 1955, 1956.

*See* also *Evasions of Postage,* 1. 2. *Inland Revenue Board. News-venders. Railways. Revenue. Transmission of Newspapers. Treasury,* The. *Unstamped Publications.*

*Price of Newspapers.* Statement of the Committee that it has been shown by the evidence that the penny stamp on each copy of a newspaper generally raises the price to the public beyond the mere addition of that sum, *Rep.* 7 ——In the event of the stamp being abolished, witness conceives it would be the duty of every paper to reduce the price exactly the amount of the stamp, *Morris* 2085, 2086. 2146——Reference to the American paper, the "New York Sun," as showing the possibility of producing a good paper at a low price, *Spencer* 2367——In the event of the abolition of the penny stamp, the London daily papers conducted with talent and supported with capital could be sold for 2*d.* or 3*d.* at a profit, *Cole* 2762, 2763——No newspaper can be published at present, such as the present morning papers, at less than the net amount which they now receive, *Smith* 2974.

*See* also *Abolition of the Duty,* 2. *American Press,* 4. *Bad Publications. Cheap Newspapers. Circulation. Literary Talent. London District. Mechanics' Institutions,* 3. *"New York Tribune." Obscene Publications. Penny Newspapers. Pernicious Publications. Size of Newspapers. "Times,"* The. *Working Classes.*

*Prices Current.* Some papers not strictly newspapers, such as "Prices Current," &c., are registered as such, and the declarations made; a portion of these papers being published without stamps, *Timm* 47——Messrs. A. B. Savory and Sons register a publication called "Savory's Price Current;" the title of it is "Savory and Sons' Price Current Newspaper;" the word newspaper merely applies to the stamp, *Rust* 3125——The same securities and obligations are entered into that are entered into by the publisher of an ordinary newspaper, *ib.* 3126–3128——It is not required by law that a "price current" should be stamped, but it is stamped in order that it may be transmitted through the Post-office, *ib.* 3129, 3130——If this circular were sent through the post without being stamped, the postage would be 4*d.*; but they would not then be sent, *ib.* 3131–3136——Could they be sent by post by putting a penny stamp on them, of course the trouble of registering would be saved, *ib.* 3137–3157. 3167–3171——Number of these papers sent out by Messrs. Savory in the course of the year; number which would probably be sent if charged for according to the full weight, *ib.* 3158–3166.

*See* also *Tradesmen's Catalogues.*

*Printing Machinery.* Superiority of the machinery used for newspaper printing in England to that used in America; Applegarth's machinery is superior to anything in use in any part of the world, *Morris* 2098–2107——Importance of superior machinery for the purpose of printing sufficient copies of the morning papers for early circulation, *Hunt* 2342——Powerful machinery employed

Report, 1851—*continued.*

*Printing Machinery*—continued.

employed in printing newspapers in America; the press of New York prints with greater rapidity than the "Times," *Greeley* 2652–2655——Description of machinery used in printing the American paper, the "Sun;" capital employed on that paper; extent of the circulation, *ib.* 2655–2660——The maintenance of the stamp on newspapers prevents mechanical improvements in the printing, by obliging the paper to be cut into certain sheets that the stamps may be put upon them, *Cole* 2793–2800.

*Printing Presses.* All printing presses used in the printing of unstamped newspapers are liable to seizure and forfeiture; proceedings which must be gone through before a warrant can be issued for their seizure, *Timm* 40–46——How far the parties whose presses have been seized have any redress if it turns out that what they have printed were not newspapers, *ib.* 45, 46.

*Proceedings of the Committee. Resumé* of the proceedings of the Committee *de die in diem, Rep.* 13–40.

*Proprietors.* If the newspaper proprietors throughout England were polled, nine out of ten would be disposed to keep the newspaper stamps and advertisement duty just as they are, *Whitty* 722.

*See* also *Abolition of the Duty. Advertisement Duty*, 2. *Competition. Partly Stamped Publications. Stamp Duties.*

*Prosecutions.* Power which the Board of Inland Revenue possesses of enforcing the law, and punishing those who infringe or evade the Act, *Timm* 37 *et seq.*——The mode of proceeding of the Board would be to sue for penalties in the Court of Exchequer, *ib.* 39——A question would then arise whether the publication was a newspaper in fact and in law; this would be a question which the judge would leave to the jury, *ib.*——The Legislature has vested the power in the Board to compromise all cases, either by paying a portion or without paying at all, *ib.* 121——In cases of doubt or difficulty the Board is advised by the Attorney and Solicitor-General, *ib.* 122.

The discretion of the Board in instituting a prosecution is governed by their estimate of the opinion the jury is likely to form of the publication, *Keogh* 514–517——The Stamp-office has a dangerous discretion as to whom they shall pick out for prosecution, and whom not, *Collett* 747–758——There have been no prosecutions under the stamp duty of late years, as all parties have ceased to publish on receiving notice from the Board of Inland Revenue, *Haywood* 2569–2584——Explanation of the threatened prosecution of Mr. Bucknall for publishing several copies of a newspaper without being stamped, *Keogh* 3069–3074.

Return of prosecutions in respect of violations of the Newspaper Stamp Acts for the three years ended September 1836, when the present Act came into operation, *App.* 499——Return of prosecutions in respect of violations of the Newspaper Stamp Acts for the three years ended 1st June 1851, *ib* 503.

*See* also *Infractions of the Law. Libel. Libellous Publications. "Narrative of Current Events." "Norwich Reformer." "Poor Man's Guardian." "Punch." "Stroud Observer."*

*Provincial*

Report, 1851—*continued.*

*Provincial Newspapers.* In the case of provincial papers, they have become more extended in circulation as they became more local in the nature of their intelligence, *Whitty* 649——Extreme facility of communication with respect to their local events and interests given to a people in a district has a good effect upon their character, by enabling them to know what they are about, and what is doing around them, *ib.* 650——It is very desirable to encourage that diffusion of the press which is created by greater facilities being afforded in the provinces instead of concentrating it all in one place, *ib.* 651.

*See* also *Local Newspapers.* *Transmission of Newspapers,* 1.

*Public,* The. The stamp is paid for by the public, in the shape of an additional charge upon the papers, *Morris* 2022, 2023.

*See* also *Price of Newspapers.* *Stamp Duties.*

*Publishers.* See *Advertisement Duty.* *Extracts from Newspapers.*

"*Punch.*" Witness is of opinion that if he were to attempt to prosecute "Punch" for being a newspaper he would be laughed out of court, *Timm* 97——"Punch," which is of small size, and under 6 *d.*, is a peculiar publication; their comments are merely a joke on the public events of the day, and it would be ridiculous to notice them with a view to prosecution, *Keogh* 515, 516. 518——Grounds on which witness asserts that this publication comes under the definition of a newspaper; it comments on the public events of the day, *Collett* 758. 760–775——"Punch" is as much a newspaper, according to the law, as the "Times" and "Morning Chronicle," *ib.* 758——Witness could produce nearly 50 papers unstamped that illegally publish news, intelligence, and occurrences, or works or observations thereon, *ib.* 910, 911——Instance of this in the case of "Punch," *ib.* 913——Complaint as to "Punch" publishing on unstamped paper, *App.* 486.

*See* also *Partly Stamped Publications.*

Q.

*Queen's Speech.* The Queen's speech is printed and published almost immediately it is delivered in the House of Parliament, without a stamp, *Morris* 2133.

R.

*Railways.* Facilities afforded by the railways for the conveyance of the daily newspapers into the country, *Cassell* 1355——The great bulk of the London press is now taken out by railways in the morning, and the Post-office very little used, *Cassell* 1355; *Morris* 2076–2078; *Cole* 2699. 2703; *Smit* 2819——In the event of the stamp duty upon newspapers being abolished, and a postage being fixed for their transmission through the post, a large proportion of the newspapers will be forwarded by railway, *Hill* 1812–1815. 1830–1832——Great number of newspapers sent by the railways at the present time for the purpose of early delivery; extra charge made by newsvenders for these early copies in the country, *Hill* 1836–1832. 1842–1851; *Morris* 2076–2078——None of the unstamped penny publications are sent through the post; they are distributed to the booksellers in the various towns by the railways, *Haywood,* 2479, 2480. 2594–2598. 2606–2613.

The

Report, 1851—*continued.*

*Railways*—continued.

The reading portion of the community has been greatly benefited by the establishment of railways, as a means of conveyance for unstamped periodicals, *Haywood* 2598——By the present arrangement the stamped newspapers that go by the railways pay for a postal privilege which they do not use, *Cole* 2704——Manner in which the newspapers are sent by railway, and cost of sending them, *Smith* 2820, 2821——The cost of conveyance by railway is paid by the agents in the country; it is very seldom that any additional charge is made for the early copy of the papers, *ib.* 2822–2826——Practice of some of the railway companies to transmit newspapers to individuals living near their lines; charge made for this accommodation, *ib.* 2827, 2828.

*See* also *Evening Papers.*

"*Ratepayer,*" The. Remarks relative to the publication of the "Ratepayer," a monthly unstamped periodical; communication received from the Board of Inland Revenue, requiring that paper to be stamped, *Anderson* 2455–2473——Since the communication from the Board of Inland Revenue the paper has been stamped, and is now a weekly newspaper, *ib.* 2462–2472.

"*Reasoner,*" The. Case brought under the notice of the Board, through witness, as a violation of the law, the "Reasoner;" particulars relative to this case, *Collett* 758.——*See* also *Party Papers.*

"*Red Republican.*" Instance of a paper called the "Red Republican," which contains political articles every week, which is unstamped, and consequently illegal, *Collett* 914, 915.——*See* also *Party Papers.*

*Reduction of the Duty.* Witness recollects when the stamp duty was reduced, the impossibility of enforcing the duty was one of the principal reasons alleged for reducing it, *Timm* 195–198——The impossibility was the want of a more stringent measure, and the want of power to search, *ib.* 198, 199——Beneficial effect of the reduction of the stamp on newspapers; it was the repeal of a heavy tax, and the substitution of a postage rate, *Russell* 1509, 1510——Advantages which the established newspapers experienced from the reduction of the stamp duty in former times, *Morris* 2141–2145——At the time of the reduction of the stamp duty on newspapers, and when the penny stamp was fixed, it was considered as a postage duty, affording newspapers a free circulation by post; it was not considered a tax, *Cole* 2695–2698. 2801.

*See* also *Abolition of the Duty,* 1. *Agents.* *Character of the Press,* 1. *Daily Papers.* *Revenue.*

*Reform Bill.* Reference to the number of unstamped newspapers issued about the time of the Reform Bill, *Collett* 737.

*Registration of Newspapers.* Section six of the Act 6 & 7 Will. 4, c. 76, enacts that no newspapers shall be printed or published before a declaration shall have been delivered in to the Commissioners of Stamps and Taxes, setting forth the correct title of the newspaper, and also the true description of the building wherein such paper is intended to be printed, and also of the building where published; and also setting forth the names, additions, and places of

*Registration of Newspapers*—continued.
of abode of the printers, publishers, and proprietors of such newspaper, *Timm* 4——The seventh section of the Act 6 & 7 Will. 4, c. 76, imposes a penalty of 50 *l.* for printing and publishing a newspaper before such declaration has been made and delivered, *ib.* 5. 37——The eighth section of the Act 6 & 7 Will. 4, c. 76, directs that a declaration shall be filed, and that certified copies of such declaration shall be admitted as evidence in all courts of law against the parties named in the declaration as the printer and publisher, *ib.* 5——Reference to a return made in 1850, of the papers published in the metropolis which are registered as newspapers, a portion whereof is published without stamps, *ib.* 47, 48——It would be competent for these parties if the Board sued them for penalties to plead that the thing was not a newspaper, though they had themselves signed the declarations and registered it as such, *ib.* 49, 50——A publication is not a newspaper in virtue of its registration, but in virtue of its contents, *ib.* 51.

One advantage of registering every newspaper is, that it affords an easy means of proving the fact of publication, *Keogh* 411, 412. 421, 422——Evidence on the subject of the return delivered in by Mr. Timm of the fifty-three registered newspapers published without stamps; they do not contain that matter upon which the newspaper duty is imposed, viz. public news, intelligence, or occurrences, *ib.* 448–452——Many of the fifty-three registered publications are of less price than 6 *d.*, and smaller in size than the size set forth, and published at less intervals than twenty-six days, but the question is, do they comment on public news, if so, they would be subject to the newspaper duty, *ib.* 505, 506. 509——With regard to the Board of Inland Revenue enforcing these conditions of high price and large size, they look to the law as it stands, *ib.* 514——If they consider it is infringed they endeavour to enforce it, giving notice to the parties of the position in which they stand, and if they resist, of course they are prosecuted, *ib.*——Way in which the return of the fifty-three registered publications was made up, *ib.* 521, 522——Enumeration of several of the monthly and weekly unstamped publications which are registered as newspapers, *Cassell* 1277.

*See* also *Advertisements. Character of the Press,* 1. *Inland Revenue Board. Libellous Publications. New Publications. Partly Stamped Publications. Postmaster-General. Prices Current.*

*Re-transmission of Newspapers.* See *Old Newspapers. Postage.*

*Revenue.* Amount derived from the stamp duty before the reduction from fourpence to a penny, and amount derived since, *Collett* 737——From that time to this the amount of revenue derived from newspaper stamps has never been so large as to be a serious matter of consideration, *ib.*——The removal of the stamp duty, and charging one penny for newspapers transmitted through the post, might affect the revenue at first, but it would ultimately prove a benefit, *Cassell* 1361——Grounds on which witness forms the opinion that the revenue would derive a benefit by the abolition of the stamp duty on newspapers, *ib.* 1361–1414——Great loss to the Post-office revenue that would result from the substitution of a penny postage on newspapers for the present stamp duty, *Russell* 1512–1515; *Hill* 1813–1816——Witness would have no objection

Report, 1851—*continued.*

*Revenue*—continued.

objection to extending free trade to newspapers were there not a question of revenue concerned, *Russell* 1615-1617——The present arrangement of newspaper stamps is a defective arrangement as regards the postal revenue, *Bokenham* 1990-1992——The chief ground upon which witness advocates the retention of the stamp duty on newspapers is, that an excellent revenue is raised without imposing any sensible burden, *Morris* 2193-2195——At the time the penny stamp on newspapers was fixed it was contemplated that the revenue arising therefrom would be considerable, *Cole* 2719——Reasons why witness does not consider that the penny stamp can be defended on fiscal grounds, *Hickson* 3193——Statement of the net produce of the stamp duty on Newspapers in the United Kingdom for the years 1848, 1849 and 1850, *App.* 483.

*See* also *Ad Valorem Duty.* *Advertisement Duty,* 2. *Inland Revenue Board.* *News,* 1. *Paper Duty.* *Postage.* *Post Office.*

"*Rugby Morning Advertiser.*" Remarks as to the publication of an unstamped paper, the "Rugby Morning Advertiser;" this contains the same description of information as the "Stroud Observer," yet it has not been suppressed, *Bucknall* 1138, 1139.

*Russell, Alexander.* (Analysis of his Evidence.)—Editor of the "Scotsman," Edinburgh paper; has been connected with the newspaper press between twelve and thirteen years, 1466-1469——Extensive circulation of the "Scotsman" newspaper; it is the most extensive in Edinburgh, 1467—The penny stamp on newspapers is, on the whole, a favourable arrangement for the press, 1471-1478. 1486 *et seq.* 1516-1538——Witness does not consider the stamp a tax, but a payment made to the Post-office for services, which could not be so efficiently performed in any other way for much more cost, 1471. 1478. 1600, 1601. 1615——There are no unstamped newspapers published in Edinburgh, nor in any part of Scotland, that witness is aware of, 1472, 1473——How far Edinburgh possesses any advantage over Glasgow and other places in Scotland from there being a stamping department established there, 1474-1477——The removal of the stamp and the substitution of a postal rate might have the effect of encouraging small local newspapers, 1479. 1487.

Improvement in the general tone of the newspaper press in Scotland of late years, 1480. 1511——The unstamped press of Scotland circulates in the form of newspapers without coming within the strict definition of a newspaper, such as "Chambers' Journal," 1481-1483——Witness is not aware of a single unstamped periodical of an evil tendency published in Scotland; cause to which this is attributable, 1482, 1483——Objections to the removal of the newspaper stamp and the substitution of a postage upon the papers, 1494-1508——Beneficial effect of the reduction of the stamp on newspapers; it was the repeal of a heavy tax and the substitution of a postage rate, 1509, 1510.

Great loss to the Post-office revenue that would result from the substitution of a penny postage on newspapers for the present stamp duty, 1512-1515——Witness does not approve of the system of allowing publishers of periodicals to stamp a portion of their impressions for the purpose of sending them through the

Report, 1851—*continued.*

*Russell, Alexander.* (Analysis of his Evidence)—*continued.* the post, 1532–1542——Witness does not see his way clear as to the adoption of an *ad valorem* duty upon newspapers or an *ad valorem* duty upon letters, 1530, 1531——Objection to allowing tradesmen's catalogues to bear the penny stamp for the convenience of transmission through the Post-office, 1539–1541——The present practice is for the Post-office to carry everything by post that bears the penny stamp; by this means the regulation of the postage is taken out of the hands of the Postmaster-general and placed in those of the Board of Inland Revenue, 1543–1546——Objectionable nature of this plan; the postage regulations should be left entirely in the hands of the Post-office, 1546.

Objections to the removal of the penny stamp, as it would have the effect of giving rise to the growth of local newspapers of an inferior quality, and the most struggling papers in the large towns would be killed off by them, 1547–1575. 1579–1595. 1606——Impossibility of newspapers being published in England as cheaply as in America, even if the stamp be abolished, 1576–1578——Amount of the postage charged on newspapers in America, 1576. 1596–1598.

Witness considers the metropolitan papers a greater advantage than local papers for the circulation of sound intelligence, 1599——Doubts as to whether the abolition of the penny stamp would lead to any increase in the number of newspapers published, 1602–1612——Witness does not look upon newspapers as a means of educating the people, 1613–1615——Witness would have no objection to extending free trade to newspapers were there not a question of revenue concerned, 1615–1617.

*Rust, Henry.* (Analysis of his Evidence.)—Witness appears before the Committee to represent Mr. A. B. Savory & Sons, 3124——They register a publication, called "Savory's Price Current;" the title of it is "Savory and Sons' Price Current Newspaper;" the word newspaper merely applies to the stamp, 3125——The same securities and obligations are entered into that are entered into by the publisher of an ordinary newspaper, 3126–3128——It is not required by law that a price current should be stamped, but it is stamped in order that it may be transmitted through the Post-office, 3129, 3130——If this circular were sent through the post without being stamped, the postage would be 4 *d.*; but they would not then be sent, 3131–3136——If they could be sent by post by putting a penny stamp on them, of course the trouble of registering would be saved, 3137–3157. 3167–3171——Number of these papers sent out by Messrs. Savory in the course of the year; number which would probably be sent if charged for according to the full weight, 3158–3166.

S.

*"Sam Sly."* See ***Libellous Publications.***

*Savory,* Messrs. See ***Prices Current.***

*Scotland.* There are no unstamped newspapers published in Edinburgh, nor in any part of Scotland, that witness is aware of, *Russell* 1472, 1473——Great improvement

Report, 1851—*continued.*

*Scotland*—continued.

improvement in the general tone of the newspaper press in Scotland of late years, *Russell* 1480. 1511——The unstamped press of Scotland circulates in the form of newspapers without coming within the strict definition of a newspaper, such as "Chambers' Journal," *ib.* 1481–1483.

*See* also *Edinburgh. Immoral Publications. Stamping Establishments.*

"*Scotsman*" *Newspaper.* Extensive circulation of the "Scotsman" newspaper; it is the most extensive in Edinburgh, *Russell* 1467.

*Scurrility.* See *American Press,* 3.

*Secretary to the Board of Inland Revenue.* All the secretarial business relating to newspapers or stamps is brought under witness's notice, *Keogh* 270, 271 ——Every letter from the Board on the subject of the newspaper press is signed by witness; he writes on the part of the Board, *ib.* 272, 273.

*Seditious Libel.* See *Libel.*

*Size of Newspapers.* Limitation as to the size of the sheets of paper stamped for newspapers, *Hill* 1767–1769——Object of limiting the superficial extent of newspapers when Lord Monteagle's Stamp Act passed, *Morris* 2071——In the event of the abolition of the stamp, and no limit being placed on the size of newspapers, papers will be published all sizes and all prices, *Haywood* 2585.

*See* also *Printing Machinery. Registration of Newspapers. Supplements to Newspapers.*

*Smith, William Henry.* (Analysis of his Evidence.)—Newspaper agent; witness's house has been engaged in the business upwards of sixty years, 2810, 2811——Considerable extent of witness's business, 2812–2818——Small proportion of the daily papers sent through the Post-office; the majority are sent by railway trains, 2819——Manner in which the newspapers are sent by railway, and the cost of sending them, 2820, 2821——The cost of conveyance by railway is paid by the agents in the country; it is very seldom that any additional charge is made for the early copy of the papers, 2822–2826——Practice of some of the railway companies to transmit newspapers to individuals living near their lines; charge made for this accommodation, 2827, 2828——Frequency of newspapers being sent through the post several times; this power of re-transmission by means of the stamp is a great convenience to the middle classes, 2829–2834. 2839–2846. 2876–2883.

The abolition of the stamp, and the charge of a penny for each re-transmission would be felt as a considerable tax, 2835, 2836——Taking off the penny stamp would lead to the establishment of a great number of local newspapers, but they would still require postal communication to bring the papers into the remote districts, 2837, 2838. 2917–2920——In the event of the stamp being abolished, it is most probable that there would be cheaper newspapers established, 2847——It would be impossible to provide newspapers for a penny, even were the stamp taken off; it would not make more difference in the price of the papers than the amount of the stamp, unless the quality was very much deteriorated, 2848–2857——Very little revenue would arise from a penny postage for the conveyance of newspapers, as the newsvenders

*Smith, William Henry.* (Analysis of his Evidence)—*continued.* venders would immediately contrive means by which the papers should be delivered at a very small cost, 2858–2873——The newsvenders would be able to establish a successful competition with the Post-office in the distribution of newspapers, 2863–2871.

Postage charge of a penny for the conveyance of newspapers within the London district; object of this charge being fixed, 2874, 2875——Statement of the number of daily papers distributed by witness's house prior to the reduction of the stamp in 1836, and since that period, showing the great increase, 2884–2889——With respect to class publications, they have the same advantages as newspapers, when stamped, although they are not obliged to stamp the whole of their impressions; witness does not consider this any hardship on the newspapers, 2890–2900——The recipients of the London newspapers in the country would not obtain their papers any cheaper from the removal of the stamp, whereas those parties to whom they are now re-transmitted free would have to pay a postage charge, 2901–2916.

Remarks relative to newspapers being kept for reference; to whatever extent papers are kept for reference, they are damnified by the penny stamp, 2921–2929——Objection of the news agents to the reduction of the newspaper stamp in 1836, in consequence of the reduction of their profits; they are also unfavourable to the removal of the penny stamp from the same cause, 2930–2934——The tendency of the abolition of the stamp would be to concentrate the news agent business into fewer hands; witness would be able to convey newspapers at a much less cost than the Post-office, 2932–2934——Evidence relative to the circulation of the daily morning and evening press in London, showing the increase and decrease of the several papers, 2935–2949. 2969–2971——The circulation of evening newspapers has greatly diminished since the establishment of railways; people in the country now get the early morning papers instead of the evening, 2948–2951.

The news agents frequently experience great difficulty in obtaining the required quantity of the "Times;" causes to which this may be attributable, 2952–2967——In the event of the abolition of the penny stamp, the "Times" would profit by it more than any other paper, 2965. 2968–2975——The abolition of the penny stamp would have very little influence upon the increase and sale of the newspapers; the price could not be reduced more than the amount of the stamp, 2972–2977——No newspapers can be published at present, such as the present morning papers, at less than the net amount which they now receive, 2974.

*Solicitor to the Board of Inland Revenue.* Witness has not exactly the control or superintendence in reference to the stamping of newspapers, *Timm* 2——But parties before they can obtain stamps for the printing of a newspaper must come before his department and enter into certain securities against libels, *ib.*——And they must also make a declaration as to the parties who are the printers, publishers, and proprietors of the paper, *ib.*——The whole of the preliminary proceedings are within witness's department, not the actual stamping, *ib.* 3.

"*Spalding*

Report, 1851—*continued.*

"*Spalding Free Press.*" Remarks relative to the "Spalding Free Press;" it is a stamped newspaper, *Watkinson* 2666–2668——Witness thought of commencing the paper unstamped; reason which led him to have it stamped, *ib.* 2669——Complaint of witness being charged postage for newspapers sent from his newspaper office to the Board of Inland Revenue at Lincoln, as he is compelled by law, with a view to their assessing the advertisement duty, *ib.* 2680–2688.

*Spencer, Rev. Thomas.* (Analysis of his Evidence.)—Clergyman of the Established Church, 2361——Opinion that the newspaper stamp is a great obstacle in the way of every movement for the diffusion of knowledge and the good of the people, 2362——Evidence generally in support of this opinion, 2363 *et seq.*——The little knowledge possessed by the working classes is attributable to their being unable to afford a newspaper, 2363——The stamp duty may be considered as a premium upon drunkenness; manner in which this is obviously the case, 2364. 2380–2383——Witness considers that newspaper reading is the most acceptable and instructive description of reading which people can possess, 2365——The abolition of the stamp would cause an enormous increase in the sale of newspapers by the reduction of the price, 2366, 2367.

Nothing would have so great an effect in improving the feelings of agricultural labourers as a reduction in the price of newspapers, 2367–2369. 2383–2391——Reference to the American paper, the "New York Sun," as showing the possibility of producing a good paper at a low price, 2367——At present all the advantages of the monopoly of the newspapers is on the side of bad men and bad principles, and the difficulty is only on the side of those who wish to do good; how witness arrives at this conclusion, 2370–2379——Difficulty experienced by the Temperance Society, or the Peace Society, in disseminating right principles among the community, from the high price of newspapers, 2370——Beneficial effects which have resulted from the circulation of Elihu Burritt's tracts in America in favour of peace, 2375, 2376——Although there are many pamphlets of a superior order, such as "Chambers' Journal," still the lower order of people will not read them; they must have a newspaper or they will not read anything, 2384–2391.

The circulation of a cheap press would tend to remove all prejudices from the minds of the people, and prevent hostility to machinery and other great improvements, 2392–2398——Inconvenience of a charge being made for the transmission of newspapers from one part of London to another; this is avoided by posting them out of the London district; this applies also to all the large towns, 2392–2394. 2399–2408——The circulation of cheap newspapers amongst the labouring classes would facilitate the transfer of labour from one part of the country to another, by making it known where labour was wanted, and where labour might be in excess, 2395, 2396——Emigration would be very much assisted by the circulation of a cheap newspaper press, 2397, 2398——It would give great additional facility if the newspapers were allowed to circulate in London for a halfpenny wrapper, 2406. 2409——Witness objects *in toto* to the stamp on newspapers as a means of transmission through the post; recommendation of a stamped halfpenny wrapper, 2410–2413. 2447.

 The

Report, 1851—*continued.*

*Spencer*, Rev. *Thomas*. (Analysis of his Evidence)—*continued.*

The abolition of the penny stamp would increase the demand for literary talent, and increase the remuneration of literary men, 2414–2417——The effect of the reduction of the taxes on knowledge, and the establishment of a cheap newspaper press, would tend greatly to improve the tone and morals of the people in general, 2417–2419——Character of the Americans and the American papers; they are superior to the English press in coming in contact with the people, 2420–2422. 2425–2445——Manner in which the newspaper press of the country would be improved by the abolition of the stamp, 2423, 2424——In this country truth labours under a disadvantage, because those who want to disseminate truth are conscientious, and will not evade the law by sanctioning the issue of cheap unstamped publications, 2446–2449——Great advantage would result from pamphlets advocating temperance and other principles being allowed to contain news, as tending to make the truth more attractive, 2450–2452.

*Spoiled Stamps.* If the stamps are spoiled, or if a newspaper becomes defunct, having on hand a certain supply of stamps, or if it changes in size, a return is made by the Stamp-office if the stamps are brought back, *Keogh* 399——If the paper is printed on, no return is made, *ib.* 400——The Stamp-office does not make any allowance for stamps in the case of spoiled papers, *Whitty* 732, 733.

*Stamp Act.* Witness would say there has not been greater difficulty in carrying out the law with regard to the stamp tax on newspapers than in carrying out the law with regard to exciseable matters or customs, *Timm* 200, 201——Conclusions witness has come to with regard to the mode in which the law is administered as to the stamping of news, *Collett* 737 *et seq.*——Carrying out the present Stamp Act literally, and with the extreme rigour of the law, would be very oppressive, not only to capitalists, but it would arrest the moral and social progress of the people, *Cassell* 1300–1306.

*Stamp Duties.* Witness has turned his attention very much to the effect of the newspaper stamp duty; the result of this consideration is, that it is most decidedly unfavourable to the community, *Whitty* 567, 568——The duty on the newspaper stamps and the advertisement duty together, put into one sum, are a considerable fiscal burden on the press, *ib.* 722–729——They fall rather on the public than on the proprietors, *ib.* 722——The penny stamp on newspapers is on the whole a favourable arrangement for the press; evidence in support of this opinion, *Russell* 1471–1478. 1486. 1488 *et seq.* 1516–1538.

Remarks relative to the various stamp duties that have been imposed on newspapers since the time of Queen Anne; the papers have grown up to their present perfection in spite of the stamp, *Hunt* 2354——Return of the number of newspaper stamps at one penny, issued to the undermentioned newspapers in England, Ireland, Scotland, and Wales, from the year 1837 to 1850, inclusive, specifying each newspaper by name, and the number of stamps issued each year to each newspaper, *App.* 524.

*See* also *Abolition of the Duty. Ad Valorem Duty. Character of the Press. Comments on News. Duty. Education,* 1. *News,* 1. *Paper Duty. Penny Newspapers. Post-office. Reduction of the Duty. Supplements to Newspapers. "Times,"* The. *Working Classes.*

*Stamped Wrappers.* See *Envelopes. Postage Labels.*

*STAMPING*

Report, 1851—*continued.*

*STAMPING ESTABLISHMENTS:*

1. *Limited Number of Stamping Places; alleged Inconveniences arising therefrom.*
2. *Opinion that no great Inconvenience arises from this Fact.*
3. *Difficulties in the way of Removing this supposed Grievance.*
4. *Papers laid before the Committee.*

1. *Limited Number of Stamping Places; alleged Inconveniences arising therefrom:*

Evidence relative to the limited number of stamping places in the United Kingdom, and the alleged inconvenience arising therefrom; nature of the complaints which have been made to the Board of Inland Revenue on the subject, *Keogh* 284. 289-295——Some years ago there was but one place for stamping, *ib.* 284——London was the only place, and then the papers in the north of England, and some of the papers in Scotland, pressed very hard to have an establishment in Edinburgh, *ib.*——This was conceded, and very shortly after Manchester was established, *ib.*——The south of England is of course supplied from London, *ib.* 291.

Witness obtains his stamps from Manchester; the selection of the place for getting them depends greatly on proximity, *Whitty* 652-654——There would be a very great advantage in having an increased number of stamp offices, *ib.* 655-659——Expenses attending the obtaining of stamped paper from Somerset House for country newspapers; establishing district offices in various parts of the country would lessen the expense, *Bucknall* 1204-1211——Manner in which the paper for the "Times" is obtained and stamped; expense to the proprietors of the newspaper in fetching the paper from the Stamp-office to their printing-office, *Morris* 2134-2140.

2. *Opinion that no great Inconvenience arises from this Fact:*

There is no doubt the necessity of sending so far for stamped paper does require newspaper proprietors to keep a larger supply of stamped paper than they would otherwise keep, *Keogh* 285——But it was conceived when the duty was reduced from 4 *d.* to 1 *d.*, that this would not be a very great evil or hardship upon the newspaper proprietors, *ib.* 285. 287——Witness does not believe that the proprietors of newspapers deal directly with the paper manufacturers for their supply of paper, but deal with the agents in London, who, if the proprietors are proprietors of country papers, forward the paper ready stamped to them, *ib.* 315-336. 364-369——So that the proprietor of a paper, say in Cornwall, would not be under the necessity of sending his paper up to London in the first instance to have it stamped, *ib.* 315-336——Even newspapers in the neighbourhood of Manchester, where there is a stamping establishment, are supplied with their paper from London, *ib.* 320. 336. 340, 341.

There may have been occasions in which delay and loss have accrued to the proprietors of newspapers from their having to get their paper stamped at a distance, but this has been from the neglect of the parties themselves, *Keogh* 342——Applications have been made by parties to be allowed in a case of sudden emergency to print upon unstamped paper, they agreeing to pay the stamp duty afterwards, *ib.* 343——Where the transaction is one that occurs for

Report, 1851—*continued.*

*STAMPING ESTABLISHMENTS*—continued.

2. *Opinion that no great Inconvenience arises from this Fact*—continued.

for the first time it is always passed over on the payment of the duties, but it would not be granted beforehand, *Keogh* 343-347. 352-363. 370. 385-389——Instances of this, *App.* 488——Short period of time taken when a person applies for stamps before he is supplied with them, *Keogh* 394, 395.

3. *Difficulties in the way of Removing this supposed Grievance:*

Evidence showing, that allowing the paper for newspapers to be stamped wherever there is a stamp-office, or a collection of excise, would be likely to lead to fraud, and would also cause a large increase of expense, *Keogh* 292, 293. 296-314. 337-339. 348-351——How far there is any distinction in the course pursued with respect to the stamping of newspapers and the stamping of deeds and bills, and documents of that kind, *ib.* 371-383——The Stamp-office only supply stamps on paper of their own to their distributors in the country; this is the only way in which the Stamp-office can be said to keep any stock of stamps, *ib.* 372, 373. 375, 376——Newspaper proprietors send their own paper to the office to be stamped, *ib.* 374——The public in London send in all their own paper and parchment, and every other thing requiring a stamp, to be stamped, just as the newspaper proprietors do, *ib.* 375——Impracticability of printing stamps for newspapers as stamps for deeds are prepared, and supplying the stamp distributors in the country with them, and allowing them to send them to the newspapers, *ib.* 384——Stamping the paper for newspapers by hand is found preferable to doing it by machinery, *ib.* 390-393.——*See* also *Edinburgh.*

4. *Papers laid before the Committee:*

Statement of the expenses connected with the stamping of newspapers in London, Edinburgh, and Manchester, as returned to the House of Commons, 28th January 1850, *App.* 484——Copy of memorial from the newspaper proprietors of Glasgow to the Lords of the Treasury, *ib.* 485.

*Starting Newspapers.* Course which must be adopted by a party contemplating the publication of a newspaper, *Timm* 33 *et seq.*——Witness delivers in a form of particulars required at the Board of Inland Revenue Office, Somerset House, previously to the printing of any newspaper, or upon any change in respect to the same, *ib.* 33-36.

*Stroud.* Average circulation of unstamped publications in Stroud; the number is very small, *Bucknall* 1161, 1162.

*"Stroud Free Press."* Witness is now engaged in the publication of a stamped paper, the "Stroud Free Press;" price and circulation of this paper, *Bucknall* 1123-1134——Evidence generally relative to witness having sent an unstamped copy of the "Stroud Free Press" to the Board of Inland Revenue, and the proceedings of the Board against witness, although no copy of that publication was sold, or ever left witness's printing-office, *ib.* 1187-1197——Reason for witness sending an unstamped copy of that paper to the Inland Revenue Board, *ib.* 1195. 1200-1203——The "Stroud Free Press" is at present carried on at a loss; could it be published without a stamp, it would yield a good profit, *ib.* 1203.

Report, 1851—*continued.*

"*Stroud Observer.*" Evidence generally as to the "Stroud Observer," and the suppression of that paper by the Board of Inland Revenue, *Bucknall* 1099 *et seq.*——Pecuniary loss to witness from the suppression of the "Stroud Observer;" extensive circulation of that paper; only three numbers were published, *Bucknall* 1099–1105. 1118, 1119. 1142. 1176——Communications which passed between witness and the Board of Inland Revenue, which led to the suppression of the "Stroud Observer," *ib.* 1106, 1107. 1113, 1114. 1135——Statement as to what passed at an interview witness had with Mr. Keogh, the Secretary of the Board of Inland Revenue, with respect to the pending prosecution for the publication of the "Stroud Observer" on unstamped paper, *ib.* 1108–1113——Witness considers that it is a great hardship on him to be prevented from publishing the "Stroud Observer," while so many unstamped papers of the same class are allowed to be published by other parties, *ib.* 1113. 1135. 1142, 1143. 1177. 1198——He would not have dropped the "Stroud Observer" had he been in a pecuniary position to have defended himself in a court of law, as he considers he had not acted illegally; it would have been a very expensive undertaking, *ib.* 1114–1117. 1163, 1164. 1171.

Extensive circulation of the "Stroud Observer" among the poorer class of operatives; the suppression of this paper was a great hardship on this class of the community, *Bucknall*, 1119, 1120. 1152–1156——It would not have paid to have stamped the "Stroud Observer;" it would not have sold at the increased price, *ib.* 1121——Loss to the revenue by the suppression of the "Stroud Observer" of the amount arising from advertisement duty; this was a large amount, considering the nature of the publication, *ib.* 1122. 1144–1146——Circulation of newspapers in Stroud; great wish among the people for a cheap local organ like the "Stroud Observer," *ib.* 1146–1154——Witness considers that from want of means to withstand the threat of the Board of Inland Revenue, he has been unjustly deprived of the profits arising from the publication of the "Stroud Observer," *ib.* 1173–1175——Though witness's publication was suppressed, richer publishers have been allowed to go on publishing precisely the same kind of works, they having the means of withstanding the threats of the Board of Inland Revenue, *ib.* 1173–1177. 1184–1186.

*Supplements to Newspapers.* The effect of the Newspaper Act, by restricting the superficial extent of letter press in newspapers, makes the stamp on supplements very onerous, *Rep.* 7——Section 5 of the Act 6 & 7 Will. 4, c. 76, directs that certain particulars shall be printed on papers that are sold as supplements to the newspapers, and that they should contain the word supplement, *Timm* 4——The stamp duty acts as a protection to the inferior class of newspapers, and tends to limit the circulation of the leading newspapers, by reason of the duty on the supplements, *Morris* 2055–2070——It is quite possible to have a uniform stamp of a fixed denomination, without reference to size; the supplement is just as much part of the paper as page No. 6, and there is no reason why a particular page should be stamped, *ib.* 2070——Calculations bearing upon the statement with regard to the effect of the stamp duty on the supplement, *ib.* 2079–2084——The stamp on the supplement has the effect of restricting the circulation of newspapers; it is a heavy burthen, and ought not to be imposed on any ground whatever, *ib.* 2165,

*Supplements to Newspapers*—continued.
2165, 2166——Whatever is done with the stamp on the newspaper itself, the stamp on the supplement ought decidedly to come off, *ib.* 2226. 2231. 2236.——*See* also "*Times,*" The.

*Sureties.* Newspaper proprietors do not give sureties for newspaper stamps; the sureties are for the duties upon advertisements, *Keogn* 398.
*See* also *Advertisement Duty,* 1. *American Press,* 1. *Libel.*

T.

*Taxes on Knowledge.* The reduction of the taxes upon knowledge would greatly improve the general tone of the press, and also the general condition of society, *Bucknall* 1250——There is no disposition amongst the people to disagree, on religious grounds, as to the propriety of removing the existing taxes on knowledge, *Bunting* 2310–2314.
*See* also *Censorship. Education.*

*Telegraphic Despatches.* See *Electric Telegraph.*

*Temperance Society.* Difficulty experienced by the Temperance Society, or the Peace Society, in disseminating right principles among the community from the high price of newspapers, *Spencer* 2370.

"*Times,*" The. Total amount paid by the "Times" for penny stamps, in- including also halfpenny stamps for supplements, *Morris* 2019–2021——Remarks relative to the stamp duty payable on supplements of the "Times;" this tends to limit the circulation, as the losses upon the supplement destroy the profit of the paper, *ib.* 2028–2050——The stamp on the supplement is extremely unjust, as it consists entirely of advertisements, on each of which a duty is paid, *ib.* 2051–2054——It is also unjust on the public, as it limits the advertisements, *ib.* 2052——Publication of an account of the opening of the Exhibition on unstamped paper, as it was published in the "Times;" it is witness's opinion that it did not require a stamp, *ib.* 2121–2133.
It is witness's conviction that if the stamp duty were removed from newspapers the commercial advantages of the "Times" would be enormous, from the increased circulation, but witness would be sorry to see the stamp abolished, as it might lead the public to patronize inferior papers, *Morris* 2225–2238——If the price of the "Times" were reduced, its circulation would be increased without its tone being lowered, *Haywood,* 2551, 2552——The news agents frequently experience great difficulty in obtaining the required quantity of the "Times;" causes to which this may be attributed, *Smith* 2952–2967——In the event of the abolition of the penny stamp, the "Times" would profit by it more than any other paper, *ib.* 2965. 2968. 2975.
*See* also *Cheap Newspapers.* "*Evening Mail.*" *Postage. Printing Machinery.* "*Punch.*" *Working Classes.*

*Timm, Joseph.* (Analysis of his Evidence.)—Solicitor to the Board of Inland Revenue, 1——Witness has not exactly the control or superintendence in reference to the stamping of newspapers, 2——But parties before they can obtain stamps for the printing of a newspaper must come before his department and enter into certain securities against libels, 2——And they must also

Report, 1851—*continued.*

*Timm, Joseph.* (Analysis of his Evidence)—*continued.*

also make a declaration as to the parties who are the printers, publishers, and proprietors of the paper, 2——The whole of the preliminary proceedings are within witness's department, not the actual stamping, 3.

Reference to the Acts of Parliament which regulate the proceedings, 4——The principal Act is the 6 & 7 Will. 4, c. 76, which imposes the present stamp duty of one penny upon newspapers, and a halfpenny upon supplements, 4——In the Schedule (A) of this Act there are the definitions of what in law are to be deemed newspapers; nature of these definitions, 4. 17–22——Detail of the various provisions of this Act (6 & 7 Will. 4, c. 76), 4–6——Any person who prints a paper liable to stamp duty as a newspaper unstamped incurs a penalty of 20*l.* for every copy, 7–9——But no penalty can be recovered beyond the copies which the Board may have in their possession, and be able to give in as evidence, 8.

The Act of the 60 Geo. 3, c. 9, provides for sureties for the payment of fines on conviction of any printer or publisher for the publication of any blasphemous or seditious libel, 10——Extension of the provisions of this Act by the 1 Will. 4, c. 73; 10–13——The whole of the Acts of Parliament bearing upon the question of the newspaper press were consolidated by the Act 6 & 7 Will. 4, c. 76, except the 60 Geo. 3, and 1 Will. 4; 14–16——Under these Acts, in no case must facts, intelligence, or occurrences, or anything that can come within the description of public news, be printed on any material without a stamp, 15. 17–22——Comments or observations may be published without a stamp, provided they are published at intervals exceeding twenty-six days, 23——They may be published without a stamp at a less interval than twenty-six days, provided they contain a quantity of paper at least equal to two sheets, each sheet containing a quantity not less than twenty-one inches in length and seventeen in breadth, and that the publication shall be published for sale at a sum not less than sixpence, 24–32.

Course which must be adopted by a party contemplating the publication of a newspaper, 33 *et seq.*——Witness delivers in a form of particulars required at the Inland Revenue Office, Somerset House, previously to the printing of any newspaper, or upon any change in respect to the same, 33–36——Power which the Board of Inland Revenue possesses of enforcing the law, and punishing those who infringe or evade the provisions of the Act, 37 *et seq.*——Every person who prints a newspaper without a stamp is liable to a penalty of 20*l.* for every copy of the same, 37, 38——The mode of proceeding of the Board of Inland Revenue would be to sue for penalties in the Court of Exchequer, 39——A question would then arise whether the publication was a newspaper in fact and in law; this would be a question which the judge would leave for the jury, 39.

All printing presses used in the printing of unstamped newspapers are liable to seizure and forfeiture; proceedings which must be gone through before a warrant can be issued for their seizure, 40–46——How far the parties whose presses have have been seized have any redress, if it turns out that what they printed were not newspapers, 45, 46——Some papers not strictly newspapers, such as prices current, &c., are registered as such and the declarations made, a portion of these papers being published without stamps, 47——Reference to a return made in 1850 of the papers published in



the

Report, 1851—*continued.*

*Timm, Joseph.* (Analysis of his Evidence)—*continued.*

the metropolis which are registered as newspapers, a portion whereof is published without stamps, 47–48——It would be competent for these parties, if the Board sued them for penalties, to plead that the thing was not a newspaper, though they had themselves signed the declarations and registered it as such, 49, 50.

A publication is not a newspaper in virtue of its registration, but in virtue of its contents, 51——Witness would say that such papers as the "Athenæum," the "Architect," &c., do not serve the purpose of newspapers generally, 52–54——The test at the Board of Inland Revenue, whether a given publication is a newspaper or not, is, whether it contains public news, intelligence, or occurrences, or comments or observations thereon, published at less intervals than twenty-six days, 55–57——The Board has never found itself in any great practical difficulty in deciding what is news and what is not, 58——Explanation of the grounds of the proceedings which have been commenced against the publishers of a "Narrative of Current Events," edited by Dickens, and nature of these proceedings, 59–66.

After parties have registered their publications as newspapers, and have obtained stamps, they may print whatever they please on these stamps, such as prices current, or catalogues of articles sold by the parties; the Board of Inland Revenue has no power of preventing this, 67–87——With respect to such publications passing free through the post, this is a question for the Post-office, 73–84——Although certain class publications such as the "Legal Observer," the "Lancet," the "Builder," &c., may sometimes contain what is strictly speaking news, still witness does not consider he could get a jury to say that they were newspapers published unstamped, 88–96. 113, 114——Witness is of opinion that if he were to attempt to prosecute "Punch" for being a newspaper he would be laughed out of court, 97——If a person extracts parts of a newspaper, and publishes them on unstamped paper, it renders him liable to a penalty of 20*l.* for every copy, if what he extracts is news, 98–101.

Case in which the publisher of the "West Riding Examiner" republished from his own paper 2,000 copies of the report of a particular trial; notice of an action was given him for the full amount of penalties, but he was let off on the payment of the small penalty of 10*l.*; 102–112. 115–121——The Legislature has vested the power in the Board to compromise all cases, either by paying a portion, or without paying at all, 121——In cases of doubt or difficulty the Board is advised by the Attorney and Solicitor-general, 122——Witness considers it the business of every one connected with the Inland Revenue Board to give notice officially to any party flagrantly violating the law, 125–127——Opinion that the "Annual Register" does not come within the scope of the law, 128–145.

Magazines have from the time that the newspaper stamp duty has been imposed, obtained a character different in some respect from that of a newspaper 146——Although they may contain news in one article, yet generally they are filled with other matter than is common to newspapers 146–148——If the decision of the court should be, that "Dickens's Household Narrative" is a newspaper, such decision would not carry with it, and include the large monthly

Report, 1851—*continued.*

*Timm, Joseph.* (Analysis of his Evidence)—*continued.*
monthly publications, such as the "New Monthly Magazine," 149–155——Their contents are totally different from Dickens's paper, 149——If witness were aware that it was a common practice in London to publish separate parts of a newspaper upon unstamped paper, he would consider it his duty to interfere in such cases, provided the matter so printed were news, 156–173.

The Board of Inland Revenue are guided in their proceedings against parties for any infractions of the law rather by what a jury would say than by their own discretion and judgment in the case, 174–178——Applications have been made from the proprietors of newspapers, who are now under the necessity of stamping every copy that they publish, to be allowed the privilege that the 53 registered newspapers enjoy, of only stamping that portion which goes by post, 179——The law prevents the Board from granting these applications, 180——Evidence showing that there is a wide distinction between the case of the proprietors who stamp all their impressions and the publications of the applicants for this privilege, as it is termed, 181–194——Witness recollects when the stamp duty was reduced; the impossibility of enforcing the duty was one of the principal reasons alleged for reducing it, 195–198——The impossibility was the want of a more stringent measure, and the want of power to search, 198–199.

Witness would say that there has not been greater difficulty in carrying out the law with regard to the stamp tax on newspapers than in carrying out the law with regard to exciseable matters or customs, 200–201——Lengthened examination on thhe subject of the prosecution pending against Dickens's "Narrative of Current Events," with the grounds for witness's coming to the conclusion that it is undoubtedly in its present form, and at the present interval of publication, a newspaper, 202–268.

*Tone of the Press.* See *Character of the Press.*

*"Town,"* The. See *Obscene Publications.*

*Tradesmen's Catalogues.* After parties have registered their publications as newspapers, and have obtained stamps, they may print whatever they please on these stamps, such as prices current, or catalogues of articles sold by the parties; the Board of Inland Revenue has no power of preventing this, *Timm* 67–87——With respect to such publications passing free through the post, this is a question for the Post-office, *ib.* 73–84——Allowing merchants to transmit their prices current and tradesmen their catalogues through the post, if stamped in the same way as newspapers, produces a large sum to the revenue, *Keogh* 523–532——These papers would not be published or transmitted to nearly the extent they now are if they had not this privilege; but this is a matter for the Post-office itself, *ib.*——Objection to allowing tradesmen's catalogues to bear the penny stamp, for the convenience of transmission through the Post-office, *Russell,* 1539–1541.

*See* also *Prices Current.*

*TRANSMISSION*

Report, 1851—*continued.*

*TRANSMISSION OF NEWSPAPERS:*

1. *How far the Stamp may be considered as an equivalent for Postal Services.*
2. *Regulations and Suggestions relative to the Transmission of Newspapers.*
3. *Evidence as to the Transmission of Papers in America.*

1. *How far the Stamp may be considered as an equivalent for Postal Services:*

Opinion of the Committee that newspapers do not practically enjoy such favourable terms for transmission by post as other printed matter, *Rep.* 8—— If the newspaper stamp were allowed to be affixed only to such copies as go through the post, it would then assume the character of a mere equivalent for postal services, *ib.*——Taking the whole number of newspapers published, a very small proportion pass through the Post-office, therefore the stamp levied for the facilities afforded by the Post-office is no advantage, but the contrary, *Cassell* 1355-1360——As far as those newspapers are concerned that are sent by post, a service is rendered for the penny stamp, *Morris* 2072-2075—— The facilities of transmission by post are valueless to most of the provincial papers, *Bunting* 2281-2291.

2. *Regulations and Suggestions relative to the Transmission of Newspapers:*

Recommendation of the Committee that immediate steps should be taken to place the regulations affecting the transmission of newspapers and other printed matter by post on a more satisfactory footing, *Rep.* 9, 10——Suggestions as to the transmission of newspapers through the Post-office, supposing the stamp to be abolished, *Collett* 930 *et seq.*——Regulations as to the transmission of newspapers by post, *Parkhurst* 1619-1623.

By a Treasury minute, dated 1838, any publication which bears a newspaper stamp is allowed to go free through the Post-office, provided it does not exceed two ounces in weight, *Hill* 1689, 1690——Great number of newspapers sent through the Post-office by the newsvenders, *ib.* 1729-1731. 1737, 1738——In the event of the stamp on newspapers being abolished, whether the papers would be dispatched through the Post-office or by other means, would depend upon the comparative excellence of the manner employed by the Post-office and the news agent, *ib.* 1851——The present effect of the stamp on newspapers is to tax all readers of papers, that a few persons choosing to send their papers through the post may do so free of charge, *Haywood*, 2599——Witness considers this unjust; a penny postage should be charged on newspapers each time they are sent through the post, *ib.* 2599-2610.

3. *Evidence as to the Transmission of Papers in America:*

Postal regulations of America for the transmission of newspapers, *Greeley* 2627-2638——The newspapers are but seldom transmitted through the post from one person to another; they are so cheap, it is not worth while, *ib.* 3025-3028——Distinction made by the Post-office in America in the charge for the

*TRANSMISSION OF NEWSPAPERS*—continued.

3. *Evidence as to the Transmission of Papers in America*—continued.

the transmission of newspapers and other printed matter; manner in which it is decided what constitutes a newspaper, *Greeley* 3037–3040.

*See* also *Circulation.* *Evasions of Postage*, 2. *Local Newspapers*, 1, 2. *London District.* *Newsvenders.* *Obliteration of Stamps.* *Old Newspapers.* *Postage.* *Postmaster-general.* *Post-office.* *Prices Current.* *Railways.* *Reduction of the Duty.* *Tradesmen's Catalogues.* *Treasury*, The *Unstamped Publications.*

*Treasury*, The. Witness has no doubt but that the Treasury have the power of making any alteration in the present regulations for the transmission of newspapers through the post, *Hill* 1793——Power of the Treasury to lay down any regulations as to the transmission of newspapers through the Post-office; they could, at their discretion, put a charge upon all newspapers, *Parkhurst* 1629–1633.

*See* also *Post-office.* *Transmission of Newspapers*, 2.

U.

*United States.* See *American Press*, 2.

*Unstamped Newspapers.* Section 22 of the Act 6 & 7 Will. 4, c. 76, authorises justices of the peace, upon information, on oath, of a suspicion that newspapers are printed without being stamped, to grant a search warrant, and if unstamped newspapers are found, the printing engines and machines may be seized and condemned as forfeited, *Timm* 5, 6——Instances of newspapers published on unstamped paper in London, Edinburgh, and Manchester, *App.* 484.

*See* also *"Dunfermline Journal."* *Extracts from Newspapers.*

*Unstamped Publications.* In the event of unstamped publications being sent through the Post-office, they are charged as letters when detected; impossibility of examining every parcel, *Parkhurst* 1639–1650——Every precaution is taken against this system of fraud that the machinery of the Post-office will allow; cases of fraud are very rare now, *Parkhurst* 1643–1651; *Hill* 1746–1748——Detection does not invariably follow cases of fraud in sending unstamped publications through the Post-office, *Hill* 1695——All unstamped publications that are detected are charged as unpaid letters; they are universally refused, and there exists no means of tracing the party who post them, *Bokenham* 1997–2003——In this country truth labours under a disadvantage, because those who want to disseminate truth are conscientious, and will not evade the law by sanctioning the issue of cheap unstamped publications, *Spencer* 2446–2449——Detail as to the name, quality, and circulation of the various

Report, 1851—*continued.*

Report, 1851—*continued.*

*Whitty, Michael James.* (Analysis of his Evidence)—*continued.*

stamp duty; the result of this consideration is that it is most decidedly unfavourable, 567, 568——Witness has published a high-priced paper and also a low-priced paper, 569, 570——The high-priced paper answered witness's purpose best; but it did not answer the public purpose so well, 571, 572——Grounds for forming the opinion that if good newspapers were cheap the buyers and readers would increase twenty or thirty fold, 573–586. 601–609.

Improper papers are read very extensively by the working and poorer classes, for the want of better; illustration of this opinion, 587–590——The publication of unstamped newspapers very much reduced the sale of the penny papers of an obscene and improper character, although these unstamped papers were not very good themselves, 590–597——If good newspapers were sold at a low price, there would be few or no bad publications issued; grounds for this assertion, 598–601——Witness considers that cheapness would have a good effect in the quality of the newspapers, 602–609. 611——If the stamp were taken off newspapers and the duty off advertisements, the papers might be sold at a penny, the same as they are in America, 610——Cheap penny papers would pay a great deal better to the proprietors than the present high-priced papers, 612.

Character of the papers published in America; nature of the talent employed on them, 613–617——Witness is aware that the London daily papers incur an immense expense for news; if sold cheap they could afford this expense, and much more, 618——No penny or twopenny paper would ever produce the income of the "Times" if the stamp duty were taken off, nor would the "Times" do it if this were done, 619——The penny stamp decidedly operates to create a monopoly, 620——The effect of abolishing the stamp and advertisement duties would be to equalize a great deal the circulation of newspapers, and to give a decided preference to the best one, 621–627——If the penny stamp, the advertisement duty, and the paper duty were taken off, papers would be published in this country at a penny, and be as well conducted as the "Times," 622——Way in which there would be a great increase in the number of papers if the duties were removed, 628–635——Still witness does not consider that the country would be inundated with cheap papers, a large capital being required to start them, 630–635——A cheap press would have the best possible effect, 636–639.

The freedom of the press in America acts as a kind of safety valve for public opinion, 640–642——The effect of the advertisement duty in a commercial town like Liverpool is most injurious, 644–648——In the case of provincial papers they have become more extended in circulation as they become more local in the nature of their intelligence, 649——Witness would say, that extreme facility of communication with respect to their local wants and interests given to a people in a district has a good effect upon their character, by enabling them to know what they are about, and what is doing around them, 650——It is very desirable to encourage that diffusion of the press which is created by greater facilities being afforded in the provinces instead of concentrating it all in one place, 651.

Witness obtains his stamps from Manchester; the selection of the place for getting them depends greatly on proximity, 652–654——There would be a very great advantage in having an increased number of stamp-offices, 655–

659——

Report, 1851—*continued.*

*Whitty, Michael James.* (Analysis of his Evidence)—*continued.*
659——In regard to moral character the American press is quite equal to our own, 660–666. 673. 691–704——Witness is aware that in this country an opinion prevails extensively adverse to the respectability of the American press, but it is an entirely wrong one, 665——As regards price, taking quantity for quantity, the price in America is less than one-third of our own, 667, 668——This is a great advantage to any community having a free constitutional government, 669——If we were free in England from the taxes on knowledge, as they are popularly called, we should have as cheap and as good a press as they have in America, and a much better one than we have now, 670–673. 691–704.

Further grounds on which witness forms the opinion that if we had a cheap press all the bad and immoral publications would be driven out of the market, 674–690. 706–721——The duty on the newspaper stamps and the advertisement duty together, put into one sum, are a considerable fiscal burden on the press, 722–729——They fall rather on the public than on the proprietors, 722——Witness would say that if the newspaper proprietors throughout England were polled, nine out of ten would be disposed to keep them just as they are, 722——The Stamp-office does not make any allowance for stamps in the case of spoiled papers, 732, 733.

*Working Classes.* Opinion of the Committee that the newspaper stamp prohibits the existence of such newspapers as from their price and character would be suitable to the means and wants of the labouring classes, *Rep.* 11——Many of the working classes now club together to take newspapers even when they do not altogether approve of them, for they feel it necessary to have something of the kind, *Collett,* 927——This has been very much the case with respect to the "Northern Star," *ib.*——There is no doubt that it is the desire of the artizans and mechanics, and the various branches of the industrial classes, to get rid of the stamp on newspapers, *Collett,* 951–953; *Bunting* 2273–2280. 2292–3309; *Haywood* 2511–2514——If the stamp were taken off they could get their newspapers at all prices, from a halfpenny up to fourpence or fivepence, *Collett* 954–964. 972–978.

The extensive sale of cheap publications shows a taste among the working classes for reading, and mental improvement, and a general desire for cheap literature, *Cassell* 1324; *Haywood* 2509, 2510——The stamp duty may be considered as a premium upon drunkenness; manner in which this is obviously the case, *Spencer* 2364. 2380–2383——Witness considers that newspaper reading is the most acceptable and instructive description of reading which people can possess, *ib.* 2365. 2384–2391——Beneficial effects would result to the population of the country from the free publication of news, *Haywood* 2526–2529——The working classes might be safely left to discriminate between the good and bad newspapers; the removal of the stamp would not lead them to patronise inferior papers, *ib.* 2541–2550.

Even though the number of stamps issued for newspapers has increased from 28,000,000 in 1836 to the enormous number of 65,000,000 at the present time, witness is of opinion that newspapers have not reached down to the comprehension of the very lowest persons who are able to read, *Hickson* 3194, 3195——The writing of the "Times" really overshoots the comprehension of the labouring classes, *ib.* 3196——Great extent to which the

Report, 1851—*continued.*

*Working Classes*—continued.

the working classes of America are subscribers to newspapers; cost of the papers, *Greeley* 3014–3024——The working classes of America do not resort to the public-houses to read the newspapers, *ib.* 3029–3031.

*See* also *Agricultural Labourers. American Press,* 2. *Bad Publications. Cheap Newspapers. Cheap Publications. Education,* 1. *Mechanics' Institutions. Monthly Publications. Penny Newspapers. Pernicious Publications. Registration of Newspapers. "Stroud Observer." Unstamped Publications.*

"*Working Man's Friend,*" The. Remarks relative to the publication entitled "The Working Man's Friend;" superior character of this work, *Cassell* 1322, 1323——In the event of the decision going against the "Household Narrative," the "Working Man's Friend" would be liable to the stamp duty; witness would be obliged in that case to increase the price of that publication, *ib.* 1331–1344——Obliging witness to stamp the "Working Man's Friend" would entirely destroy it, *ib.* 1345–1348——Were witness precluded from commenting upon the interesting public events of the day in the "Working Man's Friend," it could not be carried on successfully, *ib.* 1349–1354.